MW00856450

Syncretism in the West
Pico's 900 Theses (1486)

The Evolution of Traditional Religious and Philosophical Systems

Medieval and Renaissance Texts and Studies

Volume 167

Syncretism in the West: Pico's 900 Theses (1486)

The Evolution of Traditional Religious and Philosophical Systems

With Text, Translation, and Commentary

by

S. A. Farmer

Medieval & Renaissance Texts & Studies
Tempe, Arizona
1998

A generous grant from
Pegasus Limited for the Promotion of Neo-Latin Studies
has assisted in meeting the publication costs of this volume.

This 2016 paperback edition is a digital reproduction of the 2008 hardcover edition and may contain some imperfections.

The ISBN for this paperback edition is 978-0-86698-817-9

The CIP data below is reprinted directly from the original hardcover edition.

Library of Congress Cataloging-in-Publication Data

Farmer, S. A. (Stephan Alan)
Syncretism in the West: Pico's 900 theses (1486): the evolution of traditional religious and philosophical systems: with text, translation, and commentary / by S. A. Farmer.
p. cm. -- (Medieval and Renaissance texts and studies; v. 167)
Includes bibliographical references and index.
~~ISBN 0-86698-209-4 (alk. paper)~~
1. Pico della Mirandola, Giovanni, 1463-1494. Conclusiones nongentae. 2. Syncretism (Religion). 3. Philosophy. 4. Theology. I. Pico della Mirandola, Giovanni, 1463-1494. Conclusiones nongentae. English & Latin. II. Title. III. Series.

B785.P53C664 1998
195--dc21

98-21436
CIP

∞
This book is made to last.
It is set in Bembo,
smythe-sewn and printed on acid-free paper
to library specifications.

Printed in the United States of America

Table of Contents

TABLE OF CONTENTS

Part 2:
Text, Translation, and Commentary

"In any field find the strangest thing and then explore it."
— John Archibald Wheeler

"Clarity is achieved through breadth."
— Niels Bohr

CONCLVSIONES non diſputabūtur niſi poſt Epiphaniam. Interim publicabuntur in omnibus Italiæ Gymnaſiis. Et ſiquis Philoſophus aut Theologus etiam ab extrema Italia arguendi gratia Romam uenire uoluerit pollicetur ipſe. D. diſputaturus ſe uiatici expenſas illi ſoluturum de ſuo :. .:.

THE CONCLUSIONS will not be disputed until after the Epiphany [January 6]. In the meantime they will be published in all Italian universities. And if any philosopher or theologian, even from the ends of Italy, wishes to come to Rome for the sake of debating, his lord the disputer promises to pay the travel expenses from his own funds.

Announcement at the end of the 1486 edition of Pico's theses

Preface

Primum igitur, quod est omnium maximum, sicut ostendimus, quae sunt in omnis mundis contineri in singulis.

The first [principle], which is the greatest of all, as I have shown, is that whatever exists in all worlds is contained in each one. Pico, *Heptaplus*[1]

This study developed in conjunction with a cross-cultural model of the evolution of premodern religious and philosophical systems; a fuller account of that model, which involves a number of fields outside history, will appear in a separate volume. Important parts of that model examine the systematic changes introduced in thought by repeated attempts to reconcile traditions, by "syncretism" in a broad sense of the term.[2] Pico was the obvious candidate for a study

[1] *Opera* (1557/72: 8); hereafter cited as *Opera*; Garin, ed., *De hominis dignitate, Heptaplus, De ente et uno, e scritti vari* (Florence, 1942: 194); hereafter cited as *Scritti vari*. References to all Pico's texts besides the nine hundred theses and *Commento* will be given by book and chapter number when these exist and to the standard 1557 and 1572 Basel editions of Pico's *Opera*; except for an occasional line, pagination is identical in the two Basel editions. I have also normally provided cross-references to Garin's partial edition of Pico's works and exclusive references to his version of the *Commento*, which was based on manuscript evidence not available to the Basel editors.

[2] I adopt here the *Oxford English Dictionary*'s definition of syncretism as the "attempted union or reconciliation of diverse or opposite tenets or practices, especially in philosophy or religion." The term is applied in this study not only to reconciliations of different writers or traditions but to attempts as well to harmonize highly stratified compilations (like the Aristotelian corpus, Torah or "Book of Moses," or various Confucian texts) traditionally ascribed to a single authority. Since religious and philosophical commentators worldwide tended to apply similar reconciliative techniques to each stratum of authoritative traditions, over centuries the religious and philosophical systems that grew out of those traditions not surprisingly developed strong family resemblances East and West. Indeed, it can be shown that the evolution of the correlative (or "fractal") structures commonly associated with scholastic systems in their mature forms can be simulated by the same kinds of iterative computer models used to simulate the growth of complex systems in other fields. For

of syncretic processes in the European Renaissance, which in a sense summed up over two thousand years of earlier Western traditions. Pico's nine hundred theses[3] provide a unique window not only onto Renaissance thought but onto the growth and decline of premodern traditions as a whole.

Pico published his theses in December 1486 as part of a grand plan to debate "all teachings" and "all sects" at Rome. Pico's dispute, which was quickly banned by Pope Innocent VIII, was to be held the next year "in the apostolic senate"—before the college of cardinals—with the pope himself envisioned as supreme judge. The enormous scope of Pico's project reflected over three centuries of Western textual revivals amplified by the early printing revolution; whatever its omissions, Pico's text covers a wider range of traditions than any other known fifteenth-century work. The nine hundred theses throw light on hundreds of philosophical and theological conflicts tied to the "warring schools" of Greek, Arabic, Hebrew, and Latin scholasticism; on Renaissance Neo-Platonism and classicism (or so-called humanism) in general, in both of which Pico played a major part; on natural magic, numerology, astrology, Kabbalah, and related esoteric traditions, in which Pico's Renaissance influences were large; and on scores of other topics tied to the complex traditions of the period. If any one text provides a handbook of late fifteenth-century thought, it is this one; indeed, Pico promises a discussion "of everything knowable" (*de omni re scibili*) at more than one point in his work. It was no accident that Pico's text was the first printed book banned universally by the church.[4]

In his *Apology* for his aborted debate, Pico suggested that an *occulta concatenatio* or "hidden connection" linked theses widely scattered in his text; reconstruction of those links is anything but trivial, since Pico's text is loaded on nearly every page with traps for unwary debating opponents. Analysis has been made more difficult by massive corruption in all accessible versions of Pico's text, which in the past has made meaningful study of the theses next to impossible. The edition

---

discussion, accompanied by protocols for computational models, see Farmer and Henderson (1997); cf. also below, pp. 91–96. On parallel developments in Western and Eastern scholastic traditions, see further Cabezón, ed. (1998).

[3] The *editio princeps* of Pico's work carried no title, presumably because the theses were intended to be debated and not simply read. Given the fact that none of the titles given by tradition to the work can claim strong textual support, I have followed Pico's practice by referring indifferently to his "theses" or "conclusions," etc., without assigning a formal title to the text.

[4] On this point, see Hirsch (1967: 89).

supplied with this study as evidence attempts to provide the first reliable version of Pico's text since the exceedingly rare *editio princeps*, whose erratic punctuation raises its own barriers to his thought. My translation is the first based on trustworthy Latin sources;[5] hopefully, that translation will promote wider study of Pico's text, which to date has only been studied in a misleadingly piecemeal fashion.

§

Chapter 1 surveys the nine hundred theses, analyzes Pico's debating plans, and investigates the hidden mystical and eschatological goals of his Vatican project. Chapter 2 looks at the historical origins and systematic effects of Pico's syncretic methods; this chapter discusses ways in which "correlative systems" in general (to adopt the sinologists' terms)—including those hierarchical variations best known in the West—were shaped by the kinds of syncretic processes that operated at an accelerated rate in Pico's work; along the way this chapter discusses syncretic mechanisms that originally helped generate the monotheistic gods and abstract cosmological principles underlying those systems, which began to emerge in all advanced Eurasian societies in the middle of the first millennium BCE.

Chapter 3 analyzes some unique features of Pico's system, including those pertinent to his mystical and magical thought and to his lost *Concord of Plato and Aristotle*, which was closely tied to his aborted Vatican debate; this chapter looks more closely at the specific kinds of structures imposed on traditional thought by syncretic processes.

Chapter 4 discusses Pico's later development, which has long been the subject of heated debate. Study of Pico's later works, reinterpreted in the light of his theses, turns up unexpected signs of massive literary fraud: Extensive evidence shows that after his death Pico's later texts were heavily doctored by his nephew-editor Gianfrancesco Pico and other key figures in the conservative Savonarolan movement; indeed, strong evidence assigns a guiding role here to Savonarola himself, who—for reasons that remain obscure—obtained control of Pico's papers after the latter's sudden death in 1494.

The story of tampering and forgery in Pico's works provides a powerful

---

[5] Albano Biondi's Italian translation of the theses (1995), the first in any language, appeared after the present study was already in press. Biondi's edition and translation are based on corrupt sources and are unfortunately filled with errors, further obscuring Pico's goals in his debate. For analysis, see below, pp. 186–88.

example of a perennial premodern theme: Extreme anti-syncretic no less than extreme syncretic tendencies tended to emerge in all traditional societies suddenly inundated by newly rediscovered or foreign texts. The exaggerated growth of these tendencies in the early printing age can be linked to the final collapse of syncretic traditions that took place in the two centuries after Pico's death. Reconstruction of this part of Pico's story provides a forum for discussing what Stephen Jay Gould has labeled "the greatest intellectual transformation in modern Western thinking"[6]—the final demise, after two thousand years of continuous development, of the extreme kinds of correlative thought summed up so magnificently in Pico's work.

Part 2 of this study, as my principal evidence, contains my Latin edition of the nine hundred theses, accompanied by my English translation and commentary.

§

I want to thank the friends and colleagues who have helped me to complete this study. Thanks goes first to my good friend and recent collaborator, the sinologist John B. Henderson, for his contributions to the comparative dimensions of this work. Readers interested in the parallel development of Eastern and Western traditions should consult Henderson's *The Development and Decline of Chinese Cosmology* (1984), his *Scripture, Canon, and Commentary: A Comparison of Confucian and Western Exegesis* (1991), and his most recent study, *The Construction of Orthodoxy and Heresy: Neo-Confucian, Islamic, Jewish, and Early Christian Patterns* (1998). In a rapidly globalizing society, Renaissance scholars have much to gain and nothing to lose from expanding in comparative directions, returning to paths pioneered by Sarton many decades ago. As the studies of Henderson (1984) and Elman (1984) have suggested, even the so-called humanist movement finds powerful parallels in the work of late Ming and early Ch'ing Dynasty philologists. Those parallels are not coincidental but reflect recurrent patterns of decay and revival in all premodern literate cultures. Viewed from a cross-cultural perspective, Renaissance intellectual traditions, whose complexities remain unrivaled in premodern societies, throw light not only on the evolution of traditional Western thought but on parallel developments as well outside the West.

Research for this study began under fellowships in the early 1980's from the National Endowment for the Humanities and from the Harvard University Center

---

[6] *New York Review of Books* 38, no. 11 (13 June 1991): 11.

for Italian Renaissance Studies at the Villa I Tatti in Florence, Italy. At I Tatti I drew support from the lively mixture of fellows, research associates, official and unofficial visitors, and staff members that has long made I Tatti such a productive institution. Scholars in Florence or elsewhere, some now deceased, whose conversations were suggestive or who answered my oral or written inquiries while I conducted my research include Charles Schmitt, William Bouwsma, Eve Barsook, Gene Brucker, Salvatore Camporeale, Maury Feld, Eric Gombrich, Bill Kent, Paul Oskar Kristeller, Donald Weinstein, Charles Hope, Paola Zambelli, Daniela Mugnai, Dale Kent, Arthur Field, John Monfasani, François Secret, Alan Perreiah, and Michael Allen. I also want to thank my friends John Minton, Dan Tozzer Kemp, Kavous Behzadi, Mark Leski, and Peter Robinson for our many discussions concerning this work.

Anna Terni, formerly Chief Librarian at the Biblioteca Berenson at I Tatti, helped me locate materials critical to my early research; it was in Berenson's old library, filled with neglected Eastern curiosities as well as familiar Western texts, that the comparative dimensions of this study first took shape. Thanks goes also to the staffs of the Österreichische Nationalbibliothek, Bayerische Staatsbibliothek, the Universitätsbibliothek in Erlangen, the Vatican Library, the British Library, the Bibliothèque Nationale in Paris, the Folger Library, the Library of Congress, and the Stanford University libraries for providing key materials used in completing this study.

A special thanks goes to Karen Lemiski and the staff of MRTS for the long hours they devoted to editing and producing this book.

Thanks goes finally to those who helped me find financial support for my research in its various stages. Craig Smyth, past Director of the Villa I Tatti, found the funds to allow me to continue my work in Florence after my official tenure at that institution had ended. Without his support and encouragement, and the constant help of Nelda Ferace, Assistant Director for Administration at I Tatti, I would have found neither the means nor the courage to continue my work. I also want to thank the Child Estate Fund in Florence, to which Professor Smyth kindly directed me, for additional assistance in this period. Lewis Spitz, Lawrence Ryan, Noel Brann, and Marvin Becker helped me find financial support in earlier stages of my research. I would like finally to recall the generous support that the late Professor Jane DeGrummund gave this study at a critical juncture.

§

No study of a work as obscure as the nine hundred theses can possibly hope to be without error; given the complexity of Pico's text, any analysis should ideally take place collaboratively, drawing on the expertise of specialists in the dozens of traditions covered in Pico's work. Readers who wish to add their comments to Pico's text are invited to contact me at **www.safarmer.com/pico/**, where corrections and updates to this study will be posted as the need arises. Readers interested in the theoretical issues discussed in this work are also invited to contact me at that address.

This study frequently deviates from traditional paths in Renaissance studies, a result that I suspect might follow inevitably from any extended analysis of Pico's text. Some of these deviations are tied to the cross-cultural interests that originally drew me to the theses: Pico's text provides an ideal laboratory to study the connections between textual exegesis and the growth of correlative systems—connections that are not unique to Renaissance or premodern Western thought. (A number of extreme syncretic texts outside the West might serve as almost equally good laboratories.) Hopefully, Renaissance specialists will take anything they find useful in this book (ignoring if they wish my cross-cultural and theoretical comments, which lie at the center of the book's sequel) but will not mistake the book for what it is not—a traditional attempt to discuss Pico's thought in terms of each of the ancient, medieval, and Renaissance sources drawn on in his work. Any traditional source hunt would, in any event, soon be superceded on points of detail: No one can claim mastery over more than a small part of the traditions covered in Pico's text, which largely explains why previous studies have focused exclusively on isolated sections of the work. But as Pico himself suggested, to make real sense of his theses it is necessary to attempt a reading of the whole. Past studies that have discussed isolated sections of Pico's text—especially those sections involving magic and Kabbalah—have typically resulted in a wholesale confusion of Pico's ideas with the traditions he planned to synthesize in his debate. In the case of the Kabbalah, extraordinary efforts have been made by Pico scholars since the sixteenth century to unravel the meaning in medieval traditions of the obscure symbols of the kabbalistic *sefirot* (or emanated states of God's nature), overlooking the obvious correlations that Pico planned to make between those symbols and the equally obscure symbols of the Neo-Platonic *henads*—pagan religious constructs that (unnoted in the literature) take up almost an equal amount of space in Pico's text. Remarkably, other key sections of the theses, including the one that contains Pico's promised "new philosophy" (*philosophia nova*)—capable of resolving "every proposed question on natural and divine things"—have not been mentioned even in passing in five hundred years of Pico scholarship, despite the obvious importance of those sections for anyone hoping to decode Pico's text.

Whatever value this book has for traditional Renaissance scholars will not depend on its identification of Pico's sources (all of which he radically distorted) but on its demonstration of the systematic way in which he planned to collate those sources in his debate—the key to any comprehensive reading of Pico's thought, which must be a collective achievement. The need for collaborative work is underlined by the evidence discussed at the end of my study of massive adulterations in Pico's literary corpus, since that evidence suggests that major portions of Pico's lost texts—including his monumental *Concord of Plato and Aristotle*—can be reconstructed from the large number of plagiarized fragments preserved in the works of Pico's nephew and his Savonarolan colleagues. Philological reconstruction of this magnitude, however, is best undertaken by a number of researchers working together.

The old saying that books are not finished but abandoned is probably truer of this book than of most. This study was completed in the late 1980s; a series of mishaps delayed publication for nearly a decade. New studies published in that period have steadily improved our knowledge of Pico and similar writers outside the West; incorporation of recent findings in my notes has undoubtedly improved this book. But as five centuries of Pico scholarship attests, real dangers await those who dwell too long in Pico's distorting hall of mirrors; the work of any one scholar, no matter how incomplete, must in any event stop somewhere. It is with great pleasure and considerable relief, after a long and fascinating journey, that I see Pico off to press.

I dedicate this book with love to Linh, Brenton, and Erin.

Florence, Italy—Palo Alto, California

Part 1:

Introductory Monograph

Chapter 1: Pico's Roman Debate

Et sic in omnibus meis conclusionibus, semper occulta quaedam est concatenatio, quam forte ipsi non advertunt.

And so in all my conclusions, there is always a certain hidden connection, which they possibly do not notice. *Apology*, 1487[1]

i. General Introduction

Giovanni Pico della Mirandola, the count of Concord,[2] was twenty-three years old when he proposed his nine hundred theses for debate at Rome in late 1486. The fact that Pico planned this giant dispute is known to all Renaissance scholars, along with at least part of the story of his troubles with the church. There is high drama here: the suspension of the debate by Pope Innocent VIII; the appointment of a high-level papal commission to investigate the theses' orthodoxy; Pico's defiant publication of his *Apology* and his flight from Rome; his capture, excommunication, and imprisonment in France; the intervention of the French court and Lorenzo de' Medici on his behalf; his provisional release and escape to Florence; and so on. Parallels have been drawn to Galileo's fate nearly a hundred and fifty years later, and the story fits in nicely with old romantic images of the Renaissance.[3]

---

[1] *Opera*, 235.

[2] Concordia was a secondary feudal holding of Pico's family near Mirandola, and *Comes Concordiae* (the count of Concord) was literally Pico's aristocratic title. Both Pico and his contemporaries made much of his title as a divine sign of his holy mission as a reconciler.

[3] Resources for study of Pico's troubles with the church are found in the *Apology* and in the texts printed in Dorez and Thuasne (1897). Cf. also the *Determinationes magistrales contra conclusiones Joannis Pici* (1489) by Petrus Garsias, one of the papal commission members. Other relevant materials can be found in Berti (1859) or are signaled in the notes to Garin (1963). In the text and notes below I have suggested a few of the causes behind Pico's extended persecution by the church, but the issue is complex and interesting enough to justify a dedicated study.

No one, however, has ever made much sense of the nine hundred theses as a whole. The formal oration that Pico wrote to open his debate—the unfortunately mistitled *Oration on the Dignity of Man*[4]—is among the most read and quoted of Renaissance texts; indeed, the work has been claimed as the "manifesto of the Renaissance" by the most influential Italian scholar of the past half century.[5] But the nine hundred theses, for which the *Oration* was simply a preface, have only been studied in a piecemeal fashion—and for the most part badly.

Renaissance historians cannot be blamed entirely for this. Pico proposed his theses in part as an elaborate puzzle that he meant to solve at Rome. The theses were meant to be debated, not read: to make much sense of them, Pico's puzzle as a whole must first be deciphered. The problem has been complicated by unreliable texts—bad in the sixteenth-century versions that scholars have usually relied on, worse at times in the two modern editions—that have kept hidden that *occulta concatenatio* between theses that Pico hinted was the key to his Roman plans.[6]

Pico was already well known when he arrived in Rome in mid-November 1486 to make final preparations for his dispute. Contemporary accounts, not all of which can be dismissed as sheer hyperbole, describe him as having astonishing study habits and powers of memory.[7] Pico came from a rich and powerful aristocratic family and had the means to pursue an unusual education. He had early classicist training at his family castle and elsewhere and by 1486 had extensive literary contacts in Italy and France. He studied church law at the University of Bologna (1477–1478) and philosophy and theology in the Universities of Ferrara (1478–1479), Padua (1480–1482), Pavia (1483–1484), and Paris (1485–1486). From his sixteenth year on, Pico was in close contact with Marsilio Ficino and his Platonic circle in Florence, spending a full year in that city in 1484–1485. By the

---

[4] Judging from a letter written while he was planning his debate, Pico's original title, if he had one, was something on the order of *Oratio ad laudes philosophiae* (Oration in Praise of Philosophy). The traditional title *Oratio de hominis dignitate* first appeared ten years after Pico's death in a corrupt German reprint of his collected works. See below, pp. 18–19 n. 50.

[5] Garin, *Scritti vari*, 23. Similar sentiments were expressed earlier by Burckhardt, Gentile, Cassirer, and a legion of lesser scholars.

[6] On earlier editions, see below, pp. 183–88.

[7] E.g., we are told in his *Vita* by his nephew that hearing a poem read just once, Pico could repeat it both backwards and forwards to everyone's amazement (*Opera*, fol. 3r). Praise of extraordinary memories was a premodern commonplace, but Pico's powers were mentioned often enough by those who knew him to merit special comment. Whether or not Pico actually had an eidetic memory is another question; cf. here the evidence on how he quoted his sources, discussed later in this work.

time of his proposed debate he was an accomplished scholar in Latin and Greek, had a growing competence in Hebrew, and had begun initial studies of Arabic and "Chaldean" (Aramaic).[8] Pico moved everywhere with a train of tutors and translators, classicists and poets, and philosophers and theologians from different "schools" who advised him. From an early date his education was self-consciously aimed at collecting material from all the battling sects of his period, which he hoped to pacify in his dispute.[9]

From scattered sources we can piece together a few initial details concerning his Vatican project. The text of the nine hundred theses was printed by Eucharius Silber in Rome on 7 December 1486, following several intense months of composition. The projected length of the debate is uncertain, but we know that Pico planned to spend the full winter of 1486–1487 in Rome and that he transferred most of his large household and library there for the project. According to a papal complaint, Pico had the theses posted in various public places in the holy city and had them published "in other parts of the world." The exact sense of the last words is uncertain, but we know that Pico sent copies, or ordered them to be sent, to all Italian universities, accompanied by his famous promise to pay the traveling expenses of any philosopher or theologian willing to come to Rome to debate him. Another copy was sent to Marsilio Ficino and was discussed in his circle in Florence, and still others were given to prominent theologians of the period.[10]

---

[8] The extent of Pico's knowledge of these last three languages when he drew up his theses is still a matter of controversy. Regarding Hebrew, Pico claimed some months before publication of the text that he could "dictate a letter not yet with praise, but without fault" [possum nondum quidem cum laude, sed citra culpam epistolam dictare.] (*Opera*, 367). In later years, his knowledge of Hebrew was apparently considerable, as we shall see in a later chapter.

[9] A poem discovered by Kristeller and ascribed to Pico—a very early work, if genuine—tells us that one of the young aristocrat's goals was "pugnantes pacis sub foedera sectas ducere" [to lead battling sects under a league of peace] (Kristeller 1965: 91). A letter that Pico sent to Ermolao Barbaro two years before publication of the nine hundred theses (*Opera*, 368–69) contains Pico's first reference to the underlying harmony of Plato and Aristotle, which was to be a central theme of his debate: "So that if you look at their words, nothing is more conflicting; if at the sense, nothing more concordant." Cf. Cicero *Academica* 2.5.5; 1.4.17–18.

[10] Publication data and Pico's offer to pay travelling expenses are found in the colophon to the nine hundred theses. Other data are drawn from his letters, *Opera*, 378, 385. Innocent VIII's complaint is found in the bull reprinted in Garin, *Scritti vari*, 63–66. On the

It was apparently Pico's aim to gather at Rome as many experts as possible on the different "nations" or "sects" of thinkers (*gentes*) and their "heresiarchs" or "sect leaders" (*heresiarchae*) covered in his dispute. He referred to his conference as an "assembly" (*consessus*), "congress" (*congressus*), and—at least before his troubles with the pope—as a "council" (*concilium*). The last term is especially suggestive, since we know that the debate was to be held "in the apostolic senate"—before the college of cardinals—with Pope Innocent VIII apparently as supreme judge.[11] The dispute was to begin no sooner than the Feast of the Epiphany (January 6), symbolic date of the submission of the pagan *gentes* to Christ in the persons of the *Magi*.[12]

Intellectuals of the early printing age still depended heavily on the oral rehearsal and transmission of ideas, and public and private disputes were common. The view that disputation was a dying medieval institution, corruptly present but alien to the creative side of Renaissance thought, rests mainly on classicist propaganda over five hundred years old. A close look at the writers who promoted this view shows that their own condemnations of disputation were far from universal or absolute.[13] The formal debates held in Ficino's Platonic circle, which included

---

discussion of the theses in Florence, see the letter addressed to Roberto Salviati in Ermolao Barbaro's letters (1943: 2:8–9; also in Dorez and Thuasne 1897: 109–11). Ficino later sent his thanks to Pico for his copy of the text—for reasons that will become clear later, with rather ambivalent praise; see Ficino, *Opera* (1576: 1:880). In his *Vita* of his uncle, Gianfrancesco Pico tells us that "non pauci et quidem celebrati theologiae doctores ceu pias et mundas prius approbaverant [quas quaestiones] eisdemque subscripserant" [not a few, and indeed distinguished doctors of theology, first approved those questions as pious and upright, and gave them their written endorsement]. Apparently one of these theologians included the bishop of Reggio (*Opera*, fol. 3v).

[11] *Opera*, 323; Garin, *Scritti vari*, 134. In the section of the *Apology* that Pico borrowed from the *Oration*, the phrase "in the apostolic senate" is conspicuously dropped (*Opera*, 115). The term "council" appears only in texts antedating Pico's troubles with the church—in one of his letters (*Opera*, 382) and in the *Commento*, on which he abandoned work about the time that the theses went to press. The pope's projected role as the debate's supreme judge is implied in the wording of the preface to the second part of the nine hundred theses; a strong papal role is also suggested in the first lines of the *Apology* and in Pope Alexander VI's 1493 bull lifting Pico's excommunication. The bull can normally be found reprinted at the front of Renaissance editions of Pico's *Opera*.

[12] On the significance of these symbols in Pico's debate, see below, pp. 43–44.

[13] On favorable attitudes towards disputation in the early classicist movement, see Gilbert (1971). Formal debates played important roles in premodern traditions in the East as well as the West, although no cross-cultural studies of the genre yet exist.

classicists and scholastics both, despite occasional antiquarian trappings, are difficult to distinguish from the disputes held regularly in the medieval university or cloister.[14]

Even in the rich environment of Renaissance debates, Pico's project was immediately recognized as exceptional. Before trying to solve his Vatican puzzle, we need to look at some of the more problematic pieces that he set before us.

To start with the obvious, there was the sheer size of Pico's project, which dwarfed any earlier known examples of medieval or Renaissance debates. In the century after Pico's death, plans for giant disputes became more common, with some proposed of truly outrageous proportions. But these were clearly conceived in Pico's shadow, with their organizers mimicking him down to details in a way shocking to modern, if not to premodern, sensibilities. From what is known of these *Pici redivivi* and their debates, it is clear that none of them had a very good idea of what Pico himself had planned at Rome.[15]

The impression that Pico's project made on Renaissance intellectuals is understandable when we look at the size of more typical scholastic debates. The public dispute of even a single thesis, like those commonly posted by religious orders on the eve of religious festivals, could go on for many hours, or in some cases for days—although here, in debates that were rule-bound and formal only in

---

[14] This is evident even in Della Torre's rapid survey of debates in the Medicean-backed Platonic circle (1902: 801–3). In Landino's *De vera nobilitate* (cited here from Di Napoli 1965: 123 n. 1), which describes discussions at the home of the Medici, the links between these discussions and scholastic dispute are strongly underlined, with the University of Paris put on equal footing with the ancient schools: "Tanta erat optimorum ingeniorum atque eruditorum vis, totque eadem de re tamque variae opiniones, tanta denique subtilitate disputatae, ut intra magnificos illos lares, non modo Academiam Lycaeumque ac postremum Porticum ipsam Athenis migrasse, sed omnem Parisiensem scholam illuc convenisse putares" [The power of genius and learning there was so great, and so many and varied were the opinions on the same topic disputed with such great subtlety, that you would have thought that not only the Academy and Lyceum and finally the school of Stoics had migrated from Athens, but that the entire Parisian school had assembled there].

[15] On a few of Pico's imitators, see Garin (1947: 2:85ff.), Nardi (1958: 283ff., 399ff., and passim), Di Napoli (1965: 81–82, 123–24 n. 2), and Zambelli (1977a, 1977b). The size of these projects grew rapidly as each later figure tried to outdo Pico and his previous imitators. The champion in terms of sheer numbers, so far as I am aware, was Jacopo Mazzoni, who in 1576 published his list of 5197 theses for his upscaled version of Pico's project (see bibliography).

theory, the original topic might be quickly lost in a flurry of related questions.[16] In the toughest regular test in medieval disputation, the quodlibetal discussion—in which debaters might sometimes literally take up any question from the floor—no more than twenty or twenty-five theses were normally covered in the usual two days of debate, with the number rising only in exceptional cases.[17] In a perverted late form of the quodlibet, to whose popularity Pico unwittingly contributed, itinerant scholars would sometimes appear at court or in university towns ready to debate any question with anybody—usually shortly thereafter falling into the inquisitor's hands or slipping back otherwise into permanent anonymity. Although these were often raucous and drawn-out affairs, no evidence suggests that more topics were actually debated in them than in the theoretically more orderly university quodlibets.[18]

---

[16] This is illustrated in a bitter debate in which Pico took part held at the home of Lorenzo de' Medici in 1489. The debate involved participants from the rival Dominican and Franciscan convents attached to Santa Maria Novella and Santa Croce and was a rematch held one week after an equally nasty conflict held "as accustomed" (*ut mos est*) on neutral turf at S. Reparata on the eve of the festival of St. John the Baptist, Florence's main patron saint. Also present besides Pico at this intended pacification rite—apparently the reason for its location at Lorenzo's—were Ficino, Poliziano, and other Florentine intellectuals. The dispute began with discussion of the thesis that "The sin of Adam is not the greatest of all sins"—recalling old conflicts between the official theologians of the rival orders, St. Thomas Aquinas and Duns Scotus—but quickly turned to broader questions with accusations of heresy flying wildly on every side. Pico made an appearance in the dispute in his savored role as *Comes Concordiae*, attempting (with amusingly scant success) to reconcile the two sides using the same strategies that he had mapped out three years earlier for his Vatican debate. The battle is described in two fascinating incunabula in a bitter propaganda war between the champions of the two camps, the Dominican Nicolaus de Mirabilibus and the Franciscan Georgius Benignus (for titles, see bibliography). These two rare volumes are among our best sources for study of the social and intellectual functions of Renaissance disputation. A modern edition and translation of them would be useful.

[17] Figures based on Glorieux's studies of quodlibets from the thirteenth and fourteenth centuries (1925–35: 2:11ff.), the only period for which the genre has been studied in detail. While the topics in certain variations of these debates were sometimes drawn from lists of *quaestiones*, *conclusiones*, *assertiones*, *theses*, etc., previously submitted by the *respondens*, no earlier examples are known that approach the scope or numbers of theses found in Pico's text.

[18] The most famous earlier figure here was Ferdinand of Cordoba, Thorndike's "boy marvel" (1923–58: 4:486–87; cf. Dorez and Thuasne 1897, 44–45). Forty years before Pico, at the age of twenty, Ferdinand wandered disputing from Spain through France and

As a last example, we know of the fairly short lists of theses left us by candidates for university degrees, for whom debates fulfilled something akin to final exams. By a stroke of luck, one such earlier list that has survived is that of Petrus Garsias, who sat on the papal commission that investigated the nine hundred theses and who answered Pico's *Apology* at the personal request of Pope Innocent VIII. Pursuing his license in theology at the University of Paris, Garsias in 1478 had posted and printed under his name forty theological and ten philosophical *assertiones*, most of them drawn conservatively from the works of Thomas Aquinas. Since this was a one-day affair, it is unlikely that more than a handful were actually debated—at some point, not unlike in a modern doctoral defense, the authorities declaring themselves satisfied and enrolling Garsias's name in the book of licensees in theology.[19] Pico's later adversary was apparently thirty-five or thirty-six at the time, not untypical for someone receiving the theological license. When we consider that Pico, a twenty-three-year-old layman, had included in his conclusions an even larger number of theses from St. Thomas—most of them theological and anything but conservative in intent—one of the reasons for Pico's nasty reception at Rome becomes less mysterious, no matter how we judge the

---

Italy, in one match at the College of Navarre reportedly responding to all questions against "fifty of the most perfect masters" before a crowd of three thousand spectators. Ferdinand was later reported to speak Latin, Greek, Hebrew, Arabic, "and many more tongues," awakening suspicions of his identity with the Antichrist (Thorndike 1944: 341–43). Critics of Pico's debate attempted from the start to associate him with this perverted quodlibetal tradition, provoking his attempts in the *Oration* and *Apology* to distinguish himself from "the many in our age" who like Gorgias of Leontini in antiquity proposed to debate not on a fixed number of questions but "on all questions on all arts" (*Opera*, 117, 324; Garin, *Scritti vari*, 138). Nevertheless, the fame of Pico's project—which despite his disclaimer proposes several methods "to the investigation and understanding of everything knowable" (a point peculiarly denied by De Lubac 1974)—was apparently the largest factor in the popularity of this disputational genre in the sixteenth century. Thus one of Pico's later imitators, Tiberio Russiliano—turning Pico's disclaimer on its head—would on occasion drop his prepared list of four hundred theses to respond "to every question, something that no one but Georgias of Leontini has done!" Describing one such series of battles in 1519, Tiberio tells us "multis continuisque diebus Patavii cathedraliter publiceque disputavimus" [I disputed in Padua continuously for many days, both from a doctor's seat and publicly] before being crowned (presumably with laurel) by the Venetian patricians (Zambelli 1977a: 514–15).

[19] Garsias's text, entitled *Assertiones theologicales apud sanctum Eustachium XXVIII Aprilis disputandae per dominum Petrum Garciam* (Paris, n.d. [1478]), is reprinted in Kieszkowski's version of the nine hundred theses (1973: 101–8).

orthodoxy of the thirteen theses initially used as a pretext to attack him.[20]

Renaissance debates could be marathon affairs, but Pico's contemporaries apparently viewed the debate of nine hundred theses to be impossible. In both the *Oration* and *Apology*, however, Pico suggested that in some sense, at least, he meant to debate them all. What he had in mind is one of the key pieces of his Vatican puzzle.

Other parts of Pico's project also broke known precedents. Some of these are suggested in the structure of the theses. Pico's text is divided into two major and numerous minor sections laid out in complex numerological patterns. (For an overview of these divisions, see the charts of the theses on pp. 204–7.) The first section contains 402 theses (originally 400) divided into twenty-eight subsections representing the opinions of the *gentes* and their *heresiarchae*. The "sect leaders" in each "nation" are grouped by subtradition or paired in several other ways, at first with the aim of sharpening contrasts between their positions.[21] But the *gentes* themselves are arranged in reverse historical order, as Pico understood it: the Latin scholastics are followed by the Arabs, the Arabs by the Greeks, the Greeks by the Chaldeans, the Chaldeans by the Egyptians, and the Egyptians by the "Hebrew Cabalist wisemen."

This quasi-historical section of the text is followed by a topical division containing 498 theses (originally 500) presented according to Pico's own opinion (*secundum opinionem propriam*). The fact that Pico endorsed all the theses in this second section has never been seriously questioned. His intentions are less obvious in the first part of the text, whose historical structure was apparently unprecedented.[22] According to standard debating practice, as *respondens* in his dispute it should have been Pico's job to defend all nine hundred theses against the opposing *arguentes* or *opponentes*. At the end of the *Apology*, however, Pico claimed that the first part of the theses not only contained true opinions that he planned to defend, but likewise

---

[20] Besides the forty-five theses that Pico gives us *secundum Thomam*, the nine hundred theses include dozens of other conclusions aimed polemically at the Dominican official theologian. Further on Pico and Thomas, see below, pp. 47–49 and passim.

[21] Thus St. Thomas is juxtaposed to his master (and for Pico, Thomas's rival) Albert the Great, Giles of Rome is matched with his traditional adversary Henry of Ghent, Averroes is opposed to his predecessor and rival Avicenna, and so on.

[22] Pico emphasizes the unorthodox nature of this section in his opening preface to the text.

> many impious doctrines of the old philosophers Averroes and Alexander [of Aphrodisias] and many of others, which—although I have always professed, asserted, and proclaimed, both publicly and privately, that they are no less alien from the true and right philosophy than from the faith—contemplating a scholastic exercise in the manner of the academies, I undertook to dispute among the learned and the few, in a secret congress [inter paucos et doctos secreto congressu].[23]

Pico's disclaimer was written as his relations with the church were becoming more dangerous every day, and it is at least reasonable to suspect in it special pleading. Indeed, what had become a "secret congress" by the end of the *Apology*—which Pico claimed was written in twenty hectic nights—in the text's opening pages is clearly announced as a "public assembly"! Despite such inconsistencies, Innocent VIII eventually accepted Pico's disclaimer, which Giovanni Di Napoli reemphasized three decades ago in an influential study of Pico's thought.[24] All earlier studies, however, and even some later ones like Kieszkowski's, simply ignore Pico's words, portraying all nine hundred theses as equally representative of his views.

This problem is complicated by the fact that scores of theses in the work's historical part are in sharp conflict. Thus theses ascribed to Averroes oppose others from Avicenna; propositions given "according to Thomas" contradict theses ascribed to Albert the Great or Duns Scotus; conclusions from St. Thomas are in violent internal conflict; and so on. Since no one has ever proposed a way to distinguish what Pico endorsed in this section from what he opposed, historians who have quoted from it indiscriminately have helped give birth to a large family of warring "Pico's."[25] Partly for this reason, studies of Pico's work are in a more confused state than those of nearly any other major Renaissance thinker. No consistent interpretation of Pico's thought is possible until this part of his Roman puzzle is solved.

---

[23] *Opera*, 237.

[24] Di Napoli (1965). Innocent's bull banning Pico's debate acknowledges the distinction between the work's two parts but nevertheless objects to heretical doctrines in both sections. The bull is reprinted in Garin, *Scritti vari*, 63–66.

[25] A partial list of the scholars who have abused the evidence in this fashion includes Cassirer, Garin, Semprini, Anagnine, Dulles, Boas, Nardi, Monnerjahn, and Kieszkowski. P. O. Kristeller (1965: 60) also leaned towards the traditional view of Pico's text, but he showed greater caution on this point than earlier scholars.

Judged from just about any perspective, the scope of Pico's text is impressive. The nine hundred theses include propositions on moral philosophy, logic, metaphysics, physics, astrology, magic, numerology, theology, epistemology, physiology, and a half dozen other fields. Single propositions deal with questions as diverse as why Germans are fair in color and whether or not antipodes exist on the far side of the earth. There are theses on the figures of the syllogism, on the sins of Sodom, on the order of Aristotle's writings, on the visibility (and invisibility) of demons, and on the interpretation of dreams and prophecy. Others deal with the nature of prime matter, with the evolution of languages, with the problem of motion, with the possibility of creating mankind from "putrefaction" (decaying matter), and with the date of the end of the world.

Lists like this just scratch the surface. Answering his critics, who complained that he had needlessly piled up theses *ad ostentationem numeri*, Pico made two remarkable claims. The first was that his theses included "all the most ambiguous and controversial questions on which the principal schools battle." Far from multiplying propositions unnecessarily, he had divided his topics into as few headings as possible. Had he broken them into their finer parts, as others did, his theses would have grown into a truly incalculable number. Indeed, just one of his theses, in which he promised to reconcile Plato and Aristotle completely, could have easily been divided into six hundred headings or more.[26]

Pico did not mean for these remarks to be taken lightly. Supporting evidence can, in fact, usually be found that the opposing theses in the first part of the text were heatedly debated in one or more of the intellectual circles in which Pico moved. Part of the unique value of the theses lies in the insights they provide into these controversies, relatively few of which have ever been discussed in the historical literature.

Pico's second boast was that his text brought forward many other things that were "utterly unknown and untried" (*incognita prorsus et intentata*).[27] In this class were theses drawn from late-ancient Platonic and Aristotelian commentaries not yet widely known to Pico's classicist or scholastic contemporaries;[28] esoteric doctrines ascribed to Zoroaster, Orpheus, Mercury (Hermes) Trismegistus, Pythagoras, and other of the so-called ancient theologians (*prisci theologi*); a comprehensive

---

[26] *Opera*, 331, 124; Garin, *Scritti vari*, 162–64.

[27] *Opera*, 331, 124; Garin, *Scritti vari*, 162.

[28] The most important of these were previously unstudied texts of Simplicius and Proclus; see my introductory notes to theses 17.1–9 and 24.1–55.

system of natural magic and another of numerological prophecy; and, as the planned highlight of his debate, the outlines of what Pico announced as a "new philosophy" (*philosophia nova*), "thought out in Aristotelian and Platonic philosophy," capable of resolving "every proposed question on natural and divine things."[29]

It was in the theses as well that Pico first introduced the Cabala[30] into the mainstream of Renaissance thought. Pico's approach to this obscure Jewish mystical and magical tradition illustrates the massive preparations underlying every side of his Vatican project. In readying himself for this part of his debate, Pico commissioned Latin translations of an enormous body of Hebrew and Aramaic texts from one of his early Jewish tutors, the Christian convert Flavius Mithridates. Chaim Wirszubski, who spent over two decades analyzing the remnants of these translations, has estimated their original length as some 5,500 folio pages long—approximately fifteen times the length of the *Aeneid*.[31] These translations were begun (but, despite Wirszubski's claims, were far from completed) in the hectic six months preceding publication of the theses—while Pico also studied original Hebrew and Aramaic texts with Flavius and began studies under him of Arabic as well.[32]

In roughly the same period Pico had another of his Jewish informants, the distinguished philosopher Elia del Medigo, provide him with fresh Latin translations of previously known and unknown texts of Averroes and of other Arabic philosophers, which in the absence of the Arabic originals had survived in medieval Hebrew translations. Pico also had Elia collect and comment on a wide range of technical conflicts in Arabic philosophy that Pico meant to resolve at Rome.[33]

---

[29] See below, pp. 18–25.

[30] Throughout this study, I have used the modern transliteration "Kabbalah" or its cognates when discussing Hebrew traditions and "Cabala" (used by Pico) when speaking of the Christian transformations of those traditions that Pico introduced into Western thought.

[31] Wirszubski (1989: 11).

[32] On the degree to which Pico did or did not use Mithridates' translations, see my introductory note to theses 28.1–47. On Flavius in general, see Gaffarel (1651), Starrabba (1878), Cassuto (1918, 1934), Secret (1965), and the other studies by Wirszubski noted in my bibliography. A few additional papers are listed in Dell'Aqua and Münster (1965).

[33] On Elia and Pico's other Jewish tutors and informants, see Cassuto (1918). Some additional bibliography can be found in the notes to Dell'Aqua and Münster (1965). The location of manuscripts prepared by Elia for Pico are listed in the appendix to Kristeller (1965). Kieszkowski's long article on Elia and Pico (1964) is erratic but at present must be consulted for its textual evidence. For an update of Elia's interactions with Pico, see Mahoney (1997).

Pico's most surprising use of sources came in his handling of the Platonic tradition, whose doctrines he claimed he was submitting for the first time in many centuries to public dispute.[34] At Rome, Pico planned to propose an interpretation of the Platonic tradition that was explicitly at odds with that of Marsilio Ficino—of whom in 1486, at any rate, Pico had an extremely low opinion as both a philosopher and Platonic commentator. In his own reading of the Platonic tradition, Pico relied heavily on post-Plotinian Greek scholastics (especially Porphyry, Iamblichus, and Proclus) who had not yet been systematically discussed by Ficino; he also drew heavily on the Greek text of Plotinus's *Enneads*, which Pico thought that Ficino interpreted especially badly.[35]

The fact that intellectual conflict divided the two best-known Italian philosophers of the period has long been known to specialists on their thought, although in Renaissance studies as a whole Pico is still routinely miscast as Ficino's "disci-

[34] *Opera*, 325, 119; Garin, *Scritti vari*, 142.

[35] This despite the fact that, according to Ficino, it was Pico who years earlier had first urged him to begin translating Plotinus. Ficino is criticized openly in the *Commento* and covertly in the nine hundred theses (for evidence, see, e.g., thesis 5>31 and note), both of which were composed at roughly the same time as the *Oration*, in the last half of 1486. On Plotinus in particular, see, e.g., Pico's rude remarks at the beginning of the *Commento* (Garin, *Scritti vari*, 462) concerning the confusion of a certain "great Platonist" in interpreting a key position in Plotinus. Correspondence between Pico and Ficino in the same period again alludes obscurely to tensions between the two philosophers that in part involved Plotinus (see Kristeller 1937: 2:33–35; cf. *Opera*, 367–68). With this in mind, when in the *Oration* and *Apology* Pico praises that "divine Plotinus" who writes "with a learned indirectness of speech that the sweating Platonists (*sudantes Platonici*) scarcely understand," it does not take much imagination to guess which "sweating Platonist" Pico had most in mind (*Opera*, 325, 118; Garin, *Scritti vari*, 142). (The phrase *sudantes Platonici* is not an echo of ancient sources like Porphyry's *Life of Plotinus*, increasing the likelihood that the phrase was specifically aimed at Ficino.) It is interesting to note that shortly after the nine hundred theses were published, Ficino temporarily abandoned work on the *Enneads*; according to Kristeller, he did not take up the task again until 1489, in the meantime hastily translating previously neglected texts from Porphyry, Iamblichus, Proclus, and other representatives of the post-Plotinian Platonic tradition, which Pico had tried to stake out as his personal turf in the nine hundred theses. On Ficino's general activity in this period, see Kristeller (1937: 1:cxxvi ff.); cf. Marcel (1956), who occasionally differs with Kristeller on dating Ficino's texts. In a later study (1965: 66), Professor Kristeller comments that Pico not only first moved Ficino to translate Plotinus but that "the same may be true of some of his other later translations"—i.e., those involving the late Neo-Platonists noted above.

ple." Using the evidence in the nine hundred theses, we can uncover some of the deepest grounds of their conflicts.

Tracking the sources of Pico's text often leads us into bizarre textual terrain—underscoring the enormous distances separating Renaissance from modern views of texts.[36] Pico's theses presented "according to Zoroaster and his Chaldean interpreters," for example, can only be loosely tied to the *Chaldean Oracles* known in Greek sources to Pico's contemporaries and to modern scholars. Writing to Ficino, Pico boasted that he possessed the original "Chaldean" version of these sources, which supplied "complete and absolute" (*integra et absoluta*) what in Greek was "full of faults and mutilated" (*mendosa et mutila*).[37] Pico's claim was excitedly discussed by Renaissance classicists from the fifteenth to seventeenth centuries, but it has been overlooked by most modern students of the *Oracles*. Since the *Oracles* apparently originated in Greek, it would be interesting to know what texts Pico had in hand; in my commentary to Pico's theses, I introduce evidence that forgeries by Flavius Mithridates probably figured here.[38]

A second example is even stranger. In the section of the text devoted to the Platonists, we find eight theses attributed to "Adeland the Arab," who Pico claimed was Plotinus's fellow student in Egypt under Ammonius Saccas (third century CE).[39] Both external and internal evidence, however, clearly show that

---

[36] In judging the evidence that follows, it can hardly be claimed that Pico's textual scholarship was substandard by Renaissance criteria, since he was consistently ranked among the *best* scholars of his times by contemporaries including Marsilio Ficino, Angelo Poliziano, Ermolao Barbaro, and Aldo Manuzio. Poliziano, in fact, who is often styled the "father" of modern philology, was not only Pico's best friend but—according to Poliziano himself—his philosophical disciple as well. Pico's textual scholarship was also lavishly praised by a long line of sixteenth-century classicists and religious reformers starting with Erasmus and More. The suggestion is that Renaissance philology was far less "modern" than is frequently claimed.

[37] *Opera,* 367.

[38] See my introductory note to theses 8>1–15.

[39] See theses 21.1–8. Pico announced his discovery of these theses in a letter written to Ficino late in the summer of 1486, *Opera*, 367–68. After boasting of other Hebrew, Chaldean, and Arabic discoveries that he had recently made, Pico mentions this text as something closer to what (with typical condescension) he represents as Ficino's narrower Platonic interests: "Et quod te magis tanget, Adelandi cuiusdam, qui sub Ammonio Plotini magistro in Aegypto philosophatus est, multae sunt quaestiones" [And what concerns you more, there are many questions of a certain Adeland, who philosophized in Egypt under Ammonius, the teacher of Plotinus].

Adeland the Arab was Adelard of Bath, the twelfth-century Englishman![40] While the exact sources of this strange metamorphosis are unknown, hints exist that fragments of Adelard's writings may have come to Pico in a loose Hebrew adaptation. Here again there are reasons to suspect a sinister role for Flavius Mithridates, whose reputation in the Renaissance as something of a con man was apparently well deserved. Pico's involvement with this colorful figure—who liked to style himself as Pico's would-be but scorned lover—constitutes one of the strangest personal stories of the period, although it is one that is still far from being completely understood.[41]

---

[40] It should be noted that "Adeland" was simply a common medieval variation on "Adelard."

[41] Pico suggests that his theses from "Adeland the Arab" came from a text written in Arabic (*Opera,* 367), a language that he had begun to study with Flavius Mithridates in the summer of 1486. It is doubtful that Pico could read much Arabic by the time that he compiled the theses, however—the depth of Flavius's own command of Arabic has been questioned on solid grounds (Levi della Vida 1939: 91–97)—and it is more likely that they were drawn from one or more known Hebrew adaptations of Adelard's *Quaestiones naturales* that Pico *assumed* derived from Arabic, a common route for Arabic sources to pass into the Renaissance. Gollancz (1920) has published two versions of those adaptations—there are others—that suggest ways in which in Pico's mind, at least, Adelard could have reasonably been transformed into Plotinus's fellow student. Both these versions shift the setting of Adelard's work from England to the mysterious Middle East; the longer of the two manuscripts is filled with exotic place names (Kush, Tiberias, Tyre, Philistia, Sidon, Zoan, Rameses, Egypt, etc.) that give the text the aura of an Alexandrian mystical treatise. Adelard's metamorphosis into an Arab presumably derived from similar corruptions, following his comments concerning the "Arabic wisdom" that he acquired in Spain. The longer of the two sources that Gollancz provides refers several times to Ibn Ezra (twelfth century CE), but even if such clues were present in whatever manuscripts Pico used, at that point in his studies he could not have read them without the help of Flavius, whose predilection for twisting texts to match Pico's fancies and Flavius's own self-interests has been amply documented by Wirszubski. Since the *Quaestiones naturales* and its Hebrew adaptations both contain legitimate Neo-Platonic doctrines, and since Pico believed that Plotinus acquired his wisdom in Alexandria from Ammonius Saccas—the first writer noted in traditional genealogies of the Neo-Platonists—by premodern standards of textual attribution it would not have been unreasonable to represent Adelard as Plotinus's fellow student. It is noteworthy that at the beginning of bk. 3, chap. 15 of Pico's posthumously published *Disputations against Divinatory Astrology,* we find a long passage on the tides attributed to "Adeland out of the opinions of the Saracens"—clearly drawn this time from the Latin text of the *Quaestiones naturales.* By the time that the *Disputations* was written, however, Flavius was long out of the picture, and Pico had presumably had time to discover his earlier embarrassing error.

We know more about Pico's sources than about those of nearly any other major Renaissance thinker. We possess two inventories of his famous library, one of the most varied collections of the early printing age; much data on the manuscripts that he used; and, in a surprising number of cases, those manuscripts themselves, often accompanied by important marginal notes in Pico's own hand.[42] When joined with the theses, this evidence provides us with rare insights into the strange transformations commonly worked on their sources by Renaissance intellectuals—transformations that must be understood, in any case, to make much sense of Pico's Roman puzzle.

One final feature of Pico's theses meriting special comment is their language. Pico's text comes packed with obscure symbols, conflicting technical terms from the warring sects, and strange Neo-Latinisms of Pico's own invention. The problems in deciphering the text do not arise simply from our historical distance from the work. Innocent VIII's first bull on the theses, ordering temporary suspension of Pico's debate, also complained of the text's "new unfamiliar vocabulary" and of its "unheard of novelty of terms."[43] In order to make even the barest sense of hundreds of theses, we must first track down Pico's exact sources, or failing that attempt to reconstruct his meaning from evidence that he intentionally scattered about the text. Systematic motives lay in part behind the peculiar shifts in language in the theses, which present one of the most formidable barriers to reconstructing Pico's Roman plans.

The pope's reaction to Pico's proposed debate was swift and harsh. Much sterile discussion has arisen over the orthodoxy or heterodoxy of thirteen theses that, in an advisory judgment, the papal commission censured with varying degrees of harshness. When Innocent VIII's papal hammer came down, however it came down on Pico's project as a whole. In a bull signed 4 August 1487, but not published until four months later, Innocent complained of heretical theological theses in the text presented "according to the opinion both of the count himself and of others," and of theses that "savored" of heresy or were "offensive to pious ears." But he was particularly incensed by propositions "renovating the errors of pagan philosophers," by those "cherishing the deceits of the Jews," and by others

[42] On Pico's library, see Calori Cesis (1897) and Kibre (1936). Manuscripts used by Pico that later found their way into the Vatican libraries are surveyed by Mercati (1938) and, in the case of Mithridates' translations, are analyzed in Wirszubski's works; on this topic, see also Levi della Vida (1939). A list of extant manuscripts of Pico's writings and some once owned by him is found in the appendix to Kristeller (1965).

[43] Dorez and Thuasne (1897: 114–17).

promoting "certain arts, disguising themselves as natural philosophy, harmful to the Catholic faith and human kind, sharply damned by the canons and doctrines of Catholic doctors."[44]

In the end, it was Pico's esoteric theses that gave him the most trouble—his conclusions on the *prisci theologi* and later Greek Neo-Platonists, which interpreted pagan religious language allegorically; his Cabalistic theses, which he ironically proposed as part of a final plan to convert the Jews; and his magical theses, which, despite all disclaimers, were always open to suspicions of demonology and witchcraft. While Innocent was initially conciliatory towards Pico himself—this too later changed—his fury in condemning the nine hundred theses is impossible to mistake. All copies of Pico's text were to be burned within three days; excommunication was threatened for anyone presuming "to read, to copy, to print; or to have read, copied, or printed; or to hear others reading it in whatever fashion." Included were detailed instructions for copying Innocent's bull and having it read at Mass in every city and diocese in the Christian world.[45]

Earlier local bans of printed books are known, but Hirsch is apparently justified in labeling this the "first broad inquisitional action in the history of printing, heralding the promulgations of the *indices librorum prohibitorum.*" It was no accident that in the same year Innocent ordered the first universal prepublication review of printed books known.[46] That nearly all copies of the theses were in fact burned is suggested by the book's extreme rarity after 1487, despite an early reprint—apparently from that year—and evidence of the book's initial wide circulation. Because of Innocent's ban on discussing the text, little external evidence has survived concerning the goals of Pico's project. Our knowledge of his planned debating procedures must also be reconstructed from sparse internal evidence in the text itself.

It is one goal of this study to show that Pico's plans can nevertheless be reconstructed, drawing on four kinds of evidence: hints from Pico's other works, which

---

[44] Garin, *Scritti vari*, 64–65. Publication of the bull was delayed until December 1487, when Pico was in flight from Rome to Paris.

[45] Garin, *Scritti vari*, 65. The events leading to Pico's own excommunication are too complex to discuss here. But evidence suggests that they may indeed have included Pico's publication of the backdated *Apology* after his formal abjuration—a fact much disputed in the literature.

[46] Hirsch (1967: 89). The text of the nine hundred theses itself was never included on the *Index*, however, as is sometimes claimed. See Reusch (1883: 1:59), who is miscited on this point by Edgar Wind (1954: 412).

have not previously been studied with this end in mind; guidance from a key series of theses in which Pico sketches his promised "new philosophy" in a highly rigorous, if often rather peculiar, language; evidence from study of Pico's sources; and suggestions arising from topical rearrangements of the theses—facilitated by computerization of Pico's text—that help uncover that *occulta concatenatio* between them that he suggested was the key to decoding his Roman puzzle.

Active in the first stages of the printing revolution, Pico was a philosopher with a traditional veneration of texts and authorities—and one with a broader range of texts at hand than nearly any known writer before him. Reflecting the unique times in which he worked, Pico ranks among the most extreme syncretists in history. In the nine hundred theses we can hence search for clues to the syncretic forces that helped shape the religious and philosophical systems of thousands of years of similar thinkers, East and West.[47]

Writing a century and a quarter later, the Italian philosopher Tommaso Campanella perceptively noted that "Pico was truly a noble and learned genius, but he philosophized more in the words of others than in nature." In contrast, Campanella boasted that he himself learned more from the anatomy of an ant or herb than from all the books that had ever been written. These were the conceits of the early scientific age, and they cannot be taken literally. Campanella's magical

---

[47] Syncretic tendencies are a diagnostic feature of all scholastic traditions, and many earlier Latins scholastics like Albert the Great might be considered no less extreme in those tendencies than Pico. However, medieval figures like Albert were generally far more dependent on secondary and tertiary sources than Pico, who had access to a broad range of original Greek, Hebrew, and to a lesser extent Arabic texts not widely available to his medieval counterparts. Pico also had access to the full spectrum of high-scholastic traditions that emerged in the two centuries separating his work from Albert's and went much further than the latter writer, whose compiling tendencies were typical of earlier stages of scholastic movements, in integrating his sources in a self-consistent fashion. No premodern syncretists outside the West are known whose projects even remotely approached the scale of Pico's. Cf. here the relatively narrow range of traditions synthesized by Lin Chao-en, whom Berling (1980) represents as the archetypal syncretist of the Ming Dynasty (1368–1644). Henderson (1984: 41; 1991: 209), whose studies span over two thousand years of Chinese history, acknowledges the narrower range of Eastern as compared to Western syncretic traditions, explicitly invoking on this point the example of Pico's work. There are countless parallels in the evolution of syncretic traditions in China, India, Europe, and other premodern societies, as pointed out later in this study. But in the sheer *quantity* of traditions available for synthesis, Pico and his Renaissance contemporaries won out handily over their Eastern counterparts.

views of the cosmos were cut from the same cloth as Pico's, and in the same passage we find him claiming that he had not only read but memorized the writings of "all authorities."[48] We may hence wonder how far Campanella, locked as he wrote these lines in his Neapolitan dungeon, truly escaped the "words of others" to read directly from the book of nature.

But Campanella's sentiments were strong ones that in the long run turned out to be revolutionary. Neither Pico nor any of his contemporaries could have easily conceived them. Preparing for his Vatican debate, Pico represented a far more ancient style of thinking that was entering its final and most extreme levels of expression. In the nine hundred theses we can observe that ancient style of thought and search as well for the origins of those newer sentiments—representing one of the most profound intellectual transformations that ever took place in human history.

ii. Pico's Correlative System (His "New Philosophy")

Some first clues to Pico's debating plans are found in a section of the theses provocatively entitled "Seventy-one paradoxical conclusions according to my own opinion introducing new doctrines in philosophy," which internal evidence shows originally contained seventy-two propositions.[49] To distinguish these from another set of "paradoxical conclusions," Pico referred to this set elsewhere as his "paradoxical dogmatizing conclusions." It is in this section that we find the outlines of Pico's promised "new philosophy," which turns out to be an extreme version of a kind of correlative system associated universally with syncretic thinkers, East and West.

Pico underscored the importance of this section in a key passage of the *Oration*. The fact that Renaissance historians have routinely bypassed this passage without comment suggests how distant modern interest in the *Oration* has remained from Pico's original aims in writing the text.[50] After boasting of his in-

---

[48] Campanella, *Opere* (1956: 972).

[49] As was the case elsewhere, one thesis was removed from this section while the work was in press, almost surely for theological reasons. See thesis 9>4 and note.

[50] Modern interest in the *Oration*, following Burckhardt's lead in the nineteenth century, has almost exclusively focused on the light the work sheds on the "philosophy of man" that supposedly emerged in the period. This tendency has reinforced continued use of the mistitle *Oratio de hominis dignitate* (Oration on the Dignity of Man), which was applied to the text long after Pico's death. Pico's title, if he had one, was something on the

tended reconciliation in his debate of Plato and Aristotle, Pico makes an even more ambitious claim. He addresses the "Fathers" at Rome—the pope and cardinals and those we can consider the current "heresiarchs" of the warring schools:

> In second place, what I have thought out in Aristotelian and Platonic philosophy I have brought together in seventy-two new physical and metaphysical doctrines. If anyone holds them he will be able—unless I am wrong, which will be shown to me soon—to resolve every proposed question on natural and divine things by a far different method than we are taught by that philosophy read in the schools and cultivated by the learned of this age. Nor, Fathers, should anyone be astonished that in my first years, at a tender age at which it is hardly permitted, as some claim, for me to read the treatises of others, I wish to bring forward a new philosophy (*novam afferre velle philosophiam*). Let him praise it if it is defended, or damn it if it is refuted.[51]

Pico's "new philosophy" lay in a traditional, though highly exaggerated, Neo-Platonic framework, with special ties to those high-syncretic Platonic systems developed in antiquity after Plotinus by Porphyry, Iamblichus, Syrianus, Proclus, and related figures. Schematic versions of these pagan scholastic systems could be studied in the Middle Ages in Latin translations of Proclus's *Elements of Theology* and fragments of his other works, and indirectly in Latin versions of Pseudo-Dionysius and the anonymous *Book of Causes*, which were both closely tied to Proclus's thought. But Pico drew not only from these texts but from what remained of their earlier Greek sources—and was the first known Latin philosopher since antiquity to approach Proclus's massive *Platonic Theology* in anything

---

order of *Oratio ad laudes philosophiae* (Oration in Praise of Philosophy), as suggested in a letter written just before his debate (quoted below, p. 40). No title appears on the copy of the early draft of the work published (with some errors) by Garin (repr. 1961) from the extremely faded manuscript preserved in MS Palatino 885 of the Biblioteca Nazionale in Florence. Garin attributes the manuscript to the fifteenth century, Kristeller (1965: 113) to the sixteenth. The title *De humanae naturae praestantia dissertatio* (Discourse on the Preeminence of Human Nature) assigned to the early draft by Kristeller comes from a late catalog entry but is not given as a title in the manuscript itself. The title *De hominis dignitate*, so far as I have been able to find, first showed up in a corrupt 1504 Strassburg reprint of Pico's *Opera*, edited by Jacob Wimpheling and Hieronymus Emser. Like all other early versions of Pico's collected works, the Strassburg edition omitted the nine hundred theses, decontextualizing the *Oration* and allowing its ready transformation into a so-called humanist document.

[51] *Opera*, 326; cf. 119–20; Garin, *Scritti vari*, 146.

approximating its original exegetical spirit.[52] What makes Pico's use of these systems interesting is his heavy reliance on syncretic methods embedded in them as the grounds of his announced method "to resolve every proposed question on natural and divine things."

Leaving details for later, we need to look at only three basic (and not particularly "new") elements of Pico's "new philosophy" before approaching his underlying goals and methods at Rome.

Cosmic emanationism

In Pico's system, God did not create the universe directly but acted through a complex series of intermediaries. In the relatively simple pattern presented in Pico's "paradoxical dogmatizing conclusions," God created only the first hypostasis, which Pico indifferently labeled the "intellect," "intellectual nature," "angelic mind," "angel," or "first created mind," syncretically conflating the technical terms of a wide range of traditions.[53] The intellect then created "soul," which in turn informed the lower realms of nature. Elsewhere in the theses, when Pico attempted to harmonize more complex hierarchical concepts—the Neo-Platonic

---

[52] Petrus Balbus first translated the *Platonic Theology* for Nicholas of Cusa a few years before the latter's death in 1454; on this translation, which Pico did not use, see Saffrey (1987). It is well known that Cusanus was heavily influenced by Proclus's schematic *Elements of Theology*, which was widely available in medieval Latin versions; despite Balbus's translation, however, no evidence exists that Cusanus was much interested in the central exegetical and mythological concerns of the *Platonic Theology*, which lay at the center of Pico's theses *secundum Proclum*. The situation is more complex in respect to Marsilio Ficino, whose interests in this side of Proclus's thought have been rightly emphasized in a number of studies by Michael Allen (1983, 1984, 1987, 1989, and others). For our purposes, what appears most interesting here is that all of Ficino's translations from Proclus and other post-Plotinean Neo-Platonists, as well as the two most clearly Proclean of Ficino's own works studied by Allen (Ficino's commentaries on the *Parmenides* and *Phaedrus*), appeared *after* and not before the nine hundred theses, in which Pico first strongly underscored the views of those writers. Indeed, Pico not only claimed precedence in the *Oration* and *Apology* in debating those views—a claim whose polemical intent was not lost on Ficino—but drew more than a hundred of his theses from Proclus alone, making the latter writer by far the single most important source in the nine hundred theses. Further on Pico and Proclus, see my introductory note to theses 24.1–55.

[53] Invoking the so-called double-truth, "theologically speaking" Pico also referred to the first hypostasis using the plural forms "angels," "intelligences," or "intellects," etc. On Pico's use of the double-truth, see below, pp. 61–63.

henads, the Cabalistic *sefirot*, various levels of soul, and so on—his emanationist schemes became far more elaborate, as we shall see later.

Harmonizing his emanationism with the *creatio ex nihilo* demanded by Christian dogma presented Pico with no real problems, as one might initially expect. Earlier Latin scholastics, drawing directly or indirectly from Proclus's *Elements of Theology*, had worked out the standard reconciliation of this conflict, arguing that the creative activity of each emanated being could be rightly attributed "in some more eminent mode" to each higher entity creating it, with the chain of causation leading back to, and ultimately summed up in, God.[54] In his Vatican debate Pico planned to use this strategy to oppose Thomas Aquinas's attacks on emanationism head on.[55] In the *Commento*, Pico contemptuously dismissed Marsilio Ficino's meeker compromise between emanationism and creationism, marveling that his rival held "that according to Plato our soul is immediately produced by God, which is opposed no less to the sect of Proclus than to that of Plotinus."[56] In the *Heptaplus*, which Pico composed while he was still in deep trouble with the church, he did not hesitate to use emanationist language even in interpreting the opening creation myth in Genesis.[57]

Cosmic proportions and correspondences

Pico's was also a highly correlative system, in the sense that everything standing on any one level of reality reappeared "in some mode" on every other. The concept that "all things exist in all things in their own mode" (*omnia sunt in omnibus modo suo*) can be taken as the central principle of later Neo-Platonism, and Pico

---

[54] See Proclus's *Elements of Theology*, prop. 56, and Dodds' commentary (1963: 54, 230). Dodds cites supporting texts from Dietrich of Freiberg and Albert the Great, both of whom also used this strategy.

[55] See thesis 2.17 and note.

[56] Cf. Garin, *Scritti vari*, 466, whose edition follows variant texts that read "Porphiro" here instead of "Plotino."

[57] *Opera*, 3; Garin, *Scritti vari*, 176. Pico tells us that in Genesis Moses "de rerum omnium emanatione a deo de gradu, de numero, de ordine partium mundanarum altissime philosophatur" [philosophizes in a supreme way concerning the emanation from God of the gradation, number, and order of the parts of the world]. Scholastic reconciliations of creationism and emanationism were so common by Pico's time that his words here would have hardly raised the eyebrows of his most powerful theological critics. Craven's attempts (1981: 109) to dismiss this and other emanationist passages in Pico's work—on the implied grounds that Pico could not have held such unorthodox views—cannot be supported.

was prepared to discuss the concept repeatedly in his debate.[58] Pico represented the proportions and correspondences in the universe in a series of striking linguistic reversals typical of his *philosophia nova*:

> 3>38.[59] In souls of an inferior sort, reason exists through the mode of sense. In superior souls, sense exists through the mode of reason.
>
> 3>41. Just as common sense consists in the cognition of accidental qualities and of material quantity, so reason consists in the cognition of substantial qualities and of formal quantity—with the proportion observed that that one acts sensually, this one rationally.
>
> 3>52. Knowledge concerning God, man, and prime matter is the same, and whoever has knowledge of one will have it of the rest—with the proportion observed of the extreme to the extreme, of the middle to the extremes, and of the extremes to the middle.

Each step up the hierarchy of being was accompanied by an increase in the perfection of individual properties and by their progressive "reciprocal penetration" (*ad invicem penetratio*)[60] until the height of perfection and unity was reached in God. Like his Greek predecessors, Pico pictured this movement in mathematical terms. At Rome he planned to exploit the symmetries of the cosmos in "something else *new*, the *ancient* method of philosophizing through numbers"[61]—one of several of his methods leading to "the investigation and understanding of everything knowable." In his "paradoxical dogmatizing conclusions," Pico represented the cosmic descent from unity to multiplicity in mathematical metaphors:

---

[58] Cf. theses 24.17, 7a>30–31, 7a>35, etc. Wirszubski (1989: 100ff.) has pointed to a number of passages where a related concept (*quodlibet in quolibet*) was interpolated by Flavius Mithridates into his translations for Pico of kabbalistic texts. Wirszubski credits this concept to the influence of Nicholas of Cusa, reflecting an historiographical tradition dating back to Cassirer. The concept was, in fact, a medieval commonplace, with countless parallels in non-Western scholastic traditions. I discuss the syncretic origins and functions of the concept below, pp. 85–89.

[59] Section and thesis numbers in Pico's historical theses are separated in my edition by a period (1.1, 18.47, etc.) and in his theses given "according to his own opinion," as here, by a pointed bracket (1>1, 11>71, etc.).

[60] Cf. thesis 6>6, inspired by the Latin *Book of Causes*.

[61] *Opera*, 326, 120; Garin, *Scritti vari*, 146 (emphasis added). Pico's phrasing here reflects the common premodern equation of originality with restoral.

3>36. Just as the intellect multiplies the unity of God, so the soul quantifies and extends the multiplicity of the intellect.

Numerology aside, the problem was to find the right language to suggest the simultaneous identity and nonidentity of corresponding properties standing on different cosmological levels. One common scholastic device that Pico used was to systematically vary the adjectives or adverbs modifying some base term:

3>1. Just as propertied existence is preceded by quidditative existence, so quidditative existence is preceded by unial existence.

5>47. Providence exists statutorily in God, ordinatively in intelligence, executively in the soul, denunciatively in the heavens, determinatively in the whole universe.[62]

What this method could not easily represent were the differences in the degree of "reciprocal penetration" of properties located on different hierarchical levels. At the opposing poles of God and the soul Pico's solution was straightforward. Contradictions or contradictory things (*contradictoria*) exist only in the extended realm of the soul, but in the "unial nature"—here meaning God—all such distinctions are resolved:

3>15. Contradictions coincide in the unial nature.

3>18. The incompatibility of contradictions first shows up in the soul, since it is the first quantity, positing part beyond part.

Pico had more problems representing the intermediate level of unity in the "intellectual nature" located between God and the soul. He made several tries:

3>13. Contradictions in the intellectual nature are compatible.

3>14. Granted that the preceding conclusion is true, it is more properly said that in the intellectual nature there are no contradictions, than that they are compatible.

---

[62] Thorndike (1923–58: 4:495) singles out this thesis for particular scorn for its scholastic character. Among other ends, the distinctive rhythms, stereotyped linguistic reversals, and numerological structures found in the nine hundred theses served implicit mnemonic functions; given the complex ways in which we will find that Pico planned to "collate" theses in his debate, it is in any case certain that he memorized the text.

3>17. In the intellect there is this and that, but not this beyond that.

3>24. It cannot be said that there are ideas in the intellect, for the sake of an example that fire, water, and air are three ideas, but it must be said that they are threefold.

Pico's struggles here with language might be viewed as the *reductio ad absurdum* of an extreme linguistic realism. In fact, however, part of his aim was to point to deep limitations in language. The sharp distinctions of verbal discourse only apply to things in the soul and in the realms informed by the soul, where part exists simply "beyond part." In superior realms, these distinctions break down—in the intellectual nature partially, in God totally. Thus although correspondence of some sort exists between the soul and God, that correspondence cannot lie between individual properties in their natures—since in God these properties are indistinguishable—but only between the whole of God's "simple" unity and the "extended" unity in the soul. This idea stands behind the language of a number of strangely worded mystical theses like the following:

3>43. The act by which the angelic and rational nature is bestowed with the greatest happiness is an act neither of the intellect nor of the will, but is the union of the unity that exists in the otherness of the soul with the unity that exists without otherness.

Pico's belief that ordinary language could not represent the nature of things on the highest levels of reality explains his apparent endorsement of nominalistic views in a number of his theses given "according to his own opinion"—despite the fact that other parts of his system are in violent opposition to that tradition. It also explains his planned rejection at Rome of the universality of the law of noncontradiction ("A cannot be both A and not-A")—the foundation of traditional Aristotelian logic—which with earlier Neo-Platonizing scholastics he claimed was only valid on the lowest levels of reality.[63]

Cosmic conversion

Finally, as suggested in the mystical conclusion just quoted, Pico's "new philosophy" made much of the Neo-Platonic "conversion" or return of emanated

[63] On theses in Pico's text of a nominalist cast, see 3>2–7 and note. On his rejection of the law of noncontradiction, see thesis 2.32 and note.

beings to God—in effect the reverse of the process of emanation. Pico's mysticism did not end with his plan to debate mystical theses at Rome, which might be mistaken for a purely intellectual exercise. That mysticism was, in fact, central to the deepest goals of his debate, whose planned location at the spiritual center of the Latin world was not accidental.

iii. Syncretism and Correlative Thought: Pico's Resolution of the "Being" and "One" Controversy

The significance of Pico's "new philosophy" cannot lie simply in his adoption of these three ancient principles—emanation, proportion, and conversion—that were part of medieval thought long before the Greek sources that he used could be studied directly. What is interesting is the exaggerated way that he developed those principles. For our present purposes, the most important of them is the concept of cosmological proportion or correspondence. What finally lets us crack Pico's Roman puzzle is the utter consistency with which he applied this concept throughout his system. This consistency is nicely illustrated in Pico's reconciliation of ancient conflicts over "being" and the "one," which he treated at length in his lost *Concord of Plato and Aristotle*. In surviving sources, Pico deals with these issues most fully in *On Being and the One*, which he composed in 1491 as a preliminary sketch for the *Concord*. But he had worked out his ideas years earlier for his Vatican debate, and they can, in fact, be deduced immediately from the principles of his "new philosophy."

The central conflict here concerned whether being or the one was ontologically "prior," meaning, as Pico tells us in *On Being and the One*, which of them was "simpler" and "most universal."[64] The question in this form was first raised by ancient Platonic commentators in interpreting the *Parmenides* and related texts on the Eleatic problem of the one and the many—interpretations made especially problematic by the conflicting treatments of the question found in the Aristotelian corpus. The standard Neo-Platonic solution to the problem—that the one was superior to being—was developed at length by Proclus in his *Platonic Theology* and commentary on the *Parmenides*, and was endorsed by almost all later Neo-Platonists, including Marsilio Ficino.

It is not difficult to show that Proclus was by far Pico's most important single

---

[64] *De ente et uno* 1 (*Opera*, 241; Garin, *Scritti vari*, 388).

source in the nine hundred conclusions.[65] It is nevertheless not surprising to find him rejecting Proclus and the Neo-Platonists on this one question: Being and the one, like all other principles, must exist "in some mode" on every level of reality; indeed, the two "correspond with one another" and can be "converted"; that is, the two are coextensive and in the deepest sense identical principles.[66]

The fact that certain parts of the Aristotelian corpus similarly equate being and the one, as Pico himself tells us, has been cited by P. O. Kristeller as evidence that when Pico "attempted to reconcile Plato and Aristotle, he did not subordinate Aristotle to Plato, but rather the Neo-Platonists, and perhaps even Plato, to Aristotle."[67] More recently, Michael Allen has also pictured Pico as being committed "to reconciling Plato with Aristotle under an Aristotelian banner."[68] On this issue, these modern Ficino scholars echo Ficino himself, who near the end of his commentary on the *Parmenides*—which was largely composed to respond to Pico—complains "If only that marvelous youth [*mirandus ille iuvenis*, punning on Pico's name] had carefully considered the preceding discussions and arguments before he so confidently attacked (*tangeret*) his teacher and so securely proclaimed against the opinion of all Platonists that the divine *Parmenides* is simply [a] logical [exercise] and that Plato himself like Aristotle equated the 'one' and the 'good' with 'being'."[69] But Pico's approach here was not Aristotelian in any genuine sense, as was immediately recognized by his contemporary Aristotelian critics. Indeed, one of these critics turned Ficino's words exactly on their head and complained that on the issue of being and one, Pico was not attributing Aristotelian views to Plato but Platonic concepts to "our Aristotle."[70]

In rejecting the standard Neo-Platonic view that the one was prior to being, in fact, Pico was simply out-Platonizing his rivals, by insisting on the universality of their own central metaphysical principle—that "all things exist in all things in

---

[65] Besides the fifty-five theses that Pico gives us *secundum Proclum*—the largest number from any one writer—Pico also drew scores of other theses without attribution from Proclus's *Platonic Theology* or *Commentary on the Timaeus*, as shown in my commentary.

[66] *De ente et uno* 1 (*Opera*, 242; Garin, *Scritti vari*, 388).

[67] Kristeller (1965: 62–63).

[68] Allen (1989: 39).

[69] Ficino *Opera* (1576: 2:1164).

[70] See Pico's long polemical exchange with Antonio da Faenza, reprinted in *Opera*, 256–88. Antonio's complaint that Pico had Platonized Aristotle, which has its validity, is found on p. 257.

their own mode"—which they had abandoned in confronting an isolated exegetical problem, the claim in the *Parmenides* that the one was superior to being. Pico's rejection of the standard Neo-Platonic reading of that text—as Ficino complained, Pico argued that the "divine *Parmenides*" was simply a logical exercise—has been hailed as an anticipation of modern views of the work.[71] But Pico's ideas here arose from anything but a commitment to modern philological standards, as any reader can quickly discover for himself or herself.

What remains unexplained is the depth of Pico's commitment to the principle that "all things exist in all things in their own mode," which he upheld even when it forced him—as in this case—to abandon the most important ancient writers who supported that principle. It would, in fact, be difficult to name any other premodern thinker who applied this supreme correlative principle as widely—and indeed, as mechanically—as Pico did in the nine hundred theses, much as Leibniz was to do in a somewhat different way some two centuries later. A number of plausible reasons might be given: the strict requirements of symmetry in Pico's numerology; the analogical form of his mysticism; the key role of correlative thought in his magic; support for the concept in the Kabbalah and other esoteric traditions; and so on.

But even more important was the exegetical flexibility that the principle gave Pico in reconciling conflicting texts, especially those texts linked by tradition to the names "Plato" and "Aristotle."[72] Pico's strategy was one that shows up in

---

[71] *De ente et uno* 2 (*Opera*, 242–43; Garin, *Scritti vari*, 390ff.). For modernizing readings of the *De ente et uno*, see, e.g., Klibansky (1943) and Di Napoli (1965: 317). Most of the highly inconsistent accounts of the *De ente et uno* in the historical literature have arisen from attempts to treat the text as a systematic rather than as an exegetical treatise.

[72] It is important to note that when Renaissance writers like Pico or Ficino referred to the works of Plato and Aristotle, they included among those works many texts that not even the most conservative modern scholars would attribute to those figures; cf. here thesis and note 2>38. Taking this point further, it can be argued that the Platonic and Aristotelian canons (like all other textual canons of similar antiquity) were highly stratified school products rather than straightforward creations of single authors. The concept of textual stratification that has long been taken for granted in biblical studies and analysis of the Chinese and Indian classics, however, has yet to make much of a dent in Platonic and Aristotelian studies, due in part to the lingering influence of Werner Jaeger's and A. E. Taylor's works. Major advances in the past decade have been made in destratifying classical Taoist, Confucian, and Indian texts, and fresh research on the New Testament (especially concerning the so-called Q document) has continued that process in biblical studies. Ironically, however, in the case of the two major philosophical canons in the West—those

one variation or another in virtually every premodern commentarial tradition: Disagreements between unassailable authorities can be *immediately* resolved if we interpret their conflicting words to refer not to the same but to corresponding concepts standing on different levels of reality, or to the same concept viewed from superior or inferior hierarchical perspectives.[73]

Thus the identification of being and the one found in certain strata of the Aristotelian corpus—a view that Pico claimed that Plato no less than Aristotle upheld "in one mode"—is true if both being and the one are taken here to refer to everything that exists. The Platonic view that the one is superior to being, on the other hand—an idea that Pico predictably claimed that Aristotle also supported "in one mode"—is true if being here is taken to refer to concrete or participated being and the one to the abstract one or unparticipated unity of God. Finally, if we consider the indistinguishability of God's unity taken in itself, we can equally support the view that God is above the one, just as he transcends all other categories. Apparent disagreements between Plato and Aristotle on these issues arise from our misunderstanding of the *levels* of reality described in their works, not from any unthinkable real conflict dividing them.[74]

Pico's method here looks suspiciously like an exegetical *deus ex machina*, and that is precisely what it was—one invoked in the West by pagan writers like Proclus for one set of syncretic purposes and for still others by Christian writers like Pseudo-Dionysius, from whom Pico partially derived the examples offered above.[75] In Pico's mind, however, that method was not based on an arbitrary

---

ascribed to Plato and Aristotle—the process of destratification has hardly even begun. When these two last fortresses of traditional historiography fall, the repercussions for premodern studies in general can be expected to be profound.

[73] For examples of the use of similar strategies in non-Western traditions, see, e.g., Berling (1980), Henderson (1984, 1991).

[74] Cf. *De ente et uno* 3–5 (*Opera*, 243ff.; Garin, *Scritti vari*, 396ff.). Evidence suggests that paradoxical Western and Eastern views of the one, God, the absolute, etc., as simultaneously transcendent and immanent—or as a general *coincidentia oppositorum*—originally developed out of the repeated use of the kinds of reconciliative strategies illustrated here. Further systematic consequences of the use of such strategies are discussed in chap. 2.

[75] Dionysius's influence is especially evident in *De ente et uno* 5, where Pico tells us that in his own work "magna etiam aperitur fenestra legitimae intelligentiae librorum Dionysii qui *De mystica theologia* et *De divinis nominibus* inscribuntur" [a great window of legitimate understanding is opened on the books of Dionysius entitled *On Mystical Theology* and *On the Divine Names*] (*Opera*, 250; Garin, *Scritti vari*, 420).

series of scholastic distinctions: The terms "one," "being," "good," "beauty," "unity," and so on, when used to describe any one level of reality, can be systematically linked to the same terms used to describe every other level. So long as we remain ignorant of the deep correspondences in reality, we can easily mistake verbal conflicts in ancient texts for real conflicts. Once we acknowledge those correspondences, we find that beneath those conflicts lay a systematic element and indeed a hidden concord, reflecting the ancients' dignity as authorities living closer than us to the origins of the world and hence to primal truth.

The lesson of Pico's planned reconciliation of Plato and Aristotle can be confirmed by study of every mature scholastic and syncretic tradition known: What begins with attempts to harmonize texts or textual authorities invariably leads to increasingly correlative visions of reality.

Pico repeatedly invoked the principle *omnia sunt in omnibus modo suo* in all his major works. In the *Heptaplus* he labeled the concept the "greatest of all" cosmic principles and discovered in it the key to decoding all sacred texts.[76] The reconciliative uses of the concept show up too often in Pico's conclusions to require much additional comment here. Pico's general approach is beautifully illustrated in one of his theses presenting his "new philosophy"—aimed this time at reconciling Xenophanes and the Eleatics on the concept of the one:

> 3>70. Although there were three who said that all things are one—Xenophanes, Parmenides, and Melissus—whoever carefully scrutinizes their words will see that the one of Xenophanes is that which is one simply. Parmenides' one is not the absolute one, as is believed, but is the oneness of being. The one of Melissus is the one that possesses extreme correspondence to Xenophanes' one.

Joined syncretically, this successive trinity of *prisci theologi* unfolds the outlines of a complete correlative ontology—with Xenophanes first revealing God's oneness, then Parmenides the reflected oneness in creatures, then Melissus finally the negative oneness of nonbeing or prime matter.[77] Apparent conflicts in the ancients are harmonized, and everything is ranked neatly in historical and hierarchical order.

---

[76] Discussed below, pp. 80–81.

[77] Five years later, however, in *De ente et uno* 3 (*Opera*, 244; Garin, *Scritti vari*, 396), Pico tentatively followed Simplicius in identifying Parmenides' one with God.

iv. Cosmology and History: The Structure of Pico's Theses and the Eschatological Goals of His Vatican "Council"

We can look now at the organization of the nine hundred theses, which contains important clues to Pico's goals at Rome. Hints of peculiarities in the work's structure show up in the preface to the historical part of the text, where we are told that the theses are "proposed separately by nations and their sect leaders, but in common in respect to the parts of philosophy—as though in medley, everything mixed together."

For the structure of Pico's theses to be as haphazard as superficially appears would be anomalous, however, and not just because Pico promised to unveil a philosophical system in his debate. All Pico's other works are meticulously structured, reflecting the standard premodern view that the structures of texts should mirror the structures of the realities they represent. This idea was, in fact, at the center of a number of theses that Pico prepared for his debate.[78] Since the universe, as Pico pictured it, was ordered numerologically, not surprisingly numerology plays a prominent role in the structure of all his works. The *Heptaplus*, Pico's commentary on the first creation story in Genesis, is hence divided into seven parts of seven chapters each, mirroring the seven days of creation. *On Being and the One* and Pico's lost *Concord of Plato and Aristotle* were both planned as "decads"—divided into ten sections each—suggesting the importance of this Pythagorean "number of numbers," as Pico refers to it in the nine hundred theses.[79] Pico's unfinished *Disputations against Divinatory Astrology*, at least according to his nephew, was originally planned in thirteen books, apparently to emphasize the demonic origins of "superstition."[80] Similar numerological patterns were apparently also originally part of Pico's *Commentary on the Psalms*, which due to his unscrupulous nephew survives today only in fragments.[81]

---

[78] This principle was also applied to the order of books in a larger canon. Cf. thesis 2>38, which concerns the order of books in the Aristotelian corpus.

[79] See thesis 9>23. We find that the *Concord of Plato and Aristotle* was a "decad" in *De ente et uno* 5 (*Opera*, 249; Garin, *Scritti vari*, 146).

[80] *Opera*, fol. 4v, 411.

[81] On this work, see below, pp. 165–69. In the *Apology*, Pico tied the traditional numbering of the Psalms to their magical "power" and "efficacy" (*Opera*, 172); cf. also thesis 10>4 on the magic in the Psalms. A further hint that Pico's *Commentary on the Psalms* originally included numerological patterns is found in the fact that the work was begun simultaneously with the numerologically rich *Heptaplus*. Cf. here *Opera*, 1; Garin, *Scritti vari*, 170.

The first obvious place to search for structure in Pico's theses, then, is in the text's numerological design. The fact that the printed edition of the conclusions prepared for Pico's debating opponents was (rather perversely) unnumbered was apparently tied to Pico's debating tactics: Cross-references in the work show that his own version was numbered.[82] In any event, numerological symbolism shows up pervasively in the theses, much of it hinting at deeper mystical and eschatological goals underlying Pico's project.

The structure of the two main parts of the nine hundred theses was apparently planned around the two types of "perfect numbers" most commonly acknowledged in the West—numbers like six and twenty-eight composed of the sum of all their factors,[83] and the Pythagorean decad, which was "perfect" and "every number," as the *Apology* tells us, since beyond it we count "by repetition."[84]

From antiquity on these numbers were repeatedly juxtaposed by religious thinkers as complementary symbols of perfection and completion. Thus the famous Bapistry doors in Florence have twenty-eight panels in the north and south portals, while Ghiberti's final set facing east and the cathedral (the so-called Gates of Paradise) have ten. Reflecting similar symbolic patterns, the first or historical section of Pico's theses includes six "nations" of thinkers represented by twenty-eight "heresiarchs" or their sects; the second part of the text, presented "according to Pico's own opinion"—like the *On Being and the One* and *Concord of Plato and Aristotle* after it—originally contained ten sections, apparently to emphasize the perfection of Pico's own system.[85]

Other numerological symbols crop up frequently in the text. Since "one" was Pico's standard symbol for a *coincidentia contradictoriorum*, the first section of his theses given "according to his own opinion" appropriately contains his "paradoxical reconciliative conclusions." The first thesis of that first set, at the pinnacle of

---

[82] Cf. theses 2>58, 9>4, 11>39. Last-minute changes in the text make it difficult to know how Pico planned to use the number symbolism planted in it, although he clearly meant to reveal that symbolism in the course of his debate.

[83] I.e., $1 + 2 + 3 = 6$ and $1 + 2 + 4 + 7 + 14 = 28$. On perfect numbers in general, see Theon of Smyrna *Mathematics Useful for Understanding Plato* 1.32.

[84] *Opera*, 172. The decad was also said to be perfect since it was composed of the sum of the first four natural numbers $(1 + 2 + 3 + 4)$—the numerical correspondents of the point, line, plane, and solid, which were the geometric building blocks of the Pythagorean cosmos. Cf. thesis 10>5 and note.

[85] Pico added an eleventh section while the work was in press to replace theses apparently removed for theological reasons. See my introductory note to theses 6>1–10.

unity, proclaims the harmony of Plato and Aristotle, the central philosophical theme of Pico's debate. The final section of the work, outlining Pico's Cabalistic plan to convert the Jews, contains seventy-two theses, the number of letters in one of the most secret of the Cabala's secret names of God.[86] The first thesis of Pico's "paradoxical dogmatizing conclusions"—both literally and figuratively the first principle of Pico's "new philosophy"—is the five hundredth thesis in the text as a whole; elsewhere in the work, we find that this number symbolizes eschatological return.[87] This supports the view that Pico's *philosophia nova*, "thought out in Aristotelian and Platonic philosophy," was in fact intended as a *philosophia renovata*, returning thought to its primal but now shattered unity. Similar symbolism was also apparently intended by Pico's original inclusion of five hundred theses presented "according to his own opinion."

The seriousness with which Pico intended his numerological symbolism is suggested in an important letter that he wrote to his friend Girolamo Benevieni less than a month before his text went to press. The theses, he informed Benevieni, had recently grown from seven to nine hundred and had threatened to reach a thousand. But it was proper to halt at the "mystical" number nine hundred, Pico wrote, "for if my doctrine of numbers is correct, this is the symbol of the excited soul turning back into itself through the frenzy of the muses."[88]

Numerological patterns pervade the nine hundred theses, suggesting that other structure is hidden there. Moreover, that structure was apparently tied to some mystical and eschatological plan underlying Pico's entire project. The outlines of that plan become clearer when we recall the reverse historical order (as Pico understood it) of the first part of his text: The theses of the Latin scholastics are followed by those of the Arab, Greek, Chaldean, Egyptians, and Hebrew "nations." The importance of this sequence is suggested in both the *Oration* and *Apology*, which tell us that "all wisdom emanated from the barbarians to the Greeks, from the Greeks to us," and further in the *Apology*, where we find that the Hebrew Cabala contained "the secret declarations of God" and "the true sense of the Law received from the mouth of God" by Moses; in the *Heptaplus*, we find that Pythagoras and apparently Plato too drew deeply on this secret Mosaic wisdom.[89] Taken together, these clues suggest that Pico's historical theses were

---

[86] See 11>56–57 and notes.

[87] See 11>68–69 and notes.

[88] The letter is quoted more fully on p. 40.

[89] *Opera*, 1ff., 175–76, 325; Garin, *Scritti vari*, 142, 170–72.

meant to represent a reverse genealogy of thought—or an emanation of wisdom, as he suggests—tracing the historical flow of truth backwards in time from the warring Latins, whose theses are found at the start of Pico's text, to the harmonious agreement of *prisci theologi* and Cabalists, whose doctrines appear at the end of the text's historical part. With one of those nice symbolic touches characteristic of all his works, Pico concludes the historical part of his text with the promise to reveal the secrets of God's nature hidden in the Hebrew word *Amen*.[90]

We learn more of this "emanation of wisdom" in an early draft of the *Oration*, which differs on important points from the version published after Pico's death by his nephew. The aim of the first part of the *Oration* was to develop a formal defense of philosophy—an appropriate way to start Pico's debate—and not to celebrate the dignity of man or freedom of the will, as is commonly argued. Man is indeed free to choose his destiny—to live the life of a beast, to judge the world like the angelic Thrones, or to rise to God through love like the Serafim. But the destiny we choose depends on our state of knowledge: "For how can we judge or love what is unknown?"[91] It is for this reason that we must study philosophy, preparing ourselves for earthly rule or the mystical ascent. Pico again addresses the pope, cardinals, and assembled leaders of the schools:

> These are the reasons, venerable Fathers, that not only moved but compelled me to the study of philosophy. In order to attain it as passionately as I pursued it, I always believed that two things were of use. The first was this: to swear by the words of no one, but to study all teachers of philosophy, to examine all writings, to acknowledge all schools. I saw that to achieve this it was necessary to understand not only Greek and Latin but also Hebrew and Chaldean and the Arabic language, which I have just begun to study under Guglielmo [Flavius] Mithridates, an expert teacher of these languages. For almost all wisdom emanated from the barbarians to the Greeks, from the Greeks to us; hence in their manner of philosophizing our writers have always thought it sufficient to stand with foreign discoveries and to cultivate alien things. Sacred letters need to be sought wholly—and the more secret mysteries first—from the Hebrews and Chaldeans, then from the Greeks. The rest of the arts and all parts of

[90] Thesis 28.47.

[91] *Opera*, 316; Garin, *Scritti vari*, 112–3. Ironically, far from stressing the autonomy of the will, as is usually argued, Pico normally emphasized its blindness and total dependence on the intellect for its direction. For discussion, see below, pp. 105ff.

> philosophy the Greeks divide with the Arabs. Who can progress in these things if he does not go to them?[92]

It is no accident that Pico's "emanation of wisdom" ends abruptly with the Arabs. On the whole, in fact, the "nation" of Latin scholastics comes off rather badly in all of Pico's major works, although for systematic reasons he did not repudiate Latin scholastics entirely.[93] The *Oration* suggests two reasons for preferring older to newer sources of knowledge. The first repeats the standard Renaissance complaint about corrupt texts and translations, which badly distort the wisdom of the ancients. The second reminds us that the ancients stood closer than we do to the truth, since "we are flesh and what we know is of the earth," "our heads damned with dizziness by the sudden fall of man from heaven."[94]

Ideas like these were common in both classicist and scholastic circles in the Renaissance. What is noteworthy is the way that Pico worked these ideas into the first part of his theses, whose historical structure closely mirrors the structure of the cosmos expressed in his "new philosophy." I am not suggesting that Pico viewed the historical "emanation of wisdom" as proceeding in quite so systematic a fashion as the emanation of creation from God's nature; rigor of that sort in a philosophy of history was scarcely demanded even by Hegel. The tendency for cosmological and historical models to mirror each other was common in premodern traditions, moreover, and the possibility always exists that in Pico those parallels developed unconsciously. On the other hand, Pico's insistence that the structures of texts should reflect the structures of the realities they represent provides strong arguments against any such interpretation. Whatever the cause, the parallels between cosmological and historical emanations in the nine hundred theses are striking, ultimately providing some final clues to the goals of Pico's debate. The most important of these parallels are the following:

---

[92] Garin (1961: 236, 239–40). It is noteworthy that the reference in this passage to Mithridates, who was a criminal fugitive from the papal court, is not found in the version of the *Oration* published by Pico's nephew after his uncle's death.

[93] On Pico's criticisms of Thomas Aquinas, for example, see below, pp. 47–49. Pico repeatedly attacks Latin scholastics as a group in the *Commento*, *Heptaplus*, and in his theses given "according to his own opinion." All this suggests that Pico's famous letter to Ermolao Barbaro that in part defends the Latin scholastics (*Opera*, 351–58)—written one year before the theses—demands a careful reevaluation.

[94] Garin (1961: 236, 238); cf. *Opera*, 316, 321; Garin, *Scritti vari*, 112, 130.

1. *Movement from unity to multiplicity.* In Pico's cosmological system, as we saw earlier, the emanation of creatures proceeds from unity to multiplicity, with harmony yielding to discord the further one is from God. The emanation of wisdom in Pico's historical theses expresses a parallel movement, reflected in the conflicting theses of *gentes* and *heresiarchae* in Pico's reverse genealogy of thought. These conflicts are sharpest and most frequent at the beginning of the text with the corrupt Latins and Arabs and, after gradually diminishing, disappear totally by the end, in the harmonious concord of *prisci theologi* and Cabalists.

Similar patterns were apparently found in Pico's lost *Concord of Plato and Aristotle,* which was described in two sketches by Gianfrancesco Pico shortly after his uncle's death. In the longer of these sketches, Gianfrancesco described the *Concord* while surveying other of his uncle's works-in-progress:

> Among these above all should be numbered his *Concord of Plato and Aristotle,* which already begun he would have quickly perfected if he had survived a few more years. Indeed, he had so raised philosophy from its cradle and led it to adulthood right up to our own times, that a philosopher of our age would have desired nothing more in either Greek, or Latin, or barbarian manuscripts. He would have summoned watery Thales, and fiery Heraclitus, and Democritus enveloped by his atoms; likewise Orpheus and Pythagoras and the other ancients, through his help and grace, would have agreed with the Academy. At last the prince of philosophy—that is, Plato—bound in veils of myths and mathematical wrappings, and Aristotle, enveloped in controversies, he would have sanctified by his dexterous gifts with the faith of a future friendship. Between Averroes also and Avicenna, between Thomas and Scotus, who have long been in contention, he would have procured a truce in many matters, if not peace universally. . . . The tumult of the moderns was to have been both honored and taxed—partly for their merits, partly for their faults.[95]

The unity of thought yielding slowly to discord: The obvious parallels between the structure of the nine hundred theses and Pico's lost *Concord of Plato and Aristotle* suggest that the latter text was planned as a direct extension and presumably defense of his aborted Vatican debate. This alone was grounds for Pico's nephew

[95] *Opera,* fol. 5r. A shorter version of this sketch is found in Gianfrancesco's *Opera* (1557: 1297–98).

to suppress publication of the *Concord*, which evidence suggests was in fact finished, or all but finished, at the time of Pico's death.[96]

2. *Cosmological and historical symmetries.* The proportions and symmetries in Pico's cosmos appear most clearly when we abandon the material world and move upwards towards God. A parallel movement occurs in Pico's historical theses, where we find the conclusions of the most ancient traditions (or those like the Cabala that Pico mistook for ancient) most fully expressing the cosmic symmetries of Pico's "new philosophy." The first clear suggestion of this shift occurs at nearly the exact center of the historical section of the text, with the movement from the Arabs to the Greek Aristotelians and Platonists.[97] This shift supports Pico's claim that his system was "thought out in Aristotelian and Platonic philosophy," with the implication that the ancients grasped more clearly than the moderns the correlative nature of reality. It also helps explain why Pico's historical theses begin with the "heresiarchs" of the *via antiqua*—Albert the Great, Thomas Aquinas, John Duns Scotus, and so on—and omit completely the leaders of the *via moderna*, in whose nominalist systems, in Pico's eyes, the crystalline proportions of the cosmos had been totally shattered.[98]

3. *Numerology in cosmology and history.* Just as the emanation of creatures pro-

---

[96] See below, pp. 148 n. 42, 159, 163–64. Pico first mentions the *Concord* as an independent work in 1489, in *Heptaplus* 5.4 (*Opera*, 37; Garin, *Scritti vari*, 298). There we find that in reconciling Aristotle and Plato the *Concord*, like the nine hundred theses before it, was to deal with the whole of philosophy: "Aristotelem Platoni conciliantes universam philosophiam pro virtutibus tractandam examinandamque suscepimus" [reconciling Aristotle to Plato I shall undertake, to the best of my abilities, to treat and examine all of philosophy]. Direct textual evidence also links Pico's theses to his lost *Concord*, as we shall see in chap. 4.

[97] In the extant version of Pico's conclusions, this transition occurs at the 198th thesis; it probably was originally intended for the 200th thesis, the exact midpoint of the historical section in the text's original form.

[98] Professor Kristeller (1965: 59) has suggested that Pico's exclusion of the nominalists may have reflected the fact that Louis XI prohibited their teachings at the University of Paris in 1474. That edict was lifted in 1481, however—four years before Pico's first trip to Paris—and evidence in the *Apology* suggests that in Paris Pico had studied their doctrines intensely; we also find the nominalists attacked a number of times in Pico's theses presented *secundum opinionem propriam*. Their exclusion from the Latin *heresiarchae* thus appears to be best explained on systematic grounds.

ceeds numerologically, so too Pico's historical emanation is regulated by number. In his "mathematical conclusions" Pico suggests that his numerology provided a means for historical interpretation and prophecy no less than a grasp of "everything knowable" in the cosmic sphere. Elsewhere in the theses, Pico planned to use his numerological methods to discuss the ages of history or to calculate the date of the end of the world. Pico claimed that methods similar to his own were used by Joachim of Fiore, the most important medieval figure in a Western tradition of numerological prophecy extending from antiquity to Newton and beyond.[99] In the nine hundred theses, both the mystical ascent and the ages of the world are represented in six parallel stages, tied to a final "Sabbath" completing and uniting all the rest. Pico presumably intended to connect these six stages of history to the six *gentes* of thinkers included in his text; in any case, much other evidence ties his project to some eschatological plan.[100]

4. *Cosmological and historical shifts in language.* In Pico's "new philosophy," ordinary language can only adequately describe the inferior regions of the universe. Above, the divine mysteries are rightfully clothed in symbolic dress. Parallel to this in the historical order, the language of Pico's theses becomes increasingly symbolic as we leave rational philosophy and theology behind with the Latins and Arabs and approach the secret wisdom of the *prisci theologi* and Cabalists. At the beginning of his historical theses, Pico employs the technically precise and metaphorically restricted Latin of Western scholasticism; by the end, the text's language is almost entirely symbolic, very little of which could have meant anything to anyone at Rome but Pico himself. A transition here again takes place with the later Greeks, whose theses are expressed in a complex mix of philosophical and symbolic terms. This pattern reflects what the nine hundred theses tell us about the evolution—or, more precisely, devolution—of languages, leading us back from the corrupt languages of the moderns to the primal tongue of Hebrew and those "closely derived" from it, in which secret truths and magical powers lay hidden in the isolated shapes of letters.[101]

---

[99] Besides those examples found in his mathematical theses, cf. 10>20 on the *Orphic Hymns* and 11>9 from Pico's second set of Cabalistic conclusions. On Joachim, cf. thesis 7>10; on the Joachimite tradition, see Reeves (1969).

[100] On the mystical and eschatological concepts of Sabbath, see, e.g., theses 5>58, 11>16, and passim below.

[101] On the magical powers of Hebrew, see the theses listed in note to 28.33; cf. my discussion below, pp. 63–65, and passim in my commentary to the theses. Pico also dis-

One might argue that the text's radical shifts in language simply reflected what Pico found in his sources and were not part of any self-conscious design. But the selection and arrangement of those sources was, of course, entirely Pico's own.

5. *Cosmological and temporal emanations of the "left hand."* One parallel involves a side of Pico's system that I have not yet mentioned. Alongside the orderly emanation of reality Pico pictured an evil emanation, a "left-hand coordination" or mirror image of the first, presided over not by God but by evil demons. Pico drew this idea from his kabbalistic sources, but he thought that he also found evidence for it in the *Hermetic Corpus* and undoubtedly elsewhere, although he claimed that the doctrine was too secret to discuss at Rome.[102]

Hints of a left-hand order in history show up a number of ways in Pico's works. In the theses we not only find Old Testament kings like Solomon represented as true prefigurations or "types" of Christ, but others like Zedekiah—the king of Judah when it fell to Babylon—as false types, having a "diminished correspondence" to Christ and Solomon.[103] In the *Apology*, we discover that necromancers falsely mimic the genealogies of good magicians by tracing their bestialities and incantations to Solomon, Adam, Enoch, and "similar men." False Cabalists do the same, claiming descent for their diabolical arts from the secret wisdom revealed to Moses on the mountain.[104]

At the end of the *Disputations against Divinatory Astrology*, we find Pico tracing the historical genealogy of "superstition," following it from demonic influence in the Egyptians and Chaldeans—just as in the nine hundred theses and *Concord of Plato and Aristotle* Pico traced the genealogy of true wisdom, with its more gradual degeneration, from its origins to present times.[105] Since after Pico's death his nephew published only this anti-concord of sorts in the *Disputations* and not what remained of the *Concord* itself, Pico's later thought has sometimes been represented as a "palinode" to his earlier work.[106] I will take up this question in a later chapter, but for now it should be noted that Pico acknowledged a left-hand order

---

cusses the magic of Hebrew in an important letter written to an unknown friend shortly before the nine hundred theses went to press (*Opera*, 384–86).

[102] Cf. thesis 27.10.

[103] Cf. thesis 11>51.

[104] *Opera*, 181.

[105] See especially *Disputationes* 12, *Opera*, 717ff.; *Disputationes*, ed. Garin (1946–52: 2:485ff.).

[106] E.g., in Di Napoli (1965). See further below, pp. 142–46.

in history early in his career, explaining why in the nine hundred theses he could attack the "opinions of the Egyptians" while supporting the general idea that Egyptian sages like Mercury (Hermes) Trismegistus were privy to a secret wisdom far surpassing that of the moderns.[107]

6. *Cosmological and historical conversions.* One final parallel involves the underlying religious goals of Pico's project. In the final stage of his cosmology, it will be recalled, Pico envisioned a return of emanated beings to God, a mystical conversion of multiplicity to unity. It should be evident by this point that Pico hoped to trigger a parallel historical conversion in his Vatican debate, returning thought from its current warring state to the unity it enjoyed in the days of the ancient wisemen.

It is interesting to look at this idea in relation to Pico's mysticism, which is analyzed more fully in chapter 3. Pico's mysticism, despite numerous claims to the contrary, reflected standard medieval compromises balancing human responsibility against the need for divine grace.[108] In the technical scholastic formula that Pico adopted in the *Oration*—dropped abruptly in a sea of metaphor—grace follows "if we ourselves have first done what is in us" [si quid in nobis ipsi prius egerimus]. To do "what is in us," as Moses tells us, means that we must "prepare our path through philosophy to celestial glory while we can," ascending the four steps in the ladder of knowledge—moral philosophy, dialectics, natural philosophy, and theology—that make up the main topics of Pico's debate. Once we have climbed those steps, returning into the divine unity reflected in our souls, we will have "done what is in us," and God will reward us with the peace and mystical union that comes from a final quietistic infusion of grace.[109]

These ideas were much on Pico's mind when he composed the nine hundred

[107] For attacks in the nine hundred theses on the Egyptians, see theses 26.1–6, which immediately precede the section devoted to Mercury Trismegistus.

[108] It is common in Renaissance studies to find Pico portrayed as a voluntarist, Pelagian, or semi-Pelagian, etc., based mainly on misreadings of the opening pages of the *Oration*. See below, pp. 105ff.

[109] *Opera*, 319 and passim; Garin, *Scritti vari*, 122 and passim. Discussions of the doctrine of the *facere quod in se est*, which was attacked by Protestant reformers in the sixteenth century, can be found in Oberman (1962; 1963: 129–45 and passim; 1966: 123–41). See also Ozment (1974). Some version of this doctrine was accepted in most scholastic circles, and it was by no means limited as sometimes claimed to the so-called nominalist tradition. Cf. on this point the quotation from Thomas Aquinas below, p. 110.

theses and *Oration* in the fall of 1486. Some of the circumstances surrounding their composition are explained in an important letter, already quoted in part, that Pico sent to Girolamo Benivieni less than a month before the nine hundred theses went to press. Benivieni had recently been at Pico's retreat at Fratta, outside Perugia:

> Before you left, the doctrines to be disputed publicly by me had stopped at seven hundred. After you left, they grew to nine hundred—and unless I had drawn back, would have reached a thousand. But it was proper to halt at this number, since it is mystical. For if my doctrine of numbers is correct, this is the symbol of the excited soul turning back into itself through the frenzy of the muses [i.e., through philosophical studies]. This which I am sending you has likewise been added to the *Oration*. For since I have determined that no day should pass without my reading something of the Evangelical teachings, the day after you left these words of Christ fell into my hands: "I give you my peace, I give you my peace, I leave you peace" [cf. John 14:27]. Immediately, with a certain sudden excitation of the soul, I dictated certain things on peace in praise of philosophy (*de pace quaedam ad philosophiae laudes*) with such great speed that I often ran ahead of and upset the hand of my secretary.[110]

The section that Pico added to the *Oration* in that inspired frenzy pertains to the peace of the soul and not, strictly speaking, to the peace that he planned to bring to the warring schools. But the analogical leaps that he makes elsewhere between mystical and historical frames of reference should make us sensitive to similar movements here as well:

> Truly, Fathers, there is manifold discord in us. We have grave and internal and worse than civil wars at home. If we do not want them, if we desire that peace that so raises us to the summit that we are set among the elevated of the Lord, moral philosophy alone will utterly check and calm them. . . . Dialectic will calm the tumults of reason tossed anxiously between the inconsistencies of rhetorical language and the deceits of the syllogism. Natural philosophy will calm the quarrels and disagreements of opinion that agitate, pull apart, and lacerate the restless soul. But it will calm it in such a way as to order us to remember that nature, according to Heraclitus, is born from war—the reason that it is called "contention"

---

[110] Dorez (1895: 358).

by Homer—and because of this in natural philosophy true quiet and solid peace cannot present itself to us. This is the task and privilege of her mistress, holiest theology. To that peace theology will both point out the way and as guide lead us, who from far off seeing us hastening will cry, "Come to me you who labor, come and I will restore you, come to me and I will give you the peace which the world and nature cannot give you." Called so sweetly, invited so kindly, with winged feet like terrestial Mercuries, flying into the embrace of the most blessed mother, let us enjoy that hoped for peace, the holiest peace, the undivided bond, the friendship of one soul through which all souls not only concord in one mind that is over every mind, but in a certain ineffable mode become fully one. This is that friendship that the Pythagoreans say is the end of all philosophy. This is that peace that God makes in his heights, which the angels descending to the earth announce to men of good will, so that through it men themselves ascending into heaven may become angels. Let us wish this peace for our friends. Let us wish it for our age. Let us wish it for every house we enter. Let us wish it for our soul, so that through it she may become the house of the Lord—so that after she has cast off her uncleanliness with morals and dialectics, has adorned herself in manifold philosophy as in royal splendor, and has crowned the pinnacles of the gates with theological garlands, the king of Glory [i.e., Christ] might descend, and coming with the Father, make his stay with her. If she shows herself worthy of so great a guest—such is his immense mercy—in garments of gold like a wedding gown, wrapped in a manifold variety of sciences, she will receive her beautiful guest no longer as a guest but as a spouse.[111]

The "manifold discord" and "civil wars" in this passage refer on a primary level to conflicts in the soul but analogically point just as well to the intellectual wars that Pico planned to resolve at Rome or indeed to the military conflicts that he was then witnessing in Perugia—lamented in still another hymn to peace, this time a poem, written in this same period.[112] Similarly, the mystical "concord in

[111] *Opera*, 318; Garin, *Scritti vari*, 116–20.

[112] See Pico's letter to Baldo Perugino in Dorez (1895: 357). The "pro pace extemporaneum carmen" [extemporaneous poem on peace] mentioned in that letter has occasionally been identified with the section on peace just quoted from the *Oration*, e.g., by Garin (1961: 231). More likely, however, the reference in the letter is to Pico's poem entitled *Ad*

one mind" to which Pico refers here can hardly be divorced from the historical concord of philosophies that he sought throughout his career: Free movement between all such levels was at the heart of Pico's correlative methods, and his use of the same words to describe them can never be taken to be totally accidental. The discovery of such correspondences was, in fact, what Pico refers to in the nine hundred theses as the "method of secret analogizing" (*via secretae analogiae*).[113]

If on the mystical plane Pico's revival of ancient wisdom was meant to prepare the soul for its individual reunion with Christ, it is reasonable to ask whether on the historical plane—and indeed, on a cosmic scale—that revival was meant to prepare mankind as a whole for its final "marriage" to Christ in the Second Coming. Remarkably, a number of hints in Pico's letters and in the nine hundred theses suggest that he had something precisely like this in mind.

The biblical passage that inspired the "Ode to Peace" in the *Oration* is filled with eschatological sentiments, recalling Christ's words to his disciples before the Passion: "I give you peace, I leave you peace. Set your troubled hearts at rest, and banish your fears; you have heard me say, 'I am going away, and coming back to you'" (John 14:27–28). The mystical frenzy that overcame Pico when he read those lines visited him more than once in the hectic months before the theses went to press. In a letter written to Marsilio Ficino in September 1486, Pico announced his discovery of certain Chaldean and Arabic writings, filled with mysteries, that fell into his hands "clearly not by accident or fortuitously, but for the good of my studies by the plan of God and my guiding spirit." Those "treasure chests" (*thesauri*) contained proof that Zoroaster had predicted Christ's coming, one of many such discoveries that Pico planned to announce at Rome. It was discoveries like this that compelled him "by force" to take up study of Chaldean and Arabic as well as Hebrew—a burdensome task, but one promising "the true image of the future glory that will be revealed in us."[114]

Pico was referring here to his struggles with those languages, the key to that treasure chest of holy secrets. But his words came, again unacknowledged, from another biblical passage filled with eschatological sentiments: "I judge that the sufferings of this present time are as nothing to the future glory that will be revealed in us. . . . We know that the whole of creation has been groaning in travail

deum deprecatio (which deals with political peace in Italy), discovered and published by Kristeller (1965: 99).

[113] See thesis 10>7.

[114] *Opera*, 367–68. Cf. the version edited from a Vatican manuscript by Kristeller (1937: 2:272–73).

together until now; and not only creation, but we ourselves, who have the first fruits of the Spirit, groan inwardly as we wait for adoption as sons, the redemption of our bodies" (Romans 8:18–23).

Pico's plans for his debate uniformly suggest eschatological hopes and apocalyptic urgency: his choice of the Vatican as its site; his inclusion of theses from what he viewed as all *gentes* and their *heresiarchae*—terms rich with religious overtones; the location "in the apostolic senate" of this "council," with the pope himself as supreme judge; the inclusion in the historical theses of conclusions from six "nations" grouped in twenty-eight sections—both "perfect numbers" symbolizing perfection and completion; and so on. The concluding section of Pico's theses contains his grand plan for the final conversion of the Jews, last item on the medieval agenda before the coming of the millennium—that future Sabbath when all conflicts between all "nations" will be finally resolved. Significantly, that method was based on Pico's rediscovery of "the true exposition of the Law" revealed by God to Moses on the mountain—binding the end with the beginning, closing the circle of time.[115]

Finally, there is the clue that Pico left in the date of his debate, which was to be postponed until after the Feast of the Epiphany. As noted earlier, the Epiphany celebrated in part the submission to Christ of the *gentes* in the persons of the *Magi*—the ideal symbol for the submission of Pico's "nations" to a restored Christian philosophy and theology in his debate.[116] These symbolic associations were

---

[115] Cf. *Apology*, in *Opera*, 178. Pico underscores the religious connotations of the term *concilium* by using it to refer to the sacred Council of Elders that was supposedly held when the "true explanation of the Law" (i.e., the Cabala) was committed to writing: "Habetur autem de isto Concilio, in quo fuerunt scripti isti libri, mentio lata et diffusa apud Hebraeos in libro qui dicitur *Sederolam*, id est, *Liber saeculorum*, ubi habetur qui sederunt in Concilio, et denique totius Concilii gesta et ordo. Ex quibus omnibus satis patere potest, non esse confictum a me quod praeter Legam scriptam, Moyses veram quoque Legis expositionem a Deo acceperit, et quod illa deinceps per successionem a Moyse 70 senioribus, et ab illis aliis suis successoribus fuerit revelata" [Moreover, wide and diffuse mention of that Council in which those books were written is found among the Jews in the book called *Sederolam*, that is, the *Book of Ages*, where you can find who sat in the Council and what the order and activities of the whole Council were. From all these it is sufficiently clear that I did not invent the idea that besides the written Law, Moses also received from God the true exposition of the Law, and that this was then revealed through succession from Moses to the 70 Elders, and from them to their successors].

[116] On celebrations of the Epiphany in Florence by the Confraternity of *Magi*, sponsored by the Medici, see the texts printed in Hatfield (1970). Given Pico's close

clearly carefully chosen. The most famous line from the Office of the Epiphany at dawn supplied, in fact, the inspiration for Pico's final triumphal words on the soul's marriage to Christ, quoted earlier, in the "Ode to Peace" found in the *Oration.* That line, from the antiphon, reads: "On this day the church is joined to her celestial spouse" [Hodie caelesti sponso juncta est ecclesia].

Did Pico believe that his Vatican debate would end with the Four Horsemen of the Apocalypse crashing through the Roman skies, now that mankind—dressed "in garments of gold like a wedding gown, wrapped in a manifold variety of sciences" (cf. Revelation 19:8–9, Isaiah 61:10, etc.)—was prepared at last for its final marriage to Christ? It is impossible to know for sure. In the eschatological thought of the Renaissance it is often difficult to distinguish hard convictions, half-hopes, and heavy metaphorical play—although it was rarely ever *simply* play. In one hesitant Cabalistic calculation of the date of the end of the world, in any case, Pico's theses carry us to the year 2000.[117]

As Pico recalled Scripture elsewhere, however, no one knows for certain the date of the end of the world, and we must hold ourselves in constant readiness.[118] Pico's ability to weave a complex web of eschatological symbols around his Vatican project would have been applauded by his sympathizers for its own sake—it was a mode of expression in which Renaissance thinkers were surpassed by none—and could be taken as well as a reminder that all of us, as Moses warns us, must "prepare our path through philosophy to celestial glory while we can."

It is impossible, however, not to suspect something more here than a simple warning. No serious student of history could be much surprised by a Renaissance intellectual's belief in the impending end of the world or even by his assigning to

---

friendship with Lorenzo de' Medici, it is reasonable to assume that the Medici family's special links with the Feast of the Epiphany may have figured in Pico's choice of opening dates for his dispute.

[117] See thesis 11>9.

[118] Like most medieval and Renaissance writers, Pico was normally circumspect in his attempts to calculate the exact date of the end of the world. On this see, e.g., *Heptaplus* 7.4 (*Opera*, 53; Garin, *Scritti vari*, 352), which refers again to the end as a Sabbath. Pico wrote a book entitled *De vera temporum supputatione* (On the True Calculation of the Ages) that dealt in part with this topic; the text is referred to repeatedly in the *Disputationes* (e.g., *Opera*, 435, 554, 564; *Disputationes*, ed. Garin [1946–52: 1:122, 536, 582–84]) and again in Pico's biography by his nephew-editor Gianfrancesco Pico (*Opera*, fol. 4v). But as in so many other cases, Gianfrancesco chose not to publish the text, possibly because it contradicted the eschatological predictions of his mentor Savonarola. See further below, chap. 4.

himself a central part in the cosmic drama of history. Any medieval or Renaissance assembly—let alone one of Pico's unprecedented scale—was apt, in any case, to awaken in its participants images of the Final Assembly at the end of the world in which Christ would resolve all conflicts between all "nations."[119] Throughout the last half of the fifteenth century, as the ominous date of 1500 approached, eschatological speculation increased sharply, as suggested above all in the works of Savonarola and his followers. Even Marsilio Ficino—whose ultimate hostility towards Savonarola is well known—was hardly a stranger to eschatological thinking, and like Pico saw the divine hand guiding his own attempts to revive ancient wisdom. In one famous passage, in fact, Ficino attributed to Pico himself—animated by the ghost of Cosimo de' Medici—a guiding role in his own holy mission.[120] A saintly, prophetic, or even semi-messianic role was similarly assigned to the young count of Concord by other of his contemporaries, in a way that only the most radically modernizing historian could dismiss as sheer hyperbole.[121] Finally, as we shall see in chapter 3, in his magical theses Pico created a

[119] Thus speaking of disputations in his *Rhetorica novissima*, read to the University of Bologna in 1235, the rhetorician Buoncompagni da Signa concludes: "Wherefore, after treating of assemblies, I put an end to my labor, awaiting without horrible fear the Last Assembly in which the third Angel will sound the trumpet at whose blast heaven and earth will be moved. . . . Afterwards, indeed, the Son of God himself will appear. . . . And then all conflict of opposing counsel will cease and all contentions of controversy be solved" (Thorndike 1944: 46).

[120] Ficino *Opera* (1576: 2:1537ff.). Ficino makes much of the fact that Pico was born in the same year (1463) that Ficino began studying Plato in Greek under Cosimo de' Medici's patronage. Twenty-one years later, on the same day and indeed at almost the same hour that Ficino's translation of Plato was published [quo die et ferme qua hora Platonem edidi], Pico was moved by Cosimo's departed soul to travel to Florence to inspire Ficino to take up Plotinus. Considering the strained relations between Pico and Ficino over interpreting Plotinus, discussed earlier, this passage has some peculiar overtones.

[121] Gianfrancesco's biography of his uncle and Thomas More's free English adaption of that text follow patterns drawn from the *Lives of the Saints*, including stories of Pico's miraculous birth and youthful feats. For similar views, see the testimonials of Pico's contemporaries in *Opera*, 407ff., and the interesting letter of Baptista Spagnuoli of Mantua to Pico's nephew included in *Opera*, 387–88, which describes Pico's prophetic appearance to Baptista in a dream. Pico appears in a prophetic role in still another dream—there are a surprising number of such cases—in Giovanni Nesi's eschatological *Oraculum de novo saeculo* (1497). In his *De honesta disciplina* 3.2 (quoted here from Garin, *Scritti vari*, 81), Pietro Crinito informs us that Girolamo Savonarola compared Pico's wisdom alone in their period to that of the greatest of all the church fathers: "Et unus tu—inquit—es, Pici, aetate

portrait of *homo magus* as a kind of worldly redeemer—possessing the power to "marry the world" and to raise all nature from its fallen state.

No matter how we interpret this evidence, it can hardly be doubted that Pico pictured his Vatican council as something more than simply the largest scholastic debate in history. In the early draft of the *Oration*, Pico wrote that "there is no one who has ever existed, or who after us will exist, to whom truth has given itself to be comprehended in its entirety. Its immensity is too great for human capacity to be equal to it." These are among the most powerful lines in the *Oration*, and P. O. Kristeller has rightly called attention to their beauty.[122] But the most interesting fact about those lines has surprisingly never been emphasized: despite their power, Pico *dropped* them from his final draft.[123] There are reasons to believe that he did so for the obvious reasons. The last months before his debate were rich in major discoveries; in its final form, the nine hundred theses point more than one way to the understanding of "everything knowable." As Pico's vision of his Vatican project grew, we may well imagine that he simply viewed his words as no longer appropriate: The ancient concords had been rediscovered, and the old harmonies of things were about to be restored at Rome.

v. Collating the Theses: Pico's Debating Strategies

We can now look at how Pico meant to debate his theses. We must first further dispose of the old view that he planned to reconcile all the theses in his

nostra, qui omnium veterum philosophiam ac religionis christianae praecepta et leges percalleas, ut haec tua quidem rerum pene omnium cognitio antiquioribus illis, Hieronymo, Augustino, Basiliis, Gregoriisque ac Dionysiis, merito conferri possit" [And you alone, Pico, he said, exist in our age who fully understands the philosophy of all the ancients and the precepts and laws of the Christian religion, so that your understanding of almost all things is able to be rightly compared to that of the ancients Jerome, Augustine, Basil, Gregory, and Dionysius]. Comments like these help explain why Savonarola and his followers tried to enlist Pico's posthumous aid in bolstering their movement—in part by doctoring his published works. See below, pp. 151–79.

[122] Kristeller (1965: 84); Garin (repr. 1961: 239): "Nemo aut fuit olim aut post nos erit cui se totam dederit veritas comprehendendam. Maior illius immensitas quam ut par sit ei humana capacitas."

[123] It is also conceivable that these lines were struck out for religious reasons by Pico's nephew, who apparently tampered with other lines in the *Oration* after Pico's death; see below, p. 171 n. 108. Whether Gianfracesco believed that religious prophets like his mentor Savonarola were capable of comprehending truth "in its entirety" is an open question.

text. There is no doubt that Pico was capable at will of twisting virtually any writer into the shape of any other. We have seen preliminary evidence for this already, and we will see further evidence in later chapters. But Pico's model of history predicted discord in traditions as well as harmony, as we have seen, and when it did Pico kept a sharp eye out for conflict and planned to make much of it at Rome.

Much confusion on this point has arisen from an isolated line in the *Oration*, where we are told that besides totally reconciling Plato and Aristotle, Pico planned in his debate to point to "many places in which many opinions of Scotus and Thomas, and of Averroes and Avicenna, which are thought to be in discord, I assert to be in concord." The reference is to the first set of theses that Pico gives us "according to his own opinion," suggestively entitled "Seventeen paradoxical conclusions according to my own opinion, first reconciling the words of Aristotle and Plato, then those of other learned men who seem to strongly disagree." The first of these theses proclaims the universal harmony of Plato and Aristotle; thirteen uphold the partial agreement of Thomas, Scotus, or their schools on single issues in logic and theology (on one issue, Giles of Rome is also brought to harmony); and three others announce the agreement of Averrois and St. Thomas, or of Averrois and Avicenna, on three isolated questions in physics.[124]

The limited agreement that Pico proposed between these authorities—only Plato and Aristotle are said to be in total harmony—has often been interpreted as applying to all teachings of these writers, or even to all writers without distinction.[125] Pico's historians have been especially insistent on an impossible agreement between Pico himself and the writer he planned to attack most violently at Rome, St. Thomas Aquinas.[126] In part, at least, systematic reasons lay behind

---

[124] *Opera*, 326, 119; Garin, *Scritti vari*, 146. Cf. theses 1>1–17.

[125] Thus Randall (1962: 62): "For Pico, Plato, Aristotle, Jesus, the Cabbala, in fact everybody, really meant the same thing."

[126] Pico's supposed agreement with Thomas has been especially emphasized by Catholic historians including Dulles (1941) and Di Napoli (1965); cf. also the French theologians De Lubac (1974: 274) and Roulier (1989). Renaissance antecedents for this reading were provided by Gianfrancesco Pico, who in his spiritualized biography of his uncle (*Opera*, fol. 5v) claimed that whatever differences Pico had with Thomas early in life—an obscure allusion to Pico's troubles over his debate—Pico later told him that he disagreed with the official Dominican theologian on only "three or four out of ten thousand propositions" [adde quod ex decem millibus propositionum, tribus tantum, aut quattuor non consentire]. The fact that Gianfrancesco was heavily under the influence of the Dominican friar Girolamo Savonarola when he wrote the *Vita* was surely one factor behind this fantastic

this conflict, since Thomas's system regularly violated the cosmic symmetries critical to Pico's "new philosophy."

A sense of how polemical Pico could be can be gathered from his defense in the *Apology* of a thesis that the papal commission ruled to be "false, erroneous, heretical, and against the truth of Sacred Scriptures." In defending the thesis, which attacked Thomas on the way in which Christ descended into hell (in the three days between the Crucifixion and Resurrection), Pico admitted to difficulties in interpreting Thomas's view. But "to err on an opinion in Thomas is not to err in faith"; moreover, the origins of these difficulties lay in blatant inconsistencies in Thomas himself:

> Nor should it seem anywhere miraculous that Thomas follows one opinion in one place and another in another, for in the first book of the *Sentences* as well he follows the opinion of the Commentator [Averroes] on what can be generated from putrefaction, which he then rejects in the seventh book of the *Metaphysics* and elsewhere. Similarly, in the second book of the *Sentences* he follows the opinion of the Commentator on the [nature of] matter in the heavens, which he rejects both in the second book of *On the Heavens* and in the *Summa*. Similarly, in the fourth [book of the *Sentences*] and in his questions on Boethius's *On the Trinity*, he holds to the Commentator's way on unlimited dimensions [in prime matter], and then in his own treatise [on that subject], as is believed, and in many other places he does not hold to it. Similarly, in the first book of the *Sentences* he says that the intellect and [that which is] intelligible are understood through the same kind of action, but in the first part of the *Summa* and in the third book of the *Sentences* he holds that a reflexive action differs from a directed action. Similarly, in the [latter] work he claims that the soul of Christ as it was conjoinable to the body was like the soul of a pilgrim (*viator*), but insofar as it was conjoinable to the Word

---

claim. Gianfrancesco also quotes Pico's passing praise for Thomas in the *Heptaplus*, which was written while Pico was actively attempting to repair his differences with both the Dominicans and papacy. The extreme violence of Pico's early polemics with the Dominicans is suggested in Pico's defense of his first examined thesis in the *Apology*, in *Opera*, 125–50. On pp. 132–33 Pico attacks the vicar general of the Dominicans (cf. Dorez and Thuasne 1897: 62, 120)—one of Pico's most powerful adversaries—as a *magister rudis*, "badly disposed to the study of natural philosophy, worse to the study of metaphysics, and worst of all to the study of theology."

was like the soul of a possessor (*comprehensor*). But in the *Summa* he holds that Christ's soul totally, and in respect to everything, was like that of a *comprehensor*, and the fact that his soul did not transmit to his body the gift of splendor and the inability to suffer came from divine dispensation. He argues similarly concerning Christ's knowledge in [that] work [i.e., the *Sentences*], and otherwise in the *Summa*, and likewise on many other subjects—which shows that he followed different opinions in different places.[127]

It is not necessary here to elaborate on Pico's theological and philosophical disagreements with St. Thomas, which can be traced in my commentary on Pico's text. My object instead is simply to point to further evidence that Pico did not reduce all later writers to a philosophical mishmash where everyone agreed with everyone else. The *Oration* and *Apology* provide much evidence that in his debate Pico planned to oppose many theses no matter how they were construed. For reasons involving Pico's model of history, conflicts between schools could be expected to be sharpest in later "nations" like the Latins, whose theses are located at the start of his text. In the *Oration*, Pico discusses the role that false teachings were to play in his debate:

> If there is a sect that attacks truer teachings and ridicules the good causes of thought with false charges, in doing so it strengthens the truth and does not weaken it. Just as fire is stirred by motion, it excites and does not extinguish it. Moved by this belief, I wished to bring forth the opinions not of one set of teachings only—which would please some people—but of all teachings, so that through this comparison of many sects (*complurium sectarum collatione*), and discussion of many philosophies, the splendor of truth, which Plato recalls in his *Letters*, might shine more clearly on our souls just like the sun rising from the deep.[128]

Pico's Latin in this passage is instructive. "To judge through comparison" (*iudicare ex collatione*) was a standard scholastic formula, meant to distinguish the rational judgments of humans from the instinctive judgments of irrational animals. The underlying belief was that the truth would reveal itself, as Pico suggests in the *Oration*, once all proposed solutions to "doubtful points" were systematically col-

---

[127] *Opera*, 137.

[128] *Opera*, 325, 118–9; Garin, *Scritti vari*, 142.

lected and compared.[129] Reflecting this belief, the scholastic *quaestio* typically began with a collation of what was supposed to be all logically possible or historically proposed solutions to a problem, summarized in the opposing *sic*'s and *non*'s at the start of the question. In theory, these were to be weighed and ideally reconciled before the final "determination" of the question. Like the *disputatio* itself, the *quaestio* was the predictable byproduct of an intellectual culture that depended as heavily on memory as on writing in preserving ideas.[130] Even when the original sources of proposed solutions to a problem were lost or forgotten, their key ideas were preserved and indexed, so to speak, in writing or memory, under *quaestiones* that often remained fixed for centuries. The unorthodox historical structure of the first part of the nine hundred theses obscures the links between Pico's text and the *quaestio* genre; once Pico's theses have been regrouped topically and compared, however, much of the traditional nature of his debating plans comes to light.

In the majority of cases, Pico's theses fall into broad topical series that cut across both main divisions of the text. In some cases, these series involve no more than two or three sharply conflicting theses; in others, a dozen or more theses may be involved. In either case, the opposing theses in the historical part of the text can be viewed as traditional solutions to all those ambiguous and controversial questions that Pico promised to resolve in his debate. Pico's determination of these questions can often be located in a straightforward manner in the section of the text presented "according to his own opinion." When this is not clearly the case, his solutions to these questions can often be deduced quickly from the principles of his *philosophia nova* or from the various esoteric methodologies that he planned to illustrate in his debate. Drawing on all available evidence, in any case, we are rarely left totally in the dark as to Pico's opinions even in the problematic first part of the text, where theses that Pico supported are intentionally mixed with those that he meant to reinterpret radically or attack.

Supporting evidence that Pico meant to collate his theses in this fashion is found in the *Apology*, where he repeatedly qualifies the sense of one thesis in the light of others, and in records of contemporary disputes—including one in which we can observe Pico himself at work[131]—in which the initial theses placed in

---

[129] On the formula *iudicare ex collatione*, see the entry in Deferrari and Barry (1948: 613). It is noteworthy that in the medieval university the master in charge of disputations was sometimes referred to as a *collator*.

[130] Forms analogous to the *quaestio* can be identified in numerous non-Western scholastic traditions; unfortunately, no cross-cultural studies of the genre yet exist.

[131] See above, p. 6 n. 16.

dispute yield quickly to the debate of topically related problems. The *Oration* includes just such a collation of opinions in its formal defense of philosophy, moving rapidly through *sententiae* attributed to St. Paul, Dionysius, Jacob, Job, Moses, Plato, Pythagoras, Zoroaster, Orpheus, and other *prisci theologi*, to show that all ancient wisemen believed that philosophy provided a necessary propaedeutic to the mystical ascent.[132] The profound authority of these ancient wisemen assured their unanimity on this and other issues. Pico would have had to adjust his method only slightly in collating the warring doctrines of the later schools—letting the truth stand out from error, as he tells us, "just like the sun rising from the deep."[133]

If Pico had held his dispute, the occult links that he planted between theses would have given him a great deal of control over the direction of the debate. Along these lines, it is interesting to note that the text's opening theses, attributed to Albert the Great, are topically linked to dozens of theses scattered throughout the text central to Pico's proposed reconciliation of Plato and Aristotle. Thus the first thesis begins a long series on the complementarity of the Aristotelian and Platonic theories of knowledge; the second and third begin another on the Platonic ideas; the fourth begins a related series on the problem of matter and form; and so on. If the choice of where to begin were left to Pico's opponents—the most common scholastic procedure—and they began not unnaturally with the first theses in the text, Pico would have been able to turn the debate quickly towards his main philosophical themes.

Reconstruction of this part of Pico's plans helps us understand what he says about the size of his debate. Answering his critics on this issue, Pico did not suggest, as though this were a quodlibetal discussion of sorts, that in practice he only expected to debate a small number of theses. He instead chose to attack his critics directly:

> It remains in third place to respond to those who are offended by the great multitude of things that I have proposed, as though this burden sat

[132] *Opera*, 316ff.; Garin, *Scritti vari*, 112ff.

[133] The belief that truth might rise like fire from a collation of canonical texts was as common in Renaissance classicist as in scholastic circles. Thus nearly four decades after Pico, in *De libero arbitrio collatio* (*Opera* 1703–1706: 9:1220F), Erasmus hopes "ut superet ubique veritas, quae fortassis ex collatione Scripturarum, velut ignis ex collisione silicum, emicabit" [that truth will everywhere rise supreme, perhaps shining forth from a collation of Scriptures just like fire from the striking of flint].

> on their shoulders and whatever labor was here did not have to be endured by me alone. Certainly it is indecent and capricious to desire to set a limit to another's industry and, as Cicero says, to desire mediocrity in something that is better when it is bigger. In undertaking this venture it was necessary for me alone to succeed or fail. If I should succeed I do not see why anyone should judge it praiseworthy to excel on ten questions but blameworthy to excel on nine hundred. If I fail, if they hate me they will have reason to accuse me, or to excuse me if they love me.[134]

Although debating the theses one by one was clearly out of the question, Pico seems to suggest in this passage that in some sense he meant to debate them all. In parts of the theses where he meant to demonstrate an esoteric methodology—his means for converting the Jews, for example, or for decoding the secrets of the *prisci theologi*—Pico apparently expected to debate only enough theses to illustrate his techniques. Thus in one such section he promises to respond to seventy-four questions to "verify" his numerological methods, and in another involving magical exegesis vows no more than hints "useful to excite the minds of contemplatives."[135] It is reasonable to assume that Pico had similar plans for demonstrating his promised method for resolving "every proposed question on natural and divine things"—operating in this case on the theses from the warring schools collected in the historical part of his text. Indeed, analysis of repetitive patterns in topically related theses in the text suggests that once Pico had illustrated his system in resolving a few sets of questions, it would have been relatively simple for him to show how to apply that system everywhere else—even in theses not falling into clear-cut topical series.

In my commentary on Pico's text, I have attempted to track hundreds of occult links that Pico planted between his theses. Even though Pico could hardly have hoped in his debate to connect his theses in a totally predictable fashion, such links were critical to his disputing plans, and attempts to reconstruct them are a prerequisite to interpreting his text.

I will limit myself here to a single example of how theses from different parts of Pico's text are occultly linked. Since one of the key goals of Pico's debate was to reconcile Plato and Aristotle, not surprisingly both main sections of his text

---

134 *Opera*, 324, 117; Garin, *Scritti vari*, 138.

135 See the title to theses 7a>1–74; cf. thesis 10>1. For a stunning example of how in other cases Pico meant to "collate" far-flung esoteric theses in his debate, cf. 28.31, 11>22, 11>27.

contain dozens of theses on the Platonic theory of ideas. These theses cover an enormous range of topics drawn from fifteen hundred years of Greek, Arabic, Hebrew, and Latin scholasticism—with the logical and ontological status of the ideas as universals, with their relation to angelic and human cognition, with their ties to the divine nature, and so on. We can follow Pico's most common way of resolving these topics in a small subseries of theses on the relationship between the ideas and God's nature. The connections between theses in this series are indeed "occult" due to inconsistencies in the technical terms that Pico adopts unchanged from his sources. But this is a common problem in the nine hundred theses, and it will be useful to follow one such series to its end. Pico boasted that his text contained all the most ambiguous and controversial questions fought over by the schools, and in his view those conflicts arose in large part from equivocal uses of technical language.

Like dozens of other conflicts that Pico planned to resolve, the debate over the location of the ideas could boast over a thousand years of history. In the ancient syncretic systems closest to Pico's own thought, the ideas were located in an eternally created hypostasis subordinate to the divine nature—using Pico's terms, in the "intellect," "intelligence," "intellectual nature," "angelic mind," "angel," or "first created mind"—from which the rest of reality emanated. This view was rejected by early Christian scholastics like St. Augustine, however, who relocated the ideas directly in God, attempting this way to "save" both the eternity of the ideas and the unmediated *creatio ex nihilo* demanded by Christian dogma. Like most syncretic solutions, this one led to new problems. Location of the ideas directly in God could be interpreted as a threat to his unity, since the ideas were often represented as individual archetypes of creation; indeed, Augustine himself literally posited one idea for each created being.[136] An alternate solution, commonly associated with John Scotus Erigena (ninth century CE), attempted to get around this problem by reinterpreting the ideas as created beings located in, but not directly identified with, God's nature. But this led to still other problems, since it apparently elevated part of creation to coeternal status with God.[137]

Attempts by later Latin scholastics to avoid *both* these problems *and* Neo-Platonic emanationism led to the kinds of verbal-metaphysical compromises typical

---

[136] Cf. Gilson (1955: 74), with relevant Latin passages from Augustine provided on p. 593 n. 25.

[137] Cf. Gilson (1955: 117–19), with relevant Latin passages from Erigena's works provided on p. 611 nn. 17, 18.

universally of scholastic traditions. Thus John Duns Scotus, the official theologian of the Franciscan order, tried to resolve the problem by positing the ideas as "secondary" (and hence not eternal) objects of God's cognition. In Scotus's formulation, the ideas possessed only an "intelligible" or "relational" existence (*esse intelligibile* or *esse secundum quid*). Scotus's solution is recalled by Pico in a carefully worded thesis presented *secundum Scotum:*

> 4.2. The idea of a stone is nothing but the stone produced by the divine intellect in intelligible existence, which is existence in a relational sense (*esse secundum quid*), existing in the divine mind just as the known in the knower.

Scotus's weakening of the ontological status of the ideas led a number of later Franciscans—including the so-called prince of Scotists, Francis of Meyronnes—to return to a view closer to St. Augustine's, once again identifying the Platonic ideas immediately with God. Pico predictably kept a sharp eye out for civil wars like this in scholastic subtraditions; in the nine hundred theses he accordingly included the following thesis from book one of Francis's commentary on Peter Lombard's *Sentences*. Without knowing Pico's source, it would be difficult to spot the occult links between the theses ascribed here to Scotus and Francis, especially since Pico adopted unchanged Francis's equivocal designation of the ideas as "quiddities"—a term whose conflicting technical senses are duly cataloged in the historical part of Pico's text.[138] But Francis's break with Scotus was still hotly debated in Pico's day, and the *occulta concatenatio* between theses would have been transparent to any contemporary theologian—at least once Pico's theses were topically rearranged:

> 3.5. Quiddities [i.e., the ideas] possess their formal existence from eternity from themselves, not from something outside themselves (*non ab extrinseco*).

Pico's own views on this conflict show up hundreds of theses later, in a section of the text that he entitled "Thirty-one conclusions according to my own opinion, rather opposed to the common mode of speaking of theologians."[139] Pico's position can be predicted immediately from the principles of his "new philoso-

---

[138] See, e.g., theses 2.42, 3.8, 7.36.

[139] There are only twenty-nine theses in the surviving text; see theses 4>1–29. Evidence suggests that the two missing theological theses were removed while the work was in press.

phy": Located at the pinnacle of the hierarchy of being, God can admit in his essence neither a multitude of separate Platonic ideas nor any "primary" or "secondary" acts of cognition. The technically precise language of the following thesis was meant by Pico to undercut the views of the ideas attributed to John Scotus Erigena, John Duns Scotus, Francis of Meyronnes, and the other Latins whom Pico collectively labeled "the common school of theologians":

> 4>6. The intuition of God's knowledge is not directed formally at creatures as primary or secondary objects, as the common school of theologians says, but contemplating himself only, and nothing but himself primarily or secondarily, in a unitive and elevated manner, and with more than the power equal to the task, he knows all things.
>
> Corollary: There is no multiplicity of understandings in God, nor do creatures, as things understood, exist numerically in the divine essence as something understood, but in the innermost sense there exists but one most simple understanding.[140]

By this point, Pico's own view of the Platonic ideas will hardly come as a surprise. Like everything else in his system, Pico pictured the ideas as existing in a complex series of correlative "modes"—in God "ideally" and indistinguishably, in the first created mind "formally" and more diffusely. The fact that Pico left unexplained how the ideas unfolded from their "ideal" to "formal" modes of existence—he would have typically offered a mathematical metaphor in explanation—need not concern us here. In Pico's own eyes, at least, he had found a foolproof way to simultaneously uphold Augustine's view that uncreated ideas exist in God—without threatening God's unity or positing "eternal creatures" in his nature—and to defend the orthodoxy of his own emanationism:

> 4>3. I hold with theological truth that the ideal and formal reasons of things were first effectively devised by God formally in the first created mind.

---

[140] In reconciling warring scholastic traditions, Pico was prepared to discuss God's "properties," "attributes," "notions," and so on, as we see in his "paradoxical reconciliative conclusions," 1>2–3, 1>7. He was also apparently prepared to discuss the syncretic bonds between such concepts and the Neo-Platonic *henads*, kabbalistic *sefirot*, and similar concepts. At the deepest theological level, however, as we see in this thesis, he felt that such concepts applied linguistic distinctions far beyond their legitimate sphere; in his theological conclusions, see also thesis 4>5.

> Corollary: Where the ideas exist ideally [i.e., in God], they do not exist formally. Where they exist formally [in the first created mind], they do not exist ideally.

Pico's approach to this ancient cosmological problem illustrates the enormous—and often comical—gulfs separating premodern from modern views of language. What is crucial to note at present is that Pico did not plan to argue that Francis and Scotus were in harmony on this issue but intended to construct a correlative metaphysical framework within which the deeper grounds of their conflict could be satisfactorily "resolved." The extreme flexibility of that framework would have allowed Pico to reconcile virtually any authorities—including Scotus and Francis if his historical model had demanded it—simply by distinguishing the levels of reality intended by their concepts, just as he did in harmonizing Xenophanes and the Eleatics on the concept of the "one."[141] The simple pattern in this series of theses shows up in dozens of other sets in Pico's text. The close links between Pico's exegetical methods and his correlative system by now require no further comment.

The broader reconstruction of Pico's plans at Rome requires tortured leaps like this around the nine hundred theses—a tribute, if nothing else, to the prodigious powers of memory required in Pico's debate. Other questions about his dispute too find no easy answers. Outside of his suggestions of a papal role, for example, Pico gives us no direct evidence as to how his theses were to have been placed in debate or judged. Since Pico was technically the *respondens* at Rome, following usual procedures his opponents would normally have had first shot in the debate—raising objections to theses to which Pico would be required to "respond." In that response, Pico would have been free to make new distinctions in the theses or to bring related topics to the center of discussion.

That normal procedure was to be followed in Pico's debate can be inferred from the form of a handful of theses scattered about his text. Thus the key conclusion announcing Pico's reconciliation of Plato and Aristotle reads:

> 1>1. There is no natural or divine question in which Aristotle and Plato do not agree in meaning and substance, although in their words they seem to disagree.

---

[141] Above, p. 29.

In the *Oration* and *Apology* Pico remarks with some justice that this thesis could have "easily been drawn out into six hundred headings or more, enumerating singly all the places in which I think that they agree, others that they disagree."[142] The only reasonable way that the thesis could be debated would be through Pico's response to counter-theses proposing points on which Plato and Aristotle disagreed. Even here Pico could be expected to invoke an *occulta concatenatio* between his theses, since in many cases he could point to conclusions that suggested his anticipation of, and response to, the most likely counter-theses raised against him.[143]

The fact that Pico's opponents were apparently to have fired the first shot in the debate raises other problems. One of these involves the obscure symbolic language found in many sections of the text. When in one thesis Pico tells us that when we are uncertain as to how to proceed in a magical petition (or prayer) we should turn to the "lord of the nose," exactly who did he expect would contradict him? From Pico's sources we find that the "lord of the nose" was a symbol of the fifth of the ten kabbalistic *sefirot*, or emanated states of God's being, but no one at Rome could have possibly known this but Pico himself.[144] The presence of theses like this suggests that before debating a conclusion an *opponens* could demand an explanation of its bare sense—a declaration of its meaning *ex vi verborum*, to use the scholastic formula adopted by the papal commission and Pico himself.[145] The requirement that a *respondens* provide a brief explanation of a thesis before its formal debate was apparently standard disputation practice. The nature of these explanations is suggested by the brief formal replies that Pico provided first verbally and then in writing to the papal commission in defending the orthodoxy of his theses.[146]

Another difficulty lies in the expectation that as *respondens* in the debate, Pico

---

142 *Opera*, 331, 124; Garin, *Scritti vari*, 162–4.

143 Cf., e.g., theses 5>19 and 5>29, which suggest the complementarity of Platonic and Aristotelian theories of knowledge.

144 Cf. thesis 28.40 and note.

145 On the formula *ex vi verborum* or *ex vi sermonis*, see the proceedings of the papal commission (Dorez and Thuasne 1897: 116, 127, 129, etc.); cf. *Apology*, in *Opera*, 149, where Pico cites William of Ockham on this topic.

146 See the text in Dorez and Thuasne (1897: 114ff.). In the *Apology*, in *Opera*, 167, Pico tells us that the object of such an explanation was "to declare explicitly the force of each term advanced in the conclusion" [explicite declarare vim singulorum terminorum in conclusione positorum].

would defend all the theses in his text, a number of which he clearly did not endorse. The initial confusion of Pico's contemporaries on this point, and the continued confusion of modern scholars, has already been noted.[147] But the problem here probably lies less in the heterodoxy of Pico's plans than in modern exaggerations of the formality of scholastic disputes, which outside of special academic situations were often just as unruly and violent as their classicist critics loved to complain. Once Pico argued that he did not endorse all the theses in the historical part of his text, the pope accepted his argument without known complaint.[148] Pico's main goal was undoubtedly to get his central issues placed rapidly in dispute, and given the *occulta concatenatio* that he planted between theses, that end would not have been hindered by his unequal endorsement of the propositions in the historical part of the text. Whether an opponent began with a thesis presented "according to Thomas," "according to Averroes," or given according to Pico's own opinion, in Pico's response one could expect a rapid-fire collation of theses drawn from various sections of the text.

A hint of Pico's casual attitude towards disputational procedures is further suggested by his indifferent use of the terms *quaestiones* and *conclusiones* in referring to his theses before as well as after his troubles with the church began.[149] Given these circumstances, it would be an error to try to reconstruct too rigid a set of formal procedures for his debate—procedures that Pico probably never planned and, given the chaotic nature of scholastic disputes, could not have reasonably carried out.

---

[147] Above, pp. 8–9.

[148] Above, p. 9.

[149] Pico uses the more tentative term *quaestiones* not only in the *Apology* (e.g., *Opera*, 114), which was written at the height of his papal troubles, but also in a letter written well before publication of the theses (*Opera*, 382).

Chapter 2: Syncretism in Premodern Thought

There is layer upon layer in the words of the sages. In your reading of them, penetrate deeply. If you simply read what appears on the surface, you will misunderstand. Steep yourself in the words; only then will you grasp their meaning. Chu Hsi (twelfth century CE), *Conversations of Master Chu, Arranged Topically*[1]

If anyone more closely turns over and weighs more precisely their dissenting words—and searching more scrupulously, peeling off the skin, presses inside with a profound and penetrating mind into their deepest hiding places—he will discover in their conflicting and battling words a unity of sense beyond ambiguity. Gianfrancesco Pico on his uncle's *Concord of Plato and Aristotle*[2]

i. Syncretic Strategies

So far, we have looked at those reconciliative methods most important to Pico's disputing plans. Studying them more fully illuminates the syncretic forces that helped shape his system. Those methods were flexible and could be used to effect full or partial reconciliations of traditions. In practice, Pico often combined different methods in single theses. Here I will analyze ten basic types, looking in this section at their general character and in the next at their systematic effects. Some variation of all these methods shows up in all mature commentarial traditions, and none was Pico's own invention.

1. *Deductive reconciliations.* Pico sometimes simply ignored the apparent conflicts in his authorities and deduced harmonious views from the purported "principles"

---

[1] Gardner, trans. (1990: 129).

[2] *Vita*, in *Opera*, fol. 5r.

or "fundamentals" of their thought. This was one of his methods in bringing Scotus and Thomas, and Avicenna and Averroes, to partial agreement, in wringing Christian truths from pagan or kabbalistic sources, and in harmonizing Aristotelian with Platonic texts.[3] Precedents for many of Pico's least historical readings show up regularly in earlier or contemporary scholastic sources. Some were apparently meant as challenges to particular schools—as in theses "according to Thomas" exactly reversing Thomas's sense, or in others claiming that Alexander of Aphrodisias or Averroes upheld, and did not deny, the idea of personal immortality. We will later observe Pico using this strategy to reconcile the Averroist concept of the "unity of the intellect" with Christian dogma—an assault again on Thomas Aquinas and Marsilio Ficino, both of whom attacked that concept on religious grounds.[4]

2. *Eliminating arbitrary equivocation in terms.* Pico, like syncretists in other cultures, frequently argued that apparent conflicts in authorities arose from totally superficial differences in language. Once we moved from the "outer bark" of words to their "inner core," these conflicts would disappear. This idea is suggested in Pico's biography by his nephew, quoted at the head of this chapter, and in a number of theses worded like the following:

> 1>4. On the subject of theology, Thomas, Scotus, and Giles agree fundamentally and at root, although in its branches and on the outer surface of words each of them seems to disagree strongly with the others.

> 1>16. Averroes and Avicenna cannot disagree fundamentally on whether the physicist receives composite bodies from the metaphysician, even if they differ in their words.

The *Commento* opens with similar language: Despite conflicts in words, all ancient Platonists agree totally in sense, claiming as their principal doctrine that being exists in three "modes"—causal, formal, and participated.[5] Arguments like this help explain why Pico's historical theses include propositions using the same technical terms (like *quidditas* or *esse*) in a wide range of conflicting senses. These could be sorted out at Rome, honoring or taxing the "tumult of the moderns partly for their merits, partly for their faults"—as Gianfrancesco tells us of his

---

[3] Cf., e.g., theses 1>3, 11>27, and the examples cited passim below.

[4] Below, pp. 112–14.

[5] Garin, *Scritti vari*, 461.

uncle's *Concord*[6]—depending only on whether Pico chose to view these conflicts as real or illusory.

3. *Reading the terms of one tradition through the concepts of another.* This was one variation of Pico's deductive methods. His main inspiration for its use came from late Greek commentators like Themistius, Ammonius, and Simplicius, as suggested by the theses drawn from their works. Like these late-ancient Neo-Platonic scholastics, Pico most often applied the technique at the expense of the Aristotelian tradition, reinterpreting key Aristotelian terms in a Platonic (that is, a Neo-Platonic) fashion. We will later watch Pico using this strategy to reinterpret the Aristotelian substance/accident distinction, which he recast proportionally in line with his "new philosophy."[7] He also applied it in his Platonization of favored Latin scholastics like Albert the Great and in his Christianization of pagan and Jewish esoteric traditions.

4. *The double-truth.* Western medievalists invariably associate the double-truth with Averroes and his Latin commentators, but numerous variations of the technique show up as well in non-Western scholastic traditions.[8] Medieval Christian condemnations of the double-truth had little lasting effect, and Pico employed the strategy repeatedly in his theses without being criticized by the papal commission. Thus in his theological conclusions he invoked the method to resolve a traditional controversy over whether *aevum* or "aeviternity"—the durational state proper to angels—like eternity was continuous or like time had a beginning and end.[9] This question, which involved a number of sticky theological problems, could be treated by raising some careful technical distinctions:

---

[6] *Vita*, in *Opera*, fol. 5r.

[7] Below, pp. 97ff.

[8] Cf., among many other examples, the similar views of the double-truth developed in the three-treatise (*San-lun*) school of Buddhism. For illustrative texts, see de Bary et al., eds. (1960: 1:293–303); cf. Fung Yu-lan (1953: 2:293ff.). The double-truth was also linked to the development of dualistic views of reality in medieval Indian traditions; on this topic in Vedantic scholasticism, see Mumme (1992).

[9] The concept of *aevum* was itself a syncretic construct, arising in antiquity from reconciliations of sacred texts claiming that God alone existed in eternity with other texts placing angels or demons in that state. The conflict was resolved by distinguishing between *aeternitas per se* and *aevum*, *aeviternitas*, or *aeternitas participata*, etc.—the durational state of immutable but created beings.

> 4>28. Theologically speaking, I say that in aeviternity succession formally speaking is not intrinsically continuative, but limited. According to the philosophers, however, I state the contrary.

Pico's fullest exposition of the double-truth comes in a passage of the *Commento* that discusses a conflict among ancient Neo-Platonists over the unity of the angelic or intellectual nature:

> Some, like Proclus, Hermias, and Syrianus, and many others, place between God and the world soul . . . a large number of creatures. . . . Plotinus, Porphyry, and in general the most perfect Platonists place between God and the world soul one creature only, which they call the "son of God," since it was produced by God. The first opinion agrees more with Dionysius the Areopagite and Christian theologians, who posit an almost infinite number of angels. The second is more philosophical and agrees more with Aristotle and Plato and is followed by all Peripatetics and the better Platonists. And therefore we, having proposed to declare what we believe is the common meaning of Plato and Aristotle, shall follow this second way—having left the first, although it alone by itself is true (*benché sola per sè vera*).[10]

Pico planned to use a number of variant forms of the double-truth at Rome. Following earlier medieval precedents, he even proposed a double-truth of sorts between the medical doctrines of Aristotle and Galen.[11]

It is rarely easy to judge the precise motives behind use of the double-truth. Western scholastics undeniably did employ the strategy at times to mask heretical views, but it could be used just as well as part of an elaborate demonstration of the limits of reason. Most often, however, as in the passages just quoted, it simply provided a means to allow discussion of dangerous theological issues without prejudicing either religious or philosophical authority. Following the lead of Etienne Gilson, Western medievalists commonly argue that no one using the method literally believed in two separate truths, one philosophical and one theological. But it cannot be denied that repeated use of the technique promoted something like that view. Thus despite what the *Commento* tells us about following the "more philosophical" way on the unity of the angelic nature, as synonyms of the intellect, first created mind, angelic mind, and so on, in both the *Commento* and nine

---

[10] Garin, *Scritti vari*, 464–65.

[11] Thesis 2>76.

hundred theses we find Pico using terms like "angels" and "the angel" indiscriminately—sometimes in the same sentence—leaving the impression that these did in some way represent complementary views of reality.[12]

5. *Letter symbolism, gematria, and anagrammatic methods.* Pico came armed with more radical exegetical methods that allowed him to rewrite entire traditions when needed. He drew many of these from his kabbalistic sources, but he also found support for them in a wide range of Greek, Arabic, and Latin texts. These methods were grounded on the traditional belief that the deepest meanings of sacred texts transcended their outer sense and indeed might extend to the isolated shapes of letters. Thus in Pico's first or historical set of Cabalistic theses, we find that there is no letter or even part of a letter in the Torah that does not conceal divine secrets; in his second set, presented "according to his own opinion," Pico was prepared to unveil the Christian truths that Moses hid in the Law in the order of otherwise trivial words (like the Hebrew word for "then"), or even in single strokes of single letters (as in the closed form of the letter *mem*). Every stroke of every letter in the Torah contains Christian secrets—supplying ammunition "against the rude slander of the Hebrews," "leaving them no corner in which to hide."[13]

Pico's other esoteric methods were equally extreme. Following the fact that numbers were represented by letters in Semitic languages and Greek, various techniques commonly known as *gematria* were developed in antiquity for transforming words and texts through their numerical values. Thus the numerical values of words or letters could be added up or operated on arithmetically in other ways to hide or reveal secret messages in texts—this was the method used in Revelation 13:18 to hide the secret name of the Beast—or other messages could be concealed or uncovered by substituting one letter for another using fixed numerical procedures. These methods were employed widely in antiquity in dream analysis, mystical and prophetic exegesis, apocalyptic composition, as well as for syncretic ends, and following predictable patterns became progressively more com-

[12] For a good example of Pico's rapid shifts between singular and plural forms, see the *Commento,* in Garin, *Scritti vari,* 510.

[13] *Oration/Apology,* in *Opera,* 328, 330; 122, 124; Garin, *Scritti vari,* 154, 160. Pico's works are filled with such expressions, undermining attempts to link his syncretism to modern forms of toleration.

plex and systematic in the Middle Ages.[14] Thus Scholem notes one kabbalistic manuscript that lists seventy-two methods of *gematriot*,[15] presumably one for each of the characters in God's secret name of seventy-two letters.[16]

It is possible to reconstruct a few of Pico's word/number calculations in the conclusions, but for reasons of his own he left few hints as to where he meant to make them, and fewer still as to which technique he meant to use in any one thesis. In most but not all cases his readings had less to do with the esoteric aims of his sources than with his own syncretic goals. In one thesis he claimed that unspecified *gematria*-like techniques were the key to his syncretic fusion of natural magic and Cabala.[17]

Pico employed related esoteric methods that involved anagrammatic manipulations of Scriptures, drawn mainly from the thirteenth- and fourteenth-century writings of the Spanish kabbalist Abraham Abulafia and his commentators. In the *Apology*, Pico compared this "science of the revolution of the alphabet" (*scientia alphabetariae revolutionis*) or "art of combination" (*ars combinandi*), as he variously called it, to the method known to the Latins as the *ars Raymundi*—that is, to the anagrammatic methods of the Christian Spaniard Raymond Lull—although he conceded that "perhaps they proceed in a different mode."[18] Abulafia's methods were tied to mystical goals and only secondarily to what we would normally think of as textual exegesis. The aim was not to reconcile Scriptures with each other or with pagan traditions—although this was in part what Pico was after—but to transform the soul mystically through contemplation of the infinite depths of truth concealed in sacred texts. In the nine hundred theses, Pico suggested that his own methods could not be applied mechanically but required a state of contemplative purity, perhaps even the trancelike state assumed by Abulafia and his disciples.[19]

---

[14] These techniques seem to be nearly universal in premodern cultures; outside the West, they have survived well into modern times. Thus the Javanese novelist Pramoedya Ananta Toer has a character complain in *Footsteps* (Eng. trans. 1995: 376): "Numbers, days, even the hour, the syllables of a person's name, the year, month, the points of the compass were all given a numerical value in Javanese. Then they would be added together in some combination or another and the result used to foretell what would happen or to decide what shouldn't happen."

[15] Scholem (1974: 341–42).

[16] Cf. thesis 11>56 and note.

[17] Thesis 9>25.

[18] *Opera,* 180. On Pico and Lullism, see most recently Umberto Eco (1997).

[19] See, e.g., theses 11>12–13. On Abulafia's methods, see Scholem (1941: 119–55), who provides some useful texts in English translation. After Pico's death, his nephew

The *Heptaplus* implies that Pico's *ars combinandi* involved precise transformation rules, but in practice these reduced to more or less free permutations of letters if not indeed to automatic writing inspired by God.[20] In effect, using these techniques any required reading could be gotten from any text. Scholem points to the conviction among Renaissance Jews that six hundred thousand interpretations of the Torah existed, one for each Israelite alive when Moses received the Law. The idea was that the "great name of God" that was the Torah itself contained the same infinite depths of truth that lay hidden in his transcendent nature.[21] Pico suggests something similar when he claims that the means of reading the Law "without points"—that is, without vowel signs, in Hebrew effectively eliminating fixed divisions in words—illustrates both the manner in which sacred texts are written and God's infinite and "unial containment" of all things.[22] In an appendix to the *Heptaplus*, Pico illustrates his *ars combinandi* at length, giving us "a taste of Mosaic profundity" by making repeated anagrammatic transformations of the first word of the Torah—*Bereshit*, "In the beginning." Here we find that in that single word Moses miraculously concealed all the principles of the hierarchy of being as well as the Christian truth that God created the world through his Son the Word, the Alpha and Omega, beginning and end of the cosmos.[23]

Finally, Pico syncretically fused *gematria* with other numerological techniques in his "way of numbers" (*via numerorum*), leading "to the investigation and understanding of everything knowable." His goal here was to unite the numerological symbolism of the Pythagoreans—syncretically fused with Neo-Platonic metaphysics in deep antiquity—with *gematria* and less formal types of number symbolism in Scriptures, in the Greek and Roman church fathers, and in various scholastic and esoteric sources, in order to unveil the secret harmonies buried there.[24] Once again, enough of Pico's *via numerorum* can be reconstructed to decide on his general approach, although not always his procedures thesis by thesis.

---

claimed—supposedly on the basis of Pico's unpublished papers—that Pico abandoned the "art of Abulafia" in his later years; see below, p. 163 n. 89. As we will find is true of all Gianfrancesco's claims about his uncle's later thought, this contention must be viewed with deep skepticism.

[20] *Heptaplus*, in *Opera*, 59ff.; Garin, *Scritti vari*, 374ff.

[21] Scholem (1974: 170–72).

[22] Thesis 11>70.

[23] *Opera*, 59ff.; Garin, *Scritti vari*, 374ff.

[24] On Pico's *via numerorum*, see further theses 7>1–11, 7a>1–74, and my commentary.

His methods were again flexible enough to yield virtually any reading needed for any purpose.

6. *Standard scholastic distinction.* More prosaically, Pico planned to reconcile other authorities by applying standard verbal modifiers to distinguish those writers' real from their apparent meanings. The standard scholastic distinction shows up in all its familiar tortured forms in Pico's historical theses. Thus one thesis drawn from St. Thomas tells us that the true body of Christ exists "locally" in heaven but "sacramentally" on the altar, and so on.[25] In the *Apology*, Pico demonstrates his mastery of this ancient scholastic device at length. In those sections where he claims the most originality, however, he typically distinguishes concepts in the more elaborate correlative manner characteristic of his *philosophia nova*. He also reinterprets traditional distinctions like the Aristotelian subject/accident dichotomy in this fashion.[26]

7. *Hierarchical or correlative distinctions.* As suggested in the last chapter, these were Pico's most typical syncretic devices. While the standard scholastic distinction typically led to binary divisions of concepts—*substance* or *accident*, *real* or *intentional* existence, *speculative* or *practical* science, and so on—once organized in correlative series these could be multiplied in a nearly endless fashion, limited only by a commentator's ingenuity in inventing verbal modifiers for some base term. This method is beautifully illustrated in a thesis that contains one of the most extreme examples of hierarchical thinking known. Hyperscholastic propositions like this one, which show up frequently in Pico's theses given "according to his own opinion," underscore the vulnerability of the standard neo-Burckhardtian view of Pico as a precursor of modern ways of thinking or as an incipient critic of hierarchical thought.[27] The seven levels of reality distinguished in this thesis show up repeatedly in Pico's theses presented "according to his own opinion":

---

[25] Thesis 2.14.

[26] See below, pp. 97ff.

[27] Thus Cassirer (1927; Eng. trans. 1963: 84), echoing Giovanni Gentile, found in Pico "the modern pathos of thought"; Garin (1963: 55) saw him expressing the "conscious image of man characteristic of the modern world"; Kristeller (1972: 13–14) found him taking "one of the first steps in dissolving the notion of the great chain of being that had dominated Western thought for so many centuries."

> 5>26. Beauty exists in God as its cause, in the total intellect truly essentially totally, in the particular intellect truly partially essentially, in the rational soul truly participationally, in the visible accidents of the heavens imagerially essentially totally, in subcelestial visible qualities imagerially partially essentially, in quantities imagerially participationally. [!]

Pico most often invoked extreme correlative distinctions like these to unveil the secret concords in the ancients—his apparent object here was to harmonize ideas in the Platonic corpus with elements of his own system[28]—but these methods could be used just as well to effect full or partial reconciliations of more recent traditions. We earlier saw him applying the technique in reconciling Xenophanes and the Eleatics on the concept of the "one" and in resolving Christian conflicts over how the Platonic ideas existed in God.[29]

8. *Syncretic syllogisms.* Premodern commentators routinely gathered support for old views—and in the process generated new ones—by combining unrelated snippets of sacred texts in a systematic fashion. The assumption was that occult messages hidden collectively in those texts, and even "everything knowable," could be uncovered once those passages were combined in a syllogistic or quasi-syllogistic fashion.[30] This scissors-and-paste approach to the history of thought is nicely illustrated in a characteristic thesis from Pico's second set of Cabalistic conclusions:

> 11>24. By the response of the Cabalists to the question of why in the Book of Numbers the section on the death of Mary is joined to the sec-

[28] The thesis is an apparent attempt to translate into systematic form Diotima's metaphorical speech on beauty found in *Symposium* 210a–212a; there may also be resonances here from the discussions of beauty in the *Phaedrus*, discussed at length by late-ancient commentators like Hermias. In the thesis, Pico distinguishes seven levels of beauty to correlate these views with the seven days of creation, seven ages of history, and the seven levels of the mystical ascent distinguished in the nine hundred theses. Cf. 5>58 and my discussion below, pp. 110–12.

[29] Above, pp. 29, 53–56.

[30] Galileo's satire did not depart far from reality when Simplicio, the scholastic interlocutor in the *Dialogue Concerning the Two Chief World Systems* (trans. Drake, 1967: 108), declares that in reading Aristotle we "must be able to combine this passage with that, collecting together one text here and another very distant from it. There is no doubt that whoever has this skill will be able to draw from his books demonstrations of all that can be known; for every single thing is in them." On similar views in non-Western scholastic traditions, see Henderson (1991), Cabezón, ed. (1998).

> tion on the red calf [cf. Num. 19:2–10, 20:1], and by their exposition of that passage where Moses, in the sin involving the golden calf, said *Destroy me!* [Exod. 32:32], and by the words in the *Zohar* on that text, *And we were healed by his bruises* [Isa. 53:5], those Hebrews claiming that it was not fitting that the death of Christ should satisfy mankind's sin are inevitably refuted.[31]

The remarkable ways in which unrelated fragments of sacred texts were combined by ancient exegetes explains the origins of many of the theological concepts that passed into the religious traditions accepted by Pico. Thus the syncretic fusion of biblical references to "Wisdom, God's darling and delight," made "at the beginning, long before the earth itself" (Wisdom 9:1–18; cf. Prov. 8:22–31) with Christ's characterization in Paul and elsewhere as "the power and wisdom of God" (I Cor. 1:25), eventually led to Jesus' *literal* identification with God's creative wisdom and power. From here it was a simple step to his identification with the *Logos* or Word of God—linked to wisdom and creation in Wisdom 9:1–18, etc.—and to his eventual elevation to the "mind of God" in the scholastic Trinity. The peculiar anthropomorphization of God's *Logos* or Word was prepared by Hebrew exegetes long before it appeared in its Christian form in the Gospel according to John. Thus in a famous passage in the Book of Wisdom (18:14–17), we find the anthropomorphized Word leaping in judgment from the heavenly throne, bearing God's "inflexible decree" as his sword—"his head touching the heavens, his feet on earth."[32]

Pico's text contains a number of theses that combine unrelated fragments of biblical, Talmudic, kabbalistic, and pagan texts in this syncretic manner—harmonizing Plato and Aristotle and the *prisci theologi*, battling the Jews, and reading out secret messages hidden collectively in Scriptures using the tools of medieval logic developed precisely for exegetical ends like these.[33]

---

[31] The passage syncretically conflates the Virgin Mary with Miriam of Num. 20:1.

[32] The Book of Wisdom, traditionally attributed to Solomon, antedated by perhaps a century the works of Philo of Alexandria, who is often represented as the source of the Johannine *Logos*. The syncretic identification of one divine being with another following the paths taken here goes back to deep antiquity—e.g., to Mesopotamian traditions, where Enlil was sometimes characterized as the "Word" of Anu, or Ea as the "son of Anu," "begotten in his image"; cf. Sandars (1972: 24, 26). Evidence for such tendencies can also be found in the Egyptian pyramid texts, dating from the mid-third millennium BCE.

[33] The exegetical functions of medieval logic have unfortunately been obscured by the mathematical formalism that has dominated studies of that field for the past sixty years.

9. *Allegorization.* Pico used allegory repeatedly in the nine hundred theses to uncover the occult agreement of the *prisci theologi* and kabbalists, relying in part on the earlier readings of late Greek Neo-Platonists and the more speculative kabbalists, and in part on what in the *Commento* Pico suggested was his immediate and apparently inspired grasp of the sense of symbols.[34] He also used allegory this way in the *Oration*, *Heptaplus*, and *Commentary on the Psalms*, and planned a vast extension of the technique in his *Poetic Theology*, which he apparently never

---

Even Moody, however, who was the first scholar to translate medieval logic routinely into modern symbolic notation, was forced to acknowledge profound differences between the theoretical aims of symbolic logic and the exegetical goals of its medieval predecessor. Thus while modern logic is an "axiomatic derivation of the principles of mathematics, Medieval logic functioned as an art of language (*sermocinalis scientia*) closely associated with grammar, to be used as a means of construing authoritative texts of Sacred Scripture and of the Church Fathers and of establishing interpretations of such texts that would be logically coherent and free from contradiction" (1975: 373–74). *Sermocinalis scientia* is more precisely translated as the science or art of "speech" or "discourse"—that is, of oral disputation—which was taught in the medieval university as a branch either of logic or of rhetoric. Insofar as the premises and conclusions of medieval logic were exclusively verbal statements—and in disputation, at least, had to be held tenaciously in memory—to translate its propositions into modern symbolic notation or to treat it as a theoretical science seriously distorts its role in medieval thought. More recent scholarship has suggested that medieval interest in logical paradoxes or *insolubilia*—the most modern appearing elements of medieval logic—did not derive from speculative motives, as Moody and his followers argued, but from pedagogical ends that once again involved disputational needs. This finding further undermines the outward parallels between modern and medieval logic that have driven studies of the latter field since the 1930s.

[34] See Garin, *Scritti vari*, 556. After outlining his allegorical reading of the fable of Alcestis and Orpheus, which was aimed polemically at Ficino's commentary on the *Symposium*, Pico writes: "Quasi maraviglia mi pare che e Marsilio e ogni altro, preso dalle parole di Platone, non l'abbia inteso; e testimone me n' è la conscienzia mia, che la prima volta che mai el *Simposio* lessi, non prima ebbi finito di leggere le parole sue in questo loco, che nella mente questa verità m'apparve" [It appears nearly astonishing to me that Marsilio and all others, struck by the words of Plato, have not understood them; and my conscience testifies that the first time I ever read the *Symposium*, I had not finished reading the words in this place before this truth appeared in my mind]. Pico promises to provide a fuller interpretation of this myth "in my commentary on the *Symposium* and in my *Poetic Theology*." Pico's troubles over the nine hundred theses caused him to abandon work on both these texts, which were planned as part of his broader polemics against Ficino.

completed.[35] The syncretic functions of this method are suggested in the following thesis proclaiming the syncretic agreement of six separate traditions:

> 11>10. That which among the Cabalists is called <מטטרון *Metatron*[36]> is without doubt that which is called Pallas by Orpheus, the paternal mind by Zoroaster, the son of God by Mercury, wisdom by Pythagoras, the intelligible sphere by Parmenides.

No divine inspiration is needed to see that this "mystery" refers to the intellectual nature or angelic mind, the first created hypostasis in Pico's cosmology. In general, the ancients' secret messages frequently possess this rather pedestrian character. As the *Heptaplus* tells us of Moses' secrets in the Law, we must not expect to learn there anything that we did not already know but instead to recognize that which "gathered and concealed in a few words is scattered in the immense volumes of theologians and philosophers."[37] That is, those mysteries recovered after such agonizing exegetical efforts do little more than confirm the agreement of the ancients with each other and with true philosophy and religion. Their secrets invariably lead back to Pico's *philosophia nova* and to his interpretation of Christian truth.

Discovering the secret harmonies in the ancients was easier when Pico stumbled over real historical connections between traditions. Thus when he announced the occult agreement between the Neo-Platonic *henads* and kabbalistic *sefirot* he stood on solid ground, although he would have angrily rejected modern explanations of their connections. The *sefirot*, or emanated states of God's being, originated in ancient speculation on God's secret names and properties—systematic collections of his proper names (like his "ineffable name" YHVH in Hebrew), or attributes like his power, beauty, majesty, wisdom, compassion, love, justice, and so on—gathered up from casual references in unrelated Scriptures in deference to the secret harmonies hidden there. To form the *sefirot*, these were syncretically fused by medieval Hebrew exegetes with the gnostic *aeons*, Neo-Platonic *henads*,

---

[35] The *Poetic Theology* is mentioned in the *Commento* (see preceding note) and in parallel sections of the *Oration* and *Apology* (*Opera*, 121, 327; Garin, *Scritti vari*, 150). Scattered evidence survives that would permit a detailed reconstruction of Pico's methods in his *Poetic Theology*, which unlike earlier Renaissance works in that genre (like Boccaccio's *Genealogia deorum*) was motivated by highly systematic goals.

[36] The *editio princeps* leaves a blank space here for Pico's Hebrew. Internal evidence in the text supports the reading of *Metatron*, proposed by Wirszubski on other grounds; see my note to thesis 11>10.

[37] *Heptaplus*, 2nd Proem, in *Opera*, 6–7; Garin, *Scritti vari*, 196–98.

and similar concepts—abstract orders of transfigured demons, angels, and deities originally collected from a wide range of sources by pagan exegetes for similar syncretic purposes. Pico's identification of the *sefirot* with the *henads* was not thus simply the wild fantasy of a Renaissance syncretist.[38]

Similarly, when Pico suggested that Proclus's "guardians" (a *henadic* order) and Pseudo-Dionysius's "powers" (an angelic order) were the same, he was on track again.[39] The suspicious resemblances between Proclus's pagan orders of *henads* and Pseudo-Dionysius's Christian orders of angels provided one clue to the late date of Dionysius—claimed by tradition as Paul's disciple—whose authority in the Middle Ages was second only to the Bible's and St. Augustine's. The fight over Dionysius's authenticity, while originating in late antiquity, was not settled until near the end of the nineteenth century. Pico's eye for these connections was no less acute than those of the modern scholars who eventually stripped Dionysius totally of his authority. But what modern historians view as evidence of historical borrowing for Pico was simply further proof that the ancients shared a common revelation, concealed in diverse symbols to hide the deepest secrets from the uninitiated. Where Pico differed from his modern counterparts was not in his recognition of those connections but in the historical framework in which he set them.

Without close study of Pico's system and his sources, it is not often easy to force his theses to yield up their secrets, not even those that eventually disclose their commonplace character. Even Jesus, Pico tells us, instructed his disciples not to write down but only to communicate in secret the deepest mysteries to the most worthy.[40] Whatever Pico's later relations with Savonarola, in 1486, at any rate, true religion for Pico was the stuff of intellectuals and not of the masses. It is diverting to watch the struggles in Pico between his eagerness to reveal his hard-won knowledge and his equally strong hesitations to do so. Thus on occasion he unveils a minor mystery in full, on others concedes a bare hint to "excite the minds of contemplatives," and on still others alludes vaguely to mysteries too sacred to reveal in public.[41] How much further he planned to go at Rome is

[38] On the syncretic origins of the *sefirot* and the Kabbalah in general, see Scholem (1974: 8–86). Abundant evidence of the syncretic roots of the gnostic *aeons* can be found in the texts collected in *The Nag Hammadi Library*, ed. Robinson (1978). On the syncretic origins of the *henads*, see my discussion on pp. 85–89.

[39] Cf. thesis 10>9 and note. Pico attributes guardians in that thesis to Orpheus, but he was clearly interpreting the *Orphic Hymns* through Proclus's *Platonic Theology*, in which the guardians represented an order of *henads*.

[40] *Apology/Oration*, in *Opera*, 122, 329; Garin, *Scritti vari*, 156.

[41] Cf., e.g., theses 10>1, 27.10.

uncertain. This ancient occultist stance took on new meaning in the Renaissance, when esoteric traditions met the printing press and could indeed find their way into the hands of the "worthy" and "unworthy" without distinction.

Following Pico's views of history, not only Zoroaster, Homer, Orpheus, Pythagoras (and the other pre-Socratics), Plato, Jesus, Dionysius—and of course Moses and the Cabalists—hid their deepest secrets in obscure symbols, but so too did Aristotle, who "disguised and concealed the more divine philosophy, which the ancient philosophers veiled under tales and fables, under the mask of philosophical speculation and in the brevity of words."[42] Thus when all other methods failed, Pico was ready to interpret even the dense Greek of the Aristotelian corpus allegorically—whatever that might mean in this case—to bend Aristotle to agreement with that "divine Plato."

10. *Temporal strategies.* Finally, Pico invoked the kind of temporalized allegory or "typology" used extensively by Hebrew, Christian, and Islamic exegetes to reconcile the Old and New Testaments with each other or with the Quran—in Christian forms taking persons or events in the Old Testament as imperfect prefigurations or types of people, things, or events revealed "in the ripeness of time," usually meaning in the period of the Incarnation or the Last Things. In its most sophisticated versions, typology was set in a historical framework that envisioned a progressive movement from shadows to truth, resulting in a kind of "temporal hierarchy" in which successive types approached closer and closer to some ideal. The progressive view of history implied in typology was obviously partially at odds with the regressive models of time suggested in the nine hundred theses and in Pico's lost *Concord of Plato and Aristotle*—leaving aside, that is, the final historical conversion that he hoped would be triggered by his system. The unstable union of these ideas in a single writer was common in the Renaissance, arising from imperfect syncretic fusions of ancient regressive or cyclical models of time with the progressive typologies found in the church fathers, and above all in Augustine's *Civitas dei.*

Syncretic methods of a similar sort appear in a wide range of non-Western scholastic traditions, tied to cyclical as well as linear models of time. Even the successive incarnations of Hindu deities and Buddhas can be shown to have close genetic links to "types" in Hebrew and Christian thought—as can invocations of the Greek ages of gold, silver, bronze, and iron, or of the Chinese five phases or

[42] Thesis 11>63.

similar concepts, when used to harmonize texts.[43] Using these models, inconsistencies in authoritative texts could be explained as reflections of orderly temporal shifts in the cosmos—just as in hierarchical cosmological models similar conflicts were resolved by referring authorities' equivocal uses of terms to different levels of reality. If the heroes or giants described in sacred texts no longer exist nor men live hundreds of years, this is because we have moved from the days before the flood or the age of gold into more degenerate times; if the blood sacrifices described by Moses or similar sages are not demanded in later texts, this is because times have progressed and what is needed now are spiritual sacrifices prefigured in those ancient rites; premodern temporal no less than hierarchical models were invariably expressed in some sort of proportional or correlative form.

In various pagan esoteric sources, in the Kabbalah, and in the Latin tradition stemming from Joachim of Fiore—whose writings we have seen Pico knew—typology was combined with numerology and prophecy in a highly systematic fashion. In the nine hundred theses and *Heptaplus* Pico demonstrated his deep interests in prophetic numerology of this sort. He also composed a special treatise dealing in part with the subject, his *De vera temporum supputatione* (On the True Calculation of the Ages), now lost. In his Vatican debate Pico planned to apply his numerological methods to unveil the prophetic and eschatological secrets hidden in pagan no less than in Hebrew and Christian texts—once again drawing a harmonious sense out of highly conflicting sources.[44]

---

[43] A number of examples of the five phases as reconciliative devices are collected in Henderson (1984). The Western *locus classicus* for ages of gold, silver, bronze, and iron is Hesiod *Works and Days*, ll. 109ff. The fact that the scheme originated as a syncretic means of reconciling diverse creation myths is suggested by the fact that a fifth creation story not neatly fitting the pattern is awkwardly interpolated between the ages of bronze and iron. Syncretic fusions of diverse creation accounts also clearly lay behind pre-Columbian North American and Mesoamerican myths concerning ages of mud, wood, maize, etc. For a Quiché Maya version of the myth, see the *Popul Vuh* (trans. Tedlock, 1985). On this scheme elsewhere among the Maya, see Thompson (1970: 330ff.), and in pre-Columbian Mesoamerican culture in general, León-Portilla (1970: 30ff.). Striking examples of typology as syncretic devices can also be found in other non-Western traditions. Thus the Mahayana Buddhists routinely claimed that Hinayana doctrines foreshadowed their own views—paralleling exactly Christian or Islamic typological reconciliations of the Torah with the New Testament or Quran. On such devices among the Chinese Mahayana, see the discussion and texts in de Bary et al., eds. (1960: 1:287ff.). On syncretic traditions in general in China, see Berling (1980), Henderson (1984), and Gregory (1991).

[44] Besides the examples of this in Pico's mathematical conclusions, see also 10>20 and note.

ii. *The Syncretic Growth of Premodern Religious, Philosophical, and Cosmological Systems*

Syncretic methods like Pico's had systematic effects that were remarkably similar no matter what traditions were being fused. The historical significance of these methods lies here, since they illuminate otherwise mysterious parallels in the evolution of traditions. These effects were clearer in literate than in oral traditions, whose fluidity permitted syntheses in flexible and impermanent ways.[45] Reconciliations of literate traditions, however, required the use of formal syncretic methods like those planned by Pico for his Vatican debate. The systematic effects of these methods were cumulative and are best observed evolving in traditions over vast periods of time. But the exaggerated scale of Pico's Vatican project lets us watch some of them at work shaping his system and provides a forum for discussing their historical origins and some of their broader effects in premodern thought.

Systematic complexity

The most obvious result of the use of these methods was the sheer complexity that they introduced into systematic thought. When religious and philosophical exegetes could not harmonize the conflicting concepts of their authorities more directly, the tendency was to carve out niches for all those concepts somewhere in their systems. The results of this compilational mode of thought were much the same whether room for those concepts was created by use of a standard scholastic distinction, by some variation of the double-truth, or by the invention of cosmic correlations and hierarchical distinctions to preserve their full or partial truth.

Every compromise like this made in earlier strata of a tradition was at least potentially retained in its later stages—although the influence of a strong authority or the use of Ockham's razor might occasionally sweep an older set of distinctions aside. In the West, we can study these processes in the growth and (less frequently) decline of the complex faculty psychologies of later Latin scholasticism—the cumulative products of centuries of attempts to harmonize the psychological theories ascribed to Aristotle and Galen, the conflicting views of those theories in various Greek, Arabic, and Hebrew commentators, the partly competing ideas of patristic authorities like St. Augustine, and the still broader reconciliations of all these traditions in later scholastics like Albert the Great. The importance still

[45] See Barth's important study of preliterate cosmologies (1987); cf. Goody (1977).

assigned to these issues in the Renaissance is suggested by the scores of theses devoted to them in the nine hundred conclusions.

Similar compilational processes, as suggested in the last section, lay behind ancient and medieval collections of God's secret names and properties, which were gathered up and syncretically joined in deference to the presumed completeness and complementarity of sacred texts. Thus from attempts to unveil the secrets collectively hidden in the outwardly casual utterances of canonical works complex theologies were born. The origins of the gnostic *aeons*, Christian, Buddhist, and Hindu trinities, Neo-Platonic *henads*, kabbalistic *sefirot*, and countless analogous constructs can all be traced to compilational processes like these. Indeed, it is often possible to estimate the relative age of traditions simply by comparing the complexities of these constructs, which emerged, so to speak, out of the fossilized remains of more primitive stages of thought.

Increased abstractness: monotheism and transcendentalism

Every attempt to reconcile conflicting terms or symbols results in a depletion of their original meanings and in an increase in their formality and abstractness. The fact that reconciliations like this occurred repeatedly in premodern traditions helps explain prominent entropic features in those traditions as well as convergent patterns in their structural growth. We earlier looked at one example of such transformations in Pico's fusion of the kabbalistic *Metatron*—originally a concrete demonic power—with Orpheus's Pallas, Zoroaster's paternal mind, Hermes' son of God, Pythagoras's wisdom, and Parmenides' intelligible sphere. Pico's conflation of these concepts transformed them collectively into his abstract intellectual nature: Myth this way originally became philosophy, and symbols, metaphysical allegory.

Syncretic identifications of this sort had been occurring in literate traditions for thousands of years. Thus in the second century CE, Apuleius invoked this technique to muster religious support for the cult of Isis, just as Buddhist or Christian missionaries would later do for their religions by identifying native gods with their foreign ones or with subordinate orders of demons or saints.[46] In a famous

[46] The latter phenomenon has been studied most extensively in relation to the colonial Maya. For an overview and bibliographical guidance, see Farriss (1984: 309–19). Matteo Ricci leaned heavily on similar techniques in selling Christianity in late Ming Dynasty China. Thus in his *True Meaning of the Lord-of-Heaven,* we find that before the Buddhists corrupted them, the Chinese (like the pagan *prisci theologi* in the West) were worshipping the true Christian God. For one recent study, see Spence (1985); on Ricci's reconciliative

passage in the *Golden Ass*, Isis appears to Apuleius's protagonist in a vision:

> Behold, Lucius, moved by your prayers I am present—parent of natural things, mistress of all the elements, the first progeny of the ages, the highest of deities, the queen of infernal spirits, the first of those in heaven, the uniform visage of gods and goddesses. . . . My single divinity is venerated throughout the world in many faces, in various rites, under many names. Hence the first-born Phrygians call me Pessinuntia, mother of the gods; the autochthonous Athenians Cecropian Minerva, the sea-driven Cyprians Paphian Venus, the arrow-carrying Cretans Dictynnian Diana, the trilingual Sicilians infernal Proserpine, the Eleusinians the ancient goddess Ceres. Others call me Juno, some Bellona, some Hecate, some Rhamnusia. But the Ethiopians, illuminated by the first rays of the nascent sun god, and the Egyptians, possessors in abundance of ancient doctrine, worshipping me with the proper ceremonies, call me by my true name—Queen Isis.[47]

H. W. F. Saggs points to a similarly remarkable syncretic text from the first millennium BCE, which implies that all major Mesopotamian gods were simply hypostases of the god Ninurta:

> Your two eyes, O Lord, are Enlil and Ninlil;
> Your two lips are Anu and Antu;
> Your head is Adad, who made heaven and earth, . . .
> Your brow is Shala, his beloved spouse, who rejoices the heart;
> Your neck is Marduk.[48]

Correlations like this were not systematically "neutral." They were a powerful force in the progressive movement towards transcendentalism, ethical and religious

---

methods, see Bettray (1955). Depending on a commentator's orientation, the direction of such syncretic identifications could be reversed. Thus in Japanese traditions we alternately find various Buddhas or bodhisattvas as avatars of Shinto gods, or Shinto gods as avatars of Buddhas or bodhisattvas; in India, similar reversible relationships existed at various times between Hindu deities, Buddhas, and bodhisattvas. For discussion and some Japanese texts, see Tsunoda et al., eds. (1958: 1:263ff.).

[47] *The Golden Ass* 11.5, retranslating the Latin text in the Loeb edition, pp. 544–46. Walbank (1993: 221–22) cites a more primitive syncretic passage on Isis from the previous century; see also the related text he quotes on pp. 120–21.

[48] Saggs (1989: 289).

universality, and monotheism characteristic of all developing literate religions. Transformed by repeated syncretic fusions, no longer limited to a single location or function, local deities lost their foothold in the soil and ascended towards Mt. Olympus or the Heavenly Jerusalem. The bonds between their original concrete and later abstract manifestations were regularly spotted by later religious commentators, leading to their systematic arrangement in hierarchical or temporal series—providing added support this way for the principle of correspondence.[49]

Havelock has underlined the importance of processes like these in the original development of abstract philosophy in Greece, arising from attempts by the early pre-Socratics—viewed more accurately as exegetes than as speculative thinkers—to integrate conflicting ideas and strata in the Homeric corpus and related texts. The result was the abstract dualism that historians label the Platonic theory of ideas:

[49] For an illustration of the operation of these processes even in extreme polytheistic contexts, see chap. 42 of the so-called *Egyptian Book of the Dead.* Still earlier examples can be cited from the coffin and pyramid texts. The links between literate syncretic processes and the emergence of monotheism have been widely acknowledged by premodernists, although less often by specialists in Judeo-Christian traditions than in other fields. Proto-monotheistic tendencies in premodern India are routinely traced by Indologists to integrations of diverse or conflicting strata in early works like the Vedas; a similar thesis finds widespread support among Mesoamericanists, following Thompson's classic study of the syncretic growth in the Maya classic period of the high god Itzam Na (Itzamna) (see Thompson 1970: 209–33; cf. Taube 1992; Freidel, Schele, and Parker 1993: 46ff. and 410 n. 16). On the connections between literate syncretic processes and the emergence of monotheism in Greece, see Walbank (1993: 220–21). Much evidence, some of it discussed later, similarly suggests that Jewish monotheism and related universalistic concepts arose from attempts to reconcile conflicting strata in early Hebrew traditions, which undeniably retained numerous traces of polytheistic beliefs. Nineteenth-century anthropologists including Tylor and Frazer clearly perceived the evolutionary path linking polytheism to monotheism, if not the precise mechanisms involved in the transformation of one set of traditions into the other; suggestions concerning the literate origins of such transformations came in the same period from studies by the so-called higher critics of textual strata in the Torah. Unfortunately, the influence of these findings was blunted in the early twentieth century by the claims of conservative scholars regarding a supposedly aboriginal monotheism in the cults of various sky or firmament deities in preliterate Amerindian, African, and Australian religions. The impact of such claims on comparative religious studies is still evident in anthologies of world religious traditions like Eliade's (1967), whose selections place undue stress on so-called high gods in preliterate religions and in other ways obscure evidence of literate evolutionary processes in religious history.

> You can take a word, justice, city, courage, bed, ship, and treat it as a common name and demand a general definition of it which will cover all the possible poetic instances. But this procedure is sophisticated. It becomes possible only when the spell of the poetic tradition has already been broken. . . . But how, while still working within that tradition, can one start to extrapolate such topics and principles out of the narrative flux? The answer is that you can take similar instances and situations which are severed and scattered through different narrative contexts but which use many of the same words and you can proceed to correlate them and group them and seek for common factors shared by them all. . . . So another way of putting the mental act of isolation and abstraction is to say it is an act of integration. The saga [here, the *Iliad*] will contain a thousand aphorisms and instances which describe what a proper and moral person is doing. But they have to be torn out of context, correlated, systematized, unified and harmonized to provide a formula for righteousness. The many acts and events must somehow give way and dissolve into a single unity.[50]

Evidence suggests that the striking parallels in the emergence of abstract theology, philosophy, and cosmology in ancient Greece, India, China, and the Middle East in the middle of the first millennium BCE can be traced to exegetical processes like these[51]—promoted by the first widespread use of lightweight writ-

---

[50] Havelock (1963: 218). Strictly speaking, Havelock did not claim that the pre-Socratics were attempting to "reconcile Homer with Homer"; indeed, he correctly emphasized that the later pre-Socratics, and, even more strongly, certain parts of the Platonic corpus, represented Homer as an adversary. But Havelock's main thesis—that the abstract language of Greek philosophy was exegetically "wrung out" of the mythopoeic language of Homer (pp. 289–90)—fully supports the views I have developed here. Havelock's early stress on the importance of literacy in ancient philosophy has on the whole been received with hostility by Western classicists, who unlike specialists in Eastern traditions have been slow to acknowledge the importance of commentarial processes as an engine of religious and philosophical change. For some typical recent views, see Harris (1989). For a cross-cultural model of the part played by commentarial traditions in the evolution of religious and philosophical systems, see Farmer and Henderson (1997).

[51] It is instructive here to compare Havelock's studies of the evolution of Greek thought with Karlgren's studies of early systematic thought in China (Karlgren 1946, 1968). Havelock saw Greek philosophy rising from materials exegetically "wrung out" of Homer (see preceding note). Karlgren similarly pictured the products of the so-called Han Dynasty

ing materials, and subsequent development of stratified textual traditions, that began simultaneously in all advanced old world cultures in this period.[52] In Renaissance traditions we observe in effect the cumulative results of two thousand years of such processes, resulting in the exaggerated hierarchical and correlative forms of Pico's "new philosophy."

Pico's heavy use of correlative strategies had abstract systematic effects that clashed with a key principle of his system—the idea that concepts at the highest levels of reality reciprocally penetrate and cannot be distinguished by ordinary language. This was one reason why he claimed that the ancients hid their deepest secrets in obscure symbolic language. Following the fieldwork in Africa of Victor Turner, anthropologists commonly associate similar views of symbols with preliterate thinking. Thus Frederik Barth argues that "multivocality is a regular feature of

---

systematizers as being "worked up" from early legends and myths of the Chou era. Some of the early systematic results of such processes in China (which clearly antedated the Han Dynasty)—the generation of the abstract cosmological principles of Heaven, the Way, Principle (*li*), and so on—can be fruitfully compared to the concepts of *Logos*, *Nous*, and idea of the Good, etc., which emerged in roughly the same period in Greek thought.

[52] The old-world diffusion of lightweight writing materials has not yet been discussed in a dedicated study, nor has it been previously linked to these parallel developments. A number of Western scholars have claimed that the origins of abstract thought lay in the introduction either of the alphabet (e.g., Havelock 1963, 1982; Goody and Watt 1963; Goody 1986, 1987; Logan 1986) or of literacy in general (Goody 1977). What seems to have been critical, however, was not literacy per se, which long antedated the mid-first millennium, nor alphabetism, which never reached the Far East, but the rapid expansion in the mid-first millennium of the use of these lightweight materials—bamboo strips or silk in China (later rice paper), palm leaves or birch bark in India, and parchment or papyrus in the Mediterranean (the latter exported from Egypt on a large scale for the first time in this period)—which allowed the first broad collections of previously disparate oral and written traditions. The subsequent establishment of religious and philosophical canons, which were typically heavily stratified and hence loaded with contradictions, in turn nurtured the growth of formal commentarial traditions and the emergence of exaggerated reconciliative impulses, which helped drive structural developments in religious, philosophical, and cosmological traditions throughout the next two millennia. Studies of syncretic processes in ancient Egypt, where the use of papyrus went back as far as the third millennium, confirm and do not contradict this thesis—a claim supported by evidence of internal commentarial processes linking the pyramid and coffin texts to the *Book of the Dead*. Limitations as to who had access to lightweight writing materials—a critical issue in respect to Egyptian and Mesoamerican traditions—must be taken into account in evaluating these developments.

symbols, each having, as it were, a fan or spectrum of referents."[53] Gombrich associates similar ideas with the literate traditions of Renaissance Neo-Platonism: Symbols do not explain the mysteries so much as they move the soul to ascend upwards, where the deepest truths are grasped in an instantaneous mystical rapture.[54] Scholem similarly distinguishes symbolism from allegory in the Kabbalah: In symbols the kabbalist discovers something "which is not covered by the allegorical network: a reflection of the true transcendence. The symbol 'signifies' nothing and communicates nothing, but makes something transparent which is beyond all expression"; it is not simply "an empty shell into which another content is poured."[55]

We do catch a few glimpses of this "open" view of symbols in Pico. Thus he sometimes used different symbols to express the same idea or explained the meanings of the same symbols differently in different contexts. The implication is that symbols suggest, but cannot exhaust, the contents of the mysteries. More typically, however, Pico's compulsive correlations of symbols forced him to "fix" their meanings in a way that violated both the tenets of his own metaphysics and what were on occasion, at least, the originally looser metaphorical meanings of those symbols. At times, in fact, he argued that those meanings were built directly into the structure of the cosmos. Thus in his clearest statement of his exegetical theories, in the *Heptaplus*, we find that the symbols of the patriarchs were not arbitrary but were based on that "greatest of all" cosmic principles—the idea that everything on every level of reality is reflected "in some mode" on every other. Hence in holy texts we find divine names applied to the celestial or earthly worlds, or earthly names to divine things, and so on:

> Since they are drawn together by the chains of concord, all these worlds exchange names as well as natures with mutual liberality. From this principle (if perhaps someone has not yet perceived it) has flowed the discipline of all allegorical interpretation. Nor were the ancient Fathers able to represent correctly some things through the figures of others unless they were taught, as I have said, the occult friendships and affinities of all of nature. Otherwise there would be no reason why they should have represented one thing by this image, or that by another, rather than the contrary. But expert in all things—and moved by that Spirit who not only

---

[53] Cf. Turner (1967: 50), Barth (1987: 34).

[54] Gombrich (1978: 159–60)

[55] Scholem (1941: 27).

> knows all things, but made them—they would aptly symbolize the natures of one world through that which they knew corresponded to them in the other worlds. Therefore those who wish to interpret rightly the figures and allegorical sense of those Fathers need the same knowledge—unless the same Spirit comes to them as well.[56]

The fact that the ancients used different symbols to represent the same things could be justified (in Pico's eyes) by those authorities' esoteric aims. Apparently nothing ruled out the possibility that something be "aptly" symbolized by several things at once. By repeatedly correlating those symbols, however, Pico in effect stripped them of their metaphorical senses and transformed them into philosophical abstractions—turning them indeed into "an empty shell into which another content is poured."

Cosmic correspondences and "forced fits"

Premodern syncretists could organize their systems in a wide range of cosmological frameworks, but all these in one way or another involved the construction of elaborate cosmic proportions and correspondences, whose exegetical functions we have already analyzed at length. The mania for correspondences in systems like Pico's had some amusing side effects, illustrating another way in which those systems grew in complexity and formality: Ultimately the demands of symmetry alone could force simpler concepts into the structure of more complex ones. Thus in his second set of Cabalistic theses, Pico "adapts" the soul's operations to the structure of the ten *sefirot*—with the correspondence completed with stranger and stranger functions after he ran out of more traditional ones:

> 11>66. I adapt our soul to the ten *sefirot* thus: so through its unity it is with the first [*sefirah*], through intellect with the second, through reason with the third, through superior sensual passion with the fourth, through superior irascible passion with the fifth, through free choice with the sixth, through all these as it converts to superior things with the seventh, through all these as it converts to inferior things with the eighth, through a mixture of both of these—more through indifferent or alternate adhe-

[56] *Heptaplus*, 2nd Proem, in *Opera*, 6–7; Garin, *Scritti vari*, 192. Pico apparently believed that in his own exegeses he was aided by "the same Spirit" who aided the patriarchs; see, e.g., p. 69 n. 34.

sion than simultaneous inclusion—with the ninth, and through the power by which it inhabits the first habitation with the tenth.

The forced fit illustrated in this thesis was a common feature of both Western and non-Western syncretic traditions.[57] The Pythagoreans' addition of a counter-earth to raise the number of celestial bodies to ten—corresponding to their holy decad—is a classic example. The nine hundred theses similarly give us ten spheres—calling for some equally awkward adjustments to Aristotelian-Ptolemaic cosmology—in part for the same reasons as the Pythagoreans and in part to correlate the ten spheres with the ten *sefirot*, Ten Commandments, ten operations of the soul, and so on.[58]

Another example of a forced fit, this time diminishing and not increasing a set of distinctions, is found in the tenth of Pico's ten conclusions "according to the ancient teachings of Mercury Trismegistus the Egyptian." The thesis syncretically identifies the ten demonic "punishers" (*ultores*) Pico found in the *Corpus Hermeticum* with the "evil order of ten" in the Cabala—that is, with the "left-hand coordination" or mirror image of the *sefirot* presided over not by God but by evil demons. Unfortunately for Pico's correspondence, the *Corpus Hermeticum* lists twelve and not ten punishers, whose properties Pico unwittingly copied into his thesis. He apparently caught the discrepancy after his theses went to press. Thus in the emendations of errors at the end of the *editio princeps* we are simply told to drop two punishers from the thesis: When in doubt, Pico's text, and not the correspondence, had to go.[59]

Horizontal and vertical correspondences

Pico's correlative tendencies resulted in another subtle but important contradiction in his system. So long as he posited his correspondences horizontally—that is, on a single plane of reality—the main problem we face is the philological violence that he inflicted on his sources. But his one-to-one vertical correspondences—as in his thesis on the ten *sefirot* and ten operations of the soul—clashed as well with

[57] On forced fits in Chinese cosmology, see the index under that phrase in Henderson (1984); cf. also Porkert's study of systems of correspondence in Chinese medicine (1974). Goody (1977) discusses materials pertinent to this issue in early literate societies.

[58] See, e.g., theses 11>48–49, 11>66.

[59] This provides a striking example of premodern philological methods; see theses 27.9–10.

his emanationist metaphysics, which should have ruled out such correlations due to the progressive narrowing of the hierarchy of being as it approached unity and God. Here Pico would undoubtedly have argued that the ten *sefirot* and ten operations of the soul did not correspond in a one-to-one fashion but *proportionally* as different *multiples* or *powers* of ten—suggesting this way the different levels of unity in the two sets of concepts. This approach was not only consistent with Pico's emanationist metaphysics but was as well the usual way that this problem was handled by later Renaissance syncretists who drew on Pico's thought or its late-ancient models.[60]

In his passion for constructing correspondences, however, Pico often lost sight of this view. Indeed, his penchant for vertical correlations in the nine hundred theses, *Heptaplus*, and other major works often leaves us with the impression that the upper and lower realms constituted truly parallel and indeed numerically matching worlds. This conflict was one factor behind the ambiguous views of astrology that Pico expressed throughout his career—even in his posthumously published attack on it as a divinatory science.[61]

Syncretic processes and cosmic hierarchies: the metaphysical foundations of Renaissance magic

Syncretic systems could be organized in either hierarchical or nonhierarchical frameworks, but due to the long-range influence of the principle of correspondence, whenever hierarchy appeared in any major component of those systems, that form of organization eventually tended to be imposed on all other components.[62] One striking example of this shows up in Renaissance magic, which was grounded on the principles of what since Frazer's time has been commonly referred to as imitative or sympathetic magic.[63] In its nonliterate varieties, imitative

[60] Cf., e.g., the scaled cosmic numerology pictured in Plate 1, on p. 195 below. On these later Renaissance syncretists, see Schmitt (1966) and Heninger (1977), both of whom stress Pico's influence on these writers. Cf. also Schmitt's introduction to the 1970 reprint of Steuco's *De philosophia perennis*, a text that purportedly drew in part on Pico's unpublished papers.

[61] For discussion, see below, pp. 137–42.

[62] This is as true of non-Western as of Western thought: The view that Eastern traditions were predominately nonhierarchical or nondualistic is a romantic-era myth that will not die.

[63] *The Golden Bough*, Vol. 1, chap. 1.

magic in all periods in the West differed little from the primitive correlative magic practiced universally in preliterate societies. At its foundations lay loose metaphorical networks potentially linking every object in nature—expressed anthropomorphically, nature's "loves" and "hatreds," "sympathies" and "antipathies."[64] The shaman or magician magically tapped the powers of those networks by joining or separating those objects or their symbols, or by performing appropriate imitative rites.

In purely oral traditions little effort was made to transform these metaphorical networks into more complex formal systems: The magical power of the nonliterate shaman or sorceress was limited only by his or her ability to imagine correlative bonds between any two objects in nature. In the literate magical traditions drawn on by Pico, the situation was different. Starting in the Hellenistic era, these networks were progressively tightened and systematized, eventually fusing with the broader hierarchical cosmologies of late Greek Neo-Platonism and related traditions.[65]

Some of the syncretic forces that promoted this process in the Renaissance are illustrated in an important passage in Agrippa von Nettesheim's *De occulta philosophia*, a standard sixteenth-century handbook of magic that drew heavily on Pico's thought. In the ancient and medieval magical traditions synthesized in the Renaissance, the sympathies and antipathies of imitative magic were sometimes pictured as forces operating solely in the sublunary realm; sometimes as images of more powerful forces in the celestial, angelic, or intelligible worlds; or occasionally as reflections of still higher powers in the ideas in the mind of God. The *magus* tapped these powers by calling on some version of the ancient correlative principle that "like turns to like," the idea, to adopt Agrippa's formula, that "everything moves and converts to that which is similar" (*unaquaeque res movet et convertit ad suum simile*)—in one common variation using material or symbolic charms or baits (*illecebrae* or *illices*) to draw down higher powers into the sublunary world. The following passage underscores the syncretic processes that helped fuse these ideas into a hierarchical whole. An occult force is found in every stone and herb, Agrippa writes:

[64] Behind the universality of these ideas lay deeper correlative processes in the brain; see below, pp. 92–96.

[65] Again, the same evolutionary argument can be made for Eastern magical traditions, which were systematically elaborated (e.g., in so-called Neo-Taoist traditions) in the first few centuries of the common era.

> But from where these powers come, none of those have shown who have written immense volumes on the properties of things—not Hermes, not Bacchus, not Aaron, not Orpheus, not Theophrastus, not Thabit, not Zenothemis, not Zoroaster, not Evax, not Dioscorides, not Isaac the Jew, not Zacharias the Babylonian, not Albert, not Arnald. And yet all these men grant what Zacharias writes to Mithridates, that "a great force and the fates of men lie in the powers of stones and herbs." . . . Thus the Academics with their Plato attribute these powers to the formative ideas of things, but Avicenna attributes operations of this sort to intelligences, Hermes to the stars, Albert to the specific forms in objects. *And although these authorities seem to contradict one another, none of them, if rightly understood, departs from the truth—since all their words in most things come to the same effect.* For God is in the first place the origin and end of all powers. He gives the seal (*sigillum*) of the ideas to his ministers the intelligences, who as faithful executors impress all things entrusted to them with an ideal power using the heavens and stars as instruments. . . . And so every form and power comes *first* from the ideas, *then* from the presiding and ruling intelligences, *afterwards* from the disposing aspects of the heavens, and *next* from the disposed combinations of elements corresponding to the influences of the heavens.[66]

In the next chapter we shall see how hierarchical distinctions like these functioned in Pico's magical system, which heavily influenced Agrippa's thought and the overall course of Renaissance occultism.

Hierarchy and the Neo-Platonic tradition: the syncretic origins of the concept that "all things exist in all things in their own mode"

We have looked at the exaggerated correlative features of Pico's "new philosophy." I have suggested that it was because of the syncretic pressures on his work that Pico developed those structures in such an extreme way. One could, of course, argue that the form of Pico's system simply reflected the influences of earlier Neo-Platonic systems, especially those high-correlative systems constructed after Plotinus by Iamblichus, Syrianus, Proclus, and related writers. But even if we limited ourselves to a traditional Renaissance "source hunt," we would still need

---

[66] *De occulta philosophia* 1, chaps. 13–15 (emphasis added). I used the edition in the 1970 photoreprint of Agrippa's *Opera*, 27–30.

to explain Pico's special attraction to the late Greek Neo-Platonists as well as the origins of those writers' own extreme hierarchical and correlative tendencies. To account in a conventional way for the emergence of hierarchical-correlative thinking in the premodern West by invoking the simple formula "Neo-Platonic influences" begs the most interesting historical questions at issue.

The hypothesis that I want to introduce here is that the rigidly hierarchical forms characteristic of traditional Western thought did not originate from a mechanical fusion of Platonic and Aristotelian principles, as Lovejoy argued in *The Great Chain of Being* long ago,[67] nor from so-called speculative motives, as has been claimed more recently,[68] but from the Greek Neo-Platonists' own extensive reconciliative needs. This is not to deny that Neo-Platonic systems fulfilled numerous nonsyncretic functions, nor to ignore the preliterate roots of hierarchical and correlative thought, which can be shown to reach deep into neurobiological soil.[69] In any event, the thesis that the exaggerated hierarchical and correlative thinking of late Greek Neo-Platonism was a byproduct of syncretic processes is supported by what is known of the origins of the central metaphysical principle of that tradition—the concept, expressed in Pico's words, that "all things exist in all things in their own mode" (*omnia sunt in omnibus modo suo*).

Dodds attributed the primitive Western origins of this principle to Anaxagoras and noted that Iamblichus traced it to Numenius, and Syrianus to the Pythagoreans.[70] Pico likewise found it in Anaxagoras, "later interpreted by the Pythagoreans and Platonists," and not surprisingly thought that he discovered it in Moses as well.[71] The concept in the West emerged in fully generalized form in middle Platonism—Dodds claims that Numenius's part here was crucial—but in extant sources it did not assume a dominant role in cosmology until after Plotinus, in the highly formal scholastic systems of writers like Iamblichus, Syrianus, and Proclus. It was no accident that the fullest ancient development of the principle came in Numenius and these later writers—who were all deeply concerned with reconciliative problems—and not in Plotinus, for whom such issues were of far less importance. This distinction is highlighted when we compare the differing attitudes of these writers towards pagan myth. Plotinus, who allegorized pagan mythology

[67] Lovejoy (1936).

[68] Mahoney (1982).

[69] See below, pp. 92–96.

[70] Dodds (1963: 254, 346).

[71] *Heptaplus*, 2nd Proem, in *Opera*, 6; Garin, *Scritti vari*, 188ff.

using no fixed system and with no pressing syncretic goal, endorsed the principle that "all things exist in all things in their own mode" but did not elevate it to a central position in his ontology.[72] Much the same can be said of Pico's rival Marsilio Ficino twelve hundred years later, who in his earlier writings, at least, tended to follow the looser and more metaphorical ontology of Plotinus rather than the elaborate formal systems of late Greek Neo-Platonism closest to Pico's thought.[73]

Starting with Iamblichus, however, the principle became increasingly important to pagan Neo-Platonists of the Christian era, who invoked it repeatedly in defending the integrity of their dying pagan gods. In Pico's sources, this tendency can be followed in excruciating detail in the systematic metamorphosis of pagan deities into abstract *henads* completed in Proclus's works—a transformation undertaken, in Dodds's words, "as a last desperate attempt to carry out the policy of Iamblichus and maintain the united front of Hellenic philosophy and Hellenic religion against the inroads of Christianity." Thus Proclus believed "that the special task of the Platonic philosopher [was] the exact classification of deities," something involving "the splitting of each god into a series of gradually weakening forces, so that Zeus, for example, appears as five different gods each of whom symbolizes the 'jovial' principle on a different plane of reality."[74] Proclus's main use for this device came in reconciling conflicting texts in his religious authorities—and above all in the Platonic corpus—by assigning contradictory statements about the gods, mythopoeic symbols, or philosophical concepts to different planes of reality, where each could be said to subsist in some cosmic "mode." Pico planned to exploit this part of Proclus's system extensively in his proposed *Poetic Theology*, as suggested by much evidence in the *Commento*, *Oration*, and nine hundred theses. Thus in the *Commento*, to cite just one example, we find Pico harmonizing conflicts in pagan myths concerning Heaven (Uranus), Saturn, and Jove by

---

[72] Cf. here Dodds (1963: 254, 260 n. 2). The most extensive exegetical treatment of myth by Plotinus is found in *Enneads* 3.5, and even that is far from systematic when compared to those treatments found in later Neo-Platonic exegetes like Proclus or Hermias.

[73] This difference shows up clearly when we compare Ficino's readings of pagan myth in his early *Symposium* commentary with Pico's in the *Commento* and nine hundred theses—reflecting similar differences between Plotinus and Proclus in antiquity. On Ficino's increased dependence on post-Plotinean Neo-Platonic sources after Pico published his theses, see above, p. 20 n. 52.

[74] Dodds (1963: 259–60).

claiming that all three stood "in some mode" for the soul, angelic mind, or God himself.[75]

Historians of philosophy normally treat the allegorical symbolism of late Greek Neo-Platonism as dead weight obscuring whatever real importance lay in its systems. Thus A. C. Lloyd complains that "the reader may have less patience than Proclus had gods," and Laurence Rosán—who painfully translates the mythology of the *Platonic Theology* into a totally abstract ontology—gives scarcely a clue as to why in developing his system Proclus wasted so many thousands of pages on all those dead or dying pagan gods.[76] But what modern historians represent as "excess baggage" was, in fact, the main burden of Proclus's system. What was crucial was to defend the truth of the old religions by invoking the *henads* and similar syncretic constructs to demonstrate that every line of Platonic Scriptures was in harmony with every other.[77]

Dodds, who notes with faint interest the ability of the *henads* "to reconcile irreconcilable texts," makes light of the fact that "Homer's Olympians, the most vividly conceived anthropomorphic beings in all literature, should have ended their career on the dusty shelves of this museum of metaphysical abstractions."[78] Through this transformation, however, their lifetimes were extended by over a thousand years, giving them time to give birth to a family of metaphysical systems that did not reach their highest level of abstraction until Leibniz's *Monadology*, where almost nothing but correspondence remained and virtually no traces of the exegetical origins of those systems.[79] In the nine hundred theses we can observe

---

[75] Garin, *Scritti vari*, 470–72. Many similar examples are found in Pico's fifty-five conclusions *secundum Proclum*.

[76] Lloyd (1967: 309–10); Rosán (1949).

[77] Given the fact that Socrates and Plato were literally worshipped in the late Academy, the phrase "Platonic Scriptures" is hardly an exaggeration. On this see, e.g., Marinus's *Life of Proclus*, translated in Rosán's study (1949). Parallels can be drawn here to the worship of Confucius or Lao Tzu in late- and post-classical Chinese traditions.

[78] Dodds (1963: 267, 259–60). Dodds acknowledges that older scholars like Zeller viewed the religious functions of the *henads* as primary, however.

[79] Cf. *Monadology* 47, 48, 62, etc. Needham's attempts (1954– : 2:291ff.) to trace Leibniz's correlative tendencies to Chinese influences ignores two thousand years of independent Western developments. The fact that similar correlative systems evolved East and West undercuts any attempt to explain the origins of those systems by pointing to the influence of a privileged writer, sect, or tradition. For discussion of some of these parallel developments, see Cabezón, ed. (1998); Farmer and Henderson (1997).

a highly advanced stage of this development. Responding to intense syncretic pressures, as we have seen, Pico extended the Neo-Platonic principle *omnia sunt in omnibus modo suo* even further than his ancient, medieval, and Renaissance predecessors—deserting their ranks forthright in the key battle over being and the one.[80]

Syncretism, monotheism, and the growth of temporal cosmologies: the example of Hebrew thought

Hierarchical order was only one way in which premodern syncretists organized their systems. Those systems could also be ordered in temporal models shaped progressively, regressively, cyclically, or, as we see in Pico's thought, in various hybrid combinations of those forms. The primitive origins of these models in extrapolations from observed social or natural phenomena are obvious. The elaborate models of this kind found pervasively in mature literate traditions, however, are unknown except when borrowed in preliterate ones, suggesting again the critical importance of literate syncretic processes in their development.[81] In effecting variations in these systems, both the "temporal depth" and specific nature of their base traditions played a part. It does not take much historical imagination to see why repeated syntheses of long traditions of societies undergoing sustained social or environmental change would tend to favor linear models of time, while reconciliations of ritual traditions of sedentary agricultural peoples would just as naturally favor cyclical ones, and so on. Accidents of textual preservation and the influence of foreign traditions could, of course, complicate these patterns in any given case.

As a simple illustration of how these processes worked we can look at ancient Hebrew thought, which supplied a key part of the temporal framework adopted by Christian writers like Pico. Even the oldest biblical texts contain frequent interpolations of much later materials, as illustrated in the opening creation myth in

---

[80] Above, pp. 25–29.

[81] Goody (1968, 1977) and Barth (1987) present strong arguments that the schematic accounts of preliterate cosmologies reported by anthropologists in the tradition of Griaule (e.g., 1965) or Levi-Strauss badly distort the fluid forms of preliterate myths. Goody also underlines the error of assuming that the elaborate cosmological systems sometimes found among modern nonliterate peoples are uninfluenced by their contacts with literate civilizations.

Genesis with its fully developed transcendent and universal God.[82] Once we "destratify" those texts and rearrange them chronologically, however, it becomes clear that Hebrew traditions not only encapsulated a broad range of mythical concepts arising out of diverse social and environmental conditions but traced as well a general movement from more particularistic to more abstract religious and ethical concepts. Thus preceding the transcendent creator God and protector of "widows and orphans" emerging from the later prophets on, we find the Hebrew God in earlier concrete dress and with rather less noble moral traits as nomadic family or tribal *numen*, war god, fertility or agricultural deity, and so on—reflecting long-range social changes and local fluctuations in Hebrew history.

It is not difficult to see how in Jewish thought the gradual accumulation and canonization of conflicting oral and literate traditions, including many of foreign pagan origins, eventually gave birth through abstractive syncretic processes to more universal religious and ethical concepts that were "read back" interpolatively into those earlier traditions. Indeed, the wider the drift in religious ideas and the faster texts accumulated, the more rapidly those syncretic forces operated. Hence it is no accident that monotheism and universal ethical concepts first clearly appeared in Hebrew thought in the period of rapidly expanding literacy at the time of the later prophets, and more clearly still following the wider collections and disseminations of Hebrew canon following the so-called Babylonian captivity.[83] The syncretic forces operative here were essentially identical to those that led to the simultaneous development of abstract thought in Greece, with the crucial difference that in their syntheses Hebrew exegetes confronted a far more temporally diverse set of sources than did the Greeks, for whom the Homeric corpus provided the main if not exclusive textual base for early exegetical thinking. It is hence obvious why later Hebrew exegetes found typological strategies, and hence linear models of time, more useful than the Greeks as tools in reconciling texts.[84]

Due to the untidy historical nature of the phenomena that they tried to ex-

---

[82] The first creation account in Gen. 1:1–2:4 was added after the Babylonian captivity by the so-called Priestly redactors. The more primitive anthropomorphic creation story beginning at Gen. 2:5 derived from the much older Yahwist tradition.

[83] The fact that a literate explosion took place in Hebrew culture in this period, tied to the broadened availability of papyrus throughout the Mediterranean in the mid-first millennium BCE, is reflected in the increased number of references to scribes, writing, and scrolls in biblical strata datable on independent grounds to this period.

[84] Typology was not absent from Greek thought, however, as illustrated in the model of the development of justice suggested in the *Oresteia*. Cf. here Havelock (1978).

plain, premodern temporal models often had rougher conceptual edges than atemporal ones.[85] Allowing for this difference, however, in temporal cosmological models we simply find projected on a horizontal or durational plane what hierarchical systems pictured on a vertical or metaphysical axis. The movement from "shadows" to "truth" could be expressed either temporally or hierarchically, with which framework was favored largely depending on the specific nature of the traditions undergoing fusion.

iii. Theoretical Conclusions

No matter what their specific contents or origins, traditional religious, philosophical, and cosmological systems tended to become increasingly complex and formal over time, to make much of proportions and correspondences, and to favor hierarchical organization or its temporal analogues. The universality of these tendencies provides strong arguments against picturing those systems as products of unconditioned "speculative" thinking. In this chapter, I have suggested that cumulative syncretic processes, operating over centuries and even millennia, made those developments more or less inevitable. Pico provides a useful forum for discussing this thesis since his exaggerated syncretism illustrates so clearly the systematic consequences of those processes.

Certainly few premodern thinkers anywhere approached the past with the reconciliative passion that we find in Pico. If his system was an extreme one, however, his general approach was anything but unique. The goal of harmonizing texts and traditions was a perennial theme in all traditional literate societies; the syncretic products of earlier levels of tradition were typically fiercely defended even by those religious conservatives and classical purists who most violently opposed syncretic tendencies in their contemporaries.[86] The historical resilience of those tendencies, no matter what forces opposed them, ensured that in the long run their systematic effects evolved in a more or less predictable fashion.

---

[85] This was not universally the case, however, as we find in the highly systematic cycles-within-cycles of Chinese, Indian, or Mesoamerican views of time or in the equally systematic linear schemes found in Joachim of Fiore and related Western and Arabic writers. Numerous hints exist in the nine hundred theses, some of which we have already seen, that Pico's sevenfold division of history belonged to this general class; for further hints in this direction, see theses 10>20–21 and note.

[86] This was true even of Pico's Savonarolan opponents; see below, pp. 155–57.

The thesis that the structures of traditional religious, philosophical, and cosmological systems were largely shaped by universal ways of reconciling—and hence misinterpreting—sacred or semisacred texts seems at first sight an odd one. It becomes less peculiar once we recognize that the syntheses that gave birth to those systems simply applied to thought "fixed" in texts hierarchically abstractive and correlative processes operative at all levels of perception, language, and cognition. Even the assignment of so-called proper names involves high-level abstraction insofar as those names are applied to objects changing continuously over time: The distinction between concrete and abstract terms out of which ancient dualistic and correlative thought originally evolved is a relative one.[87]

Neurobiological evidence has accumulated in the past two decades that the neural assemblies underlying all perceptual and cognitive systems are organized in multilayered correlative (or topographical) maps—that hierarchical and correlative processes are fundamental to *all* human thinking.[88] Once sacred traditions began to accumulate in literate form, the application of these processes to reconciling conflicting textual traditions—which were paradoxically thought to hide unified meanings or even the "secret thoughts of God"—helped lift thought by its bootstraps, so to speak, to exaggerated hierarchical and correlative levels not attainable in the less stable ebb and flow of oral traditions. The differences between the fluid metaphorical models of preliterate peoples and the increasingly rigid correlative

---

[87] The view that syncretic processes—viewed here as neurobiological phenomena—played a key role in the growth of abstract thought was first expressed by the German psychologist Heinz Werner. See, e.g., Werner (1948). Many of Werner's ideas on abstract symbol formation can be supported by modern selectionist or "Darwinian" models of neurobiological function. See here Edelman (1987); cf. Deacon (1997), who explicitly acknowledges his debt to Werner's work.

[88] For a recent summary, see Stein and Meredith (1993). Other materials relevant to correlative brain processes can be found in Gazzaniga, ed. (1995), Edelman (1987), Churchland (1986: 412ff.), Pellionisz and Llinás (1985), and many other recent studies. On some of the cultural implications of correlative brain processes, see Brown's pioneering work (1991). Recent studies of synesthesia—the pathological condition in which subjects literally "hear" colors or "taste" sounds, etc. (see, e.g., Cytowic 1989, 1993; Baron-Cohen and Harrison, 1997)—provide further evidence that correlative systems have deep neurobiological foundations. For a survey of some of the structural symmetries in cortical architecture underlying correlative brain processes, see Mountcastle's classic paper (1978). Experimental work by Goldman-Rakic (e.g., 1987) throws light on some of the dynamic processes involved in topographical or correlative communications between different brain regions; see also the discussion of Merzenich's work in the final note to this section.

systems of literate ones, on this view, arose simply from the greater diversity and "fixedness" of literate as opposed to oral traditions. Those differences were byproducts of what Goody in another context has labeled literacy's amplifier effect: A written source "forces one to consider contradiction"; it "can be inspected in much greater detail, in its parts as well as in its whole, backwards as well as forwards, out of context as well as in its setting."[89] It was at this heightened level of literate awareness that conflicts in sacred traditions first gave rise to demands for extensive formal reconciliation, resulting in the birth of the abstract philosophical, theological, and cosmological systems that began to emerge with the first widespread dissemination of lightweight writing materials in the middle of the first millennium BCE. These developments were followed over the next two thousand years by wave after wave of commentarial traditions, most with strong reconciliative tendencies, which added cumulatively if somewhat unevenly to correlative religious, philosophical, and cosmological systems whose complexities reached the same order of magnitude, East and West, by the later Middle Ages.

By the time of Pico's proposed Vatican debate, the cumulative effects of over two thousand years of syncretic processes had reached their most extreme levels ever. In the nine hundred theses scores of the earlier correlative principles of the warring subtraditions of Latin, Arabic, and Hebrew scholasticism, of Greek Neo-Platonism and Aristotelianism, and of a wide range of esoteric traditions—Neo-Pythagorean numerology, "Chaldean" and "Orphic" magic, pseudo-Hermetic mysticism and pseudo-Mosaic kabbalism—each the product of the repeated inbreeding of traditions of still greater antiquity, merged to give birth to the abstract concept of cosmological correspondence at the center of Pico's "new philosophy." The cumulative pressures of thousands of years of reconciling books and traditions eventually led to the elevation of the ultimate syncretic strategy as "the greatest of all" cosmic principles. Exegesis had completed its metamorphosis into cosmology; correspondence now lay at the very essence of reality: "Whatever exists in all worlds is contained in each one"!

Similar high-correlative systems emerged out of the mature syncretic traditions of late traditional China, India, and other non-Western societies.[90] The sugges-

---

[89] Goody (1977: 44, 109).

[90] It is noteworthy that sinologists (e.g., Berling 1980, Henderson 1984: 136) commonly place the highpoint of Chinese syncretic thinking in the Ming Dynasty, and Indologists the peak of Indian syncretism in the early Moghul period—both exactly contemporaneous with the European Renaissance. Earlier syncretic highpoints in China and India likewise existed simultaneously with the great period of Western syncretism that extended from the

tion that all these systems were byproducts of repeated syncretic inbreeding finds strong theoretical support from an unexpected direction: As Mandelbrot and his followers have elegantly shown in the last fifteen years, correlative (or "fractal") structures of exactly the sort found in these systems can be expected in any evolving system modified by an extended series of recurrent (or "iterative") transformations. Indeed, when sixteenth-century commentators translated Pico's verbal symmetries and correspondences into visual form, the results were diagrams whose fractal structures are often immediately apparent (see Plate 1 on p. 195). The existence of cross-cultural parallels in the growth of correlative systems has profound implications for emerging mathematical and computer models of cultural evolution.[91]

---

last third of the first millennium BCE to the end of classical antiquity. Partial desynchronization in the growth of Eastern and Western correlative traditions followed in later periods from variations in the impact of the so-called barbarian invasions, from differences in literate technologies, and from variations in demographics and institutional controls over information flows; nevertheless, by the later Middle Ages the structural complexities of Eastern and Western cosmological traditions had reached roughly comparable levels. (The greater diversity of traditions available in the Mediterranean region, paradoxically arising in part from the deeper fragmentation of traditions that occurred in the West during the barbarian invasions, gave Western scholastics something of an edge here.) Sarton (1927–48) underscored a number of these structural parallels as far back as the 1920s, but the paths that he pioneered in comparative studies were largely abandoned by later generations of Renaissance scholars, due in part to ethnocentric forces unleashed by World War II.

[91] Mandelbrot himself was fascinated by the fractal-like systems that he found in Leibniz and in the so-called great chain of being (Mandelbrot 1983: 405ff., 419). Misled by older historical studies (above all, Lovejoy's), Mandelbrot apparently viewed those correlative systems as unique and accidental products of Western thought; he hence failed to search for the iterative mechanisms that his own work suggests might drive the growth of such systems. Once those mechanisms have been identified in repetitive exegetical processes, the possibility arises of simulating the structural evolution of those systems using standard models of fractal growth. The obvious tuning parameter in building such models is the rate of information flow within and between traditions, which is sensitively dependent on developments in communication technologies and related demographic and institutional factors. If that rate remains similar in two isolated streams of tradition, mathematical models predict that the systematic complexities of those traditions will remain similar in successive historical periods—as was roughly the case when we compare Eastern and Western cosmological constructs in each period following the middle of the first millennium BCE. Mathematically related models of self-organized criticality (Bak, Tang, and Wiesenfeld 1988; Bak and Chen 1991) have interesting applications in modeling the collapse of correlative cosmologies in later periods of the Eastern and Western printing revolutions, when rates of information flow increased by several orders of magnitude over

Syncretic processes and developments in literate technology were not the only forces that affected the evolution of premodern traditions. The growth of these traditions was regulated as well by institutional constraints on information flows, by attacks by religious conservatives and classical purists, by empirical discoveries, and by accidents in textual preservation and related factors. The progressive tendency towards abstractness and proportion in later strata of these traditions, moreover, was often countered by injections of more primitive preliterate and anthropomorphic levels of thought—as witnessed in the complex interplay of abstract philosophy and folk religion in popular Taoism, in Mahayana Buddhism, and in Western and Eastern cults of the saints.

But a consideration just of long-range historical patterns suggests one remarkable conclusion. Havelock has argued that the pre-Socratics' integration of conflicting concepts in the Homeric corpus led them to take "the vital step of expressing the idea of integration itself, as a governing principle of their method"—projecting into the structure of the cosmos (as in the Heraclitan *Logos*) those abstract mental processes brought to consciousness by their own exegetical acts. In the far broader commentarial systems that evolved over the next two thousand years, we find correlative models of reality that increasingly reflected not just isolated acts of textual exegesis but the cumulative history of many centuries of such acts—with the abstract cosmological principles and transcendent gods of Eastern and Western scholastics, born out of repeated syncretic inbreeding, suggesting in a sense the furthest limits of those acts. And one thinks here of the Aristotelian image of God as "thought thinking thought"—but here it was man trapped in this vicious circle, cogitating and recogitating his earliest anthropomorphic projections in texts and in attempting to harmonize those texts building ever more complex hierarchical and correlative models of reality that as traditions grew and further inbred came to reflect nothing more clearly than the nature of his own neurological processes.[92]

---

those found in earlier periods. For a broader discussion of these issues and descriptions of applicable computer simulations, see Farmer and Henderson (1997).

[92] On this point, see also the recent paper by the distinguished mathematical biologist A. L. Goldberger (1996), who similarly pictures premodern correlative or fractal structures as an "externalization of the fractal properties of our physiology in general, and of our neural architectures and neuro-dynamics, in particular." The view that the dynamic properties of premodern correlative systems are external reflections of neural processes finds extensive support in recent neurobiological discoveries. A famous series of experiments conducted by Merzenich and his colleagues in the last fifteen years (surveyed in Merzenich et

What was needed to overthrow the views of books, traditions, and authorities underlying these developments was not the rediscovery of particular ancient traditions, as is sometimes suggested, but the unprecedented opportunities for disseminating and comparing those traditions that emerged in later stages of the printing revolution. We will return to this problem at the end of this study in reviewing certain radical shifts—or apparent ones—in Pico's later thought. In part to measure the depth of those shifts, in the next chapter we will first look more closely at that exaggerated correlative system that Pico planned to unveil in his grand debate "of everything knowable" at Rome.

al. 1990) suggests that hierarchically linked brain maps reorganize themselves in ways that are strikingly similar to those pictured in premodern correlative systems, in which all "higher" and "lower" realms of reality were believed to change in harmony. See the diagram of hierarchical brain processes in Edelman (1987: 173), who suggestively remarks that "changes in any one level must result in readjustment of all 'linked' levels"—words that could be adopted unchanged to describe the dynamics of virtually any premodern cosmological system. The implication of this and other recent neurobiological discoveries, especially those related to correlative (or topographical) brain maps, is that sufficient evidence is currently available to identify the neurobiological grounds of imitative magic, animistic religious thought, and other primitive correlative concepts including the universal microcosm/macrocosm theme. When this evidence is combined with detailed models of how these concepts were successively transformed in literate traditions, we possess the foundations for the first testable cross-cultural model of the evolution of premodern religious and philosophical systems. Mathematical models of the self-organization of complex systems current in evolutionary biology (see, e.g., Kauffman 1993) have suggestive uses here; the claim that such models can add nothing to our understanding of systems as complex as those found in premodern religious and philosophical traditions is groundless; indeed, those systems, if anything, are significantly *less* complex than those systems already being modeled by theoretical biologists. For further discussion, see Farmer and Henderson (1997). The links between neurobiology, transformations in literate technologies, and processes of cultural evolution are the subject of the sequel to this book.

Chapter 3: Deciphering the 900 Theses

> When something is proposed for debate, a proposition is put forward that is brief and concise and unexplained, implying in its words and senses numerous difficulties to be resolved in the battle of the dispute itself. For if everything there were explained, there would be no need for disputation.
> *Apology*, 1487[1]

The nine hundred theses are loaded with ambiguities that Pico meant to resolve in the course of his debate. His views in such cases can often be grasped immediately once all topically related theses have been collated and compared. Others require a more detailed commentary. In this chapter we will look at four closely related examples of the latter sort: at Pico's syncretic reading of the Aristotelian substance/accident distinction and at his epistemological, mystical, and magical theories. Pico's ideas on these topics throw further light on his syncretic methods and on the particular forms imposed by those methods on his system.

i. Pico's Syncretic Reading of the Substance/Accident Distinction

A large number of the nine hundred theses invoke the traditional Aristotelian distinction between substance and accident—roughly speaking, the difference between the essential "appleness" of an apple and its contingent sweetness or tartness. The theses also employ these terms in a wider but still traditional sense to distinguish other primary and secondary features of objects or concepts. Occasionally, however, especially when expounding his "new philosophy," Pico hierarchicalized this age-old distinction in an idiosyncratic fashion. Predictably, this tendency shows up most often in his "paradoxical dogmatizing conclusions":

[1] *Opera*, 148.

> 3>23. Just as substantial forms exist in the second world through the mode of accidents, so accidental forms exist in the first world through the mode of substances.
>
> Corollary: Just as in the first world there is nothing white, but there is whiteness, so in the second world there is no fire, but things on fire.

Linguistic reversals like this, as we have seen, were one of Pico's favorite devices for representing the idea of cosmic proportion or correspondence. The thesis simply restates, if in rather unusual terms, the conventional Neo-Platonic view that the "true" substance of any object lies in the intellectual realm ("the first world"), while the material realm informed by soul ("the second world") contains only secondary images of that substance. Support for this reading shows up in the *Heptaplus*, where we find that the Platonists, "imitators always of Hebrew learning," maintained

> that every species that exists in matter should be attributed more to the condition of an accident than to that of a true substance. Those things legitimately claim that title for themselves that exist per se, that are supported by themselves, and that are what they are by true reason, unmixed with and little polluted by foreign things.[2]

Pico's further develops his view of the substance/accident distinction in his "paradoxical dogmatizing conclusions":

> 3>59. Wherever some nature exists composed out of many natures remaining in it in act, the nobler always subsists in it substantially, the others accidentally.

The implication here is that, depending on the situation, the same nature can be viewed as either a substance or an accident—an idea with obvious reconciliative uses. Applying this principle, we can quickly harmonize two of Pico's theses that seem to be in blatant conflict:

> 3>61. The whole substance of the rational soul is the intellectual part.
>
> 2>65. Granted that the intellective power in us is an accident, in angels it is a substance.

---

[2] *Heptaplus* 1.3, in *Opera* 13–14; Garin, *Scritti vari*, 212–14.

The conflict disappears once we understand Pico's proportional view of the substance/accident distinction: The intellectual part of the soul is rightly viewed as the soul's substance; but in respect to the angel's superior intellect, the soul's intellective power, which derives from the angelic intellect, has only an accidental status. This view fit in nicely with Pico's emanationism and gave him the flexibility that he needed to reconcile inconsistent uses of the terms substance and accident in his authorities.

Pico's Neo-Platonized view of the substance/accident distinction had some interesting side effects, including one that brought him into dangerous conflict with the church. Medieval theologians like St. Thomas argued that in special cases, at least, accidents could exist independently from their substances. In the doctrine of "separable accidents" they found a way to explain how in the Eucharist the appearances or accidents of the bread or wine could remain while their substance was replaced by the body and blood of Christ. Since Pico viewed accidents as inferior images of substance, however, he was forced to reject the doctrine of separable accidents in its usual form.[3] He dealt with part of this question in a number of his "eighty philosophical conclusions dissenting from the common philosophy":

> 2>49. To posit a distinction between snubness in noses and whiteness or similar accidents through this—that one is separable and the other inseparable from a given subject—is fallacious.
>
> 2>50. The distinction that appears to exist between the preceding accidents originates solely from the voluntary imposition of names.
>
> 2>51. It is necessary to say according to Averroes that substance belongs to the intrinsic quiddity of an accident, and this opinion is in total harmony with both Aristotle and philosophy.
>
> 2>78. Accidents should in no mode be called beings, but *of* being.

Denials of the separability of accidents were repeatedly condemned in the Middle Ages, and Pico's threat to the orthodox view of the Eucharist would have been obvious to any contemporary theologian. The fact that Pico anticipated trouble on this point is suggested by his inclusion of the two following theological theses that proposed ways of upholding the Eucharist without recourse to separa-

---

[3] Pico wavered on this point after being pressed by the papal commission. See the *Apology*, in *Opera*, 229–31, 239.

ble accidents. Predictably, both theses were violently attacked by the papal commission:

> 4>1. Whoever says that an accident cannot exist unless it exists in something can uphold the sacrament of the Eucharist, even maintaining that the substance of the bread does not remain as the common way holds.
>
> 4>2. If the common way is maintained concerning the possibility of assumption (*suppositionis*) in respect to any creature, I say that without the conversion of the bread into the body of Christ, or the annihilation of the breadness, the body of Christ can exist on the altar in accordance with the truth of the sacrament of the Eucharist. This is said speaking of what is possible, however, not of what is so (*non de sic esse*).

Pico's wording here was obviously tentative, something that he stressed heavily in defending—and sometimes bending—his views on this issue in the *Apology*. To complicate interpretation further, from another thesis attacked by the papal commission it is clear that Pico did not personally endorse the view that God could assume any nature—and certainly not an inanimate substance like bread.[4] Nevertheless, the fact that the "common way" of theologians upheld that view, as Pico saw it, was one argument that he planned to make in claiming that the Eucharist could be maintained without recourse to separable accidents. Pico's inclusion of dangerous theses like these is best explained by his anticipation of theological objections to his Neo-Platonized view of the substance/accident distinction—illustrating again the systematic way that he expected that his theses would stand together (or fall) in his debate.

One further side of Pico's reinterpretation of the substance/accident distinction is central to his epistemological and mystical theories, which we will look at later in this chapter. One question that was fiercely debated for over a thousand years by Greek, Arabic, Hebrew, and Latin scholastics concerned whether or not intelligible images (*species intelligibiles*)—images of universal concepts—were necessary to thought.[5] The question was closely tied to the substance/accident problem,

---

[4] See thesis 4>13 and note.

[5] The question originally arose from commentaries on *De anima* 3.7, which argues that the soul always thinks in images. *Species intelligibiles* are usually rendered literally as "intelligible species" to emphasize their links with the logical and metaphysical concepts of genus and species. Those links were attenuated in Pico's thought, however (see, e.g., theses 2>2–3 and notes), and I have hence avoided the cognate in my translation.

since intelligible images were often represented as secondary modifications or "accidents" of the intellect.

Medieval historians have generally approached this topic as a purely epistemological issue, since scholastic discussions of intelligible images most frequently arose in commentaries on the *De anima* and related texts, following Aristotle's view (as interpreted by various Arabic, Jewish, and Latin scholastics) that intelligible images were abstracted by the "active intellect" from phantasmata or sensible images (*species sensibiles*) and subsequently "impressed" on the "passive" (or "possible") intellect.[6] But as was common in scholastic conflicts, opposing views on this issue were also guided by implicit metaphysical and theological assumptions, as well as by professional commitments to the interpretations of venerated earlier commentators. In general, the more narrowly a writer identified with the Aristotelian tradition, the more apt he was to argue that intelligible images were necessary to thought, while writers like Pico associated more closely with the Platonic tradition tended to take the opposite position. Earlier authorities like Averroes and Albert the Great were regularly lined up by debaters on both sides of the question; in this case, however, Platonizers like Pico had to ignore much evidence in those writers' Aristotelian commentaries and were forced to seek support in other of their works not tied to the Aristotelian corpus.[7]

On systematic grounds it is not difficult to guess Pico's view on this problem. Since in Pico's thought faculties and properties progressively interpenetrate as we ascend the hierarchy of being, in the intellectual nature we expect to find a close union between the intellect and the intelligible—between what does the thinking and what is thought. The implication is that intelligible images cannot exist in the intellect (or "intellective soul") in any distinct fashion, nor can they be interpreted as mere accidents of its substance. Pico's views here are again detailed in his "eighty philosophical conclusions dissenting from the common philosophy," which cover a number of technical sides of this question:

> 2>53. If Thomas says that according to Aristotle accidents exist in intelligences, he contradicts not only Aristotle but himself.

---

[6] See the series of propositions listed in note to thesis 1.1.

[7] E.g., in the nine hundred theses Pico claims that both Averroes and Albert denied that *species intelligibiles* are abstracted from phantasmata, contradicting numerous passages in those writers' Aristotelian commentaries; cf. theses 1.1, 2>31. Pico could find partial support for this view in Albert's commentaries on Pseudo-Dionysius's works and on other non-Aristotelian texts.

2>72. Anyone who doubts that one thing is produced more truly and substantially from what is intelligible and from the intellect than from matter and material form is not a philosopher.

2>73. Holding the opinion on the intellective soul that the Commentator [Averroes] maintains, it seems rational to me to claim that the soul is the subject of no accident. And although I will defend this position as true, I take no position on whether he held it.[8]

Pico did not deny a place for sensual abstraction or even intelligible images in his epistemology: as we shall see in a moment, his syncretic theory of knowledge predictably made room for both Aristotelian and Platonic approaches to this problem. In the last thesis quoted, we find hints that Pico's views on this question were critical to his interpretation of the Averroistic concept of the "unity of the intellect"—discussed later in this chapter—which he boasted that he intended to reconcile at Rome with the Christian view of personal immortality.

ii. Reconciling Plato and Aristotle: Pico's Theory of Knowledge

I will limit myself here to a bare sketch of Pico's theory of knowledge, directing readers to the nine hundred theses and to my commentary for details. Pico planned to reconcile the conflicting theories of knowledge found in the Aristotelian and Platonic canons using an age-old compilational or hierarchical strategy: Aristotle's stress on sensual abstraction and Plato's on the soul's innate knowledge reflected their complementary interests in "natural" and "divine" things; but both ancient authorities would agree that daily or ordinary knowledge depends on sensual abstraction and that knowledge in its most elevated state totally transcends the senses.[9] Pico's position here can be illustrated quickly:

---

[8] Pico evidently meant to deduce this view from the purported principles of Averroes's thought, ignoring Averroes's explicit statements on the subject. On this exegetical strategy, see above, pp. 59–61.

[9] Belief in the complementarity of the Platonic and Aristotelian theories of knowledge can be traced in antiquity to middle Platonism and found numerous Renaissance adherents like Ficino, who claimed that Aristotelian studies were preparatory to the inner mysteries of Platonism. Reflecting this idea, Raphael in his famous "School of Athens" has Plato holding the *Timaeus* and pointing upwards, while Aristotle grasps the *Ethics* and spreads his arm over the world. This approach was equally prominent in non-Western scholastic traditions, e.g., in the *Sutra of Hui Neng* (Tang Dynasty, Eng. trans. 1969: 86–87), where it was

5>29. It should not be believed that in Plato's teachings any soul understands through an inspection of ideas, except when it arrives at that state that is the supreme grade of contemplative perfection.

Corollary: They err who believe that according to Plato those things that we daily know and understand, we know in the light of the ideas.

3>40. Not only Platonic philosophers, but even among the Peripatetics, in whom it is less apparent, the followers of Averroes have to concede that the soul can acquire a perfect knowledge of everything knowable through a purgatorial path, without any other study or investigation, through a single moderate and easy collation of, and direction of attention towards, intelligibles possessed from above.

Daily knowledge depends on the abstraction of universal images (*species universales*) from sensible images or phantasmata—a process in which both the "exterior" and "interior" senses play a part—which are in turn utilized by the "rational part of the soul," which Pico syncretically identifies with the Aristotelian possible intellect.[10] In discussing daily knowledge, however, Pico meticulously avoids the phrase "intelligible images"[11] and, in fact, denies that acquisition of these more elevated universals involves the rational part of the soul; in the soul's rational part we find the operations of "composition" and "discourse" but not the abstractive operation placed there by the "common school of all Latin philosophizers."[12] Once we grasp Pico's implied distinction between "universal" images and "intelligible" images, we can reconcile several theses given "according to his own opinion" that again appear—and were clearly meant to appear—to be in conflict:

2>1. A universal image can be abstracted immediately from an image existing in an exterior sense.

2>31. That intelligible images are not abstracted from phantasmata, I assert both as true and as the opinion of the Commentator and of Albert.

---

applied to reconciling the Buddhist "Gradual" and "Sudden" schools—the former pertinent "to wise men of the inferior type," the latter (not surprisingly, Hui Neng's sect) "to those of the superior type." But as Western syncretists would say of the truths of Aristotle and Plato, in the deepest sense the doctrines of both sects were one and the same.

[10] See thesis 5>19.

[11] See the previous section.

[12] See thesis 2>77 and note.

Pico's broader theory of knowledge can be reconstructed from close study of the nine hundred theses, supplemented by scattered clues in his other works; that theory depends heavily on the views of substance and accident that we looked at in the previous section. In the *Apology*, we find that the soul has no intrinsic knowledge except an *intelligere abditum* or "hidden understanding" of itself. In defending this position before the papal commission, Pico invoked the authority of St. Augustine and Henry of Ghent.[13] Ordinary or daily knowledge derives from sensual abstraction, as we have seen, while divine knowledge is attained when the purged soul rises mystically to its intellectual part or the "partial" intellect, and from there to the "angelic" or "total" intellect, to which the partial intellect is correlatively linked, which subsequently "informs" the soul with *species intelligibiles*. Following Pico's view of the substance/accident distinction, however, these images are then completely absorbed in the soul's undivided substance and can hence no longer be considered distinct entities or "accidents" in the soul. The transformational processes involved here explain why in the following series of theses Pico can claim that the soul, whose initial knowledge is limited to self-consciousness, through self-inspection can eventually attain a knowledge of all things. The apparent contradictions in these theses were clearly intended as debating traps for Pico's opponents:

> 3>60. The soul understands nothing in act and distinctly except itself.
>
> 3>63. Although in the soul there exists in act an intellectual nature, through which it convenes with the angel, just as a rational nature exists in it, through which it is distinguished from that, there is nothing intrinsic in it through which it is able, without an appropriate image, to understand something distinct from itself.
>
> 3>66. Through external information the soul can arrive at this: that it understands all things indivisibly through its substantial form.
>
> 3>62. The soul always understands itself, and understanding itself in some way understands all beings.[14]

---

[13] *Opera*, 235; Dorez and Thuasne (1897: 137).

[14] As in dozens of similar cases, Pico's carefully worded puzzle cannot be solved using Kieszkowski's edition, which gratuitously replaces "external" (*extrinsicam*) with "internal" (*intrinsecam*) in thesis 3>66.

Pico's efforts to reconcile the Platonic and Aristotelian theories of knowledge normally led to the kinds of metaphysical complexities generally associated with syncretic systems. On occasion, however, Pico's passion for symmetry led him to simplify sets of distinctions introduced by earlier commentators for their own exegetical ends. Thus, wielding Ockham's razor, Pico deemphasized, although predictably enough he did not fully repudiate, a complex series of interior mental faculties introduced by earlier writers to harmonize conflicting references in Aristotle, Galen, and their expositors to the soul's powers. The following theses refer to the faculty of common sense[15] and to various internal senses distinguished by a long line of Greek, Arabic, Hebrew, and Latin commentators:

> 2>30. Common sense is not distinct from the sense of sight, hearing, smell, taste, and touch.
>
> 2>58. I assert both as true and as the opinion of Aristotle and Plato that just as the sensitive power of common sense does not differ in subject, that is, as a thing, from the sensitive powers of the exterior senses, as my thirtieth conclusion stated, so neither do the phantastic or imaginative, judgmental, and memorative powers differ from the sensitive powers of the interior senses.

The apparent aim of these theses was to maintain the maximum possible symmetry between the exterior and interior senses—a view tied again to Pico's correlative views of reality.[16]

iii. "Freedom of the Will"? Pico's Mysticism and the Syncretic Origins of Some Ancient Religious Paradoxes

Pico's theory of knowledge was closely tied to his views of the relative powers of the intellect and will—a topic discussed continuously, and with little significant development, from ancient times through the Renaissance. Scholars earlier in this century made much of supposed Renaissance innovations in these discussions,

---

[15] On the *sensus communis*, see note to thesis 1.10.

[16] By deemphasizing but not abolishing the faculties of common sense, the imagination, the memorative powers, etc., Pico could heighten the correspondences between the "outer" and "inner" senses, while leaving his options open if these faculties were upheld by an unassailable authority.

confusing premodern with nineteenth-century views of the will and led by the belief, to quote the thesis of one representative scholar, that "the Italian Renaissance, conceived essentially along Burckhardtian lines, was accompanied by a powerful assertion of a philosophy of will by leading representatives of Italian humanism and among philosophical circles influenced by them."[17]

Pico's ideas on the will can hardly remain undiscussed in any study of his work, since he has so often been represented as the archetypal Renaissance voluntarist or "philosopher of will." That view, supported by misreadings of the *Oration*, or rather its first few pages, is ironic, since in many ways Pico leaned heavily towards the opposing intellectualist camp. One of his theological conclusions was, in fact, judged "erroneous and savoring of heresy" by the papal commission precisely for claiming that not even religious dogmas could be accepted by a pure act of will, but first had to pass intellectual tests.[18]

We earlier glimpsed part of Pico's apparent intellectualism in the *Oration*, where it played a key role in the defense of philosophy that he planned to make in opening his debate. The will is indeed "free"—we will look later at ambiguities in Pico's use of the term—but the will cannot love or judge what it does not know; it is for this that we must study philosophy, directing the will in its mystical ascent or worldly rule.[19] Pico similarly emphasized the will's blindness and dependence on cognition for its direction in the *Commento*, *Heptaplus*, *Commentary on the Psalms*, and elsewhere.[20] Pico even attributed similar views, which were linked closely to the Platonic tradition, to the Aristotelian whom he most regularly attacked in the theses—St. Thomas Aquinas:

5>46. When Plato says that only the unwilling sins, he only means what

---

[17] Trinkaus (1970: 1:xx). The confusion is between premodern views of the will as a faculty of desire or choice and romantic and existentialist views of it as an unconditioned creative power. The latter views have no genuine medieval or Renaissance antecedents other than those involving God's creative powers. This confusion was prominent in studies of Renaissance views of man (the latter supposedly voluntaristic in a modern sense) expressed earlier in this century by Gentile, Cassirer, Semprini, Garin, Kristeller, Haydn, Trinkaus, Rice, Yates, and other scholars in the Burckhardtian tradition.

[18] See thesis 4>18 and note.

[19] See above, pp. 39ff.

[20] For one especially clear expression of Pico's intellectualism, see the *Commento* (Garin, *Scritti vari*, 491–93), which was composed about the same time as the *Oration*.

Thomas maintains, namely that there can be no sin in the will, unless there is a defect in reason.[21]

As is common in syncretic systems, however, things do not end here so simply, and Pico cannot any more be classified as a simple intellectualist than as a voluntarist. A broader perspective on his views comes in a series of theses that deals with the traditional theological question of whether man's greatest "felicity" (or happiness) exists in the intellect or the will. Once again, Pico's ideas here can be predicted immediately from the principles of his "new philosophy": Since faculties interpenetrate as we rise in the hierarchy of being, at the top of that hierarchy distinctions between the intellect and will are devoid of meaning; man's "greatest happiness" is achieved only when the participated unity of the soul is fully absorbed into the absolute unity of God. This view is succinctly expressed in a key mystic thesis, quoted earlier for different purposes, that shows up in Pico's "paradoxical dogmatizing conclusions":

> 3>43. The act by which the angelic and rational nature is bestowed with the greatest happiness [literally, "felicitated with the greatest felicity"] is an act neither of the intellect nor of the will, but is the union of the unity that exists in the otherness of the soul with the unity that exists without otherness.

The French theologian Henri De Lubac (who, along with other Catholic scholars, has violently attacked neo-Burckhardtian readings of Pico) has argued that this thesis demonstrates Pico's total indifference to the "superficial" medieval intellect/will debate.[22] In fact, however, the thesis refers only to the soul's state at the height of mystical union. For man still in search of God—for the *viator* or

---

[21] Pico also represented Aquinas as an intellectualist in a number of other theses; see note to 2.12.

[22] De Lubac (1974: 175–76). Other Catholic scholars who have similarly attacked the dominant neo-Burckhardtian image of Pico include Dulles (1941), Di Napoli (1965), Craven (1981), and Roulier (1989). Many of their criticisms of this tradition have been valid; unfortunately, the result of their works has been the creation of an image of an orthodox or even Thomistic Pico that is no less distant from the historical reality. In contrast, one other Catholic historian, Englebert Monnerjahn (1960), argued for the opposing view that Pico's unorthodox views helped pave the way for the Protestant Reformation. What is clear in all this is that historians of many persuasions have been able to hang their hats on Pico's work—in large part because of the inherent ambiguities in the nine hundred theses.

"pilgrim"—distinctions between the intellect and will were real ones, and Pico believed that they had to be considered in the mystical ascent. De Lubac aside, Pico accordingly included several dozen theses in his text that directly related to this issue.[23]

In respect to the lowest levels of the mystical ascent, as we saw earlier, Pico appears to be a straightforward intellectualist: The will is blind and totally dependent on some cognitive power for its direction. As the soul climbs upwards, however, and faculties begin to interpenetrate, Pico's position becomes increasingly difficult to classify. This problem is nicely illustrated in two of Pico's theological theses, where for the sake of debate he temporarily adopts the "common way" on mystical happiness:

> 4>24. Holding to the common way of theologians, that happiness exists in the intellect or in the will, I state two conclusions, of which the first is this: The intellect could not attain happiness unless an act of will existed, which in this is more powerful than that act of intellect.
>
> 4>25. The second conclusion is this: Granted that an act of intellect formally attains the essence of an object bestowing happiness, because its act concerning that is an act of happiness, formally it possesses it from an act of will.

Carefully worked ambiguities like these, which were always handy in reconciling authorities, show up again in Pico's resolution of the related question of the roles played by free will and grace in achieving salvation. Renaissance scholars here too (or, at least, those in the Burckhardtian tradition) have regularly represented Pico as a voluntarist or even Pelagian.[24] In fact, however, the compromise that Pico struck on this issue placed him squarely in the mainstream of medieval theology, which was forced on dogmatic grounds to uphold the conflicting beliefs that God was omnipotent and omnibenevolent but that man was nonetheless

---

[23] The most important of these are listed in my note to thesis 2.12.

[24] As an extreme example, Haydn (1950: 349–50) found in Pico a concept of human freedom "as autonomous as in Sartre's Existentialism" and "as free as the Pelagian heresy"—one that recognized "no restraint in its determination almost literally to storm the ultimate citadel." It is interesting to note that such readings of Pico became especially popular between the World Wars; like Sartre's views of freedom, the popularity of such claims can partially be considered a reaction to historical events that *shattered* traditional beliefs in human dignity.

morally responsible for his own salvation or damnation. Despite his supposed special interests in human freedom, nowhere does Pico show much interest in the paradoxes involved in the simultaneous acceptance of these views.[25]

Pico's most typical compromise on this issue can be followed in a series of theses interpreting the words of 1 Tim. 2:4 that "God wills [or 'desires'] that all men be saved" (*deus vult omnes homines salvos fieri*). This text provided a standard forum for discussion of the free will/divine omnipotence problem from ancient through medieval times, receiving special attention in Peter Lombard's twelfth-century *Sentences*, which (as suggested in Pico's theses) remained the standard theological textbook well into the Renaissance.[26] Scholastic reconciliations of 1 Tim. 2:4 with other Scriptures stressing man's responsibility for his own salvation predictably ended in fine distinctions being drawn between different acts of willing (or different "wills") in God. The fact that Pico planned to follow well-worn paths in resolving this question is suggested in the following theses from his theological conclusions. It is noteworthy that the orthodoxy of these theses, unlike those of an intellectualist cast, was never questioned by the papal commission:

4>21. Not every [act of] will of God's benevolence is effective.

4>22. The words of the Apostle stating that *God wills that all men be saved* should be understood in a positive sense [only] of the antecedent will of the benevolence of God.

4>23. The antecedent will can be described like this: The antecedent will of God is that by which God gives to someone the natural or antecedent powers by which he can achieve something. With him God is prepared to co-act if the other wills it, nor will he manifest the contrary to him with the command or advice to do it, permitting him freely to will to achieve his own salvation.

By the time of Pico's proposed Vatican debate, the exegetically convenient concept of divine "co-action" was well over a thousand years old. We must in-

[25] At Rome he planned to resolve conflicts between freedom and necessity in a traditional hierarchical or modal fashion; see the conclusions listed in my note to thesis 24.2.

[26] *Sentences* 1, *d.* 46. The slow demise of the influence of the *Sentences* is a complicated issue—tied to questions involving Renaissance classicism, the Reformation and Counter-Reformation, and the printing revolution—that has never been satisfactorily discussed. The fact that no English translation has ever been published of this extraordinary work, which was one of the most commented upon texts in human history, is remarkable.

deed prepare ourselves for grace by "doing what is in us"—to recall Pico's words in the *Oration*—but the natural power to prepare ourselves comes itself from a previous act of grace.[27] Pico's views here do not depart significantly even from those of St. Thomas Aquinas, whose wonderfully ambiguous formula can be recalled from the *Summa*:

> When man is said "to do what is in him," this is said to be in man's power as he is moved by God.... It is the part of man to prepare his soul, since he does this through his own free will. And yet he does not do this without the help of God moving him, and drawing him to himself.[28]

Other sides of Pico's mysticism must be pieced together from evidence scattered widely in the theses, confirmed again by discussions in other of his works. The mystical ascent takes place in seven steps, corresponding to the seven days of creation, seven ages of cosmic history, and seven grades of beauty that Pico found in the universe. Ascent of these steps involves a progressive interiorization of knowledge—"reflexive knowledge," in Pico's terms—with a steplike shift in the soul from the sensual to rational to intellectual faculties. Pico's inclusion of exactly nine hundred theses, it will be remembered, was meant to symbolize this general movement of the "excited soul turning back into itself through the frenzy of the muses"—that is, through the guidance of philosophical studies.

In the *Commento*, Pico distinguishes seven stages of the mystical ascent, presenting his interpretation of the traditional Platonic ladder of love.[29] In the first step, the particular beauty of an object is perceived by the senses and is desired for itself. In the second step, this sensual beauty is made more spiritual by the soul's inner powers but still remains distant from its source. In the third step, the soul separates concrete images from all their particularities and "considers the proper nature of corporeal beauty in itself," contemplating the "universal beauty of all bodies understood together." Many Latin Aristotelians, Pico tells us, believed that so long as the soul was attached to the body it could not achieve a more perfect knowledge than this. But he promised that in his council (*concilio*)—his Vatican

---

[27] On the medieval doctrine of the *facere quod in se est*, see above, p. 39 n. 109.

[28] *Summa q.* 109, *art.* 6, *ad* 2, 4: "Cum dicitur homo facere quod in se est, dicitur hoc esse in potestate hominis secundum quod est motus a deo.... Hominis est preparare animum, quia hoc facit per liberum arbitrium: sed tamen hoc non facit sine auxilio dei moventis et ad se attrahentis."

[29] Pico's ideas here were put forward as a sketch for his projected commentary on the *Symposium*, planned as part of his general polemics against Ficino. See above, p. 69 n. 34.

debate—he would demonstrate that this view was "alien from the mind of Aristotle and from almost all Arabic and Greek Peripatetics."[30]

Corporeal beauty plays a role in only these first three steps. In the fourth of the seven steps, the soul considers the vision of universal corporeal beauty that it obtained in the last step, and noting that everything corporeal is particular,

> concludes that this universality does not proceed from a sensible exterior object but from its own intrinsic light and power. Hence it speaks to itself: "If this beauty only appears to me in the shadowy mirrors of natural phantasms through the strength of my own light, certainly it is reasonable that looking in the mirror of my own substance, divested of all clouds and dark material, I ought to see all such things more clearly." And so, turning into itself, it sees the image of ideal beauty that it participates from the intellect . . . ; and this is the fourth step, the perfect image of celestial love.[31]

In the fifth step, building on this interior or "reflexive" knowledge, the soul rises from its rational to its intellectual part, and the "celestial Venus" (the intellect or angelic mind) reveals herself to it in her own image—although not yet with the "total plenitude of her beauty," since this cannot be contained in the soul's particular or "partial" intellect. Finally, through love (or will) the soul unites its partial intellect to the universal intellect or angelic mind, the "first of creatures, the ultimate and universal lodging of ideal beauty." And achieving this union in the sixth step

> its journey ends, nor is it permitted to move further into the seventh—as it were, the Sabbath of celestial love—but there, as at its one end, it ought to rest blissfully at the side of the first Father, the source of beauty.[32]

The *Commento*, which repeatedly sidesteps sensitive theological issues, gives few hints as to the nature of this "Sabbath" of the soul that lies at the top of, or transcends, the ladder of love. In one passage, however, Pico suggests that the Platonists believed that at the summit of man's intellect the soul "immediately

---

[30] Garin, *Scritti vari*, 567–68. Pico attributes the power of abstraction here to the active intellect, contradicting views that he developed in the theses; see above, p. 103. However, he repeatedly stressed that the opinions in the *Commento* were aimed at a popular audience—and were hence largely meant to be noncontroversial.

[31] Garin, *Scritti vari*, 568–69.

[32] Garin, *Scritti vari*, 569.

conjoins with God"; similarly, in the *Oration* we find that in his highest mystical state man is "made one spirit with God," that "God and he are one," or that in that state "we shall not be ourselves, but he himself who made us."[33] The implication is that the Sabbath of the soul refers to a final quietistic union with God that comes to us once we have "done what is in us" and can achieve no more through our own powers.[34]

That a final quietism was integral to Pico's mysticism is further suggested by his sudden shifts from active to passive language whenever he describes the higher stages of the mystical ascent. There the soul is "drawn," "possessed," "intoxicated," "consumed," "inspired," "illuminated," "perfected," or even—as we found earlier—"felicitated" by God. Further support for this interpretation is found in the following thesis on the *Protagoras*, which was one of Pico's main sources for his famous opening myth in the *Oration*. The six (or seven) steps to which the thesis refers by now should have a familiar ring:

> 5>58. That hunt (*venatio*) of Socrates in the *Protagoras* can be appropriately divided this way into six grades: so that the first is the existence of external matter, the second particular immaterial existence, the third universal existence, the fourth rational existence, the fifth particular intellectual existence, the sixth total intellectual existence. In the seventh, in the Sabbath, as it were, one must desist from the hunt.

§

One final side of Pico's mysticism merits extended comment. Pico claimed that in its highest mystical state the soul was totally fused with God; even beneath that state, to recall the *Oration*, we find the mystic attaining "the friendship of one soul through which all souls not only concord in one mind which is over every mind, but in a certain ineffable mode become fully one."[35] Fifteenth-century theology left much room for poetic license, and Pico's contemporaries would have found these words no more daring than the equally metaphorical claim in the *Commento* that the mystic might eventually rest "blissfully at the side of the first Father."

---

[33] *Commento*, in Garin, *Scritti vari*, 479; *Oration*, in *Opera*, 315, 316, 320; Garin, *Scritti vari*, 106, 112, 124.

[34] Cf. above, pp. 39ff.

[35] Quoted above, p. 41.

Modern scholars have interpreted these lines more literally, however, with Edgar Wind, for one, making much of Pico's supposed "doctrine of mystical self-annihilation" or "self-destruction."[36] Others, including Bruno Nardi and Eugenio Garin, have stressed the links between Pico's views and Averroes's concept of the "unity of the intellect"—the idea that the powers of the intellect are not differentiated in individuals. This view was heatedly attacked by Christian philosophers from Thomas Aquinas to Marsilio Ficino for its apparent denial of the soul's personal immortality; one of the main goals of Ficino's *Platonic Theology* was, in fact, to refute Averroes's authority on precisely these grounds.[37]

Recalling Pico's frequent opposition to both Aquinas and Ficino, it is not surprising to find him boasting that in his Vatican council he planned to reconcile Averroes's concept of the unity of intellect totally with Christian orthodoxy. The following theses show up in Pico's forty-one conclusions *secundum Averroem*. Although not explicitly presented as Pico's own opinion, the views expressed here go far beyond anything found in Averroes's own writings, and judging from Pico's wording, his personal endorsement of these views appears to be certain. Along the way, Pico attacks the fourteenth-century Averroist John of Jandun—the leading commentator on the Commentator—whose views of Averroes were still much in vogue in the fifteenth century:

> 7.2. The intellective soul is one in all men.
>
> 7.3. Man's greatest happiness is achieved when the active intellect is conjoined to the possible intellect as its form. This conjunction has been perversely and incorrectly understood by the other Latins whom I have read, and especially by John of Jandun, who not only in this, but in almost all questions in philosophy, totally corrupted and twisted the doctrine of Averroes.
>
> 7.4. It is possible, upholding the unity of the intellect, that my soul, so particularly mine that it is not shared by me with all, remains after death.

Pico apparently viewed his planned reconciliation of Averroism and Christianity as one of the high points of his Vatican council; if his position can be reconstructed, we would expect evidence for it in that section of the theses where he

---

[36] Wind (1968: 63).

[37] Nardi (1949), Garin (1937). For Ficino's arguments, see *Theologia Platonica*, bk. 15.

planned to introduce his "new philosophy." And indeed, buried deep in his "paradoxical dogmatizing conclusions," we find one particularly strangely worded thesis that seems a likely candidate to achieve that goal. The conclusion pertains to what Pico labeled the *ipseitas* or "self-identity" of created beings. Insofar as it can be translated at all into meaningful English, it reads:

> 3>20. The self-identity (*ipseitas*) of each and every thing is then most itself (*ipsa*) when in itself all things exist in such a way that in itself all things *are* itself.

As is suggested in several related theses, this conclusion refers to the "true" substance of created beings in the intellectual nature, where everything exists most fully in a state of "reciprocal penetration." It is in that nature, to quote a nearby conclusion on Anaxagoras, that "the greatest mixture coincides with the greatest simplicity."

It is not difficult to see how Pico could apply this thesis to reconcile the unity of the intellect with Christian views of personal immortality: In Pico's system, the soul's *ipseitas* or self-identity is paradoxically *most* preserved when it *loses* that identity in the intellectual nature—where "all things exist in such a way that in itself all things *are* itself." Here internal contradictions are reconciled even to the point that personal identity and intelligible unity—Anaxagoras's "mixed" and "unmixed"—are one and the same. One reason why Pico labeled these propositions "paradoxical conclusions" at this point becomes all too painfully clear. His method of reconciling conflicting doctrines was based as usual on what from a modern, if not from a premodern, perspective appears to be a simple linguistic trick.[38]

Beyond the unity of intellect, it will be recalled, Pico posited a final "Sabbath of the soul," where the individual was fully absorbed in God's nature. No evidence has survived as to how Pico planned to reconcile this view with the orthodox Christian concept of personal immortality. By this point, however, it should be clear that if pressed on this point, Pico had available an extensive arsenal of syncretic techniques that would have allowed him harmonize the most flagrant doctrine of self-annihilation with what he would claim was a wholly orthodox concept of personal immortality. In Pico's syncretic universe, identity and non-identity, multiplicity and unity, mystical self-annihilation and personal immortality, in some prodigious way could always be shown to be one and the same.

---

[38] For other approaches to the unity of intellect question, see 7.2–4 note.

iv. Pico and the Syncretic Origins of Renaissance Magic: Further Problems in the Yates Thesis

I will end my sketch of Pico's theses by looking at his magical system, which was closely tied to his mystical and eschatological thought. Pico's papal troubles and the complexities of the theses discouraged from the start any general discussion of the goals of his debate. But the esoteric side of his work was studied intensely for nearly two hundred years after his death, with scores of writers from Johann Reuchlin and Agrippa von Nettesheim to John Dee, Giovanni Della Porta, Francesco Patrizi, Robert Fludd, and Athanasius Kircher plagiarizing mercilessly from Pico's magical and Cabalistic theses or from his discussions of natural magic and Cabala in the *Oration* and *Apology*.[39]

The fullest interpretation of Pico's magic to date is found in a key chapter of Frances Yates's classic study, *Giordano Bruno and the Hermetic Tradition* (1964). Part of this side of Yates's work was deeply indebted to the analysis of Renaissance magic of her longtime colleague at the Warburg Institute in London, D. P. Walker, who was in turn heavily influenced by an earlier Warburg study by Panofsky and Saxl.[40] Yates's interpretation of Pico's magic depended heavily on the traditional view of Pico as Ficino's "disciple." In Yates's formulation, Pico first adopted Ficino's "natural magic" and then added to this his own "Cabalistic magic," which completed the foundations of all later Renaissance magical traditions.[41] While other sides of Yates's reading of Renaissance magic have been heavily criticized by other scholars (especially the role she assigned in it to so-called Hermetism), her views of Pico's magic and its links to Ficino's work have

[39] The many surviving manuscripts that contain extracts from Pico's magical and Cabalistic theses illustrate the special interest that Renaissance intellectuals took in this side of his thought. On some of these manuscripts, see Kristeller (1965: 107–23). The fact that Renaissance *magi* borrowed extensively from Pico without attribution has ironically caused some scholars to underestimate Pico's influence on Renaissance magic. Thus in his long chapter on Renaissance natural magic, which does not mention Pico, Shumaker (1972: 111–12, 137–38) summarizes a key passage from Giovanni Della Porta's *Magia naturalis* and another from Agrippa von Nettesheim's *De occulta philosophia* without recognizing that both were plagiarized nearly verbatim from Pico.

[40] Walker (1975), Panofsky and Saxl (1923). The latter study was written while the Warburg was still located in Germany.

[41] Yates (1964: 84ff.). Brian Copenhaver's study (1997) of magic in Pico's Cabalistic theses, which arrived while I corrected proofs of this book, is referred to briefly in my commentary on Pico's text.

been repeatedly cited as hard historical fact.[42] Due to the extraordinary influence of this side of Yates's model, it will be necessary to approach Pico's magic in part through a criticism of her study.[43] Pico's syncretic system drew on an enormous range of Western magical traditions, making it difficult to provide any comprehensive view of this side of his thought except through a thesis-by-thesis discussion, some of which is provided in my commentary. My primary object in this section is to clear the way for a fresh reading of the theses by correcting misconceptions about Renaissance magic rooted far too deeply to be ignored. One of my subsidiary aims will be to provide evidence that we will need in chapter 4, which discusses Pico's apparent *repudiation* of magic in his posthumously published *Disputations against Divinatory Astrology*. At the end of this section, I will discuss the role that magic played in the eschatological goals of Pico's debate.

Yates's model of the origins of early Renaissance magic

Following earlier Warburg scholars, Yates associated Renaissance *magia naturalis* rather narrowly[44] with the particular brand (or brands) of astrological magic found in Marsilio Ficino's *De vita coelitus comparanda* (On Obtaining Life Celestially)—the last of the three treatises in Ficino's medical compilation *De vita*.[45]

---

[42] Yates's view of Pico's magic is accepted without question in frequently cited studies of Renaissance occultism like Keith Thomas's (1971) and in numerous textbook accounts of Renaissance thought. The most thorough criticism of Yates's views of Renaissance magic is found in Westman and McGuire (1977); see also Copenhaver (1987, 1988), Vickers, ed. (1984). Trinkaus (1970), the only writer to seriously challenge Yates's view of Pico's magic, does so on historiographical grounds (pitting "humanism" against "Hermetism") and without analysis of the nine hundred theses.

[43] Every student of Renaissance thought is deeply indebted to Yates's studies, and it is unfortunate that it is necessary to criticize her views in the following pages. The fact that after more than three decades any serious analysis of Pico's magic must still begin with a discussion of Yates's views is a tribute to the importance of her work.

[44] On other sides of Renaissance magic, including its metaphysical foundations, see above, pp. 83–85.

[45] Below, I used the 1498 Venetian edition, reprinted in 1978 with a listing of variant readings from later editions and notes and a bibliographical essay by the late Martin Plessner. Plessner underlined a number of peculiarities in Yates's reading of the *De vita coelitus comparanda*, including some serious mistranslations. On the *De vita*, see now the critical edition and translation by Kaske and Clark (1989). Kaske and Clark accept the traditional view that Pico was Ficino's "disciple" (p. 57) and hence do not discuss the conceptual ties

Yates traced the origins of the revival of magic she pictured in the Renaissance to Ficino's translation in 1463 of the *Corpus Hermeticum*, whose religious associations "rehabilitated" medieval magic, turning "that old dirty magic" into the "learned" and "religious" magic of the later *De vita coelitus comparanda*.[46] As Ficino's disciple, Pico "imbibed from Ficino his enthusiasm for *magia naturalis* which he accepted and recommended much more forcibly and openly than did Ficino," adding to this his own "Cabalistic magic," which tapped forces "beyond the natural powers of the universe," invoking "angels, archangels, the ten sephiroth which are names or powers of God, God himself, by means some of which are similar to other magical procedures, but more particularly through the power of the sacred Hebrew language." By fusing Ficino's natural magic with his own Cabalistic magic, in Yates's eyes, Pico completed the basic arsenal of the Renaissance magician. Pico's *Oration*—his preface to his Roman debate—was, in fact, "the great charter of Renaissance Magic, of the new type of magic introduced by Ficino and completed by Pico."[47]

Yates attempted to tie Pico's magic to the growth of modern technological attitudes. Behind this side of her thesis lay another version of the romantic theme that "Renaissance man" developed a powerful "philosophy of will":

> It was now dignified and important for man to operate; it was also religious and not contrary to the will of God that man, the great miracle, should exert his powers. It was this basic psychological reorientation towards a direction of the will which was neither Greek nor mediaeval in spirit, which made all the difference.[48]

According to Yates, Pico thus brought mankind to a critical turning point in history:

---

between Pico's earlier magical writings and Ficino's later ones. In the same place, they also endorse the view that following his troubles with the church "Pico soon renounced magic and such astrology as he had ever believed in." We will look at the remarkable origins of this traditional view in the final chapter of this study.

[46] Yates (1964: chaps. 1–5, especially pp. 17–19, 41, 80, 107). Yates does not attempt to explain the twenty-six year interval between Ficino's translation of the *Corpus Hermeticum* and the appearance of his only magical work, the *De vita coelitus comparanda*.

[47] Yates (1964: 84–86).

[48] Yates (1964: 156). On the "will" theme in Renaissance historiography, see above, pp. 105ff.

> The profound significance of Pico della Mirandola in the history of humanity can hardly be overestimated. He it was who first boldly formulated a new position for European man, man as Magus using both Magia and Cabala to act upon the world, to control his destiny by science. And in Pico, the organic link with religion of the Magus can be studied at its source.[49]

Problems in Yates's view of Pico's magic

Analyzing Yates's claims more closely will help us define the precise nature of Pico's magic, preparing us for a fresh look at his magical texts. I will limit myself to discussing five problems in Yates's thesis:

1. *Pico wrote his magical works before Ficino wrote his.* The first problem involves an unfortunate chronological oversight. The fact that no one has made much of it in the thirty years of debates over Yates's work underscores the power of the traditional view that Pico was Ficino's disciple: The *De vita coelitus comparanda*—Ficino's only magical treatise, and our sole source of information concerning his *magia naturalis*—was not written until some two-and-a-half years after Pico introduced his own magical thought in the nine hundred theses, *Oration*, and *Apology*.[50] One might argue that Pico learned his *magia naturalis* from Ficino through their personal contacts in Florence. But in the period in which Pico composed his three magical texts, in the fall and winter of 1486–1487, he was not near Florence, nor had he spent more than a month there at the most since mid-1485.[51] Ficino and Pico did keep in touch part of this time through letters and intermediaries. But relations between them in this period were at their lowest point ever, as we find from their letters and from the criticism that Pico aimed at Ficino in

---

[49] Yates (1964: 116).

[50] Part of book 1 of *De vita*, which contains no magic, was apparently written as early as 1480, but the rest including the *De vita coelitus comparanda* was not composed before the summer of 1489. See Kristeller (1937: 1:lxxxiii ff.), Kaske and Clark (1989).

[51] Pico left Florence for the University of Paris in the summer of 1485, returning to Italy in late March or early April 1486. After a brief stop in Florence, he was in Arezzo by 10 May 1486, where he became involved in a famous scandal—the so-called rape of Margherita—that ended with the death of a number of Pico's retainers, with Pico's brief imprisonment in Arezzo, and with his temporary retirement to Perugia and nearby Fratta, where he composed the *Commento*, the *Oration*, and nine hundred theses. Pico had no face-to-face contact again with Ficino until 1488.

the *Commento*, *Oration*, and nine hundred theses, which were all written in the fall and winter of 1486–1487.[52]

If Pico did learn his natural magic from Ficino, then, he must have done so at a minimum some four years before Ficino wrote his only magical work. Assuming that Ficino's views on magic were the same in 1485 as in 1489—a doubtful assumption, given his well-known vacillations on the subject[53]—from what we know of relations between the two writers, the *last* thing we would expect in 1486 would be to find Pico endorsing those views. Support for this interpretation shows up in the nine hundred theses, where Pico brags of the magic that he "first discovered" in the *Orphic Hymns*—another apparent slap at Ficino, who had composed an earlier, nonmagical, commentary on the *Hymns* of which Pico certainly had knowledge.[54] Further evidence on this point shows up in the *Heptaplus*, where Pico rejects magic using astrological talismans, whose use Ficino endorsed a few months later in the *De vita coelitus comparanda*.[55] Ficino in fact alludes to the *Heptaplus* in that text, and hence was aware of Pico's attack, which came in a

---

[52] For some of this criticism, see above, pp. 12–13 and passim. Their relationship was clearly already sour, however, since earlier in 1486 Ficino wrote a satirical apology for Pico's tragic misadventures in Arezzo (see previous note) that Pico could not have found remotely amusing. For this text, see Kristeller (1937: 1:56–57).

[53] On disagreements over Ficino's views of astrology and celestial magic in different periods, see Michael Allen (1984: 183 n. 27). Walker, whose opinions Allen endorses, tells us flatly (1975: 53) that the *De vita coelitus comparanda* "is the only work where [Ficino] recommends magic that he evidently practiced himself."

[54] On Ficino's commentary, see my introductory note to theses 10>1–31. Pico's boast is made in his title to that section of the text.

[55] *Heptaplus* 2.7, in *Opera*, 22; Garin, *Scritti vari*, 244. Pico writes: "Quare neque stellarum imagines in metallis, sed illius, id est, Verbi Dei, imaginem in nostris animis reformemus. Neque a caelis aut corpore aut fortuna, quae nec dabunt, sed a Domino caeli, Domino bonorum omnium, cui data omnis potestas in caelo et in terra, et praesentia bona quatenus bona sunt, et veram aeternae vitae felicitatem quaeramus" [Therefore let us not form images of stars in metals, but images of him, that is, the Word of God, in our souls. Let us not seek from the heavens goods of the body or fortune, which they will not give; but from the Lord of heaven, the Lord of all goods, to whom is given every power in heaven and on earth, let us seek both present goods—insofar as they are good—and the true happiness of eternal life]. It should be noted that the views that Pico endorses here, which were written while he was trying to repair his relations with the church, are in no way incompatible with the magic discussed in the nine hundred theses, which (Yates's claims aside) did not involve astrological talismans. On the latter point, see my commentary to theses 9>24–25.

period in which the two philosophers *were* in regular contact.[56] If Pico and Ficino triggered a magical revival in this period—a claim that we will look at shortly—then it must have been Pico and not Ficino who started it. Pico himself, in fact, pointedly suggests something like this more than once in the nine hundred theses and *Apology*.[57]

2. *Pico's did not view Mercury (Hermes) Trismegistus as a magician.* Another problem in Yates's model (one by now widely recognized) involved what she pictured as the Hermetic sources of that revival. We can leave aside the question here, which has been discussed by other scholars, of how far Ficino's own magic was Hermetic, except to note the large number of non-Hermetic magical sources cited in the *De vita coelitus comparanda* (Galen, al-Kindi, Albumasar, Thabit, Haly, Avicenna, Albert the Great, Arnald of Villanova, Peter of Abano, etc.) or to recall that Ficino claimed that his work was part of his commentary-in-progress on Plotinus—a work that Ficino tells us was begun at Pico's urging.

Attempts to identify Pico's *magia naturalis* with Hermetism—a tradition that Pico closely associated with Ficino—rest on even less solid grounds. In the *Oration* and *Apology* Pico provides us with a long list of magicians who might be reasonably viewed as the sources of this side of his thought. In this class "among the moderns" Pico singles out three writers who had "scented out" *magia naturalis*—al-Kindi in the ninth century and William of Paris (William of Auvergne) and Roger Bacon in the thirteenth.[58] The *Apology* also mentions one of Pico's contemporaries—*not* Ficino, but a mutual friend, Antonius Chronicus (Antonio Vin-

[56] At the end of June 1489, we find them together at the scholastic debate at Lorenzo de' Medici's house discussed above, p. 6 n. 16. By September of that year, Ficino, like Pico two-and-a-half years earlier, was writing his own ecclesiastical *Apology* for his magic—printed at the end of the *De vita*—which concludes in part with a mock plea for help from his "Phoebus" Pico, who he knew could slay this "poisonous Python" (Ficino's ecclesiastical opponents) rising from the swamp "with a single shot" (p. 186). Given Pico's ongoing troubles with the church—Innocent VIII made it clear in that year that he viewed the *Heptaplus* as no less heretical than the nine hundred theses—it is impossible to miss the irony in Ficino's words.

[57] Thus in the *Apology* (*Opera*, 180–81), Pico boasts that he was "first among the Latins" to mention Cabala, which he linked with magic, and in the nine hundred theses claimed that he was the first to discover magic in the *Orphic Hymns*.

[58] *Opera*, 328, 121; Garin, *Scritti vari*, 152.

ciguerra)—as someone who had mastered natural magic in Pico's own day.[59] The *Apology* elsewhere associates magic with still another "modern," Albert the Great.[60] Pico further lists as ancient magicians—drawing this time from Pliny, Apuleius, Porphyry, and similar late-ancient sources—Homer, Pythagoras, Empedocles, Democritus, Plato, Zalmosis, Zoroaster, Eudoxus, Hermippus, Apollonius of Tyana, Plotinus, and several minor Pythagoreans.[61] He also makes much in the nine hundred theses, *Oration*, and *Apology* of his "discovery" of magic in the *Orphic Hymns* and Cabala.[62]

What is remarkable in these lists is that virtually the only prominent *priscus theologus* who is *not* listed as a magician is Hermes Trismegistus![63] The one clear reference to Hermetic magic in Pico's early works—a negative one—shows up in the *Apology*, where Pico repeats a complaint from William of Auvergne's *De universo* concerning the Egyptians' use of illegal magic invoking demons. Going to Pico's source, we find that William's target was a famous passage on enticing demons into idols found in the Hermetic *Asclepius*—a text that Yates viewed as a central catalyst in the Renaissance magical revival.[64] Significantly, none of the ten conclusions that Pico attributes in his theses to Mercury Trismegistus contains any of the astrological magic that Ficino associated with that figure.[65] Finally, in Pico's posthumously published *Disputations against Divinatory Astrology*, magical works attributed "by some" to Hermes are treated with scorn.[66]

Given the wide range of magical texts already available in the Middle Ages—including the long list of Greek, Arabic, and Latin authors provided by Pico and the ancient and medieval medical, astrological, and philosophical sources cited by Ficino—it is not clear in what way a magical revival was needed in the Renais-

---

[59] *Opera*, 121. Like several other personal references, this one is suspiciously dropped from the parallel section of the *Oration* published by Pico's nephew after his uncle's death. Cf. *Opera*, 328; Garin, *Scritti vari*, 152.

[60] *Opera*, 169.

[61] *Apology/Oration*, in *Opera*, 120–21, 327–28; Garin, *Scritti vari*, 150.

[62] On Cabala and magic, cf. *Apology* (*Opera*, 166–80, 239) and the evidence discussed in my commentary on the theses.

[63] This is the most amusing evidence that we have of the Pico-Ficino rift: Pico was not prepared to acknowledge Hermes Trismegistus, whom Pico closely linked with Ficino, as a real magician.

[64] *Opera*, 169; Yates (1964: 41).

[65] Cf. theses 27.1–10.

[66] Below, p. 145. As we shall see later, however, Savonarolan adulterations in the *Disputations* may have factored in passages like these.

sance. If as evidence for such a revival we point to the expanded magical syntheses of the later Renaissance that included Cabala, then again it was Pico and not Ficino who must be credited with having started it.[67] Obviously, fresh Renaissance translations of Greek magical and theurgic treatises already indirectly underlying medieval magic, the most important translated by Ficino after Pico's proposed debate,[68] added fuel to the enthusiasm for the occult in the later Renaissance. This was especially true as the printing press made wide distribution of these sources and their broader syntheses in magical handbooks like Agrippa von Nettesheim's possible for the first time.[69] But this phenomenon was not dependent on the recovery of any privileged set of Hermetic (or non-Hermetic) texts. This interpretation is confirmed by the enormous popularity in the later Renaissance of the same medieval Arabic and Latin magical treatises that lay at the foundations of much of Pico's and Ficino's magical systems—works attributed to al-Kindi, William of Paris, Albert the Great, Roger Bacon, and so on—which apart from the absence in them of Cabala are virtually indistinguishable from Renaissance magical texts. A number of these medieval treatises were, in fact, first printed in the sixteenth century and gained unprecedented circulation in an appendix to Agrippa von Nettesheim's popular magical handbook.[70]

---

[67] Ficino, who knew no Hebrew, defers to Pico on matters related to Jewish thought in the *De vita coelitus comparanda*, chap. 22 (repr. 1978: 168). Indeed, echoes of Pico's concept of the mystical Sabbath, which had Talmudic and kabbalistic roots, show up in the previous chapter of Ficino's text (p. 160).

[68] These included selections of relevant materials from late-Greek Neo-Platonic texts already drawn on by Pico in the nine hundred theses, *Apology*, and *Oration*—including Porphyry's *De abstinentia*, Iamblichus's *De mysteriis* and *Vita Pythagorae*, and a fragment from Proclus that Ficino entitled *De sacrificiis et magia*. All these translations were apparently completed in 1489—the same year as the *De vita coelitus comparanda* and two-and-a-half years after publication of the nine hundred theses. Cf. here Kristeller (1937: 1:cxxxii ff.) and the somewhat different chronology given by Marcel (1958). For the role of these works as sources of Ficino's magic, see Walker (1975: 36ff.); cf. also Copenhaver (1987).

[69] On Agrippa and Renaissance magic, see above, pp. 84–85.

[70] Vol. 1 of Agrippa's *Opera* (repr. 1970), which contains the *De occulta philosophia*, is bound with a dozen or so other medieval and Renaissance magical tracts including a commentary on book 30 of Pliny's *Historia naturalis* which (like so many other Renaissance magical texts) plagiarizes heavily from Pico's *Oration* or *Apology*. The work also includes other magical treatises attributed to medieval and Renaissance figures including Gerhard of Cremona, Peter of Abano, and Abbot Trithemius.

3. *The mechanisms of Pico's natural magic differed from Ficino's.* Another part of Yates's model involves the mechanisms that she associated with natural magic—above all, given the stress she put on Ficino's text, mechanisms of a celestial sort. Following Walker, Yates pointed to the *spiritus mundi* or "world spirit" as the medium by which celestial powers flowed into the terrestrial realm. Part of Western magic was indeed "spiritual magic" of this sort (to adopt here Walker's terms),[71] especially the medical-magical traditions adopted in Ficino's medical compilation, in which the *spiritus mundi* provided a handy link between the celestial world and the quasi-physical spirits binding body and soul in Greek, Arabic, and Latin medicine. But the *spiritus mundi* was only one of a large number of mechanisms used to explain these interactions.[72] Numerous ancient, medieval, and Renaissance magical tracts refer vaguely to stellar rays (*radii*) or influences (*influxus*) without mentioning the *spiritus mundi* at all. Others ignore the problem of transmission completely, considering the mere existence of cosmic correspondences as a sufficient explanation for the magical powers found in the world. In other texts, interactions between the celestial and terrestrial worlds are depicted in a quasi-mechanical fashion, with direct contact between the Aristotelian-Ptolemaic spheres, ending in the derived motion of the lunar orb, "churning" the four sublunary elements and hence transmitting celestial effects into the material world. Still other works, tied less directly to astrological models, invoke the Neo-Platonic "vehicle" (or "body of the soul") as a magical bond between man and the Platonic "world soul" (*anima mundi*), which penetrated the whole of the created realm.[73] Other treatises, which are strikingly similar in a wide range of Eurasian cultures, develop

---

[71] Those terms are a bit misleading, since in Renaissance magical texts the words "spiritual magic" or "spiritual science" generally referred to magic involving angels and demons and not to magic transmitted through the *spiritus mundi*. On this in Pico, e.g., see the *Apology*, in *Opera*, 172.

[72] The *spiritus mundi* and closely related concepts (the Chinese *ch'i*, Indian *prana*, Christian *spiritus sanctus*, etc.) all originated in primitive concepts of divine breath inherited from preliterate animistic traditions. In their abstract manifestations in literate times, these concepts became useful devices to rationalize the transmission of magical forces in the cosmos; invocation of such devices was neither necessary nor universal, however; as artifacts of more fundamental correlative processes in the brain (see pp. 92–96 above), interactions in imitative magic could be pictured as being transmitted through any number of cosmic media—or through no medium at all.

[73] On the Neo-Platonic "vehicle," which Pico syncretically links with still another magical mechanism (the "sense of nature" of Latin scholastics), see thesis and note 5>45.

elaborate theories of musical-magical resonances that link heaven and the earth.[74]

This list of mechanisms could be greatly expanded. In a typical syncretic fashion, Renaissance magical treatises commonly collected conflicting or partially conflicting accounts of magical transmission from older sources and combined them with varying degrees of systematic consistency. Much evidence shows that Pico's nine hundred theses and Ficino's *De vita coelitus comparanda*, despite their many other differences, both fall squarely in this category.[75]

Given its extreme syncretic nature, the text of the nine hundred theses predictably invokes a large number of magical mechanisms: the Neo-Platonic "vehicle" or body of the soul, cosmic or stellar "influxes," and many others. Curiously, however, one mechanism that does *not* show up in Pico's text is the *spiritus mundi*, which according to Walker and Yates lay at the center of Ficino's *magia naturalis*.[76] Indeed, the only reference in the whole of the nine hundred theses to "spirits" (other than demonic or theological ones) comes in the following two "mathematical conclusions":

> 7>7. Just as medicine chiefly moves the spirits that rule the body, so music moves the spirits that serve the soul.
>
> 7>8. Medicine heals the soul through the body, but music the body through the soul.

---

[74] For some interesting comparative evidence, see DeWoskin's study (1984) of resonance theory in Chinese magic, where we find the cosmic *ch'i* and musical forces playing roles similar to those assumed by the *spiritus mundi* and similar concepts in Western musical magic.

[75] Thus in the *De vita coelitus comparanda* we find celestial "influxes" or "rays" sometimes linked with the *spiritus mundi*, sometimes with the Aristotelian "quintessence," and sometimes with the Platonic *anima mundi*. Cf., e.g., chaps. 1–4, 16. Walker (1975: 13 n. 1) concedes that Ficino was "somewhat inconsistent" on the nature of the *spiritus mundi* but nonetheless, like Yates after him, treats Ficino's doctrine of celestial influences as a product of systematic rather than syncretic processes. This is also apparently Copenhaver's view (1988). Once we recognize that the text is a compilation, as Ficino himself tells us, the inconsistencies in the work become totally understandable.

[76] It is doubtful that this omission throws light on the Pico-Ficino rivalry: The *spiritus mundi*, as we have seen, was only one of many alternate magical mechanisms, and nothing suggests that in 1486 Pico associated it specifically with Ficino. Given the central role that historians have assigned to the *spiritus mundi* in Renaissance magic, however, it is noteworthy that the concept played no role in the three earliest magical texts—Pico's nine hundred theses, *Oration*, and *Apology*—that we have from any major Renaissance figure.

These theses are themselves noteworthy, since they demonstrate that Pico believed that music—which he associated with one at least one kind of magic[77]—operated on the soul through its quasi-physical "spirits," another idea that has been claimed as original to Ficino's later magical work.[78] This minor point aside, however, these theses do not suggest that the *spiritus mundi* played any role in Pico's magical thought. In his posthumously published *Disputations against Divinatory Astrology*, it is true, Pico does speak of a "celestial spirit" (*caelestis spiritus*)—if not a *spiritus mundi*—that transmits forces of some sort into the lower world. Yates, citing Walker, claims that the *Disputations* repeats "what is practically Ficino's theory of astral influences borne on a 'celestial spirit'," and based on that claim proposes a sweeping reinterpretation of the *Disputations*—which explicitly, at least, attacks magic—as a hidden defense of "Ficinian 'astral magic'" and "a vindication of Magia naturalis."[79] Walker himself, however, whom Yates miscites on this point, noted a critical distinction between Pico's *caelestis spiritus* and Ficino's *spiritus mundi*—a distinction that in Walker's eyes, at least, rendered Pico's version of that concept useless in magic. Due to the infirmity of the lower world, Pico's "celestial spirit" could affect sublunary objects in only a general way; all individual properties arose from unpredictable material differences in nature. Walker writes:

> One could not, therefore, on [Pico's] view, say that any particular herb, sound or food was more solarian or venereal than any other, nor use [Pico's *caelestis spiritus*] to transform one's own spirit, as Ficino proposed; nor could one consider oneself as specially subject to the influence of any one planet.[80]

My object here is not to claim that Pico repudiated all forms of celestial magic—we will later see that he did not—but to provide further evidence that his concept of *magia naturalis* was significantly different from the *magia naturalis* discussed in Ficino's later work.

---

[77] See, e.g., Pico's theses on the *Orphic Hymns* (10>1–31).

[78] Walker (1975: 24ff.).

[79] Yates (1964: 114–15). On the *Disputations* and magic, see below, pp. 142–45. Pico's apparent repudiation of magic in that text could have arisen from several causes that we will examine later, including Savonarolan tampering with Pico's text.

[80] Walker (1975: 25ff.). Walker rather overstates the case, however, at least in respect to Pico's early thought, as suggested in theses 5>9–12. Important ambiguities in Pico's discussions of astrological correspondences are analyzed in chap. 4, below.

4. *Yates misread Pico's views of magic and Cabala.* Yates oversimplified other important parts of Pico's magical thought, including his views of "practical Cabala," or what Yates labeled "Cabalistic magic" (a phrase not used by Pico himself Starting from the assumption that Pico's *magia naturalis* was celestial magic like Ficino's, Yates argued that his practical Cabala "attempted to tap the higher spiritual powers, beyond the natural powers of the universe," invoking for magical ends angels, archangels, and the powers of "God himself."[81]

Pico did distinguish the powers of Cabala from those of natural magic, but that distinction did not involve a simple identification of *magia naturalis* with astrological powers or Cabala with higher ones. Instead, as we would expect from his syncretic system, Pico acknowledged many different *types* of natural magic and Cabala that possessed complex and overlapping roles. Thus while Pico hints that one kind of Cabala invoked intellectual or angelic powers,[82] as Yates tells us, he also discusses at length another part "that concerns the powers of celestial bodies." He also tells us that one side of his *magia naturalis* involved "the powers and activities of natural agents"—that is, sublunary forces—suggesting again that his natural magic did not deal solely with the celestial or astral realm.[83] Moreover, Pico went to extraordinary lengths—for obvious reasons, given the location of his planned debate at the Vatican—to deny that the *magus* had direct access to God's power, except in the general sense that God was the ultimate source of all magic.[84]

Pico addressed these issues in his defense of the following thesis—in Renaissance times, the most notorious in the text—that was judged to be "false, erroneous, superstitious, and heretical" by Innocent VIII's papal commission:

> 9>9. There is no science that assures us more of the divinity of Christ than magic and Cabala.

Yates tells us that "what exactly he meant by this amazing statement is nowhere fully explained," although she speculates that the thesis might be tied to a concept "of the Eucharist as a kind of Magia."[85] In fact, however, Pico explained his views on this issue in detail in the *Apology*, on two pages that Yates cites four

---

[81] Yates (1964: 84). On magic in the Cabala, see also the notes on Wirszubski (1989) and Copenhaver (1997) in my commentary.

[82] Cf. theses 9>16–18, 11>12 and notes; *Apology*, in *Opera*, 172.

[83] *Apology*, in *Opera*, 172.

[84] Cf. thesis 9>6.

[85] Yates (1964: 105–6). If Yates were right, this would have been a particularly hard sell for Pico at Rome.

times for other purposes.[86] Our certainty concerning Christ's divinity comes from the way in which he performed miracles (*ex modo faciendi miracula*). And the fact that Christ performed miracles, and did so supernaturally, is known to us exclusively through the testimony of Scripture. If, however, any human sciences can help us *confirm* Christ's divinity, these are natural magic and that part of Cabala that is not a revealed science. The rest of Pico's defense distinguishes sharply between the powers of natural magic and God's divine powers—presumably why Yates chose not to cite this passage in her study:

> For [to know] this, that Christ's miracles testify to us his divinity, it is first necessary to recognize that they were not accomplished through any natural power but only through the power of God. Second, it is necessary to know that Christ had that power from himself and not from anything else. In [regard to] the first [point], no human science can help us more than that which understands the powers and activities of natural agents, and their mutual applications and proportions, and their natural strengths, and recognizes what they can and cannot do through their own power. And among the human sciences, the science that knows the most about this is the one that I call "natural magic"—on which my conclusions were posited—and that part of the Cabala that concerns the powers of celestial bodies. Because through these it is known that those works that Christ performed could not be done by means of natural powers.[87]

The fact that Pico originally planned to defend his thesis on Christ's divinity in this pedestrian fashion—and was not backtracking in the *Apology* to save his skin—is confirmed by the wording of the two theses that immediately precede it in his magical conclusions. The second of these (the orthodoxy of the first was never questioned) was reluctantly admitted by the papal commission to be "true and tolerable," although it complained that the thesis could easily "be taken to a bad sense, since it is connected with magical things":[88]

> 9>7. The works of Christ could not have been performed through either the way of magic or the way of Cabala.

---

[86] *Opera*, 171–72. (Yates 1964: 89 n. 1, 90 n. 1, 105 n. 2, 106 n. 2). The first of these notes provides us with a long Latin quotation that covers every point discussed on those pages except this one.

[87] *Opera*, 172.

[88] Dorez and Thuasne (1897: 136).

> 9>8. The miracles of Christ are the most certain argument of his divinity, not because of the things that he did, but because of the way in which he did them (*non ratione rei facta, sed ratione modi faciendi*).

In conclusion, it should be noted that Pico believed that one part of Cabala drew down not only celestial powers but powers in the intellectual or angelic nature as well; evidence also shows that Pico thought that part of natural magic tapped celestial as well as sublunary forces. Recognition of hierarchical distinctions of power in both natural magic and Cabala was a predictable feature of Pico's syncretic system and is repeatedly suggested in the theses themselves. With this granted, the evidence shows that the two central claims in Yates's reading of Pico's magic—her identification of his *magia naturalis* with Ficino's celestial magic and her association of his "practical Cabala" exclusively with powers "beyond the stars"—are both fundamentally in error.

5. *Pico's magic was not operative in any simple sense.* One final problem in Yates's interpretation of Pico's magic lies in her picture of its goals and historical significance. Like Walker before her, Yates admitted that much of Pico's magic was more concerned with regenerating the soul than with material manipulation of the world. But she also claimed that Pico "formulated a new position for European man" in his magic, endorsing operational views of nature that paved the way for modern science.

One problem in this interpretation arises from its assumptions about what Pico and other Renaissance *magi* meant by magical "works." One side of Renaissance magic—although this was equally true of ancient and medieval magic—could be plausibly linked to modern science insofar as it aimed in some way at improving the conditions of human life. We only need to think here of the medical magic in the ancient and medieval medical works drawn on by both Pico and Ficino.[89] Outside of this clearly operative side of magic, however, Renaissance writers also used the term magical "works" to describe different ways of acquiring occult

[89] Pico apparently practiced "magic" of this sort himself, as Petrus Crinitus tells us in a suggestive passage of his *De honesta disciplina* (see Kibre 1936: 101). Here we find that when the classicist Ermolao Barbaro came down with the plague in Rome, Pico sent his friend a magical antidote that he reportedly "concocted from the oil of scorpions and the tongues of asps and other poisons of the same sort." Kibre points out (pp. 101–8) that a surprisingly large segment of Pico's library consisted of Greek, Latin, and Arabic medical treatises, most of which would have discussed magic of one sort or another.

knowledge, sought for contemplative or prophetic reasons more often than for material ends.[90] One such type of "magic" involved esoteric means of textual exegesis; thus Pico's theses on the Orphic hymns are entitled "Thirty-one conclusions according to my own opinion on understanding the Orphic hymns according to magic, that is, the secret wisdom of divine and natural things first discovered in them by me."[91] Pico's meaning is suggested in the following theses:

> 10>20. Through the seven hymns attributed to the paternal mind—to Protogonos, Pallas, Saturn, Venus, Rhea, Law, and Bacchus—a knowledgeable and profound contemplator can predict something about the end of the world.
>
> 10>21. The work of the preceding hymns is nothing without a work of Cabala, whose property it is to practice every formal quantity, continuous and discrete.

The magical "work" in these theses—which apparently involved *gematria* or other word-number translations to calculate the seven ages of the world (one symbolized by each "god" in 10>20)—refers to prophetic exegesis and not to material operations of any quasi-technological sort. Much of Pico's magic was clearly of this variety and can be included in the "practical part of natural science" that he identified with *magia naturalis* only in the sense that it involved an esoteric means of reading texts. Indeed, Pico apparently viewed any exegetical method that yielded secret wisdom as just as magical as the celestial magic discussed by Yates.

The *Oration* and *Apology* provide us with further information on this contemplative brand of magic. It was evidently this kind that Pico had in mind when, drawing on Porphyry, he tells us that in the Persian language *magus* means "interpreter and worshipper of divine things."[92] This natural magic seeks out "the hid-

---

[90] In his attack on Pico's theses, Petrus Garcias (1489: H4v) adopted a succinct definition of magic (probably not original to him) that carefully balanced the prophetic and material sides of magic—and which probably could have been accepted by Pico himself: "Magia secundum communiter loquentes est ars cognoscendi et divinandi occulta faciendique magna et mirifica in natura" [Magic according to the common way of speaking is the art of knowing and divining hidden things and of making great and wonderous things in nature].

[91] Title to theses 10>1–31.

[92] *Opera*, 327, 120; Garin, *Scritti vari*, 148; cf. Porphyry *De abstinentia* 4.16.

den wonders in the recesses of the world, in the bosom of nature, in the store-rooms and secrets of God." And contemplation of this leads to religion. For this magic

> excites the admiration of the work of God so that thus prepared, love, faith, and hope must surely follow. For nothing moves anyone more to the worship of God than diligent contemplation of the *mirabilia* of God. So that when we have fully explored these wonders through this natural magic that I speak of, animated more ardently to worship and love of the Maker, we shall be compelled to sing: "The heavens are full, all the earth is full of the majesty of thy Glory!" [Isa. 6:3].[93]

And here we can recall that for Pico, natural philosophy—of which natural magic was the "apex and summit" (*apex et fastigium*)—was the third of the four types of studies (moral philosophy, dialectic, natural philosophy, and theology) that prepared man for the mystical ascent.[94] A great deal of evidence suggests that much of Pico's magic—probably most of it—concerned this contemplative magic rather than any crass material operations in the world.

This notwithstanding, Pico does suggest that certain parts of natural magic involve material operations—including, as was true of one part of Cabala, operations of an astrological kind:

> 9>5. No power exists in heaven or earth seminally and separated that the magician cannot actuate and unite.

Operative goals of some kind are also suggested in the following conclusions:

> 9>3. Magic is the practical part of natural science.

> 9>4. From that conclusion and the forty-seventh paradoxical dogmatizing conclusion, it follows that magic is the noblest part of natural science.

Here Pico was referring to what in the final version of his text was his forty-sixth "paradoxical dogmatizing conclusion," which reads:

> 3>46. Given any practical object, the operation that acts on it (*quae eum practicat*) is nobler than that which contemplates it, if all other things are equal.

---

[93] *Opera*, 328, 121–22; Garin, *Scritti vari*, 152–54.

[94] *Apology*, in *Opera*, 170. Cf. above, pp. 39ff.

Taken together, these theses seem not only to condone but to require us to work magic in the world. But it is a mistake to think that such operations have much in common with modern science. Later Renaissance *magi* living on the edge of the scientific revolution, like Giovanni Della Porta, might have considered magic as a way for man "to control his destiny through science," to recall Yates's words. But we have seen too much of Pico to expect to find him supporting this view. Why should "divine" man, who was capable of union with God, become involved in the material realm?

The answer to this question underlines a profound difference between typical premodern and modern attitudes towards nature. The *magus*, as Pico pictured him, was not a transformer of nature but its "minister." Following the principle that "every inferior nature is governed by whatever is immediately superior to itself," mankind, according to Pico, is ruled by the lowest order of angels and in turn is entrusted with governing the material world. Once the soul has been elevated by philosophical studies to the contemplative seat of the Cherubim, it is prepared to rise to God like the Serafim and descend to the world like angelic Thrones, "well instructed and prepared, to the duties of action."[95]

The operative side of Pico's magic is best interpreted in terms of the traditional concepts of cosmic fall and redemption, which are discussed in a Christological context in the *Heptaplus*.[96] Just as the whole universe was corrupted by the fall of man—a result of the cosmic correspondences in the "man the microcosm" concept—so following his mystical purification *homo magus* receives the power to raise fallen nature with himself, to "actuate" and "unite" the cosmos, "to marry the world"—just as Christ "marries" the soul prepared by philosophy for the mystical ascent.[97] The suggestion is that the operative side of Pico's magic was linked to a general plan for cosmic salvation—a view fitting in perfectly with the eschatological goals of his Vatican debate.

This interpretation finds strong support in the following magical theses linking the "man the microcosm" concept—implied in the first and last theses in the series—with the soul's mystical redemption and with the magician's actuation, union, and marriage of the world:

> 9>10. What man the *magus* makes through art, nature made naturally making man [i.e., the whole cosmos is united in his nature].

---

[95] *Commento*, in Garin, *Scritti vari*, 539–40; *Oration*, in *Opera*,.316; Garin, *Scritti vari*, 112.

[96] *Heptaplus* 5.7, in *Opera*, 40; Garin, *Scritti vari*, 304ff.

[97] Cf. above, pp. 41–46.

9>11. The miracles of the magical art exist only through the union and actuation of those things that exist seminally and separated in nature.

9>12. The form of all magical power comes from the soul of man standing, and not falling.

9>13. To operate magic is nothing other than to marry the world.

9>14. If there is any nature immediate to us that is either simply rational, or at least exists for the most part rationally, it has magic in its summit, and through its participation in men can be more perfect. (785)

Summary and conclusions

In Pico's magic, we find a wide range of magical ideas joined in the hierarchical and correlative patterns typical of syncretic systems. The complexities of these broad and often only partially synthesized systems are underlined by the difficulties that historians have had in interpreting their details. The main problem in the standard account of Pico's magic, advanced by Frances Yates over three decades ago, lay in its equation of Pico's *magia naturalis* with Ficino's celestial magic in the *De vita coelitus comparanda*—an equation arising from the traditional view that Pico was Ficino's "disciple." As we have seen in this section, Pico's magical writings antedated Ficino's by several years, developed a view of "natural magic" that was significantly different from Ficino's, and from the start included a wider range of magical traditions (including Cabala) than that found in Ficino's later magical works.

Whether it is useful to speak with Yates of a Renaissance magical revival at all is an open question. If we insist that such a revival started with Pico and Ficino, then all evidence points to the nine hundred theses as its public starting point. The many different kinds of magic and Cabala discussed in Pico's theses suggest that his magic was rather more complex and varied than suggested by Walker or Yates. Finally, Yates's claim that Pico's magic prepared the way for scientific attitudes towards the world—simply a new twist on an old Burckhardtian theme—is difficult to reconcile with the views that Pico advances of the *magus* as cosmic priest. The stress that Pico placed on those views provides further suggestions that his planned Vatican council did not aim simply at a restoration of knowledge—but ultimately at the regeneration of the entire cosmos.

Chapter 4: Pico and Anti-Pico

Giovanni Pico, the brother of my father Galeotto ... . promised to reconcile both philosophies, those of Plato and Aristotle. . . . I, however, . . . seek not to reconcile but to refute the entire doctrine of the *gentes*. G. F. Pico, *An Examination of the Vanity of the Doctrine of the* Gentes *and of the Truth of Christian Teachings*

"If you want to destroy the error, destroy the book." Medieval proverb quoted in the *Disputations against Divinatory Astrology*[1]

i. The Decline of Syncretic Traditions

It is no paradox that it was at nearly the same time that correlative systems like Pico's reached their height of complexity that their historical importance began to decline. The same technology that produced the flood of books that fed Pico's system in the long run broke the stranglehold of books over systematic thought. And with that shift the syncretic impulse diminished and correlative systems lost their preeminent place in history. The inertial forces of tradition did not allow that impulse to die quickly. Indeed, Pico's Renaissance and early-modern admirers, from Reuchlin, Agrippa, and Steuco in the fifteenth and sixteenth centuries to Fludd and Kircher in the seventeenth, in many ways lived in the greatest Western period of syncretic and correlative thought ever.[2] One can recall here the part played by correlative thinking in Kepler's or Newton's works. But as these same writers illustrate, by the 1600s correlative thought had become increasingly open to empirical correction and its motives tied less narrowly to "saving" texts. If correlative systems had not yet evolved into the purely heuristic models of modern science, from the early seventeenth century on those systems retreated steadily

[1] G. F. Pico, *Opera* (1557, 2:1026); later references will be given without the publication date; Pico, *Opera*, 428; Garin, ed., *Disputationes* (1946–52: 1:96); hereafter cited as *Disputationes*.

[2] On Western syncretic traditions in these centuries, see Schmitt (1966) and Heninger (1977), both of whom stress Pico's seminal role in those traditions.

from the mainstream of thought, degenerating eventually into the purely romantic occultism of the nineteenth century. Insofar as early-modern philosophers like Vico, Herder, or Hegel can be classified as syncretists, their aim was less that of harmonizing conflicting texts than of systematizing a rapidly expanding body of historical knowledge judged independently of textual authority. Their correlative systems and reconciliative methods can be usefully compared to Pico's, but the motives that drove them were of a far less bookish and exegetical order.

The decline of correlative systems was obviously tied to the growth of those mechanistic models of reality that, starting in the sixteenth century, increasingly challenged and eventually displaced them. The role of printing in disseminating those models and promoting modern science in general has been discussed at length by others.[3] But it would be appropriate here to survey important internal developments in correlative traditions, likewise tied to printing, that also played a role in promoting that shift.

As we see in Pico, printing made more sources more widely available than at any earlier stage of Western history, encouraging syncretically minded thinkers to incorporate increasingly broad bodies of traditions into their systems and rendering those systems progressively open to philological and scientific attack. With each leap in complexity, those systems retreated further and further from the original sense of the traditions involved in their synthesis and from any views of nature even remotely suggested by empirical observation. Moreover, due to the increasingly systematic correspondences resonating in those systems, any assault on any one part of them—whether of a political, religious, empirical, or philological nature—potentially, at least, became an attack on them as a whole.[4]

Printing also provided opponents of correlative systems with the tools needed to dismantle those systems permanently on philological grounds. Despite the obvious dependence of those systems on books and exegesis, their long-range survival paradoxically depended on the relative inaccessibility of books. The oratorical and disputational rituals of premodern times served crucial mnemonic functions for intellectuals who even in privileged cases like Pico's rarely had access to the full range of sources they viewed as authoritative. How often the "texts" that Pico set out to reconcile were inventions of reconstructive memory—a situation obviously

---

[3] E.g., by Eisenstein (1979).

[4] As King James I supposedly put it to the Puritans, "No Bishop, no King." It can be argued that mathematical models of self-organized criticality, developed to describe systems in similarly sensitive states, can be applied to model the collapse of correlative systems; for references, see p. 94 n. 91.

easing any syncretic task—is underscored by the fact that numerous citations in Pico's theses can be shown to be loose paraphrases rather than exact quotations: Pico's famous eidetic memory, like those commonly ascribed to premodern intellectuals elsewhere, can be shown on hard textual evidence to have been an illusion.[5] The arguments of this twenty-three-year-old prodigy who proposed to reconcile from memory *all* the conflicts in *all* the works of Plato and Aristotle—including many texts that not even the most conservative modern classicist would ascribe to those figures—let alone his harmonization of texts ascribed to Moses, Orpheus, Pythagoras, Mercury Trismegistus, Dionysius, Zoroaster, "Adeland the Arab," and similar mythical or semimythical figures, could not stand for long once those works could be routinely compared line by line by any disinterested scholar.

The premodern intellectual's tedious work of memorization encouraged correlative and syncretic tendencies in more than one way. As Yates and others have shown, among their other functions, correlative systems served critical mnemonic ends, discussed in a Western textual tradition that stretched from antiquity through early modern times.[6] Common sense alone dictates that writers who spent much of their lives memorizing and reciting the words of authorities were not likely candidates for original thinking. Conversely, the diminished role played by memorization as the printing revolution progressed contributed to the freer and less bookish views of reality that became increasingly common in the early modern period. Neurobiological evidence too suggests that the rote memorization at the heart of traditional education would encourage the stereotyped trains of ideas, dampened originality, and general adhesion to textual authority typical of traditional thinkers.[7]

It is important to distinguish the successful assault launched on syncretic traditions once the printing revolution was well on course from those more vocal, but far less fundamental, attacks made on them by Renaissance classicists and religious

---

[5] All memory processes are currently viewed as being reconstructive in nature, and hence all so-called eidetic or photographic memories as illusory. See, e.g., Rumelhart, McClelland, et al. (1986: 1:79ff.). The heightened memory abilities of synesthetes and *idiot savants*, which are accompanied by major cognitive deficits, are a separate issue.

[6] Yates (1966), Spence (1985). A comparative study of mnemonic techniques outside the West is needed.

[7] On the role of repetition in memory formation on the neurobiological level, see, e.g., the papers in Gazzaniga, ed. (1995). Byrne and Berry, eds. (1989) and Black (1991) also provide good overviews.

reformers. The periodic emergence of textual revivals aimed at purifying sacred or semisacred traditions of purported imperfections was a diagnostic feature of all traditional societies. In general, however, the philological polemics hurled by religious reformers and textual purists at their opponents were invoked for highly selective religious and professional ends—and rarely if ever with the simple goal of unraveling the historical meanings of texts.

Anyone tempted to stress the "modernity" of Renaissance philology is encouraged to review the motley band of fictional authorities paraded through the nine hundred theses, which summed up what in Pico's acutely educated opinion were the major traditions known in his day. Pico's intimate ties with Lorenzo de' Medici, Marsilio Ficino, Ermolao Barbaro, Angelo Poliziano, and Aldo Manuzio, as well as the admiration expressed for Pico's scholarship by Reuchlin, Erasmus, More, Zwingli, and dozens of later classicists and religious reformers, suggests that Pico's brand of textual scholarship was much closer to the *best* of the period than Renaissance scholars like to concede. Despite their wide reading of ancient texts and early development of scientific editing tools, the classicists' views of traditions, books, and authorities were far more similar to those of their scholastic opponents than their own propaganda claimed.[8] Besides noting the magical views of texts that permeated classicist and reformer no less than scholastic circles,[9] we can recall here Pico's and Ficino's strange exegeses of Platonic and Aristotelian texts—which were in few legitimate senses sounder than those of earlier scholastics—or ask why

[8] The same can be said of the classicists' counterparts in Ming and early Ch'ing Dynasty China, whose philological criticism is also often placed in too modern a light. See, e.g., Elman (1984), whose views of the philological achievements of Ming and Ch'ing *literati* are similar to those claimed for Renaissance classicists.

[9] Some obvious magical elements in Renaissance views of books are rarely emphasized. Thus the case of bibliomancy—divination by randomly opening sacred books—in Petrarch's famous account of his ascent of Mt. Ventoux is rarely mentioned, with the message that Petrarch gleaned from Augustine's *Confessions* at the summit ("And men go to admire high mountains . . . and desert themselves") mistaken for a mere literary device. But extensive evidence shows that throughout his life Petrarch believed that he was in direct contact through this and other esoteric means with St. Augustine, his guardian saint. The implied subjective magic in classicist memorization and repetition of ancient *sententiae*—which is reminiscent at times of monks chanting holy texts—too is rarely noted. In formal religion, leaving aside the obvious magic in the Mass, in saint worship, etc., one can finally point to the implied magic in the shared belief of classicists, scholastics, and religious reformers that grace passed literally into the elect on hearing the Word. For analogues of all these phenomena in non-Western societies, see the papers in Goody, ed. (1968).

the philological weapons that Valla, Erasmus, or Luther launched with such fury against their scholastic opponents were never applied to the pseudo-Pauline and patristic sources on which their own religious ideas were based.

Until well into the sixteenth century, what tended to separate classicist, reformer, and scholastic views of texts, besides professional disagreements and matters of style, was not the issue of whether or not all wisdom could be located somewhere in the past—that was a truth few premodern intellectuals anywhere questioned—but where exactly in the complex labyrinths of history that truth was found. In respect to whatever traditions they took as authoritative, classicists and religious reformers alike exhibited syncretic tendencies that were hardly less extreme than those of their scholastic adversaries. Even Erasmus marveled at how truth might arise from a collation of holy texts like sparks from the striking of flint.[10] Similar views show up even in supposed Renaissance skeptics like Pico's nephew-editor Gianfrancesco Pico, who judged from any modern perspective endorsed a picture of reality nearly as syncretic—and certainly no less credulous—than the one of his uncle's that he set out so single-mindedly to destroy.

ii. The Disputations against Divinatory Astrology: *Pico's "Palinode" to Syncretism?*

Pico died in Florence at the age of thirty-one on 17 November 1494, the same day that the armies of Charles VIII of France entered the city, ending sixty years of Medicean rule and ushering in the violent Savonarolan era in Florentine history. Pico's death had been preceded by two years by Lorenzo de' Medici's and by a month and a half by Angelo Poliziano's, their close companion. The story of Pico's death has long symbolized the end of a major cultural and political era in Renaissance history.[11]

The eight years that had passed since Pico's aborted Vatican debate were not uneventful ones in his life. This was a period of nearly continuous struggle with Pope Innocent VIII, ending only when Innocent's successor—Alexander VI, a

---

[10] *Opera* (1706, 9: 1220F). See above, p. 51 n. 133.

[11] Pico's death and Charles VIII's entry into Florence as the twin sign of a new age was first suggested in a 1495 letter of Ficino's (Pico, *Opera*, 405). Gianfrancesco Pico claimed that the French king, who had known Pico in France, rushed two physicians to Pico's bedside with letters written in the king's own hand (*Opera*, fol. 7v).

Pico family ally—lifted Pico's excommunication in 1493. Despite his papal troubles, Pico found time in these years for intense textual studies, most of them conducted in Florence or in the villa at Fiesole that Lorenzo de' Medici gave to Pico after the latter's return from his humiliating flight to France. In this period Pico composed the *Heptaplus*, *Commentary on the Psalms*, *On Being and the One*, *On the True Computation of the Ages*, *Concord of Plato and Aristotle*, *Disputations against Divinatory Astrology*, and a number of other works.[12] Pico also spent much time in these years in formal disputations, despite the denials found in Gianfrancesco's biography of his uncle.[13] Pico's mastery of Semitic languages, and especially Hebrew, advanced in this period far beyond the levels he reached under Flavius Mithridates' strange tutorship preceding the publication of the nine hundred theses.[14]

The question of whether Pico's views changed radically in his later years is of interest in testing the model of syncretic processes introduced in this study. Both the syncretic attitudes that helped shape correlative traditions and the philological views that helped destroy them depended on a systematic comparison of texts and authorities. Where early modern philologists differed from their medieval and Renaissance predecessors lay in the thoroughness with which that comparison could be undertaken, and this depended in large part on the opportunities for continuous access to those texts. If the exaggerated correlative tendencies in Pico's theses represent a *reductio ad absurdum* of the syncretic impulse—an early product of the marriage of the printing revolution to Western thought—it would not be surprising to find in Pico's later works a marked decrease in those tendencies, given the obvious philological weaknesses of his system, the heavy criticism hurled at that system by his enemies, and the breadth of Pico's own philological and textual resources, which arguably exceeded those of any other intellectual of his day. If evidence of such a shift can be found, Pico's work might qualify as a

---

[12] The fate of Pico's later writings, most of which are lost, is traced later in this chapter.

[13] For Pico's involvement in one dispute in these later years, see above, p. 6 n. 16. For other reports of Pico's involvement in disputations, see the references in Kristeller (1965: 60 n. 95).

[14] E.g., the *Disputations* mentions a translation from Hebrew of an astrological text that Pico apparently made in 1493 (1, *cap. unicum*, in *Opera*, 423; *Disputationes* 1:80). Other suggestions of Pico's improved knowledge of Semitic languages are found in surviving fragments of his *Commentary on the Psalms* and in a letter from 1492 that discusses Hebrew books that had briefly fallen into his hands (*Opera*, 360).

microcosm of Renaissance thought not only in the sense that his early works attempted to sum up the central traditions of the period but as well in that his later works anticipated the course of their eventual decline.

Apparent evidence that such a shift may have taken place shows up in Pico's posthumously published *Disputations against Divinatory Astrology*. Curiously, that evidence is not found in the text's main arguments, which are in total harmony with the cosmological ideas that Pico introduced eight years earlier in the nine hundred theses. Pico never doubted that influences of some sort flowed from the heavens to the earth. The question was how those influences operated. Were these influences specific enough to allow predictions of individual events on earth, or were they of a more general nature that precluded exact predictions?

Pico's answer to that question does not differ in the *Disputations* from the answer given in his early works: Due to the elevated nature of the *caelum* and to the material corruption of the lower world, detailed astrological predictions are not possible. Pico's nine hundred theses discussed celestial forces and astrological magic of various types, but none of them endorsed, or even bothered to discuss, the horoscopal brands of astrology most directly attacked in the *Disputations*. The theses suggest that a man may possess from the planets certain predisposing traits—a Mercurial, Venereal, Martial, Jovial, or Saturnian temperment, and so on—but knowing these traits will not permit us to predict in detail the course of his life. One of Pico's theses (7a>74) suggests the possibility that in the heavens "all things are described and signified to anyone knowing how to read them"; and the text's final thesis (11>72) informs us that "true astrology" teaches us to read the secrets in nature or the "book of God." But nowhere does Pico imply that these truths pertain to individual events and not to general cosmological principles, which even the *Disputations* tells us can be read out in the heavens.[15]

The central arguments against divinatory astrology in the *Disputations* are based, in fact, on the same cosmological principles that Pico had planned to introduce at Rome. These ideas are developed most fully in book 3 of the *Disputations*, the theoretical heart of Pico's text. What the astrologers represent as occult powers descend to the earth through celestial "motion," "light," and "heat"—archetypal principles that should not be confused with *ordinary* motion, light, and heat.[16]

---

[15] For Pico's conclusions on astrology, see my note to thesis 22.4–8. The same basic views of astrological influences inform the *Commento*, nine hundred theses, *Heptaplus*, and *Disputations*. In the *Commento*, e.g., see Garin, *Scritti vari*, 570.

[16] By repeating without elaboration Pico's claim that celestial actions were limited to the effects of "motion," "light," and "heat"—i.e., without explaining the special sense in

What the heavens contain is the "union" of these and all other terrestrial properties; indeed, the "manifold unity" of the heavens is the most perfect worldly reflection of the "simple unity" that is God. It is thus true in one sense that correspondences bind the heavens and the earth; but what exists in a unified way in the heavens is reflected diffusely in the terrestrial world, ruling out the one-to-one correspondences needed for predictive astrology. Characteristically, Pico is a bit vague on the way in which the *unitas multiplex* of the heavens unfolds into the terrestrial *mixtio* of matter and form:

> The diversity of those [occult powers] does not derive from any constellation, but from the diversity of the *mixtio*, from whose varying proportions one form or another springs forth (*dissultat*). And this pertains to the dignity of heaven: that those things divided in multiplicity in the inferior order are collected in the superior in a simple state of act and elevated way. . . . Now celestial bodies distribute everything equally, no matter how various or manifold, through their single gift of light and heat. That gift, communicated now more, now less, by the stars in succession (*ex serie*), produces in those things an order among themselves rather than diversity. Nor need we inquire further what that gift is, nor its property. I have already often said that it needs no one to demonstrate it, for it is that which reveals itself and everything else with itself—that is, that light evident to all, which issuing from corporeal motion and inspiring heat, suggests to us the occult mystery of God, symbolizing in its motion the power, in its light the wisdom, in its heat the love by which that first God, the first of all I say, just as the *caelum* is the first among all bodies, moves, illuminates, creates, perfects, and conserves all things. . . . For take away [the *caelum*] with its heat, and the peony will not aid epileptics, nor the hyacinth stop the flow of blood, nor rhubarb draw out bile. And just as everything operating in us would stop if not excited by the warmth of our internal heat, so the power of those bodies and the heat itself of living things would stop if they were not nourished and in turn conjoined by celestial heat.[17]

Once again, cosmic proportion rules. Pico does not deny the existence of all

---

which Pico used those terms—a number of earlier scholars, including Cassirer and Garin, confused Pico's ideas with those of a much later scientific era.

[17] 3.24, in *Opera*, 510–11; *Disputationes*, 1:386–88.

celestial correspondences—his correlation of the three Persons of the Trinity (God's power, wisdom, and love) with the archetypal motion, light, and heat of the *caelum* is obvious enough—nor, as his last two sentences suggest, even all magical forces. Pico's continued adhesion to the correlative principles of his "new philosophy" is demonstrated more fully in a later passage:

> It does not seem that the nature of the *caelum* can be more clearly and briefly explained than by saying that the *caelum* is the unity of all bodies. For there is no multitude that does not depend on its unity, nothing in the universe that does not derive from what is one as from its fountainhead. . . . Although there are many such principles, this manifold unity (*multiplex unitas*), as it were, ultimately refers back to the most simple unity (*ad simplicissimam unitatem*) of the first Principle. For in this way every number exists in some way in unity, the whole state in the king, the whole army in its commander. So every power and every perfection of each aggregate exists in its principle. But what in that aggregative condition, so to speak, is divided, defective, imperfect, and disjoined, flourishes in its head in the singular complex of a limitless unity, pure, efficacious, and perfect. From here it follows that nothing of an inferior body is found in its head, but the whole body nevertheless is said to subsist in the head. Similarly, what is first among those things that exist, the ineffable God, is at once *none* of those things that exist and simultaneously *all* things through his eminence as the first nature and through his absolute power. Now from what principle does the genus of corporeal things depend except on that body that is first in place and dignity? But that is the *caelum*. Therefore what I have said is true: that the *caelum* is the unity of all bodies, and all things belonging to other bodies can be denied of it, and all can likewise be affirmed of it. *Denied* since what is formed in those bodies, which is individual, multiple, and imperfect, has various ends, and the *caelum* has neither the nature of form nor diversity. *Affirmed* since it includes all those things simultaneously—not through the potentiality of matter, but through the vastness of its power and through its sublimity as the original nature.[18]

The point, recalling the principles of Pico's *philosophia nova*, is simply that just as God unites in himself all natures absolutely, so too the *caelum* as the first physi-

[18] 3.25, in *Opera*, 512–13; *Disputationes*, 1:392–94 (emphasis added).

cal body unites in itself all inferior natures: "All things exist in all things in their own mode." Indeed, one striking passage in the *Disputations* claims that every star literally enfolds in itself every power of every fallen body: "Est igitur in virtute cuiuslibet stellae virtus omnis corporum caducorum" [Every power of fallen bodies therefore exists in the power of every star]. The difference between the occult virtues of one or another celestial body—for despite what Pico says about the unity of the *caelum*, he clearly acknowledges in it hierarchical distinctions—is that superior bodies contain these powers "in a far more united and elevated fashion."[19]

In his typical syncretic and paradoxical fashion, Pico again manages to have it both ways: Enfolding in a unitary fashion all inferior natures, the *caelum* (like God himself) may be said at once to correspond with *everything* and simultaneously with *nothing*—letting Pico "save" his correlative system while denying the one-to-one correspondences needed for predictive astrology.

Evidence of apparent conceptual shifts in the Disputations

If the main arguments of the *Disputations* reflect the familiar proportions of the nine hundred theses, suggestions from another direction exist of radical changes in Pico's thought. Absent from the *Disputations* are all suggestions of Pico's early *theologia poetica*, which had claimed that Christian truths lay hidden everywhere in pagan myths. Indeed, the *Disputations* ridicules the allegorical symbolism of the astrologers, originating in "corrupt philosophy and the fables of the poets," which they had the audacity to suggest (as Pico himself had repeatedly suggested in his earlier works) issued from the "finger of God."[20] The text even attacks the Hebrew *magistri*—apparently the kabbalists—who tried to convince those with "credulous eyes" that the strokes and characters of "their alphabet" could be found in the stars.[21] And we recall here how even years after his aborted debate Pico himself found magic in "their alphabet"—the holy alphabet invented by Moses, in whose every twist and turn one could literally discover every secret, natural or divine.[22]

---

[19] 3.25, in *Opera*, 513; *Disputationes*, 1:394.

[20] 8.5, in *Opera*, 656; *Disputationes*, 2:274.

[21] 8.5, in *Opera*, 654–55; *Disputationes*, 2:269.

[22] On the magic of the Hebrew language, see my note to thesis 28.33. Pico expanded on these ideas in an appendix to the *Heptaplus* and in an important letter that he wrote just before publication of the nine hundred theses (*Opera*, 384–86). In that letter he argues that

There are many similar surprises in the text. We have seen that numerological correspondences run through every side of Pico's works. While isolated passages in the *Disputations* acknowledge numerological and even musical principles in reality, others ridicule the "mathematical fictions" of the astrologers and Pythagoreans—that latter who, believing that everything came in tens, created a counter-earth to "fill out" the number of celestial spheres to reach their holy decad (*ut denarius eorum numerus impleretur*).[23] And we can recall here how in the nine hundred theses Pico himself had repeatedly invoked the decad (one of two "numbers of numbers" in his magical theses) for similar reasons—proposing ten celestial spheres for their symmetries with the ten *sefirot*, ten Hermetic-Cabalistic *ultores*, ten chief *henads* or "unities" in the Neo-Platonists, ten functions of the soul, and so on. Indeed, the structure of the nine hundred theses, *On Being and the One*, and lost *Concord of Plato and Aristotle* all reflected the cosmic secrets of this most perfect of "perfect numbers."[24] The *Disputations*, however, hesitates to speculate even on whether eight, nine, or ten celestial spheres exist.[25]

Even more startling are the views of magic in the *Disputations*, which the text traces back to diabolical influences in the Chaldeans and Egyptians. The Chaldean and Egyptian *gentes* were little prone to wisdom, the *Disputations* argues, as anyone can see who considers the backwards inhabitants of those regions today. Nor should anyone be misled by the fact that as a youth Pico had himself been deceived by those nations, led astray by the testimony as to their supposed wisdom in Plato and other ancient writers. All in all, the Egyptians and Chaldeans were much devoted to idolatry and superstition but not much given to philosophy.[26] It was from their foul demon worship that "magic arose, which is nothing but a complex of idolatry, astrology, and superstitious medicine, which I have refuted one by one with other superstitions in my books *On the True Faith against Its Seven Enemies*."[27]

The last sentence appears abruptly in the last book of the *Disputations* in that book's current form. The views expressed there are especially peculiar since nothing in the text's main arguments requires rejection of the idea that magical power

---

the letters in the Hebrew alphabet could not have changed since the time of Moses, since if they had, they would have lost their magical power.

23 5.2, in *Opera*, 554; *Disputationes*, 1:536.

24 Above, pp. 30ff.

25 8.1, in *Opera*, 643; *Disputationes*, 2:235.

26 12.2, in *Opera*, 719; *Disputationes*, 2:492–94.

27 12.6, in *Opera*, 729; *Disputationes*, 2:525. On the *Seven Enemies*, see further below.

can be drawn in some way from the stars. Early in the work, Pico attacks the talismanic astral magic that Ficino had endorsed, but Pico had already rejected that brand of celestial magic early in his career.[28] Especially curious is the failure in the *Disputations* to distinguish "natural" and "demonic" magic—or even astrological magic and the many other types of *magia naturalis* that Pico had defended so vigorously in the nine hundred theses, *Oration*, and *Apology*.

Compounding this problem, the *Disputations* contains numerous passages that offer potential support for the kinds of celestial magic that Pico endorsed in his early works. Thus early in the text, Pico argues that differences in the "nobility" of inferior matter determine how much or how little of astral influences are captured on the earth—a view commonly advanced in ancient and medieval magical texts. Moreover, Pico's work argues that the *unitas multiplex* of the heavens is not distributed uniformly on the earth but "in succession" (*ex serie*), producing in inferior things "an order among themselves rather than a diversity"—another position that could be easily turned to magical ends. Another passage, again recalling Pico's early magical writings, argues that Saturn and Jupiter "do the same thing, but one in one mode, the nobler in a nobler and more elevated mode." One might claim that different celestial bodies contain different properties—and hence, one might infer, might be tapped by the *magus*—insofar as they "contract" differently the heavens' uniform formative power.[29] Nowhere does the *Disputations* draw out the obvious magical implications of these ideas. But the work's arguments leave plenty of room, if Pico wanted it, to allow him to support both the astrological and nonastrological types of magic that he endorsed in his early works.[30]

Nevertheless, attack magic the *Disputations* does—and with a vengeance. Roger Bacon, "that great patron of astrology"—and one of Pico's main magical sources in the nine hundred theses—is attacked especially harshly for his acceptance of spurious authorities.[31] Albert the Great, another of Pico's early magical sources, is praised for abandoning his interests in magic in his later life—the parallels we are meant to draw between Albert's and Pico's lives are clear—

[28] See above, pp. 123–26. Francis Yates's association of Pico with talismanic magic was based on misreadings of the Latin in several key magical theses; see theses 9>24–25 and notes.

[29] 2.25, in *Opera*, 514; *Disputationes*, 1:398–400.

[30] See also the first of the long passages from the *Disputationes* quoted earlier in this section, on p. 140.

[31] 1, *cap. unicum*, in *Opera*, 419; *Disputationes*, 1:64–66.

spending his last holy years locked in the cloister.[32] Moreover, we find, magical works ascribed to Albert such as the *Speculum astronomiae*, like similar astrological texts attributed to St. Thomas and other authorities, were not by Albert at all.[33] The text hurls special scorn at the Egyptians and Chaldeans—ridiculing Zoroaster's writings, for example, in which eight years earlier Pico had found the doctrine of original sin and prophecies of Christ's Incarnation. "Who was more powerful in antiquity in astrology, in magic, and in all superstition than Zoroaster?" And yet Zoroaster was killed in battle by Ninus, the first king of Assyria, who was neither an astrologer nor magician.[34] Mercury (Hermes) Trismegistus—or more precisely, the astrological works attributed to him "by some"—is also treated with contempt, as are standard magical authorities like al-Kindi. The secret magic that the nine hundred theses, *Oration*, and *Apology* discovered in Orpheus and the other *prisci theologi* and Cabalists is mentioned nowhere in the text.

Historians have long argued over whether or not Pico's thought changed radically in his later years. No firm answer to this question was possible until a clearer picture existed of the nine hundred theses, Pico's most important philosophical text. Anyone comparing Pico's theses closely with the *Disputations* is forced to admit the appearance of profound intellectual changes in the latter work—profound enough to support Di Napoli's claim, aimed against Garin and others, that the *Disputations* contained a virtual "palinode" to Pico's early work.[35] Curiously, those changes left untouched the basic principles of Pico's *philosophia nova*, which remained essentially the same in the *Disputations* as in his theses. What Pico had apparently abandoned instead were important corollaries to his system, including the most extreme instances of his early numerological thinking and his views of the authority of the *prisci theologi* and Cabalists. Most surprising of all were Pico's apparent shifts on magic, which were closely linked to his general views of the world. For the early Pico, as we have seen, the *magus* was not an astrologer but a cosmic priest, intent on redeeming all of fallen nature with himself. For Pico to abandon magic implied a major shift in what earlier generations of historians liked to refer to as his "philosophy of man."

---

32 12.7, in *Opera*, 729–30; *Disputationes*, 2:528.

33 1, *cap. unicum*, in *Opera*, 427 (which refers to an alternate title for the *Speculum*) and passim; *Disputationes*, 1:94 and passim.

34 12.2, in *Opera*, 713; *Disputationes*, 2:474. There may be some question of which Zoroaster Pico had in mind here, however. Cf. *Oration/Apology*, in *Opera*, 121, 327; Garin, *Scritti vari*, 150.

35 Di Napoli (1965).

What remains unclear are the origins of these changes. Was Pico's system collapsing under its own weight, the victim of his early philological and syncretic excesses? Or did these changes come from another source? It is to this question, the most important that remains in our attempts to reconstruct Pico's thought, that we will turn in the two concluding sections of this study.

iii. Other Readings of the Disputations

Hints can be found in the *Disputations* of Pico's growing sophistication on textual questions, including questions on which he had blundered spectacularly in his early career. Thus the *Disputations* quotes the twelfth-century *Quaestiones naturales* of Adelard of Bath—a writer hilariously transformed in Pico's theses into Plotinus's fellow student—conspicuously and at length in the original Latin text.[36] I earlier suggested that Flavius Mithridates, Pico's first tutor in Hebrew, Aramaic, and Arabic, played a role in Adelard's bizarre displacement in space and time. Similarly, evidence suggests that Flavius's forgeries probably lay behind Pico's boast that he possessed the original "Chaldean" text of the *Chaldean Oracles*, which he attributed to Zoroaster.[37] By the time that he wrote the *Disputations*, however, Pico's proficiency in Semitic languages had grown under tutors who were far more trustworthy than Flavius, and Pico had presumably had time to discover his early embarrassing errors. One suspects a trace of personal apologetics in the long discussions in the *Disputations* of the botched translations, corrupt manuscripts, and forged texts underlying the occult arts:

> Now since the things claimed by [the astrologers] cannot be confirmed by reason—whether they themselves believe that they are true or only want them believed by others—they attribute fabulous books of this sort to the most famous and ancient men, and so with fictitious authorities trap others in their error. The book *On the Properties of Elements*, which deals with grand conjunctions, is of this sort, as is the *Book of Secrets* dedicated to Alexander [the Great], which they ascribe to Aristotle through no fault or responsibility of that great philosopher. Similarly, the magicians circu-

[36] Pico identifies the source of the long quotation that opens *Disputationes* 3.15 as "Adeland drawing on the opinions of the Saracens" [Adelandus ex opinionem Saracenorum]. The theses, on the other hand, identify the same author as "Adeland the Arab," supposedly Plotinus's third-century contemporary. See my discussion above, pp. 13–14.

[37] Above, p. 13. See further my introductory note to theses 8>1–15.

> late the books entitled *On the Cow* by Plato, and those they call the *Institutes*, filled with the most detestable illusions and fictions, not less alien from Plato than those beggars themselves are from Plato in goodness and wisdom. Similarly, in times past the so-called gnostic heretics ascribed books to Zoroaster to make their heresies seem respectable by invoking Zoroaster's antiquity. But Porphyry showed with many arguments that those books were not by Zoroaster but were recent and forged.[38] Those unskilled in humane letters (*humaniorum litterarum rudiores*), even if otherwise learned, can be easily deceived and defrauded by lies like these—although those who thoroughly understand the nature and style of authorities can immediately distinguish adulterated from authentic works. But the astrologers' fictions and what has come down to us of the superstitious arts are so far from all resemblance to the truth that this is obvious to anyone who is even moderately learned.[39]

While from a theoretical perspective it would be attractive to imagine Pico's system bursting apart here at its philological seams, other possibilities must be considered. The *Disputations* was a polemical tract, and as Pico himself tells us in the text, following the conventions of the disputation it was his job to raise every conceivable weapon against his opponents, even denying positions that he might normally concede.[40] The claim that an opponent's texts were corrupt, his translations distorted, and his authorities spurious was standard fare long before the advent of Renaissance classicism; the fact that a Renaissance writer made such complaints should never be naively mistaken for evidence that his own scholarship was more reliable. In any case, while a growth in Pico's philological sophistication may explain some of the conceptual shifts in the *Disputations*, the text's adherence to disputational conventions must also be taken into account.

Other possibilities cloud the interpretive picture. It would be possible to argue that the *Disputations* was a pseudopalinode of sorts—similar to that reputedly found in Agrippa von Nettesheim's antimagical *De vanitate scientiarum*—aimed at deflecting criticism of Pico's eagerly awaited (and clearly far more dangerous) *Concord of Plato and Aristotle,* which we know was closely linked to his aborted Vatican

---

[38] Porphyry *Life of Plotinus* 16.

[39] 1, *cap. unicum*, in *Opera,* 419; *Disputationes*, 1:64.

[40] 4.1, in *Opera,* 520; *Disputationes*, 1:421. This chapter of Pico's work throws considerable light on Renaissance disputational practices and invites closer study.

debate.[41] The same role may also have been played by the treatise or treatises entitled *On the True Faith against Its Seven Enemies*—if in fact such a text (or texts) ever existed.[42] Certainly there is enough ambiguity in the *Disputations* to make such a reading plausible. If part of that ambiguity was intentional, Pico's apparent rejection of magic, the *prisci theologi*, and the Cabala in the *Disputationes* might be

---

[41] See the discussion above, pp. 35–36.

[42] On the *Concord of Plato and Aristotle*, see, e.g., *Disputations* 3.4 (*Opera*, 460; *Disputationes*, 1:208), which refers to the *Concord* as though it were already completed. We have testimony regarding the *Seven Enemies*, of which Gianfrancesco claimed that the *Disputations* was simply one section, in the latter text and in Gianfrancesco's biography of his uncle, which provides what Gianfrancesco claims to be a general outline of the work. According to Pico's nephew, the *Seven Enemies* was meant to attack the enemies of the church "with their own weapons." One part was devoted to attacking impious philosophers, who scorned religion and only adored natural reason; another used the Old Testament and the "proper armaments of the Judaic school" (presumably the Cabala) against the Hebrews; another attacked "the Quran of Mohammed"; another (the *Disputations*) dealt with divinatory astrology; and a final part looked one by one at various superstitions including "hydromancy, geomancy, pyromancy, soothsaying, and other inanities of that kind" (*Opera,* fol. 4v). The claim that Pico meant to attack the enemies of the church "with their own weapons"—an idea repeatedly suggested in the nine hundred theses, *Oration*, and *Apology* in reference to the Jews and the Cabala—implies that despite the polemical tone of its title, the *Seven Enemies* may not have differed as much from the nine hundred theses or *Concord of Plato and Aristotle* as Gianfrancesco would like us to believe. Indeed, Gianfrancesco's description of the work, which may have drawn from a lost introductory fragment, at times sounds remarkably like Pico's public challenge years earlier to debate the opinions of the *gentes* and their *heresiarchae* in Rome. ("Hos itaque septem quasi duces," Gianfrancesco relates, "sub quibus reliqui velut gregarii continentur, propriis eorum armis conflicturus ad congressum citaverat" [And so these seven as leaders, under which the rest are contained as soldiers, he would have summoned to battle (*ad congressum*) to defeat them with their own weapons].) (Whether Pico planned another "congress" in a literal sense is an interesting question.) Another reference to the *Seven Enemies*—this time emphasizing the *Disputations* as a prelude "in that bitter sevenfold fight against the enemies of the church" can be found in a letter of Gianfrancesco's dated 1 June 1494 (five months before Pico's death) in Gianfrancesco's *Opera* (2:1285–86). Tentatively accepting this date as authentic, and recognizing that the *Seven Enemies* may have been meant to offer theological cover for Pico's *Concord of Plato and Aristotle*, leads me to doubt whether anything ever existed of the former text besides the extant portions of the *Disputations* and whatever Gianfrancesco possessed of Pico's works on the Cabala. In any case, if substantial parts of such a work did exist, and the text were as polemical as Pico's nephew claimed, from what we know of Gianfrancesco's editorial policies (see below), it is the one work of Pico's that we can be certain that Gianfrancesco *would* have published.

reconcilable in some way with the more dangerous views found in his lost *Concord of Plato and Aristotle,* which appears to have carried on the central themes of the nine hundred theses.[43]

In this interpretation, the fact that the *Disputations* never distinguishes "natural" from "demonic" magic—a distinction that Pico was careful to make in all his early works—might be taken as a hint that, under whatever name, Pico continued to support the religious and contemplative forms of magic that he had planned to discuss at Rome. As Pico tells us in the *Apology*, "This name 'magic' is an equivocal name." In the same text he declares, "I am no magician!"—with the unstated qualification that he only meant that he did not practice magic of the demonic sort.[44] Reflecting similar unstated reservations, the apparent attacks in the *Disputations* on the Egyptians and Chaldeans might simply reflect Pico's assaults in the theses on those Egyptians and Chaldeans in history's evil "emanation"—the temporal analogue of the "left-hand" emanation in the cosmic sphere.[45] The same might be true of the criticism directed in the *Disputations* against the Hebrew *magistri*—recalling the attacks in the *Apology* on those Jews who "falsely polluting divine things with false and vain superstitions" supported demonic magic by invoking the sacred name "Cabalist," citing the fabricated authority of Adam, Solomon, Enoch, and "similar men."[46] Anyone doubting that Pico was capable of intentional duplicity of this sort only needs to recall the subtle debating traps planted on virtually every page of the nine hundred theses. The theological disaster that followed publication of that text, and the work's close ties with the still unpublished *Concord of Plato and Aristotle*, gave Pico an obvious motive for seeking whatever intellectual cover the *Disputations against Divinatory Astrology* might provide. The normally close links in premodern thought between astrology and magic, and the fact that from his earliest days Pico had good systematic reasons of his own for rejecting divinatory astrology, made the *Disputations* an obvious text in which to pursue such a strategy.

---

[43] See above, pp. 35–36, and the evidence on the *Concord* discussed later in this chapter.

[44] *Opera,* 169, 116.

[45] Above, pp. 38–39.

[46] *Opera,* 181. It is interesting that the word "Cabala" does not appear even once in the *Disputations*. Recognizing that similar references were removed from the *Commento* after Pico's death, I suspect that Gianfrancesco or one of his associates was responsible for this omission. In any event, other evidence suggests that Pico never abandoned his interest in Cabala.

The traditional view of Pico "under the influence of Savonarola"

One more possible reading of the *Disputations* needs to be mentioned. An old historical tradition, drawing on Gianfrancesco Pico's spiritualized biography of his uncle, has pictured the apparent changes in Pico's later thought as evidence of a sudden religious conversion—most commonly said to have occurred "under the influence of Savonarola." The fact that Gianfrancesco's *Vita* was transparently based on hagiographical models does not by itself invalidate that interpretation. The image of the precocious but worldly youth abandoning the world following a sudden religious experience was strong enough in the Renaissance to guarantee that life often imitated art. In the wake of his ongoing troubles with the church, the premature death of his two closest friends, Lorenzo de' Medici and Angelo Poliziano, and the rapidly deteriorating political climate in Florence, it would hardly be surprising at the end of his life to find in Pico a more pessimistic view of the world than the one he had held at the time of his planned Roman debate.

Nor can Pico's links to Savonarola be minimized. We know that it was Pico himself who persuaded Lorenzo de' Medici to recall the fiery Dominican preacher to Florence a final time in 1490, an event that ironically contributed heavily to the Medicis' fall from power. Contemporary accounts show us Savonarola praising Pico as the only intellectual of the period equal to St. Jerome, St. Augustine, and other church fathers, debating with him over the value of pagan philosophy, and ultimately burying him in Savonarola's San Marco, wrapped in death, at least, in the habits of the Dominican order. Many of Pico's companions from the old Lorenzean circle—indeed, nearly all of them except Ficino—appear, moreover, after Pico's death in the Savonarolan vanguard, the so-called *piagnoni* or "weepers," who drastically transformed Florence before Savonarola was finally executed in 1498.[47]

The evidence we have of Pico's later religious views and his interactions with Savonarola is, however, far from unambiguous. The portraits of the later Pico drawn even by avid *piagnoni* like Giovanni Nesi and Pietro Crinito more often remind us of the bold magician-priest of the nine hundred theses—who was literally prepared "to marry the world"—than of the self-effacing Christian of his nephew's *Vita,* where we find the humble (and even self-flagellating!) Pico vowing to wander barefoot preaching the simple word of Christ once his current literary projects were complete.[48] Suggestions, in fact, exist of serious conflict between

[47] On Florence in this period, see Weinstein (1970).

[48] *Opera,* fols. 6r, 7r.

Pico and Savonarola, reflected in accusations by Giovanni Sinibaldi, one of Savonarola's closest associates, that Pico had deceived Savonarola on his religious views at the end of his life.[49] In publicly eulogizing Pico, moreover, Savonarola—unlike Ficino—placed the philosopher in purgatory and not in heaven for breaking a supposed vow to join Savonarola's order before his death.[50]

Finally, it should be noted that the old story that has been rehashed for centuries to illustrate Savonarola's influence on Pico—that Pico's hair literally stood on end when Savonarola preached—derives from no more credible source than Savonarola himself. Savonarola included the story, long after Pico's death, in an eleventh hour appeal to Pico's old family ally, Pope Alexander VI, just before Savonarola's final (and ultimately fatal) break with the church.[51] As we shall see in the next section, Savonarola's attempts to enlist Pico's posthumous support in his cause had extensive precedents—drastically affecting the contents of Pico's surviving works.

iv. Evidence of Posthumous Tampering in Pico's Works by Gianfrancesco Pico, Savonarola, and Their Associates

Which interpretation of Pico's later thought is the correct one? As Pico's textual resources grew, did his work anticipate in miniature the decline of syncretic-correlative traditions, as I have modeled it? Did the apparent shifts in his thinking reflect the polemical character of the *Disputations*? Were they part of an elaborate pseudopalinode? Did they result from a genuine religious conversion, related or not to Savonarola's influence? Is there some truth in more than one of these interpretations? Unfortunately, these questions cannot be answered in a simple fashion. The problem lies in textual problems even more serious than those found in the nine hundred theses, one of the most difficult of Renaissance works. For evidence

---

[49] These accusations are found in a marginal note of Sinibaldi's to Dominico Benivieni's *Trattato . . . in defensione e probazione delle dottrine e profezie predicate da frate Jeronimo da Ferrara* (1496) (Treatise . . . in Defense of the Integrity of the Doctrines and Prophecies Preached by Friar Girolamo Savonarola). See Ridolfi (4th ed., 1974: 147, 549). Cf. Garfagnini (1997).

[50] *Prediche sopra aggeo*, ed. Firpo (1965: 104). Savonarola's eulogy is reported in much elaborated form by Gianfrancesco Pico in his *Vita* of his uncle, *Opera*, fol. 7v. Ficino places Pico in heaven about the same time that Savonarola was putting him in purgatory, in a letter from 1495 included in Pico's collected works (*Opera*, 405).

[51] For the relevant passage (from Savonarola's *Compendium revelationum* [Compendium of Revelations]), see Weinstein (1970: 70).

shows that after his death Pico's writings were doctored—and doctored heavily—by his Savonarolan editors for religious and political ends.

The story of how and why that doctoring took place has more twists and turns than any fictional mystery faced by Umberto Eco's scholastic-detective William of Baskerville. It involves one of the most violent propaganda wars of the early printing revolution, the temporary fall of Italy's leading political family, unrestrained religious fanaticism, a case of torture, and Pico's murder or purported murder by his secretary (it is quite likely that his secretary was framed). It also involves at least one conspirator with a twisted psychological profile—Pico's nephew—and a coverup as outrageous as any in recent political memory. The fact that the mystery itself exists has escaped the general attention of Renaissance historians, although over the past century tantalizing bits and pieces of evidence have periodically surfaced in out-of-the-way scholarly journals.

The figure most immediately responsible for the tampering was Pico's nephew Gianfrancesco Pico, a philosopher himself of sorts and the most influential of Savonarolan propagandists. But the story involves other prominent *piagnoni* as well, and compelling evidence suggests a major role in the drama for Savonarola himself. To discuss the story fully would take a study at least as long as the present one. Even a partial unraveling of the mystery, however, throws new light on one of the most obscure periods in Florentine history.

Gianfrancesco Pico as his uncle's editor

Immediately after hearing of Pico's death, his nephew rushed to Florence with the self-appointed task of becoming his uncle's editor and literary executor. His motive, or so he claimed one year later, was simply to prevent the destruction of Pico's works:

> Although his will had not yet been opened and his heir was not known, nevertheless his book chests were opened so I could turn over and inspect all his works. I saw in his discarded papers (*in cartaceis illis*) and dispersed codices the incredible study of the man, all kinds of treatises, and conceptions admirable beyond the capacities of the human mind. It is true that in collecting his writings his negligence should not be praised, for because of this all his works were scattered and dispersed. But of this another time.[52]

[52] *Opera*, 288.

When the will was opened, Gianfrancesco found to his dismay that he was not named Pico's heir. All Pico's books and other movable goods were left to Gianfrancesco's uncle and hated enemy—Antonmaria Pico—who was involved in extended military conflicts with Gianfrancesco and Gianfrancesco's father Galeotto (Pico's eldest brother) for control of the family territories.[53] This did not deter Gianfrancesco from his editorial ambitions, however. Over the next three years he apparently had unlimited access to Pico's unpublished papers, which, to the permanent detriment of Pico's literary fortunes, fell for unknown reasons into the hands of Savonarola and the Dominican friars at San Marco in Florence. There Pico's papers remained, or supposedly remained, until February 1498, when Antonmaria sold whatever was left of them along with Pico's books to Cardinal Domenico Grimani, who had them shipped to Rome.[54] Drawing in part on these papers, assisted by his tutor and personal physician, Giovanni Mainardi (another ardent Savonarolan), in 1496 Gianfrancesco published two volumes of his uncle's writings in Bologna, which have provided the foundations for all later versions of Pico's collected works.[55]

---

[53] Pico's will and codicil, transcribed from documents in Florentine archives, can be found in C. Milanesi (1857: 85–94). The will and part of the codicil are reprinted in Calori Cesis (1897: 21ff.) and in Italian translation in Poletti (1987). Cf. also the corrections to Calori Cesis and the other sources listed in Kibre (1936: 17–18). On the armed struggles between Galeotto Pico and his brother Antonmaria, see Ceretti (1878). For a summary of Gianfrancesco's battles for Mirandola and Concordia after his father's death, see Schmitt (1967).

[54] There is nothing in Pico's will or codicil suggesting that Pico's books and papers be held at San Marco, but we know that that is where they were when Antonmaria's agents sold them in 1498. See the passage from Antonio Pizzamano, Cardinal Grimani's agent, cited in Calori Cesis (1897: 76) and Kibre (1936: 5 n. 4). Calori Cesis's claim, based on an anonymous chronicler of the Pico family, that the books were willed to the Dominicans of San Marco is in clear conflict with the evidence in Pico's will; see here also Kibre (1936: 17). There are a number of unsolved mysteries involving Pico's will, books, and unpublished papers that call for closer scrutiny, especially given what we know about posthumous tampering in Pico's works. On the fate of Pico's books in Rome, see Mercati (1938) and Levi Della Vida (1939).

[55] On Mainardi, whose part in this work was considerable, see Zambelli (1965) and the collection of studies in *Atti del Convegno internazionale per la celebrazione del V centenario della nascita di Giovanni Manardo 1462–1536* (1963). Raspanti (1997) has recently claimed, without evidence, that the second volume of Pico's collected works, which contains the *Disputationes*, was, in fact, published one year before the first volume. On this claim, see my discussion below, pp. 175–76 n. 121. For reasons that will become clear later, all dates involving the *Disputationes* must be approached with deep skepticism.

Given what they knew of Pico's literary output, more than one of Pico's friends hinted at their deep disappointment in Gianfrancesco's edition. The first volume contained Gianfrancesco's spiritualized biography of his uncle; the *Heptaplus* and *Apology*, which had been printed in Pico's lifetime; the *Oration* and *On Being and the One*, which had circulated widely in manuscript; a tiny selection of Pico's correspondence (opening with three letters to the ambitious Gianfrancesco, who until then was totally unknown); and some fragments from some anomalous moral and religious tracts, which we will discuss later. The second volume contained twelve of what Gianfrancesco claimed were thirteen planned books of the *Disputations against Divinatory Astrology*, which were reportedly transcribed from Pico's papers by Mainardi and Gianfrancesco with remarkable speed after Pico's death.[56]

The omissions in the 1496 edition are extensive—the nine hundred theses and *Commento* are only the most obvious examples—but despite promises made for decades, Gianfrancesco never published another line under his uncle's name before his own death some four decades later.[57]

To understand Gianfrancesco's editorial work, we need to look more closely at his peculiar relations with his uncle. Although the elder Pico was only six or seven years Gianfrancesco's senior, from their letters it appears that Pico took a paternal if distant interest in his nephew, to which Gianfrancesco initially responded with something akin to open hero-worship. While Gianfrancesco liked to boast of his close personal ties to his uncle, the evidence suggests that at Pico's death Gianfrancesco was far from qualified to act as either his biographer or editor. A few examples will make this clear. Describing a epistolary battle that Pico had had with the philosopher Antonio da Faenza over the *On Being and the One* several years

[56] On their transcription, see the letter from Gianfrancesco Pico to Baptista Spagnuoli of Mantua (G. F. Pico, Opera, 2:1340–42). The dates of this letter are uncertain, but the current consensus is that the *Disputationes* was transcribed and the *Vita* composed by February 1495—scarcely three months after Pico's death (see, e.g., Zambelli 1965: 219–20 and n. 40 and Garin's preface to the 1971 reprint of Pico's *Opera*). Once again, however, for reasons discussed later, there are grounds to call all dates involving the *Disputationes* into question. In any event, Cavini (1973: 134) dates Gianfrancesco's letter to February 1496, not 1495—a redating that to me seems highly probable.

[57] For a brief biography of Gianfrancesco, see Schmitt (1967). The reprints of Pico's works that Gianfrancesco later saw to press added no new texts to the original 1496 edition. Zambelli's claim (1977a, 1977b) that the nine hundred theses were included in the 1518 Venetian edition published by Gianfrancesco is in error.

before Pico's death, Gianfrancesco admitted that he only knew by "rumor" of his uncle's book, despite the fact that it had circulated widely in manuscript for several years. In continuing Pico's polemics with Antonio, Gianfrancesco showed no real understanding of his uncle's views, adding to them mainly "many things as testimony from great authorities" for the benefit of unnamed critics and the unlearned.[58] Again, shortly after his uncle's death, Gianfrancesco wrote excitedly to Pico's friend and spiritual advisor, the Carmelite General Baptista Spagnuoli of Mantua, of a translation of Ptolemy's *Centiloquium* with an anti-astrological commentary that he found in Pico's papers, only to be gently admonished by Baptista that the texts were presumably simply the well-known works of Giovanni Pontano—which were pro-astrological to boot. Pico's historians have universally agreed with Baptista, but Gianfrancesco did not bother to correct his claim in his *Vita* of his uncle: hardly a propitious start for his editorial career.[59]

Dozens of errors in Gianfrancesco's *Vita*, many of them apparently intentional, others rooted in blatant ignorance, have misled historians for five centuries: Gianfrancesco falsely claims that Pico stayed a year in Rome waiting to start his debate, never mentioning his humiliating flight to France or imprisonment (*Opera*, fol. 3v); transforms the vehemently anti-Thomistic Pico into the Dominican's pious defender (fol. 5v); is off by several years as to when Pico wrote the *Heptaplus*, which was then his best-known work (fol. 4r); and falsely claims that Pico abandoned poetry, burning his Italian and Latin poems after a sudden religious conversion (fol. 4r). It is especially revealing that the *Vita* nowhere mentions Pico's close personal ties with Lorenzo de' Medici or the Medici family—something to be kept in mind when we consider the political motives behind Gianfrancesco's editorial hatchetwork.[60] The stories in the *Vita* of Pico's miraculous birth and childhood feats are borrowed directly from the lives of the saints (especially St. Ambrose).[61]

Problems of a different kind arise out of Gianfrancesco's philosophical perspectives, which were violently opposed to his uncle's. Charles Schmitt, who has written the fullest account yet of Gianfrancesco's work, notes that despite Gianfrancesco's claims to being a simple defender of Pico's work, "if the truth be

---

[58] *Opera*, 289–90.

[59] G. F. Pico, *Opera*, 2:1341, 1353.

[60] Gianfrancesco's silence on Lorenzo de' Medici and Gianfrancesco's role as a Savonarolan propagandist have also been suggestively linked by Kristeller (1965: 77 n. 185).

[61] *Opera*, fol. 3r.

known, philosophically, at least, he was his uncle's bitterest opponent."[62] Every premodern society that experienced rapid expansions in textual knowledge gave birth not only to extreme syncretic tendencies but to equally extreme reactions in the opposite direction. Some version of Tertullian's complaint, "What has Athens to do with Jerusalem!" has been raised in every traditional society in periods of intense cultural fusion: Avicenna found his antithesis in al-Ghazali, St. Thomas in St. Bonaventure, the Neo-Confucian scholastics in their classicist critics. If Pico illustrates the syncretic extremes fostered by the early Western printing revolution, in his nephew we find his inverse image—a fanatical anti-syncretist who, through a perverse symmetry in history, held the fate of Pico's works in his hands.

Gianfrancesco's first philosophical treatise, *On the Study of Human and Divine Philosophy*, was composed the same year that Gianfrancesco saw Pico's works off to press. Despite lavish words concerning his uncle's genius, the work violently attacks the ancient philosophers whose reconciliation with Christian thought was Pico's lifelong goal. Two-and-a-half decades later, with countless similar attacks in between, Gianfrancesco raised the same theme in his longest work, *An Examination of the Vanity of the Doctrine of the* Gentes *and of the Truth of Christian Teachings*, whose main theme can be gathered from its title and from the quotation given at the opening of this chapter. The work was Gianfrancesco's anti-concord, as it were—one whose links with his uncle's lost *Concord of Plato and Aristotle* were anything but casual, as we shall see later.

Gianfrancesco Pico is commonly represented as a philosophical "skeptic," placed in a tradition linking Montaigne with Galileo and Gassendi and other anti-systematic writers of the scientific revolution.[63] But the skeptic label is extremely misleading, as is evident when we scan the long list of Gianfrancesco's supplications to the saints, the Virgin Mary, and his own guardian angel, or his treatises on witchcraft or on the powers of supernatural prophecy, which along with his Savonarolan propaganda make up the vast bulk of his work.[64] Taken out of context, Gianfrancesco's use of skeptical arguments from Sextus Empiricus or Cicero might have potentially encouraged genuine skeptical attitudes in the sixteenth century; his actual influence in this direction, however, if it existed at all, was very

---

[62] Schmitt (1965: 313). See also Schmitt's monograph on Gianfrancesco (1967).

[63] See, e.g., Schmitt (1965, 1967), Popkin (1979).

[64] The fullest catalog of Gianfrancesco's writings is found in the appendix to Schmitt (1967).

slight.[65] Gianfrancesco's goals were far removed from the "suspension of belief" of the ancient skeptic; nor, given his virulent defense of the authority of Christian philosophers like Pseudo-Dionysius or St. Thomas, can he even be said to have "invoked reason to destroy reason," as has been claimed of other medieval skeptic-fideists.

To understand Gianfrancesco's thought, it is less important to note the particular ideas that he attacked or supported—for despite his supposed skepticism, he uncritically endorsed a wide range of philosophical concepts—than to identify the authorities with whom he associated those ideas. In Gianfrancesco's works every weapon conceivable—philological assault, pseudo-Pyrrhonian skepticism, or simple *ad hominem* ridicule—was mustered to attack what he saw as unwanted pagan influences in Christian thought. What belies the skeptic label is the fact that he just as ardently wielded the same weapons in defending venerated Christian writers—no matter how deeply, at an earlier level of tradition, the ideas of those writers reflected those very same pagan influences. Above all, Gianfrancesco's goal was to defend what he pictured as the absolute infallibility of Scripture, which to quote his mentor Savonarola, "we are obliged to believe is true right down to the 'last iota,' and to approve all that it approves and to condemn all that it condemns because it was written by God and cannot be in error."[66]

No matter how opposed he was to his uncle's ideas, for decades Gianfrancesco continued, when convenient, to represent himself as a humble defender and continuer of Pico's work. Thus immediately following Pico's death, Gianfrancesco not only took up his uncle's abandoned polemics with Antonio da Faenza—involving Pico's plans to reconcile the two greatest pagans of all—but wrote a defense as well of his uncle against Petrus Garsias's *Determinationes magistrales*, a work that Pico himself had chosen to ignore. Ironically, Gianfrancesco's attitudes towards magic, Cabala, and the other esoteric arts—the targets of Garsias's most violent attacks—were far closer to Garsias's than to Pico's.[67] Further, attempting to supplement the Italian epitome that Savonarola wrote of the *Disputations*—a summary

---

[65] See here Popkin (1979: 21).

[66] Savonarola, *Trattato contra li astrologi*, ed. Garfagnini and Garin (1982: 278).

[67] Gianfrancesco's attack on Garsias, which was apparently written in 1495 or 1496, has been lost and is not listed in Schmitt's catalog of Gianfrancesco's writings. Among other places, Gianfrancesco mentions the work in an important letter to Lilio Gregorio Giraldi that lists his works (G. F. Pico, *Opera*, 2:1365, 1369).

written for political motives that we will explore later—Gianfrancesco wrote his own epitome of Pico's text in the scholastic or "Parisian style," intended for those who were learned but unequal to Pico's classical Latin.[68]

Over time, Gianfrancesco's confusion of his works with his uncle's reached fantastic proportions. Repeated pleas came to him from Baptista Spagnuoli to preserve every fragment of Pico's works—the products, Baptista argued, of the greatest thinker of their age. In one letter Baptista tells that he had dreamt of Pico stammering—his point is clear enough—and continues emotionally: "I tell you what Christ said to the Apostles: 'Gather the fragments lest they perish!'"[69] Gianfrancesco enthusiastically responded that he would collect every line; for years he repeated Baptista's suggestion that if nothing else he would gather Pico's unpublished works in piecemeal form, as in Gellius's *Attic Nights* or Clement of Alexandria's *Stromata*.[70] At times Gianfrancesco hinted that he would one day publish a more elaborate compilation of Pico's writings illuminated by his own commentaries, or pictured his thought intertwined even more intimately with his dead uncle's—"common to both... by him begun, by me perfected"[71]—in what he peculiarly represented as their common philosophical goal. "Not only shall I give form to Pico's material with my form," he boasted to Ercole Strozzi in late 1496, "but I will also add some materials: cementing the two together with my glue, I will supplement what is omitted and draw together what is diffuse."[72]

Although Gianfrancesco fluctuated wildly on this point, there is no doubt that when he wrote these lines he had far more than fragments of Pico's unpublished works in his hands. In the same letter to Strozzi, Gianfrancesco boasted that by that time he had already extracted "perhaps three hundred chapters of the worthiest things" from his uncle's unpublished papers, which, although still in a disordered state, he intended to polish stylistically and publish.[73] Based on the average

---

[68] Gianfrancesco promised to write such a work in his *De studio divinae et humanae philosophiae*, which was written in 1496 (G. F. Pico, *Opera*, 2:23). The work is either the same, or closely related to, the *Quaestio de falsitate astrologiae* that Gianfrancesco wrote around 1510. For an edition, see Cavini (1973). Not surprisingly, given what we will see in a moment, like Gianfrancesco's *De rerum praenotione*, on which it was based, the *Quaestio de falsitate astrologiae* often plagiarizes long sections of Pico's works nearly verbatim.

[69] Pico, *Opera*, 388.

[70] G. F. Pico, *Opera*, 2:24, 1346.

[71] G. F. Pico, *Opera*, 2:1346.

[72] G. F. Pico, *Opera*, 2:1330.

[73] For the text containing this claim, see the following note.

length of the 142 chapters that Gianfrancesco and Mainardi had earlier transcribed from the *Disputations*, this left Gianfrancesco with the equivalent of over 650 folio-sized printed pages from this part of his uncle's works—by no means an unreasonable figure, given the apparent speed with which Gianfrancesco and Mainardi had transcribed his attack on astrology.

Besides these disordered chapters—and the distinction is crucial—Gianfrancesco admitted to possessing an even larger segment of Pico's unpublished works. He confided to Strozzi: "I believe that I can draw out not a little (*nonnihil*) of the *Concord of Plato and Aristotle*, and likewise many things against heretics, against the Hebrews, and many things on the *Psalms*, which are collected in order, where you can recognize Pico's incredible genius."[74] The works "against the Hebrews" presumably refer to Pico's extended writings on the Cabala—writings alluded to in the *Heptaplus* and other texts—a tradition that Pico consistently portrayed as a weapon against the Jews. Whatever the full scope of Pico's writings transcribed by Gianfrancesco and his tutor—and they were to have access to *all* his papers until early 1498—by late 1496 they already possessed, besides the three hundred chapters of fragments that Gianfrancesco mentions, significant portions, and arguably full texts, of the *Concord of Plato and Aristotle*, *Commentary on the Psalms*, and other of Pico's most important unpublished works.

[74] G. F. Pico, *Opera*, 2:1329–30. "Nam trecenta forte rerum capita dignissimarum excerpsimus, rerum inquam duntaxat nudarum atque etiam informium, quae pro virili laborabimus ut specie induantur, hoc est, orationis luce splendescant. Sed nullo ordine posita sunt, eumque penitus refugiunt. Praeterea nonnihil de Platonis Aristotelisque concordia depromere posse arbitramur, pleraque item adversus haereticos, adversus Hebraeos, multa in Psalmos, quae ordine collocata sunt, ubi incredibile Pici ingenium agnosces." In an important letter to Giovanni Mainardi (G. F. Pico, *Opera*, 2:1299–1300), we find that it was the older and more capable Mainardi who originally made the excerpts from Pico's works, which by the time of Gianfrancesco's letter, which was written in 1495 or 1496, Gianfrancesco had already begun to polish for publication. Predictably, Gianfrancesco started with a chapter entitled *De discentium erroribus* (About the Errors of Those Learning), where Mainardi would find nothing substantial left out, "or certainly little according to my opinion, but you will discover many and various things added, not so much in regard to the style or to explain those matters, but to augment and amplify them" [addita cum multa tum varia deprehendes, non tam ad orationis filum resque ipsas explicandas, quam ad eas augendas et amplificandas]. He sent the expanded fragment to Mainardi to see if his method of "amplifying" his uncle's works pleased his tutor. None of these fragments, however, let alone the longer texts mentioned by Gianfrancesco, ever made it into print—at least not under Pico's name.

In the decades to come, Gianfrancesco blatantly equivocated about which of these texts he had in his hands. In an undated letter written to Emperor Maximilian I, who had asked about Pico's Cabalistic writings, Gianfrancesco complained—despite his earlier boasts about transcribing Pico's works—that of these he possessed not a single fragment, citing as an excuse his uncle Antonmaria's sale of Pico's original papers years earlier.[75] In 1505 he wrote in much the same vein to Thomas Wolf, although here once again he inconsistently hinted of spectacular future projects that would unite his own work and his uncle's.[76] Promises of future publications of Pico's works show up in letters that Gianfrancesco wrote as much as a decade or more later.[77]

Gianfrancesco complained repeatedly in these years of Pico's difficult hand and of manuscripts that he repeatedly portrayed as being torn, riddled with corrections, and nearly illegible.[78] The difficulty of Pico's handwriting can be confirmed by manuscript evidence, but Gianfrancesco's complaints lose much of their force when we consider that Pico is known to have dictated much of his work to his secretary Cristoforo di Casale (on whom later), and by the apparent speed with which Gianfrancesco and Mainardi transcribed the massive *Disputations*, which Gianfrancesco too predictably complained was brought to light "ab exemplari liturato multasque in partes discerpto" [from a copy that is erased and in many places torn].[79] Considering the enormous mass of Pico's texts that Gianfrancesco admits that he and Mainardi had transcribed by 1496, it is difficult not to view these complaints as a mask for other motives for not publishing Pico's works in their original form.

---

[75] G. F. Pico, *Opera,* 2:1294–95.

[76] G. F. Pico, *Opera*, 2:1346.

[77] E.g., in a letter to Lilio Gregorio Giraldi (apparently written in 1516; see note 107 below), Gianfrancesco claims—rather astonishingly, given the late date at which he made it—"Quae autem nondum instaurata, haec habetur: in Psalmos commentaria, in quibus reficiendis assiduam operam impendimus; et multae quoque schedae fragmentorum, quae si faverit Omnipotens, collecturum me spero, ne pereant" [These things are at hand which are still not yet repaired: the commentaries on the Psalms, on whose restoration I am working incessantly, and also many pages of fragments, which, if the Almighty permits, I hope to collect, lest they perish]. G. F. Pico, *Opera*, 2:1365.

[78] See, e.g., his *Vita* of his uncle, in *Opera*, fol. 5r.

[79] G .F. Pico, *Opera*, 2:1340. Cf. *Disputationes*, 1:26.

A list of Pico's works suppressed by his nephew

The list of Pico's texts suppressed by Gianfrancesco is a long one. Not one line of Pico's Cabalistic writings, *Concord of Plato and Aristotle*, nor (except for one gloomy religious poem of dubious authenticity) Pico's large corpus of Latin and Italian poetry made it into Gianfrancesco's edition of his uncle's works. The same year that edition appeared, the ever-dour Gianfrancesco bragged that he himself had not opened a book of secular poetry in nearly five years.[80] No part of Pico's *Commentary on the Psalms* made it into the work, except for an anomalous fragment of even more doubtful authenticity.[81] The text of the nine hundred theses too was left out of Gianfrancesco's edition; indeed, Gianfrancesco badly twisted Pico's words from the *Apology* to make it appear that Pico himself had wished the book to go unread.[82] Gianfrancesco reluctantly published the *Oration* only following "the repeated urgings of the most famous men," burying it deep in the 1496 edition with Pico's other "works of lesser care," as he called them, without once mentioning in his foreword the spectacular Roman debate for which the text was composed.[83] Indeed, Gianfrancesco repeatedly expressed his deep contempt for public debates as well as for Cabala, numerological speculation, natural magic, the *prisci theologi*, formal theology and metaphysics, pagan philosophy—and just about everything else of interest in his uncle's works.

Gianfrancesco also kept the *Commento* out of his edition, suggesting that perhaps he would someday publish the work in a Latin translation, but certainly not in the Italian original, lest Pico's arcane teachings "be brought before the eyes of

---

[80] G. F. Pico, *Opera*, 2:18. On Pico's poetry, which—despite Gianfrancesco's claims—Pico continued to rework throughout his life, see Kristeller (1965, 1975). Also missing from Pico's *Opera* are a number of other writings mentioned by Pico or his nephew as completed works, including the *De vera temporum supputatione* (On the True Calculation of the Ages), which dealt with calculations of the date of the end of the world that may not have pleased the Savonarolans, and texts like Pico's commentary on the Book of Job, which contained magical references.

[81] See below.

[82] *Opera*, fol. 2v. Gianfrancesco claims in the *Vita* that Pico told his readers "to read the *Apology*, but to pass over unread the little book of unexplained conclusions" [ut Apologiam legerent, libellum vero ipsum conclusionum inexplicitarum praeterirent illectum]. What Pico *actually* said was that no one should read the conclusions unless he had *first* read the *Apology* [haec nisi prius attigerit]—a very different point (*Opera*, 237)!

[83] *Opera*, 313.

the vulgar and be made generally accessible" (*maxime pervia*).[84] Predictably enough, Gianfrancesco never published such a translation, although one manuscript—reportedly copied from one of Savonarola's personal notebooks—has survived that contains Latin excerpts from the *Commento*; whether these were made from the Italian original or from a lost Latin translation is unknown.[85] This is not the only evidence of Savonarolan interest in the *Commento* after Pico's death. As Garin showed many decades ago, in 1500 Girolamo Benivieni, on whose Platonic love poem the *Commento* provided a nominal commentary, plagiarized long sections from Pico's text for his own commentary on his poetry, which he had hastily Christianized in the 1490s under Savonarola's influence. Interestingly enough, Benivieni dedicated the work to Pico's nephew and editor, who had apparently encouraged Benivieni in his plagiarized use of Pico's text.[86] In 1519 Benivieni's publisher—not surprisingly, rather over Benivieni's objections—printed Pico's original version of the *Commento* in Benivieni's collected works, with a number of references to the Cabala and other theological topics, as well as repeated criticisms of Ficino, removed by an unknown hand.[87] In Gianfrancesco's reprint edition of his uncle's works from the previous year we find no trace of this important text, which included a number of references to Pico's planned council at Rome.

---

[84] *Opera*, fol. 4r–v.

[85] Biblioteca Nazionale di Firenze, Manus. Conv. Sopp. D.8.985, fol. 208r ff. The excerpts are preceded in rubrics by an abbreviated title that Garin (repr. 1961: 204) expands to read *Ex libro co[ncord]ia Jo. de Mirand.*—implying that the work contained excerpts from Pico's lost *Concord of Plato and Aristotle*. Reexamination of the manuscript, however, demonstrates that these passages are in fact Latin translations from the Italian *Commento*—a possibility that Garin had noted in passing (p. 205)—pointing to the more natural expansion of *Ex libro co[mmentar]ia Jo. de Mirand.* Garin uses these excerpts to argue that radical changes had taken place in Savonarola's attitude towards Plato late in life (cf. pp. 201–2)—a judgment dependent on an unfortunate misprint in the critical edition of Savonarola's sermons on *Exodus* (sermon 22 dates from March 1498 and not March 1488, as Garin reports it). Whether or not Savonarola was, in fact, the translator of these excerpts probably cannot be known for certain, although to my knowledge the attribution has not been questioned.

[86] Garin, *Scritti vari*, 10–18. See also *Commento di Hieronymo Benivieni cittadino fiorentino sopra a più sue canzone et sonetti dello amore et della bellezza divina* (Florence, 1500). On Benivieni's Christianization of his love poetry and his role as a Savonarolan propagandist, see Weinstein (1970).

[87] Garin, *Scritti vari*, 10–18, 445–49. The latter pages reprint the introductory letters to the first printed edition of the *Commento* (Benivieni, *Opere* [1519]).

Gianfrancesco's plagiarized use of Pico's unpublished works

The fact that Gianfrancesco suppressed his uncle's most important unpublished texts does not mean that he found no use for them himself. Gianfrancesco's two longest treatises, the *De rerum praenotione* and the *Examen vanitatis*, like Benivieni's commentary before them, both drew heavily from Pico's unpublished works. The same is apparently true of several of Gianfrancesco's less well-known treatises, including the *De providentia dei contra philosophastros*.[88] Garin has called attention to Gianfrancesco's use in the *De rerum praenotione* of anti-magical writings that Pico's nephew claimed were found in Pico's papers; whether Gianfrancesco's representation of Pico's views here was faithful is far from clear.[89] Gianfrancesco's use of his uncle's papers in his own major work—his *Examination of the Vanity of the Doctrine of the* Gentes *and of the Truth of Christian Teachings*—was even more distorting: It can be shown that Gianfrancesco's attack on the *gentes* drew at length from Pico's defense of the *gentes* in his lost *Concord of Plato and Aristotle*! In one key chapter, in fact, Gianfrancesco gives us a long account of Pico's "modal" view of the Platonic theory of ideas, discussed earlier in this study, which Gianfrancesco uses to attack Aristotle—exactly reversing his uncle's views.[90] A number of theses in that chapter follow the exact sequence of ideas found in the nine hundred theses— providing further evidence of the close links between Pico's aborted Vatican council and his *Concord of Plato and Aristotle*.[91]

---

[88] On the links between the latter treatise and Pico's *Concord of Plato and Aristotle*, see *Examen vanitatis* 6.15 (G. F. Pico, *Opera*, 2:1231). On further plagiary in Gianfrancesco's works, see n. 68 above.

[89] *De rerum praenotione* 4.3 summarizes what Gianfrancesco claimed were his uncle's mature views on the demonic origins of "superstition"—including magic and the "art of Abulafia," which figured prominently in the nine hundred theses and appendix to the *Heptaplus*. In *De rerum praenotione* 7.2 (G. F. Pico, *Opera*, 2:629ff.), Gianfrancesco argues at even greater length—on demonstrably false grounds—that his uncle rejected *magia naturalis* totally in his later life. Gianfrancesco claimed that Pico's early endorsement of *magia naturalis* hinged on his acceptance as a youth of divinatory astrology—a kind of astrology that Pico supported in none of his early works—and that he hence must have withdrawn that endorsement once he rejected astrology in the *Disputations*. A deeper flaw in Gianfrancesco's argument lay in his assumption that for Pico *magia naturalis* exclusively meant celestial magic, which we have again seen was not the case.

[90] G. F. Pico, *Examen vanitatis* 6.15, in *Opera*, 2:1231–6. Gianfrancesco in fact admits here that he is drawing from the *Concord of Plato and Aristotle*—of which decades earlier he had boasted that he possessed "not a little."

[91] Just as in Pico's theses (above, pp. 53–56), in *Examen vanitatis* 6.15 we find a "collation" of conflicting views on the location of the Platonic ideas—whether they resided in

The textual evidence is incontrovertible: Gianfrancesco plagiarized extensive materials from his uncle's lost *Concord of Plato and Aristotle* to produce his anti-concord in the *Examination of the Vanity of the Doctrine of the* Gentes—providing an ironic twist on his boast that he would "perfect" the work his uncle had begun. The *Examen vanitatis* even contains traces of the original historical structure of the *Concord*, suggesting that Pico's lost masterpiece was at Gianfrancesco's side as he turned its arguments on its head to produce his concerted attack on philosophy—permanently wedding, as he had always promised, his literary fortunes with his dead uncle's.

Gianfrancesco even offered what appears to be an apology of sorts for his editorial tampering.[92] My uncle had a mild and serene disposition, Gianfrancesco wrote in the *Vita*, and he told me once that only one thing could move him to anger—that certain book chests (*scrinia*) should perish that were stuffed with the results of his night labors and vigils. But since he turned all his efforts to work on behalf of God the highest and the church, Gianfrancesco goes on, I began to sense that even the destruction of these books would no longer anger him. "O happy mind, which at last could be held down by no adversity!" Gianfrancesco continues:

> He held human glory for nothing and would often tell me that fame was of some use to the living but of little to the dead. And I know that he valued his own teachings only insofar as they served some use to the church by eliminating and exploding hateful errors. Indeed, I even sensed that he had reached that height of perfection that he cared little if his *Commentationes* [the title that Gianfrancesco gave to the 1496 edition of Pico's works] were not made public under his own name—but only that that which was brought out under the name of "Pico" should bring some benefit to men.[93] [!]

Evidence of forgery in Pico's works

The evidence of textual suppression and literary theft is indisputable. Was

God or in the "first mind," etc.; a discussion of the related questions of whether "man is generated from man" (see thesis 1.3 and note); of whether forms preexist in prime matter (thesis 1.4); and so on.

[92] Passages like this lead me to think that the *Vita* was not completed until 1496—not early 1495, as is usually claimed. See also above, note 56.

[93] *Vita*, in *Opera*, fol. 6r–v.

Gianfrancesco guilty of forgery as well? The question brings us back to the problem of interpreting Pico's supposed repudiation of the *prisci theologi*, natural magic, esoteric numerology, and the Cabala in his later writings. Certainly it was not necessarily a matter of forging whole texts, for which in the case of the *Disputations*, at least, there was no need. Given that work's unpolished and polemical nature, the same end could have been achieved through heavy-handed editing or through the interpolation of an occasional line—with Gianfrancesco fulfilling his promise to "supplement what is omitted and draw together what is diffuse," to recall his plans for Pico's "fragments." Gianfrancesco himself tells us that he and Mainardi "repaired" the *Disputations*, which was "called back from destruction" from a manuscript that Gianfrancesco claimed was so illegible that it often seemed to be written in some language other than Latin.[94] Even Garin, who in general pictured Gianfrancesco as Pico's faithful editor, was forced to admit that the 1496 Bologna edition did not appear without "some probable revisions" (*qualche probabile ritocco*). Garin cited as evidence Antonio da Faenza's pleas that Gianfrancesco tone down Pico's polemics with him over *On Being and the One*.[95] Zambelli too, who has published an important study on Mainardi, acknowledges that Mainardi's work on Pico's texts, which at first was greater than Gianfrancesco's, involved something more than just simple transcription. But Zambelli too has explicitly denied that Mainardi or Gianfrancesco meant to change the sense of Pico's texts.[96]

Although no manuscripts of the *Disputations* have survived to allow us to test Gianfrancesco's editorial policies, Pico's nephew has left us with striking evidence of how his heavy-handed editing—if editing was all that was involved in this case—did change Pico's sense. That evidence is found in the commentary on Vulgate Psalm 15 (Psalm 16 in the Hebrew text) and some related fragments that Gianfrancesco printed "under the name of 'Pico'" in Pico's collected works. It will be remembered that for decades after Pico's death Gianfrancesco claimed that he possessed and might someday publish "many things" on the Psalms "collected in order" in his uncle's papers. While Gianfrancesco never fulfilled this promise—leaving aside what passes for Pico's commentary on Psalm 15 in the Bologna

---

[94] See Gianfrancesco's introductory letter in Garin's edition of the *Disputationes*, 2:26; cf. Gianfrancesco's remarks in the *Vita*, *Opera*, fol. 5r, and in a letter to Baptista Spagnuoli of Mantua (G. F. Pico, *Opera*, 2:1340).

[95] See Garin's preface to the 1971 reprint of Pico's *Opera*. Antonio's request is found in Pico, *Opera*, 310.

[96] Zambelli (1965: 219–20; 1983: personal communication).

edition—substantial manuscript fragments of his uncle's *Commentary on the Psalms*, whose authenticity on both linguistic and conceptual grounds is indisputable, have survived to give us a good sense of the nature of that work. Parts of Pico's commentaries on the 6th, 10th, 11th, 17th, 18th, 47th, and 50th Psalms (following the Vulgate numeration) are found in manuscripts copied by the same hand dispersed today in Berlin, Paris, Ferrara, Cremona, and the United States. Garin surveyed these fragments—not citing the Cremona manuscript—in an article written many decades ago. Pico's commentary on Psalm 47 was edited by Ceretti in the nineteenth century from another manuscript in Modena; indications in an ancient catalog entry suggest that the Modena manuscript earlier lay in the Mirandolan archives.[97]

It is not necessary to read very far into these fragments before recognizing why Gianfrancesco suppressed them. Pico's *Commentary on the Psalms*, like all his other works before it, is filled with admiring references to the *prisci theologi* and to Hebrew and Chaldean wisdom. Its exegetical methods are closedly linked to the Cabalistic methods dealt with in the nine hundred theses, a work that Gianfrancesco wholeheartedly loathed. Pico's *Commentary on the Psalms* also contains detailed discussions of Latin, Greek, Hebrew, Aramaic, and Arabic linguistic questions which—whatever their real profundity—clearly went far beyond Gianfrancesco's meager philological depths.[98] When we recall the claim in the *Apology* that the traditional numbering of the Psalms reflected their efficacy "in spiritual and celestial science"—that is, in magic[99]—we need hardly guess why Gianfrancesco left Pico's *Commentary on the Psalms* "to the judgment of the dust" (*in arbitrio della polvere*), as Girolamo Benivieni tells us was his aim and was certainly Gianfrancesco's concerning the far less dangerous *Commento*, which at least did not offer extended commentaries on Christian Scripture.[100]

It is revealing to compare these manuscript fragments with the commentary on Psalm 15 that found its way into the 1496 Bologna edition. It can be easily

---

[97] On the extant fragments of the *Commentary on the Psalms*, see the appendix in Kristeller (1965). Cf. Garin (1961: 241–53), Ceretti (1895). A critical edition of Pico's text, edited by Antonino Raspanti, appeared after the present study was already in press. I have briefly discussed Raspanti's views in the notes below.

[98] Unlike his uncle, Gianfrancesco knew no Hebrew, let alone Arabic or Aramaic. In a letter written many years after Pico's death, Gianfrancesco admitted to his failed attempts to learn Hebrew from the son of one of Pico's Jewish tutors (G. F. Pico, *Opera*, 2:1371).

[99] *Apology*, in *Opera*, 172; On the Psalm's magical powers, see also thesis 10>4.

[100] *Commento*, in Garin, *Scritti vari*, 447–48.

demonstrated, again on both linguistic and conceptual grounds, that the dim-witted moral commentary on Psalm 15 passed "under the name of 'Pico'" in Gianfrancesco's edition cannot in anything approximating its present form have been written by Pico.[101] And if this is true, the same is true of the three sets of spiritual "rules" printed along with that text (*Twelve Rules Partly Exciting, Partly Directing, Man in Spiritual Battle*; the *Twelve Arms of Spiritual Battle*; and the *Twelve Conditions of a Lover*), and of the *Commentary on the Lord's Prayer* "rediscovered" and published under Pico's name in the sixteenth century. Whether or not all these texts issued from the same hand—evidence suggests that the *Commentary on the Lord's Prayer* may be an even clumsier forgery based on these earlier spurious texts—conceptually and linguistically they form a close-knit piece with the commentary on Psalm 15 printed in the 1496 Bologna edition.[102]

---

[101] The commentary on Psalm 15 printed in Pico's *Opera* is written in a highly simplified version of scholastic Latin, or the so-called Parisian style; the genuine manuscript fragments of Pico's *Commentary on the Psalms* are composed in the syntactically distinct classical or Roman style of most of Pico's other works. The commentary on Psalm 15 includes no discussion of the original Hebrew text; the surviving manuscript fragments of Pico's commentary are full of such discussions and contain as well long analyses of Greek, Arabic, Aramaic, and Latin linguistic questions. The manuscripts of Pico's *Commentary* are packed with symbolic readings of a Cabalistic or quasi-Cabalistic type like those found in the nine hundred theses and *Heptaplus*; such readings are again totally absent from the commentary on Psalm 15 inserted in Pico's *Opera*.

[102] In his *Vita, Opera*, fol. 5r, Gianfrancesco mentions a commentary by Pico on the Lord's Prayer and "around fifty rules for living well" that he claims that Pico would have expanded into many chapters had he lived. The relationship between the later work and the three sets of *Twelve Rules*, *Twelve Arms*, and *Twelve Conditions of a Lover* printed in the 1496 Bologna edition is unknown, as are the fortunes of the *Commentary on the Lord's Prayer* mentioned by Gianfrancesco, which is not found in any of the editions of Pico's collected works printed in Gianfrancesco's lifetime. The *Commentary on the Lord's Prayer* printed in Pico's late Renaissance *Opera* apparently first appeared as a separate book printed by Nicolaus de Benedictis in Bologna; the book is undated, although Di Napoli (1965) argues that it did not appear before 1521. It was presumably this edition that G. Regino used in his Italian translation of the work, "in these days newly come to light" [in questi giorni novamente venuta a luce], which appeared in Venice in 1523. The Bologna text was also presumably the basis of a later Latin edition (Venice, 1537) and for the Latin versions found in later Renaissance editions of Pico's *Opera*. Both the *Commentary on the Lord's Prayer* and the three sets of *Twelve Rules*, etc., are written in the same highly simplified scholastic Latin found in the pseudo-Pichean commentary on Psalm 15—clearly distinguishing them from the genuine manuscript fragments of Pico's *Commentary on the Psalms*, which are written in the syntactically and semantically distinct "Roman style." All these spurious

Even if these works were by Pico, the evidence would point to an earlier date for all of them than the early 1490's, undermining the traditional view that they illustrate shifts that took place in Pico's thought "under the influence of Savonarola."[103] Especially annoying in these works is their monotonous recital in their highly simplified Latin of the hackneyed Thomist theme that God is the *summum bonum*—exactly what we would expect if they were written not by Pico but by some moderately educated Dominican friar.[104] Ironically, due to Pico's enormous reputation as a philosopher, these spurious works were the most popular writings ascribed to Pico throughout the Reformation period, when virtually any text sounding the ancient *contemptus mundi* theme found an enthusiastic audience. Along with the gloomy *Deprecatoria ad deum* that Gianfrancesco attributed to his uncle (the only poem that Gianfrancesco included in Pico's corpus) and two hortatory letters addressed from Pico to his nephew, these texts were repeatedly printed, together or separately, in French, German, English, and Italian versions throughout the sixteenth century—translated in the north by such well-known

---

works are closely tied by recurring verbal motifs unlike anything found elsewhere in Pico's works—e.g., by repeated references to God as the *summum bonum*, to the moral dangers of *superbia*, etc.—which suggest that they either came from the same hand or were meant to appear as though they did. The *Commentary on the Lord's Prayer* (*Opera*, fol. a2v) even refers directly to the commentary on Psalm 15 ("ut diximus in expositione Psalmi 'Conserva me Domine' . . .")—not coincidentally, one suspects, since it was the only such commentary attributed to Pico in print—and at times not very cleverly takes up the language of the later work nearly verbatim. Until an exhaustive analysis of all these works is made it will not be possible to pinpoint their exact sources, but these stylistic features of the works, as well as their total lack of linguistic learning, clearly demonstrate that in their final form they cannot be ascribed to Pico.

[103] It is known that Pico began his *Commentary on the Psalms* at the same time as the *Heptaplus* (see the first proem of the latter work, *Opera*, 1; Garin, *Scritti vari*, 170)—beginning in 1488, two years before Savonarola was recalled to Florence. Given the close linguistic and conceptual ties between the commentary on Psalm 15, *Commentary on the Lord's Prayer*, and *Twelve Rules*, etc., even if we assumed that these works were legitimate, we would have to date them around the same time as the *Heptaplus* as well. In any event, no evidence besides *a priori* assumptions concerning "the intense rhythm of Pico's religious life in his final days"—to translate Garin (*Scritti vari*, 45)—lies behind the traditional attribution of these works to Pico's later years.

[104] It is important to remember that while Pico's papers were being edited they were held by Savonarola and the Dominicans at the Convent of San Marco in Florence. Apparently, the Dominicans eventually got more than their fair share of revenge on Pico for his attacks on them in the nine hundred theses and *Apology*.

Christian "humanists" as Robert Gaguin, Jakob Wimpheling, Thomas More, and Thomas Elyot.[105]

While the surviving fragments of Pico's *Commentary on the Psalms* also contain large sections of moral exegesis, these are far more complex, both linguistically and conceptually, than the simple moral commentary on Psalm 15 found in Pico's printed works. Unlike that text, moreover, all these fragments offer elaborate multileveled readings of Scripture like those found in the nine hundred theses and *Heptaplus*.[106] Until an exhaustive comparison of these fragments is made with the commentary on Psalm 15, the possibility must be left open—although it seems a slim one indeed—that the latter work and the closely related *Twelve Rules, Twelve Arms, Twelve Conditions*, and even more suspicious *Commentary on the Lord's Prayer* in *some* earlier form reflected *something* from Pico's hand. For now, the question must be left open as to whether those texts were out-and-out forgeries, intentional misattributions, or simply the products of Gianfrancesco's brutal editorial hand. But considering their simplistic Latin and total lack of linguistic learning, we can be certain that if they did originate with Pico, by the time they made it through Gianfrancesco's editorial sieve they were as far removed from Pico's thought as any forgeries could be.[107]

---

[105] On these translations, see Kristeller (1965: 76) and the list of manuscripts in the appendix to his study. Wimpheling may also have been responsible for the famous mistitle "Oration on the Dignity of Man." See above, pp. 18–19 n. 50.

[106] See, e.g., the allegorically rich, and in part Cabalistically inspired, readings in Pico's moral commentary of Psalm 47, which was demonstrably composed by Pico. Cf. Ceretti (1895: 108ff.), Raspanti, ed. (1997: 202–32).

[107] Antonino Raspanti's edition of Pico's *Commentary on the Psalms* (1997) appeared after this book was already in press. Since Raspanti's views diverge on important points from my own, I would like to add a brief note here on our differences. Raspanti is not insensitive to the sharp conflicts between the Psalm 15 commentary printed in Pico's collected works and the early manuscript fragments of his *Commentary*, which do not cover Psalm 15. Nevertheless, constrained by the traditional assumption that Gianfrancesco was Pico's trustworthy editor, Raspanti is forced to argue that the Psalm 15 commentary "enjoys an indisputable authority, since it was taken directly from the autograph" [gode di indubbia autorità, perché tratta direttamente dall'autografo] (Raspanti 1997: 31)—a claim made despite the fact that no autograph has survived. Raspanti offers two explanations (p. 37) for the radical differences between the printed text and what we find in the manuscripts. The first suggests that, faced by the enormous linguistic difficulties in Pico's *Commentary*, in 1496 Gianfrancesco was forced by practical considerations—including his own linguistic inadequacies—to limit himself to publishing the simple Psalm 15 commentary. In passing, Raspanti grants that this decision may have had something to do with Gianfrancesco's

Chapter Four

A summary of Gianfrancesco's textual adulterations

To sum up the evidence so far: Gianfrancesco not only intentionally distorted his uncle's biography but also suppressed from Pico's collected works a number of his most important published and unpublished texts. These included the *Commento* and nine hundred theses, extensive sections (and quite possibly full manuscripts) of Pico's *Commentary on the Psalms, Concord of Plato and Aristotle, On the True Calculation of the Ages*, and extended writings on the Cabala; all but one poem—assuming, that is, that the pessimistic *Deprecatoria ad deum* is authentic—from Pico's large body of Latin and Italian poetry; and in addition "perhaps three hundred chapters of the worthiest things" that Gianfrancesco transcribed from other of Pico's unpublished papers held by Savonarola at San Marco. Moreover, Gianfrancesco plagiarized extensive portions of those writings, including key sections of the *Concord of Plato and Aristotle*, for purposes diametrically opposed to his uncle's, and encouraged Girolamo Benivieni's similar plagiarized use of the *Commento*. Gianfrancesco

---

involvement with the Savonarolan movement. Unfortunately, this explanation does not tell us why the commentary on Psalm 15 differs so radically from the surviving manuscript fragments. Raspanti therefore proposes another tentative hypothesis: Perhaps the commentary on Psalm 15 was not originally part of Pico's *Commentary on the Psalms* at all, but in Pico's mind belonged more to writings of an "edifying" (*edificante*) and "exhortatory" (*parenetico*) sort. Considering the enormous linguistic differences separating the Psalm 15 commentary from Pico's other writings—leaving aside, that is, the three sets of spiritual "rules" and the *Commentary on the Lord's Prayer*, which are of similar dubious authenticity—it is difficult to be persuaded by these arguments. What is missing in Raspanti's analysis is any discussion of the duplicitous ways in which Gianfrancesco treated all his uncle's texts—a problem that we have seen extends far beyond the *Commentary on the Psalms*. Raspanti never asks the obvious question: If the surviving manuscripts of Pico's *Commentary* were careful copies of the original made at Gianfrancesco's court—as Raspanti argues on good grounds was the case—and Gianfrancesco was Pico's faithful editor, why did he renege on his repeated promises to publish those fragments? Finally, it is important to note that Raspanti's assignment (1997: 37) of an earliest date of 1520 to the extant manuscripts of Pico's *Commentary*, following suggestions in a letter to Lilio Gregorio Giraldi in Gianfrancesco's Opera (1365–69), is clearly mistaken, since Schmitt long ago (1967) noted other versions of Gianfrancesco's works that place that letter as early as 1514. Cavini (1973: 133) questions Schmitt's 1514 dating but cites other sources that date the letter to 1516. More to the point, given Gianfrancesco's misrepresentations elsewhere concerning the *Commentary*, the odds are high that despite that letter Pico's text was originally transcribed by Gianfrancesco or Mainardi as much as twenty years earlier—before 1498, when all of Pico's original papers were (or were supposed to be) shipped to Rome.

further inserted into Pico's collected works, or allowed someone else to insert there, a commentary on Psalm 15 and the closely related *Twelve Rules*, *Twelve Arms*, and *Twelve Conditions of a Lover* that, whatever their origins, like the *Commentary on the Lord's Prayer* "rediscovered" in the sixteenth century, in their present form cannot be ascribed to Pico. To justify his editorial tampering, moreover, from the start Gianfrancesco argued that *any* use of Pico's works was justified so long as those works served some religious end.

By now, it should be evident that no text of Pico's that Gianfrancesco printed or reprinted can be assumed to be free of adulterations of some kind. Comparison even of Gianfrancesco's edition of the *Oration* with the work's early draft and with the parallel sections of the *Apology* suggests the existence there of minor but noteworthy editorial tampering.[108] If in this case Gianfrancesco was restrained by the fact that the most controversial sections of the *Oration*, dealing with magic and the Cabala, were printed in the *Apology* long before Pico's death, much evidence shows that he did not exercise the same restraint in handling Pico's previously unpublished texts.

Pico's "palinode" in the Disputations: *real or apparent?*

To return a final time to the original problem in this chapter: Was Gianfrancesco responsible for Pico's apparent palinode to the *prisci theologi*, natural magic, esoteric numerology, and Cabala in the *Disputations*? The text of the *Disputations* is obviously difficult, and no definitive answer can be currently given to this question. But given Gianfrancesco's abysmal record everywhere else as his uncle's editor, coupled with other evidence as to Pico's positive interests in his last years

[108] E.g., one passage praising Flavius Mithridates, one possibly ironic reference to Ermolao Barbaro, and one passage praising the magical knowledge of Pico's friend Antonius Chronicus—found in the early draft of the *Oration* or in the section of the *Apology* that parallels the *Oration*—are suspiciously left out of the *Oration* as Gianfrancesco printed it. Similarly, clear associations between rational or celestial souls and demons found in the early draft of the *Oration* are missing from the version of that text printed by Gianfrancesco; a striking reference to "the *magi*" in the early draft becomes "the Persians" in Gianfrancesco's edition; and so on. Given the nature of these changes, which are strikingly similar to those found in the first printed edition of Pico's *Commento*, it is all but certain that they originated from Gianfrancesco's hand and not his uncle's.

in the esoteric arts,[109] the burden of proof by this point surely lies with anyone who argues that serious tampering in the *Disputationes* did not take place. It might be difficult to determine for sure whether key isolated lines in the *Disputations*—like those condemning magic in a wholesale manner—were interpolated or doctored, or to guess where Gianfrancesco cut out compromising materials from the work.[110] But the question of whether or not longer interpolations are found there is susceptible to hard scientific test. The formulaic ways in which Renaissance authors handled word order and other elements of Latin style, as well as wide variations in the technical jargon found in their works, make computer tests of textual authenticity easier to apply here than in most places where they have been used. Even superficial comparison of Pico's distinctive "Roman" and "Parisian" styles with Gianfrancesco's laborious and slow-moving Latin suggests that any longer interpolations in the *Disputations* from Gianfrancesco's hand might be distinguished by computer analyses of invariant syntactic features in their works. A large enough textual base of the writings of Giovanni Mainardi and Girolamo Savonarola—whose role in this story we will turn to in a minute—exists to make computer comparisons of their works with Pico's possible as well.

Savonarolan political motives in Gianfrancesco's editorial tampering

In passing I have suggested a few of the motives behind Gianfrancesco's editorial hatchetwork. Among the most important were his personal ambitions—in later years, fed by some ill-concealed bitterness over his uncle's greater fame—and his genuine hatred of Pico's views, which apparently turned out to be rather different from what Gianfrancesco expected when he began his editorial career. But in the case of the *Disputations*, political motives alien to everything else known of Pico's thought also played a part. Whatever Pico's original reasons were for composing the *Disputations*, by the time that the work was finally printed, twenty months after his death, the text figured in a violent propaganda war fought for enormous political stakes. At the center of battle lay Savonarola's claims that he possessed a divine mandate to rule Florence using his supernatural prophetic

---

[109] See, e.g., Pietro Crinito, *De honesta disciplina* 2.2 and 1.7; Giovanni Nesi, *De oraculo novo* (1497: fol. 34r and passim); and the letter to G. F. Pico from Pico's friend Baptista Spagnuoli of Mantua, printed in Pico's *Opera*, 387.

[110] Simply by eliminating any distinction in the text between demonic and natural magic—something involving no more than the suppression of an occasional line—Pico's sense could have been drastically transformed.

powers. The argument that astrological or other "natural" means of prophecy existed became the rallying point of Savonarola's enemies, especially those stragglers left in the largely depopulated Medicean camp.

Even before Pico's death, Savonarola had cited Pico's unfinished *Disputations* in support of his polemics with the astrologers, which had long preceded his takeover of Florence. Years later, in the heat of political battle, both camps would argue that Pico had begun his treatise under Savonarola's influence or that in writing it had sought the Dominican's "council and advice."[111] Whatever truth (if any) lay in these claims, there is no doubt that after the *Disputations* was printed, the work was repeatedly used to support Savonarola's Florentine political agenda. The argument that the astrologers had predicted the arrival of false prophets in the city was a standard claim of Savonarola's opponents, who added that Savonarola's horoscope predicted his tendencies to heretical views.[112] Against these arguments Savonarola and his followers could cite the claims in the *Disputations* that astrology and all natural forms of prophecy were inspired by evil demons, who hoped to undercut the supernatural prophecy that lay behind Savonarola's claims to political power.[113] The fact that Savonarola's views were apparently supported by the man reputed to be the most brilliant philosopher of the age—one whose early ties to the Medici and earlier support of "natural" prophecy of some sort were well known—lent those views extra weight, counterbalancing whatever arguments issued from the Medicean camp.

In the two years following publication of the *Disputations*, a flood of printed treatises, pamphlets, and open letters appeared in Florence on the prophecy ques-

---

[111] Cf., e.g., Giovanni Nesi (1497), Lucio Bellanti (1498: fol. q2r).

[112] See Lucio Bellanti (1498: fol. s7r).

[113] See, e.g., 12.6, in *Opera*, 728; *Disputationes*, 2:522: "Noverunt scilicet improbi daemones (sic non solum a nostris, sed a Platonicis quoque nuncupati), noverunt, inquam, sub una superstitione quantum mundo veneni propinarent, quod cum altius in venas penetrasset, primum quidem fidem adimeret religioni, summo hominum bono, quasi de caelo pendente fatali necessitate, quasi nulla miracula, nulla divinitus praecognitio futurorum, sed vi constellationum omnia provenirent" [Doubtless wicked demons (so they are called not only by me, but by the Platonists as well) knew—they knew, I say—how much poison they propagated in the world under one superstition, so that when it penetrated deeply into the veins, it stripped faith from religion, the highest good of man—as if all things came from the necessity of fate, depending on the heavens; as if no miracles existed, no foreknowledge of future things through divine means; but everything came from the force of constellations]. Suggestions of longer Savonarolan interpolations are especially strong in passages like this in the last book of the *Disputations*.

tion—almost all written in support of, or opposition to, Pico's text. Considering the enormous political stakes involved in this controversy, it is not surprising that Gianfrancesco Pico and his fellow *piagnoni* suppressed or altered as many of Pico's works as possible that contradicted their claims. Through Gianfrancesco's editorial manipulations, the eminently apolitical Pico was posthumously made to join Savonarola's camp.

Savonarola's role in adulterating Pico's works: the postdated Trattato

It is interesting to look at Savonarola's part in this drama. It was in Savonarola's convent at San Marco, it will be recalled, that Pico's papers, along with his books, were apparently held in trust throughout the period in which Gianfrancesco and Mainardi transcribed them. We know from Gianfrancesco's own testimony, moreover, that in the period in which he was editing (and doctoring) his uncle's works that he repeatedly sought Savonarola's advice: The evidence that survives reveals the elder Pico as Savonarola's aristocratic patron and debating opponent, but for the younger Pico the Dominican was the infallible spokesman and prophet of God.[114] Nor can there be any doubt that while Gianfrancesco edited Pico's papers that Savonarola also consulted them and tried to enlist their help in his political cause. It was presumably in this period that Savonarola (if Garin is correct that the latter was the transcriber) made his Latin excerpts from Pico's unpublished *Commento*—excerpts that, interestingly enough, break off abruptly at passages of an astrological cast.[115] It was at this time as well that Savonarola composed his fiery *Trattato contra li astrologi* (Treatise against the Astrologers), which while represented by Savonarola as a simple epitome of Pico's work, went much further—for obvious reasons—than the *Disputations* in attacking all "natural" forms of prophecy.[116]

Serious questions exist concerning the composition date of the *Trattato*, which

---

[114] On the elder Pico's relations with Savonarola—which, if anything, saw Pico in the dominant role—see Crinito's *De honesta disciplina* 2.2. Gianfrancesco's views of Savonarola are expressed at length in his biography of the Dominican and in his numerous other Savonarolan works; see the long list of Gianfrancesco's writings in Schmitt (1967). Cf. also Garfagnini (1997).

[115] On these excerpts, see above, p. 161 and n. 85.

[116] See, e.g., *Trattato*, 3.6, ed. Garfagnini and Garin (1982: 360–70), which finds no extended parallel in the extant text of the *Disputations*. The fact that Savonarola found time to write this work in the midst of his worst political troubles underscores the importance of the astrology controversy throughout Savonarola's period of rule in Florence.

Savonarola claimed in his proem was written *after* the *Disputations* went to press; an internal reference in the text further suggests a composition date in 1497, the year following Gianfrancesco's publication of Pico's text.[117] Savonarola's word has been accepted at face value by Villari, Schnitzer, Ridolfi, and more recently by Garfagnini and Garin, coeditors of the critical edition of the *Trattato*.[118] Against this long-held view, the unambiguous evidence exists that Gianfrancesco already referred to the *Trattato* as a completed work in his *De studio divinae et humanae philosophiae*, which was written in 1496.[119] Years ago, moreover, Zambelli noted potential evidence in an ancient manuscript catalog, acknowledged but not explained by the recent editors of the *Trattato*, that at least two manuscripts of Savonarola's epitome may have existed as early as 1495[120]—the same year that Gianfrancesco Pico and Mainardi reportedly transcribed the *Disputations*, but long before the work apparently went to press.[121] While the exact composition date

[117] Savonarola writes in the proem: "The book of disputations of Count Giovanni Pico della Mirandola against these superstitious astrologers having now been published, and having read it . . ." [Ora, essendosi pubblicato el libro delle disputazioni del Conte Giovanni Pico dalla Mirandola contra questi superstiziosi astrologi e avendolo letto . . .]. In 3.4 of the same work (ed. Garfagnini and Garin, 1982: 351), we are told "we are in the year 1497" [siamo nell'anno .M.CCCCLXXXXVII].

[118] See Zambelli (1965: 247–48) and the *Nota critica* in the *Trattato*, ed. Garfagnini and Garin (1982: 402).

[119] See G. F. Pico, *Opera*, 23, where the reader is told that what Pico had done in the *Disputationes* "easily appears out of the epitome that the distinguished man Girolamo Savonarola has written in the vernacular language to make the work available to the unlearned" [facile apparet ex Epitomate quod Hieronymus Savonarola vir celeberrimus conscripsit et vernacula lingua ut ineruditis opem ferret].

[120] Zambelli (1965: 247–48).

[121] Until recently, the publication date of the *Disputationes* has been universally given as 16 July 1496. The first edition of the work, published in Bologna by Benedictus Hectoris, gives us a date one year earlier—"anno salutis mcccclxxxxxv die vero xvi Julii"—but this has generally been considered a misprint, since the two pages of *errata* at the end of that text twice print the date of the printer's privilege for Pico's collected works (7 July 1496). Moreover, the first volume of that collection, which was published on 20 March 1496, promises the imminent future publication of the *Disputationes*. External evidence for a 1496 publication date is also contained in a letter from Gianfrancesco Pico to Thomas Wolf, dated 24 November 1505, which states that Pico's book against divinatory astrology was "repaired" (*reparata*) and published by Gianfrancesco nine years earlier (G. F. Pico, *Opera*, 1344). On these points, cf. the *Catalogue of Books Printed in the XVth Century Now in the British Museum* (London, 1908–62: 6:843); Garin, *Scritti vari*, 89; Valenziani (1950:

of the *Trattato* remains uncertain, the evidence clearly suggests that the treatise was completed well before the end of 1496, and possibly a full year before Pico's text was printed; moreover, this fact was intentionally obscured in Savonarola's "epitome" of Pico's work—as we would expect if, in fact, Savonarola was involved in doctoring the original.

Given the sum of evidence—Savonarola's enormous political stakes in the astrology controversy, his control of Pico's papers and profound influence over their editors, his distorted use of the *Disputations*, and the apparent postdating of the *Trattato*—the question that remains is not whether or not, but how deeply, Savonarola was involved in doctoring Pico's works. Further answers to this question might arise from a more careful comparison than has been made to date of the *Trattato* with the *Disputations* as Gianfrancesco printed it.

---

335); Zambelli (1965: 221 n. 41); Di Napoli (1965: 303 n. 18); and Garin's introduction to the modern reprint of Pico's Basel *Opera* (Turin, 1971). In apparent opposition to these views, in his recent edition of Pico's *Commentary on the Psalms*, Antonino Raspanti (1997: 35) states without qualification that the *Disputationes* was published on 16 July 1495, adding that the rest of Pico's works were printed the following year. Since Raspanti makes these claims without discussing the problem of the printer's privilege, Gianfrancesco Pico's letter to Thomas Wolf, or the works of these earlier scholars, it is impossible to know whether his dating is a simple slip or is backed by new but uncited evidence. In an earlier note in his edition, Raspanti (1997: 31 n. 46) refers to a recent study of Pico's incunabula by E. Cigola (cited as *Bibliografia di Giovanni Pico: Centimento e localizzazione dei manoscritti e delle edizioni a stampa* [Parma, 1994], but said still not to be in print) that conceivably provides support for Raspanti's dating; unfortunately, Raspanti does not report Cigola's views fully enough to judge whether or not this is the case. Given the problem of Savonarola's postdated *Trattato*, the question of the publication date of the *Disputationes* is not a trivial one. While assignment of a putative 1495 date to the text—long before Pico's other collected works—might render the postdating of the *Trattato* somewhat less incriminating, the same evidence would also further underscore the Savonarolan motives behind Gianfrancesco's editorial work, given what we know of the political importance of the astrology issue in Savonarolan Florence. Such an early publication date—scarcely eight months after Pico's death—would also throw into further doubt Gianfrancesco's complaints concerning the nearly illegible nature of the massive manuscript on which that work was supposedly based. In any event, given the other evidence discussed in this chapter, it is clear that any revision of the accepted publication date of the *Disputationes* must be backed by solid evidence, with special attention paid to sources besides those originating from Gianfrancesco Pico, Savonarola, and others in their party.

Was Pico poisoned?

The most spectacular mystery remains. In August 1497, at the exact height of the astrology controversy, a group of Medicean sympathizers tried to wrest control of Florence out of Savonarola's hands. Among the participants were five of the most prominent citizens of Florence and a number of lesser figures, including most notably Cristoforo di Casale (or Cristoforo da Casalmaggiore), who served as Pico's secretary and amanuensis throughout much of his career.[122] Late that month the Venetian patrician and diarist Marin Sanudo, who had close contacts with Gianfrancesco and the *piagnoni*, repeated the claim from his secretary in Bologna that "among the other things that [Cristoforo] confessed under torture was that he had hastened the death of his patron, since he poisoned him—something that up until now had not been known."[123] In the edition of Poliziano's collected works published the following year—interestingly enough, underwritten by Sanudo himself—flattering references to Cristoforo and his brother Martin, another of Pico's longtime retainers, were clumsily removed by an unknown hand.[124] If one Poliziano scholar is right, that hand belonged to none other than Gianfrancesco Pico, who, assisted again by Giovanni Mainardi, was at that time busily preparing Poliziano's collected works for the press[125]—a fact that, given what we know of Gianfrancesco's and Mainardi's editorial policies, raises unpleasant new questions for specialists on Poliziano's works.

Nothing further is known at present of Cristoforo's role in the anti-Savonarolan conspiracy of 1497. Whether his reported confession did occur—let alone whether Pico was poisoned, and by whom and why—remains an open question.[126] What cannot be doubted is that with Cristoforo out of the picture there

---

[122] For background on this conspiracy, see Weinstein (1970: 282ff.). Cristoforo's part in this conspiracy is suggested in the diaries of Marin Sanudo, Vol. 1, columns 714–15, 726—evidence first spotted by Dorez (1899). Cristoforo's advice was, not surprisingly, sought by Gianfrancesco Pico early in his editorial work; see Gianfrancesco's comments in Pico's *Opera*, 289, 310.

[123] Sanudo, Vol. 1, column 726: "Et che quel Cristofalo di Caxale, olim cancelier dil conte Zuam di la Mirandola, tra le altre cosse che 'l confessò a la tortura, chome havia fato accelerar la morte al suo patron, perhochè lo tosegoe. La qual cossa fin qui è stata incognita."

[124] See the evidence first uncovered by Dorez (1899), augmented and reinterpreted by Cotton (1962).

[125] Cotton (1962).

[126] Dorez (1898, 1899), who never questioned the validity of Cristoforo's confession under torture, speculated that he murdered his lifelong friend and patron (1) for personal

were no longer any known hostile witnesses to the extraordinary literary fraud perpetrated by Gianfrancesco Pico, Savonarola, and their associates.

Final mysteries

In Pico's later life, mystery adds to mystery, and many of the questions raised in this chapter must for now remain unresolved. What were Pico's views in his last days of Savonarola's political ambitions? Did Pico repudiate the magical and esoteric arts as fully as the *Disputations* hints—and as Savonarola suggests more fully in the postdated *Trattato*? If that repudiation occurred, why is Pico shown defending those arts against Savonarola in Pietro Crinito's *De honesta disciplina*, and why—in Giovanni Nesi's equally Savonarolan *De oraculo novo*—do we find the dead philosopher in a Hermetic vision praising the Cabala's prophetic powers? What is the full story behind Giovanni Sinibaldi's bitter complaint that Pico deceived Savonarola on his religious views at the end of his life? How much of Pico's *Concord of Plato and Aristotle* and other lost texts can be reconstructed from the plagiarized fragments scattered throughout his nephew's works? How did the pseudo-Pichean *Commentary on Psalm 15*, *Twelve Rules*, *Twelve Arms*, *Twelve Conditions*, and *Commentary on the Lord's Prayer* come to be credited to Pico? Was it really a coincidence that Pico died on the very day that Charles VIII entered Florence—ending in the fall of the Medici and Savonarola's ascent to political power? What is the real story behind Cristoforo di Casale's supposed confession that he poisoned his longtime friend, patron, and companion? To what extent was Savonarola involved in torturing Pico's secretary—let alone in the remarkable literary fraud to which of all hostile voices Cristoforo alone could have offered authoritative testimony?

Answers to many of these questions presumably lie buried in the public and private papers from the 1490s preserved in the Florentine Archivio di Stato and elsewhere, in hints in Savonarola's works and those of his closest friends and

gain, since Cristoforo and his brother were minor beneficiaries in Pico's will; and (2) to ingratiate himself with the Medici, who in Dorez's eyes viewed Pico as a traitor for associating with Savonarola. Dorez never considered the possibility that the portrait of Pico "under the influence of Savonarola" was cooked up by Savonarola and the *piagnoni* for propagandistic ends. Kibre (1936: 16–17 n. 28)—apparently misreading Dorez (1898, 1899)—tells us that "suspicions that Pico had been poisoned have been shown to be groundless." No known evidence supports this view. For further speculations on these issues, see Poletti (1987).

enemies, and above all in the still largely unexplored works of the nefarious anti-Pico of our story—Pico's nephew-editor Gianfrancesco Pico della Mirandola. Any determination of what changes, if any, actually occurred in Pico's later thought would shed new light on the Savonarolan years in Florence and—from a theoretical angle—on issues related to the decline of the thousands of years of syncretic traditions summed up so magnificently in Pico's nine hundred theses.[127]

We may end by recalling the advice given to Pico's nephew five hundred years ago by the Carmelite General Baptista Spagnuoli of Mantua—who had a far better understanding of the scope of Pico's thought than modern scholars studying the mangled remains of his works: "Collect everything! Let us hear the dead man talking! We may learn more from him who is silent than from those who are now speaking—from nature's great experiment in youthful genius, the miraculous ornament of our age!"[128]

There is much interesting work left to be done.

---

[127] Additional historical questions that need to be studied include how far Pico's troubles with Pope Innocent VIII, his associations with Savonarola, and his editorial mishandling by Gianfrancesco were linked to the extended battles between Pico's brothers Galeotto (Gianfrancesco's father) and Antonmaria over control of Mirandola and Concordia. Conflicts over these territories involved the papal court (where Pico's brother Antonmaria spent many years in exile), the imperial court (which backed Galeotto and Gianfrancesco against Antonmaria and the papacy), and even the Florentine government, since Antonmaria, who by right inherited Pico's papers, was employed as a condottiere fighting Florence in the same year that Gianfrancesco and his Savonarolan associates were doctoring Pico's works for their own political purposes. The role that Giovanni Pico played in these political conflicts before his death is worth close study, as is his part in the conflict between Savonarola and the Medici after the death of Lorenzo de' Medici. For some preliminary evidence on these issues, see the documents published in Milanesi (1857), Berti (1859), and Ceretti (1878).

[128] G. F. Pico, *Opera*, 2:1353.

Part 2:

Text, Translation, and Commentary

Introduction to the Edition

i. History of the Text

The nine hundred theses were published by Eucharius Silber in Rome on 7 December 1486, as we read in the colophon of the text. All surviving manuscripts of the theses derive directly or indirectly from that first printed edition, an unusual but by no means unique case in the Renaissance. Evidence exists that Pico himself made extensive changes in the text shortly before, and apparently while, the work was in press.[1] The conceptual nature of key emendations of errors listed at the back of the 1486 edition suggests that Pico also had a hand in correcting the text after it was printed, pointing to the *editio princeps* again as our final authority for the work. Kieszkowski's claim that the manuscript that served as the model for that edition is extant is based on spurious evidence, to which I will turn in a moment.

The *editio princeps* became exceedingly rare immediately after Innocent VIII's orders to burn the work the following year. A reprint edition appeared sometime later in Ingolstadt, identified by its type as coming from Lescher's press. The work has traditionally been assigned to 1487, presumably before the publication of the papal ban.[2] The edition's obvious errors suggest that Pico did not play a role in its publication, nor could the text have possibly derived from any authoritative earlier manuscript.

The nine hundred theses were not printed again until 1532, in an edition that De Pina Martins identified with a Parisian press.[3] Zambelli's claim that the theses were reprinted by Gianfrancesco Pico in the 1518 Venetian edition of Pico's *Opera*—they were, in fact, omitted from all his editions of his uncle's works—is a

[1] See my introductory note to theses 6>1–10 and passim in my commentary.

[2] Cf. Valenziani (1950: 336), Kieszkowski (1973: 3). I used a microfilm of this reprint preserved in the British Library (IA 13505). The tentative 1487 date assigned to the work is reasonable, since that is apparently the only year that Lescher's press is known to have been active.

[3] De Pina Martins (1976).

slip.[4] The 1532 editors apparently had access to both the Silber and Lescher incunabula, or (more likely) to later handwritten copies of them, following one edition or the other in a haphazard fashion. Collation of these incunabula with the 1532 text shows that the editors of the latter work did not have access to any manuscripts antedating these early printed editions. The classicist and antischolastic leanings of the 1532 editors—extremely poor editorial credentials in this case—are illustrated in their preface to the short extract from the *Apology* reprinted in their edition, where they complain that in the omitted parts Pico "only spars scholastically with his adversaries" [tantum scholastice cum adversariis agit]. The 1532 edition was the first to number Pico's theses (an implied numbering system is found in the *editio princeps*), beginning a new count in each subsection of the text. The influence of the 1532 edition on the later history of Pico's text is suggested by the fact that this numbering system was adopted by all later editors of the work. In the present edition, this numbering system is supplemented by section numbers to facilitate cross-referencing of Pico's theses.[5]

The theses were next printed in the 1557 Basel and Venetian versions of Pico's *Opera*, which were the first editions of his collected works to include the text. Both these editions closely follow the corrupt 1532 edition, with a few speculative changes added by their own classicist editors. In the Basel edition, this led on occasion (as with the addition of a spurious *non*) to an exact reversal of Pico's sense.[6] Reprints in 1572 and 1601 of the Basel edition until recently remained the most commonly cited versions of Pico's text. A final Renaissance edition, apparently based on one of the Basel reprints, was included in an anthology of philosophical texts compiled by N. Hill of London, published in Paris in 1601 and in Geneva in 1619. The theses are not included in Garin's standard editions of Pico's works, which were issued in 1942 and 1946–1952. The Latin editions of Kieszkowski (1973) and Biondi (1995), the first modern versions of Pico's theses, are discussed in the following section.

Besides these printed editions, four complete manuscripts of Pico's theses are

[4] Zambelli (1977a, 1977b).

[5] On the numbering system used in this edition, see p. 22 n. 59. The lack of a simple cross-referencing device accounts for many of the difficulties that scholars have traditionally had in discussing Pico's text.

[6] See, e.g., thesis and note 3.3.

known.[7] Close study of these manuscripts demonstrates, as Garin suggested over a half century ago, that all of them are posterior to the 1486 text.[8] Two of these manuscripts are preserved in the Österreichische Nationalbibliothek in Vienna. The first, Codex Vindobonensis Palatinus 5516, which is undated, contains a close copy of the 1486 text (see Plate 2). The manuscript's marginalia provide no evidence, as Kieszkowski claims in his edition, that this manuscript contains a prepublication copy of Pico's text sent to a fifteenth-century theologian; indeed, those marginal notes include quotations from printed sources that were not published until after Pico's death. The spurious 1486 date that Kieszkowski assigns to the text derives from the scribe's partial duplication of the colophon found in the *editio princeps*. The fact that this manuscript exists at all illustrates the interest shown in Pico's text between 1487 and 1532, when printed copies of it were exceedingly rare. But the manuscript throws no independent light on the text as Pico conceived it.

Codex Latinus 14708 of the Österreichische Nationalbibliothek contains another copy of the theses dated 1501 at the end. Collation of this manuscript with the 1486 version also shows its obvious derivation from the first printed edition.

In Munich, at the Bayerische Staatsbibliothek, a third copy of the theses is preserved in Codex Latinus Monacensis 11807. The colophon tells us that the manuscript was copied in Ingolstadt in 1518. The work closely follows the reprint edition of Pico's text published three decades earlier in that city, with various changes added from one or more handwritten copies or printed editions of Pico's text.

A last manuscript, Codex Latinus 646 at the Universitätsbibliothek in Erlangen, requires special comment, since Kieszkowski, who based his edition on this manuscript, claimed that it contained Eucharius Silber's personal copy of the text. Again, however, on internal evidence it can be quickly demonstrated that the Erlangen manuscript derived from, and was not the model for, Silber's 1486 edition—as Garin and Kristeller both noted long before Kieszkowski's edition went to press.[9] As in the case of other handwritten copies of Pico's text, the Erlangen manuscript contains corrections based on later printed editions or derivative manu-

---

[7] A number of other manuscripts survive of Pico's magical and Cabalistic theses, all based on earlier printed sources. On these manuscripts, see the appendix to Kristeller (1965).

[8] Garin, *Scritti vari*, 54.

[9] Garin, *Scritti vari*, 54; Kristeller (1965: 109–10). See also the discussion in Wirszubski (1989: 209–12) and below, n. 25. The nature of the Erlangen manuscript's corruptions further suggests that it was probably a later and not first-generation copy of the *editio princeps*.

scripts—apparently one reason why Kieszkowski failed to recognize it immediately as a copy of the *editio princeps*. In the extremely corrupt Erlangen manuscript, the the colophon of Silber's edition survives only in part, concluding with the words "Opera venerabilis viri Eucharii Silber alias Franck" (see Plate 3). It was on the grounds of this spurious evidence that Kieszkowski claimed that the manuscript contained Silber's personal copy of the text.

ii. The Modern Editions of Kieszkowski and Biondi

Of Kieszkowski's edition, which appeared in 1973, not much further needs to be said. De Pina Martins, who collated Kieszkowski's version with the 1532 Paris edition (which De Pina Martins mistook as authoritative) noted over a hundred discrepancies between the two texts, including in Kieszkowski's an enormous number of elementary grammatical errors.[10] Comparison of Kieszkowski's work with the authoritative first edition places his efforts in an even less favorable light. In his text entire words, phrases, and even whole sentences disappear without a trace or are transposed into the wrong conclusions; the order of theses is sometimes gratuitously inverted; and the sense of many others is obscured by eccentric punctuation and impossible syntax. Collation of Kieszkowski's text with the *editio princeps* turns up errors in well over three hundred theses in his edition; three conclusions disappear entirely and, by even the most conservative estimate, thirty or forty others are mangled beyond recognition.

These problems cannot all be blamed on Kieszkowski's erratic choice of the Erlangen manuscript as the basis for his edition. Review of his apparatus shows his unreliability in reporting variant readings even in the easily accessible Basel editions. The source notes in Kieszkowski's edition are almost uniformly misleading, as are his strange conjectures as to which non-Latin terms Pico intended for the blank spaces left by the printers in the *editio princeps*.[11] All in all, Kieszkowski's edition, which (despite earlier critiques by De Pina Martins and Wirszubski) is still often cited as the standard text,[12] is far more corrupt than the sixteenth-century editions that it was meant to replace.

---

[10] De Pina Martins (1976).

[11] In 11>6, for example, which pertains to "the three great four-letter names of God" in Kabbalah, Kieszkowski fills in the blanks with three Hebrew names *none* of which has four letters.

[12] E.g., by McGinn (1994).

Kieszkowski's influence also remains alive in Albano Biondi's recent version of Pico's text, which was published in 1995. Misled by Kieszkowski's claims about the Erlangen manuscript, Biondi ignores the *editio princeps* and adopts Kieszkowski's text as the grounds of his edition, attempting to emend Kieszkowski's errors using the corrupt version of the theses found in the 1557 Basel *Opera*. Biondi's attempted "compromise" (*compromesso*)[13] between Kieszkowski and the Basel edition has predictable results. Corruption due to Kieszkowski's misreadings of the Erlangen manuscript and other derivative texts, to speculative emendations in the Basel edition, or to errors transmitted from the 1487 reprint to the 1532 edition, on which the Basel version was based, are passed on in silence by Biondi, whose edition does not provide a critical apparatus or even minimal explanatory notes. Biondi also adopts without discussion Kieszkowski's erroneous claims concerning the Greek words omitted from the 1486 edition (as in theses 22.10 and 5>18) and the speculative conjectures concerning missing Hebrew made by the sixteenth-century Christian Cabalist Archangelus de Burgonovo. One thesis (1>11) drops out of Biondi's edition completely; others (like 1>10 and 2>33) are misreported due to Biondi's failure to consult the list of errors provided at the back of the *editio princeps*.

Biondi's Italian translation introduces further misreadings of Pico's text, especially in those sections employing symbolic language or scholastic terms. Thus in thesis 2>34 Biondi mistranslates the technical scholastic phrase *minima naturalia*, which refers to lower limits of divisibility in nature, as "*Piccoli Trattati naturali*"—the Italian title of Aristotle's *Parva Naturalia* or "Minor Natural Works."[14] The mistranslation obscures an important *occulta concatenatio* between Pico's thesis and one in opposition earlier in the text from St. Thomas.[15] In the opening preface to the theses, Pico's *gentes* and *heresiarchae*, referring to the "nations" and "sect leaders" whose theses are collected in the first part of his text, are transformed by Biondi into *pagani filosofi* (pagan philosophers) and *maestri stessi dell'eresia* (teachers of heresy or heads of heresies)—despite the fact that the first of the *gentes* we meet are not pagans but Latin scholastics, and the first *heresiarchae* are not heretics but Albert the Great, Thomas Aquinas, Duns Scotus, and other orthodox Christian theologians. In this case, Biondi's mistranslation distorts our interpretation of Pico's

---

[13] Biondi (1995: 4).

[14] Biondi (1995: 70).

[15] Cf. 2.27 from Thomas and 2>34 from Pico's own opinions.

entire text.[16] When the punctuation in Kieszkowski's edition or the Basel version is corrupt (as in theses 24.18 and 24.55 from Proclus), Biondi badly misreads Pico's sense, showing that he did not check ambiguous readings against Pico's sources or use the clues to the meaning of the theses found in closely related conclusions. In other cases, when Biondi does not understand Pico's Latin, he simply leaves key phrases untranslated (as in theses 4>5 and 4>7) or gives a overly literal translation that makes Pico's text appear even more obscure than it is.[17]

The massive corruption in Kieszkowski's and Biondi's editions would be less of a problem if each of Pico's theses was meant to stand on its own. Because of the *occulta concatenatio* that links theses in the text, however, even minor errors in one thesis can throw off the interpretation of large parts of Pico's text[18]— reinforcing the old view that the nine hundred theses are a hodgepodge of disconnected doctrines and that Pico had nothing systematic in mind in his meticulously planned Vatican debate.

---

[16] Biondi (1995: 6–7). The fact that by *gentes* Pico had "nations" and not pagan philosophers in mind is suggested at the start of his preface, where he announces his plan to debate his own opinions and those of the "wise Chaldeans, Arabs, Hebrews, Greeks, Egyptians, and Latins"—the latter clearly referring to Latin scholastics, not to Latin pagans, whom are rarely alluded to in Pico's text. Pico's text reads (Biondi punctuates it slightly differently): "Sunt autem disputanda dogmata, quod ad gentes attinet et ipsos heresiarchas seorsum posita, quod ad partes philosophiae promiscue, quasi per satyram, omnia simul mixta." Biondi translates: "Le posizioni di pensiero sottoposte a discussione sono presentate a parte quando si tratta di filosofi pagani e dei maestri stessi dell'eresia, ma sono presentate assieme senza distinzione, quasi nello stile misto della satira, quando si tratta di partizioni della filosofia" [The opinions submitted for discussion are presented separately when they concern pagan philosophers and teachers of heresy, but all together and indistinctly, in the satire's mixed style, when they concern the divisions of philosophy]. Besides other problems with Biondi's translation (e.g., his interpretation of the phrase *per satyram*), this reading conflicts with the existing organization of Pico's text, which groups pagan and Christian philosophers in the same manner (by "nation" or "sect") and contains no divisions at all that refer to *maestri dell'eresia*.

[17] Thus in theses 25.13–14, which refer to number symbolism in the cosmos, Biondi translates the mathematical terms "numerus planus aequilaterus" (square number) and "numerus linearis" (prime number) literally—using the Italian equivalents of "equilateral plane number" and "linear number"—which makes it impossible to interpret Pico's sense.

[18] In thesis 3>66, for example, Kieszkowski's misrepresentation of a single word (replacing *intrinsicam* for *extrinsecam*) prevents interpretation of a complex series of "paradoxical dogmatizing conclusions" that are critical to reconstucting Pico's theory of knowledge.

iii. The Present Edition

The current edition is based on identical copies of the *editio princeps* preserved in the British and Vatican Libraries.[19] In my apparatus, I have noted variant readings from the 1487 Ingolstadt reprint—the principal source, via the 1532 Parisian edition, of the most important errors found in later versions of Pico's text. I have not attempted in the apparatus to list the hundreds of errors found in the later manuscripts and printed editions of Pico's text; when further corruption introduced in these texts is of historical interest, it is noted in my commentary. During preparation of this edition, the *editio princeps* was collated with the four derivative manuscript copies of Pico's text, with the 1487, 1532, two 1557, and 1572 editions, with Kieszkowski's text, and (after my edition was in press), with Biondi's Latin and Italian versions of the theses. Leaving aside questions of punctuation, the only improvement on the Latin text of the 1486 edition found in any later work shows up in the correction of a few trivial typographic errors or idiosyncratic uses of the diphthong first made in the 1487 reprint; all these corrections are noted in my apparatus.

The use of punctuation was not standardized in the late fifteenth century, making the interpretation of even printed texts at times an arduous task. This problem is especially troublesome in the nine hundred theses, where the shift of a single comma can radically alter Pico's sense.[20] The fact that Pico himself did not have total control over final punctuation of his text is suggested at numerous points in the *editio princeps*, where the punctuation seems at times to have been

---

[19] The *editio princeps* consists of thirty-six unnumbered leaves; the body of the text contains thirty-five lines of text arranged in a single column. A space is left for the initial capital at the start of the text to be filled in later by hand; similar spaces are left elsewhere in the work for Greek, Hebrew, and (in one case) Aramaic terms. The London example is listed in the catalog of the British Library as measuring 195 x 119 mm; Albareda (cf. Kieszkowski 1973: 3) represents the Vatican exemplar as measuring 198 x 120 mm. The work does not carry a title, apparently because the theses were meant to be debated and not simply read. Pico's theses are contained on folios 1r–35r, followed immediately by the printer's colophon. 35v contains an announcement of the terms of the debate (including Pico's promise to pay traveling expenses for his opponents) followed by the printer's register. 36r contains the *Emendationes errorum*, which evidence suggests were at least in part drawn up by Pico himself; on this, see passim in my commentary to the text.

[20] Pico actively exploited this fact in defending himself before the papal commission, changing the punctuation of his theses as it suited the needs of his defense. See, e.g., my note to thesis 4>8.

tossed randomly (and sometimes maliciously) by the printers at the printed page. Predictably, the worst cases of mispunctuation show up in those sections of the text that contain Pico's most obscure technical and symbolic language.[21] Given this problem, in scores of cases I have been forced to trace Pico's exact sources before punctuating or translating his theses; indeed, as the corruptions in Biondi's edition suggest, it is not possible to produce any reliable edition or translation of Pico's text without first tracking down hundreds of his direct and indirect sources.

In repunctuating Pico's text, I have transformed the two main punctuation marks in the *editio princeps*—the medieval colon and period, which served a number of overlapping functions—into modern commas, semicolons, colons, and periods as needed. I have also (sparingly) changed lower-case letters into capital letters, or vice versa, when inconsistencies in the 1486 text seriously detract from Pico's sense. Every alteration made in the punctuation of the *editio princeps* is signaled in my text by the use of special symbols (see the transformation rules on page 209) or by notes in my apparatus, allowing readers to check my punctuation against the original. Throughout, I have proceeded with great caution in altering Pico's text, since suggestions exist that many of the ambiguities in his work (as well as many of his deviations from his sources) were intentional.[22]

With few exceptions, I have left orthography in my edition as it stands in the original, acting on the assumption that useful evidence may lie buried there. Supporting this view, study of otherwise trivial shifts in the text's orthography provides good evidence of major alterations made in Pico's text while it was already in press.[23] The one exception that I have made in my edition to not standardizing (or classicizing) this side of Pico's work lies in my silent expansion of common

[21] Cf., e.g., my punctuation in thesis 24.18 with the punctuation found in the *editio princeps*, which can be reconstructed using the transformation rules provided on p. 209 of my edition.

[22] Attempts to "correct" Pico's text in light of his sources were a common cause of the corruption found in sixteenth-century editions of the theses. Outside of using those sources as a guide to punctuating Pico's text, it would be an error for any modern editor to follow the same course, since we know that Pico frequently distorted his sources for polemical and reconciliative purposes (see, e.g., thesis 27.9 and note). These transformations, in fact, constitute some of the most interesting sides of Pico's work.

[23] See my introductory note to theses 6>1–10. Some of the text's variant spellings and transliterated forms also throw light on Pico's esoteric thought; on this, see, e.g., thesis 11>57 and note.

Latin abbreviations, which occur frequently in the *editio princeps*. The few cases of possible ambiguity in those abbreviations are noted in my apparatus.

It is not always easy to distinguish intended quotations in the *editio princeps*, although the 1486 edition occasionally indicates a presumed direct quotation by capitalizing its initial letter. Study of Pico's sources, however, suggests that even these passages were more often than not loose paraphrases rather than exact quotations; the implication is that Pico frequently quoted from memory, a common practice until well into the modern era.[24] Given this problem, while I have occasionally italicized presumed quotations in my translation when this clarifies Pico's sense, I have not tried to distinguish (as Pico clearly did not) the complex mix of free and literal translations, close and not-too-close paraphrases, and direct and indirect quotations that he often crammed into single theses. On rare occasions, I have also introduced italics into the Latin or English texts when this has seemed necessary for emphatic purposes; throughout it should be kept in mind that no such punctuation appears in the original.

Finally a word on the work's missing Greek, Hebrew, and Aramaic terms. Eucharius Silber, like most other fifteenth-century printers, was only equipped to print letters in the Latin alphabet. The *editio princeps* accordingly leaves blank spaces for non-Latin terms to be filled in later by hand (see Plates 4 and 5). Unfortunately, no copies of the nine hundred theses have survived (if any besides the original ever existed) that supply these missing terms.[25] In a few cases, Pico transliterated Hebrew words into Latin before or after these blank spaces, allowing us to fill in those spaces quickly with the appropriate words. Studies of Pico's sources have in a few other cases permitted reliable reconstruction of this part of his text. Only Kieszkowski and Biondi have claimed to have fully reconstructed this part of Pico's theses, filling in the lacunae (or those they did not overlook)[26] with highly conjectural, and sometimes patently absurd, Hebrew and Greek. In the following edition the spaces for missing terms are set out between pointed brackets. Except where hard evidence exists concerning what goes in between, I have left these spaces blank and have not engaged in speculative reconstructions, which could adversely affect our reading of closely related theses in the text.

---

[24] This evidence also puts to rest the old claim that Pico had an eidetic memory.

[25] As Wirszubski (1989: 210–11) points out, the Erlangen manuscript that Kieszkowski claimed as the printer's copy not only omits these terms but frequently leaves out the blank spaces as well—further evidence that the manuscript could not have been the model for the *editio princeps*.

[26] See my notes to theses 5>18 and 8>11.

iv. On the Translation and Commentary

The nine hundred theses are a translator's nightmare—helping explain why five hundred years passed before any complete translation made it to print. Once the hardest part of the job is accomplished, and Pico's sense is established, putting the theses into some kind of modern prose is trivial; making them readable is not. Pico's scholastic language, unlike his classical Latin, was not meant to be eloquent but precise; at times the text's recurrent patterns and stereotypical linguistic reversals (as in 3>38 or 5>26, etc.) give the impression of being computer-generated prose. Any translation that adheres narrowly to Pico's literal sense sounds absurdly alien in English; any translation that deviates even normal distances from the literal threatens to obscure the *occulta concatenatio* linking different parts of Pico's text. In my translation I have often had to settle for an uneasy balance between the unusual demands for consistency imposed by the text and the goal of putting Pico's scholastic prose into something remotely resembling modern English. My highest priority at all times has been to make the intellectual content of the theses as transparent as possible.

My commentary on Pico's text has three main objects: to elucidate Pico's technical and symbolic language; to underline the conceptual links between theses to facilitate analysis of his thought; and to point to supporting evidence for the model of syncretic processes introduced in my study. Throughout I have had to settle on a high degree of compression in discussing hundreds of complex philosophical, theological, and cosmological issues; for obvious reasons, I have not been able to present anything more than a preliminary commentary on the text. My textual notes are usually fullest for the first conclusion in a topical series, where I normally list all or a representative sample of conceptually related theses; commentary on later theses is often limited to a simple cross-reference to that initial note.

One of the subsidiary goals of my commentary has been to provide an overview of Pico's use of sources. Here my goals have been constrained by limitations of space, and I have often had to restrict myself to a general analysis of the issue without providing a detailed thesis-by-thesis discussion. Given sufficient space, it would be possible to say a great deal more about the origins of a number of theses in the historical part of Pico's text. In some cases, it is possible to follow Pico as he moves page by page through certain texts, drawing theses from various scholastic commentaries on Peter Lombard's *Sentences* or from favorite Greek sources like Proclus's *Platonic Theology* or *Commentary on the Timaeus.* But these are special cases; it is important to recognize that not all or even most of the nine hundred theses can be traced unambiguously to single sources. Many of Pico's theses express opinions assigned to authorities by common consent. Others turn those opinions intentionally on their heads, apparently as challenges to rival philosophers or warring schools. Evidence also exists that Pico drew some of his theses from epitomes, anthologies or florilegia, or even wholly from oral sources. The latter was the case, for example, in respect to at least some of the materials on Arabic and Hebrew thought that Pico collected from Elia del Medigo, Flavius Mithridates, or his other Jewish informants. Other of Pico's theses combine materials from his sources in a highly idiosyncratic fashion, making it impossible again to point to one passage or another as his immediate source. This was the case in many of the theses that Pico drew from his Neo-Platonic sources, where he often compressed ideas spread out over dozens of pages in Proclus's *Platonic Theology* and similar texts into the exaggerated correlative forms characteristic of his own thought.

In cases like this, any full discussion of Pico's sources would need to trace his transformations of those materials thesis by thesis and suggest as well what changes awaited them following their "collation" with topically related materials in the course of his dispute. Given the enormous space that any such analysis would require, in my commentary I have generally avoided long source discussions of individual theses and have focused instead on the more critical issue of what systematic connections Pico planned to make between theses in his debate.

PLATE 1

An abstract cosmological diagram meant in part to interpret Pico's numerological and Cabalistic theses. From Nicolas LeFèvre's French translation of the *Heptaplus* (1579) (bound with Francesco Giorgio, *De harmonia mundi totius cantica tria*). The correlative (or fractal) structure of Pico's system is evident in the scaled circles-within-circles representing different ontological levels of his system. Note the interplay between the two "perfect numbers" 28 and 10, which played a central role not only in Pico's emanational theories but in his syncretic model of history and in the eschatological structure of the nine hundred theses. The numerological scheme here should be compared with theses 25.12 and 5>1 (see also the notes to those theses)—which too deal with the geometrical progressions found in the cosmological descent of the one to the many. LeFèvre sums up the fractal principles underlying Pico's system with words traditionally though imprecisely credited to Anaxagoras: "All things exist in all things, and all individuals in all individuals."

By permission of the British Library, 692.f.17, e6v.

QVANT A CE QVE CHACVN DES TROIS *mondes est pourueu de sa racine, quarré & Cube, tout ainsi que l'Vniuers, comme il apparoist par les nombres qui sont hors les rondeaux, par là peux-tu entendre l'Armonie & conuenance de tout, & comme peut estre vray le dire d'Anaxagore, qui mettoit* omnia in omnibus & singula in singulis.

Ceste suitte de nombres procedant de 1. a. 28. second nombre parfaict & Cube du 3. declare le secret & mystere de l'ame & du mõde descript & demõstré par Platon au Timée.

Note le mystere des lettres Hebraiques, chacune desquelles vaut autant que le nombre qu'elle a pres de soy enclos dans vn petit rõd.

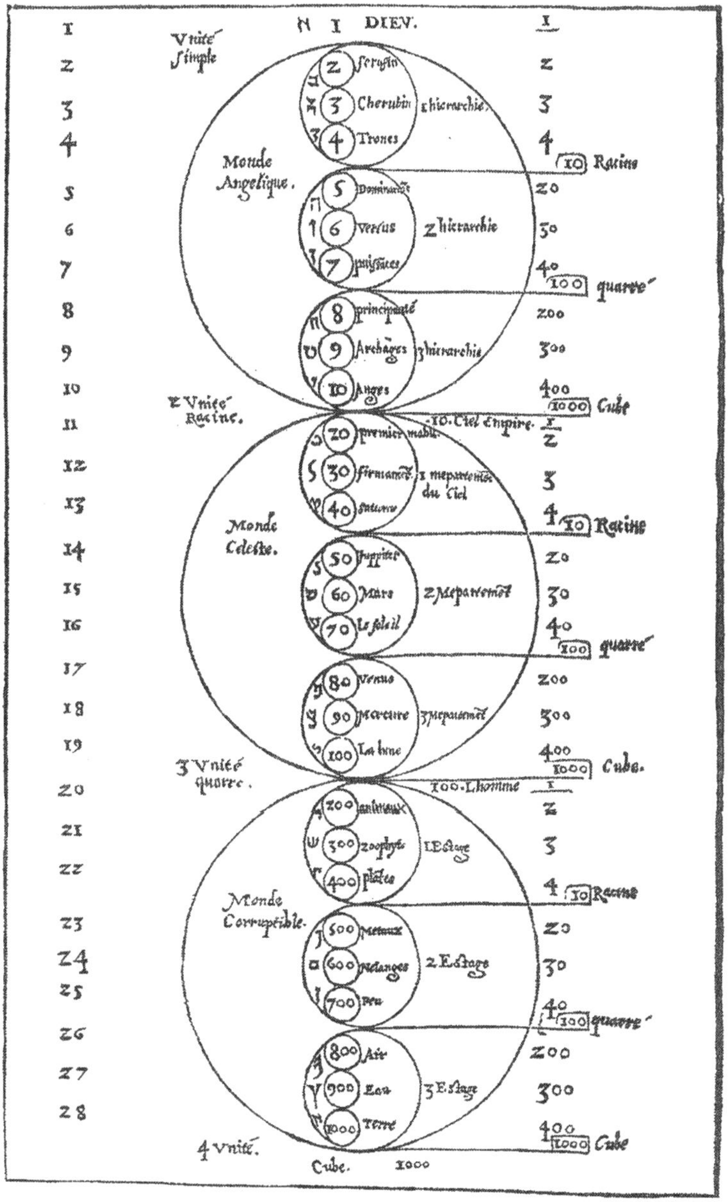

PLATE 2

The beginning of Codex Vindobonensis Palatinus 5516, the best of several surviving manuscripts of the nine hundred theses copied from the 1486 printed edition.

Vienna, Österreichische Nationalbibliothek, Cod. 5516, fol. 1r.
By permission.

DE ADSCRIPTIS NV̄ERO NONIGẼTIS: DIALETICIS: MORALIBVS PHYSICIS: Mathematicis: Methaphysicis: Theologicis: Magicis: Cabalisticis: cũ suis: tũ sapientũ Chaldeorũ: Arabum: Hebreorũ: Grecorũ: Aegyptiorũ: Latinorũq; placitis disputabit publice Johannes Picus Mirandulanus cõcordie Comes: in quibus recitandis nõ Romane linguae nitorem, Sed celebratissimorũ Parisiensiũ disputatorũ dicendi genus est imitatus: propterea q eo nostri temporis philosophi plerique omnes utunt. Sũt autẽ disputanda dogmata: quo ad gentes attinet et ipsos heresiarchas seorsũ posita: quo ad partes phie promiscue quasi per satyrã oĩa simul mixta

¶ Conclusiones secũdum doctrinã latinorũ philosophorũ et theologorum Alberti magni: Thomae Aquinatis: Henrici Gandauẽn: Iohannis Scoti: Egidii Romani: et Francisci de Maironis.

¶ CÕCLVSIONES SCDM ALBERTV̄ NV̄ERO.XVI

¶ Species intelligibiles nõ sunt necessarię: et eas ponere nõ est bonis Peripateticis consentaneum.

¶ Corruptis omnibus indiuiduis speciei humanae hec ẽ uera. homo est animal

¶ Hec est in quarto modo dicendi per se. homo est homo

¶ In quolibet pũcto materiae sunt per habitũ inchoationis potestatiuum essentiae om̃ formarũ naturaliũ materię coeterne secũdũ philosophos, concreate secundũ fidem

¶ Forma in intensione et remissione nõ uariat̃ sm̃ essẽtia; sed sm̃ esse

¶ Anima separata intelligit per species sibi a principio sui esse concreatas: quibus dũ est in corpore aut nunq̃ aut raro utitur.

¶ Sonus fertur secundũ esse reale usq; ad principiũ nerui auditiui.

¶ Lumen nõ habet in medio nisi esse intentionale.

¶ Organũ auditus est neruus expansus ad concauũ auris.

¶ Obiectũ per se et proprie sensus communis ẽ magnitudo ut bene dixit Auicenna.

Plate 3

At the end of the text of the nine hundred theses preserved in Universitätsbibliothek Erlangen Codex Latinus 646, which derives from the *editio princeps*, the colophon from the printed text survives only in part, giving the words *Opera venerabilis viri Eucharii Silber alias Franck*. Supported by this spurious evidence, Kieszkowski based his 1973 edition of the nine hundred theses on this derivative manuscript, mistaking it for the printer's handwritten copy of the text. Kieszkowski's claims concerning the corrupt Erlangen manuscript were accepted by Albano Biondi, who based his 1995 Latin and Italian versions of Pico's text on Kieszkowski's edition. The text above the surviving fragment of the colophon, written in a different hand, is an addition by a later annotator of Pico's promise to pay the traveling expenses to Rome of would-be debators, which was left out of the Erlangen manuscript by the original copyist.

Top portion of Universitätsbibliothek, Erlangen, Codex Latinus 646, fol. 38r.
By permission.

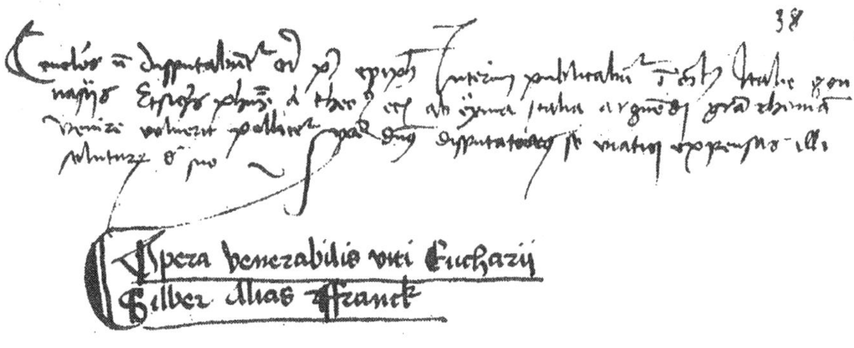
38

Opera venerabilis viri Eucharij
Silber alias Franck

PLATE 4

Folio 9r from the *editio princeps*. Note the paragraph marks separating theses, whose numbering was implied but not provided in the original text. The blank spaces in the middle of the page are for non-Latin terms (in this case Greek) to be filled in later by hand. Cf. the thesis at the top of the page, loosely drawn from Iamblichus's *De mysteriis*, with thesis 23.1 from my edition. The handwritten insertion in the text is a correction by an early reader following the *Emendationes errorum* at the end of the edition.

By permission of the British Library, IB 18857, fol. 9r.

¶ Intellectus speculatiuus est forma separata quantum ad rem & ad modum: practicus separata: quantum ad rem coniuncta: quantum ad modum anima rationalis coniuncta sm rem separata sm modum: Inrationalis coniuncta sm rem & sm modum.

¶ Opifex sensibilis mũdi septimus est hierarchiæ intellectualis.

¶ Corporalis natura est in intellectu immobiliter: in animo ex se primo mobiliter: in animali ex se mobiliter participatiue: in coelo aliunde ordinate: infra lunã aliũde mobiliter inordinate.

¶ Elementa in octo coeli corporibus coelesti modo bis inueniuntur: quæ quis inueniet si retrogrado ordine in illa bina numeratione processerit.

¶ Super hunc mundum quem uocant Theologi   est alius quem uocant   & super hunc alius quem uocant

¶ Cum excellenter ad intellectum assimilatur anima fit in uehiculo motus perfecte circularis.

¶ Nulla est uis coelestium astrorum quantum est in se malefica.

¶ Qui finalem causam diluuiorum incendiorumq; cognouerit: hæc potius   .i. purgationes q̃ corruptiones uocabit.

¶ Cum dicit Plato in mundi medio positam animam: de inparticipata anima debet intelligi: quam ideo in medio dicit positam: quia æqualiter omnibus adest ab omni respectu & particulari habitudine liberata.

CONCLVSIONES SECVNDVM PROCLVM NVMERO .LV.

¶ Quod est in intelligibilibus terminus & infinitum: est in intellectualibus mas & femina: in supermundanis idemtitas & alteritas: similitudo & dissimilitudo. In anima circulatio eiusdem & circulatio alterius.

¶ A saturniis legibus eximuntur dei qui contentiui & perfectiui sunt: A Iouiis legibus dei saturnii: A fatalibus legibus omnis anima uiuens intellectualiter. Legi aũt adrastiæ omnia obediunt.

¶ Dei appellatio simpliciter absolute uni competit qui est deus deorum: simpliciter non absolute cuilibet supersubstantialium: sm essentiam: intellectualium cuilibet sm participationem ani-

Plate 5

The end of folio 28r and beginning of 28v in the *editio princeps*, with the arrow indicating a blank space after the word *Lictor*. The space was apparently left to be filled in later with an Aramaic term, suggesting that Pico may indeed have used, as he claimed, a "Chaldean" text in drawing up his theses on the so-called *Chaldean Oracles*. In my commentary, I argue that forgeries by Pico's tutor Flavius Mithridates were probably involved here (see note to thesis 8>11).

By permission of the British Library, IB 18857, fols. 28r, 28v.

¶ Per canem nihil aliud intelligit zoroaſter : q̃ partem inrationalem animæ & proportionalia: quod ita eſſe uidebit qui diligenter dicta omnia expoſitorum conſiderauerit: qui & ipſi ſicut
& zoroaſter enigmatice loquuntur.

¶ Dictum illud zoroaſtris ne ex eas cum traſit Lictor

28r/28v

perfecte intelligetur per illud Exodi quando ſunt prohibiti Iſra
helite exire domos ſuas in tranſitu angeli interficientis primoge
nita ægyptiorum.
¶ Per Syrenam apud Zoroaſtrem nihil aliud intrlligas q̃ partem animæ rationalem.

Chart of Pico's Historical Theses

Pico's first 400 theses,[1] which have a quasi-historical structure, take us from the warring Latin scholastics to the (mostly) harmonious ancients; Pico's agreement with traditions increases as we move backwards through the text in time (downwards through this chart). To reconstruct Pico's views in this part of the text, all topically related theses must be collated with the last 500 theses given "according to his own opinion." The historical structure of this part of the text, as shown in chapter 1, mirrors the emanational principles of Pico's correlative cosmology, or so-called *philosophia nova.*

"Nations" or Sects (*gentes*)	**"Heresiarchs" or Sect Leaders**	**Section #[2]**	**# of theses**
The Latins Sect leaders include the official theologians of the Dominicans, Franciscans, and Augustinians. The language of this section is abstract and philosophical, and the section is filled with conflicting theses, reflecting Pico's model of history.	Albert the Great	1.	16
	Thomas Aquinas	2.	45
	Francis of Meyronnes	3.	8
	John [Duns] Scotus	4.	22
	Henry of Ghent	5.	13
	Giles of Rome	6.	11
		115 Total	

The Arabs Wars still rage among the sect leaders, but the Arabs also deal increasingly with "higher" matters, including proofs of the existence of God and celestial issues beyond the understanding of the Latin scholastics.	Averroes	7.	41
	Avicenna	8.	12
	al-Farabi	9.	11
	"Isaac of Narbonne"	10.	4
	Abumaron (Avenzoar)	11.	4
	Moses of Egypt (Maimonides)	12.	3
	"Mohammed of Toledo"	13.	5
	Avempace	14.	2
		82 from the Arabs, 197[3] Total	

[1] 402 after some hasty last-minute revisions.

[2] Assigned by the present editor but implied in the *editio princeps*.

[3] Probably originally 199 or 200, implying that two or three earlier theses were dropped at some point from the Latins and Arabs.

"Nations" or Sects (*gentes*)	**"Heresiarchs" or Sect Leaders**	**Section #**	**# of theses**
The Greek Peripatetics The correlative structure of the cosmos becomes clearer as we move into the second half of the historical part of the text, and the wars between sect leaders lessen in intensity.	Theophrastus Ammonius Simplicius Alexander of Aphrodisias Themistius	15. 16. 17. 18. 19.	4 3 9 8 5
		29 from the Greek Peripatetics, 226 Total	

The Platonists From this point on only a few "civil wars" are evident among later Neo-Platonists; Pico's language becomes increasingly symbolic (and obscure) as we approach the ancient wisemen.	Plotinus "Adeland the Arab" Porphyry Iamblichus Proclus	20. 21. 22. 23. 24.	15 8 12 9 55
		99 from the Platonists, 325 Total	

"Nations" or Sects (*gentes*) No sect leaders are identified among the most ancient "nations," which are largely in agreement.		
Pythagorean mathematics	25.	14
Chaldean theologians	26.	6
Mercury Trismegistus the Egyptian	27.	10
Hebrew Cabalist wisemen Pico announces his rediscovery of the secret wisdom revealed orally to Moses on the mountain. The section ends with mystical speculation on the word *Amen*.	28.	47
	77 from the ancient sages, 402 Total	

Chart of Theses according to His Own Opinion

The 500 theses[1] in this part of the text were originally divided into ten sections; an eleventh was added while the book was in press to replace theses removed for doctrinal reasons (see the introductory note to theses 6>1–10).

Abbreviated Title and Section Description	Notes	Section #[2]	# of theses
Paradoxical reconciliative conclusions. The first thesis in this set promises to reconcile all of Plato and Aristotle; the rest aim to reconcile various Arabs and Latins on isolated issues, but not *in toto*.	The first thesis has numerological significance	1>	17
Philosophical conclusions dissenting from the common philosophy. Resolves numerous standard scholastic conflicts.		2>	80
Paradoxical conclusions introducing new doctrines in philosophy. Introduces Pico's *philosophia nova*, capable of resolving "every proposed question on natural or divine things." The correlative structures here are typical of syncretic systems worldwide.	The first thesis of this section = 500, a symbol for Pico of mystical return	3>	71[3]
Theological conclusions opposed to the common mode of speaking of theologians. Fiercely attacks St. Thomas; contains most of the theses attacked by the papal commission.		4>	29[4]

[1] 498 after some hasty revisions.

[2] Assigned by present editor but implied in the *editio princeps*.

[3] One thesis was removed shortly before or while the work was in press.

[4] Two theses were apparently removed while the work was in press.

Abbreviated Title and Section Description	Notes	Section #	# of theses
Conclusions on the doctrine of Plato. Contains only 62 theses, we are told, since Pico's first reconciliative thesis "takes it upon itself to discuss the entire doctrine of Plato." This section contains many covert attacks on Marsilio Ficino.	The first thesis in this section = 600	5>	62
Conclusions on the *Book of Causes*. Inserted while in press to replace other theses apparently withdrawn for doctrinal reasons.		6>	10
Conclusions on mathematics (numerology). One of three or four of Pico's methods leading to a grasp of "everything knowable."	Does thesis 700 have numerological significance?	7> 7a>	11 74
Conclusions on Zoroaster and his Chaldean commentators. Supposedly based on Chaldean texts.		8>	15
Conclusions on magic. This section precedes Ficino's magical writings by several years and is sharply distinguished from them.		9>	26
Conclusions on understanding the Orphic Hymns according to magic. Much of the magic here is exegetical and prophetic in nature.	Does thesis 800 have numerological significance?	10>	31
Cabalistic conclusions confirming the Christian religion. The Jews are converted "with their own weapons" and mankind is prepared for its final eschatological reunion with Christ.	Thesis 900 has numerological significance	11>	72[5]
		498 Subtotal, 900 Total	

[5] This section apparently originally contained seventy-one theses.

Guide to Textual Symbols, Titles, and Punctuation

1. ¶ = the start of a new section or thesis in the 1486 edition; replaced at the beginning of theses in the present edition by section and thesis numbers.

2. Section and thesis numbers in Pico's historical theses (theses 1.1 to 28.47) are separated in the current edition by a period; theses given "according to his own opinion" (theses 1>1 to 11>72) are separated by a pointed bracket.

3. Folio numbers in the *editio princeps* are given between pointed brackets in the Latin text; page breaks are indicated in the Latin text by a slash (/).

4. Numbers in parentheses given in the English text = consecutive thesis numbers, which are provided every five theses.

5. Running titles provided at the top of each page in the current edition are not found in the *editio princeps*; all other titles are found in the 1486 text.

The exact text of the *editio princeps* (except for unambiguous abbreviations) can be reconstructed from this edition by using the following transformation rules:

Current Edition		**1486 Edition**
commas or semi-colons	→	colons
colons or periods	→	periods
underlined punctuation (, or : or ; or .)	→	no punctuation in the *editio princeps*
underlined letters (sed, Iove, Phedrus) (used sparingly)	→	reverse upper/lower case in 1486 edition (Sed, iove, phedrus)
subscript line between words (sed_ego)	→	superfluous colon, omitted in the modern edition
< >	→	blank space left for Greek, Hebrew, or Aramaic words in the 1486 edition

Exceptions: On rare occasions, colons in the *editio princeps* are retained in the current edition or are transformed into modern periods; in a few other cases, periods in the 1486 edition are transformed into modern commas or are dropped from the text; all these exceptions are noted in the critical apparatus.

DE ADSCRIPTIS NVMERO NONINGENTIS, DIALECTICIS, MORALIBVS, PHYSICIS, MATHEMATICIS, Methaphysicis, Theologicis, Magicis, Cabalisticis, cum suis, tum sapientum Chaldeorum, Arabum, Hebreorum, Graecorum, Aegyptiorum, latinorumque placitis disputabit publice Iohanes Picus Mirandulanus Concordie Comes; in quibus recitandis non Romanae linguae nitorem, sed celebratissimorum Parisiensium disputatorum dicendi genus est imitatus, propterea quod eo nostri temporis philosophi plerique omnes utuntur. Sunt autem disputanda dogmata, quod ad gentes attinet et ipsos heresiarchas seorsum posita, quod ad partes philosophiae promiscue, quasi per satyram, omnia simul mixta.

1486 space left for initial capital | quo ad gentes attinet . . . quo ad partes philosophie | *Emendationes errorum,* corrige: quod ad gentes attinet . . . quod ad partes philosophiae | 1487 text emended *sic*

PREFACE. "splendor of the Roman language" = classical or so-called humanist Latin. "style of speaking of the most celebrated Parisian disputers" = the *stilus Parisiensis,* medieval or scholastic Latin. "*per satyram*" (*per saturam*) = as in a bowl of fruit, in a mixture or medley; the words *satura* and *satira* or *satyra* ("satire," as Biondi reads it) were etymologically linked by ancient grammarians, and their orthography was often confused. It is important to recall that the first twenty-eight subsections of the text giving the opinions of others included theses that Pico meant to attack as well as endorse. In order to establish his views on any one issue, topically linked theses in the historical part of his text need to be collated with the theses given "according to his own opinion." At Rome, Pico planned to reveal the occult links between

First Preface

The following nine hundred dialectical, moral, physical, mathematical, Metaphysical, Theological, Magical, and Cabalistic opinions, including his own and those of the wise Chaldeans, Arabs, Hebrews, Greeks, Egyptians, and Latins, will be disputed publicly by Giovanni Pico of Mirandola, the Count of Concord. In reciting these opinions, he has not imitated the splendor of the Roman language, but the style of speaking of the most celebrated Parisian disputers, since this is used by almost all philosophers of our time. The doctrines to be debated are proposed separately by nations and their sect leaders, but in common in respect to the parts of philosophy—as though in a medley, everything mixed together.

---

theses and, ultimately, in the cosmos and history, paving the way (or so he hinted) for Christ's return; see above, pp. 30–46. The phrase "proposed separately by nations [or sects] and their sect leaders [or heresiarchs]" is Pico's way of stressing the unorthodox historical organization of the first part of his text; on Biondi's reading, which takes *gentes* and *heresiarchae* to refer to pagan philosophers and heretics, see pp. 187–88 above. Note that Pico's "nations" are not listed in his preface in reverse historical order, as they appear in the text itself. Other discrepancies show up in the preface to Pico's theses presented "according to his own opinion," suggesting that both prefaces were written before a final revision of the text. Internal evidence of further revisions while the book was already in press is discussed in my introductory note to theses 6>1–10.

¶Conclusiones secundum doctrinam latinorum philosophorum et theologorum Alberti Magni, Thomae Aquinatis, Henrici Gandauensis, Iohannis Scoti, Egidii Romani, et Francisci de Maironis.

CONCLVSIONES SECVNDVM ALBERTVM NVMERO .XVI.

1.1. Species intelligibiles non sunt necessariae, et eas ponere non est bonis peripateticis consentaneum.

1.2. Corruptis omnibus indiuiduis specie humanae haec est uera: homo est animal.

1.3. Haec est in quarto modo dicendi per se: homo est homo.

Section title. 1487 Francisci de maronis

CONCLUSIONS ACCORDING TO THE LATINS. This section includes what Pico viewed as the principal doctrines of the *heresiarchae* or "sect leaders" of the Latin *via antiqua*. The reasons for Pico's omission of the nominalists or *moderni* are discussed above, p. 36. In line with Pico's views of history, doctrinal conflicts are sharper and more numerous in the Latins than in the more ancient *gentes* we encounter as we move backwards in time through Pico's text. While Pico's title lists the Latin *heresiarchae* here in chronological order, they are presented differently in the text, apparently to heighten contrasts between "warring schools."

CONCLUSIONS ACCORDING TO ALBERT. Albert the Great, unlike St. Thomas Aquinas, is generally treated sympathetically in all Pico's works. Links exist between theses in this section and materials in Albert's commentary on the *De anima* and other Aristotelian works, his *Summa de creaturis* (especially the section entitled *De homine*), and his *Summa theologiae*. More precise sources are difficult to pinpoint due to Pico's habit of turning Albert's views on their head. A number of theses in this section are opposed to others in the following section from Aquinas, suggesting that in compiling them Pico may have drawn on secondary sources like the *Concordantie Thome et Alberti* (Concordance of Thomas and Albert) found in his library (Cesis 1897: 45; Kibre 1936: 203).

The Latins: Albert the Great

¶Conclusions according to the doctrine of the Latin philosophers and theologians Albert the Great, Thomas Aquinas, Henry of Ghent, John Scotus, Giles of Rome, and Francis of Meyronnes.

SIXTEEN CONCLUSIONS ACCORDING TO ALBERT.

1.1. Intelligible images are not necessary, and it is not fitting for good Aristotelians to posit them. (1)

1.2. With all individuals of the human species destroyed, this holds true: Man is an animal.

1.3. This is in the fourth mode of speaking per se: Man is man.

1.1. Pico's first thesis reverses Albert's accustomed view, apparently for polemical reasons. The thesis starts a long topical series on the origins of "intelligible images" (higher universals) that is closely linked to Pico's planned reconciliation of Plato and Aristotle. See my discussions above, pp. 100–104. In Pico's historical theses, some in conflict, cf. 2.39, 7.15, 8.4, 10.2, 15.3, 21.1–3. For Pico's views, see 21.3, 2>1, 2>31, 2>77, 3>40, 3>60–66.

1.2. Standard scholastic formula for affirming the independence of species and genera from individuals (explaining the reading of "destroyed" rather than "corrupted"). Biondi translates: "Essendo corrotti tutti gli individui della specie umana, é vera la proposizione: l'uomo é un essere animato," which destroys Pico's sense. The origin of the discussion goes back to Aristotle *Metaphysics* 7.14–15, which attack the Platonic theory of ideas. Conflicting historical theses include 2.45 and 7.19 from Thomas and Averroes. See also 2>35 from Pico's theses. Pico believed that from the limited standpoint of human knowledge it was legitimate to view species and genera as having independent existences, but viewed from a higher perspective, these were mere "beings of reason." Cf. 2>2–3, 3>2–7 and notes.

1.3. Commentators on *Posterior Analytics* 1.4 distinguished four modes in which a predicate could be ascribed to a subject in a "proper" or per se sense. The fourth mode referred to a subject's essential cause; the thesis thus means "Man is the cause of man"; it is tied to a diffuse series of theses on the ideas as causative principles.

1.4. In quolibet puncto materiae sunt per habitum inchoationis potestatiuum essentiae omnium formarum naturalium, materiae coeternae secundum philosophos, concreatae secundum fidem.

1.5. Forma in intensione et remissione non uariatur secundum essentiam, sed secundum esse.

1.6. Anima separata intelligit per species sibi a principio sui esse concreatas, quibus dum est in corpore aut nunquam aut raro utitur.

1.7. Sonus fertur secundum esse reale usque ad principium nerui auditiui.

1.8. Lumen non habet in medio nisi esse intentionale.

1.9. Organum auditus est neruus expansus ad concauum auris.

1.10. Obiectum per se et proprie sensus communis est magnitudo, ut bene dixit Auicenna. <1r/1v>

1.4. "habit" here = an infused property created with matter but not included in its formal definition. The thesis reflects one variation of Pico's view that all things are contained in some way in all things. In Pico's theses, cf. especially 2>54, 3>52. Pico's endorsement of Albert's views on "inchoate forms" is confirmed in *Heptaplus* 1.2. The pure potentiality of such forms is suggested in 1.16. The double-truth in this thesis apparently reflects Pico's views, not Albert's.

1.5. The "intension and remission of forms" in scholastic language pertained to alteration in the technical Aristotelian sense, i.e., to an increase or decrease in accidental qualities over time (the reddening of an apple, alterations in position or motion, etc.). Cf. 2.27, 2>34. Pico's views on such issues were highly conservative. Cf. 7>5, where he complains about the mathematical treatment of such matters by the so-called *moderni*.

1.6. Like 1.1, tied to Pico's harmonized Aristotelian/Platonic theory of knowledge. Closely related theses include 18.6, 20.10, 20.12, 21.1–3. In Pico's theses given "according to his own opinion," cf. 3>40, 5>19, 5>29–30, 5>54.

1.4. In every point in matter the essences of all natural forms exist in a habit containing the power of generation—co-eternal with matter according to the philosophers, co-created according to faith.

1.5. A form in intension and remission does not vary in essence, but in existence. (5)

1.6. A separated soul understands through images that were co-created with it at its origin, which while it is in the body it either never or rarely uses.

1.7. Sound is carried with real existence right up to the beginning of the auditory nerve.

1.8. Light in a medium has only intentional existence.

1.9. The organ of hearing is the nerve extended to the aural cavity.

1.10. The object per se and properly speaking of common sense is magnitude, as Avicenna correctly stated. (10)

1.7–8. Cf. 8.9–10, 9.9–10. Arising from commentary on Aristotle *De anima* 2.7–8. For Albert, the greater "intentionality" (or "spirituality") of light as compared to sound was shown by the fact that sounds are affected by winds but colors are not; all sensual images become "spiritual" once they pass *through* the senses, however. In medieval debates, this thesis was usually tied to broader issues involving sensual abstraction.

1.9. *Re* Aristotle *De anima* 2.8. In general, locating the sensual organs involved conflicts between Aristotelians and followers of Galen. Cf. 8.11 from Avicenna. In 2>76 Pico posits a kind of double-truth in reconciling a related conflict between these two authorities.

1.10. Commenting on *De anima* 2.6, 3.1. "Objects of common sense" or "common sensibles" included everything (like magnitude) perceived by more than one sense organ. Arguments arose over how many of such objects existed and whether or not a special faculty, the *sensus communis*, was needed to perceive them. Pico planned an extended discussion. Cf., e.g., 10.3, 13.3, and from Pico's theses, 2>30, 2>58, 3>41.

1.11. Stat speciem cuius dicimur reminisci esse totaliter deperditam et abolitam.

1.12. Non introducitur uegetalis anima ante sensualem, nec sensualis ante rationalem, sed tota simul.

1.13. Licet ad receptionem speciei concurrat sensus passiue, ad iudicandum tamen de sensibili actiue concurrit.

1.14. Corpus mobile est subiectum scientiae naturalis.

1.15. Corporis in eo quod corpus consideratio ad methaphysicum spectat.

1.16. Potentia respectiua materiae non addit supra materiam rem, sed rationem.

1.11. "image" here = image of God. Cf. Albert *Summa theologiae, pars* 2, *q.* 87, *membrum* 5 (Borgnet edition): Although it is true to say that original sin was repaired by grace, "the most sublime state in general is the state of innocence, in which a nature is depressed by neither fault nor punishment." In 9>12 and elsewhere Pico suggests a contrary view, and *Heptaplus* 7.1 (*Opera,* 49; Garin, *Scritti vari,* 340) tells us that through grace man's nature can be "restored to its pristine dignity." Given the excessive claims that have been made on this issue in the past, it is important to emphasize that Pico's views on human dignity were based solidly on ancient and medieval tradition and were not unique to Pico or Renaissance thought.

1.12. On the unity of the soul, cf. in the historical theses 2.41, 7.31, 20.5. For Pico's views on this issue and metaphysical unity in general, see note 2.23 and 4>7 from Pico's theological theses.

1.11. It holds true that the image that we are said to recall is totally lost and abolished.

1.12. The vegetative soul is not introduced before the sensual soul, nor the sensual before the rational soul, but the whole is introduced at once.

1.13. Granted that sense agrees passively in receiving an image, it agrees actively in judging a sensible object.

1.14. Moveable body is the subject of natural science.

1.15. The consideration of body as it is body pertains to the metaphysician. (15)

1.16. A potentiality in respect to matter does not add substance to matter, but reason.

1.13. For Albert every sense had both an active and passive element, an idea that Pico found appealing due to the symmetry it suggested with the structure of higher cognitive powers. Related historical theses, some in conflict, include 8.10, 10.3, 17.1, 17.7. Thesis 2>1 suggests that Pico believed that inferior universals were abstracted directly by the senses.

1.14–15. On scholastic conflicts over the objects of "natural science" (physics) and/or metaphysics, cf. 2.42, 7.20, 7.38. Pico's usual hierarchical means of resolving such conflicts is illustrated in 3>9. Other linked theses include 1>16, 2>61.

1.16. Apparently meant to qualify Albert's sense in 1.4. Pico often used the final thesis from a "sect leader" to qualify earlier theses from that figure; cf. 4.22 and note from Scotus, 7.41 from Averroes. The dichotomy *res/ratio* (substance/reason) normally distinguished something existing concretely from its formal possibility or idea.

CONCLVSIONES SECVNDVM THOMAM NVMERO .XXXXV.

2.1. Si spiritus a filio non procederet, a filio non distingueretur.

2.1. 1487 Si spiritussanctus

CONCLUSIONS ACCORDING TO THOMAS. On Pico's opposition to Thomas, see above, pp. 47–49 and passim. The order of these theses suggests that the first half or so were drawn from Thomas's commentary on the *Sentences*, with the rest inspired by his *De ente et essentia* and various Aristotelian commentaries. Only the last two conclusions were apparently drawn from the *Summa theologiae*. Pico here often opposes Thomas's views to those attributed in other sections to Albert, Scotus, Giles of Rome, and Averroes. He also includes theses to point out inconsistencies in Thomas's thought. A copy of Petrus Bergomensis's *Concordantiae conclusionum in quibus Thomas de Aquino videtur sibi contradicere* (1476) (Concordance of Conclusions in Which Thomas Aquinas Seems to Contradict Himself) was apparently in Pico's library (Kibre 1936: 203) and may have been used in compiling this section. Pico's theological conclusions (theses 4>1–29) and numerous other conclusions presented "according to his own opinion" are highly anti-Thomistic—clearly one of the reasons behind Pico's troubles with the Dominican order and the church.

FORTY-FIVE CONCLUSIONS ACCORDING TO THOMAS.

2.1. If the Spirit did not proceed from the Son, it would not be distinguished from the Son.

2.1. Starts a complex series on the distinction of Persons in the Christian Trinity, drawn from medieval commentaries on book 1 of Peter Lombard's *Sentences*. Cf. in the historical theses 3.1–2, 4.3, 5.2–4, 6.1, 6.4. Pico planned to resolve some of the conflicts in these theses in 1>2–3, 1>7. Pico's view of distinctions in the divine nature was extremely problematic. On the one hand, in his theological theses (cf. especially 4>5, 4>26–27 and notes) he tried to distance himself from such distinctions, arguing (in line with his *philosophia nova*) that God's nature was indivisible. On the other hand, he was constrained on dogmatic grounds to accept the basic notion of the Trinity, and in esoteric sections of his text he intended to link other distinctions made by Christian theologians in the divine nature to similar divisions in the *henads* of post-Plotinian Neo-Platonism (theses 24.1–55), the kabbalistic *sefirot* (theses 28.1–47, 11>1–72; cf. also the *Apology* [*Opera*, 173]), and other non-Christian traditions.

2.2. Processus spiritus sancti temporalis attenditur secundum dona gratiae gratum facientia.

2.3. Contingens rerum quae sunt, erunt, aut fuerunt, existentia ideo deo ab aeterno fuit infallibiliter nota, quia fuit aeternitati eius praesentialiter praeposita.

2.4. Contingentia ad utrumlibet futurorum cognitorum a deo simul stat cum infallibilitate diuinae scientiae.

2.5. Quodcunque contingens deus sciuit esse futurum, necessario sciuit illud esse futurum.

2.6. Ex diuina bonitate potest sumi ratio praedestinationis aliquorum et reprobationis aliorum, et sola diuina uoluntas est ratio quod istos reprobet et illos eligat in gloriam.

2.7. Licet dei uoluntas consequens semper impleatur, non tamen necessitatem rebus uolitis generaliter imponit.

2.8. Nec habens gratiam potest, etiam de potentia dei absoluta, deo non esse acceptus ad uitam aeternam, nec non habens esse acceptus.

2.9. Opus ab anima charitate formata elicitum meretur aeternam gloriam decondigno.

2.2. 1487 facientis

2.6. 1486, 1487 summi

2.2–9. On various sides of the divine omnipotence/free will problem. On the theses involving grace, cf. 4.1, 4.11, and 4.13 from Scotus, which involved bitter conflicts between the Domi-

2.2. The temporal procession of the Holy Spirit is extended with the gifts of grace making one gracious [to God].

2.3. The contingent existence of things that are, will be, or were, has been known infallibly to God for all eternity, because it was set out presentially in his eternity.

2.4. Contingency in respect to future events known by God is consistent with the infallibility of divine knowledge. (20)

2.5. Everything contingent that God knew would happen, he knew necessarily that that would happen.

2.6. The reason for the predestination of some and the rejection of others can be located in God's goodness, and the divine will alone is the reason why he rejects those and elects the others to glory.

2.7. Granted that God's will subsequent to an act is always fulfilled, it does not impose necessity universally on those things willed.

2.8. Neither can one who has grace, even through the absolute power of God, not be accepted by God to eternal life, nor can one who does not have it be accepted.

2.9. A work elicited from the soul shaped by charity merits eternal glory through its worth. (25)

---

nicans and Franciscans. Pico's own views on grace, free will, and salvation are expressed in 4>21–23 and are discussed above, pp. 39, 108–110. In general, Pico posited hierarchical distinctions between different levels of necessity and freedom; see the theses listed in 24.2 note.

2.10. Potuerunt tres personae diuinae simul suppositare unam naturam.

2.11. Virtutes morales et cardinales remanebunt in patria post resurrectionem. <1v/2r>

2.12. Beatitudo est essentialiter in actu intellectus.

Correlarium: Nec fruitio, nec aliquis actus uoluntatis, est essentialiter beatitudo.

2.13. Sacramenta noue legis sunt causa gratiae, non solum sine qua non, sed per quam.

2.14. Verum corpus Christi est in coelo localiter, in altari sacramentaliter.

2.15. Impassibilitas corporum post resurrectionem erit ex pleno dominio animae super corpus.

2.15. 1486 domino | 1487 dominio

2.10. Involves the limits of divine power. Cf. 2.8, 2.20, 4.13, 18.4. Thomas, Scotus, and other Latins adhering to what Pico referred to as the "common way of theologians" held that everything was in God's power that did not involve a logical contradiction. In *Sentences* 3, *d.* 1, *q.* 2, *art.* 4 Thomas thus argued that while it would be impossible for all three Persons to assume human nature simultaneously as *one* Person—since this contradicts what we mean by a "person"—no contradiction would be involved if God had assumed one nature as *three* Persons. Pico himself dispensed with the principle of noncontradiction in respect to the divine nature; see 2.32 note.

2.11. One of a diffuse set of theses on the virtues. Cf. 2.34, 4.10, 5.8, 5.10, 20.8–9, 20.11, 25.8–10. Pico planned to resolve conflicts here by positing hierarchical distinctions between different "modes" of the virtues. In 7a>70 he planned to use his numerological methods to resolve one such issue.

2.10. The three divine Persons were capable of simultaneously assuming one nature.

2.11. The moral and cardinal virtues will remain in heaven after the Resurrection.

2.12. Beatitude exists essentially in an act of intellect.

Corollary: Neither enjoyment, nor any act of will, is essentially beatitude.

2.13. The sacraments of the New Law are the cause of grace, not only as its necessary condition, but as its means.

2.14. The true body of Christ exists in heaven locally, on the altar sacramentally. (30)

2.15. The inability of bodies to suffer after the Resurrection will follow from the soul's full domination over the body.

2.12. First of a long series of theses on the relative powers of intellect and will in achieving mystical happiness or "beatitude." Also tied closely to the series on the "unity of intellect" problem that starts at 7.2–4. Pico represents St. Thomas as an intellectualist again in 2.19, 2.28, 2>74, and 5>46. Related historical theses, a few in conflict, include 3.3, 17.3, 20.7, 24.44, 28.44. For Pico's own views, cf., e.g., 3>43, 5>48, 7a>51 (to be resolved "through numbers"), and 10>23–24, 10>31, and 11>17 (expressed in highly symbolic language). On this issue, see my detailed discussion above, pp. 105–110.

2.13–14. "New Law" = New Testament. Other theses on the sacraments, not all in one series, include 4.14–15, 4>1–2, and 4>10. 2.14 is discussed at length in the *Apology*, in *Opera*, 183ff. See also 2.20 note.

2.15. In debates between Dominicans and Franciscans, this issue was closely tied to the question of Christ's *impassibilitas* or "inability to suffer," raised in 4.12 from Scotus. The *Apology* (*Opera*, 137; quoted above, pp. 48–49) charges Thomas with inconsistency on the latter issue.

2.16. Christus in ultimo iudicio iudicabit non solum in natura humana, sed etiam secundum naturam humanam.

2.17. Licet defendi possit quoquomodo creaturam posse creare, rationabilius tamen est credere potentiam creandi creaturae communicari non posse.

2.18. Aeuum est subiectiue in angelo beatiori.

2.19. Non potest esse peccatum in uoluntate, nisi sit defectus in ratione.

2.20. Non potest per dei potentiam idem corpus esse simul in diuersis locis.

2.21. Non est sub eadem specie angelorum plurificatio.

2.22. Deus per speciem non uidetur, sed ipse per suam essentiam intellectui applicatur ut species intelligibilis.

2.22. 1487 Deus in patria per speciem

2.16. This view was attacked by Scotus, who argued that judgment belonged to Christ more as God than as man. A link here was usually made in scholastic debates to the question of whether Christ possessed one or two concrete states of existence or *esse*—one Thomist-Scotist conflict that Pico planned to resolve in his debate. Cf. 4.4, 1>5.

2.17. The thesis pertains to emanationism, which Thomas viewed as heretical. Pico's opposing view is discussed in the *Apology* (*Opera*, 189) and above, pp. 20–21. Related historical theses include 7.5, 8.7–8, 11.1, 13.5, 26.3. In 7a>7 and 7a>26 Pico planned to discuss different aspects of emanationism through his "way of numbers."

2.18. On the syncretic origins of *aevum* or "aeviturnity"—an intermediate state between time and eternity—see above, p. 61 n. 9. "exists subjectively" = exists in a metaphysical substance. The concept of *aevum* was sometimes expanded into a larger hierarchical series of durational states, as we find, e.g., in 9>16–18. Related theses on time and *aevum* in the historical conclusions include 5.6, 24.50. In Pico's theses, cf. 5>37–40, 6>1. In 4>28 Pico invokes a double-truth to resolve a related issue.

2.19. See note 2.12. Cf. especially 5>46 from Pico's own opinions.

2.16. Christ in the Last Judgment will judge not only in human nature, but also according to human nature.

2.17. Granted the proposition that a creature can create can be defended in some way, it is more rational to believe that the power of creation cannot be communicated to a creature.

2.18. Aeviturnity exists subjectively in more beatified angels.

2.19. There can be no sin in the will, unless there is a defect in reason. (35)

2.20. Not even through God's power can the same body exist simultaneously in different places.

2.21. No multiplicity of angels exists in the same species.

2.22. God is not seen through an image, but through his essence he is accommodated to the intellect as an intelligible image.

2.20. On the limits of God's power, see 2.10 note. In *Sentences* 4, *d.* 10, *q. unica*, *art.* 1 we find Thomas tying this proposition to the view upheld in 2.14.

2.21. Cf. 2>44 and note. Since Thomas insisted on the total immateriality of angels, and since matter in his system provided the principle of individuation (thesis 2.26), each angel was necessarily a unique species unto itself. Pico rejected these views on the grounds of cosmic correspondence, arguing that matter existed in the angelic nature no less than in lower natures. In the *Commento* (Garin, *Scritti vari*, 472) he postponed discussion of the question of whether matter was the same on every level of reality; in the nine hundred theses he planned to settle the issue in his usual "modal" fashion, as we find in 2>68. In 7a>48 he intended to argue the same question proportionally through his "way of numbers." Cf. also 8.3, 14.1, and 11>67 on the nature of the matter in the *caelum*. Pico's Basel editors emended *plurificatio* in 2.21 to the more classically sounding *purificatio*, making it impossible to reconstruct Pico's views in this series.

2.22. Cf. Thomas *Sentences* 4, *d.* 49, *q.* 2, *art.* 1. Pico presumably planned to collate this thesis with others involving distinctions between God's transcendent and revealed natures. Cf., e.g., 28.35 and related theses on the Cabalistic "garment."

2.23. Vnum supra ens non addit nisi priuationem diuisionis.

2.24. Subiectum et propria passio realiter distinguuntur.

2.25. Forma generatur per accidens.

2.26. Materia signata est principium indiuiduationis.

2.27. Eadem est numero qualitas a principio alterationis usque ad finem.

2.28. Tota libertas est in ratione essentialiter.

2.29. In generatione substantiali fit resolutio usque ad materiam primam.

2.30. Ens dicit immediate decem conceptus ita inter se unitos ut non unius sint, sed ad unum.

2.23. Part of a key series on metaphysical unity. Related historical theses include 2.30, 3.7, 7.32, 15.2, 24.45. In Pico's own theses, cf. 2>55, 2>63–64, 3>1, 3>4, 3>29. In general, Pico argued that while several forms could enter into the composition of one being, these were ultimately fused in its undivided substance. This series is also tied to those beginning at 1.12 and 2.24. On the "being" and "one" issue in general, see above, pp. 25–29.

2.24. Starts a complex series on the substance/accident distinction. A *propria passio* = a property that is not part of the essence or formal definition of a subject or substance; it nevertheless belongs "inseparably" to that subject since it is in that subject alone that the property exists (a standard example was "snubness" in noses). On metaphysical grounds, Pico rejected all distinctions between "separable" and "inseparable" accidents; see above, pp. 99–100. Related theses include 2.35–36, 7.37, 9.8, and from Pico's opinions, 2>49–51, 2>78. Cf. also the theses on metaphysical unity listed in the previous note.

2.25. Related to the previous thesis. Cf. Thomas's *Commentary on the Metaphysics* 7.7, where we find that existence per se does not belong to forms, since forms are only found in composition with matter. Forms can thus only be said to be generated "accidentally." Cf. also 2.29, 2.43.

2.23. The one adds nothing to being except privation of division.

2.24. A subject and an accident proper to it are really distinguished. (40)

2.25. Form is generated accidentally.

2.26. Specified matter is the principle of individuation.

2.27. A quality remains the same in number from the beginning to the end of an alteration.

2.28. All freedom exists essentially in reason.

2.29. In the generation of substances decomposition occurs all the way to prime matter. (45)

2.30. Being immediately signifies ten concepts so interunited that they are not *of* one thing, but refer *to* one thing.

2.26. "Specified matter" or *materia signata* = matter determined and limited by form. Opposed to 4.6 from Scotus. On Pico's opposed view of individuation, see 3>20.

2.27. Cf. 1.5, 2>34, and notes. Thomas denied that limits to divisibility, or "natural *minima*," existed in qualities. He therefore claimed that alteration took place in a single movement without passing through a successive series of states. Pico's opposing views are suggested in 2>34.

2.28. See 2.12 note.

2.29. Thomas, who believed that matter could not exist without form (cf. 2.25, 2.43), and who posited only one substantial form in each created nature, claimed that the generation of any new substance necessitated the destruction of any previous form found in its matter. Pico upheld the opposing view that matter had a distinct form of its own preceding the substantial form. On the *forma corporeitatis* or "material form," cf. 16.1–2, 2>12, 2>70.

2.30. In the series on metaphysical unity. See 2.23 note.

2.31. Essentia et existentia in quolibet creato realiter distinguuntur.

2.32. De eadem re nullo modo actu distincta extra animam possunt uerificari contradictoria.

2.33. Materia nullum dicit actum entitatiuum positiuum.

2.34. Nulla uirtus moralis praeter iustitiam est subiectiue in uoluntate.

2.35. Haec propositio: Homo est risibilis, non est in secundo modo / dicendi per se. <2r/2v>

2.36. Duo accidentia solo numero differentia non sunt in eodem subiecto.

2.37. Grauia et leuia a nullo alio motore mouentur quam uel a generante uel a remouente prohibens.

2.38. Grauia potius seipsis, quam a seipsis mouentur.

2.31. Starts a long series. Whether Thomas in fact posited a "real distinction" between essence and existence was hotly debated since the late thirteenth century. The essence/existence controversy was especially difficult due to the many inconsistencies that existed in the use of these terms. Cf. here 7.35 from Averroes (which clashes with this thesis), 7.36, 8.6. Pico's formula in 3>11 was meant to reconcile such conflicts.

2.32. "distinct outside the soul" = distinguished in a real or extramental sense. Cf. Thomas *Commentary on the Metaphysics* 2.7–11, 11.5–6. At issue is the metaphysical form of the law of noncontradiction ("A cannot be both A and not-A"), one of the foundations of Aristotelian logic. Thomas argued that to predicate contradictions in a single object would eradicate all distinctions between separate beings. In Pico's view, however, contradictions coincided on higher levels of reality, partially invalidating the law of contradiction. Cf., e.g., 3>13–18, 3>20, and 7a>16–17 (the last of these argued through the "way of numbers"). See also my discussion above, p. 24.

2.33. Cf. 7.21, 8.6, 18.3, 2>52. The question involved whether the matter of created beings was or was not part of their formal essence or definition—an issue on which Pico sided with Thomas, Averroes, and Alexander of Aphrodisias vs. Avicenna.

2.31. Essence and existence are really distinguished in everything created.

2.32. Contradictions that are actually distinct outside the soul can in no way be verified of the same object.

2.33. Matter in entities does not signify any positive state of act.

2.34. No moral virtue except justice exists subjectively in the will. (50)

2.35. This proposition: *Man is capable of laughter*, is not in the second mode of speaking per se.

2.36. Two accidents differing only in number cannot exist in the same subject.

2.37. Heavy and light things are moved by no mover other than one imposing or removing a restraint.

2.38. Heavy things are moved more *with* themselves, than *by* themselves.

2.34. See 2.11 note. Opposed to 4.10 from Scotus, who placed the virtues in the will or "superior appetite."

2.35. On "modes of speaking" in general, see note 1.3. The second mode = predication of a *propria passio* or "proper accident" (explained in note 2.24). The thesis was apparently meant as a challenge to the Thomist school, since the formula *homo est risibilis* was Thomas's standard *example* of the "second mode of speaking."

2.36. Series starts at 2.24. Except in special cases like the Eucharist, Thomas argued that accidents drew their existence and unity from the substances in which they inhered. Hence to speak of two identical accidents in a single unifying subject implied a contradiction.

2.37–38. Cf. Thomas *Commentary on the Physics* 7.8. First of a series of theses on the Aristotelian principle that "everything that moves is moved by another." Related historical theses, most in conflict, include 4.18, 6.11, 7.12, 7.22. Cf. in Pico's theses 2>36–37, and 7a>44. A related series on celestial motion starts at 7.7–8.

2.39. Phantasma est agens secundarium et instrumentale in productione speciei intelligibilis.

2.40. Difficultas intelligendi et ex parte ipsius intellectus et ex parte ipsius intelligibilis prouenire potest.

2.41. Potentiae animae ab anima realiter distinguuntur.

2.42. Quiditates in particulari a methaphysico non considerantur.

2.43. Implicat contradictionem, materiam esse sine forma.

2.44. Non est ponenda in deo idea materiae primae.

2.45. Non sunt ponendae ideae generum.

2.39. "phantasms" = sensual images. Part of the series starting at 1.1. See that note.

2.40. Cf. 4.19–20, 7.25, 11.4. The question on difficulties in understanding arose in exegeses of *Metaphysics* 2.1, which (translating the most common medieval Latin version) reads: "But perhaps, since a difficulty exists in two modes, its cause is not in things but in us. For just as the eyes of a bat ["owl" in Pico, see 7.25 note] stand to the sun, so too the intellect of our soul stands to those things that in all of nature are most evident." This passage was the *locus classicus* for scholastic discussions of the limits of human understanding. The insignificance of those limits for Pico is illustrated in 3>40, which provides his commentary on thesis 7.25 from Averroes.

2.39. A phantasm is a secondary and instrumental agent in the production of an intelligible image. (55)

2.40. Difficulties in understanding can originate both from the part of the intellect and from the part of the intelligible object.

2.41. The powers of the soul are really distinguished from the soul.

2.42. Individual quiddities are not considered by the metaphysician.

2.43. For matter to exist without form implies a contradiction.

2.44. The idea of prime matter should not be posited in God. (60)

2.45. Ideas of genera should not be posited.

2.41. Series starts at 1.12. See that note.

2.42. See 1.14–15 note. There is a further tie with 4.7–8 from Scotus; cf. also 2>5–6.

2.43. Cf. 2.25, 2.29, and notes.

2.44. Linked to the preceding thesis. Cf. *Summa* 1*a*.15, 3 *ad* 3: One can argue that the idea of matter exists in God, but not in a distinct way from the idea of the composite of matter and form.

2.45. Drawn from the same source as the previous thesis. Series starts at 1.2.

CONCLVSIONES SECVNDUM FRANCISCVM NVMERO .VIII.

3.1. Ideo haec est falsa: Essentia generat, quia essentia est ultimate abstracta, et generat formaliter praedicatur.

3.2. Potest uideri essentia sine personis, et una persona sine alia.

3.3. Voluntas potest non frui ostenso obiecto fruibili.

3.4. Ens denominatiue dicitur de deo.

3.5. Quiditates habent ab aeterno suum esse formale a se, non ab extrinseco.

3.6. Nulla diffinitio adaequat diffinitum.

CONCLUSIONS ACCORDING TO FRANCIS. Francis of Meyronnes (d. after 1328), the "prince of Scotists." Most of these theses were meant to illustrate the "civil warfare" among the Franciscans. In his *conclusiones conciliantes* (theses 1>1ff.) Pico suggests that the conflicts between Thomas and Scotus were exaggerated by their disciples, so Francis's placement between the two in Pico's theses has apparent symbolic significance. Pico was drawing here from book 1 of Francis's commentary on the *Sentences* and conceivably from the *Tractatus de formalitatibus*, a compilation drawn from Francis's works. Copies of both works were in Pico's library. In 2>60 Pico sharply criticizes one of the logical concepts put forward by Francis.

3.1–2. "*The essence*" = the abstract nature of God considered independently of the Persons. Pico apparently planned to correlate God's "essence" with the kabbalistic *Ein-Sof* and similar concepts in pagan traditions. Cf. 2.1 note, 11>4 note. In a more conventional sense, however, Pico denied that God had an "essence"; see note to 2>47–48.

3.3. Series starts at 2.12. Pico's Basel editors added a gratuitous *non* to this thesis ("The will is not able not to enjoy"), turning Francis into an intellectualist. Cf. especially 4.5 from Scotus.

EIGHT CONCLUSIONS ACCORDING TO FRANCIS.

3.1. This is false: *The essence generates,* because the essence is totally abstract, and *generates* is predicated formally.

3.2. The essence can be seen without the Persons, and one Person without another.

3.3. The will is able not to enjoy when shown an enjoyable object.

3.4. Being is predicated of God in a derivative way. (65)

3.5. Quiddities possess their formal existence from eternity from themselves, not from something outside themselves.

3.6. No definition is adequate to the thing defined.

3.4. To predicate *denominative* ("through naming") in this context = to predicate something accidentally or derivatively, as opposed to substantially; see Pico's use of this term in *Opera*, 282. The thesis is opposed to 4.7 from Scotus.

3.5. "Quiddities" = literally the "whatnesses" of things, referring in Francis to the ideas in the mind of God. Cf. Francis *Sent.* 1, *d.* 42, *q.* 2; *d.* 46, *q.* 3. Opposed to 4.2 from Scotus; see my discussion above, p. 54. Thesis 3.5 is also strongly linked to 5.9 from Henry of Ghent. Other common scholastic uses of "quiddity" referred to material essences (e.g., 2.42) or to the ideas reflected in "intelligences" (e.g., 7.36). Pico intended to distinguish these senses hierarchically in his debate. 11>58 (see note) may possibly throw further light on Pico's views on this issue.

3.6. One of several theses with strong nominalistic overtones. Cf. 7.41, 13.1, 2>2–3, 2>46, 3>2–7, and my notes to the last of these theses.

3.7. Pluralitas formalitatum stat cum idemtitate reali.

3.8. Esse non est de quiditate dei, sed dicitur de eo in secundo modo.

3.8. 1487 Esse non de est quiditate

3.7. Series starts at 2.23. A "formality" or "formal distinction" was a Scotist compromise between a "real distinction," pertaining to things that were viewed as being metaphysically separable, and a "rational distinction," pertaining to things said to be separable only in the realm of thought. As a compromise position, formal distinctions were said to be metaphysically real but inseparable from the objects in which they were found even by God. Formalities were invoked by the Scotists and later scholastics as reconciliative devices to harmonize texts that emphasized

3.7. A plurality of formalities is consistent with real identity.

3.8. Existence does not belong to the quiddity of God, but is predicated of him in the second mode.

God's unity with others positing distinctions in his nature (as in the Trinity), to reconcile works stressing the unity of the soul with others emphasizing its individual powers, and so on. For Pico's views, see theses and notes 2>66, 3>56, and 3>58.

3.8. For the second mode of speaking or predication, see notes 2.35, 2.24. God's *esse* or existence here is idiosyncratically represented as a "proper accident" of his nature—a view clashing with ideas associated with Scotus. Cf. Francis *Sent.* 1, proem, *q.* 6.

CONCLVSIONES SECVNDVM IOHANEM SCOTVM NVMERO .XXII.

4.1. Charitas non est distinctus habitus ab habitu gratiae, quo mediante spiritus sanctus animam inhabitat.

4.2. Idea lapidis non est aliud quam lapis productus a diuino intellectu in esse intelligibili, quod est esse secundum quid, existens in mente diuina sicut cognitum in cognoscente.

4.3. Qui dixerit personas in diuinis absolutis proprietatibus distingui, catholicae ueritati non repugnabit. <2v/3r>

4.4. In Christo fuerunt duo esse.

4.5. Praxis est operatio alterius potentiae ab intellectu, apta nata conformiter elici rationi rectae ad hoc: ut sit recta.

CONCLUSIONS ACCORDING TO SCOTUS. Theses here are opposed to others from Francis, Henry of Ghent, and especially St. Thomas. Pico meant to resolve some of these conflicts in his "paradoxical reconciliative conclusions." Unless otherwise noted, references are to the *Ordinatio* (Scotus's commentary on the *Sentences*) in the incomplete Vatican edition of his *Opera omnia*.

4.1. Cf. 2.9 from Thomas. A "habit" here = a modification of a substance that predisposes it to act in a particular way. The apparent deterministic implications of this thesis are modified in 4.22 (see note). Cf. *Ord.* 1, *d.* 17, *p.* 1, *q.* 1–2.

4.2. Cf. *Ord.* 1, *d.* 35, *q. unica*, e.g., *n.* 32. Opposed to 3.5 from Francis. Discussed above, p. 54. See also 5.9.

TWENTY-TWO CONCLUSIONS ACCORDING TO JOHN SCOTUS.

4.1. Charity is not a distinct habit from the habit of grace, through the mediation of which the Holy Spirit inhabits the soul. (70)

4.2. The idea of a stone is nothing but the stone produced by the divine intellect in intelligible existence, which is existence in a relational sense, existing in the divine mind just as the known in the knower.

4.3. Whoever says that Persons in God are distinguished by absolute properties will not contradict the Catholic truth.

4.4. In Christ there were two existences.

4.5. A practical act is an operation of a different power from that of the intellect, suited by nature to be elicited by right reason in conformity to this: that it be right.

4.3. Series starts at 2.1. In scholastic Latin, the phrase *in divinis* is often best translated simply as "in God." On this, cf. Deferrari and Barry (1948: 333–34). For this thesis, cf. Scotus *Ord.* 1, *d.* 8, *p.* 1, *q.* 4. In Scotus, "absolute properties" are formally distinct (see note to 3.7). The Thomists attacked Scotus on this issue, arguing that distinctions between Persons could only be characterized as "relations." Pico planned to reconcile the two schools on this issue in 1>2.

4.4. Cf. Scotus *Ord.* 3, *d.* 6, *q.* 1 (Wadding edition), and thesis 2.16 from Thomas and note. Since Christ united two natures or distinct essences in one Person, did he possess two *esse* or existences as well? Pico planned to reconcile Scotists and Thomists on this problem in 1>5. Some clues to his approach can be gathered from the *Apology*, in *Opera*, 187.

4.5. Tied to the series beginning at 2.12. Pico adopts similar technical language in 2>25.

4.6. Vnumquodque indiuiduum est indiuiduum per propriam differentiam indiuidualem, quae dicitur hecheitas.

4.7. Ens dicitur de deo et creatura uniuoce in quid.

4.8. Ens de suis passionibus et ultimis differentiis quiditatiue non praedicatur.

4.9. In Christo non fuit scientia acquisita.

4.10. In appetitu superiore ponendae sunt uirtutes.

4.11. Gratia est subiectiue in uoluntate, non in essentia animae.

4.12. Corpus Christi ex se fuit impassibile.

4.13. De potentia dei absoluta possibile est culpam originalem deleri sine infusione gratiae.

4.14. Post passionem Christi potuerunt cerimonialia ueteris legis sine peccato obseruari.

4.6. "haecceity" = the "thisness" of something, a "formal distinction" that differentiates each created individual from all others. See 2.26 for St. Thomas's view of individuation and 3>20 for Pico's.

4.7–8. Cf. *Ord.* 1, *d.* 3, *p.* 1, *q.* 1–2, especially *n.* 26ff.; *q.* 3, especially *n.* 131ff. Reflects the most important Thomist-Scotist conflict that Pico planned to resolve at Rome. Scotus interpreted Thomas as holding that metaphysics dealt exclusively with "individual quiddities"—a view that for Scotus undercut all metaphysical knowledge, which for him concerned being *qua* being. Scotus consequently argued that the being of God and creatures was "univocal" (identical) and not merely "analogical," as Thomas claimed. The fact that for Scotus the resultant concept of being was transcendental—devoid of all particular determinations—is reflected in the formula in 4.8. Pico's rejection of Scotus's reading of Thomas is suggested in 2.42 and 2>5, and in 1>14 he planned to reveal the hidden agreement of the two theologians. These two theses are also tied to conflicts involving Francis of Meyronnes in 3.4 and 3.8 and Henry of Ghent in 5.9.

4.6. Each individual is individual through its own individual difference, which is called its haecceity. (75)

4.7. Being is predicated of God and creature in the same way in respect to its quiddity.

4.8. Being is not predicated quidditatively of their properties and specific differences.

4.9. There was no acquired knowledge in Christ.

4.10. The virtues should be posited in the superior appetite.

4.11. Grace exists subjectively in the will, not in the essence of the soul. (80)

4.12. Christ's body was incapable by nature of suffering.

4.13. It is possible through the absolute power of God for original sin to be eradicated without an infusion of grace.

4.14. After the Passion of Christ the ceremonies of the Old Law could be observed without sin.

4.9. Cf. *Ord.* 3, *d.* 14, *q.* 3 (Wadding edition). Another issue dividing the Scotists and Thomists. Cf. Thomas *Summa* 3*a*.11–12. In the *Apology* (*Opera*, 137; quoted above, pp. 48–49), Pico charged Thomas with inconsistency on this topic.

4.10. Opposed to 2.34 from Thomas.

4.11. Cf. *Ord.* 2, *d.* 26, *q. unica* (Wadding edition). Thomas upholds the opposite view in *Sent.* 2, *d.* 26, *q.* 1, *art.* 3.

4.12. Cf. 2.15 and note.

4.13. Opposed to 2.8 from Thomas. On the limits of divine power, see 2.10 note.

4.14. Cf. *Ord.* 4, *d.* 3, *q.* 4, *n.* 13–20 (Wadding edition). "Old Law" = Old Testament. In opposition to Thomas, e.g., *Summa* 1*a*2*ae*.103, 4.

4.15. Per haec uerba precise (Hoc est corpus meum), non expressis uerbis precedentibus, scilicet pridie quam pateretur, non potest consecrari.

4.16. Relatio creaturae ad deum est idem realiter fundamento, distincta formaliter et ex natura rei.

4.17. Quaelibet alia relatio a fundamento realiter distinguitur.

4.18. Aliquid potest mouere seipsum de actu uirtuali ad actum formalem.

4.19. Actus intelligendi ab obiecto et intellectu tanquam duobus agentibus partialibus, ut quod causatur.

4.20. Actus intelligendi nobiliori modo causatur ab intellectu quam ab obiecto, quodcunque sit obiectum, modo non sit beatificum.

4.21. Substantia non cognoscitur per speciem propriam.

4.22. Habitus actum producit ut causa partialis effectiua.

4.15. 1486 predentibus.scilicet | 1487 precedentibus scilicet

---

4.15. For other theses on the sacraments, see 2.13–14 note. Cf. especially 4>10 from Pico's theological theses. The thesis illustrates what from a modern perspective can be considered the word magic in the Eucharist. For Pico's views on the magical power of language, see, e.g., theses 9>19ff.

4.16–17. Raised by Scotus in a long discussion vs. Henry of Ghent in *Ord.* 2, *d.* 1, *q.* 4–5. The thesis begins an elaborate series on the nature of "relations" in scholastic philosophy. In Pico's historical theses, cf. 5.11–13, 6.1, 7.24, 7.39, 13.1 (all from the Latins or Arabs). The issue involved a delicate theological problem: The existence of creatures depends on their relations with God, but how can such relations exist without detracting from God's transcendence? In 4.16, Scotus resolves this problem by invoking a "formal distinction" (see note 3.7). Pico's strategy in resolving this issue is suggested in the technical language of 2>62 (see note). Another problem was epistemological: Do the relations between things posited in the realm of thought

4.15. Through these precise words, *This is my body*, with the preceding words unexpressed, namely, *On the day before he suffered*, the Consecration cannot take place.

4.16. The relation of a creature to God is identical in a real sense to the grounds of that relation, but is distinct formally and viewed from that creature's nature. (85)

4.17. Every other relation is distinguished in a real sense from its grounds.

4.18. Anything is capable of moving itself from a state of virtual act to formal act.

4.19. An act of understanding is caused by the object and the intellect as though by two partial agents.

4.20. An act of understanding is caused in a nobler way by the intellect than by the object, whatever that object is, unless it is beatific.

4.21. Substance is not known through a special image. (90)

4.22. A habit produces a state of act as a partial effective cause.

---

coincide with the metaphysical foundation of those relations—with their grounds or *fundamentum*—or are the grounds and those relations distinct (and relations hence mere "distinctions of reason")? Pico's quasi-nominalist views here are suggested in 2>46 and 3>33.

4.18. Series on motion starts at 2.37–38 from Thomas (in conflict with this thesis). "virtual act" = state of potentiality.

4.19–20. Cf. 2.40 and note.

4.21. Pico's opposing view is expressed in 3>57.

4.22. Cf. *Ord.* 1, *d.* 17, *p.* 1, *q.* 1–2, *n.* 32–45 and 69–70. Involves the issue of free will. A habit can act as a "second" but not as a "first" cause of a moral action, otherwise that action would not be free. The thesis hence qualifies the sense of 4.1.

CONCLVSIONES SECVNDVM HENRICVM GANDAVENSEM NVMERO .XIII.

5.1. Datur lumen superius lumine fidei, in quo Theologi uident ueritates theologicae scientiae.

5.2. Paternitas est principium generandi in patre. <3r/3v>

5.3. Processiones distinguuntur in diuinis penes intellectum et uoluntatem.

5.4. Ista propositio non est concedenda: essentia est pater filii.

5.5. Demones et animae peccatrices patiuntur ab igne, in quantum calidus est, afflictione eiusdem rationis cum ea qua affliguntur corpora.

5.6. Operationes angelorum mensurantur tempore discreto.

5.7. Angeli intelligunt per habitum scientialem sibi connaturalem.

5.8. Irascibilis et concupiscibilis ita distinguuntur in appetitu superiori sicut in inferiori.

Section title. 1487 henricum gandanensem

5.4. colon retained from 1486 edition

CONCLUSIONS ACCORDING TO HENRY OF GHENT. Pico's library contained both major works of Henry (d. 1293)—his *Summa theologica* and *Quodlibeta*—and apparently a compilation of his writings. See the index in Kibre (1936).

5.1. One of numerous theses on illuminationism. Cf., e.g., 6.7, 7.1, 4>16, 5>3. Cf. also 10.1, 11.2 and note.

5.2–4. Series starts at 2.1.

5.5. Commenting on Peter Lombard *Sentences* 4, *d.* 44, *q.* 6–7. Pico's interest here was presumably in the metaphysical correspondences between physical and spiritual operations.

THIRTEEN CONCLUSIONS ACCORDING TO HENRY OF GHENT.

5.1. A light exists superior to the light of faith, in which theologians see the truths of theological science.

5.2. Paternity is the principle of generation in the Father.

5.3. Processions are distinguished in God according to intellect and will.

5.4. This proposition must not be conceded: The essence is the Father of the Son. (95)

5.5. Demons and sinful souls suffer from a fire, insofar as it is hot, by an affliction of the same proportions as that by which bodies are afflicted.

5.6. Operations of angels are measured in discrete time.

5.7. Angels understand through a knowing habit that is co-natural with them.

5.8. The irascible and sensual passions are distinguished in the superior appetite just as in the inferior.

5.6. Series starts at 2.18. Cf. especially 6>1. Pico discusses this issue in the *Apology* (*Opera,* 128).

5.7. A *habitus connaturalis* = a habit or infused property created simultaneously with a nature but not included in its formal definition or essence. One of a number of closely related theses on the knowledge of angels (or intelligences, intellects, the intellectual nature, angelic mind, etc.). In the *Commento* (Garin, *Scritti vari,* 480), Pico boasted that he would resolve this issue in his Roman "council" and in his planned commentary on Plato's *Symposium*. Cf., e.g., 6.7, 7.17, 18.7, and in Pico's own theses, 5>41 and 7a>28–29 (using the "way of numbers").

5.8. Cf. note 2.11. "irascible"/"sensual" passions = two broad classes of emotions, the first referring to passions including fear, hope, sorrow, anger, etc., the second to passions involving sensual desire. Cf. 2.34, 4.10, 25.9, 7a>70 (using the "way of numbers").

5.9. Habere aliquiditatiuam et diffinibilem realitatem commune est figmentis et non figmentis.

5.10. Amicitia est uirtus.

5.11. Ratitudo formaliter cuiuslibet creati est respectus.

5.12. Ad hoc, ut sit mutuitas realis relationis, requiritur quod fundamentum ex sua natura ordinetur ad aliud, tanquam ad suam perfectionem.

5.13. Relatio non distinguitur a fundamento realiter.

5.9. See 4.7–8 and note. For an overview of this conflict between Scotus and Henry, see Gilson (1955: 449). There is also a strong link here with 3.5 from Francis of Meyronnes.

5.9. To possess a quidditative and definable reality is common to created and uncreated things. (100)

5.10. Friendship is a virtue.

5.11. The rectitude of everything created is formally a relation.

5.12. For mutuality to exist in a real relation, it is required that the grounds of that relation from its nature be subordinated to another, as it were to its perfection.

5.13. A relation is not distinguished in a real sense from its grounds.

5.10. Cf. note 2.11.

5.11–13. Series starts at 4.16–17. See my note to those theses.

CONCLVSIONES SECVNDVM EGIDIVM ROMANVM NVMERO .XI.

6.1. Potentia generandi in diuinis_nec est essentia diuina precise et absolute sumpta, nec relatio uel proprietas, nec constitutum ex ambobus, nec alterum istorum cum inclusione alterius, sed est essentia cum modo relatiuo.

6.2. Theologia nec est practica nec speculatiua, sed affectiua.

6.3. Deus sub ratione glorificatoris est subiectum in Theologia.

6.4. Pater et filius non solum duo spirantes, sed etiam duo spiratores dici possunt.

6.5. Angeli non fuerunt creati in gratia.

6.6. Ideo angelus est obstinatus et inpenitens, quia subtracti sunt ei diuini impetus speciales.

6.7. Superior angelus illuminat inferiorem_non quia ei uel obiectum presentet luminosum, uel quod in se est unitum illi particulariset et diuidat, sed quia inferioris intellectum confortat et fortificat. <3v/4r>

CONCLUSIONS ACCORDING TO GILES OF ROME. Giles or Aegidius of Rome (ca. 1247–1316), official theologian of the Augustinians. Pico here draws directly or indirectly from Giles's commentary on the *Sentences* and from several of his Aristotelian commentaries, most of which were found in Pico's library. A number of these conclusions oppose St. Thomas, whose lectures Giles reportedly attended at the University of Paris from 1269 until 1272.

6.1. See notes 2.1, 4.16–17.

6.2–3. Starts a series on the formal object of theology. Cf. 1>4 (reconciling Thomas, Scotus, and Giles), 2>27, 3>8, 7a>37 (using Pico's *via numerorum*), and 11>3 (involving the Cabala). Formal discussion of this question derived from Peter Lombard *Sentences* 1, prologue.

ELEVEN CONCLUSIONS ACCORDING TO GILES OF ROME.

6.1. The power of generation in God is not the divine essence taken separately and absolutely, nor a relation or property, nor constituted from both, nor one of those with the inclusion of the other, but is the essence in a relational mode. (105)

6.2. Theology is neither practical nor speculative, but affective.

6.3. God under the aspect of glorifier is the subject in theology.

6.4. The Father and the Son can be called not only two *who spirate*, but also two *spirators*.

6.5. Angels were not created in grace.

6.6. The [fallen] angel is obstinate and impenitent, because specific divine forces were withdrawn from it. (110)

6.7. A superior angel illuminates an inferior not because it presents to it a luminous object, or because it particularizes and divides for the other what is united in itself, but because it strengthens and fortifies the intellect of the inferior.

6.4. Series starts at 2.1. "*spirantes*"/"*spiratores*" (from *spirare*, to breathe) = terms applied to the first two Persons of the Trinity as they gave rise to the procession of the Holy Spirit. St. Thomas, unlike Giles, had used the participle *spirantes* in this context but not the substantive *spiratores*, since he believed that this implied too strong a distinction between the Persons. The conflict illustrates nicely the metaphysical importance that could be attached to minute grammatical distinctions in scholastic traditions.

6.5–6. Again anti-Thomistic. Cf. Thomas *Summa* 1*a*.62, 3 and 1*a*.64, 2.

6.7. On illuminationism, see note 5.7.

6.8. Sensus gustus, ut gustus est, non solum saporabile, sed humidum percipit.

6.9. Calor, si sit etiam separatus, ignem generare poterit.

6.10. Ad hoc, quod aliqua scientia alteri non subalternetur, sufficit quod faciat reductionem ad per se nota in suo genere abstractionis.

6.11. Dato uacuo, si aliquid in eo moueatur, in instanti mouebitur.

6.9. 1486 seperatus

6.8. Commenting on Aristotle *De anima* 2.10. Cf. 13.4, 2>59 and note.

6.9. Commenting on Aristotle *De generatione et corruptione* 1.10, whose sense was much disputed. Apparently tied to 2>67, which concerns the same text.

6.10. The premodern antecedent of Gödel's second theorem, arising from commentaries on Aristotle *Posterior Analytics* 1.9–10. The idea was that an interlocked hierarchy of sciences existed, with each operating independently from its superiors only when it restricted its questions to issues of a derivative sort. Cf. 7.14 from Averroes, 12.2 and note.

6.8. The sense of taste, since it is taste, not only perceives what has flavor, but what is moist.

6.9. Heat, even if separated, can generate fire.

6.10. For any science not to be subordinated to another, it is sufficient that it be reduced to those things known per se in its own genus of abstraction.

6.11. Given a vacuum, if anything should be moved in it, it will be moved instantaneously. (115)

6.11. Series begins at 2.37–38. Again opposed to Aquinas, who claimed that if a vacuum existed a heavy body would move at a finite speed to its "natural place." In Giles's view, since according to Aristotle velocity was proportional to applied force and inversely proportional to resistence, when the resisting medium was removed, motion would occur instantaneously. For an analysis of Giles's view with relevant texts, see Moody (1975: 161–88).

¶Conclusiones secundum doctrinam Arabum qui ut plurimum peripateticos se profitentur: Auenroem, Auicennam, Alpharabium, Auempacem, Isaac, Abumaron, Moysem, et Maumeth.

CONCLVSIONES SECVNDVM AVENROEM NVMERO .XLI.

7.1. Possibile est prophetia in somnis per illustrationem intellectus agentis super animam nostram.

CONCLUSIONS ACCORDING TO THE ARABS. How much Arabic Pico knew when the nine hundred theses were published is uncertain, although he was then studying that language, along with Hebrew and Aramaic, with Flavius Mithridates. Pico's primary expert on Arabic thought was Elia del Medigo, who supplied Pico with much of the material for this section. For a recent summary of Pico's ties with Elia, with updated bibliography, see Mahoney (1997). In line with his views of history, Pico found less harmony in Arabic thought than in more ancient *gentes,* as we find in the many conflicting theses in this section. The order of "sect leaders" given here was apparently intended to underscore internal conflicts in the Arabic "nation."

CONCLUSIONS ACCORDING TO AVERROES. Although Pico on the whole admired Averroes, earlier historians like Nardi who labeled Pico an Averroist seriously overstated the case. Cf. Pico's complaint concerning heretical doctrines in Averroes's thought, quoted above, p. 9. Most of the theses in this section involve well-known "doubtful points" arising out of interpretation of Averroes's Aristotelian commentaries, most of which Pico knew in medieval

¶Conclusions according to the doctrine of the Arabs, who for the most part profess to be Periphatetics: Averroes, Avicenna, al-Farabi, Avempace, Isaac, Abumaron, Moses, and Mohammed.

FORTY-ONE CONCLUSIONS ACCORDING TO AVERROES.

7.1. Prophecy in dreams is possible through the illumination of the active intellect over our soul.

Latin translations. Others were drawn from the epitomes on technical issues in Arabic philosophy compiled for Pico by Elia del Medigo, or from Elia's translations for Pico (from Hebrew versions) of works like Averroes's *Quaestiones in Priora Analytica*. Some sources relevant to Elia, printed with works by the fourteenth-century Averroist John of Jandun, are found in *Joannis de Gandavo Summi Averroiste subtilissime questiones in octo libros Aristotelis De physico auditu . . . his annectuntur questiones Helie Hebrei Cretensis De primo motore, De efficientia mundi, De esse et essentia et uno, eiusdem annotationes in plurima dicta Commentatoris* (Venice, 1544). For the location of manuscripts of Elia's works used by Pico, some with notes in Pico's handwriting, see Kristeller (1965: 117, 118–19, 120). For other sources, see Mahoney (1997).

7.1. Originates in commentaries on Aristotle *De divinatione per somnum*. Cf. 21.4–6 and 27.7. For other theses on illuminationism, see note 5.1. A close study of the issue of dreams and prophecy in medieval and Renaissance times is needed.

7.2. Vna est anima intellectiua in omnibus hominibus.

7.3. Foelicitas ultima hominis est cum continuatur intellectus agens possibili_ut forma; quam continuationem et latini alii quos legi et maxime Iohanes de Gandauo peruerse et erronee intellexit, qui non solum in hoc, sed ferme in omnibus quaesitis Philosophiae, doctrinam Auenrois corrupit omnino et deprauauit.

7.4. Possibile est tenendo unitatem intellectus, animam meam, ita particulariter meam ut non sit mihi communis cum omnibus, remanere post mortem.

7.5. Quodlibet abstractum dependet a primo abstracto in triplici genere causae, formalis, finalis, et efficientis.

7.6. Impossibile est eandem speciem ex propagatione et ex putrefactione generari.

7.3. 1486 Johanes de Gandago | 1487 Johannes de gandago

7.2–4. On the problem of the "unity of intellect," cf. 3>67–69 and my discussion above, pp. 112–14. Arises from commentary on *De anima* 3.5, for medieval scholastics probably the most hotly debated Aristotelian text. Discussion of 7.4 would have also involved theses 17.9 from Simplicius and 18.1 from Alexander of Aphrodisias. Cf. also 7.3 with 20.7 from Plotinus and with 3>43 from Pico's own opinion. The series can also be linked to the series on the intellect/will and mystic happiness starting at 2.12. "John of Jandun" (1286–ca. 1328) = the most important commentator on the Commentator. John, who is attacked again in 2>36, was criticized earlier by Elia del Medigo and by later philosophers like Agostino Nifo influenced by Pico. For discussion and references, see Mahoney (1997). Long after Pico's death, Nifo attributed to Pico a resolution of the unity of intellect problem linked to the works of Albert the Great (Mahoney 1992, 1997: 143ff.). The metaphorical language that Nifo ascribes to Pico is not closely related to anything in the theses, although the underlying approach that Nifo discusses can be roughly tied to 3>67–69.

7.2. The intellective soul is one in all men.

7.3. Man's greatest happiness is achieved when the active intellect is conjoined to the possible intellect as its form. This conjunction has been perversely and incorrectly understood by the other Latins whom I have read, and especially by John of Jandun, who not only in this, but in almost all questions in philosophy, totally corrupted and twisted the doctrine of Averroes.

7.4. It is possible, upholding the unity of the intellect, that my soul, so particularly mine that it is not shared by me with all, remains after death.

7.5. Everything abstract depends on what is first abstract in the threefold genus of formal, final, and efficient causes. (120)

7.6. It is impossible for the same species to be generated from propagation and from putrefaction.

7.5. "what is first abstract" for Averroes = God, who created the individual intelligences that for Averroes served as the ends of motion of the celestial spheres. In the series on emanationism listed in 2.17 note. Opposed especially to 8.7–8 from Avicenna, with whose views Pico identified on this question.

7.6. "putrefaction" = decaying matter. Opposed to 8.5 from Avicenna. The thesis arises from discussion of Aristotle *De generatione animalium* 3.11 and related texts.

7.7. Deus primum mobile non solum ut finis, sed ut uerum efficiens et proprius motor mouet.

7.8. Quilibet motor coeli est anima sui orbis, faciens cum eo magis unum substantialiter, quam fiat ex anima bouis et sua materia.

Correlarium: Anima coeli prius dat suo orbi esse nobile et perfectum quam ei det motum. <4r/4v>

7.9. Coelum est corpus simplex, non compositum ex materia et forma.

7.10. Tres modi per se sunt ad demonstrationem utiles: primus, secundus et quartus.

7.11. In omni demonstratione praeterquam in demonstratione simpliciter fieri potest circulatio.

7.12. Grauia et leuia mouent se per accidens mouendo medium per se.

7.10. 1486 utiles.Primus.Secundus

7.7–8. "*primum mobile*" = the first movable body, the highest celestial sphere. Begins a series on the motion of the "heavens" or *caelum*. Closely related theses include 15.1, 15.4, 18.2, 18.5, 2>19, and 2>36–37. The issue throughout the series is whether "God himself," "separate intelligences," or "celestial souls" were responsible for the motion of the heavens. In 2>19 and 2>36 from his own theses Pico not surprisingly makes room for all three views. The series starting at 7.7–8 is closely related to the series on the nature of matter in the *caelum* that begins at 7.9 and to the general series on motion starting at 2.37–38. It is interesting to note that Pico did not include any opinions on celestial motion from the Latins, whose views on this issue he held in contempt (cf. 2>36–37).

7.7. God moves the *primum mobile* not only as its end, but as its true efficient and proper mover.

7.8. The mover of each heaven is the soul of its sphere, creating something more substantially one with it than is made from a cow's soul and its matter.

Corollary: The soul of each heaven gives noble and perfect existence to its sphere before it gives it motion.

7.9. Heaven is a simple body, not one composed out of matter and form.

7.10. Three per se modes are useful in demonstration: the first, second, and fourth. (125)

7.11. Circularity can occur in every type of demonstration except simple demonstration.

7.12. Heavy and light things move themselves accidentally, moving the medium per se.

7.9. Cf. in this series 7.13, 7.40, 8.3, 14.1, 15.1, 23.4, 7a>10, and 11>67. The point of 7.9, drawn from Averroes *De substantia orbis* 1–2 (or from Elia del Medigo's commentary on that work, which was written for Pico), is not to deny a material or formal element to the *caelum* but to claim that their fusion is too close for us to speak of them as separate entities. Cf. 2>55.

7.10–11. Part of a diverse set of theses on demonstration originating in various chapters of Aristotle's logical treatises. For "per se modes" (of "speaking" or "predication"), see 1.3 note, which explains the fourth or "causal" mode. The first and second modes refer respectively to the properties that define an object and to that object's "proper accidents" (see notes 2.24, 2.35). Other related theses include 9.1, 9.4–5, 19.4, 19.5, and, from Pico's opinions, 2>32, 2>33, 3>48, 7a>59. Note that Pico's only mention in these theses of the Latins, whose views on logic he sharply criticized, was negative (thesis 2>33).

7.12. Series starts at 2.37–38. See my note to those theses.

7.13. Coeli non sunt idem in genere, diuersi in specie, ut credidit Auicenna.

7.14. Nulla scientia probat suum subiectum esse, nec partem principalem sui subiecti.

7.15. Vniuersalia sunt ex parte rei in potentia tantum, actu autem per operationem animae.

7.16. Dimensiones interminate sunt coeternae materiae, praecedentes in ea quamlibet formam substantialem.

7.17. Quaelibet intelligentia praeter primam non intelligit nisi primam.

7.18. Nulla est uia ad probandum simpliciter abstractum esse, praeter uiam aeternitatis motus.

7.19. Quicquid est in genere_est corruptibile.

7.20. Subiectum Methaphysicae est ens in eo quod ens.

7.21. Diffinitiones substantiarum naturalium_materiam non dicunt nisi consecutiue.

7.13. Series starts at 7.9. Can also be correlated with the series on genus/species starting at 1.2.

7.14. Series starts at 6.10.

7.15. Series starts at 1.1.

7.16. Part of a conflict between Averroes and St. Thomas to be reconciled at 1>13. In the *Apology* (*Opera*, 137; quoted above, pp. 48–49), Pico cited this as one of many issues on which Aquinas was inconsistent. Pico also planned to deal with this problem in 7a>23 using his "way of numbers."

7.17. "the first" in Averroes = God. Cf. 5.7 and note.

7.13. The heavens are not the same in genus, different in species, as Avicenna believed.

7.14. No science proves that its subject exists, nor the principal part of its subject.

7.15. Universals exist in things only potentially, but in act through an operation of the soul. (130)

7.16. Unlimited dimensions are coeternal with matter, preceding in it every substantial form.

7.17. Every intelligence except the first understands nothing but the first.

7.18. No way exists to prove absolutely that the abstract exists, except the way of eternal motion.

7.19. Whatever exists in genus can be destroyed.

7.20. The subject of metaphysics [or of the *Metaphysics*] is being insofar as it is being. (135)

7.21. The definitions of natural substances only include matter in a consequential way.

7.18. Starts a series on proofs concerning the existence and nature of the "unmoved mover," "the abstract," "the first," "God," etc. Cf. 12.1, 12.3, 2>11 (especially pertinent to this thesis), 2>43, 2>57, 3>42. It is again noteworthy that Pico included no theses from Latin scholastics on this issue. In 7a>1 he promised to prove God's existence through his "way of numbers."

7.19. Series starts at 1.2. My reasons for translating *corruptible* as I have here are given in my note to that thesis. Cf. especially 2>35 from Pico's own opinions.

7.20. Series starts at 1.14–15.

7.21. Series starts at 2.33. Opposed especially to 8.6 from Avicenna. "*consecutive*" = sequentially or consequentially, in the manner of a series, as opposed to causally; see Deferrari and Barry (1948: 212).

7.22. Demonstratio septimi Physicorum, quod omne quod mouetur_mouetur ab alio, est demonstratio signi et nullo modo causae.

7.23. Nulla potentia actiua quae sit mere neutra et indifferens ad agere uel non agere potest ex se determinari ad alterum agendum.

7.24. Vnum relatiuorum conuenientissime per reliquum definitur.

7.25. Exemplum Aristotelis in secundo Methaphysice, de nicticorace respectu solis, non denotat impossibilitatem, sed difficultatem, alioquin natura aliquid ociose egisset.

7.26. Propositio necessaria quae ab Aristotele in libro Priorum contra possibilem et inuentam distinguitur, est illa quae est ex terminis necessariis.

7.27. Ad dispositionem termini necessarii, requiritur ut sit terminus per se unus.

7.28. Cum Aristoteles dixit ex maiori necessaria et minore inuenta/concludi conclusionem necessariam, intelligendum est de minore quae est inuenta per se, necessaria per accidens. <4v/5r>

7.22. Series starts at 2.37–38.

7.23. Buridan's ass (which long antedated Buridan), starving between two perfectly equidistant bales of hay. The *locus classicus* for discussion was Aristotle *De caelo* 2.13 (295b32). The thesis has strong intellectualist implications; it is linked to the series starting at 2.12 on the intellect/will problem.

7.24. See note 4.16–17.

7.25. Part of an important series starting at 2.40; the relevant Aristotelian text is quoted in my note to that thesis. Related historical theses include 4.19–20, 11.4. *Nycticorax* is a Latin transliteration of the Greek "night-raven," which is how Lewis and Short translate the word. Liddell and Scott give us "long-eared owl," citing as their authority passages in *Historia animalium* 592b9, 597b23, 619b1 associating night-ravens and owls. Confusing things further,

7.22. The demonstration in the seventh book of the *Physics*, that everything that is moved is moved by another, is a demonstration from effects, and in no way from the cause.

7.23. No active power that is purely neutral and indifferent as to whether to act or not act can, by itself, determine to do one or the other.

7.24. One term of a relation is appropriately defined by the rest.

7.25. Aristotle's example in the second book of the *Metaphysics*, concerning the owl observing the sun, refers not to an impossibility but difficulty, otherwise nature would have done something purposelessly. (140)

7.26. The necessary proposition that Aristotle distinguishes in the *Prior Analytics* from possible and contingent propositions is that which is constructed out of necessary terms.

7.27. For a term to be established as necessary, it is required that the term be per se one.

7.28. When Aristotle said that a necessary conclusion can arise from a major necessary and minor contingent proposition, this should be understood of a minor proposition that is contingent per se, necessary accidentally.

---

the Oxford English Dictionary tells us that *nycticorax* was a "night-heron (formerly also called the night-raven)." I have settled for metaphorical reasons (since the series deals with wisdom) on "owl." Finally, it can be noted that the standard Greek text of Aristotle has "bat," *nycteris* (*vespertilio* in Aristotle's Latin translations), and not "night-raven," *nycticorax*.

7.26–28. The first of a number of theses commenting on various chapters of the *Prior Analytics*. Pico was apparently drawing in part on the translation that Elia del Medigo made for him of Averroes's *Questions* on that work. Cf. 8.1–2, 8.12, 9.6, 9.7. It is noteworthy that Pico again included no theses on this topic from the Latins, whose views on logic he sharply criticized. Serious study of "higher" matters—numerology, theories of celestial motion, proofs of God, etc.—rightly began only with the Arabs, as Pico suggested in the *Oration*.

7.29. Sub aequinoctiali non potest esse habitatio naturalis uiuentibus.

7.30. In coelo est naturaliter dextrum, et illud non mutatur quamuis partes orbis mutentur.

7.31. Qui ponit animam formam complexionalem_negat causam agentem.

7.32. Vnum methaphysicum_dicit priuationem diuisibilitatis_non actu, sed aptitudine.

7.33. Vnum methaphysicum est fundamentum unius arithmetici.

7.34. Numerus precise ita reperitur in abstractis sicut in materialibus.

7.35. Essentia uniuscuiusque rei et suum existere_idem sunt realiter.

7.36. Quiditas et essentia diuersificantur in quolibet praeter primum.

7.37. Substantia est prior accidente non solum natura,_ sed tempore.

7.29. In Columbus's notes on Pierre d'Ailly's *Ymago mundi*, which Columbus was reading about the time of Pico's proposed debate, we find that the discoveries of the Portuguese below the equator were just then beginning to be recognized even in maritime circles—a suggestion of how slowly information could travel in the late fifteenth century. Cf. Grant, ed. (1974: 631 n. 38).

7.30. Commenting on *De caelo* 2.2. The thesis involves discussion of the general movement of the heavens from east to west (disregarding the retrograde motions of the planets). Tied to 2>39, which involves a closely related issue.

7.31. Series starts at 1.12. Tied further to the theses on the "unity of intellect" problem raised in 7.2–4.

7.32. Series starts at 2.23. "*aptitudine*" = a proneness or inclination towards some state.

7.29. Below the equator there can be no natural habitat for living things.

7.30. In heaven a right-hand side exists naturally, and that does not change no matter how much the parts of a sphere change. (145)

7.31. Whoever posits the soul as a complex form denies the active cause.

7.32. The metaphysical one refers to privation of divisibility not in act, but in inclination.

7.33. The metaphysical one is the grounds of the arithmetic one.

7.34. Number is found in abstract things just as in material things.

7.35. The essence of each thing and its existence are really the same. (150)

7.36. Quiddity and essence are different in everything except the first.

7.37. Substance is prior to accident not only in nature, but in time.

7.33. The first of a large number of theses involving the theory of numbers and proportions. Pico again included no theses on these topics from the Latins, whom he felt paid too little attention to the proportional structure of reality. Cf. especially, besides the previous thesis and the next, 2>64 from Pico's own opinions.

7.34. Pico would have denied any strong form of this thesis, following an emanationist distinction that he makes later in the text between "formal numbers" (belonging to the intellectual realm) and "material numbers." Cf. 24.5 from Proclus, 25.1–2 from Pythagoras, 3>24–26 and 9>23 from Pico's own opinions. On "formal numbers," see 7>9 and note.

7.35–36. On the essence/existence controversy, see note 2.31. On "quiddities," see note 3.5. "the first" in Averroes = God.

7.37. Series starts at 2.24.

7.38. De materia ut materia est considerat physicus.

7.39. Essentia cuiuslibet intelligentiae est substantialiter ad aliquid.

7.40. Dato per impossibile quod daretur materia quae corruptionis principium non esset, adhuc si coelum ex tali materia et forma esset uere compositum, aeternum esse non posset.

7.41. Finis non causat finaliter secundum suum esse conceptum, sed secundum suum esse reale.

7.38. Series starts at 1.14–15.

7.39. On "relations," see note 4.16–17. Cf. especially 3>19 from Pico's theses.

7.40. Series starts at 7.9. Pico himself posited different grades or "modes" of matter on different levels of reality.

7.38. The physicist considers matter as it is matter.

7.39. The essence of each intelligence exists substantially in a state of relation.

7.40. It is granted as impossible that matter can exist that is not the principle of corruption. Moreover, even if the heavens were truly composed out of such matter and form, they could not be eternal. (155)

7.41. An end does not act as a final cause according to its conceived existence, but according to its real existence.

7.41. Cf. 3.6 note. Pico apparently planned to use this thesis to qualify others in this section on final causality, e.g., 7.5, 7.7. The concluding theses in several other sections (e.g., those involving Albert the Great and Duns Scotus) were to be used in similar qualifying ways.

CONCLVSIONES SECVNDVM AVICENNAM NVMERO .XII.

8.1. Praeter syllogismum cathegoricum et hypotheticum, datur genus syllogismorum compositiuorum.

8.2. Licet in nullo syllogismo qui sit actu uel potentia cathegoricus ex duabus negatiuis concludi possit, potest tamen hoc fieri in syllogismo compositiuo, ut scilicet ex duabus negatiuis concludatur.

8.3. In coelo est materia eiusdem rationis cum materia inferiorum.

8.4. Non potest in anima esse notio intelligibilis sine actuali intellectione.

8.5. Possibile est hominem ex putrefactione generari.

8.6. Essentia rei_materiam propriam et formam complectitur.

8.1. 1486 hypoteticum | 1487 hipoteticum

CONCLUSIONS ACCORDING TO AVICENNA. The *Oration* and *Apology* speak of "something divine and Platonic" in Avicenna, and Pico's theses "according to his own opinion" endorse a number of Avicenna's most characteristic doctrines. In *De ente et uno* 8, however, Pico complains that Avicenna "in many places interpolated the philosophy of Aristotle, leading to the great wars fought by him with Averroes." The majority of these theses seem to have been drawn second-hand from Averroes's attacks on Avicenna and from the epitomes and commentaries on Arabic philosophy that Pico commissioned from Elia del Medigo.

8.1–2. See note 7.26–28.

TWELVE CONCLUSIONS ACCORDING TO AVICENNA.

8.1. Besides categorical and hypothetical syllogisms, there exists the genus of composite syllogisms.

8.2. Although in no syllogism that in act or potential is categorical can anything be concluded from two negative propositions, this, namely, that something can be concluded from two negatives, can occur in a composite syllogism.

8.3. In heaven matter exists of the same kind as the matter of inferior things.

8.4. An intelligible notion cannot exist in the soul without actual intellection. (160)

8.5. It is possible to generate man from putrefaction.

8.6. The essence of an object is composed of its own matter and form.

8.3. Series starts at 7.9. See also note 2.21. Opposed to 14.1 from Avempace and 11>67 from Pico's own opinions.

8.4. Series starts at 1.1.

8.5. Opposed to 7.6 from Averroes. See that note.

8.6. See 2.33 and note. Opposed to 7.21 from Averroes.

8.7. Prima substantia prior est qualibet substantia habente habitudinem ad operationem transeuntem, quaecunque sit illa, alicuius causae siue formalis, siue materialis, siue efficientis, siue finalis.

8.8. Ab uno simplici, in fine simplicitatis, non prouenit nisi unum. <5r/5v>

8.9. Odor secundum esse reale et non intentionale usque ad sensum multiplicatur.

8.10. Propositio dicens quod sensibile supra sensum positum non facit sensationem, non est uera nisi per accidens.

8.11. Organum odoratus sunt caruncule mamillares in anteriori cerebri parte constitutae.

8.12. Nec particularis affirmatiua possibilis conuertitur semper in affirmatiuam possibilem, nec necessaria particularis affirmatiua in necessariam, ut credidit Aristoteles.

8.10. 1486 dicens que sensibile | *Emendationes errorum,* corrige: dicens quod sensibile | 1487 text emended *sic*

8.7–8. In the series on emanationism beginning at 2.17. Opposed in particular to 7.5 from Averroes. The sense of 8.8 is clarified in the *Commento* (Garin, *Scritti vari*, 465–66): From a perfect cause (God) there can only come a single perfect effect (the intellectual nature), from which the rest of reality emanates. Pico claims to have arguments for this view superior to Avicenna's. In the same passage, he ridicules Ficino for claiming that Plato believed that the soul was created immediately by God rather than through emanational processes.

8.9. Cf. 1.7–8 and note. The scholastic view that sensual images were "multiplied" in a medium (cf. 3>57) is striking enough to justify a literal translation.

8.7. The first substance is prior to every substance capable of transitive operation, whatever that is [and] of whatever cause, whether formal, or material, or efficient, or final.

8.8. From the simple one, within the limits of simplicity, only one thing can originate.

8.9. Odor is multiplied with real and not intentional existence right up to the senses. (165)

8.10. The proposition stating that a sensible object placed beyond the senses does not create sensation is only true accidentally.

8.11. The organ of smell consists of the mamillary bodies, located in the anterior part of the brain.

8.12. Particular possible affirmative propositions do not always convert into possible affirmative propositions, nor particular necessary affirmatives into necessary ones, as Aristotle believed.

8.10. Tied to the series on the "active senses" starting at 1.13. Cf. also 1.7–8 and note.

8.11. Cf. 1.9 and note. "mamillary bodies" = small nuclei in the brain's limbic system, currently believed to be involved in memory formation and in the integration of emotional and cognitive data.

8.12. See note 7.26–28. Commenting on *Prior Analytics* 1.2–3. Much discussion of the "convertibility" of propositions (see note 3>48) passed between Pico and Elia del Medigo in 1486, as we see in Elia's letter to Pico written on the eve of Pico's debate. See the text in Kieszkowski, ed. (1964).

CONCLVSIONES SECVNDVM ALPHARABIVM NVMERO .XI.

9.1. Primum quod est necessarium in demonstratione non est quod diffiniuit Aristoteles primo Posteriorum, sed sic debet definiri: Primum est illud quod ita est uniuersalius subiecto, ut tamen de subiecti genere non praedicetur.

9.2. Diffinitio generis quam dedit Porphyrius mala est, sed sic debet diffiniri: Genus est quod duorum uniuersalium est uniuersalius.

9.3. Summum hominis bonum est perfectio per scientias speculatiuas.

9.4. Cum dicit Aristoteles omnem doctrinam et omnem disciplinam fieri ex praeexistenti cognitione, intelligende sunt per doctrinam et disciplinam cognitio diffinitiua et argumentatiua.

9.5. Intentio dici de omni secundum Aristotelem est talis quod praedicatum dicitur de subiecto, et de omni eo quod est subiectum actu uel potentia, possibilitate contingentiae, non necessitatis.

9.1. colon retained from 1486 edition

9.2. 1486 dabit Porphyrius | *Emendationes errorum*, corrige: dedit | 1487 text emended *sic*

9.5. 1486 que praedicatum | *Emendationes errorum*, corrige: quod praedicatum | 1487 text emended *sic*

CONCLUSIONS ACCORDING TO AL-FARABI. Al-Farabi, d. 950 CE, the first major Arabic philosopher. The majority of these theses were inspired by al-Farabi's logical commentaries, which Pico knew in medieval Latin translations. For this side of al-Farabi's work, see the studies of Rescher listed in my bibliography.

9.1. See note 7.26–28.

ELEVEN CONCLUSIONS ACCORDING TO AL-FARABI.

9.1. The first thing that is necessary in a demonstration is not what Aristotle defined it as in the first book of the *Posterior Analytics*, but it should be defined like this: The first is that which exists more universally than the subject, but is not predicated of the genus of the subject.

9.2. The definition of genus that Porphyry gave is bad, and it should be defined this way: The genus is what of two universals exists more universally. (170)

9.3. Man's highest good is perfection through the speculative sciences.

9.4. When Aristotle says that all doctrine and all learning comes from preexisting knowledge, by *doctrine* and *learning* understand knowledge arising from definitions and arguments.

9.5. According to Aristotle, an *intention predicated of all* is such that the predicate is attributed to a subject, and to all that the subject is in act or potentially, with possible contingency, not necessity.

9.2. Tied to the series on genus/species starting at 1.2. The reference is to Porphyry *Isagoge* 2, which was normally read in Boethius's translation.

9.3. Series starts at 2.12. In the proem to *Heptaplus* 7 Pico tells us that al-Farabi dealt exclusively with "natural" and not "supernatural" happiness.

9.4. See note 7.10–11. Commenting on *Posterior Analytics* 1.1 (71a1). Cf. in Pico's theses 2>21.

9.5. See 7.10–11 note. An "*intention predicated of all*" = a concept holding for every possible case. Commenting on *Posterior Analytics* 1.4.

9.6. Qui crediderit intentionem dici de omni esse aliam ab ea quam dixit praecedens conclusio defendere non potest Aristotelem a Theophrasto, quod ex maiori necessaria et minori inuenta sequatur conclusio necessaria.

9.7. Possibile quod diffinit Aristoteles in libro Priorum_est commune ad possibile et ad inuentum, ut contra distinctum necessario.

9.8. Non potest intelligi accidens,_ etiam in abstracto,_ non intelligendo subiectum. <5v/6r>

9.9. Species sunt in medio, medio modo inter esse spirituale et materiale.

9.10. Quelibet species secundum esse spirituale_est formaliter cognitio.

9.11. Actualis cognitio sensus communis apprehendentis phantasma ut sensibile_est somnium.

9.6. Elia del Medigo discussed Theophrastus's views here via Averroes's commentary, responding to an inquiry from Pico just before his debate (Kieszkowski, ed. 1964: 65–66). The text in question in the second part of the thesis is *Prior Analytics* 1.22 (40a1). For related theses, see note 7.26–28.

9.7. See note 7.26–28. Commenting on *Prior Analytics* 1.13.

9.6. Whoever believes that an *intention predicated of all* is different from what the preceding conclusion stated cannot defend Aristotle from Theophrastus, who claimed that from a major necessary and a minor contingent proposition a necessary conclusion should follow.

9.7. The possible proposition that Aristotle defines in the *Prior Analytics* is common to possible and contingent, as distinct from necessary propositions. (175)

9.8. An accident cannot be understood, even in the abstract, without understanding its subject.

9.9. Images in a medium exist in an intermediate way between spiritual and material existence.

9.10. Every image that has spiritual existence is formally a cognition.

9.11. A dream is an actual cognition of common sense apprehending a phantasm as a sensible object.

9.8. Series starts at 2.24. Al-Farabi here is again opposing Porphyry, who supposedly first introduced the distinction between "separable" and "inseparable" accidents at issue in this series. Cf. *Isagoge* 6.

9.9–10. Series starts at 1.7–8. See that note.

9.11. Series starts at 7.1. Also tied to the two preceding theses.

CONCLVSIONES SECVNDVM ISAAC NARBONENSEM NVMERO .IIII.

10.1. Ponere intellectum agentem non est necessarium.

10.2. Intentio prima est quiditas rei obiectiue relucens in intellectu.

10.3. Motus est sensibile commune, a sensu exteriori absque actione alterius uirtutis cognoscibile.

10.4. Corpora coelestia non largiuntur formaliter inferioribus nisi caliditatem.

CONCLUSIONS ACCORDING TO ISAAC OF NARBONNE. Anagnine, Di Napoli, and Kieszkowski identify Isaac with Isaac Israeli the Elder (d. ca. 955 CE), whose *De definitionibus* and *De elementibus* were known to Pico in medieval Latin translations. Isaac, however, was normally referred to as an Egyptian, leaving the tag "of Narbonne" here something of a puzzle. Narbonne was a Jewish intellectual center in the Middle Ages, and the name "Isaac Narbonensis" would in any event have been a common one: we have, e.g., a famous Talmudist from the twelfth century named "Abraham ben [son of] Isaac of Narbonne" (Sarton 1928–48: 2:476–77). Elsewhere Pico refers to the works of the Spanish astrologer Isaac Israeli the Younger (d. in Toledo after 1330) and several times to an unidentified "Isaac the Persian" (*Opera*, 9, 672).

FOUR CONCLUSIONS ACCORDING TO ISAAC OF NARBONNE.

10.1. It is not necessary to postulate an active intellect. (180)

10.2. A first intention is the quiddity of a thing objectively reflecting in the intellect.

10.3. Motion is an object of common sense, knowable by an exterior sense without the action of any other power.

10.4. Celestial bodies do not distribute anything formally to inferior bodies except heat.

10.1. See 11.2 note.

10.2. "first intention" = concept referring a concrete object, as opposed to a "second intention" (like genus or species), usually said to arise from reflection on a "first intention." Tied to the series on universals starting at 1.1. Pico rejects the realist views implied here in 2>2–3.

10.3. In the series starting at 1.10 and 1.13. Cf. especially 13.3.

10.4. Commenting on Aristotle *Meteorology* 1.3 (340a12ff.). Cf. 11.3. Pico's own views emerge in 2>42 (see note).

CONCLVSIONES SECVNDVM ABVMARON BABYLONIVM NVMERO .IIII.

11.1. De nulla re quae in mundo sit actu corruptibilis habet deus solicitudinem.

11.2. Intellectus agens nihil aliud est quam deus.

11.3. Coelum calefacit inferiora per lumen suum super ea cadens.

11.4. Actus ipsi intellectus intrinsece, res autem intellecte extrinsece, dicuntur uerae uel falsae.

CONCLUSIONS ACCORDING TO ABUMARON THE BABYLONIAN. "Abumaron" (or "Abhomeron") = Abu Marwan Ibn Zuhr = Avenzoar (d. 1161/62), a well-known physician-philosopher of the twelfth century. Kieszkowski's edition falsely identifies him with the ninth-century astrologer Abu Ma 'shar (Albumasar), misciting Munk and Steinschneider. Pico is probably drawing here from Averroes's discussions of Ibn Zuhr, although he could also be approached through a Latin translation of his *Taysir*, his most famous medical work. The first printed edition of that text, which appeared in 1490/91, found its way into Pico's library.

11.1. Tied to the series on emanationism beginning at 2.17. Cf. especially 8.7–8 from Avicenna. For Pico, in general it is the soul that has care for corruptible things (cf., e.g., 5>50).

FOUR CONCLUSIONS ACCORDING TO ABU-MARON THE BABYLONIAN.

11.1. God has care for nothing in the world that in act is corruptible.

11.2. The active intellect is nothing but God. (185)

11.3. Heaven heats inferior things through its light falling over them.

11.4. Acts of intellect are called true or false intrinsically, the things understood extrinsically.

11.2. Opposed to 10.1. In *Heptaplus* 4.2 we find that the underlying issue here concerned whether God himself or the intellectual nature was the source of the soul's illumination, tying these theses to the series starting at 5.1. In a famous essay, Cassirer (1942, repr. 1968: 26) represented 11.2 as Pico's own opinion, not bothering to mention the conflicting thesis found just five theses earlier (in 10.1). Cassirer's essay illustrates the problems that arose in older studies that cited Pico's theses out of context: Taking both 10.1 and 11.2 as equally representative of Pico's views, we would have apparent evidence of his atheism!

11.3. See note 10.4.

11.4. Tied to the series starting at 2.40.

CONCLVSIONES SECVNDVM MOYSEM AEGYPTIVM .III.

12.1. Demonstratio octaui Physicorum, a Aristotele ad probandum primum motorem adducta, aliquid probat speciale primo.

12.2. Scientia methaphysicae non est una scientia.

12.3. Simplicitas primi et omnimoda immaterialitas probari non potest per causalitatem efficientem motus, sed per finalem tantum.

CONCLUSIONS ACCORDING TO MOSES THE EGYPTIAN. Moses = Moses Maimonides, d. 1204 CE. Pico was drawing from the *Dux neutrorum*, the medieval Latin translation of Maimonides' *Guide for the Perplexed*. The fact that Pico could casually group the most famous Jewish philosopher in history with the Arab "nation" is of historical interest. In 11>63 we find Pico claiming that Cabalistic mysteries lay hidden underneath Maimonides' philosophical prose.

12.1. Series starts at 7.18. The "something particular" is the Aristotelian principle that "matter does not move itself," discussed in the series beginning at 2.37–38. Drawn from *Guide* 2, intro., prop. 25.

THREE CONCLUSIONS ACCORDING TO MOSES THE EGYPTIAN.

12.1. The demonstration in the eighth book of the *Physics*, brought forward by Aristotle to prove the existence of the first mover, first proves something particular.

12.2. The science of metaphysics is not one science.

12.3. The simplicity and total immateriality of the first cannot be demonstrated through the efficient but only through the final causality of motion. (190)

12.2. Cf. the series starting at 1.14–15, 6.10. Thus the *Guide* claims that metaphysics does not stand alone but borders on and must be preceded by the study of physics (cf. Friedländer's trans., 2d ed. 1904: 4).

12.3. Series starts at 7.18. Cf. *Guide* 2.1. "the first" in Pico's source = First Cause = God.

CONCLVSIONES SECVNDVM MAVMETH TOLLETIVM NVMERO .V.

13.1. Relatio nullam rem dicit extra animam.

13.2. Species rerum representatiue sunt reductiue in praedicamento in quo sunt res representate.

13.3. Sensibilia communia proprias species ad sensus multiplicant, distinctas a speciebus sensibilium propriorum. <6r/6v>

13.4. Sensus tactus non est unus sensus.

13.5. De nulla re an existat potest quaerere aliquis artifex specialis.

CONCLUSIONS ACCORDING TO MOHAMMED OF TOLEDO. Di Napoli peculiarly identified Mohammed with the Persian mathematician al-Khwarismi, Kieszkowski with Meir ben Todros Abulafia (a different figure from Abraham Abulafia, from whom Pico drew his *revolutio alphabetariae*). Pico's actual source is unknown. Writing to Ficino a few months before publication of the nine hundred theses, Pico spoke of letters in Arabic of this writer falling into his hands (*Opera*, 367).

13.1. Series begins at 4.16–17. Cf. especially 2>46 and 3>33 from Pico's opinions. For other theses with nominalistic overtones, see note 3.6.

FIVE CONCLUSIONS ACCORDING TO MOHAMMED OF TOLEDO.

13.1. Relation refers to nothing outside the soul.

13.2. The representative images of things exist reductively in the predicate in which those things are represented.

13.3. Objects of common sense multiply their own images to the senses, distinct from the images of objects of the individual senses.

13.4. The sense of touch is not one sense.

13.5. Of no object can one ask whether a special creator exists. (195)

13.2. In contrast with the previous thesis, this one implies an extreme linguistic realism. Cf. especially the opposing view in 3>2 from Pico's own opinions.

13.3. Series starts at 1.10.

13.4. Commenting on *De anima* 2.11. Cf. 6.8, 2>59 and notes.

13.5. In the series on emanation starting at 2.17.

CONCLVSIONES SECVNDVM AVEMPACEM ARABEM NVMERO .II.

14.1. In coelo est materia alterius rationis a materia inferiorum.

14.2. Lux et color essentialiter non differunt.

CONCLUSIONS ACCORDING TO AVEMPACE THE ARAB. Ibn Bajjah, d. 1138/39. Pico's immediate source here was apparently Averroes, who often cites Avempace. Shortly before his debate Pico attempted unsuccessfully to get further information from Elia del Medigo on Avempace's *De anima*, the indirect source for the second of these theses. See the letter in Kieszkowski, ed. (1964: 74).

TWO CONCLUSIONS ACCORDING TO AVEMPACE THE ARAB.

14.1. In heaven matter exists of a different kind from the matter in inferior things.

14.2. Light and color do not differ in essence.

14.1. Series starts at 7.9. Directly opposed to 8.3 from Avicenna.

14.2. Commenting on *De anima* 3.5. The underlying issue involves the relationship between the passive and active intellects. Cf. 17.8 from Simplicius, which involves the same text.

¶Conclusiones secundum graecos qui peripateticam sectam profitentur: Theophrastum, Ammonium, Simplicium, Alexandrum, et Themistium.

CONCLVSIONES SECVNDVM THEOPHRASTVM NVMERO .IIII.

15.1. Si coelum inanimatum esset, esset quocunque animato corpore ignobilius, quod dicere impium est in philosophia.

15.2. Quiditas est sola forma.

15.3. Ita se habet intellectus agens ad producenda intelligibilia in possibilem intellectum, sicut se habet forma artis ad producendas formas in materiam artis.

15.4. Deus mouet coelum ut finis.

Section title. colon retained from 1486 edition.

CONCLUSIONS ACCORDING TO THE GREEK PERIPATETICS. In line with his model of history, Pico viewed Aristotle's Greek commentators far more sympathetically than either the Latin or Arabic scholastics. From this midpoint in the historical part of Pico's text, suggestions emerge more frequently of the cosmic proportions developed in his so-called *philosophia nova*. The "civil wars" in sects from this point on are not entirely eliminated, but they become increasingly muted. It should be noted that the degree to which late-ancient Aristotelian commentators like Simplicius or Themistius can be legitimately classified as Peripatetics is questionable, since the lines between Platonists and Aristotelians in post-classical times were virtually nonexistent. I have not entered here into the specialized controversy over the exact stages by which study of Aristotle's Greek commentators was renewed in the 1480s and 1490s, discussed at length by Nardi, Mahoney, and others. Figures besides Pico involved in this revival, all tied in complex ways, included Ermolao Barbaro, Nicoletto Vernia, Elia del Medigo, Girolamo Donato, and later, Agostino Nifo. Much of the activity centered around the University of Padua. For an updated bibliography, see the notes in Mahoney (1997).

¶Conclusions according to the Greeks who profess the Peripatetic sect: Theophrastus, Ammonius, Simplicius, Alexander, and Themistius.

FOUR CONCLUSIONS ACCORDING TO THEOPHRASTUS.

15.1. If the heavens were inanimate, they would be more ignoble than any animate body, which it is impious to say in philosophy.

15.2. Quiddity is the only form.

15.3. The active intellect produces intelligible objects in the possible intellect, just as the form of an art produces forms in the material of that art. (200)

15.4. God moves the heavens as their end.

CONCLUSIONS ACCORDING TO THEOPHRASTUS. Aristotle's pupil and successor as the head of the Lyceum, d. ca. 286 BCE. For Theophrastus in the Renaissance, see Schmitt (1971: 239–322). Two and possibly three of these theses were drawn directly or indirectly from reputed fragments of Theophrastus's *Metaphysics*. No copy of that treatise is listed in known inventories of Pico's library. Latin scholastics in addition knew something of Theophrastus's doctrine of the active and passive intellects via Themistius's *Paraphrase of De anima*, which Pico read in Ermolao Barbaro's translation, which was printed in 1481.

15.1. Apparently a deduction from Theophrastus *Metaphysics* 2. In the series on celestial motion starting at 7.7–8. Cf. especially 2>19 from Pico's theses.

15.2. Probably again loosely drawn from the *Metaphysics*. In the series on metaphysical unity starting at 2.23.

15.3. Series starts at 1.1. Suggestively, Pico gives a highly Platonized view of the epistemology of Aristotle's most important disciple.

15.4. Cf. *Metaphysics* 1. Like the first thesis in this section, in the series starting at 7.7–8.

CONCLVSIONES SECVNDVM AMMONIVM NVMERO III.

16.1. Diffinitio de anima data ab Aristotele in qua dicitur: Anima est actus corporis, cum de rationali, de qua principaliter datur, intelligitur, accipienda est causaliter non formaliter.

16.2. Anima rationalis non unitur immediate corpori organico.

16.3. Cum dicit Aristoteles quod oportet prima principia semper permanere, nihil aliud intendit nisi quod in qualibet transmutatione reperiuntur.

CONCLUSIONS ACCORDING TO AMMONIUS. Not the better-known Ammonius Saccas (third century CE), but Ammonius the son of Hermias, a disciple of Proclus (late fifth century CE) and reputed master of Simplicius, John Damascene, and John Philoponus. From what is known of Ammonius's writings, it is evident that Pico was drawing on second-hand sources, most probably Simplicius's works.

THREE CONCLUSIONS ACCORDING TO AMMONIUS.

16.1. The definition of the soul given by Aristotle, which says, *The soul is the act of the body*, when it is understood of the rational soul, for which it is chiefly given, should be accepted causally, not formally.

16.2. The rational soul is not united immediately to the organic body.

16.3. When Aristotle says that it is necessary that first principles remain forever, he is referring to nothing but that which is found in every transmutation.

16.1–2. Commenting on Aristotle *De anima* 2.1–2. Pico could cite these theses to back his view (normally linked with Avicenna, though not in the theses) that a *forma corporeitatis* or "material form" preceded the substantial form. Cf. 2.29 note and 2>12, 2>70.

16.3. "that which is found in every transmutation" = prime matter. Commenting on Aristotle *Physics* 1.7, which deals with the number of "first principles" in nature. Pico's views emerge in 3>50–51.

CONCLVSIONES SECVNDVM SIMPLICIVM NVMERO .VIIII.

17.1. Cognoscere actum suum non est commune cuilibet sensui exteriori, sed humanis sensibus est speciale.

17.2. Aristoteles in tertio libro De anima non tractat nisi de parte rationali.

17.3. Cum anima in se perfecte redit, tunc intellectus agens ab intelle/ctu possibili liberatur. <6v/7r>

17.4. Eadem pars rationalis, ut seipsam exiens, dicitur intellectus possibilis; ut vero est talis ut se ipsam ut possibilis est possit perficere, dicitur intellectus agens.

17.5. Eadem pars rationalis, ut extra se uadens et procedens perficitur speciebus quae in ipsa sunt, ut manens est dicitur intellectus in habitu.

17.6. Sciri potest ex praecedentibus conclusionibus quare intellectus agens quandoque arti, quandoque habitui, quandoque lumini, assimilatur.

17.2. 1486 in libro | *Emendationes errorum*, corrige: in tertio libro | 1487 in libro tertio

---

CONCLUSIONS ACCORDING TO SIMPLICIUS. Sixth-century commentator on Aristotle. Pico was apparently drawing from the original Greek text of Simplicius's commentary on *De anima*, a copy of which was in his library (Kibre 1936: 179). Nardi (1958: 345–442) claimed that Pico was the first Latin writer in the Renaissance to use the text, which had a large impact on later Renaissance scholasticism. On this issue, cf. Nardi with the studies cited in Mahoney (1997: 143 n. 73).

17.1. Commenting on Aristotle *De anima* 3.2. On Pico's view of the soul's self-consciousness, see 3>60 and note.

NINE CONCLUSIONS ACCORDING TO SIMPLICIUS.

17.1. To know its own activity is not common to every outer sense, but is unique to the human senses. (205)

17.2. In the third book of *On the Soul* Aristotle only deals with the rational part.

17.3. When the soul returns perfectly into itself, the active intellect is freed from the possible intellect.

17.4. The same rational part, as it moves outside itself, is called the possible intellect. But as it is such that it is able to perfect itself as possible, it is called the active intellect.

17.5. The same rational part, which advancing and proceeding outside itself is perfected by images that exist in itself, as it dwells within is called the intellect in habit.

17.6. It can be known from the preceding conclusions why the active intellect is sometimes compared to an art, sometimes to a habit, sometimes to light. (210)

17.2–6. Aimed at harmonizing the epistemological and theological conflicts implied in *De anima* 3.5. Tied to the series on mystical beatitude or happiness starting at 2.12. Pico presumably intended to resolve the apparent conflict between 7.3 (from Averroes) and 17.3 (from Simplicius) by pointing to the distinctions in 17.4–6.

17.7. Passio a sensibili facta_in organo solo, sensatio_in anima sola, recipitur.

17.8. Sicut lumen colores non facit colores, sed praeexistentes colores potentia uisibiles, facit actu uisibiles, ita intellectus agens non facit species cum non essent prius, sed actu praeexistentes species potentia cognoscibiles, facit actu cognoscibiles.

17.9. Cum dicit Aristoteles non recordari nos post mortem quia passiuus intellectus corrumpitur, per passiuum intellectum, possibilem intellectum intelligit.

17.7. Series starts at 1.13.

17.8. Commenting on *De anima* 3.5. Connected to the series starting at 1.1. Cf. also 14.2 and note.

17.7. An impression produced by a sensible object is received in the organ only, a sensation in the soul only.

17.8. Just as light does not make colors colors, but makes preexisting colors, visible potentially, visible in act, so the active intellect does not make images that did not previously exist, but makes images preexisting in act, knowable potentially, knowable in act.

17.9. When Aristotle says that we do not remember after death because the passive intellect is destroyed, by the passive intellect he means the possible intellect.

17.9. Commenting again on *De anima* 3.5. Cf. especially 7.4, 18.1. For Pico's view of the "possible intellect," see 5>19.

CONCLVSIONES SECVNDVM ALEXANDRVM APHRODISEVM NVMERO .VIII.

18.1. Anima rationalis est immortalis.

18.2. Cuilibet coelo praeter animam quae mouet eum efficienter, propria assistit intelligentia, quae illum mouet ut finis, ab anima tali secundum substantiam omnino distincta.

18.3. Nullam diffinitionem, etiam naturalem, ex Aristotelis sententia ingreditur materia.

18.4. Deus nec mala nec priuationes intelligit.

18.5. Numerus abstractorum de quo agit Aristoteles in duodecimo Methaphysicae, non est numerus motorum, sed numerus intelligentiarum, quae sunt fines motus.

18.6. Cum dicit Aristoteles nono Methaphysicae separata et diuina aut totaliter sciri a nobis, aut totaliter ignorari, intelligendum est de ea cognitione quae his contingit qui iam ad summam intellectus actuationem peruenerunt. <7r/7v>

18.2. 1486 preter | substrantiam

CONCLUSIONS ACCORDING TO ALEXANDER OF APHRODISIAS. Alexander, fl. 200 CE. On Alexander's fortunes in the Renaissance, see Cranz (1960: 77–135; 1971: 411–22). Pico's library contained a number of works attributed to Alexander, both in Greek and in medieval Latin translations. He could also draw from the discussions of Alexander in Averroes and other second-hand sources.

18.1. Cf. especially 7.4, 17.9. Revolves again around *De anima* 3.5. Pico reverses the usual reading of Alexander's views as reported by Averroes. Pico was possibly drawing from the spurious second book of Alexander's commentary on *De anima*, including the section entitled *De intellectu*. For an analysis of a later scholastic conflict on this topic at the University of Padua involving Nicoletto Vernia and Agostino Nifo, both of whom were linked to Pico, see Mahoney (1969).

EIGHT CONCLUSIONS ACCORDING TO ALEXANDER OF APHRODISIAS.

18.1. The rational soul is immortal.

18.2. Besides the soul that moves it efficiently, every heaven is assisted by its own intelligence that moves it as its end, totally distinct in substance from that soul. (215)

18.3. Matter enters into no definition, even a natural one, in the thought of Aristotle.

18.4. God understands neither evils nor privations.

18.5. The number of the abstract things that Aristotle discusses in the twelfth book of the *Metaphysics* is not the number of movers, but the number of intelligences, which are the ends of motion.

18.6. When Aristotle in the ninth book of the *Metaphysics* says that separated and divine things are either totally known or totally unknown to us, this should be understood of that cognition achieved by those who have finally attained the highest actuation of the intellect.

18.2. Series starts at 7.7–8.

18.3. Series starts at 2.33.

18.4. Commenting on *Metaphysics* 12.9, which deals with the nature of divine thought. Later in the nine hundred theses, Pico claims that Aristotle did not deal with God until *Metaphysics* 12.10—a point that he would undoubtedly raise in debating this thesis; see 3>44 and note. The thesis can also be collated with the series on the limits of divine power beginning at 2.10. Books 6ff. of Alexander's commentary on the *Metaphysics,* from which Pico apparently drew this and the next three theses, are usually viewed as spurious.

18.5. Series starts at 7.7–8. Commenting on Aristotle *Metaphysics* 12.8. Cf. also 3>44 and note.

18.6. Series starts at 1.6.

18.7. Sicut primus intellectus inter omnes intellectus primo se intelligit, alia secundario, ita ultimus intellectus inter omnes intellectus primo alia a se, et seipsum secundario intelligit.

18.8. Methaphysicus et dialecticus aeque de omnibus disputant, sed ille demonstratiue, hic probabiliter.

18.7. Series starts at 5.7.

18.7. Just as the first intellect among all intellects first understands itself, and other things secondarily, so the last intellect among all intellects first understands things different from itself, and itself secondarily. (220)

18.8. The metaphysician and the dialectician equally dispute about all things, but the first one demonstratively, the second probabilistically.

18.8. Cf. Aristotle *Prior Analytics* 1.1; *Topics* 1.1; and the wording in 3>9 from Pico's theses. Some material on this question gathered for Pico by Elia del Medigo is cited in Kieszkowski (1964: 52–55).

CONCLVSIONES SECVNDVM THEMISTIVM NVMERO .V.

19.1. Intellectus possibiles qui illuminantur tantum plures sunt; agentes participati illuminantes et illuminati plures quoque sunt; agens illuminans tantum unus.

19.2. Intellectus agens illuminans tantum credo sit illud apud Themistium quod est matatron in cabala.

19.3. Scientia de anima est media inter scientias naturales et diuinas.

19.4. Praeter duas species demonstrationis quia quas ponit Aristoteles, tertia alia ponenda est, et est cum una proprietas per coeuam proprietatem demonstratur.

19.5. Propositio est per se cum uel subiectum diffinit praedicatum, uel praedicatum subiectum, uel ambo diffiniuntur per idem tertium.

19.1. 1486 illuminati.Plures quoque sunt.agentes

CONCLUSIONS ACCORDING TO THEMISTIUS. Themistius, d. 388 CE. Drawn from Ermolao Barbaro's translation of Themistius's *Paraphrases* of the *De anima* and *Posterior Analytics*. The work was first printed with related texts in 1481. Pico praises the translation in a 1484 letter to Ermolao and in his polemics with the Aristotelian Antonio da Faenza; see *Opera*, 376, 268. As is true in the case of other late-ancient Aristotelian commentators, it is difficult to know whether to label Themistius as an Aristotelian or Platonist. Pico heatedly rejected the latter view in his polemics with Antonio da Faenza (*Opera*, 268).

FIVE CONCLUSIONS ACCORDING TO THEMISTIUS.

19.1. There are many possible intellects that are illuminated only. There are also many participated active intellects that are illuminating and illuminated. But there is only one active intellect that is illuminating only.

19.2. I believe that the active intellect that is illuminating only in Themistius is the same as *Metatron* in the Cabala.

19.3. The science of the soul is intermediate between the natural and divine sciences.

19.4. Besides the two types of demonstration from effects that Aristotle posits, a third other should be posited, which demonstrates one property through a coeval property. (225)

19.5. A proposition is per se when either the subject defines the predicate, or the predicate the subject, or both are defined by the same third term.

19.1–2. Adumbrates the cosmic correspondences typical of Pico's "new philosophy." *Metatron* = originally a demonic power (cf. Scholem 1974: 377–81), syncretically transformed by Pico into a philosophical principle. See also 11>10 and above, pp. 70, 75.

19.3. Since the soul mediates between the intellectual and material worlds.

19.4. "coeval property" = a "convertible property." See 3>48 and note. For other related theses, see 7.10–11 note.

19.5. Commenting on *Posterior Analytics* 1.4. On per se propositions, see note 1.3. Other related theses are listed in 7.10–11 note.

¶Conclusiones secundum doctrinam philosophorum qui Platonici dicuntur: Plotini Aegiptii, Porphyrii Tyrii, Iamblici Chalcidei, Procli Lycii, et Adelandi Arabis.

CONCLVSIONES SECVNDVM PLOTINVM NVMERO .XV.

20.1. Primum intelligibile non est extra primum intellectum.

20.2. Non tota descendit anima quum descendit.

20.3. Omnis uita est immortalis.

20.2. 1486, 1487 qum

CONCLUSIONS ACCORDING TO THE PLATONISTS. The inclusion of "Adeland the Arab" in this section violates the orderly emanation of wisdom through "nations" suggested in the *Oration* and *Apology*. Pico's emphasis in his title on the diverse geographical origins of the Platonists was an apparent attempt to skirt this problem by representing Platonism as a universal school of sorts independent of any one "nation." Translations of none of the Greek Neo-Platonists covered in this section were published by Marsilio Ficino before the nine hundred theses went to press, supporting Pico's boast in the *Oration* and *Apology* that he was the first philosopher in centuries to publicly debate their views. Certainly few theses in this section (especially those attributed to Proclus) have much in common with the lists of topics covered in earlier medieval debates. By this point in the text, the lines between Pico's views and those of his sources are thinning, but we still occasionally see him underlining "civil wars" between various Platonic sect leaders. Later in the theses, he also occasionally criticizes the doctrines or Platonic exegeses of Plotinus, Proclus, and other Neo-Platonists; see, e.g., 5>36, 5>51.

CONCLUSIONS ACCORDING TO PLOTINUS. Pico drew up these theses six years before Ficino published his translation of the *Enneads*, which Pico had urged the older philosopher to undertake in 1484. Sears Jayne (1984: 180) claims that Pico read Ficino's translation in 1486—which parts and under what circumstances Jayne does not say. But evidence suggests that Pico had not had access to whatever existed of that translation when the two philosophers fell out

¶Conclusions according to the doctrine of the philosophers who are called Platonists: Plotinus the Egyptian, Porphyry of Tyre, Iamblichus the Chalcidean, Proclus of Lycia, and Adeland the Arab.

FIFTEEN CONCLUSIONS ACCORDING TO PLOTINUS.

20.1. The first intelligible object does not exist beyond the first intellect.

20.2. The whole soul does not descend when it descends.

20.3. All life is immortal.

---

in the fall of that year, as suggested in a letter from Ficino to Pico dated 8 September 1486 (Kristeller 1937: 1:cxxvi). (But see now http://www.safarmer.com/pico/plotinus.html.) Further on Pico, Ficino, and Plotinus, see p. 12 n. 35. It is noteworthy that the theses that Pico ascribes to Plotinus are much more perfunctory than those that he gives us from Proclus, underlining the deeper systematic affinities between Pico's thought and the latter writer's—rather the reverse of the situation with Ficino. The fact that the theses here are often Neo-Platonic commonplaces makes it difficult at times to pinpoint their exact sources. While Pico drew from various parts of Plotinus's text, after the first few theses he apparently depended most heavily on the tractates found in *Enneads* 1.

20.1. Similar to the views presented by Pico in 2>72, 3>37, and elsewhere. Apparently drawn from *Enneads* 5.5.1ff.

20.2. Cf. theses 21.1–3 from "Adeland the Arab." The most relevant tractates in the *Enneads* are 4.8.1ff., which have affinities with 5>50 from Pico's Platonic theses.

20.3. Cf. *Enneads* 4.7.14. Pertinent to ancient debates over whether all souls or only rational souls are immortal. Cf. below, 27.5–6, 3>47, 5>36 (in part in opposition to Plotinus). For a discussion of Platonic, Aristotelian, and Neo-Platonic texts helpful in approaching this series of theses, see Dodds (1963: 306–8, 315ff.).

20.4. Anima quae peccauit uel in terreno uel in aereo corpore post mortem bruti uitam uiuit.

20.5. Anima irrationalis est idolum animae rationalis, ab ea dependens sicut lumen a sole.

20.6. Ens, uita, et intellectus in idem coincidunt.

20.7. Foelicitas hominis ultima est cum particularis intellectus noster totali primoque intellectui plene coniungitur. <7v/8r>

20.8. Ciuiles uirtutes_uirtutes simpliciter non sunt appellandae.

20.9. Non fit assimilatio ad diuina per uirtutes etiam purgati animi nisi dispositiue.

20.10. In ratione similitudines rerum sunt et species, in intellectu uere ipsa entia.

20.11. Consumatae uirtutis est etiam primos motus amputare.

20.4. Cf. 21.8, 5>51 (opposing Plotinus), 8>4 and note. Cf. *Enneads* 1.1.11ff.

20.5. Series starts at 1.12. In the *Commento* (Garin, *Scritti vari*, 560–61), Pico uses a similar light-metaphor to explain how sensitive and vegetative souls derive from the rational soul, "as is proven in the *Timaeus*." Possibly derived from *Enneads* 1.1.12; cf. also 4.8ff.

20.6. Conflicts with 24.46 from Proclus. Tied to the series on metaphysical unity starting at 2.23. Cf. especially *Enneads* 6.9.9.

20.7. Latin scholastic terminology syncretically imposed on Plotinus by Pico. Series starts at 2.12. Cf. especially 7.3 from Averroes and 3>43 from Pico's own opinions. Probably deduced from *Enneads* 1.4.

20.4. The soul that sinned in either a terrestrial or aerial body lives the life of a beast after death. (230)

20.5. The irrational soul is an image of the rational soul, depending on it just like light on the sun.

20.6. Being, life, and intellect coincide in the same thing.

20.7. Man's greatest happiness exists when our particular intellect is fully conjoined to the first and total intellect.

20.8. Civil virtues should not be called virtues in an absolute sense.

20.9. Assimilation to God even of a purged soul does not occur through the virtues except in a preparatory sense. (235)

20.10. In reason the likenesses and images of things exist, but in the intellect their very being.

20.11. It is the height of virtue to cut off even first motions.

20.8. For other theses on the virtues, see note 2.11. Drawn from *Enneads* 1.2.1ff. The idea is that different "modes" of the virtues exist, but only those that link us to God are virtues *simpliciter*—i.e., virtues in an absolute sense.

20.9. Cf. 20.11, 20.14–15. Drawn from *Enneads* 1.2.4ff. Reflects the quietism that Pico himself found at the height of the mystical ascent; for discussion of the latter topic, see above, pp. 39ff., 111–12.

20.10. Cf. 20.12, 21.1–3. Series starts at 1.6. Could have been drawn from a number of tractates in the *Enneads*, e.g., 1.4.10.

20.11. The allusion is to the circular motion of the soul found in the *Timaeus*, etc. For Plotinus, the soul in its highest state attains total rest; cf. *Enneads* 6.9.8ff. Cf. the contrasting view in 23.6 from Iamblichus.

20.12. Improprie dicitur quod intellectus ideas inspiciat uel intueatur.

20.13. Quae necessaria animali sunt, necessaria possunt dici, sed non bona.

20.14. Sicut accidentalis foelicitas animaduersione indiget, ita substantialis foelicitas per carentiam animaduersionis non solum non deperditur, sed roboratur.

20.15. Homo qui ad foelicitatem iam peruenit per frenesim aut litargiam ab ea non impeditur.

20.12. Due to the unity of the intellect and intelligible suggested in 20.1. Cf. 5>29–30 from Pico's own opinions and the conclusions listed in note 20.10. Among other tractates from which Pico could have derived this, see especially *Enneads* 1.2.6.

20.13. Presumably since matter for Plotinus is privation of "the good." Most likely drawn from *Enneads* 1.8.6, etc.

20.12. It is improperly said that the intellect inspects or contemplates ideas.

20.13. What things are necessary to an animal can be called necessary, but not good.

20.14. Just as accidental happiness demands attention, so substantial happiness not only is not lost, but is strengthened, by a neglect of attention. (240)

20.15. A man who has finally reached happiness will not be held back from that by frenzy or lethargy.

20.14–15. Cf. note 20.9. Series starts at 2.12. Pico's source for 20.15 is apparently *Enneads* 1.4.3ff. The idea in the original is that the soul's happiness is independent of the body's state of health or disease. The normal scholastic view of "frenzy" and "lethargy," on the other hand, was that such extreme psychological states impeded the soul's cognitive powers. Cf., e.g., Thomas *Summa* 1*a*.84.7c.

CONCLVSIONES SECVNDUM ADELANDVM ARABEM NVMERO .VIII.

21.1. Intellectus agens nihil est aliud quam pars animae quae sursum manet et non cadit.

21.2. Anima habet apud se rerum species, et excitatur tantum ab extrinsecis rebus.

21.3. Ad complementum praecedentis conclusionis, quam non solum Adelandus, sed omnes Mauri dicunt, dico ego illas species actu et substantialiter esse in parte quae non cadit, et recipi de nouo et accidentaliter in parte quae cadit.

CONCLUSIONS ACCORDING TO ADELAND THE ARAB. Pico's source here was apparently a loose Hebrew adaption of Adelard of Bath's twelfth-century *Quaestiones naturales*; see above, p. 14. The fact that Pico believed that Adeland was Plotinus's fellow student (third century CE) is confirmed by the placement of these theses between the sets ascribed to Plotinus and his disciple Porphyry. Further evidence that Adelard of Bath was Pico's ultimate source lies in the reference in 21.5 to Thabit the Chaldean (Thabit ibn Qurra, d. 901 CE), whose *Liber*

EIGHT CONCLUSIONS ACCORDING TO ADELAND THE ARAB.

21.1. The active intellect is nothing but the part of the soul that dwells above and does not fall.

21.2. The soul has within itself the images of things, and is only excited by external things.

21.3. To complete the preceding conclusion, which not only Adeland but all Moors declare, I say that those images exist in act and substantially in the part that does not fall, and are received anew and accidentally in the part that falls.

---

prestigiorum, which we know that Adelard translated, presumably came bound with whatever text Pico had in his hands. Pico would probably have known Thabit's approximate dates, and we can only assume that in his confusion over Adelard he confused Thabit as well with some earlier figure.

21.1–3. Cf. the series starting at 1.1, 1.6. Pico's own voice is clearly apparent in 21.3.

21.4. Maior pars rerum quae in somnis innotescunt aut per purgationem animae, aut per indemoniationem, aut per meram spiritus reuelationem innotescunt.

21.5. Quod scribit Tabet Chaldeus de dormitione super ępar in reuelatione somniorum recte intelligetur si ad hoc dictum dicta Platonis in Timeo concordauerimus.

21.6. Quia sicut dixit Abdala‸ videre somnia est fortitudo imaginationis, intelligere ea est fortitudo intellectus, ideo qui uidet ea ut plurimum non intelligit ea.

21.7. Anima est fons motus et gubernatrix materiae.

21.8. Transcorporationem animarum crediderunt omnes sapientes Indorum, Persarum‸ Aegyptiorum‸ et Chaldeorum. <8r/8v>

21.7. 1486 guberrnatrix

21.4–6. Cf. 7.1 and note. In *Timaeus* 71d–72c the liver is represented as the site of the irrational soul, which during sleep, illness, or divine possession receives inspired images from the intellect. Those who *have* visions are hence not in the proper mental state to *interpret* them. On Thabit, see the opening note to this section. The identity of "Abdalla" is uncertain. The famous opening quotation in the *Oration*—"Nothing is more miraculous than man!"—is similarly ascribed to an unidentified "Abdalla the Saracen."

21.4. The greatest part of the things that are learned in dreams are learned either through the purification of the soul, or through demonic possession, or through the pure revelation of spirit. (245)

21.5. We can correctly understand what Thabit the Chaldean writes about sleeping over the liver in the revelation of dreams if we unite this saying to the words of Plato in the *Timaeus*.

21.6. Since, as Abdalla said, to see dreams takes strength of imagination, to understand them strength of intellect, it follows that those who see them for the most part do not understand them.

21.7. The soul is the source of motion and governess of matter.

21.8. All Indian, Persian, Egyptian, and Chaldean wisemen believed in the transmigration of souls.

21.7. Series on motion start at 2.37–38 and 7.7–8.

21.8. See 20.4 and note.

CONCLVSIONES SECVNDVM PORPHYRIVM NVMERO .XII.

22.1. Per patrem apud Platonem intelligere debemus causam quae a seipsa totum effectum producit; per factorem eam quae materiam accipit ab alio.

22.2. Opifex mundi est supermundana anima.

22.3. Exemplar non est aliud quam intellectus ipsius opificis animae.

22.4. Omnis anima participans uulcanio intellectu seminatur in lunam.

22.5. Ex praecedenti conclusione elicio ego cur omnes Teutones bonae corporaturae et albi coloris.

22.6. Ex eadem conclusione elicio cur omnes Teutones apostolicae sedis sint reuerentissimi.

22.7. Sicut Apollo est intellectus solaris, ita Aesculapius est intellectus lunaris.

22.8. Ex praecedenti conclusione elicio ego cur luna in ascendente dat sanitatem nato.

CONCLUSIONS ACCORDING TO PORPHYRY. The theses here on the creation myth in the *Timaeus* derive from reports of Porphyry's views found in Proclus's commentary on that work (ed. Diehl, 3 vols., 1903–1906). Pico also drew from the Greek texts of Porphyry's fragmentary *Sententiae ad intelligibilia ducentes* (ed. Mommert, 1907) and from the *De abstinentia animalium* (ed. Nauck, 1886). Kristeller (1937: 1:cxxxii ff.) argued that all of Ficino's translations of Iamblichus, Porphyry, and Proclus dated from 1488, two years after publication of Pico's theses. Marcel (1956: 487ff.) claimed that Ficino's translation of Porphyry dated from 1486, but even if that date were correct, no evidence suggests that Pico had read it. The texts of all these translations were first printed in 1497, several years after Pico's death.

TWELVE CONCLUSIONS ACCORDING TO PORPHYRY.

22.1. By the father in Plato we should understand the cause which from itself produces every effect; by the maker that which receives matter from the other. (250)

22.2. The demiurge of the world is the supermundane soul.

22.3. The exemplar is nothing but the intellect of that demiurgal soul.

22.4. Every soul participating in the vulcanic intellect is seminated on the moon.

22.5. From the preceding conclusion I deduce why all Germans are large in body and white in color.

22.6. From the same conclusion I deduce why all Germans of the apostolic seat should be the most reverent. (255)

22.7. Just as Apollo is the solar intellect, so Aesculapius is the lunar intellect.

22.8. From the preceding conclusion I deduce why the moon in ascending gives health at birth.

22.1–3. Drawn from Proclus *In Timaeum* (Diehl 1:300). A reading of the emanational symbols that Pico found here can be constructed by comparing these theses with 23.2 from Iamblichus, 24.18 from Proclus, 3>21 and 5>2 from Pico's opinions, etc.

22.4–8. Adapted by Pico from Proclus *In Timaeum* (Diehl 1:147, 159), which pits Porphyry against Iamblichus. The first of many theses involving astrological correspondences. It is important to note that none of these endorses the horoscopal types of astrology attacked most sharply in the *Disputations*. On this, see my discussion above, pp. 139ff. In thesis 22.6, "apostolic seat" = the papacy. In 22.7, "Apollo"/"solar intellect" = Pico's "total" or "angelic" intellect; "Aesculapius"/"lunar intellect" = the passive intellect or "reason" (cf. 5>19)—throwing light on Pico's mystical riddle in 22.8. Other theses with astrological elements include 23.7, 5>9–12, 5>34, 7a>74, 11>72, with many others in Pico's magical and Cabalistic theses.

22.9. Duplex est malorum demonum genus; alterum animae sunt et substantiales demones; alterum materiales potentiae et accidentales demones.

22.10. Duplex genus demonum de quibus dixit secundum Porphirium praecedens conclusio nihil credimus esse aliud quam membrorum legem et potestates harum tenebrarum, de quibus apud Paulum, quamuis de quiditate et substantia harum potestatum eos non credo conuenire.

22.11. Plato in principio tractatus Timei de extremis tantum determinat, id est de eo quod uere est nullo modo genitum, et de eo quod uere genitum nullo modo ens. De mediis nihil, quorum alterum ens et genitum, alterum genitum et ens.

22.12. Deus ubique est quia nullibi est, intellectus ubique est quia nullibi est, anima ubique est quia nullibi est; sed deus ubique et nullibi respectu omnium quae post ipsum; intellectus autem in deo quidem est, ubique autem et nullibi respectu eorum quae post ipsum. Anima in intellectu et deo, ubique autem et nullibi respectu corporis.

22.9–10. Cf. *De abstinentia* 2.38–40; Rom. 7:23; Col. 1:13. *De abstinentia* 2.39 likewise considers the issue of the visibility and invisibility of demons raised by Pico in 5>43–44.

22.9. There are two kinds of evil demons; one consists of souls and substantial demons; the other of material powers and accidental demons.

22.10. I believe that the two kinds of demons of which the preceding conclusion spoke according to Porphyry are nothing but the *law of members* and *powers of this darkness* in Paul, although I do not believe that they agree on the quiddity and substance of these powers.

22.11. In the beginning of the *Timaeus* Plato only defines the extremes, that is, that which truly is in no mode begotten, and that which truly begotten is in no mode being. Of middle natures he says nothing, of which one is being and begotten, the other begotten and being. (260)

22.12. God is everywhere because he is nowhere, the intellect is everywhere because it is nowhere, the soul is everywhere because it is nowhere. But God is everywhere and nowhere in respect to all things that are after him. The intellect is indeed in God, but is everywhere and nowhere in respect to those things that are after it. The soul is in the intellect and God, but is everywhere and nowhere in respect to the body.

22.11. Compare with 5>15 from Plato, 6>8 from the *Book of Causes*. Interpreting Proclus *In Timaeum* (Diehl 1:219). For Pico "the extremes" in this thesis = God and prime matter; "middle things" = the intellectual and rational natures. Neither of these phrases is found in Pico's source. The proportional form of the thesis too goes far beyond Porphyry, at least as Proclus represents him.

22.12. Aphorizes material found in *Sent. ad intelligibilia ducentes*, 1.31. Pico refers to this thesis again in 11>29 from his last set of Cabalistic theses. Cf. also 27.3–4.

CONCLVSIONES SECVNDVM IAMBLICVM NVMERO .VIIII.

<8v/9r>

23.1. Intellectus speculatiuus est forma separata quantum ad rem et ad modum; practicus separata_quantum ad rem, coniuncta_quantum ad modum; anima rationalis coniuncta secundum rem, separata secundum modum; inrationalis coniuncta secundum rem et secundum modum.

23.2. Opifex sensibilis mundi septimus est hierarchiae intellectualis.

23.3. Corporalis natura est in intellectu immobiliter, in animo ex se primo mobiliter, in animali ex se mobiliter participatiue, in coelo aliunde ordinate mobiliter, infra lunam aliunde mobiliter inordinate.

23.4. Elementa in octo coeli corporibus coelesti modo bis inueniuntur, quae quis inueniet si retrogrado ordine in illa bina numeratione processerit.

23.1. 1487 rationalis coniuncta secundum rem et secundum modum

23.3. 1486 aliunde ordinate: | *Emendationes errorum*, corrige: aliunde ordinate mobiliter | 1487 text emended *sic*

CONCLUSIONS ACCORDING TO IAMBLICHUS. Some of these conclusions were again drawn from Proclus's commentary on the *Timaeus*, which preserves fragments of Iamblichus's lost commentary on that text. For a useful collection of these fragments, see Dillon, ed. (1973). All or most of the rest were drawn loosely from the first book of *De mysteriis*, parts of which Ficino translated into Latin two years after Pico published the nine hundred theses. *De mysteriis* purports to answer a polemical letter from Porphyry to Iamblichus's disciple Anebo, providing evidence of "civil warfare" in the Platonic camp that predictably caught Pico's eye. The striking proportions in these theses, like those in the preceding section from Porphyry, again go far beyond what we find in Pico's sources.

23.1. Deduced from more diffuse material in *De mysteriis* 1.3. The punctuation in the *editio princeps* is especially garbled in this thesis.

NINE CONCLUSIONS ACCORDING TO IAMBLICHUS.

23.1. The speculative intellect is a separated form in regard to substance and mode [of operation]. The practical intellect is separated in regard to substance, conjoined in regard to mode. The rational soul is conjoined according to substance, separated according to mode. The irrational soul is conjoined according to substance and mode.

23.2. The demiurge of the sensible world is the seventh of the intellectual hierarchy.

23.3. Corporeal nature exists in the intellect immovably, in the first soul through itself movably, in the animal soul through itself movably participatively, in heaven through another movably in an orderly way, below the moon through another movably in a disorderly way.

23.4. The elements are found in the eight heavenly bodies in two celestial modes, which anyone will find if he proceeds in reverse order through that numeration of *Binah*. (265)

23.2. Cf. Proclus *In Timaeum* (Diehl 1:308). Some related theses are listed in note 22.1–3. "intellectual hierarchy" = one of the *henadic* orders in Proclus (see opening note to next section). Saffrey and Westerink (1978: 3:ix ff.) claim that the *henads* originated with Proclus's master Syrianus, but cf. Dodds (1963: 346) and Dillon (1973: 412ff.), who trace them back much earlier. Dillon, like Pico, finds evidence of the *henads* in Iamblichus.

23.3. Systematizes diffuse material from *De mysteriis* 1; cf., e.g., chaps. 9, 17–18. The proportional language is again Pico's and is not found in Iamblichus.

23.4. In the series on the *caelum* starting at 7.9. Apparently inspired by *De mysteriis* 1.17. "*Binah*" = "intelligence," the third of the kabbalistic *sefirot* or "numerations," which are of late-medieval origins and are obviously not mentioned by Iamblichus. Pico evidently meant to derive the two "celestial modes" of the elements from *Binah* using his *revolutio alphabetariae* or some form of *gematria*. On these, see above, pp. 63–66. Hints as to Pico's sense here can be gathered from 11>67 in his Cabalistic theses.

23.5. Super hunc mundum, quem uocant Theologi < >, est alius quem uocant < >, et super hunc alius quem uocant < >.

23.6. Cum excellenter ad intellectum assimilatur anima, fit in uehiculo motus perfecte circularis.

23.7. Nulla est uis coelestium astrorum quantum est in se malefica.

23.8. Qui finalem causam diluuiorum incendiorumque cognouerit, haec potius <καθάρσεις>, id est purgationes, quam corruptiones uocabit.

23.9. Cum dicit Plato in mundi medio positam animam, de inparticipata anima debet intelligi, quam ideo in medio dicit positam, quia aequaliter omnibus adest, ab omni respectu et particulari habitudine liberata.

23.7. 1487 malefitia

23.5. Kieszkowski, followed by Biondi, fills in the blanks from Proclus's *Elements of Theology* with the impossible triad ὄν, ζωή, νοῦς ("being," "life," "intellect")—valid concepts in later Greek Neo-Platonism, as we see in 20.6 and 24.46, but clearly not the three worlds intended here. Pico was again probably drawing from book 1 of *De mysteriis*—the "theologians" are presumably the Egyptian, Chaldean, and Assyrian priests discussed in that work—where much space is spent distinguishing the higher realms of the gods from the middle world of demons and heroes, etc. The exact terms that Pico had in mind, however, are unknown.

23.5. Over this world, which the theologians call < >, there is another that they call < >, and over this another that they call < >.

23.6. When the soul is assimilated to the intellect in an elevated fashion, motion in the vehicle becomes perfectly circular.

23.7. There is no force in the celestial stars that in itself is evil.

23.8. Whoever knows the final cause of deluges and conflagrations will call these <*katharseis*>, that is, purifications, rather than destructions.

23.9. When Plato says that the soul is placed in the middle of the world, this should be understood of the unparticipated soul, which he says is placed in the middle, because freed from every relation and particular location, it equally approaches all things. (270)

23.6. Drawn from Proclus *In Timaeum* (Diehl 2:72). On the "vehicle" or Neo-Platonic "body" of the soul, see note 5>45. The thesis is evidently meant to clash with 20.11 from Plotinus.

23.7. Drawn from *De mysteriis* 1.18, which pertains to astrology and magic. Cf. the theses listed in note 22.4–8.

23.8. Quoting Proclus on the destruction of Atlantis from *In Timaeum* 1 (Diehl 1:119), whose Greek I have inserted in the text. In Diehl's edition the Egyptian to whom these words are ascribed is not Iamblichus, whose interpretation of the destruction of Atlantis is given some forty-five lines earlier, but the Egyptian priest of *Timaeus* 22b ff.

23.9. Cf. 5>7 from Pico's opinions.

CONCLVSIONES SECVNDVM PROCLVM NUMERO .LV.

24.1. Quod est in intelligibilibus terminus et infinitum, est in intellectualibus mas et femina, in supermundanis idemtitas et alteritas, similitudo et dissimilitudo. In anima circulatio eiusdem et circulatio alterius.

24.2. A Saturniis legibus eximuntur dei qui contentiui et perfectiui sunt; a Iouiis legibus dei Saturnii; a fatalibus legibus omnis anima uiuens intellectualiter. Legi autem Adrastiae omnia obediunt.

24.1. 1487 terminis

CONCLUSIONS ACCORDING TO PROCLUS. All but a handful of these theses were drawn from Proclus's massive syncretic masterpiece, his *Platonic Theology*. Pico was apparently working from the Greek text; in any case, his technical translations differ markedly from those found in the one known fifteenth-century translation of the text, made by Petrus Balbus for Nicholas of Cusa (see above, p. 20 n. 52). Most of this section concerns the complex orders of deanthropomorphized gods or *henads* at the center of Proclus's system, which Pico planned to correlate with the kabbalistic *sefirot* and similar syncretic concepts in other esoteric traditions. As Pico represents him, Proclus assigned the gods of the Platonic corpus to three superior metaphysical orders following the "one"—the "intelligible trinity," "intelligible-intellectual trinity," and "intellectual hebdomad"—followed by the three inferior orders of "supermundane gods," "twelve gods of the *Phaedrus*," and "mundane gods." (Reflecting the syncretic nature of Proclus's own system, all these orders had a large and confusing number of alternate names as well.) Below these six orders came four inferior orders of "angels," "demons," "heroes," and "souls" constructed along similar hierarchical lines. Proclus pictured each member (or "unity" or *henad*) of these orders as having further triadic orders subordinate to it; each could as well be systematically linked with concrete images from Platonic myths (the "celestial circumference," "supercelestial place," "slaughter of the gods," etc.) or with abstract philosophical concepts drawn from other Platonic or pseudo-Platonic works ("the whole," "limit," "the extremes," etc.). Proclus's goal was to demonstrate that every line of Platonic Scriptures was in total harmony with every other—with the supreme syncretic principle that "all things exist in all things in

FIFTY-FIVE CONCLUSIONS ACCORDING TO PROCLUS.

24.1. What in intelligibles is limit and infinite, in intellectuals is male and female; in supermundanes identity and otherness, similitude and dissimilitude; in the soul the revolution of the same and the revolution of the other.

24.2. The gods who are conserving and perfecting are exempt from the laws of Saturn. The Saturnian gods are exempt from the laws of Jove. Every soul living intellectually is exempt from the laws of fate. But all things obey the law of Adrastia.

---

their own mode" (cf. 24.17) ensuring that in times of special exegetical need any god, mythopoeic image, or abstract concept could stand for every other. In his debate Pico planned to correlate this material further with the ten kabbalistic *sefirot*, with Pseudo-Dionysius's hierarchies of angel, and related syncretic constructs—invariably distinguished in sets of threes, tens, or their multiples—that Pico found in the "Chaldean Theologians," Pythagoras, Mercury (Hermes) Trismegistus, Zoroaster, Orpheus, etc. As in his theses from Porphyry and Iamblichus, Pico went far beyond Proclus in the symmetries and proportions of his language, compressing dozens of pages of Proclus's thought into his own rigid correlative forms. Pico nevertheless gives us a surprisingly rich and accurate picture of Proclus's "gods," whose symbolism often surpasses in obscurity even the symbolism of Pico's Cabalistic theses.

A note on references: Chapter numbers in the 1618 Portus edition and in the edition of the *Platonic Theology* by Saffrey and Westerink (6 vols., 1968–) do not always coincide. For the sake of uniformity, references here are given to the page numbers in Portus's edition, which are reprinted in bold type in the upper left-hand margin of Saffrey/Westerink.

24.1. Ordering for syncretic ends traditional dichotomies found in the *Philebus*, *Sophist*, *Parmenides*, *Timaeus*, and other Platonic or pseudo-Platonic dialogues.

24.2. Systematizing material from Proclus *Theologia Platonica* 4 (pp. 205–6), which attempted to harmonize various passages in the *Gorgias*, *Laws*, *Timaeus*, and *Phaedrus*. "Adrastia" (cf. *Phaedrus* 248c) = Proclus's symbol for the "mode" of necessity pertaining to the "intelligible trinity." Part of a large series of theses distinguishing hierarchical levels of necessity and freedom. Cf. 2.3–7, 26.2, 28.12, 1>15, 2>14–15, 5>27, 5>35, 5>47, 6>10, 10>29.

24.3. Dei appellatio simpliciter absolute uni competit, qui est deus deorum; simpliciter non absolute cuilibet supersubstantialium; secundum essentiam intellectualium cuilibet; secundum participationem ani/mis diuinis; secundum contactum et coniunctionem demonibus; secundum similitudinem animis humanis. <9r/9v>

24.4. Contentiua proprietas est medii ordinis secundae trinitatis, qui in Phedro coelestis dicitur circumductus.

24.5. In intelligibilibus non est numerus, sed multitudo, et numerorum causa paternalis ac maternalis; in intellectualibus uero est numerus secundum essentiam et communicatiue multitudo.

24.6. Idem est quod dicitur alteritas in Parmenide, et supercoelestis locus in Phedro.

24.7. Per unum, plura, totum, partes, finitum, infinitum, de quibus in Parmenide, habemus intelligere secundum ordinem trinitatis intelligibilis intellectualis, secundum illius ordinis trinariam diuisionem.

24.8. Quod in Phedro dicitur dorsum coeli, in Parmenide dicitur unum; quod ibi profundum coeli, hic totum; quod ibi axis coeli, hic terminus.

24.7. 1487 intelligibilibus intellectualibus

24.3. Apparently systematizing material from *In Timaeum* (Diehl 3:202ff.).

24.4. Drawn from *Theologia Platonica* 4 (p. 209). "second trinity" = the "intelligible-intellectual order." Pico here associates the second *henad* or "unity" of that order with a phrase from the charioteer myth, *Phaedrus* 246a ff. For Ficino's later reading of that myth, see Allen (1981).

24.5. Systematizes material from *Theologia Platonica* 4 (pp. 222–23). Obscure hints here can be found concerning the form of Pico's emanationist numerology. Cf. 7.34 and note, 24.11.

24.6. Systematizes material from *Theologia Platonica* 4 (pp. 198–200). Much of the *Theologia Platonica* is concerned with reconciling the abstract language of the *Parmenides* with the mythopoeic language of the *Phaedrus*. The reference here is to the first of the three main orders of Proclus's "intelligible-intellectual gods."

24.3. The name of God applies simply and absolutely to one, who is the God of gods; simply not absolutely to anything supersubstantial; according to essence to anything intellectual; according to participation to divine souls; according to contact and conjunction to demons; according to similitude to human souls.

24.4. The conserving property belongs to the middle order of the second trinity, which in the *Phaedrus* is called the celestial circumference.

24.5. In intelligibles number does not exist but multitude, and the paternal and maternal cause of numbers; but in intellectuals number exists according to essence and multitude communicatively. (275)

24.6. What is called otherness in the *Parmenides* and supercelestial place in the *Phaedrus* is the same.

24.7. By the one/many, whole/parts, finite/infinite, in the *Parmenides*, we have to understand the second order of the intelligible-intellectual trinity, following the triple division of that order.

24.8. What in the *Phaedrus* is called the back of heaven, in the *Parmenides* is called the one. What is there called the depth of heaven, is here called the whole. What is there called the arch of heaven, is here called limit.

24.7. Drawn from *Theologia Platonica* 4 (p. 235). The claim is that each of the three main suborders of the middle member of the "intelligible-intellectual trinity" corresponds to one pair of contraries in the *Parmenides*.

24.8. Drawn from *Theologia Platonica* 4 (pp. 237–38), once again correlating the abstract language of the *Parmenides* with the mythopoeic language of the charioteer myth in the *Phaedrus*. The terms here refer again to the middle order of Proclus's "intelligible-intellectual trinity." Cf. 28.27 and note.

24.9. Tertium ordinem secundae trinitatis per tres terminos exprimit Plato: extrema, perfectum, et secundum figuram.

24.10. Intellectuales dii uniones habent ab uno primo; substantias ab intelligibilibus; uitas perfectas et contentiuas, generatiuas diuinorum, ab intelligibilibus et intellectualibus; intellectualem proprietatem a seipsis.

24.11. Sicut intelligibiles dei uniformiter omnia producunt, ita intelligibiles intellectualesque trinaliter, intellectuales autem ebdomatice.

24.12. Inter extremales paternos deos, Saturnum et Iouem, mediat necessario Rhea per proprietatem uitae foecundae.

24.13. Secunda trinitas ebdomadis intellectualis est trinitas curetum, quos uocat theologia intemeratos deos.

24.14. Proprium curetum est reddere opus paternae trinitatis immaculatum: mansionem primi, processum secundi, illustrationem tertii.

24.9. colon retained from 1486 edition

24.12. 1486 proprieratem

24.14. colon retained from 1486 edition

24.9. *Theologia Platonica* 4 (p. 238), with each term symbolizing one subordinate order under the third principal *henad* or "unity" of the "intelligible-intellectual trinity."

24.10. Drawn from *Theologia Platonica* 5 (pp. 247–48).

24.11. Compresses material from *Theologia Platonica* 5 (pp. 249ff.).

24.9. Plato represents the third order of the second trinity through three terms: the extremes, the perfect, and according to figure.

24.10. The intellectual gods possess their unities from the first one; their substances from intelligibles; their perfect and conserving lives, generative of divine things, from intelligibles-and-intellectuals; the intellectual property from themselves. (280)

24.11. Just as the intelligible gods produce all things uniformly, so intelligibles-and-intellectuals do so in trinities, but intellectuals in hebdomads.

24.12. Between the extreme paternal gods, Saturn and Jove, Rhea necessarily mediates through the property of fertile life.

24.13. The second trinity of the intellectual hebdomad is the trinity of guardians, which theology calls the undefiled gods.

24.14. It is the property of the guardians to impart the immaculate work of the paternal trinity: the indwelling of the first, the procession of the second, the illumination of the third.

24.12. Cf. *Theologia Platonica* 5 (pp. 253, 265ff.). "Rhea"/"Saturn"/"Jove" here = "the paternal trinity" = the first three principal orders (out of seven) of Proclus's "intellectual hebdomad."

24.13–14. *Theologia Platonica* 5 (pp. 253ff.). "trinity of guardians" = the fourth through sixth main orders of the "intellectual hebdomad." "theology" here = "Orphic theology"; cf. 10>1–31. "paternal trinity" = first three prime orders of the "intellectual hebdomad" (see previous note).

24.15. Per deorum cedes tragice a theologis septima unitas discretiua intellectualis ebdomadae designatur.

24.16. Eadem quae Rhea dicitur ut Saturno coexistens secundum suam summitatem, ut Iouem producit et cum Ioue totales et partiales deorum ordines, dicitur Caeres. <9v/10r>

24.17. Licet ut tradit theologia distinctae sint diuinae hierarchiae,_ intelligendum est tamen omnia in omnibus esse modo suo.

24.18. Sicut paternalis proprietas est solum in intelligibilibus, ita conditoria siue factiua solum in deis nouis;_ paterna simul et conditoria_in exemplari intelligibili;_ conditoria_et paterna in opifici.

24.19. Quaecunque uel deorum uel naturae operationes duplices sunt,_ immanentes et transeuntes; per immanentes seipsum unumquodque continet_et quae in ipso sunt rationes;_ per transeuntes ad exteriora se conuertit.

24.20. Post intellectualem ebdomadem ordinandi sunt immediate supermundani dei a partibus uniuersi exempti, et incoordinabiles ad hunc mundum, et secundum causam eum undique circumplectentes.

24.18. 1486 paterna inopificia. | 1487 paterna inopifitia.

24.15. Cf. *Theologia Platonica* 5 (pp. 324ff.). The "theologians" = Orphic theologians. "seventh divided unity" = last of the seven main *henads* or "unities" in the "intellectual hebdomad."

24.16. *Theologia Platonica* 5 (p. 267). "Rhea"/"Saturn"/"Jove" = see 24.12 note. Illustrates the reconciliative principle of "all in all" introduced in the next thesis. Cf. 28.3 from Pico's first set of Cabalistic conclusions.

24.17. *Theologia Platonica* 5 (p. 275). For the syncretic origins of this concept, see above, pp. 85–89.

24.18. *Theologia Platonica* 5 (pp. 275ff.). Cf. 22.1–3, 23.2, etc. The punctuation in the *editio princeps* and all later editions of Pico's text is especially corrupt. I have reconstructed Pico's sense in the light of nearby theses and the extended text from Proclus from which the thesis was

24.15. By the *tragic slaughter of the gods* theologians refer to the seventh divided unity of the intellectual hebdomad. (285)

24.16. The same thing that is called Rhea as it coexists at its summit with Saturn, as it produces Jove, and with Jove the total and partial orders of the gods, is called Ceres.

24.17. Granted, as theology teaches, the divine hierarchies are distinct, it should be understood that all exist in all in their own mode.

24.18. Just as the paternal property exists only in intelligibles, so the productive or formative property exists only in the new gods; the paternal and productive property simultaneously in the intelligible exemplar; the productive and paternal property in the demiurge.

24.19. All operations of either the gods or nature are of two kinds, immanent and transitive; through immanent operations each thing contains itself and whatever reasons exist in itself; through transitive operations it converts to external things.

24.20. After the intellectual hebdomad one should immediately place the supermundane gods, who are removed from the parts of the universe, and who are both incoordinable with this world and who encircle it everywhere as its cause. (290)

---

drawn. Meant to reconcile apparent conflicts over the identity of the "father" and the "demiurge," etc., in the *Timaeus* by distributing them to different hierarchical orders. "new gods" = alternate name for Proclus's "mundane" (or "junior" or "sublunary") gods (24.36ff.). "intelligible exemplar" = third main *henad* of the "intelligible trinity." "demiurge" here = third god in the first or "paternal trinity" of the "intellectual hebdomad" ("Jove" in thesis 24.12).

24.19. The sense in the *editio princeps* is again garbled due to mispunctuation. Drawn loosely from *Theologia Platonica* 5 (p. 283). Pico expresses Proclus's views in very alien Latin scholastic terms. Cf. 2>9–10, 3>19.

24.20. Drawn from *Theologia Platonica* 6 (p. 344), in this rare case a near quotation.

24.21. Proprium est supermundanorum deorum assimilare et tradere entibus compassionem illam et inuicem communionem, quam habent ex similitudine unius ad alterum.

24.22. Licet assimilatiuum ducalium, de quibus dixit praecedens conclusio, proprium sit, appropriatur tamen medio ordini trinitatis suae primo ordine, intellectualibus deis immediate secundum substantiam coniuncto, et tertio secundis generibus se commiscente.

24.23. Iupiter de quo in Gorgia, non est ille qui est uniuersalis conditor, tertius inter intellectuales, sed summus et primus inter ducales.

24.24. Ducalis trinitatis Iupiter est substantificatiuus, Neptunnus uiuificatiuus, Pluto conuersiuus.

24.25. Quadruplex est fabrica: prima uniuersalia uniuersalium ex toto perornat; secunda uniuersa quidem sed particulariter; tertia secundum diuisa secundum uniuersalitatem; quarta partes particulariter contexit uniuersalibus.

24.21. 1486, 1487 super mundanorum

24.22. 1486 coniuncto.& tertio

24.25. colon retained from 1486 edition

24.21. Drawn from *Theologia Platonica* 6 (pp. 345ff.). Providing, e.g., magical sympathy between the lower and higher worlds.

24.22. Attempts to systematize material from *Theologia Platonica* 6 (p. 354), where Proclus tells us that the assimilative property belongs most perfectly to the middle order of "leaders" or "supermundane gods."

24.21. It is the property of the supermundane gods to assimilate and transmit to beings that sympathy and reciprocal communion that they possess from their similarity to one another.

24.22. Granted that assimilation is a general property of the leaders, of whom the preceding conclusion spoke, it is attributed to the middle order of its trinity through the first order, conjoined immediately to the intellectual gods according to substance, and through the third, which intermixes with subordinate genera.

24.23. Jupiter in the *Gorgias* is not he who is the universal creator, third among the intellectuals, but is the highest and first among the leaders.

24.24. Jupiter is the substantifier of the trinity of leaders, Neptune the vivifier, Pluto the converter.

24.25. The fabric [of the universe] is fourfold: the first is adorned with the universals of universals totally; the second with universals indeed, but particular ones; the third with division and universality; the fourth weaves particular parts to the universals. (295)

24.23–24. Drawn from *Theologia Platonica* 6 (pp. 355–57). "universal creator" = the demiurge in 24.18 and Jove in 24.12. Jupiter in 24.23 is distributed to different levels of reality for reconciliative ends.

24.25. Following the language of *Theologia Platonica* 5 (p. 269).

24.26. Iupiter, Neptunnus, et Pluto, Saturni regnum partientes, a Saturno Regnum non accipiunt nisi per medium conditoris Iouis.

24.27. Sub primo ducalis trinitatis est esse substantiale, omnis anima nobilis generationi non subdita, primum mobile, ignis et suprema aeris pars, quae super terram crescunt, et pars orientalis. <10r/10v>

24.28. Sub secundo ducalis trinitatis est uita et generatio, omnis anima sub generationem ueniens, erraticae spherae, aqua et infima aeris pars, quae sub antra minerae et terremotus, media pars terrae et circa centrum.

24.29. Sub tertio eiusdem ordinis est specialium diuisionum conuersio, animarum purgatio, sphera actiuorum et passiuorum, terra cum terrestribus, quae circa Tartarum, et pars occidentalis.

24.30. Et si secunda trinitas deorum supermundanorum tota dicatur Proserpina, tamen prima eius unitas apud graecos dicitur Diana, secunda Persephone, tertia Minerua; apud barbaros uero, prima Hechate, secunda anima, tertia uirtus.

24.27. 1486 substantiale. Omnis

24.28. 1486 generatio. Omnis

24.30. 1486 Thesis split in two following *persephone*, corrected in *Emendationes errorum* | 1487 text emended *sic*

24.26. Drawn from *Theologia Platonica* 6 (pp. 360ff.). "Jupiter"/"Neptune"/"Pluto" = the chief *henads* of the order of Proclus's "leaders" or "supermundane gods." "Saturn" here = the first of the "intellectual gods." "creator Jove" = the third of that order, apparently the same as "Jove" in 24.12, the "demiurge" in 24.18 and 24.39ff., and the "universal creator" in 24.23!

24.26. Jupiter, Neptune, and Pluto, dividing the kingdom of Saturn, did not receive the kingdom from Saturn except through the mediation of creator Jove.

24.27. Under the first of the trinity of leaders is substantial existence, every noble soul not subject to generation, the *primum mobile*, fire and the highest part of the air, those things that rise above the earth, and the eastern part.

24.28. Under the second of the trinity of leaders is life and generation, every soul subject to generation, the erratic spheres, water and the lowest part of the air, those things beneath mineral caves and earthquakes, and the middle part of the earth and that which exists near the center.

24.29. Under the third of the same order is the conversion of particular divided things, the purification of souls, the sphere of the active and passive, the earth with terrestrial things, those things around Tartarus, and the western part.

24.30. Although the whole second trinity of supermundane gods is called Proserpina, its first unity among the Greeks is called Diana, the second Persephone, the third Minerva; but among the barbarians, the first is called Hecate, the second is called soul, the third, virtue. (300)

24.27–29. Systematizes much more diffuse material from *Theologia Platonica* 6 (pp. 367–69), which deals with the assimilative functions of the "leaders" "Jove," "Neptune," and "Pluto" in the previous theses. These theses thus have apparent magical implications.

24.30. Systematizes material from *Theologia Platonica* 6 (pp. 370–72). The "barbarians" in Proclus and Pico normally refer to the "Chaldeans."

24.31. Secundum precedentem conclusionem ex Procli mente potest exponi unum ex dictis Zoroastris secundum quod apud Graecos legitur, quanquam apud Chaldeos aliter et legitur et exponitur.

24.32. Tertia trinitas deorum supermundanorum dicitur Apollo, et conuersiuum ei appropriatur.

24.33. Trinitatem Proserpinae comitantur a latere trinitas custoditiua et conseruatiua.

24.34. Duodecim dei de quibus in Phedro dei sunt medii inter supermundanos et mundanos, uinculum illorum.

24.35. Dei de quibus in Phedro in quatuor trinitates sunt distinguendi: Opificatiuam, Custoditiuam, Vitalem, et Conuersiuam.

24.36. Quatuor sunt exercitus iuniorum deorum. Primus habitat a primo coelo usque ad principium aeris; secundus inde usque ad dimidium aeris. Tertius inde usque ad terram.

24.37. Cuilibet istorum proportionaliter correspondet quadruplex exercitus Angelorum, Demonum, et Animarum.

24.35. colon retained from 1486 edition

24.31. Reflecting Pico's claim that he possessed the *Chaldean Oracles* in an original Chaldean text. See above, p. 13, and my introductory note to theses 8>1–15.

24.32. Drawn from *Theologia Platonica* 6 (pp. 376ff.).

24.33. Drawn from *Theologia Platonica* 6 (pp. 381ff.). "Proserpina" = the second trinity of "supermundane gods" (cf. 24.30). Proclus correlates that trinity here with an inferior reflection of the "guardians," the second order in the "intellectual hebdomad" (24.13–14).

24.34. Drawn from *Theologia Platonica* 6 (pp. 394ff.), referring to the twelve celestial gods of the charioteer myth in the *Phaedrus* (cf. note 24.4).

24.31. From the preceding conclusion from the mind of Proclus, one of Zoroaster's sayings can be explained as it is read among the Greeks, although among the Chaldeans it is read and explained differently.

24.32. The third trinity of the supermundane gods is called Apollo, and the property of conversion is attributed to it.

24.33. The custodial and conserving trinities accompany the trinity of Proserpina at its side.

24.34. The twelve gods in the *Phaedrus* are the medium between the supermundane and mundane gods, the bond between them.

24.35. The gods in the *Phaedrus* should be distinguished into four trinities: demiurgal, custodial, vital, and converting. (305)

24.36. There are four [*sic*] armies of the junior gods. The first inhabits the region from the first heaven up to the beginning of the air; the second from there to the middle of the air; the third from there to the earth.

24.37. To each of these proportionally correspond the four [*sic*] armies of angels, demons, and souls.

24.35. Drawn from *Theologia Platonica* 6 (p. 400). See previous note.

24.36–37. Unfinished "forced fits"? (The phrase "quadruplex exercitus" in 24.37 clearly refers to four armies and not four divisions in three armies; cf. the use of *triplex* in 25.6.) "junior" gods = "mundane" or "new" or "sublunary" gods = the lowest of divinities in Proclus properly speaking. In *Theologia Platonica* 6 Proclus breaks off before discussing them, but they are surveyed at length in *In Timaeum* 5 and passim in his other works. The fact that Pico inserted them here shows how closely he followed Proclus's system. Following *In Timaeum* 5 (Diehl 3:165)—a likely source—the missing term in 24.37 is "heroes," third order in the demonic triad of angels, demons per se, and heroes that precedes the orders of souls. On "heroes," cf. further 10>22.

24.38. In per se uiuente apparet primo quaternitas_unius, entis, unius entalis, et entis unialis.

24.39. Opifex, ad quaternitatem respiciens per se animalis, quatuor fabricat partes principales mundi.

24.40. In quantum opifex ad exemplar formae unius in per se uiuente respicit, primam partem corporis mundani facit. <10v/11r>

24.41. Inquantum opifex in forma unius uidet unum unius essentialis, facit deos mundanos illius partis; inquantum ens unius essentialis, facit angelos in eadem parte; in quantum uidet unum entis unialis, facit demones ibi; inquantum esse entis unialis, animalia ibidem facit.

24.42. Facit opifex alias partes proportionaliter ad suarum formarum exemplaria sicut de primo est dictum; nec opportet explicare, quia quilibet sciens_ uiam analogizandi ex se poterit deducere.

24.43. Ad sapiens, pulchrum, bonumque dominum_per intellectum, amorem, et fidem ascendimus.

24.44. Sicut fides quae est credulitas est infra scientiam, ita fides quae est uere fides est supersubstantialiter supra scientiam et intellectum, nos deo immediate coniungens.

24.45. Sicut non omne corpus, sed perfectum anima participat, ita non omnis anima sed perfecta intellectu participat; omnia tamen uno participant.

24.38–42. Systematizing material from *Theologia Platonica* 3 (pp. 171–72). "that which lives per se" = the "per se animal" = Proclus's designation, interpreting the *Timaeus*, for the third order of the "intelligible trinity" (the "intelligible exemplar" in 24.18). As in 24.18, the "demiurge" here = third of the seven chief members in the "intellectual hebdomad"—labeled "Jove," "universal creator," or "creator Jove" in other theses (cf. 24.26 note).

24.38. In that which lives per se there first appears the four divisions of the one, of being, of being one, and of one being.

24.39. The demiurge, regarding the four divisions of the per se animal, fabricates the four principal parts of the world.

24.40. Insofar as the demiurge regards the exemplar of the form of the one in that which lives per se, he makes the first part of the body of the world. (310)

24.41. Insofar as the demiurge in the form of the one sees the oneness of what is essentially one, he makes the mundane gods from that part. Insofar as he sees the being of what is essentially one, he makes angels in the same part. Insofar as he sees the oneness of one being, he makes demons there. Insofar as he sees the existence of one being, he makes animals in the same place.

24.42. The demiurge makes the other parts proportionally in accordance with the exemplars of their forms, just as was said of the first. Nor is it necessary to explain this, since any knowing person can deduce the method of analogizing for himself.

24.43. To a wise, beautiful, and good Lord we ascend through intellect, love, and faith.

24.44. Just as faith that is credulity is below knowledge, so faith that is truly faith exists supersubstantially over knowledge and intellect, conjoining us immediately to God.

24.45. Just as not every body, but only the perfect, participates in soul, so not every soul, but only the perfect, participates in intellect. All, however, participate in the one. (315)

24.43–44. Series starts at 2.12. Drawn from *Theologia Platonica* 4 (pp. 193–94). In Pico's source, "faith" is represented as a quietistic mystical power that imparts a "unial silence" to the soul—a position in harmony with Pico's own mystical views.

24.45. Drawn from *Theologia Platonica* 3 (pp. 127ff.). Like the next thesis, tied to the series on metaphysical unity starting at 2.23.

24.46. Sicut secundum causalitatis ambitum, ita secundum nature et gradus sublimitatem haec per ordinem se inuicem excedunt: Anima, Intellectus, Vita, Ens, et Vnum.

24.47. Omnis ordo medius manet in antecedente stabiliter, et in se firmat consequentem.

24.48. Sicut prima trinitas post unitatem est omnia intelligibiliter, commensurate, et finiformiter, ita secunda trinitas est omnia uitaliter, uere, et infinitiformiter. Tertia est omne secundum mixti proprietatem et pulchriformiter.

24.49. Prima trinitas manet tantum, secunda manet et procedit, tertia post processum conuertit.

24.50. Aeuum est supra per se animal in secunda et media trinitate.

24.51. Sicut intelligibilia causae sunt uniuersarum serierum, ita intellectualia diuisionum secundum genera communia, supermundana differentium secundum speciem; mundana differentium secundum indiuiduum.

24.52. Per supercoelestem locum habemus intelligere quod de secun/da trinitate plus est intelligibile quam intellectuale; per subcoelestem concauitatem quod magis intellectuale quam intelligibile. Per coelum id quod aeque utroque participat. <11r/11v>

24.51. 1487 universarum spetierum

24.46. Drawn from *Theologia Platonica* 3 (p. 129). Apparently clashes with 20.6 from Plotinus. Pico himself would not agree in any absolute sense that the "one" was superior to "being." See above, pp. 25–29.

24.47. Apparently deduced from *Theologia Platonica* 3 (pp. 133–34). Cf. the wording in 6.7.

24.48. Systematizes material in *Theologia Platonica* 3 (p. 142), which deals with the three main trinities of "intelligible gods" immediately following Proclus's "one."

24.46. Just as in the sphere of causality, so in the sublimity of nature and grade, these surpass each other in turn: soul, intellect, life, being, and the one.

24.47. Every middle order dwells stably in that which precedes it, and fortifies in itself that which follows it.

24.48. Just as the first trinity after unity is all things intelligibly, commensurately, and finitely formed, so the second trinity is all things vitally, truly, and infinitely formed. The third is everything according to the property of mixture and beauteously formed.

24.49. The first trinity dwells inwardly only, the second dwells inwardly and proceeds, the third, after procession, converts.

24.50. Aeviturnity exists over the per se animal in the second and middle trinity. (320)

24.51. Just as intelligibles are the causes of universal series, so intellectuals are the causes of divisions in shared genera; supermundanes of differences in species; mundanes of differences in individuals.

24.52. By supercelestial place we have to understand what of the second trinity is more intelligible than intellectual; by supercelestial cavity what is more intellectual than intelligible; by heaven that which participates equally in both.

24.49. Systematizes material in *Theologia Platonica* 3 (p. 143), which refers again to the three main trinities of "intelligible gods." Cf. the wording in 11>59 from Pico's Cabalistic theses.

24.50. Pico's interpretation of *Theologia Platonica* 3 (p. 148). "per se animal" = symbol of the third order of the "intelligible trinity" (cf. 24.38–42 and note). *Aevum* or "aeviturnity" = symbol in Proclus of the second main trinity of the "intelligible gods" as well as a durational state. Cf. the series beginning at 2.18.

24.51. Drawn from *Theologia Platonica* 3 (p. 171).

24.52. Drawn from *Theologia Platonica* 4 (pp. 186ff.), assigning different mythopoeic terms from the charioteer myth in the *Phaedrus* (cf. note 24.4) to each main *henad* in the "intelligible-intellectual trinity."

24.53. Quaecunque de supercoelesti loco in Phedro affirmatiue dicuntur, de eo dicuntur non ut simpliciter primum, sed ut habet ante se superiora genera quibus participat. Quaecunque negatiue dicuntur, dicuntur ut analogice se habet ad primum bonum, quod est absolute caput omnium, non determinati ordinis huius uel illius.

24.54. Ambrosia est analoga termino, et nectar infinito.

24.55. Sicut intellectus perfectus ab intelligibilibus quaerendus est, ita uirtus sursum ductiua ab intellectualibus; operatio absoluta et sequestrata a materia ab ultramundanis; uita alata a mundanis; expressio diuinorum uera ab angelicis choris; repletio eius, quae a diis est aspirationis, a bonis daemonibus.

24.55. 1486 sequaestrata

24.53. Systematizing material from *Theologia Platonica* 4 (pp. 197–98), concerning the charioteer myth in the *Phaedrus*. "supercelestial place" here applies in one "mode" to the first *henad* of the "intelligible-intellectual trinity," and in another to God.

24.53. Whatever in the *Phaedrus* is spoken affirmatively of supercelestial place does not refer to that which is first in a simple way, but to that which has higher genera before it in which it participates. Whatever is said negatively of it refers analogically to the first good, which is the absolute head of all things, not of a limited order of this or that.

24.54. Ambrosia is the analog of limit, and nectar of the infinite.

24.55. Just as a perfect understanding should be sought from intelligibles, so the power that leads upwards should be sought from intellectuals; an operation that is absolute and cut off from matter from the ultramundanes; a winged life from the mundanes; the true expression of the divine from the angelic choirs; its fulfillment, whose inspiration comes from the gods, from good demons. (325)

24.54. *Theologia Platonica* 4 (p. 202). "ambrosia/nectar" = the food fed by the charioteer to his horses in the *Phaedrus* (cf. 24.4 note). "limit/infinite" = cf. 24.1.

24.55. Predictably finds in Proclus six steps in the mystical ascent. Cf., e.g., 5>26, 5>58. The punctuation is badly garbled in the *editio princeps*. Alterations in the punctuation in the last part of the thesis can lead to slight changes in the sense of the text.

CONCLVSIONES SECVDVM MATHEMATICAM PYTHAGORAE NVMERO .XIIII.

25.1. Vnum, alteritas, et id quod est sunt causa numerorum: Vnum unitorum, alteritas generatiuorum, id quod est substantialium.

25.2. In participatis numeris alie sunt species numerorum, alie specierum uniones.

25.3. Vbi unitas punctalis cadit in alteritatem binarii, ibi est primo triangulus.

25.4. Qui .i.ii.iii.iiii.v.xii. ordinem cognouerit, prouidentiae distributionem exacte tenebit.

25.5. Per Vnum, Tria, et Septem, scimus in Pallade unificatiuum discretionis, causatiuam et beatificatiuam intellectus potestatem.

25.1. colon retained from 1486 edition

25.4. punctuation of numbers retained from 1486 and 1487 eds.

CONCLUSIONS ACCORDING TO THE MATHEMATICS OF PYTHAGORAS. The complex mixture of numerology and emanation theory found in these theses suggests that Pico was drawing from late Greek sources—once again, primarily Proclus—and not from more common Latin numerological sources like Nichomachus, Boethius, Isidore of Seville, or Rabanus, etc. This section should be compared as a whole with theses 7>1ff. from Pico's own own opinions. References to Proclus's *Theologica Platonica* are again to the pagination in Portus's 1618 edition (see my opening note to theses 24.1–55).

25.1. "unities" here = "monads," the archetypal forms of number in the Pythagorean tradition (cf., e.g., Plato *Philebus* 15b). Drawn from Proclus *Theologica Platonica* 4 (p. 229).

25.2. Cf. Proclus *Theologia Platonica* 4 (pp. 233–34), which distinguishes "monadic numbers"—archetypal forms of specific numbers (the triad, pentad, heptad, etc.)—from more universal "divine numbers" that unite those forms.

FOURTEEN CONCLUSIONS ACCORDING TO THE MATHEMATICS OF PYTHAGORAS.

25.1. The one, otherness, and that which is are the cause of numbers: the one of unities, otherness of generative numbers, that which is of substantial numbers.

25.2. In participated numbers some are images of numbers, others the unions of images.

25.3. When the unity of a point falls into the otherness of what is binary, the first triangle exists.

25.4. Anyone who understands the progression i, ii, iii, iiii, v, xii will exactly grasp the distribution of providence.

25.5. In one, three, and seven, we recognize in Pallas the unification of divided things, and the causative and beatifying power of the intellect. (330)

25.3. Possibly a deduction from Proclus *Theologia Platonica* 4 (p. 240).

25.4. Pico presumably planned to correlate these numbers with the six emanational levels that he distinguished elsewhere in the theses, e.g., in 24.55, 5>26, 5>58. Conceivably adapted from Proclus *In Timaeum* (Diehl 1:136), where we find the world divided by the demiurge according to the "duad, triad, tetrad, pentad, hebdomad, and dodecad" (i.e., 2, 3, 4, 5, 7, 12). If this was, in fact, Pico's source, he added a 1 to the series (found in the preceding and following text) and dropped the 7—presumably to maintain his preferred sixfold scheme. It may be significant that all these numbers add up to 27, or 3 cubed; for a closely related thesis, see 5>1.

25.5. Cf. Proclus *In Timaeum* (Diehl 1:151). "Pallas" = symbol of the intellectual nature. On the number 7 as a symbol of the "beatifying power of the intellect," see also 11>55—illustrating how consistent Pico's symbolism was throughout the theses.

25.6. Triplex proportio Arithmetica, Geometrica, et Harmonica, tres nobis Themidos filias indicat: Iudicii, Iusticiae, Pacisque existentes symbola. <11v/ 12r>

25.7. Per secretum radii recti, reflexi,_ et refracti in scientia perspectiue, triplicis naturae admonemur_intellectualis, animalis,_ et corporalis.

25.8. Ratio ad concupiscentiam habet proportionem diapason.

25.9. Irascibilis ad concupiscentiam habet proportionem diapente.

25.10. Ratio ad iram habet proportionem diatessaron.

25.11. Iudicium sensus in musica non est adhibendum, sed solius intellectus.

25.12. In formis numerandis non debemus excedere quadragenarium.

25.13. Quilibet numerus_planus aequilaterus animam symbolizat.

25.14. Quilibet numerus linearis symbolizat deos.

25.6. colon retained from 1486 edition

25.9. 1486 a diapente | *Emendationes errorum,* dele a quia superflue ponitur | 1487 text emended *sic*

25.14. 1486 Qilibet

25.6. Drawn from Proclus *In Timaeus* (Diehl 2:198). "Themis" = divine justice, with her three daughters symbolizing her inferior properties.

25.7. In 11>37 from his Cabalistic theses, Pico similarly associates the intellectual nature with "right" or "straight" lines.

25.8–10. For other theses on the virtues, see note 2.11. The correlation of virtues with musical harmonies was a premodern commonplace.

25.11. Since the study of musical proportion prepares the soul for "higher things." Cf., e.g., Plato *Republic* 7 (530d ff.).

25.6. The three kinds of proportion—arithmetic, geometric, and harmonic—indicate to us the three daughters of Themis, existing as symbols of judgment, justice, and peace.

25.7. By the secret of straight, reflected, and refracted rays, in the science of perspective, we are reminded of the threefold nature of intellectual, animate, and corporeal things.

25.8. The proportion of reason to sensual passion is an octave.

25.9. The proportion of irascibility to sensual passion is a fifth.

25.10. The proportion of reason to anger is a fourth. (335)

25.11. The judgment of the senses should not be used in music, but only of the intellect.

25.12. In numbering forms we should not exceed forty.

25.13. Every square number symbolizes the soul.

25.14. Every prime number symbolizes the gods.

25.12. Cf. 5>1 and note. On elaborations of similar ideas by Pico's Renaissance followers, see Heninger (1977: 92–96) and Plate 1 above, p. 195. In short, the number 4 (the Pythagorean limit of physical extension) and its multiples by 10 fixed emanational limits. Forty could hence be viewed as a limit on the number of corruptible forms. Copenhaver (1997: 234ff.) speculates that the thesis may also involve the closed *mem* in Hebrew, the letter equivalent of 40. Pico conceivably may have planned such a correlation, although the only mention of the closed *mem* in the theses (11>41) is in a non-numerological context.

25.13. Cf. 5>1. "every square number" = literally "every plane equilateral number." Cf. above, pp. 32, 40, where we find that the square number 900 (30 x 30) symbolized "the excited soul turning back into itself through the frenzy of the muses"—which explains why Pico included exactly 900 theses in his text.

25.14. "prime number" = literally "linear number" = any number divisible only by itself, and hence an apt symbol for indivisible divine powers. Cf., e.g., Theon of Smyrna *Mathematics Useful for Understanding Plato* 1.6 (not Pico's source).

CONCLVSIONES SECVNDVM OPINIONEM CHALDEORVM THEOLOGORVM NVMERO .VI.

26.1. Ordo separatorum principialis non est primus, ut putant aegyptii, sed super eum est ordo fontalis, unialiter superexaltatus.

26.2. Fatum non est necessitas primae potentiae seminalis, sed est intellectualiter participata habitudo animalium rationum, indeclinans a superioribus, ineuitabilis ab inferioribus.

26.3. Substantiales rerum uisibilium qualitates non a uirtute separata particulari, ut credunt aegyptii, sed a primo receptaculo fontis luminum per animalem splendorem dependenter resultant.

26.4. Animae partiales non immediate ut dicunt aegyptii, sed mediantibus totalibus animis demoniacis, ab intellectuali splendore illuminantur.

26.5. Coordinatio intelligibilis non est in intellectuali coordinatione ut dixit Amosis aegyptius, sed est super omnem intellectualem hierarchiam in abysso primae unitatis, et sub caligine primarum tenebrarum, inparticipaliter abscondita.

26.6. Quicquid est a luna supra, purum est lumen, et illud est substan/tia orbium mundanorum. <12r/12v>

26.6. 1486, 1487 prum

CONCLUSIONS ACCORDING TO THE OPINION OF THE CHALDEAN THEOLOGIANS. All these conclusions were probably loosely drawn from Greek Neo-Platonic sources, although Pico claimed to have original Chaldean sources at his disposal. See my opening note to theses 8>1–15. In any event, Pico would have associated the various "orders" mentioned here with Proclus's *henads*, with the kabbalistic *sefirot*, and similar syncretic constructs.

26.1. Like other theses in this section, emphasizes emanational principles vs. "the Egyptians," who the Neo-Platononists accused of acknowledging only particular natures. Cf. on this the polemical letter to Anebo (supposedly written by Porphyry) answered by Iamblichus in *De mysteriis*.

SIX CONCLUSIONS ACCORDING TO THE OPINION OF THE CHALDEAN THEOLOGIANS.

26.1. The principal order of separated things is not the first order, as the Egyptians suppose, but over it exists the fontal order, unitively exalted over all. (340)

26.2. Fate is not the necessity of the first seminal power but is an intellectually participated habit of animate reasons—unbending in respect to superior things, inevitable in respect to inferior things.

26.3. The substantial qualities of visible things do not reflect downwards from a particular separated power, as the Egyptians believe, but from the first receptacle of the font of light, through animate splendor.

26.4. Partial souls are not illuminated immediately by the splendor of intellect, as the Egyptians say, but through the mediation of total demonical souls.

26.5. The intelligible order does not subsist within the intellectual order, as Ahmose the Egyptian said, but over the whole intellectual hierarchy, unparticipatively hidden in the abyss of the first unity, and under the cloud of the first darkness.

26.6. Whatever exists from the moon upwards is pure light, and that is the substance of the mundane spheres. (345)

26.2. On hierarchical modes of necessity, cf. 24.2 and note.

26.3. "first receptacle of the font of light" = the intellectual nature; "animate splendor" = the world soul. The thesis provides a strong affirmation of emanationism. See 2.17 note.

26.4. Cf. *In Timaeum* (Diehl 3:269), although there is no mention there of the Chaldeans or Egyptians. *Re* illuminationism.

26.5. Cf., e.g., 11>35. "Ahmose" presumably = Ahmose II (or Amasis II), d. 525 BCE, ideal priest-king mentioned in *Timaeus* 21e.

26.6. Cf. 2>41.

CONCLVSIONES SECVNDVM PRISCAM DOCTRINAM MERCVRII TRISMEGISTI AEGYPTII NVMERO .X.

27.1. Vbicunque uita, ibi anima; ubicunque anima, ibi mens.

27.2. Omne motum corporeum, omne mouens incorporeum.

27.3. Anima in corpore, mens in anima, in mente uerbum, tum horum pater deus.

27.4. Deus circa omnia atque per omnia; mens circa animam, anima circa aerem, aer circa materiam.

27.5. Nihil est in mundo expers uitae.

27.6. Nihil est in uniuerso passibile mortis uel corruptionis.

Correlarium: Vbique uita, ubique prouidentia, ubique immortalitas.

27.7. Sex uiis futura homini deus denuntiat: per Somnia, Portenta, Aues, Intestina, Spiritum, et Sibyllam.

Section title. 1487 omits *numero*

27.7. colon retained from 1486 edition

CONCLUSIONS ACCORDING TO MERCURY TRISMEGISTUS THE EGYPTIAN. Pico was drawing here from Ficino's translation of the *Corpus Hermeticum*, which was first printed in 1471. On Pico and Mercury (or Hermes) Trismegistus in general, see above, pp. 120–21, 145.

27.1. "soul"/"mind" = associated in Pico with the "rational" and "intellectual" natures.

TEN CONCLUSIONS ACCORDING TO THE ANCIENT DOCTRINE OF MERCURY TRISMEGISTUS THE EGYPTIAN.

27.1. Wherever there is life, there is soul. Wherever there is soul, there is mind.

27.2. Everything moved is corporeal, everything moving incorporeal.

27.3. The soul is in the body, the mind is in the soul, the Word is in the mind, and the Father of these is God.

27.4. God exists around all and through all things. The mind exists around the soul, the soul around the air, the air around matter.

27.5. Nothing in the world is devoid of life. (350)

27.6. Nothing in the universe can suffer death or destruction.

Corollary: Life is everywhere, providence is everywhere, immortality is everywhere.

27.7. God announces the future to man in six ways: through dreams, portents, birds, intestines, spirit, and the Sibyl.

27.2. Two interconnected series on motion begin at 2.37–38, 7.7–8.

27.3–4. Cf. 22.12.

27.5–6. Cf. 20.3 and note.

27.7. Cf. 7.1, 21.4–6, etc.

27.8. Verum est_quod non perturbatum, non determinatum, non coloratum, non figuratum, non concussum, nudum, perspicuum, a seipso comprehensibile, intransmutabile bonum,_ ac penitus incorporeum.

27.9. Decem intra unumquemque sunt ultores: ignorantia, tristitia, inconstantia, cupiditas, iniustitia, luxuries, inuidia, fraus, ira, malitia.

27.10. Decem ultores,_ de quibus dixit secundum Mercurium praecedens conclusio, uidebit profundus contemplator correspondere male coordinationi denariae in cabala_et praefectis illius,_ de quibus ego in cabalisticis conclusionibus nihil posui,_ quia est secretum.

27.9. colon retained from 1486 edition | 1486 luxuries: deceptio: . . . ira: temeritas: | *Emendationes errorum*, dele dictiones deceptio: temeritas: quas superflue ponuntur | 1487 text emended *sic*

27.8. Reference to God's transcendent nature. Cf. 11>35, etc.

27.8. What is true is not perturbed, not determined, not colored, not fashioned, not agitated, but is naked, transparent, comprehensible through itself, intransmutably good, and fully incorporeal.

27.9. Within each thing there exist ten punishers: ignorance, sorrow, inconstancy, greed, injustice, lustfulness, envy, fraud, anger, malice.

27.10. A profound contemplator will see that the ten punishers, of which the preceding conclusion spoke according to Mercury, correspond to the evil order of ten in the Cabala and its leaders, of whom I have proposed nothing in my Cabalistic conclusions, because it is secret. (355)

27.9–10. Twelve "punishers" in the *Hermetic Corpus* and the *editio princeps,* which Pico reduced to ten in his *Emendationes errorum* to maintain his correspondence. See my discussion above, p. 82.

CONCLVSIONES CABALISTICE NVMERO .XLVII. SECVNDVM SECRETAM DOCTRINAM SAPIENTVM HEBREORVM CABALISTARVM, QVORVM ME / MORIA SIT SEMPER IN BONVM.

<12v/13r>

CONCLUSIONS ACCORDING TO THE SECRET DOCTRINE OF THE HEBREW CABALIST WISEMEN. This is the first of Pico's two sections on the Cabala; for the second, given "according to his own opinion," see 11>1–72. On my use of the terms "Kabbalah" and "Cabala," see p. 11 n. 30.

On Pico's Hebrew sources: All these theses were drawn from late-medieval texts, although Pico believed that they derived from oral traditions traceable back to Moses. The late Chaim Wirszubski (1989) argued that Pico took all but ten or so from Flavius Mithridates' Latin translation of Menahem Recanati's Hebrew *Commentary on the Pentateuch* (early fourteenth century). Wirszubski claimed that the rest came from up to seven other kabbalistic texts translated for Pico by Mithridates, whose peculiar relations with his patron are discussed above, pp. 11–14. The sources that Wirszubski prints in his study are useful tools in helping us decode this part of Pico's text; however, Wirszubski's claim about Pico's dependence on Mithridates' translations is seriously flawed. Pico's reliance on Recanati's commentary in some form has been recognized for centuries; however, Mithridates' lost translation of that work, which is only known to us via Gaffarel's descriptions from the seventeenth century (in his edition of Pico's theses, Kieszkowski confuses Mithridates' lost text with a later translation of Recanati in Bibliothèque Nationale MS Lat. 598), included references to Pico's real or rumored troubles with Innocent VIII (see Gaffarel 1651: 5–6), demonstrating that Mithridates' translation was not completed until many months *after* Pico's theses went to press; on this, see also Secret (1965: 181). The same evidence also shows that Mithridates did not accompany Pico to Rome (wisely, since Flavius was a criminal fugitive from the papal court) and hence could not have been involved in Pico's final preparations for his debate. Unfortunately, none of these problems are mentioned in Wirszubski's study, which was completed by his editors after his death; peculiarly, however, that study (1989: 16–18) uses essentially the same evidence to argue that the *other* translations that Gaffarel saw in the manuscript containing Mithridates' version of Recanati were not completed until after the theses were published—and hence could not have been used by Pico to prepare for his debate. All these findings seriously undermine Wirszubski's central argument, which would be unlikely on any grounds, that the huge mass of translations that Flavius reportedly made for Pico (according to Wirszubski, some 5,500 folio-sized pages) was written almost entirely in the six months between May and November 1486—exactly in time to provide Pico's exclusive sources for his Cabalistic theses. Also undercutting this thesis are the obvious discrepancies between the translations or transliterations of technical terms in Pico's text and those found in the surviving translations by Mithridates (see, e.g., my notes to theses 28.2

FORTY-SEVEN CABALISTIC CONCLUSIONS ACCORDING TO THE SECRET DOCTRINE OF THE HEBREW CABALIST WISEMEN, WHOSE MEMORY SHOULD ALWAYS BE HONORED.

---

and 28.14) and the fact that Mithridates' translations throw little light on Pico's second set of Cabalistic theses given "according to his own opinion." There is no doubt that Pico drew on Recanati's commentary in some form in the present section, as has been known since Gaffarel's day. He also used several other Hebrew texts that Mithridates translated at some point; indeed, we know that Pico provided Mithridates with many of those texts himself, including the Hebrew manuscript that contained Recanati's commentary. But, despite three-and-a-half centuries of discussion, the question is far from settled as to what extent in compiling these theses Pico relied on Mithridates' translations; on Pico's first-hand readings of Recanati and other Hebrew manuscripts that he owned, read with the help of Mithridates or Pico's other Jewish contacts; on extracts made by Mithridates or others, including Elia del Medigo (who is not mentioned in Wirszubski's book); or on oral instruction, which we know played a big role in Pico's intellectual life. The intriguing story of Pico, the Kabbalah, and Pico's early Jewish tutors deserves a full reexamination, drawing more carefully than has been the rule in the past on the rich but treacherous mass of evidence that has accumulated on this topic over the past five centuries.

Pico and kabbalistic symbolism: Pico's interests in the obscure symbolism of the Kabbalah—which correlated with abandon the names and properties of the Hebrew god with the six (or seven) days of creation, the names or activities of the patriarchs, the four winds, the four directions, the letters and shapes of the Hebrew alphabet, and so on—in large part lay in the correspondences that Pico found there with closely related symbolism in Proclus and other late ancient and medieval sources (e.g., the correspondences between Proclus's *henads* and the kabbalistic *sefirot*). Unfortunately, this comparative side of Pico's work has largely been ignored in the five hundred years of studies of Pico's Cabalistic theses, which have generally been analyzed in isolation from the rest of his text. The flexibility of kabbalistic symbolism, coupled with Pico's extreme syncretic tendencies, warn us against identifying Pico's reading of that symbolism too closely with that found in his sources. Conversely, the fact that many kabbalistic symbols show up in a wide range of medieval texts underlines the difficulty of pinpointing Pico's exact sources even when we find parallels to his use of those symbols in one or more kabbalistic texts. Past studies of Pico and the Kabbalah, including Wirszubski's, have regularly confused Pico's intentions with those found in his purported sources, leading to gross misinterpretations of his objectives in his Roman debate: In some ways, there is much *less* to Pico and the Kabbalah than meets the eye. In the following notes, I have tried to pay as much attention to the links between theses in this and other sections of Pico's text as to the meaning of kabbalistic symbols in medieval sources, which at most provide a rough starting point in interpreting Pico's sense.

28.1. Sicut homo et sacerdos inferior sacrificat deo animas animalium irrationalium, ita Michael sacerdos superior sacrificat animas animalium rationalium.

28.2. Nouem sunt angelorum hierarchiae_quarum nomina Cherubim, Seraphim, Hasmalim, Haiot, Aralim, Tarsisim, Ophanim, Tephsarim, Isim.

28.3. Quamuis nomen ineffabile sit proprietas clementiae, negandum tamen non est quin contineat proprietatem iudicii.

28.4. Peccatum Adae fuit truncatio regni a caeteris plantis.

28.5. Cum arbore scientiae boni et mali, in qua peccauit primus homo, creauit deus saeculum.

28.2. 1486 nomina.Cherubim.Seraphim.Hasmalim . . . etc. | 1487 hagot | 1486, 1487 Tephsraim

28.4. 1486 coeteris

28.5. 1486 soeculum

28.1. Pico explicitly points to a mystical reading of this conclusion in thesis 11>11. The two texts that Wirszubski claims as Pico's sources (1989: 21–22) refer to the symbolism of the *sefirot*, but neither of them touch on mystical issues.

28.2. Pico gives nine rather than the usual ten hierarchies of kabbalistic angels, undoubtedly to correlate them with Pseudo-Dionysius's nine orders of Christian angels. The transliterations of angelic names and their order in Pico's thesis differ radically from those found in Mithridates' translation of the *Corona Nominis*, which Wirszubski (1989: 22–23) claims as Pico's "likeliest direct source." Translating Mithridates' Latin (retaining his exact orthography in respect to the angels) we find the angelic names are "hisim . . . ; Malachim or tafsarim . . . ; hirin or Tarsisim; Aralim; xeraphim; ofannim; cherubim; aioth; chisse or asmallim; and a tenth [that] is holy"—a very poor match with Pico's text.

28.1. Just as man and the inferior priest sacrifices to God the souls of irrational animals, so Michael the superior priest sacrifices the souls of rational animals.

28.2. There are nine hierarchies of angels, whose names are the Cherubim, Serafim, Hasmalim, Haiot, Aralim, Tarsisim, Ofanim, Tefsarim, Isim.

28.3. Although the ineffable name is the property of clemency, it should not be denied that it contains the property of judgment.

28.4. The sin of Adam was the severing of kingdom from the other shoots.

28.5. With the tree of the knowledge of good and evil, in which the first man sinned, God created the world. (360)

28.3. "ineffable name" = YHVH, normally associated with the sixth of the ten *sefirot* or emanated states of God's nature. "clemency"/"judgment" = usual properties of the sixth and fifth *sefirot* respectively. The point is Pico's standard one that all divine properties exist in some way on every hierarchical level—a view that allows him later in the theses to associate Christ with no less than four or five different *sefirot*. Cf. this thesis with 24.16–17 from Proclus. Wirszubski (1989: 23) provides a passage from Mithridates' translation of the *Liber combinationum* that, in this case, seems a good candidate to be Pico's source.

28.4. Cf. 28.36. "kingdom" = the tenth *sefirah*. "shoots" = allusion to a common kabbalistic association (found in the *Zohar*, Recanati, and other sources) of the *sefirot* with the "tree of paradise." Adam's "severing of the shoots"—cutting off the lowest *sefirah* ("kingdom") from the higher ones—was a standard symbol for the origins of sin. Cf. here Scholem (1974: 124), Wirszubski (1989: 24–25).

28.5. The *sefirot* again as the "tree of paradise." The idea is that God viewed transcendentally (the kabbalistic *Ein-Sof*) created the world through his manifested nature (the ten *sefirot*). Cf. 11>35–36, etc.

28.6. Magnus aquilo fons est animarum omnium simpliciter, sicut alii dies quarundam et non omnium.

28.7. Cum dicit Salomon in oratione sua in libro Regum: Exaudi o_coelum, per coelum lineam uiridem debemus intelligere quae gyrat uniuersum.

28.8. Animae a tertio lumine ad quartam diem, et inde ad quintam descendunt, inde exeuntes corporis noctem subintrant.

28.9. Per sex dies geneseos habemus intelligere sex extremitates aedificii procedentes a Bresith, sicut procedunt cedri a Libano.

28.8. 1486 luminae | 1487 lumine

28.6. On the emanation of souls in the Kabbalah, see Scholem (1974: 152–64). "days" = days of creation, which Pico correlated with different *sefirot* in different contexts; cf., e.g., 28.8, 11>37. "north" or the "north wind" (*aquilo*) was a regular kabbalistic symbol of the fifth *sefirah*, which is its apparent sense in 11>47 and elsewhere in Pico's text. But Wirszubski (1989: 25) is correct in suggesting that the "great north" or "great north wind" (*magnus aquilo*) in this thesis, for which no medieval parallels are known, may have a different sense. Indeed, if we compare this thesis with 28.8 (see note), we find that the *magnus aquilo* refers to the third *sefirah*, "intelligence," which Pico normally associated with his "intellectual nature." Pico could have linked this thesis to others in his text dealing with the "unity of the intellect" issue; cf., e.g., theses 3>67–69 and note.

28.7. Cf. 1 Kings 8:32ff. "green line" = standard kabbalistic symbol for the third *sefirah*, "intelligence." There is an occult link between this thesis and 22.12 from Porphyry (see 11>29 and note). Wirszubski (1989: 26) cites two texts from Mithridates that mention the "green line," but neither of these throws light on Pico's sense in these linked conclusions.

28.6. The great north wind is the source of all souls simply, just as the other days are the source of some of them and not all.

28.7. When Solomon says in his prayer in the Book of Kings, *Hear O heaven,* by heaven we should understand the green line that circles the universe.

28.8. Souls descend from the third light to the fourth day, and from there to the fifth, from which departing they steal into the night of the body.

28.9. By the six days of creation we should understand the six extremities of the edifice proceeding from *Bereshit,* just as cedars proceed from Lebanon.

28.8. "light"/"day" when found together in medieval Hebrew texts = symbols of the superior three and inferior seven *sefirot.* Thus the "third light" = *Binah* or "intelligence," which Pico most commonly associated with his intellectual nature. Wirszubski (1989: 26–29) gives a long argument based on Mithridates' translations that Pico identified the "fifth day" here idiosyncratically with the tenth *sefirah.* Further on Pico and the emanation of souls, cf. 28.6, 28.41.

28.9. "edifice" = the lower seven *sefirot* (cf. 11>48). In medieval sources, the "six extremities" normally refer to the fourth through ninth *sefirot.* "*Bereshit*" = "in the beginning" (Gen. 1:1), a decontextualized biblical term normally associated with the second *sefirah, Hokhmah,* the wisdom by which God created the world. In his second set of Cabalistic theses, Pico predictably reads *Hokhmah* as a symbol for Christ, the second Person of the Trinity in Christianity and the "Wisdom of the Father." Cf. also 28.25.

28.10. Rectius dicitur quod paradisus sit totum aedificium quam quod sit decima, et in medio eius est collocatus magnus Adam, qui est Tipheret.

28.11. Dictum est ex Heden exire fluuium qui diuiditur in quatuor capita, ad significandum quod ex secunda numeratione procedit tertia, quae in quartam, quintam, sextam, et decimam diuiditur.

28.12. Verum erit omnia pendere ex fato, si per fatum, fatum supremum intellexerimus.

28.13. Qui nouerit in Cabala mysterium portarum intelligentiae, cognoscet mysterium magni Iobelei.

28.14. Qui nouerit proprietatem meridionalem in dextrali coordinatione, sciet cur omnis profectio Abraam semper fit uersus austrum. <13r/13v>

28.10. "paradise"/"whole edifice" = the entire *sefirot* system. "*Tiferet*" = the sixth *sefirah*, interpreted as the "middle" in one of several medieval schemes as follows (adapted from Scholem 1974: 107):

	1. *Keter* (crown)	
3. *Binah* (intelligence)		2. *Hokhmak* (wisdom)
5. *Din* (judgment)		4. *Hesed* (love or piety in Pico)
	6. *Tiferet* (beauty)	
8. *Hod* (majesty)		7. *Nezah* (endurance)
	9. *Yesod* (foundation)	
	10. *Malkhut* (kingdom)	

All these names in Pico and his sources had a number of alternate forms. In general, the whole system could be pictured anthropomorphically as the "great man" or "great Adam"—with the head the first *sefirah*, the arms the fourth and fifth, the torso the sixth, the genitals the ninth, etc.—or the great Adam could be identified with the centrally placed *Tiferet*, man-the-microcosm standing for the rest. The function of *Tiferet* as a cosmic mediator explains why in his second set of Cabalistic theses Pico repeatedly associates that *sefirah* with Christ.

28.10. It is more correctly said that paradise is the whole edifice than that it is the tenth; and in its middle is set the great Adam, who is *Tiferet*. (365)

28.11. It is said that a river flows from Eden that is divided into four branches, to signify that from the second numeration proceeds the third, which is divided into the fourth, fifth, sixth, and tenth.

28.12. It will be true that all depends on fate, if by fate we understand supreme fate.

28.13. Whoever knows in the Cabala the mystery of the gates of intelligence will understand the mystery of the great jubilee.

28.14. Whoever knows the southern property in the right-hand order knows why every journey of Abraham was always towards the south.

28.11. Alluding to Gen. 2:10–14. "numeration" = literal translation of the Hebrew *sefirah*. On the symbolism of the four rivers of paradise, see further the *Oration* (*Opera*, 321; Garin, *Scritti vari*, 128), where, citing "Zoroaster," Pico identifies the rivers in Genesis with the four sciences needed to prepare man for the mystical ascent—moral philosophy, dialectic, natural philosophy, and theology.

28.12. Different "modes" of fate here are presumably identified with different *sefirot*. Cf. the long list of related theses given in note 24.2 from Proclus.

28.13. Cf. especially 11>68–69. "gates of intelligence" = standard symbol for the third *sefirah*, *Binah* or "intelligence" (cf. 11>69). "great jubilee" = eschatological return of the world to *Binah*, "mother of the world" (cf. Scholem 1974: 336). Pico presumably would have correlated this thesis with others in his text involving eschatological issues, e.g., 10>20–21.

28.14. Alluding to Gen. 12:9. "southern property"/"Abraham" = standard symbols of the fourth *sefirah*, "love" or "piety" in Pico. The "right-hand order" distinguishes the emanation of the true *sefirot* from the evil "left-hand order" mirroring it. See above, pp. 38–39 and Scholem (1974: 55 and passim); see also the similar phrasing in 11>37. Wirszubski (1989: 32–33) cites a long passage from Mithridates' translation of Gicatilla's *Portae Iustitiae* to try to show that the phrase "right-hand order" is simply a redundant symbol for the fourth *sefirah*. But Pico's language differs radically from what we find in Mithridates' translation, which uses the word *dextra* but says nothing about the *dextralis coordinatio* or "right-hand order." On Abraham's journeys as symbols of the mystical ascent, see also the *Oration* (*Opera*, 321; Garin, *Scritti vari*, 128).

28.15. Nisi nomen Abraam <אברהם>‸ id est he addita‸ fuisset, Abraam non generasset.

28.16. Omnes ante Moysen prophetarunt per ceruam unicornem.

28.17. Vbicunque in scriptura fit mentio amoris maris_et feminae_nobis mystice designatur coniuncto Tipheret et Chieneseth Israhel, uel Beth et Tipheret.

28.18. Qui media nocte cum Tipheret copulabitur, prospera erit ei omnis generatio.

28.19. Eadem sunt litterae nominis cacodemonis qui est princeps mundi huius et nominis dei Triagrammaton, et qui sciuerit ordinare transpositionem deducet unum ex alio.

28.17. 1487 chienseth

28.18. 1487 Quia media nocte

28.15. Alludes to Abraam's renaming in Gen. 17:5 as "Abraham." In medieval sources (and elsewhere in the theses) "Abraham" is represented as a symbol of the fourth *sefirah*, "love" or "piety" in Pico. Underlying this thesis is the general idea that God created the world through the twenty-two letters of the Hebrew alphabet and the ten *sefirot*—taken collectively, the "thirty-two paths of wisdom" in 28.26, 11>58. Pico would have linked this thesis with a number of others on the magical powers of Hebrew, e.g., 9>19ff.

28.16. Wirszubski (1989: 34) argues that *cerva unicornis* derives from Mithridates' translation of the Hebrew *ayalah* ("hind," a symbol of the tenth *sefirah*) by *cerva vel unicornis*. Whatever Pico's source, his underlying point is that Moses drew on higher levels of the divine nature in his prophecies. Cf. also 28.45 and note.

28.15. If Abraham's name had not been <אברהם>, that is, with *he* added, Abraham would not have procreated. (370)

28.16. All before Moses prophesized through the one-horned stag.

28.17. Everyplace in Scriptures that the love of a male and female is mentioned designates to us mystically the conjunction of *Tiferet* and *Keneset Israel*, or of *Bet* and *Tiferet*.

28.18. All the procreation of whoever copulates in the middle of the night with *Tiferet* will be prosperous.

28.19. The letters of the name of the evil spirit who is the prince of this world and of the three-letter name of God are the same, and whoever knows how to order the transposition can deduce one from the other.

28.17. The association of male and female with superior and inferior *sefirot* was a kabbalistic commonplace; their mating was viewed as a symbol of mystical and/or eschatological union or the original creation of the world through the *sefirot*. "*Tiferet*"/"*Keneset Israel*" = name/symbol of the sixth and tenth *sefirot* respectively. "*Bet*" = Hebrew letter (the first letter in the Torah), which in medieval traditions was normally correlated with the third *sefirah*, *Binah* (intelligence). Pico presumably linked this thesis with others dealing with the union of *henads* in Proclus's thought (theses 24.1–55) and similar concepts in other esoteric traditions.

28.18. "*Tiferet*" = the sixth *sefirah*, identified with the "great Adam" in 28.10. The thesis has mystical and magical overtones, suggesting the soul's union with the purified man-the-microcosm; cf. 9>10ff. from Pico's magical theses. Christ is often associated with the sixth *sefirah* in Pico's second set of Cabalistic theses, reinforcing the thesis's mystical sense.

28.19. Wirszubski (1989: 36) quotes a passage from Mithridates' translation of a commentary on the *Book of Creation* that suggests, as we would expect, that this transformation involved word-letter equations (*gematria*). On *gematria*, see above, pp. 63–66. The thesis reflects the close relationship between the parallel "right" and "left-hand" orders in kabbalism.

28.20. Cum fiet lux speculi non lucentis sicut speculi lucentis, erit nox sicut dies, ut dicit Dauid.

28.21. Qui sciet proprietatem quae est secretum tenebrarum, sciet cur mali demones plus in nocte quam die nocent.

28.22. Licet fiat multiplex coordinatio curruum, tamen inquantum attinet ad phylacteriorum mysterium duo sunt currus ordinandi, ita ut ex secunda, tertia, quarta, quinta, fiat unus currus, et sunt quatuor phylacteria quae induit Vau; et ex sexta, septima, octaua, et nona fit secundus currus, et sunt phylacteria quae induit ultima He.

28.23. Supra proprietatem penitentiae non est utendum uerbo dixit.

28.24. Cum dixit Iob, qui facit pacem in excelsis suis, aquam intellexit australem et ignem septentrionalem, et praefectos illorum de quibus non est ultra dicendum.

28.21. 1487 in die

28.22. 1486 phylatteriorum . . . phylatteria . . . phylatteria | 1487 philatteriorum . . . philatteria . . . philatteria

28.24. 1486 Cum dixit.Iob.qui

28.20. "mirror not shining"/"shining mirror" = common symbols of the tenth and sixth *sefirot. "Night will be just like day"* = Psalm 139:12. The eschatological sense of this thesis is reinforced in 11>54, especially when we recall Pico's regular association of Christ with the sixth *sefirah.* The passages from Recanati cited by Wirszubski help us interpret Pico's text, but they cannot be claimed as Pico's direct sources.

28.21. "secret of darkness" = symbol of the fifth *sefirah, Din* (judgment), associated with God's stern retribution. Cf., e.g., 11>13.

28.22. "chariot" (*merkabah* in Hebrew) = see Scholem (1941: 40ff.; 1974: 10–14). The principal allusion is to the animated chariot in Ezek. 1:4ff., rendered plural in antiquity by centuries of attempts to harmonize earlier commentaries on that text with each other and with other Hebrew and pagan chariot myths (including the famous charioteer myth in the *Phaedrus*). In Pico, different "chariots" refer to "divine," "middle," and "sensible" natures; cf. 11>2 and note.

28.20. When the light of the mirror not shining becomes just like that of the shining mirror, then *Night will be just like day*, as David says. (375)

28.21. Whoever knows the property that is the secret of darkness knows why evil demons injure more at night than in day.

28.22. Granted that many orders of chariots can be produced, insofar as the mystery of phylacteries is concerned, two chariots should be constructed: so that from the second, third, fourth, and fifth, one chariot is made, and these are the four phylacteries covered with *Vav*; and from the sixth, seventh, eighth, and ninth, a second chariot is produced, and these are the phylacteries covered with the final *He*.

28.23. Over the property of penitence the words *he said* should not be used.

28.24. When Job said, *Who makes peace in his heights*, he meant the southern water and the northern fire, and their commanders, of whom nothing more should be said.

"phylacteries" = amulets worn for devotional, mystical, and/or magical purposes, covered by or containing sacred texts or letters. "*Vav*"/"*He*" = the last two letters in the "ineffable name" YHVH. These letters were symbolically associated with different *sefirot* in different texts. On this last point, see Scholem (1974: 111).

28.23. "property of penitence" = reference to the third *sefirah*, alternately named *Teshuvah* (penitence) or *Binah* (intelligence). The thesis alludes to the fact that (1) in medieval traditions, different *sefirot* were symbolically associated with different stages of creation in Gen. 1:1ff.; and (2) that the words "God said" only appear in that account with the creation of light, another symbol for Pico for "intelligence." Pico would have presumably tied this thesis to his belief that language cannot adequately describe the highest levels of reality. Cf. also 11>31 and note.

28.24. Cf. Job 25:2. "southern water"/"northern fire" = common symbols of the fourth and fifth *sefirot*; cf. here 11>45 and note. If we follow a passage from the *Sefer ha-Bahir* cited by Wirszubski (1989: 41), the commanders of the "southern water" and "northern fire" = the archangels Michael and Gabriel. On the mystical significance of Michael, and hence presumably of this thesis, cf. 28.1 and 11>11.

28.25. Idem est bresith, id est in principio creauit, ac si dixisset in sapientia creauit.

28.26. Quod dixit Anchelos chaldeus becadmin, id est cum aeternis uel per aeterna, triginta duas uias sapientiae intellexit.

28.27. Sicut congregatio aquarum est iustus, ita mare ad quod tendunt omnia flumina est diuinitas.

28.28. Per uolatile quod creatum est die quinta, debemus intelligere angelos mundanos qui hominibus apparent, non eos qui non apparent nisi in spiritu.

28.29. Nomen dei quatuor litterarum, quod est ex mem, sade, pe, et sa/de, regno Dauidis debet appropriari. <13v/14r>

28.30. Nullus angelus habens sex alas unquam transformatur.

28.26. 1486, 1487 becadmim | 1487 cum eternis vel paterna

28.25. "*Bereshit*"/"wisdom" = common symbols for *Hokhmah*, the second *sefirah*. In his second set of Cabalistic conclusions, Pico frequently associates this *sefirah* with Christ, the "Wisdom of the Father" in the New Testament and the Second Person of the Trinity in scholastic traditions. Cf. also 28.9.

28.26. Onkelos = Onkelos the Proselyte, traditional author of the Aramaic version of the Torah known as the *Targum Onkelos* (early common era). He is mentioned often by Moses Maimonides and many other medieval sources known to Pico. "thirty-two paths of wisdom" = idea found in the proto-kabbalistic *Sefer Yetzirah* (Book of Creation) and later texts that God created the world using the combined magical power of the twenty-two letters of the Hebrew alphabet and ten *sefirot*. Cf. also 9>19ff. from Pico's magical conclusions, 11>58.

28.25. *Bereshit*, that is, *in the beginning* he created, is the same as if he had said, he created *in wisdom*. (380)

28.26. Because Onkelos the Chaldean said *becadmin,* that is, with eternal or through eternal things, he showed that he understood the thirty-two paths of wisdom.

28.27. Just as the *gathering of waters* is the just, so the *sea to which all rivers run* is divinity.

28.28. By the winged creatures who were created on the fifth day we should understand the mundane angels who appear to men, not those who do not appear except in spirit.

28.29. The four-letter name of God that is made out of *mem, tzade, pe,* and *tzade* should be attributed to the kingdom of David.

28.30. No angel having six wings is ever transformed. (385)

28.27. "*gathering of waters*" (Prov. 10:25)/"the just" = symbol/alternate name of the ninth *sefirah*. "*sea to which all rivers run*" (Eccl. 1:7)/"divinity" = *Shekhinah*, "divine presence" = symbol/alternate name of the tenth *sefirah*. See further the text from Recanati quoted by Wirszubski (1989: 42). The thesis symbolically correlates isolated texts from Hebrew Scripture just as Pico's theses from Proclus (e.g., 24.8) correlate isolated texts from the Platonic corpus. The original object in both cases was to demonstrate the secret harmonies in those sacred texts.

28.28. Referring to Gen. 1:20, implying a hierarchy of angelic powers like that found in 6.7, etc. Cf. also 28.30. Which *sefirah* here = "the fifth day" is unclear; cf. 28.8 note.

28.29. "kingdom of David" = the tenth *sefirah*. "*mem tzade pe tzade*" is generated when each letter in the "ineffable name" YHVH (normally associated with the sixth *sefirah*) is replaced by the corresponding letters when the Hebrew alphabet is *reversed;* this was one form of Pico's so-called *revolutio alphabetariae*. See Anagnine (1937: 160), Wirszubski (1989: 43–44).

28.30. Like 28.28, apparently suggesting further distinctions in the angelic orders.

28.31. Data est circumcisio ad liberationem a uirtutibus immundis quae in circuitu ambulant.

28.32. Ideo circumcisio fit octaua die, quia est superior quam sponsa uniuersalizata.

28.33. Nullae sunt litterae in tota lege quae in formis, coniunctionibus, separationibus, tortuositate, directione, defectu, superabundantia, minoritate, maioritate, coronatione, clausura, apertura, et ordine, decem numerationum secreta non manifestent.

28.34. Qui intellexerit cur sit dictum quod Moyses abscondit faciem suam, et quod Ezechias uertit facies suas ad parietem, sciet quae esse debeat orantis habitudo et dispositio.

28.35. Nulla res spiritualis descendens inferius operatur sine indumento.

28.36. Peccatum Soddomae fuit per truncationem ultimae plantae.

28.37. Per secretum orationis antelucanae, nihil aliud debemus intelligere quam proprietatem pietatis.

28.31. The passage that Wirszubski (1989: 44) quotes from Recanati associates the ritual of circumcision with Psalm 12:9 (Vulgate 11:9), "In circuitu impii ambulant" [the impious walk in a circle]. For a beautiful example of Pico's Christian Cabalism—and of the systematic links between widely separated theses in Pico's text—this thesis should be read with 11>22 and 11>27.

28.32. "eighth day" following Wirszubski's (1989: 45) reading = the ninth *sefirah*. "universalized bride" = symbol of the tenth *sefirah*.

28.33. A close reading of Recanati's Hebrew text; see Wirszubski (1989: 45–46). "numerations" = the *sefirot*; see note 28.11. The thesis reflects Pico's general views of the mystical and magical powers of Hebrew. Cf. 28.47, 2>80, 3>55, 9>22, etc.

28.34. Cf. Exod. 3:6; 2 Kings 20:2–3 (Vulgate Malachim 20:2–3). The thesis can be correlated with others suggesting that God at his highest lies beyond human understanding, implying the need at the highest stages of the mystical ascent to reject ordinary forms of knowledge. Cf., among many other theses, 26.5, 11>35. On Pico's mystical ideas, see above, pp. 39ff., 105–14.

28.31. Circumcision was given to free us from the impure powers that circle about.

28.32. Circumcision occurs on the eighth day, because it is superior to the universalized bride.

28.33. There are no letters in the whole Law which in their forms, conjunctions, separations, crookedness, straightness, defect, excess, smallness, largeness, crowning, closure, openness, and order, do not reveal the secrets of the ten numerations.

28.34. Whoever understands why it is said that *Moses hid his face*, and that *Hezekiah turned his face to the wall*, knows what should be the condition and disposition of someone praying.

28.35. Nothing spiritual, descending below, operates without a garment. (390)

28.36. The sin of Sodom came from severing the last shoot.

28.37. By the secret of early morning prayer, we should understand nothing but the property of piety.

28.35. Referring, e.g., to the *sefirot* as the "garments" of the *Ein-Sof*, God's transcendental nature. Cf. also Pico's language in 28.44, 8>8–9, 11>22, 11>35–36. Comparison should also be made with 2.22 from St. Thomas. The concept expressed in this thesis was a medieval commonplace, and the passage cited by Wirszubski (1989: 46) cannot be claimed as Pico's direct source.

28.36. Gen. 18:20ff. On the symbolism of the "severing of the shoots," see 28.4 and note.

28.37. "early morning prayer" = allusion to Abraham's early rising in Gen. 19:27. "piety" = the fourth *sefirah* (see the following two theses), normally symbolized by "Abraham." Presumably, Pico would have used theses like this to underline the affinities between the *sefirot* system and the Neo-Platonic *henads* (or similar structures). For the style of this thesis, cf., e.g., 24.6, 24.15.

28.38. Sicut extrinsecus timor est inferior amore, ita intrinsecus est superior amore.

28.39. Ex praecedenti conclusione intelligitur cur in Genesi a timore laudatur Abraam, quem tamen scimus per proprietatem pietatis omnia fecisse ex amore.

28.40. Quotienscunque ignoramus proprietatem a qua est influxus super petitione quam petimus, ad dominum naris recurrendum est.

28.41. Omnis anima bona_est anima noua ueniens ab oriente.

28.42. Ideo Ioseph ossibus tantum sepultus est et non corpore, quia eius ossa erant uirtutes et militie arboris superioris uocati Sadich influentis ad terram superiorem.

28.43. Ideo Moysis sepulchrum nemo nouit, quia exaltatus est in Iobeleo superiore, et super Iobeleum misit radices suas.

28.38–39. Gen. 20:11. On commentarial debates over the relative superiority of fear or love of God in medieval kabbalism, see Scholem (1974: 175). Pico's thesis resolves the problem in typically syncretic fashion by distinguishing hierarchical "modes" of fear. Following the complex correspondences in the *sefirot* system, these different modes of fear could be associated with *sefirot* above and below the fourth—*Hesed* ("love" or "piety" in Pico), symbolized by "Abraham." On the association of fear with "Isaac" (the object of Abraham's intended sacrifice) and the fifth *sefirah*, see 10>10 and note. For Pico's apparent source in Recanati, see Wirszubski (1989: 47–48).

28.40. "lord of the nose" in the *Zohar* (the most important medieval kabbalistic text) = the fifth *sefirah*, one of whose alternate names was *Gevurah* or "power." Cf. the materials cited by Wirszubski (1989: 48). On "petitions" (or prayer) in Cabala, which in Pico included an astrological element, cf. further 11>50 and note. Another magical reference to the fifth *sefirah* is suggested in 10>10 (see note).

28.38. Just as outer fear is inferior to love, so inner fear is superior to love.

28.39. From the preceding conclusion it is known why in Genesis Abraham is praised for his fear, although we know through the property of piety that he did all things out of love.

28.40. Whenever we do not know the property from which an influence exists over a petition we are making, we should turn to the lord of the nose. (395)

28.41. Every good soul is a new soul coming from the east.

28.42. Only Joseph's bones were entombed, and not his body, because his bones were the powers and armies of the superior tree called *Tzaddik*, which sends its influences over the superior earth.

28.43. No one knew the tomb of Moses, because he was raised in the superior jubilee, and over the jubilee he sent his roots.

28.41. Wirszubski (1989: 49) cites a passage from the *Sefer ha-Bahir* that associates "east" with the seventh *Sefirah*. In the *Sefer Yetzirah* (Book of Creation), however, which Pico knew (see, e.g., *Opera*, 385), "east" is associated with the sixth *sefirah*, the "great man," one of Pico's regular symbols for Christ. Whatever Pico's source, the main idea here is that different grades of souls derive from different levels of the *sefirot* system, as we also find in 28.6. Cf. with theses like 24.27 from Proclus.

28.42. "*Tzaddik*" = "the just," alternate name for the ninth *sefirah*, normally correlated with "Joseph." In 11>21 Pico represents "the just" as a typological symbol for Christ. "superior earth" = symbol of the tenth *sefirah*. On Pico's sources, see the following note.

28.43. "superior jubilee"/"jubilee" = apparent references to the third *sefirah* (*Binah*, "intelligence") and the sixth (*Tiferet* or "beauty," the "great Adam"). Cf. here 28.13 and the hints in 28.17. On *Binah* as the "great" or "superior" jubilee, see further Scholem (1974: 120). Like other theses in this section, theses 28.42–43 derive from Recanati's commentary, but no evidence exists for Wirszubski's claim (1989: 50) that Pico was using Mithridates' translation of the work, which was not completed until after Pico's text was published.

28.44. Cum anima comprehenderit quicquid poterit comprehendere, et coniungetur animae superiori, expoliabit indumentum terrenum a se, et extirpabitur de loco suo et coniungetur cum diuinitate. <14r/14v>

28.45. Sapientes Israhel post cessationem prophetiae per spiritum, prophetarunt per filiam uocis.

28.46. Non punitur Rex terrae in terra, quin prius humilietur militia coelestis in coelo.

28.47. Per dictionem AMEN ordo habetur expressus quomodo numerationum procedant influxus.

28.46. 1487 ponitur

28.44. "superior soul" here presumably = the "intellectual nature." "garment" = see 28.35 and note. "divinity" in Pico's Cabalistic theses normally = *Shekhinah* (divine presence), alternate name for the tenth *sefirah*. Cf. 28.27 and the text from Recanati's Hebrew commentary provided by Wirszubski (1989: 50). Pico could have correlated this thesis with dozens of mystical theses in his text.

28.45. Following the passage from Recanati cited by Wirszubski (1989: 51), "spirit"/"daughter of the voice" = higher and lower modes of prophecy flowing from "kingdom," the tenth and lowest *Sefirah*. The scheme fits in with the general view seen in Pico's historical theses, which envisions a systematic degradation of wisdom over time.

28.44. When the soul comprehends whatever it can comprehend and is conjoined to the superior soul, it will strip its terrestrial garment from itself, and be uprooted from its place, and be conjoined with divinity.

28.45. After prophecy through the spirit ceased, the wisemen of Israel prophesized through the daughter of the voice. (400)

28.46. The king of the earth will not be punished on earth, unless the celestial army is first humiliated in heaven.

28.47. In the word AMEN we find the exact order by which the influences of the numerations proceed.

28.46. Both texts that Wirszubski (1989: 51) proposes as potential sources emphasize the favorite Pichean theme that proportion exists between higher and lower realms, expressed here in an eschatological context. The misreading of *ponitur* for *punitur* in the 1487 reprint was followed by all later Renaissance editors of Pico's text.

28.47. Reflecting the general idea that mystical secrets lay hidden in the primal language, Hebrew. Cf. 28.33 and note. 11>65 throws further light on Pico's sense in this thesis. The underlying views here can be correlated with Pico's theses from Proclus on the powers of the "leaders" and other *henads*, e.g., 24.27–29, etc.

Conclusiones numero quingentae secundum opinionem propriam, quae denaria diuisione diuiduntur in Conclusiones Physicas, Theologicas, Platonicas, Mathematicas, Paradoxas dogmatizantes, Paradoxas conciliantes, Chaldaicas, Orphicas, Magicas, et Cabalisticas. In quibus omnibus nihil assertiue uel probabiliter pono, nisi quatenus id uel uerum uel probabile iudicat Sacrosancta Romana ecclesia, et caput eius benemeritum Summus pontifex INNOCENTIVS Octauus cuius iudicio, qui mentis suae iudicium non summittit, mentem non habet.

CONCLVSIONES PARADOXAE NVMERO .XVII. SECVNDVM PROPRIAM OPINIONEM, DICTA PRIMVM ARISTOTELIS ET PLATONIS, DEINDE ALIORVM DOCTORVM CONCILIANTES QVI MAXIME DISCORDARE VIDENTVR.

1>1. Nullum est quaesitum naturale aut diuinum in quo Aristoteles et Plato sensu et re non conueniant, quamuis uerbis dissentire uideantur.

Second Preface. 1486 Cabalisticas: In quibus

SECOND PREFACE. In its current form, the second half of the *editio princeps* is divided into eleven and not ten sections that contain 498 theses, suggesting again that the text was altered shortly before and/or while in press (see my introductory note to theses 6>1–10). Pico's disclaimer at the end of the preface suggests that his theological troubles were not totally unexpected.

Five hundred conclusions according to his own opinion, which are divided in ten sections into Physical, Theological, Platonic, Mathematical, Paradoxical Dogmatizing, Paradoxical Reconciliative, Chaldaic, Orphic, Magical, and Cabalistic conclusions. In all these I propose nothing assertively or tentatively unless it is judged true or probable by the sacred Roman Church and its deserved head, the supreme Pontiff INNOCENT the Eighth—to whose judgment, anyone who does not submit the judgment of his own mind, has no mind.

SEVENTEEN PARADOXICAL CONCLUSIONS ACCORDING TO MY OWN OPINION, FIRST RECONCILING THE WORDS OF ARISTOTLE AND PLATO, THEN THOSE OF OTHER LEARNED MEN WHO SEEM TO STRONGLY DISAGREE.

1>1. There is no natural or divine question in which Aristotle and Plato do not agree in meaning and substance, although in their words they seem to disagree.

PARADOXICAL RECONCILIATIVE CONCLUSIONS. On this section, see above, pp. 47ff.

1>1. Cf. Cicero *Academica* 2.5.15; 1.4.17–18. Aristotle's philosophical views are mildly criticized in 2>40, 2>42, 3>28, 3>45, 3>48, 5>42, and 7>5, raising some questions about Pico's meaning here. But cf. 11>63, where we find that Aristotle's deepest truths lay hidden *beneath* his philosophical prose. On how Pico planned to debate this thesis, see above, pp. 56–57.

1>2. Qui dicunt innascibilitatem esse positiuam proprietatem constituentem patrem in esse hypostatico incommunicabili, ab opinione sancti doctoris,_ a qua multum secundum uerba uidentur discordare,_ nihil discordant.

1>3. De ponenda sexta notione,_ quae est inspirabilitas,_ non debent discordare Thomistae et Scotistae,_ si recte suorum doctorum funda/menta introspiciunt. <14v/15r>

1>4. De subiecto Theologiae fundamentaliter et radicaliter concordant Thommas,_ Scotus,_ et Egidius, quamuis in ramis et uerborum superficie quilibet eorum a quolibet dissentire plurimum uideatur.

1>5. De quaestione illa,_ Vtrum sit unum esse in Christo_aut plura esse, dico Scotum et Thomam non discordare.

1>6. De distinctione ex natura rei non debent discordare Thomistae et Scotistae, si suos doctores fundamentaliter intelligant.

1>7. De attributorum distinctione non discordant Thommas et Scotus.

1>4. 1486 Egidius.Quamuis

1>5. 1486 esse.Dico

1>2. "Those who say" = Scotus and the Scotists. *Innascibilitas* or "inability to be born" = distinguishing trait assigned to the first Person of the Trinity by Augustine and other late-ancient scholastics. "incommunicable hypostatic existence" = existence specific to a divine Person. "holy doctor" = St. Thomas Aquinas. *Re* Peter Lombard *Sentences* 1, *d.* 28, *q.* 1. Along with 1>3 and 1>7, in the series on the Trinity listed in note 2.1. Cf. especially 4.3 from Scotus.

1>3. "notion" = distinguishing mark by which a divine Person is known to finite beings. "Inspirability" = the "notion" specific to the Holy Spirit. Cf. 6.4 and note.

1>2. Those who say that the inability to be born is a positive property establishing the Father in incommunicable hypostatic existence do not disagree with the holy doctor's opinion, with which verbally they seem to disagree greatly.

1>3. On positing the sixth notion, which is inspirability, Thomists and Scotists should not disagree, if they rightly examine the principles of their doctors. (405)

1>4. On the subject of theology, Thomas, Scotus, and Giles agree fundamentally and at root, although in its branches and on the outer surface of words each of them seems to disagree strongly with the others.

1>5. On this question, *Whether there is one existence in Christ or more than one,* I say that Scotus and Thomas do not disagree.

1>6. On distinctions in natural things Thomists and Scotists should not disagree, if they understand their doctors fundamentally.

1>7. On distinctions between attributes [in God] Thomas and Scotus do not disagree.

1>4. Reconciling the official theologians of the Dominicans, Franciscans, and Augustinians. "Giles" = Giles or Aegidius of Rome, theses 6.1–11. "On the subject of theology" = on its specific object as a science, commenting on Peter Lombard *Sentences* 1, prologue. Cf. 6.2–3 and note for related theses.

1>5. *Re* Peter Lombard *Sentences* 3, *d.* 6. See 4.4 and note.

1>6. On distinctions in general, see 3.7 note.

1>7. Series starts at 2.1. Cf. 1>2–3, Thomas *Sentences* 1, *d.* 2, *q.* 1, *art.* 2–3. Fine lines were drawn between God's "properties," "relations," "attributes," "notions," etc., when needed to harmonize authorities or texts. Pico rejected this kind of theologizing in a number of his theological conclusions, 4>1–29.

1>8. In hoc articulo preciso a suis appendiciis: Vtrum angelus potuerit diuinam aequalitatem simpliciter appetere,_ non discordat Thomas et Scotus.

1>9. In materia quid prius cognoscatur magis an minus uniuersale concordant Thommas et Scotus, qui maxime in ea discordare existimantur; de qua pono infrascriptas tres conclusiones ex utriusque mente.

1>10. De re nominaliter concepta,_ primus conceptus qui habetur_est conceptus rei conceptae proprius et conuertibilis.

1>11. De re definitiue concepta,_ primus conceptus qui habetur est conceptus uniuersalissimus.

1>12. In distinctissima cognitione,_ ultimo nota nobis sunt praedicata maxime uniuersalia.

1>13. Opinio Commentatoris de dimensionibus interminatis_principiis et fundamentis doctrinae Sancti Thomae nihil repugnat.

1>14. In materia de obiecto intellectus non discordat,_ ut creditur, sed concordat Thommas et Scotus.

1>10. 1486 est conceptus universalissimus. | *Emendationes errorum*, corrige: est conceptus rei conceptae proprius et convertibilis. | 1487 text not emended

1>11. 1487 est conceptus rei conceptus proprius et convertibilis

---

1>8. *Re* Peter Lombard *Sentences* 2, *d.* 5.

1>9–12. The 1487 reprint of Pico's text, followed by every later editor (including Kieszkowski and Biondi) misread the emendation of errors in the *editio princeps* and switched key portions of 1>10–11. Biondi's edition (1995) in addition omits the Latin text of 1>11 entirely. On these conclusions, cf. 3>2ff. from Pico's "paradoxical dogmatizing conclusions."

1>8. In this article taken from their commentaries [on the *Sentences*], *Whether an angel can desire divine equality in a simple sense,* Thomas and Scotus do not disagree. (410)

1>9. On the problem of what that is more or less universal is first known, Thomas and Scotus agree, who on this are thought to strongly disagree. On this I propose the following three conclusions from the minds of both of them.

1>10. Of a thing conceived nominally, the first concept that is had is the proper and convertible concept of the thing conceived.

1>11. Of a thing conceived definitionally, the first concept that is had is the most universal concept.

1>12. In the most distinct knowledge, the predicates that are most universal are known to us last.

1>13. The opinion of the Commentator on unlimited dimensions contradicts none of the principles and fundamentals of the doctrine of Saint Thomas. (415)

1>14. On the problem of the object of the intellect, Thomas and Scotus do not disagree, as is believed, but agree.

1>13. Involves the question of whether or not dimensions exist in prime matter conceived independently of form. Cf. 7.16 from Averroes. In the *Apology* (above, p. 48) Pico charged Thomas with inconsistency on this issue.

1>14. On the central Thomist/Scotist debate over the way in which "being" is an object of the intellect. Cf. 2.42, 4.7–8 and notes, 2>5–6.

1>15. In quaestione de contingentia ad utrumlibet in materia de casu et fortuna, re et fundamentaliter non discordant Auenrois et Auicenna, licet superficie tenus et in uerbis eorum oppositum appareat.

1>16. An corpus compositum accipiat physicus a methaphysico, discordare fundamentaliter non possunt Auenrois et Auicenna, et si uerbis discrepent. <15r/15v>

1>17. De modo quo angeli sint in loco, non differunt Thommas et Scotus.

1>15. *Re* Aristotle *Physics* 2.4–6. In the series listed at 24.2 note. Cf. especially 2>14–15.

1>16. Series begins at 1.14–15.

1>15. On the question of contingency in respect to alternate events, in the matter of chance and fortune, Averroes and Avicenna do not disagree fundamentally and in substance, although on the surface and in their words the opposite appears to be true.

1>16. Averroes and Avicenna cannot disagree fundamentally on whether the physicist receives composite bodies from the metaphysician, even if they differ in their words.

1>17. On the way in which angels exist in place, Thomas and Scotus do not differ.

1>17. Pico discusses this problem in the *Apology* (*Opera*, 131ff.), attacking the views of Thomas found in *Sentences* 1, *d.* 37. At issue is the question of whether angels, which for Thomas were totally incorporeal, existed locally in space or only through their "operations." Cf. the related question in thesis 4>8, which was attacked by the papal commission.

CONCLVSIONES PHILOSOPHICE SECVNDVM PROPRIAM OPINIONEM NVMERO .LXXX. QVE LICET A COMMVNI PHILOSOPHIA DISSENTIANT, A COMMVNI TAMEN PHILOSOPHANDI MODO NON MVLTVM ABHORRENT.

2>1. Potest a specie in sensu exteriori existente immediate abstrahi species uniuersalis.

2>2. Intentio secunda est ens rationis, habens se per modum formae qualitatiue, ab operatione intellectus proueniens consequutive, non effectiue.

2>3. Nec prima intentio nec secunda intentio alicubi sunt subiectiue.

2>4. Est deuenire in corporibus ad aliquid quod ita corporaliter locat quod corporaliter non locatur, et illud est ultima sphera, sicut in intelligibilibus est deuenire ad aliquid quod ita intelligibiliter locat, quod nullo modo locatur, et illud est deus.

Correlarium: Non est quaerendum quomodo ultima sphera locatur, sed absolute concedendum quod non locatur.

EIGHTY PHILOSOPHICAL CONCLUSIONS DISSENTING FROM THE COMMON PHILOSOPHY. As suggested in the full title of this section, these theses do not develop the "new method" promised in Pico's *philosophia nova*, which is presented in the next section. They instead put forward what Pico viewed as controversial points of view on standard scholastic issues.

2>1. Series starts at 1.1. On harmonizing the apparent conflict between this thesis and 2>31, see above, p. 103.

2>2. "second intention" = a universal concept like "genus" arising from reflection on "first intentions," referring to concepts of concrete objects. Cf. 10.2. "originating consecutively, not effectively, from an operation of the intellect" = since a second intention, as we saw in the preceding thesis, is a distinction of reason, which for Pico was an inferior reflection of the intellect. Tied to the next thesis and to the broader series of theses starting at 1.2.

Philosophical Conclusions Dissenting from the Common Philosophy

EIGHTY PHILOSOPHICAL CONCLUSIONS ACCORDING TO MY OWN OPINION, WHICH WHILE DISSENTING FROM THE COMMON PHILOSOPHY, DO NOT DEPART RADICALLY FROM THE COMMON METHOD OF PHILOSOPHIZING.

2>1. A universal image can be abstracted immediately from an image existing in an exterior sense. (420)

2>2. A second intention is a being of reason, existing in the mode of a qualitative form, originating consecutively, not effectively, from an operation of the intellect.

2>3. Neither a first intention nor a second intention exists anywhere subjectively.

2>4. In corporeal things, you eventually reach something that locates things physically in such a way that physically it is not itself located, and that is the highest sphere—just as in intelligible things you eventually reach something that locates things intelligibly in such a way that it is not itself located in any sense, and that is God.

Corollary: You should not ask in what way the highest sphere is located, but it must be absolutely conceded that it has no location.

2>3. "exists anywhere subjectively" = possesses existence (*esse*) anywhere in a metaphysical subject. The idea is that both concrete and abstract concepts of entities are "beings of reason." The implied nominalism here is clarified in 3>2–7. Cf. also 2>5–6.

2>4. Closer than any other thesis in this section to the proportional forms of Pico's "new philosophy." The Neo-Platonic inspiration of this thesis is apparent when we compare 22.12 from Porphyry.

2>5. Singulare non intelligitur ab intellectu, nec secundum ueritatem, nec secundum etiam opinionem Aristotelis, Commentatoris, et Thommae.

2>6. Licet intellectus non intelligat singulariter, ab ipso tamen est quod perfecte cognoscatur singulare.

2>7. Quaelibet res, quaecunque sit illa, in puritate sui esse constituta est intelligens, intellectus, et intellectum.

2>8. Ex praedicta conclusione habetur quare materia sit principium incognoscibilitatis et intellectus agens cognoscibilitatis.

2>9. Illa dicitur actio immanens quae non est subiectiue in illo quod passiue per eam denominatur, et per hoc distinguitur a transeunte.

2>10. Omnis alius modus praeter eum quem dixit praecedens conclusio est insufficiens ad distinguendum actionem immanentem a transe/unte. <15v/16r>

2>11. Cum dicit Auenrois non esse aliud medium ad probandum abstractum praeter aeternitatem motus, non intelligit de quocunque abstracto, sed de eo quod ultimato gradu abstractionis est abstractum a corpore.

2>12. Esse corporeum non habet res ab aliqua forma substantiali uel gradu formae substantialis.

2>8. 1486 cognoscibilitatis:

2>5–6. Cf. Thomas Aquinas *Summa* 1*a*.5,2 and the theses tied to 2.42. The implied view in 2>6 is that individuals can be known by "reason," which is an inferior reflection of the intellect. Cf. also 2>1–3.

2>7–8. "in the purity of its existence" = as it exists in the intellectual or angelic nature. Cf. 3>49, 7a>5, and 7a>42 (the last two answered through the "way of numbers"). I have not translated *intellectus agens* here as "active intellect" since Pico rarely used that phrase in respect to his own theory of knowledge.

2>5. Nothing individual is understood by the intellect, neither according to truth nor acccording to the opinion of Aristotle, the Commentator, and Thomas.

2>6. Granted that the intellect does not understand individuals, from it something exists that knows individuals perfectly. (425)

2>7. Every thing, whatever it is, situated in the purity of its existence, is that having intellect, intellect itself, and that intellected.

2>8. From the preceding conclusion it is known why matter is the principle of unknowability, and the intellect the agent of knowability.

2>9. That operation is called immanent that does not exist subjectively in that which is passively designated by it, and through this it is distinguished from a transitive operation.

2>10. Every way besides the one that the preceding conclusion states is insufficient to distinguish an immanent from a transitive operation.

2>11. When Averroes says that there is no way to prove that the abstract exists except through the eternity of motion, he does not mean this of everything abstract, but of that which in the highest grade of abstraction is abstract in respect to body. (430)

2>12. Corporeal existence does not depend on any substantial form or grade of substantial form.

2>9–10. Cf. 24.19 from Proclus. "does not exist subjectively in" = does not possess metaphysical existence in.

2>11. Cf. 7.5, 7.18 and notes. Pico himself generally argued that even angels (or the intellectual nature) included a material component, implying that "the highest grade of abstraction" here refers to God. Averroes, on the other hand, took the ends of celestial motion to be separate intelligences, which I assume are probably what Pico has in mind in his thesis. Arguably, he intended for debating purposes to leave his sense ambiguous.

2>12. Suggesting against Aquinas that a *forma corporeitatis* or material form precedes the substantial form. Cf. 2.29 and note, 16.1–2, 2>70.

2>13. Sex transcendentia quae ponit communis doctrina_a iunioribus latinis sunt efficta; ea et graeci peripatetici, et princeps eorum Aristoteles nescit.

2>14. Necessarium est apud Aristotelem primam causam mouere de necessitate.

2>15. Impossibile est_et omnino irrationale apud Aristotelem omnia euenire de necessitate, respectu cuiuscunque causae illa necessitas accipiatur.

2>16. Tractatus suppositionum ad logicum non pertinet.

2>17. Non potuit mundus esse a deo ab aeterno efficienter efficientia uera, quae est reductio de potentia ad actum.

2>18. Potuit produci, et fuit de facto secundum Aristotelem et Commentatorem productus, ab aeterno mundus a deo efficientia quae est naturalis fluxus et effectualis consequtio.

2>19. Qui negat coelum esse animatum, ita ut motor eius non sit forma eius, non solum Aristoteli repugnat, sed totius philosophiae fundamenta destruit.

2>20. In actibus nostri intellectus non est successio ratione potentiarum sensitiuarum et deseruientium, ut credunt moderni, sed eo: quia rationalis est.

2>13. "later Latins" in Pico's theses = medieval scholastics in general, not just the so-called *moderni* or nominalists. "transcendentals" = principles transcending the ten Aristotelian *praedicamenta* or categories of determined being—in Aquinas, *res*, *aliquid*, *unum*, *verum*, and *bonum*, with *ens* sometimes added as a sixth (cf. Deferrari and Barry 1947: 1110). For Pico's Platonic notion of transcendentals, which (in the light of thesis 1>1) Pico would presumably attribute to Aristotle as well, cf. 5>8.

2>14–15. With the conflict resolved by invoking hierarchical "modes" of necessity. Cf. the long list of connected theses given in note 24.2.

2>16. *Treatise on Supposition* = the first of the seven treatises in *De proprietatis terminorum*, the last of the seven tracts in the standard medieval textbook in logic, Peter of Spain's (Pope John XXI's) *Summulae logicales* (mid-thirteenth century). Pico himself occasionally used the language of "supposition theory," illustrated in 4>10 and note, but on the whole he viewed breaks with traditional Aristotelian logic (other than his own) with disdain. Cf., e.g., 2>60. 2>17–18.

Philosophical Conclusions Dissenting from the Common Philosophy

2>13. The six transcendentals that the common teaching posits were invented by the later Latins. The Greek Peripatetics, and their prince, Aristotle, did not know them.

2>14. It is necessary according to Aristotle that the first cause moves things necessarily.

2>15. It is impossible and totally irrational according to Aristotle that everything should happen necessarily, no matter what cause that necessity is referred to.

2>16. The *Treatise on Supposition* does not pertain to logic. (435)

2>17. The world could not exist efficiently from God from eternity with true efficiency, which is a movement from potentiality to act.

2>18. The world could be produced, and was in fact produced according to Aristotle and the Commentator, from eternity by God with an efficiency that produces a natural flow and effectual succession.

2>19. Anyone who denies that heaven is animate, so that its mover is not its form, not only contradicts Aristotle but destroys the foundations of all philosophy.

2>20. In the acts of our intellect succession does not exist through the sensual and subordinate powers, as the moderns believe, but through this: because it is rational.

2>17–18. Aimed at reconciling Aristotelian texts claiming that the world was eternal with others arguing that all efficient causality was directed towards a state of rest or act. Pico was prepared to invoke a double-truth in denying the eternity of the world "theologically speaking," however. Cf. here 4>28.

2>19. Series starts at 7.7–8. Cf. especially 15.1, 2>36–37.

2>20. For Pico's sense, cf. 5>37ff. The "moderns" here = Latin scholastics in general, not just the nominalists or so-called *moderni*.

2>21. Notitia de nouo acquisita fit ex praecedenti cognitione tanquam ex termino a quo, et tanquam ex causa effectiua partiali, formali, directiua, et tanquam ex causa praedisponente materiali.

2>22. Ille habitus est practicus qui est formaliter regulatiuus alicuius operationis habituati.

2>23. Habitus habet esse practicum et speculatiuum ab obiecto relato ad subiectum in quo est. Intellectus autem dicitur practicus uel speculatiuus a fine quem sibi proponit habituatus. <16r/16v>

2>24. Habitus practicus a speculatiuo finibus distinguitur.

2>25. Praxis est operatio quae non est formaliter cognitio, et potest esse recta_et non recta, rectificabilis per habitum,_ ut per partiale rectificationis effectiuum quo practicans habituatur.

2>26. Practicum et speculatiuum sunt differentiae accidentales habitus.

2>27. Theologia uiatoris,_ ut uiatoris est, simpliciter practica dicenda est.

2>28. Totam medicinam practicam esse, et ut uerum asserimus, et ut consonum dictis ac sententiae Auenrois.

2>29. Logica est practica.

2>21. 1486 omits paragraph mark (numbers in the present edition) that normally signal a new thesis

2>23. 1486 est: Intellectus

2>26. 1486 differentie accidentalis habitus | *Emendationes errorum*, corrige: differentiae accidentales habitus | 1487 text not emended

---

2>21. Commenting on *Posterior Analytics* 1.1 (71a). Other theses on demonstration are listed in note 7.10–11. Cf. in particular 9.4.

2>21. New knowledge can arise from preceding knowledge as its starting point, as its partial effective, formal, and directive cause, and as its predisposing material cause. (440)

2>22. That habit is practical that formally regulates some operation in a conditioned subject.

2>23. A habit has its practical and speculative existence from the object related to the subject in which it exists. But the intellect is called practical or speculative from an end that the conditioned subject proposes to itself.

2>24. A practical habit is distinguished from a speculative habit by its ends.

2>25. A practical act is an operation that is not formally knowledge, and it can be right or wrong, rectifiable by a habit, as when an acting subject is rectified by a partial effective habit.

2>26. Practical and speculative properties are accidental differences of habits. (445)

2>27. The theology of a pilgrim, since it *is* that of a pilgrim, must simply speaking be called practical.

2>28. All medicine is practical, and I assert this as both true and as consonant with the words and opinion of Averroes.

2>29. Logic is practical.

2>22–29. Texts in the Aristotelian tradition regularly began with a discussion of the "speculative" or "practical" nature of the sciences under consideration. Relevant to these theses, cf., e.g., Aristotle *De anima* 433a16ff., *Nichomachean Ethics* 1139a27ff. For 2>25, cf. 4.5. The "theology of a pilgrim" in 2>27 is "practical" since that theology is simply a means to a mystical end—not a speculative end in itself. See above, pp. 107–108.

2>30. Sensus communis non est distinctus a sensu uisus, auditus, odoratus, gustus, et tactus.

2>31. Non dari species intelligibiles a phantasmatibus abstractas et ut ueram, et commentatoris et Alberti sententiam, asserimus.

2>32. In omni quaestione per demonstrationem scibili, oportet praecognoscere quid subiecti et passionis, non intelligendo per quid, quid nominis, ut intelligunt expositores, sed quid rei.

2>33. Possibilis est regressus a causa ad effectum negatione quam somniat Burleus.

2>34. Tenentes minima naturalia in qualitatibus, non propterea habent negare motum alterationis fieri in tempore successiue.

2>35. Necessarium est tenere secundum Auenroem quod forma generis sit realiter alia a forma speciei, nec oppositum stat cum principiis doctrinae suae.

2>32. 1486 per quid. quid nominis

2>33. 1486 absque negatiõe | 1486 *Emendationes errorum,* ubi scribitur : absque negatõe (*sic*) : corrige: negatione | 1487 absque negotiatione

---

2>30. In the series listed at 1.10 note. Cf. especially 2>58.

2>31. Series starts at 1.1 from Albert, which is closely linked to this thesis. Cf. also 2>1 and note and my discussion of Pico's theory of knowledge on pp. 102–105.

2>32. Concerns *Posterior Analytics* 1.1. Related theses are listed in note 7.10–11.

2>33. Burleus = English scholastic, d. ca. 1343. Like the last thesis, in the series on demonstration starting at 7.10–11. Pico's text is in doubt due to problems in the *Emendationes errorum,* which at first sight seem to do nothing but expand an unambiguous abbreviation. The speculative correction in the 1487 reprint, which was silently adopted in all later editions, at first sight seems plausible, since *negotiatio* had a legitimate technical sense in late-medieval logic; for references, see Jardine (1988: 686–93). However, that term does not show up in Burleus's commentary on *Posterior Analytics,* where we would expect to find it; nor are there any suggestions supporting this emendation in Pico's works. As I tentatively interpret it, the list of errors is not trying to make (but botching) a correction of the word *negatione,* as the 1487 editors apparently

Philosophical Conclusions Dissenting from the Common Philosophy

2>30. Common sense is not distinct from the sense of sight, hearing, smell, taste, and touch.

2>31. That intelligible images are not abstracted from phantasmata, I assert both as true and as the opinion of the Commentator and of Albert. (450)

2>32. In every question knowable through demonstration it is necessary to recognize first what belongs to the subject and to its properties—not understanding by what, what name, as the commentators understand it, but what thing.

2>33. It is possible to move from cause to effect [even] with the negation that Burleus dreams of.

2>34. Those holding that natural *minima* exist in qualities do not, because of this, have to deny that alteration occurs successively in time.

2>35. It is necessary to hold according to Averroes that the form of the genus is really different from the form of the species, nor is the opposite consistent with the principles of his teachings.

---

believed. Leaving aside the trivial inconsistency in the abbreviation of *negatione*, I think the list of errors is simply telling us to remove *absque* from the thesis. Support for this reading shows up in Burleus's comments on *Posterior Analytics* 1.13, the *locus classicus* for discussion of this type of demonstration. In that chapter, Burleus discourses at length about what he idiosyncratically labels *ignorantia secundum negationem* or *ignorantia negationis* (ignorance due to negation or a deficiency), arguing that faulty demonstrations follow from distortions in sensual knowledge. Burleus concludes that "from beginning to end, if any sense is deficient it is necessary that the knowledge that is acquired naturally from that sense be deficient." Pico claimed that in man's highest state "everything knowable" could be acquired without sensual input (cf. 3>40, 3>60–66), explaining his cryptic (and sarcastic) language in this thesis. The original *absque* in ths thesis presumably arose from Burleus's confusing use of negative terms in his Aristotelian commentary.

2>34. The thesis opposes the views of Thomas Aquinas; for the meaning of the thesis, see 2.27 and note. "natural *minima*" = limits to divisibility; "alteration" = in the technical Aristotelian sense, a change in accidental qualities over time. Cf. here 1.5 and note.

2>35. Series starts at 1.2.

2>36. Demonstratio Aristotelis in .vii. Physicorum, quod omne quod mouetur mouetur ab alio, nihil probat eorum quae uel Thommas, uel Scotus, uel Egidius, quem sequitur Iohanes de Gandauo, uel Gratiadeus, uel Burleus, uel alii quos ego legerim intendunt, sed tantum quod optime dixit Commentator, a latinis omnibus expositoribus male intellectus, et est quod in quolibet moto motor est alius a mobili uel secundum naturam uel secundum subiectum.

2>37. Demonstratio .vii. Physicorum probat euidenter quod coelum non mouetur a se, datis principiis Auenrois ueris utique et firmissimis.

2>38. Ordo librorum naturalis philosophiae ab Aristotele tradite est iste: Liber Physicorum, coeli et mundi, de generatione, metheororum,/mineralium, de plantis, de generatione animalium, de partibus animalium, de progressu animalium, de anima, tum libri qui dicuntur parui naturales. <16v/17r>

Correlarium: Qui librum de anima sextum naturalium uocant, ab Aristotelis mente omnino discordant.

2>39. Omnis uia saluans dictum Aristotelis quod uenti orientales sint calidiores occidentalibus, praeter uiam animationis coeli, est friuola et nulla.

2>38. 1486 ab Aristotle est iste | *Emendationes errorum,* interpone: ab Aristotle tradite est iste | 1487 text emended *sic*

2>36–37. Completes the series begun at 2.37–38. For John of Jandun and Burleus, see notes 7.2–4 and 2>33. Gratiadeus = Gratia dei d'Ascoli, mid-fourteenth-century Dominican, whose *Quaestiones in libros Physicorum Aristotelis in studio Patavino disputatae* (Questions on the *Physics* of Aristotle Disputed in the University of Padua) was printed two years before the nine hundred theses. Copies of the works of all the writers listed in 2>36, including the last figure, show up in the inventories of Pico's library. "with the principles of Averroes assuredly granted as true and firm" = Pico is not claiming adherence here to everything that Averroes says; his point is that the views ascribed to Averroes in 2>36 are consistent with the outwardly conflicting principles attributed to him elsewhere, e.g., in 7.7–8 and 7.9.

Philosophical Conclusions Dissenting from the Common Philosophy

2>36. Aristotle's demonstration in book 7 of the *Physics*, that everything that is moved is moved by another, proves none of those things that either Thomas, or Scotus, or Giles, whom John of Jandun follows, or Gratiadeus, or Burleus, or any of the others whom I have read maintain, but only what the Commentator said best, something badly understood by all Latin commentators, and that is: *In everything moved the mover is different from the movable object either in nature or in subject.* (455)

2>37. The demonstration of book 7 of the *Physics* clearly proves that the heavens do not move themselves, with the principles of Averroes assuredly granted as true and firm.

2>38. The order of the books of natural philosophy transmitted by Aristotle is this: *Physics*, *On Heaven and the Earth*, *On Generation*, *Meteorology*, *On Minerals*, *On Plants*, *On the Generation of Animals*, *On the Parts of Animals*, *On the Motion of Animals*, *On the Soul*, and then the books called the *Minor Natural Works*.

Corollary: Those who call *On the Soul* the sixth of the natural books disagree totally with the mind of Aristotle.

2>39. Every means used to save the dictum of Aristotle—that east winds are hotter than west winds—besides the means involving the animation of heaven, is frivolous and empty.

2>38. The idea is that the order of an authority's corpus, like each work singly, should reflect the order of reality. Many of the works listed here would not be ascribed to Aristotle by even the most conservative classicists. "Those who call" = apparently followers of Avicenna; cf. the work known in Latin as *Opus egregium De anima, qui sextus naturalium Avicene dicitur,* first printed in Pavia ca. 1485. Both manuscript and printed copies were in Pico's library (Kibre 1936: 143, 221, 253).

2>39. On *Meteorology* 2.4–6. Elia del Medigo defended Averroes on this issue in his correspondence with Pico while the latter was preparing for his debate; see Kieszkowski, ed. (1964: 70–72). We find in that text that this conclusion is closely tied to thesis 7.30.

2>40. Nec ab Aristotele nec ab expositoribus adducte rationes de salsedine maris sunt sufficientes, nec potest ulla maxime stante mosaica ueritate sufficientior assignari, quam causalitas eiusdem uniuersalis prouidentiae quae et in terra discooperitionem operata est.

2>41. Nulla pars coeli differt ab alia secundum lucidum et non lucidum, sed secundum magis et minus lucidum.

2>42. Modus ab Aristotele datus quomodo calefiant inferiora a superioribus nullo modo rectus apparet.

2>43. Haec duo stant simul, et ambo credo simul esse uera, et quod ratio Auenrois in commento ultimo primi Physicorum contra Auicennam concludat, et quod, cum hoc, rationes Auicennae ad probandum primum principium sunt bonae et efficaces.

2>44. Si intelligentias esse in genere secundum Aristotelem dixerit Thommas, non minus sibi quam Aristoteli repugnabit.

2>45. Si unitas generis non est solum ex parte concipientis, sed etiam ex parte concepti, necesse est quaecunque sunt in eodem genere logico esse in eodem genere physico.

2>40. Pico is not necessarily rejecting the standard naturalistic solutions to this problem, discussed in *Meteorology* 2.1–3 and its commentaries, but is only suggesting that such solutions are theologically "insufficient."

2>41. Cf. 26.6 and the following thesis and note. Semprini (1920) solemnly declared that this thesis was "an anticipation of modern scientific theory."

2>42. Cf. 10.4, 11.3, and the preceding thesis. Aristotle *Meteorology* 1.3, which is a heavily stratified text, offers several explanations of the interaction between the celestial and terrestrial worlds. The most prominent is the quasi-mechanical view that the celestial substance "inflames by its motion whatever part of the lower world is nearest to it, and so generates heat" (rev. Oxford trans.). Pico's views of this topic are discussed above, pp. 123–25.

Philosophical Conclusions Dissenting from the Common Philosophy

2>40. The arguments proposed by neither Aristotle nor his commentators concerning the saltiness of the sea are sufficient, nor can any more sufficient one be assigned, with the truth of Moses firmly standing, than the causality of the same universal providence that reveals itself on the earth.

2>41. No part of heaven differs from another in being bright or not bright, but in being more or less bright. (460)

2>42. The manner given by Aristotle as to how inferiors are heated by superiors appears in no way to be correct.

2>43. These two things are consistent, and I believe that both are equally true: Both what Averroes concludes in his last comment on the first book of the *Physics* against Avicenna and, along with this, Avicenna's arguments to prove the existence of the first principle, are good and effective.

2>44. If Thomas says that according to Aristotle intelligences exist in genus, he contradicts himself no less than Aristotle.

2>45. If the unity of the genus not only exists in the conceiver, but as well in what is conceived, it is necessary that all things in the same logical genus be in the same physical genus.

2>43. Series begins at 7.18. Material pertinent to this question can be found in the long letter that Elia del Medigo wrote to Pico in the fall of 1486. For that text, see Kieszkowski, ed. (1964: 68ff.).

2>44. Thomas followed Avicenna on this point in *Sentences* 2, *d.* 3, *q.* 1, *art.* 5. Pico presumably planned to argue that Thomas was inconsistent here since Thomas also insisted that intelligences (or angels) lacked the individualizing property of matter. If two or more intelligences existed in the same genus or species, they would hence be indistinguishable. Cf. 2.21 and note.

2>45. Pico himself would have rejected the conditional realist premise of this thesis; cf. on this point 2>2–3 (see notes), 3>2ff.

2>46. Scientia est realiter relatiua, et scibile ad eam per accidens refertur.

2>47. Tenendo communem modum doctorum, quod scilicet de deo aliquid formaliter praedicetur, dico duas conclusiones proximas, quarum haec est prima: quod solus deus ita est substantia, quod nullo modo est non substantia.

2>48. Secunda: Deus ideo non est in genere quia est substantialiter substantia.

2>49. Ponere differentiam inter simitatem et albedinem aut consimilia accidentia per hoc, quod illud separabile sit, illud inseparabile/a certo subiecto, fictitium est. <17r/17v>

2>50. Differentia quae inter suprascripta accidentia apparet ex sola uoluntaria nominum impositione originatur.

2>51. Necessarium est dicere secundum Auenroem quod substantia est de intrinseca quiditate accidentis, et est opinio et Aristoteli et philosophiae maxime consona.

2>48. 1486 colon retained from 1486 edition

2>49. 1487 fictiuum

2>50. 1486 voluntate | *Emendationes errorum*, corrige: voluntaria | 1487 text emended *sic*

2>46. Series starts at 4.16–17; on "relations," see my note to those theses. Cf. especially 3>33, where Pico also upholds a conceptual or nominalistic view of the lower levels of human knowledge.

2>47–48. Pico would again emphatically deny the premise of these theses, which he accepts momentarily only to draw a controversial conclusion from the "common way." His underlying target was again Thomas Aquinas; cf. Thomas *Sentences* 1, *d.* 8, *q.* 4, *art.* 2–3. See also Pico's polemical exchange on this issue with the Aristotelian Antonio da Faenza (*Opera*, 269), where

Philosophical Conclusions Dissenting from the Common Philosophy

2>46. [Human] knowledge is really relational, and what is knowable is referred to it accidentally. (465)

2>47. Holding the common way of doctors, namely that something can be formally predicated of God, I state the two following conclusions, of which this is the first: that only God is so fully substance; that in no sense is he not substance.

2>48. Second: God does not exist in a genus, because he is substantially substance.

2>49. To posit a distinction between snubness in noses and whiteness or similar accidents through this—that one is separable and the other inseparable from a given subject—is fallacious.

2>50. The distinction that appears to exist between the preceding accidents originates solely from the voluntary imposition of names.

2>51. It is necessary to say according to Averroes that substance belongs to the intrinsic quiddity of an accident, and this opinion is in total harmony with both Aristotle and philosophy. (470)

Pico argues *contra Thomam* that "God does not exist in a genus, for genera are the essences of things, but God neither is an essence nor has an essence" [Deus sub nullo genere sit; genera enim rerum essentiae sunt, Deus autem nec essentia est, nec essentiam habet].

2>49–51. Series starts at 2.24. On the substance/accident problem and "inseparable" accidents, see above, pp. 97ff. The concept of "snubness" in noses as a standard example of an inseparable accident derives from Aristotle *Physics* 1.3 (186b22), *De anima* 3.7 (431b13), and similar texts.

2>52. In definitione substantiarum naturalium non esse ponendam materiam,_ et Auenroi et Alberto consentanea sententia est.

2>53. Si Thommas dixerit in intelligentiis secundum Aristotelem esse accidentia, non Aristoteli modo, sed sibiipsi contradicet.

2>54. Iste propositiones sunt concedende ut omnino uere: Materia prima fit asinus, bos, et similia.

2>55. In composito materiali non sunt duae praecisae entitates et distinctae, sed una entitas.

2>56. Sonum non ex motu aeris intercepti inter duo corpora se percutientia, ut tenet Aristoteles_et expositores eius, sed ex contactu tali talium uel talium corporum, talem uel talem sonum causari,_ dico.

2>57. Rationes quas adducunt peripatetici ad probandum quod in causis essentialiter ordinatis non eatur in infinitum, non conuincunt de necessitate falsitatem positi.

2>58. Virtutem sensitiuam sensus communis,_ sicuti non a uirtutibus sensitiuis sensuum exteriorum,_ ut dixit conclusio .xxx.,_ ita nec a uirtutibus sensitiuis sensuum interiorum, phantastica_siue imaginatiua, cogitatiua,_ et memoratiua, subiecto, id est re,_ differre, et ut ueram_et ut Aristotelis Platonisque sententiam asserimus.

2>56. 1486 intercoepti

2>52. Series begins at 2.33.

2>53. In the same series as 2>49–51.

2>54. The thesis pertains to the concept of "inchoate forms" raised in 1.4 from Albert the Great; see my note to that thesis.

Philosophical Conclusions Dissenting from the Common Philosophy

2>52. Matter should not be posited in the definition of natural substances, and this opinion is in agreement with both Averroes and Albert.

2>53. If Thomas says that according to Aristotle accidents exist in intelligences, he contradicts not only Aristotle but himself.

2>54. These propositions should be conceded as totally true: Asses, cows, and similar things arise from prime matter.

2>55. In a material composite there are not two separate and distinct entities, but one entity.

2>56. I say that sound is not caused by the motion of the air forced out by two striking bodies, as Aristotle and his commentators maintain, but that such or such a sound is caused by the contact of such or such bodies. (475)

2>57. The arguments that the Peripatetics bring forward to prove that in ordering essential causes one should not proceed to infinity do not necessarily demonstrate the falseness of what is proposed.

2>58. I assert both as true and as the opinion of Aristotle and Plato, that just as the sensitive power of common sense does not differ in subject, that is, as a thing, from the sensitive powers of the exterior senses, as my thirtieth conclusion stated, so neither do the phantastic or imaginative, judgmental, and memorative powers differ from the sensitive powers of the interior senses.

2>55. Pico's series on metaphysical unity begins at 2.23.

2>56. *Re De anima* 2.8. Cf. the series beginning at 1.7–8.

2>57. *Re* Aristotle *Metaphysics* 2.2, which argues that to accept an infinite chain of formal causes would be to deny the existence of a first cause. Related theses are listed in 7.18 note.

2>58. Cf. 2>30 and above, p. 105. Series starts at 1.10.

2>59. Dico omnes qualitates elementorum symbolas_esse diuersarum specierum.

2>60. Si qua est ponenda figura quarta syllogismorum, illa est ponenda quam Galienus ponit, non quam et Franciscus Maironis et Petrus Mantuanus pueriliter confinxerunt; rectius est tamen nullam ponere.

2>61. De materia ut ex ea per se fiunt res tractare methaphysicum, physicum autem ut ex ea res fiunt per accidens,_ habemus dicere secundum doctrinam Aristotelis.

2>62. Dictio exclusiua,_ addita uni relatiuo, correlatiuum non excludit.

2>63. Non debet concedi partem in toto quantitatiuo a suo toto esse / aliquo modo actu distinctam. <17v/18r>

2>64. Opinio quae Auicennae ascribitur,_ quod illud unum_quod cum ente conuertitur sit unum quod est principium numeri, et ita consequenter quod unaquaeque res sit una per intentionem additam essentiae suae,_ si non est necessario uera, est tamen probabilis et defendetur a me.

2>59. "qualities of the elements" = the contraries (hot/cold, dry/moist, etc.) underlying the four elements fire, air, water, and earth. See, e.g., Aristotle *De generatione et corruptione* 2.2ff. Cf. this thesis with 6.8, 13.4.

2>60. Francis of Meyronnes = see theses 3.1–8. Peter of Mantua = logician, d. ca. 1400. His *Logica* was first published in 1483 in Venice. "figures" = specific patterns of terms in syllogisms. The Aristotelian corpus only acknowledged three figures; the fourth apparently arose from later exegeses on Theophrastus's commentary on *Prior Analytics* 1. The tradition (supposedly false) that Galen upheld a fourth figure is reported by Averroes in his commentary on *Prior Analytics* 1.8 and 1.23. Further evidence is found in this thesis of Pico's disdain for medieval Latin logical traditions. Cf. 2>16.

2>59. I say that all qualities of the elements are represented by different images.

2>60. If a fourth figure of the syllogism must be posited, one should do so as Galen does it, not as it was childishly fabricated by Francis of Meyronnes and Peter of Mantua. It is more correct, however, to posit none.

2>61. According to the teachings of Aristotle we have to say that the metaphysician deals with matter as things are produced from it per se, but the physicist as things are produced from it accidentally. (480)

2>62. An exclusive statement, added to one term of a relation, does not exclude a correlation.

2>63. It should not be conceded that a part in a quantitative whole is in any mode distinct in act from its whole.

2>64. The opinion that is attributed to Avicenna—that that one which is convertible with being is the one that is the principle of number, and consequently that each thing is one through an intention added to its essence—if it is not necessarily true, is nevertheless probable, and will be defended by me.

2>61. Series begins at 1.14–15. Cf. especially 1>16.

2>62. Series starts at 4.16–17. "exclusive statement" = a statement including terms like "only" that restricts a predicate to a single subject. See the discussion in Peter of Spain's *Summulae logicales* 7.7. Pico's formula here would allow him, e.g., to reconcile texts attributing total transcendence to God or the intellectual nature with other texts claiming that the existence of lower beings depended wholly on their relations with these higher entities. Cf., e.g., 3>19.

2>63–64. In the series on metaphysical unity listed in note 2.23. For 2>64, cf. 7.33 from Averroes. Pico had discussed this material at length with Elia del Medigo, as the latter reports in his *De esse et essentia et uno*. For this text, see my opening note to theses 7.1ff. See also Mahoney (1997: 134).

2>65. Licet potentia intellectiua in nobis sit accidens, in angelis tamen est substantia.

2>66. Formalitas est actualitas apta per se perficere possibilem intellectum.

2>67. Si ex concursu elementorum fiat mixtum, quocunque modo ponantur elementa manere immixto,_ fiet mixtum ex elementis_ut ex materia digesta,_ a calido spirituali_uaporoso eleuato ab eis.

2>68. In omnibus infra deum eadem est materia secundum essentiam, diuersa secundum esse.

2>69. Quiditates physicarum naturarum,_ adequato concepto et proprio,_ concipi possunt sine accidentibus, siue a methaphysico siue a physico considerentur.

2>70. Corpus organicum,_ quod est materia animae_et ponitur in diffinitione eius ab Aristotele,_ est corpus et organicum per formam essentialiter distinctam ab anima eum perficiente.

2>71. Secundum omnes philosophos dicendum est deum necessario agere quicquid agit.

2>65. See my discussion above, pp. 98–99.

2>66. "Formality" = see 3.7 note. "possible intellect" for Pico = "the rational part of our soul" (cf. 5>19). Since Pico restricted the use of the word "formal" or related terms to the intellectual nature, he would deny vs. the Scotists the reality of "formalities" in God. Cf. 3>5 and adjacent conclusions. Cf. also 3>58.

2>67. *Re* commentary on Aristotle *De generatione et corruptione* 1.10. The thesis is tied to 6.9, which involves the same text.

2>68. See note 2.21.

2>69. In the series on the substance/accident distinction listed in note 2.24. Cf. also the series beginning at 1.14–15.

Philosophical Conclusions Dissenting from the Common Philosophy

2>65. Granted that the intellective power in us is an accident, in angels it is a substance.

2>66. A formality is an actuality appropriate per se to perfect the possible intellect. (485)

2>67. If, out of a combination of elements, a mixture is made—in whatever unmixed mode the elements are said to remain—the mixture is produced out of those elements just as matter is digested, by a vaporous spiritual heat raised out of them.

2>68. In all things below God matter is the same in essence, different in existence.

2>69. The quiddities of physical natures can be conceived without accidents through an adequate and unique concept, whether considered by the metaphysician or by the physicist.

2>70. The organic body, which is the matter of the soul and is included in its definition by Aristotle, is a body and organic through a form essentially distinct from the soul perfecting it.

2>71. According to all philosophers it must be said that God necessarily does whatever he does. (490)

2>70. Commenting on *De anima* 2.1–2. On the *forma corporeitatis* or "material form," see note 2.29. Cf. especially 16.1–2, 2>12. Pico apparently further planned to correlate the "organic body" of the soul with the Neo-Platonic "vehicle" of the soul. On this, cf. 23.6, 5>45 and note.

2>71. Cf. 2>14–15. The phrase "according to all philosophers" alerts us to an implicit double-truth here. On Pico's use of the double-truth, see above, pp. 61–63. On his hierarchical or "modal" means of resolving conflicts over freedom and necessity, cf. the theses listed in note 24.2.

2>72. Qui dubitat ex intelligibili et intellectu magis uere et substantialiter fieri unum quam ex materia et forma materiali, non est philosophus.

2>73. Tenendo opinionem de anima intellectiua quam tenet Commentator, uidetur mihi rationabiliter tenendum illam animam nullius accidentis esse subiectum; et positionem hanc tanquam ueram defendam, quanquam utrum hoc ille tenuerit, ego non definio.

2>74. Dico secundum Thommam dicendum esse in actu reflexo intellectus consistere beatitudinem nostram.

2>75. Diffinitio naturae coelestia comprehendit, et ly_et copulatiue tenetur et non disiunctiue.

2>76. Sicut quilibet philosophus habet dicere quod uirtutes sensitiue / sunt in corde, ita quilibet medicus habet dicere_quod sint in cerebro. <18r/18v>

2>77. Quod dicitur a communi schola philosophantium omnium latinorum de prima operatione intellectus_error est, quia non est alia operatio partis rationalis quam illae duae quas ipsi secundam et tertiam ponunt, compositio scilicet et discursus.

2>75. 1486 & ly : & copulatiue tenetur | 1487 et li. et copulative tenetur

2>77. 1486, 1487 scola

2>72. Pico's series on metaphysical unity begins at 2.23. Pico ascribes the view affirmed here to Averroes in *Heptaplus* 3.2 (*Opera*, 25; Garin, *Scritti vari*, 254). Anyone who doubts the claim made in Pico's thesis may not be a philosopher, but he may be a theologian, since theologians posit a multitude of angels, *henads*, etc., in the intellectual nature. See my discussion of the double-truth referred to in the previous note.

2>73. In the series on the substance/accident distinction listed in note 2.24.

2>74. "reflexive act of the intellect" = the intellective soul contemplating itself. Cf. 5>59, 10>26, etc. In the series starting at 2.12. It is important to note that Pico represents this as Thomas's view, not as his own, which is expressed most fully in 3>43.

PHILOSOPHICAL CONCLUSIONS DISSENTING FROM THE COMMON PHILOSOPHY

2>72. Anyone who doubts that one thing is produced more truly and substantially from what is intelligible and from the intellect than from matter and material form is not a philosopher.

2>73. Holding the opinion on the intellective soul that the Commentator maintains, it seems rational to me to claim that that soul is the subject of no accident. And although I will defend this position as true, I take no position on whether he held it.

2>74. I say that according to Thomas it must be said that our beatitude consists in a reflexive act of the intellect.

2>75. The definition of nature includes celestial things, and the bond between them is conjunctive, not disjunctive.

2>76. Just as every philosopher has to say that the sensitive powers exist in the heart, so every physician has to say that they exist in the brain. (495)

2>77. What the common school of all Latin philosophizers says about the first operation of intellect is in error, because there is no other operation of the rational part than those two that they themselves place second and third, namely composition and discourse.

2>75. Denies the sharp break between the sublunary and celestial worlds affirmed by many Latin scholastics. There was nothing modern in Pico's view, which can be traced back to *De caelo* 1.1ff. Pico's view also found support in a number of late-ancient commentators including John Philoponus and Averroes.

2>76. A secular variation of the double-truth introduced to harmonize Aristotle and Galen. Similar compromises are found in many earlier works, e.g., Roger Bacon *Opus Maius*, tr. Burke, 2:428–29. A syncretic text entitled *De concordia inter Aristotelem et Galenum* (On the Concord between Aristotle and Galen) was well known in the medieval period.

2>77. "first operation of intellect" = sensual abstraction, which for Pico was the function of the lower parts of the soul. Series begins at 1.1. Cf. 2>1, 2>31, and above, p. 103.

2>78. Accidentia nullo modo debent dici entia, sed entis.

2>79. Sex principia sunt formae absolutae.

2>80. Siqua est lingua prima et non casualis, illam esse Hebraicam multis patet coniecturis.

2>78. Series starts at 2.24.

2>79. Presumably tied to the six levels of created reality that show up repeatedly in the theses. Cf., e.g., 5>26, 5>58.

Philosophical Conclusions Dissenting from the Common Philosophy

2>78. Accidents should in no mode be called beings, but *of* being.

2>79. Six principles are absolute forms.

2>80. If a first and not accidental language exists, it is clear through many conjectures that it is Hebrew.

2>80. Cf. 28.33 note.

CONCLVSIONES PARADOXE NVMERO .LXXI. SECVNDVM OPINIONEM PROPRIAM NOVA IN PHILOSOPHIA DOGMATA INDVCENTES.

3>1. Sicut esse proprietatum praeceditur ab esse quiditatiuo, ita esse quiditatiuum praeceditur ab esse uniali.

PARADOXICAL CONCLUSIONS INTRODUCING NEW DOCTRINES IN PHILOSOPHY. The locus of Pico's *philosophia nova* or "new philosophy"; see my discussion above, pp. 18–25 and passim. This section contains the kinds of correlative structures that we can expect in any religious, philosophical, or cosmological tradition subjected to repeated syncretic inbreeding. The main difference between these theses and the previous ones that "do not depart radically from the common method of philosophizing" lies in this section's striking proportional forms.

Paradoxical Conclusions Introducing New Doctrines in Philosophy

SEVENTY-ONE PARADOXICAL CONCLUSIONS ACCORDING TO MY OWN OPINION INTRODUCING NEW DOCTRINES IN PHILOSOPHY.

3>1. Just as propertied existence is preceded by quidditative existence, so quidditative existence is preceded by unial existence. (500)

3>1. The first lines of the *Commento* (Garin, *Scritti vari*, 461) similarly tell us that it is the "principal dogma" of the Platonists (and, by implication, of Aristotle) that everything created has three modes of existence—"participated," "formal," and "causal." The first thesis of this section can thus be considered, in both the literal and figurative senses, as the first principle of Pico's system, which he tells us was "thought out in Aristotelian and Platonic philosophy." It is presumably no accident that in the final version of Pico's text as a whole this is the five hundredth thesis, a number that for Pico symbolized completion and return (cf. 11>68 and note).

3>2. Non possumus dicere quod de re precisissime sumpta aliquid praedicetur praedicatione proprie dicta.

3>3. Qui attingit rem in diffinitione_attingit rem in alteritate.

3>4. Solus ille qui attingit rem in precisione suae unionis_attingit rem ut est ipsa.

3>5. Quanto unusquisque modus cognitionis est eminentior, tanto in intellectu disproportionato imperfectior euadit et illi inutilior.

3>6. Sicut cognitio per demonstrationem habita homini, pro communi statu quem hic experimur, est perfectissima cognitio, ita simpliciter inter cognitiones est imperfectissima.

3>7. Sicut deus est simpliciter cognitio totius esse, ita intellectus est diffinitio totius esse, et anima scientia totius esse.

3>8. Si theologia theologice tradatur, erit ut de primo subiecto de eo quod est unialiter unum, et de quolibet quod est secundum suum esse uniale tanquam de subiecto secundario.

3>9. Vera methaphysica, tradita methaphysicaliter, est de quolibet quod est uera forma ut de primo subiecto, et de quolibet quod est secundum suum esse formale tanquam de obiecto secundario, in modo procedendi demonstrationem negligens.

3>2–7. The idea in this series is that logical and linguistic distinctions belong exclusively, but nevertheless properly, to the inferior realms of cognition and reality. The views expressed here illustrate the inadequacy of traditional labels such as "realist" or "nominalist" when applied to premodern philosophers and their hierarchical systems. Both elements can commonly be found at different levels of those systems—as we see, e.g., when we compare the apparent nominalist sentiments in 3>2–7 or 2>2–3 with the apparent realist views expressed in 2>80, 5>26, 5>53, etc.

3>2. We cannot say of a thing accepted in its most precise sense that anything is predicated by predication properly speaking.

3>3. Anyone who attains a thing in definition attains the thing in otherness.

3>4. Only he who attains a thing in the separateness of its unity attains the thing as it is itself.

3>5. Insofar as each mode of knowledge is more eminent, in understanding something disproportionate it abandons what is more imperfect and less useful to itself.

3>6. Just as knowledge through demonstration, due to the general state that we experience here, is the most perfect knowledge had by man, so simply speaking among all knowledge it is the most imperfect. (505)

3>7. Just as God simply speaking is the knowledge of all existence, so the intellect is the definition of all existence, and the soul the science of all existence.

3>8. If theology is treated theologically, it will deal as its first subject with that which is unially one, and with whatever exists in a unial fashion as its secondary subject.

3>9. True metaphysics, treated metaphysically, deals with whatever is a true form as its first subject, and with whatever exists formally as its secondary object, in its methods disregarding demonstration.

3>8. In the series listed at 6.2–3 note. Pico's "modal" or hierarchical strategy of resolving such issues is nicely illustrated in this and the following thesis.

3>9. Series starts at 1.14–15. Cf. also 18.8 and note. Demonstration apparently belongs to the realm of logic, as Pico viewed it, and not to metaphysics.

3>10. Sicut in creatura non ualet consequentia: Est ens, ergo est, ita / in deo non ualet: Est, ergo est ens. <18v/19r>

3>11. Eadem res in creatura ratione suae actualitatis dicitur esse, et ratione suae determinationis dicitur essentia.

3>12. Sicut angelus necessario componitur ex essentia et esse, ita anima necessario componitur ex substantia et accidente.

3>13. Contradictoria in natura intellectuali se compatiuntur.

3>14. Licet sit uera praecedens conclusio, tamen magis proprie dicitur quod in natura intellectuali non sint contradictoria, quam quod se compatiantur.

3>15. Contradictoria coincidunt in natura uniali.

3>16. Rationabiliter posuit Aristoteles in suis scientiis primum principium de quolibet dici alterum contradictoriorum, et de nullo simul.

3>17. In intellectu est hoc et illud, sed non est hoc extra illud.

3>18. Ideo in anima apparet incompossibilitas contradictoriorum, quia est prima quantitas, ponens partem extra partem.

3>10. On this thesis, see Pico's polemical discussion with Antonio da Faenza, *Opera,* 267–68.

3>11. Series starts at 2.31. "*determinatio*" = the definiteness or determinacy of a thing, i.e., what the thing is. Pico's "modal" distinction was apparently meant to resolve the essence/existence controversy.

3>12. Following Pico's view of the substance/accident distinction, "substance"/"accident" in the soul = its intellectual and rational parts. Cf. the wording in 3>59 and 3>61 and my discussion above, pp. 98–99.

Paradoxical Conclusions Introducing New Doctrines in Philosophy

3>10. Just as in a creature the inference *It is a being, therefore it exists*, is invalid, so in God *He exists, therefore he is a being*, is invalid.

3>11. In created beings, the same thing is called existence in respect to its actuality and essence in respect to its determinacy. (510)

3>12. Just as an angel is necessarily composed out of essence and existence, so the soul is necessarily composed out of substance and accident.

3>13. Contradictions in the intellectual nature are compatible.

3>14. Granted that the preceding conclusion is true, it is more properly said that in the intellectual nature there are no contradictions, than that they are compatible.

3>15. Contradictions coincide in the unial nature.

3>16. In his sciences Aristotle rationally posited that the first principle of everything, and simultaneously of nothing, is called the opposite of contradictions. (515)

3>17. In the intellect there is this and that, but not this beyond that.

3>18. The incompatibility of contradictions first shows up in the soul, since it is the first quantity, positing part beyond part.

3>13–18. See above, pp. 23–24. Thesis 3>15 is regularly cited (originally by Cassirer and most recently by Wirszubski) as evidence of the influence on Pico of Nicholas of Cusa's *coincidentia oppositorum*. In fact, the idea expressed both by Pico and by Cusanus was a scholastic commonplace; its syncretic origins are discussed above, pp. 85–89. On the implications of this part of Pico's metaphysics for traditional logic, cf. 2.31 and note. In 3>16, "the first principle of everything"/"of nothing" = God and prime matter. Cf. the wording in 3>52, 3>70.

3>19. Vnumquodque in natura intellectuali habet a sua intelligibili unitate et quod quodlibet sibi uniat, et quod immaculatam ac inpermixtam sibi suam seruet proprietatem.

3>20. Ipseitas uniuscuiusque tunc maxime est ipsa, cum in ipsa ita sunt omnia, ut in ipsa omnia sint ipsa.

3>21. Per praedictas conclusiones intelligi potest quae sit omiomeria Anaxagorae, quam opifex intellectus distinguit.

3>22. Nemo miretur quod Anaxagoras intellectum appellauerit immixtum, cum sit maxime mixtus, quia maxima mixtio coincidit cum maxima simplicitate in natura intellectuali.

3>23. Sicut formae substantiales in secundo mundo sunt per modum accidentium, ita formae accidentales sunt in primo mundo per modum substantiarum.

Correlarium: Sicut in primo mundo non est album sed albedo, ita in secundo mundo non est ignis, sed igneum.

3>19. 1486 habet' (typographical error not = habetur) | 1487 habet

---

3>19. Tied to the series on "relations" discussed in 4.16–17 note. Cf. especially 7.39, 2>62 and note (which suggests how Pico planned to use this doctrine).

3>20. See my discussion above, pp. 113–14. In the series on the principle of individuation, which includes 2.26 from Thomas Aquinas and 4.6 from Scotus.

Paradoxical Conclusions Introducing New Doctrines in Philosophy

3>19. Everything in the intellectual nature possesses from its intelligible unity both what unites each thing to itself and what conserves for itself its immaculate and unmixed property.

3>20. The self-identity of each and every thing is then most itself, when in itself all things exist in such a way that in itself all things *are* itself.

3>21. Through the preceding conclusions one can understand what Anaxagoras's *homoeomeria* is, which the demiurge of the intellect distinguishes. (520)

3>22. Let no one marvel that Anaxagoras called the intellect unmixed, although it is greatly mixed, since the greatest mixture coincides with the greatest simplicity in the intellectual nature.

3>23. Just as substantial forms exist in the second world through the mode of accidents, so accidental forms exist in the first world through the mode of substances.

Corollary: Just as in the first world there is nothing white, but there is whiteness, so in the second world there is no fire, but things on fire.

3>21–22. "*homoeomeria*" = the original homogeneous state of things in Anaxagoras, the Western prototype of the principle that "all things exist in all things in their own mode." Pico's reference to the demiurge in 3>21 and his phrasing in 3>22 suggests that he was drawing from some Neo-Platonizing commentary on Aristotle *Physics* 3.4 (203a20ff.).

3>23. "second world"/"first world" = the rational or animate nature (or the material world informed by that nature)/the intellectual nature. Discussed above, p. 98.

3>24. Non potest dici quod in intellectu ideae, uerbi gratia, ignis, aquae, et aeris sint tres ideae, sed oportet dicere quod sunt ternarius.

3>25. Nisi destruamus naturam intellectualem, non possumus intelligere ideas numerari, nisi per intimationem ideae numeri per re/liquas, sicut est cuiuslibet per omnes. <19r/19v>

3>26. Ex praecedentibus conclusionibus potest intelligi qui sit formalis numerus, quem dixit Pythagoras esse principium omnium rerum.

3>27. Quinque ponenda sunt prima praedicamenta: Vnum, Substantia, Quantitas, Qualitas, et Ad aliquid.

3>28. Rectius ad quinque suprascripta reducitur entium diuersitas quam ad decem quae Architas primum, deinde Aristoteles posuit, uel quinque quae ponit Plotinus, uel ad quatuor quae ponunt stoici.

3>29. Ratio predicamenti unius est absoluta praecisio ab omni extraneo.

3>30. Ratio praedicamenti substantiae est unita perfectio inparticipatae substantiae.

3>31. Ratio praedicamenti quantitatis est extrapositio partis ad partem.

3>32. Ratio praedicamenti qualitatis est ueritas denominationis per inherentem participationem.

3>33. Ratio praedicamenti ad aliquid est esse imaginarium.

3>27. 1486 praedicamenta.Vnum.Substantia.Quantitas.Qualitas & Ad aliquid.

3>24–26. On "formal" numbers, see 7>9 note. Other related theses are listed in note 7.34.

3>27–33. *Re* Aristotle *Categories* and related texts. Archytas = Archytas of Tarentum, Pythagorean philosopher of the first half of the fourth century BCE. Pico's idiosyncratic categories or

Paradoxical Conclusions Introducing New Doctrines in Philosophy

3>24. It cannot be said that there are ideas in the intellect, for the sake of an example that fire, water, and air are three ideas, but it must be said that they are threefold.

3>25. Without destroying the intellectual nature, we cannot understand that ideas are numbered, except as the idea of number is intimated by the rest, just as the idea of each thing is intimated by all.

3>26. From the preceding conclusions it can be understood what formal number is, which Pythagoras said is the principle of all things. (525)

3>27. Five primary categories should be posited: oneness, substance, quantity, quality, and relation.

3>28. The diversity in beings is more correctly reduced to the five preceding categories than to the ten that Archytas first, then Aristotle, posited, or to the five that Plotinus proposes, or to the four that the Stoics posit.

3>29. The category of oneness pertains to the absolute separateness of something from everything external.

3>30. The category of substance pertains to the perfection of something united to unparticipated substance.

3>31. The category of quantity pertains to the positioning of part beyond part. (530)

3>32. The category of quality pertains to the truth of naming through inherent participation.

3>33. The category of relation pertains to imagerial existence.

---

praedicamenta are closely related to his own emanational system. Cf., e.g., 3>31 with 3>18, and this whole series with 3>1ff.

3>34. Nullum est praedicatum formale inparticipatum_quod partialiter praedicari non possit de intelligentia.

3>35. Sicut de solo intellectu uere dicitur quod est ignis, et quod est aqua, quod est motus, et quod est status, ita de sola anima uere dicitur quod frigefit,_ quod calefit, quod stat,_ quod mouetur.

3>36. Sicut intellectus dei unitatem multiplicat, ita anima intellectus multitudinem quantificat et extendit.

3>37. Primum intelligibile cum primo intellectu, et primum scibile cum primo sciente,_ coincidit.

3>38. In animis deterioris notae est ratio per modum sensus; in animis sublimioribus est sensus per modum rationis.

3>39. Dictum illud mirabile illius barbari,_ nympharum et demonum consortis,_ de .clxxxiiii. mundis in figura triangulari cum tribus unitatibus angularibus_et una media constitutis,_ rectissime intelligetur si ab unitate intelligibili trinitatem intellectualem, animalem,_ et seminalem,_ et principalium mundi partium per primum sphericum numerum computationem,_ intellexerimus.

3>34. Since the intellectual nature "in some mode" contains all things.

3>35–38. Further examples of the proportions and correspondences in Pico's system. For 3>37, cf. 20.1 from Plotinus, 2>72 from the previous theses, etc. As I have interpreted it, *movetur* in 3>35 = moves itself.

3>39. Interpreting an obscure anecdote in Plutarch's *De defectu oraculorum* 21–22. Pico adapts his reading loosely from Proclus's equally obscure reading of that anecdote in the latter's commentary on the *Timaeus* (Diehl 1:454–55). The problem lay in harmonizing what Plutarch said about 184 worlds (183 in the standard edition) with *Timaeus* 31b–c, which claimed that the demiurge created only *one* world. Proclus and Pico predictably reconciled the texts by interpreting Plutarch's worlds as symbols of different levels of reality. The world here is symbolized by an equilateral triangle. At its center lies one monad or "unity" representing the generative

Paradoxical Conclusions Introducing New Doctrines in Philosophy

3>34. There is no formal unparticipated predicate that cannot be partially predicated of an intelligence.

3>35. Just as only of the intellect is it truly said that it is fire, that it is water, that it is motion, and that it is place, so only of the soul is it truly said that it cools, that it heats, that it stands, that it moves.

3>36. Just as the intellect multiplies the unity of God, so the soul quantifies and extends the multiplicity of the intellect. (535)

3>37. The first intelligible object coincides with the first intellect, and the first knowable object with the first knower.

3>38. In souls of an inferior sort, reason exists through the mode of sense. In superior souls, sense exists through the mode of reason.

3>39. That miraculous saying of that barbarian, the companion of nymphs and demons, concerning 184 worlds constructed in a triangular figure with three unities at the angles and one in the middle, is most properly interpreted if we understand that the intellectual, animate, and seminal trinities derive from intelligible unity, and recognize by means of the first spherical number the computation of the principal parts of the world.

---

principle of the "intelligible nature." Three more "unities" are assigned to the three angles of that triangle, which for Pico represent the archetypes of the "intellectual," "animate," and "seminal" (physical) worlds. Finally, 60 "unities," apparently representing particular forms in nature, are assigned to each of the three sides of the triangle, yielding the needed total of 184. "the first spherical number" = 5, which for Pico had eschatological significance; see note 11>63. "the principal parts of the world"—60 in Proclus's text—is computed by multiplying "the first spherical number" by 12, which Proclus tells us is the number of heavenly spheres. How Pico interpreted that number is unknown, but cf. the suggestive positioning of the number 12 in thesis 25.4 from "the mathematics of Pythagoras." How Pico planned to debate this astonishing piece of numerological exegesis, which has little in common with conventional scholastic questions, is anyone's guess. See 5>1 for a closely related conclusion.

3>40. Posse animam per uiam purgatoriam, absque alio studio uel in/uestigatione, per solam modicam et facillimam collationem et aduertentiam super iam desuper habita intelligibilia, perfectam omnium scibilium scientiam acquirere, non solum Platonici philosophi, sed etiam inter Peripateticos, hi de quibus minus uidetur, Auenrois sequaces habent concedere. <19v/20r>

3>41. Sicut se habet sensus communis in cognitione accidentalium qualitatum et quantitatis materialis, ita se habet ratio in cognitione substantialium qualitatum et quantitatis formalis, seruata proportione, quod ille sensualiter, haec rationaliter, agit.

3>42. Infinitas dei per superexcedentiam ad esse intellectuale et uiam mysticae theologiae probari potest, et ad id probandum omnis alia uia inefficax est.

3>43. Actus quo foelicitatur natura angelica et rationalis ultima foelicitate, nec est actus intellectus, nec uoluntatis, sed est unio unitatis quae est in alteritate animae cum unitate quae est sine alteritate.

3>44. Aristoteles in libro Methaphysicae de deo non tractat nisi in ultimo capitulo duodecimi quod incipit: Considerandum est etiam utronam modo uniuersum habet bonum.

3>42. 1486 super excedentiam | *Emendationes errorum*, corrige: per superexcedentiam | 1487 text emended *sic*

3>40. *Re* Pico's reconciliation of the Platonic and Aristotelian theories of knowledge. See above, pp. 102–105. Series begins at 1.6.

3>41. Cf. above, p. 22. On the faculty of "common sense," see 1.10 note.

3>42. For related theses, see 7.18 note. "the method of the *Mystical Theology*" = Pseudo-Dionysius's "negative way." See *Mystical Theology*, especially chap. 3.

Paradoxical Conclusions Introducing New Doctrines in Philosophy

3>40. Not only Platonic philosophers, but even among the Peripatetics, in whom it is less apparent, the followers of Averroes have to concede that the soul can acquire a perfect knowledge of everything knowable through a purgatorial path, without any other study or investigation, through a single moderate and easy collation of, and direction of attention towards, intelligibles possessed from above.

3>41. Just as common sense consists in the cognition of accidental qualities and of material quantity, so reason consists in the cognition of substantial qualities and of formal quantity—with the proportion observed that that one acts sensually, this one rationally. (540)

3>42. The infinity of God can be demonstrated through his transcendence of intellectual existence and through the method of the *Mystical Theology*, and every other method to prove it is ineffective.

3>43. The act by which the angelic and rational nature is bestowed with the greatest happiness is an act neither of the intellect nor of the will, but is the union of the unity that exists in the otherness of the soul with the unity that exists without otherness.

3>44. Aristotle in the book of *Metaphysics* does not write about God except in the last chapter of the twelfth book, which begins: *It must also be considered in which of two ways the universe possesses the good.*

3>43. Series begins at 2.12. See above, pp. 107–108.

3>44. Reference to *Metaphysics* 12.10, meant to "save" Aristotle from problematic passages in *Metaphysics* 12.8–9 that refer in the plural to "unmoved movers" (implying polytheism) or that deal with the limits of divine thought. Pico would typically have claimed that the real subjects of these passages were "intelligences" or "celestial souls" and not God. Cf. 18.4–5 and notes.

3>45. Ordo librorum Methaphysicae post naturales, eo modo quo eos ordinauit Aristoteles, secundum nullum processum, siue compositiuum siue resolutiuum, potest esse rectus.

3>46. Dato quocunque obiecto practicabili, nobilior est operatio quae eum practicat quam quae eum contemplatur, si caetera sint paria.

3>47. Melius potest saluare textus Aristotelis qui dicit omnem animam esse immortalem, quam qui dicit omnem animam esse mortalem.

3>48. Praeter tria demonstrationis genera, quia, propter quid, et simpliciter, quae ponunt Aristoteles et commentator, datur quartum genus demonstrationis quae dici potest demonstratio conuertibilitatis, fortius omnibus praedictis.

3>49. Magis improprie dicitur de deo quod sit intellectus uel intelligens, quam de anima rationali quod sit angelus.

3>46. 1486 coetera

3>47. 1486 salvari | 1486 *Emendationes errorum*, corrige: salvare | 1487 text not emended

---

3>45. Since, as we discovered in the last thesis, God is not discussed until *Metaphysics* 12.10, the order of those books violates the natural order of reality and hence cannot be correct. Cf. 2>38 and note.

3>46. Discussed in relation to Pico's magic on pp. 130–31.

3>47. Cf. the theses listed in note 20.3.

3>48. Series starts at 7.10–11. Cf. especially 19.4. "convertibility" = interchangeability in either a metaphysical or terminological sense, like "being" and the "one" in Pico's system; see above, pp. 25–29. Closely tied to Pico's correlative views of reality.

3>45. The order of the books of *Metaphysics* after the natural books, in that manner in which Aristotle ordered them, according to no method, either synthetic or analytic, can be correct.

3>46. Given any practical object, the operation that acts on it is nobler than that which contemplates it, if all other things are equal. (545)

3>47. Anyone who says that every soul is immortal can save the text of Aristotle better than anyone who says that every soul is mortal.

3>48. Besides the three types of demonstration that Aristotle and the Commentator posit—demonstration through effects, demonstration through causes, and simple demonstration—there exists a fourth genus of demonstration, more powerful than all those, which can be called demonstration through convertibility.

3>49. It is more improperly said that God is intellect or that which has intellect, than that the rational soul is an angel.

3>49. Cf. 7a>5–6, which Pico planned to demonstrate through this "way of numbers." One of the thirteen theses attacked by the papal commission. In his formal reply to the commission, Pico argued that the thesis conformed to the "mode of speaking of Dionysius [i.e., Dionysius's 'negative way'], who claimed that it should not be said of God that he is either 'intellect' or the 'intelligible' or similar things." The commission responded that the thesis was "false and can be taken to a heretical sense." Cf. Dorez and Thuasne (1897: 137) and the *Apology* (*Opera*, 234–35).

3>50. Sola materia sufficit ad id saluandum, cuius gratia Aristoteles et alii philosophi priuationem inter principia naturalia posuerunt.

Correlarium: Priuatio non est ponenda inter principia natu/ralia. <20r/20v>

3>51. Tria sunt principia rerum naturalium: materia, motus, et forma.

3>52. Eadem est scientia de deo, homine, et materia prima, et qui de uno scientiam habuerit, habebit et de reliquis, seruata proportione extremi ad extremum, medii ad extrema, et extremorum ad medium.

3>53. Qui primam materiam negat, nec sensui contradicit, nec rationem physicam negat.

3>54. Ad probandum primam materiam esse, magis certificat uel uia numerorum, uel uia catholicae philosophiae, quam ulla ratio physica in qua sensus habeat introitum.

3>55. Qui ordinem hebraicae linguae profunde et radicaliter tenuerit, atque illum proportionabiliter in scientiis seruare nouerit, cuiuscunque scibilis perfecte inueniendi normam et regulam habebit.

3>51. colon retained from 1486 edition

3>55. 1486 linguae profundae | 1487 lingue profunde

3>50–51. See 16.3 and note. Privation is rejected as a natural principle since it implies a sharp break in the proportions of the universe (see the next thesis). Pico hence posits that matter exists in some "mode" on every level of reality. Pico's rejection (on the grounds of cosmic correspondence) of the idea of total immateriality constitutes one of his main breaks with the Platonic tradition and with Latin scholastics like Thomas Aquinas.

3>52. *Re* Pico's correlative views of reality. See above, p. 22. See also the following note.

Paradoxical Conclusions Introducing New Doctrines in Philosophy

3>50. Only matter can save that for the sake of which Aristotle and other philosophers posited privation among the natural principles.

Corollary: Privation should not be posited among the natural principles.

3>51. There are three principles in natural things:.matter, motion, and form. (550)

3>52. Knowledge concerning God, man, and prime matter is the same, and whoever has knowledge of one will have it of the rest—with the proportion observed of the extreme to the extreme, of the middle to the extremes, and of the extremes to the middle.

3>53. Anyone who denies [the existence of] prime matter neither contradicts sense nor denies any physical argument.

3>54. To prove that prime matter exists, either the way of numbers or the method of universal philosophy is more certain than any physical argument into which sense enters.

3>55. Whoever profoundly and radically grasps the order of the Hebrew language, and knows how to preserve that order proportionally in the sciences, will possess the rule and pattern of perfectly discovering everything knowable.

3>53–54. "way of numbers" = see 7a>45. "method of universal philosophy" = reasoning based on cosmological correspondences of the sort suggested in 3>52, which link all levels of reality; cf. Pico's use of the same language in 11>2. This method is apparently identical, or closely related, to the Neo-Platonic "method of the extremes and middle" that that Pico speaks of elsewhere, e.g., in 5>15.

3>55. Refers to the correlative foundations of Pico's *revolutio alphabetariae,* noted in 11>2. See my discussion above, pp. 63–66. Cf. also the theses listed in note 28.33.

3>56. Praeter distinctionem rei et rationis ponenda est distinctio tertia, quam ego appello inadequationis.

3>57. Species inimicitiae quae a lupo ad ouis aestimatiuam multiplicantur, non accidentis alicuius, sed substantiae species sunt.

3>58. Formalitas est adaequatum obiectum intellectus.

3>59. Vbicunque datur aliqua natura composita ex pluribus naturis actu in ea remanentibus, semper in ea nobilior est substantialiter, aliae accidentaliter.

3>56. On distinctions in general, see note 3.7. Pico's *distinctio inadequationis* can be interpreted via theses 3>2–7, which suggest that distinctions that are deemed "adequate" objects of knowledge for lower cognitive faculties might be "inadequate" for higher ones. In 2>66 and 3>58, Pico reinterprets the Scotist formal distinction in this framework.

3>57. On the multiplication of sensual images or phantasmata in a medium, see 8.9 note. "estimative faculty" = the instinctive faculty of attraction and repulsion in animals, analogous to the judgmental (or cogitative) power in rational souls (cf. 2>58); the sheep and wolf were standard

Paradoxical Conclusions Introducing New Doctrines in Philosophy

3>56. Besides the real and rational distinctions, a third distinction should be posited, which I call the distinction of inadequacy. (555)

3>57. The images of hostility that are multiplied from the wolf to the estimative faculty of the sheep are not images of any accident, but images of substance.

3>58. A formality is an adequate object of the intellect.

3>59. Wherever some nature exists composed out of many natures remaining in it in act, the nobler always subsists in it substantially, the others accidentally.

---

examples. Series on substance/accident starts at 2.24; cf. also 4.21. The thesis pertains in particular in this series to Pico's rejection of the idea of "separable" accidents; see my discussion above, pp. 99–100.

3>58. Cf. 2>66, 3>56, and notes.

3>59. Series begins at 2.24. Discussed above, pp. 98–99.

3>60. Nihil intelligit actu et distincte anima, nisi se ipsam.

3>61. Tota substantia animae rationalis est pars intellectualis.

3>62. Anima seipsam semper intelligit, et se intelligendo quodammodo omnia entia intelligit.

3>63. Quamuis in anima ita sit actu natura intellectualis per quam cum angelo conuenit, sicut est natura rationalis per quam ab eo distinguitur, nihil tamen intrinsecum est in ea, per quod possit sine propria specie aliquid a se distinctum intelligere.

3>64. Intellectualis natura, quae est in anima rationali supra naturam rationalem, praecise differt a natura intellectuali pura sicut differt pars a toto.

3>65. Quia intellectus animalis differt ab intellectu intellectuali ut pars media, non ut pars tantum, ideo intellectuali totalitati magis parificatur. <20v/21r>

3>66. Potest anima per extrinsecam informationem ad hoc deuenire, ut omnia per substantialem suam formam indiuisibiliter intelligat.

3>63. 1486 distinguitur. Nihil

3>60–66. Key propositions in Pico's theory of knowledge. See my discussion above, p. 104. 3>60 was among the thirteen theses attacked by the papal commission.

Paradoxical Conclusions Introducing New Doctrines in Philosophy

3>60. The soul understands nothing in act and distinctly except itself.

3>61. The whole substance of the rational soul is the intellectual part. (560)

3>62. The soul always understands itself, and understanding itself in some way understands all beings.

3>63. Although in the soul there exists in act an intellectual nature, through which it convenes with the angel, just as a rational nature exists in it, through which it is distinguished from that, there is nothing intrinsic in it through which it is able, without the appropriate image, to understand something distinct from itself.

3>64. The intellectual nature that exists in the rational soul over the rational nature differs from the pure intellectual nature precisely as the part differs from the whole.

3>65. Because the animate intellect differs from the intellectual intellect as the mean part, not simply as a part, it is equated more to the total intellect.

3>66. Through external information the soul can arrive at this: that it understands all things indivisibly through its substantial form. (565)

3>67. Cuilibet seriei animarum unus correspondet purus intellectus.

3>68. Omnes animae coelestes in primo intellectu unum sunt.

3>69. Rationabile est secundum philosophiam omnem seriem animalem in proprio beatificari intellectu; quod tamen non assertiue sed probabiliter dictum sit.

3>70. Cum tres fuerint qui dicerent omnia esse unum: Zenophanes, Parmenides, et Melissus, uidebit qui diligenter eorum dicta perscrutabitur, Zenophanis unum illud esse quod est simpliciter unum. Vnum Parmenidis non unum absolute ut creditur, sed ens unum. Vnum Melissi esse unum habens ad unum Zenophanis extremalem correspondentiam.

3>71. Empedocles per litem et amicitiam in anima nihil aliud intelligit quam potentiam sursum ductiuam et deorsum ductiuam in ea, quas ego credo proportionari in scientia sephirot aeternitati et decori.

3>70. 1486 perscrutabitur.Zenophanes

3>67–69. "celestial souls" = the rational souls inhabiting heavenly bodies. On the problem of the "unity of the intellect," cf. 7.2–4 from Averroes. For Pico's means of resolving this issue, see above, pp. 112–14. Pico was swimming here in very dangerous theological waters. If he ran into trouble, he clearly planned to argue that 3>69 was not proposed "according to theology" or in anything but a "probable" way.

Paradoxical Conclusions Introducing New Doctrines in Philosophy

3>67. To every series of souls there corresponds one pure intellect.

3>68. All celestial souls are one in the first intellect.

3>69. It is rational according to philosophy to say that every series of souls is beatified in its own intellect. This, however, is not stated assertively but as a probability.

3>70. Although there were three who said that all things are one—Xenophanes, Parmenides, and Melissus—whoever carefully scrutinizes their words will see that the one of Xenophanes is that which is one simply. Parmenides' one is not the absolute one, as is believed, but is the oneness of being. The one of Melissus is the one that possesses extreme correspondence to Xenophanes' one.

3>71. By strife and friendship in the soul Empedocles means nothing but the power leading upwards and leading downwards in it, which I believe is proportional in the science of the *sefirot* to eternity and adornment. (570)

3>70. Discussed above, p. 29.

3>71. For Empedocles, cf. Diels frags. 16ff. "eternity" and "adornment"= symbols for Pico for the seventh and eighth *sefirot*. Compare the functions of the "seventh" and "eighth" suggested in 11>66.

CONCLVSIONES IN THEOLOGIA NVMERO .XXXI. SECVNDVM OPINIONEM PROPRIAM, A COMMVNI MODO DICENDI THEOLOGORVM SATIS DIVERSAM.

4>1. Qui dixerit accidens existere non posse nisi inexistat, Eucharistiae poterit sacramentum tenere etiam tenendo panis substantiam non remanere ut tenet communis uia.

4>2. Si teneatur communis uia de possibilitate suppositationis in respectu ad quamcunque creaturam, dico quod sine conuersione panis in corpus Christi uel paneitatis anihilatione, potest fieri ut in altari sit corpus Christi secundum ueritatem sacramenti Eucharistiae; quod sit dictum loquendo de possibili, non de sic esse.

4>1. 1486 inexistat.Eucharistiae

THEOLOGICAL CONCLUSIONS. Two theological theses were apparently removed from Pico's text during a hasty last-minute revision, most probably when the work was already in press; on this last point, see my introductory note to theses 6>1–10. Nine of the thirteen theses attacked by the papal commission came from this section, which was immediately suspect since it was composed by a layman—and a twenty-three-year-old layman at that—and not a licensed theologian. Most of the implied questions underlying these theses can be located in the vast medieval commentarial tradition on Peter Lombard's *Sentences*, in which Pico was steeped. Much evidence shows that in his formal replies to the commission and in the *Apology* Pico backtracked on the more dangerous views expressed in his theses; in any event, the evidence in the *Apology* and in the notarial record of Pico's verbal and written replies to the commission must be approached with greater caution than shown in past analyses of these texts, e.g., by Di Napoli (1965) and Craven (1981). Once again, we find Thomas Aquinas in this section as Pico's prime opponent.

4>1. Along with the next thesis, pertinent to Peter Lombard *Sentences* 4, *d.* 11–12. The thesis is discussed above, pp. 99–100, in respect to Pico's rejection of separable accidents. The lack of punctuation in the *editio princeps* in the last part of Pico's thesis (insertion of a comma after *remanere*, as found in many later editions, radically alters the sense of the original) leaves Pico's views ambiguous—apparently intentionally so. In rejecting the concept of separable accidents,

Theological Conclusions Opposed to the Common Mode of Speaking

THIRTY-ONE [TWENTY-NINE] CONCLUSIONS IN THEOLOGY ACCORDING TO MY OWN OPINION, RATHER OPPOSED TO THE COMMON MODE OF SPEAKING OF THEOLOGIANS.

4>1. Whoever says that an accident cannot exist unless it exists in something can uphold the sacrament of the Eucharist, even maintaining that the substance of the bread does not remain as the common way holds.

4>2. If the common way is maintained concerning the possibility of assumption in respect to any creature, I say that without the conversion of the bread into the body of Christ, or the annihilation of the breadness, the body of Christ can exist on the altar in accordance with the truth of the sacrament of the Eucharist. This is said speaking of what is possible, however, not of what is so.

Pico almost surely believed that the substance of the bread did *not* remain after the Consecration. When attacked on this point, however, in the *Apology* he argued that this part of his thesis (i.e., without a comma after *remanere*) only took issue with the specific *manner* in which the "common way" said that the substance remained. Pico also backtracked in the *Apology* (*Opera*, 229ff.) on his view that accidents cannot be separated from their substances—understandably, given the dangers that he faced when he wrote the text.

4>2. See the preceding thesis and note. Another thesis attacked by the papal commission. Cf. Pico's verbal response in Dorez and Thuasne (1897: 135) with his expanded reply in the *Apology*, in *Opera*, 181–98, 239–40. In his defense of his thesis, Pico heavily underscores its hypothetical nature: We can avoid the inconveniences of the doctrine of transubstantiation (i.e., those involving "separable accidents") if we accept the view of the "common way" that God can assume any nature. Hence in the Eucharist Christ might be pictured as assuming the nature of the bread just as he assumed human nature in the Incarnation. Again, however, this pertains only to a "possible sacrament," not to the Eucharist as it was actually established by God. The difficulty of determining Pico's real views here are evident when we compare this thesis with 4>13, which explicitly *rejects* the idea that God can assume any nature.

4>3. Ideales rerum formalesque rationes effectiue a deo in prima creata mente formaliter primo reperiri, cum theologica ueritate tenemus.

Correlarium: Vbi ideae sunt idealiter, ibi non sunt formaliter; ubi sunt formaliter, ibi non sunt idealiter.

4>4. Si ponamus deum cognoscere creaturas ut obiectum secunda/rium suae intuitionis, ut communiter ponitur, dico quod pater prius producit uerbum quam creaturas cognoscat. <21r/21v>

4>5. Attributales perfectiones nec in deo, nec secundum se quiditatiue sumptae, dicunt diuersas rationes in recto, et principaliter diffinibiles uel descriptibiles.

4>6. Intuitus diuinae cognitionis ad creaturas tanquam obiecta primaria uel secundaria formaliter non terminatur, ut dicit communis schola theologorum, sed se tantum et nihil aliud a se intuens primarie nec secundarie, unitiue et eminenter, et plus quam aequipollenter, omnia cognoscit.

Correlarium: Non est aliqua multitudo intellectorum in deo, nec creature ut intellecte ponunt in numerum cum diuina essentia ut intellecta, sed est penitus unum simplicissimum intellectum.

4>7. Tria transcendentia in quibus consistit imago_non dicunt diuersas rationes in recto, et principaliter diffinibiles uel descriptibiles.

4>3. 1486, 1487 repperiri

4>6. 1486 tantum.& nihil | 1486 primariae nec secundariae | 1487 primarie nec secundarie

---

4>3. Sets up a "modal" or hierarchical framework to resolve conflicts concerning the location and existential status of the ideas. See my detailed discussion above, pp. 53–56.

4>4, 4>6. On the simplicity of God's understanding. See again above, pp. 53–56. *Re* Peter Lombard *Sentences* 1, *d.* 35 and 36. It is critical to note that Pico was not personally endorsing the premise of 4>4. His apparent object was to show that if we were to accept the common

Theological Conclusions Opposed to the Common Mode of Speaking

4>3. I hold with theological truth that the ideal and formal reasons of things were first effectively devised by God formally in the first created mind.

Corollary: Where the ideas exist ideally, they do not exist formally. Where they exist formally, they do not exist ideally.

4>4. If we posited that God knows created things as a secondary object of his intuition, as is commonly proposed, I say that the Father would have to produce the Word before he knew created things.

4>5. Neither in God nor in themselves taken quidditatively do attributal perfections rightly signify different concepts, and especially none that can be defined or described. (575)

4>6. The intuition of God's knowledge is not directed formally at creatures as primary or secondary objects, as the common school of theologians says, but contemplating himself only, and nothing but himself primarily or secondarily, in a unitive and elevated manner, and with more than the power equal to the task, he knows all things.

Corollary: There is no multiplicity of understandings in God, nor do creatures, as things understood, exist numerically in the divine essence as something understood, but in the innermost sense there exists but one most simple understanding.

4>7. The three transcendentals in which the image consists do not rightly signify different concepts, and especially none that can be defined or described.

---

view (e.g., in Scotus) that God knows creatures as a "secondary object" of his knowledge, we could not claim that God's knowledge was eternal—invalidating the coeternity of the Father and the Word (i.e., the Son). It is interesting that the papal commission let this anti-Scotist thesis pass without comment, unlike Pico's anti-Thomistic conclusions.

4>5, 4>7. On distinctions in God, cf. 1>2–3, 1>7 and notes. "three transcendentals"/"the image" = image of the three Persons of the Trinity in the human soul. Cf., e.g., *Sentences* 1, *d.* 3. Tied to the series on the unity of the soul starting at 1.12. Also relevant to Pico's mysticism (cf., e.g., 3>43).

4>8. Christus non ueraciter et quantum ad realem presentiam descendit ad inferos ut ponit Thommas et communis uia, sed solum quo ad effectum.

4>9. Licet ita mihi uideatur probabile, non est tamen pertinaciter asserendum quod anima Christi per alium modum nobis ignotum non potuerit in infernum descendere.

4>10. Illa uerba (hoc est corpus, etc.), quae in consecratione dicuntur, materialiter tenentur non significatiuae.

4>11. Si teneatur communis uia quod actu intellectus attingatur deus, dico duas sequentes conclusiones, quarum haec est prima: quod uidentes uerbum, eo actu quo essentiam diuinam attingunt, creaturas non attingunt nisi eminenter, equipollenter ad formalem cognitionem, equipollentia non actus sed obiecti.

4>12. Beati duplicem habent cognitionem de creaturis, eas formaliter attingentem, quarum altera illatiue est, ex ea qua uerbum attingunt, altera secundum quam in re creata creaturam contemplantur.

4>9. 1486 ignotum potuerit | *Emendationes errorum*, corrige: non potuerit | 1487 text emended *sic*.

4>11. 1486 cognitionem. Equipollentia

4>8. *Re* Christ's "harrowing of hell" between the Passion and Resurrection. The punctuation in the *editio princeps*, as in 4>1, appears to be intentionally ambiguous. Cf. Thomas Aquinas *Sentences* 3, *d*. 22, *q*. 2. In his oral response to the papal commission, Pico first argued that since it was only the soul of Christ that descended into hell—his body remained in the tomb—and since the soul was a "separated substance" for which no local motion was possible, Christ could only descend into hell in the sense that he worked effects there. See Dorez and Thuasne (1897: 121–22). The commission (p. 127) unanimously ruled that Pico's thesis was "false, erroneous, heretical, and against the truth of Sacred Scriptures." Following this judgment, in a long technical section in the *Apology* (*Opera,* 125–50, 237–38), Pico shifted tactics by claiming that he did *not* reject the notion that Christ as a "real presence" descended into hell—as his thesis seemed to say—but only claimed that the cause (*ratio*) of Christ's "real presence" was his operation and not what Thomas claimed. Pico's response on this question in the *Apology* contains his most violent attacks on the Thomists and Dominican order.

Theological Conclusions Opposed to the Common Mode of Speaking

4>8. Christ did not truly and in respect to his real presence descend into hell as Thomas and the common way propose, but only in effect.

4>9. Although it seems probable to me, it should not be obstinately asserted that the soul of Christ could not have descended into hell in another way unknown to us.

4>10. Those words: *This is my body*, etc., which are spoken in the Consecration, are held in a material and not indicative sense. (580)

4>11. If the common way is held that God is attained through an act of intellect, I state the following two conclusions, of which this is the first: that those seeing the Word, by that act by which they attain the divine essence, attain created beings in an elevated way that is equivalent to formal knowledge—equivalent not to an intellectual act but to the object itself.

4>12. The blessed have a twofold knowledge of created beings, attaining them formally, of which one follows from their attainment of the Word and the other from their contemplation of the creature in the created thing.

4>9. Evidence that Pico recognized the theological dangers in 4>8 as he originally proposed it. The papal commission ignored Pico's disclaimer, however.

4>10. Cf. *Sentences* 4, *d.* 8. Cf. also 4.15 above. Shows Pico's use of late medieval "supposition theory"; see 2>16 and note. Explained briefly: To posit something "materially" was equivalent in modern usage to placing quotation marks around it, while to posit something in an "indicative sense" was to propose it absolutely. Pico's point is that if the formula of the Eucharist were not posited *materialiter* (or "recitatively," as Pico puts it in the *Apology*), then "this is my body" would refer to the body of the priest and not to Christ. The commission's hostility towards Pico is reflected in its judgment that this apparently innocuous thesis was "scandalous and contrary to the common opinion of holy doctors."

4>11–12. *Re* commentary on *Sentences* 4, *d.* 49 and 50. It should be recalled that Pico himself did not hold the "common way" on attaining God, which for him transcended an ordinary act of intellect; cf. 3>43 and my discussion above, pp. 107–14.

4>13. Non assentior communi sententiae theologorum dicentium posse deum quamlibet naturam suppositare, sed de rationali tamen hoc concedo.

4>14. Nec crux Christi nec ulla imago adoranda est adoratione latriae, etiam eo modo quo ponit Thommas. <21v/22r>

4>15. Si non peccasset Adam, deus fuisset incarnatus, sed non crucifixus.

4>16. In quo lumine Iohanes Apocalipsim uidit, in eo Apocalipsim non intellexit.

4>17. Primum peccatum angeli fuit peccatum omissionis, secundum peccatum luxuriae, tertium peccatum superbiae.

4>13. Note that this thesis contradicts the premise of 4>2. In his oral response to the papal commission (Dorez and Thuasne 1897: 124), Pico argued on the authority of Henry of Ghent that his thesis was not true because of any insufficiency in God but because natures below the rational nature were not "assumable" (*suppositabilis*). The commission found that the thesis "derogates from divine omnipotence, and this savors of heresy." In the *Apology* (*Opera*, 159–66, 238) Pico prudently backtracked, arguing that his thesis did *not* claim that God could not assume any nature—as it seems to say—but only disagreed with the way that the "common opinion" argued that this was possible.

4>14. Pertinent to Thomas Aquinas *Sentences* 3, *d.* 9, *q.* 1, *art.* 2, *ad quaestiunculas* 2, 4. In the notarial record of Pico's oral interrogation (Dorez and Thuasne 1897: 123), Pico invoked the authority of Henry [of Ghent] and "Varto" [?] in claiming that the image of the Cross was only owed the "adoration of reverence" (*adoratio hyperduliae*) and not the "adoration of veneration" (*adoratio latriae*)—two of a larger series of distinctions between different levels of "worship,"

4>13. I do not agree with the common opinion of the theologians saying that God can assume any nature, but I concede this of the rational nature.

4>14. Neither the cross of Christ, nor any image, should be adored with the adoration of veneration, even in that way that Thomas proposes.

4>15. If Adam had not sinned, God would have been incarnated, but not crucified. (585)

4>16. In that light in which John saw the Apocalypse, he did not understand the Apocalypse.

4>17. The first sin of the angel was the sin of omission, the second the sin of voluptuousness, the third the sin of pride.

"veneration," "reverence," "service," etc., due God, the Virgin, saints, images, relics, and so on. The commission (p. 128) found the conclusion "scandalous, offensive to pious ears, and against the usage of the universal church." In the *Apology*, in *Opera*, 155–59, 238, Pico cited the authority of Henry of Ghent, Durandus, Robert Holkot, and others on this issue—including "commonly all Scotists"—against St. Thomas.

4>15. Opposes the view of Thomas in *Sentences* 3, *d.* 1, *q.* 1, *art.* 3.

4>16. On the vision of the saints discussed in commentaries on Peter Lombard *Sentences* 4, *d.* 49, and related texts. Cf. 4>11–12.

4>17. Opposing the view of Thomas in *Sentences* 2, *d.* 5, *q.* 1, *art.* 3, where the "first sin" is represented as pride.

4>18. Dico probabiliter, et nisi esset communis modus dicendi theologorum in oppositum, firmiter assererem; assero tamen hoc dictum in se esse probabile, et est: quod sicut nullus opinatur aliquid ita esse praecise quia uult sic opinari, ita nullus credit aliquid esse uerum praecise_quia uult credere id esse uerum.

Correlarium: Non est in potestate libera hominis credere articulum fidei esse uerum_quando placet, et credere eum esse falsum quando sibi placet.

4>19. Nisi essent dicta sanctorum quae in manifesto sui sermonis uidentur dicere oppositum, firmiter assererem hanc et sequentem conclusionem; assero tamen eas probabiles esse et defendi posse rationabiliter, quarum prima est quod peccatum mortale in se est malum finitum.

4>20. Secunda est quod peccato mortali finiti temporis non debetur pena infinita secundum tempus, sed finita tantum.

4>19. 1486 rationabiliter. quarum

4>18. Pertinent to *Sentences* 3, *d.* 23–24. Cf. my discussion of the intellect/will controversy above, pp. 105–14. The notarial record has Pico telling the papal commission that "although every act of belief is said to be truly 'in our power,' this is not, however, in accordance with a tyrannical command of the will. For with the judgment of reason standing in opposition, the will cannot desire this [act]" (Dorez and Thuasne 1897: 124). The commission (p. 129) found this intellectualist thesis to be "erroneous and savoring of heresy." In the *Apology*, in *Opera*, 224–29, 239, Pico moderated his views somewhat, although in his extended discussion of authorities it is difficult to decide on this final position.

THEOLOGICAL CONCLUSIONS OPPOSED TO THE COMMON MODE OF SPEAKING

4>18. I state as a probability, and if the common way of speaking of theologians were not in opposition I would assert firmly; nevertheless, I assert that this saying is probable in itself: that just as no one holds an opinion that something is so precisely because he wills to hold that opinion, so no one believes that something is true precisely because he wills to believe that it is true.

Corollary: It is not in the free power of man to believe that an article of faith is true when it pleases him and to believe that it is false when it pleases him.

4>19. If sayings of the saints did not exist whose language seemed to clearly state the opposite, I would firmly assert this and the following conclusion. I nevertheless claim that they are probable and can be defended rationally, the first of which is: that a mortal sin in itself is a finite evil.

4>20. The second is: that for a mortal sin of a finite time an infinite temporal penalty is not due, but only a finite penalty. (590)

4>19–20. Appears to oppose Thomas Aquinas *Sentences* 4, *d.* 46, *q.* 1, *art.* 3. In his response to the papal commission on 4>20 (4>19 only briefly enters the discussion), Pico claimed that his thesis did not apply to those remaining impenitent in mortal sin—they would indeed be punished for all eternity—but only to those who had lived in sin but had repented (Dorez and Thuasne 1897: 122–23). The papal commission, after interrogating Pico at length, found that his response added "error to error" and unanimously judged his thesis and response to be "false, erroneous, and heretical" (pp. 127–28).

4>21. Non omnis uoluntas dei beneplaciti est efficax.

4>22. Dictum Apostoli dicentis_Deus uult omnes homines saluos fieri positiue de uoluntate beneplaciti antecedente intelligenda est.

4>23. Voluntas antecedens sic potest describi: Voluntas dei antecedens est illa qua deus dat alicui naturalia uel antecedentia quibus potest aliquid consequi, cui deus paratus est coagere si alius uelit, nec sibi contrarium manifestabit cum praecepto uel consilio exequendi, permittens eum libere uelle agere ad consequutionem suae salutis.

4>24. Tenendo communem uiam theologorum, quod foelicitas sit in intellectu uel in uoluntate, dico duas conclusiones, quarum prima est haec: quod intellectus ad foelicitatem non perueniret nisi esset actus uoluntatis, qui in hoc est ipso actu intellectus potior. <22r/22v>

4>25. Secunda conclusio est haec: Licet actus intellectus formaliter foelicitantis attingat obiecti essentiam, tamen quod actus suus circa illum actus sit foelicitatis, formaliter habet ab actu uoluntatis.

4>23. 1486 consequtionem

4>21–23. Pertains to *Sentences* 1, *d.* 46–48. See my discussion above, pp. 109–10. Cf. also 2.2–9 from Thomas.

THEOLOGICAL CONCLUSIONS OPPOSED TO THE COMMON MODE OF SPEAKING

4>21. Not every [act of] will of God's benevolence is effective.

4>22. The words of the Apostle stating that *God wills that all men be saved* should be understood in a positive sense [only] of the antecedent will of the benevolence of God.

4>23. The antecedent will can be described like this: The antecedent will of God is that by which God gives to someone the natural or antecedent powers by which he can achieve something. With him God is prepared to co-act if the other wills it, nor will he manifest the contrary to him with the command or advice to do it, permitting him freely to will to achieve his own salvation.

4>24. Holding to the common way of theologians, that happiness exists in the intellect or in the will, I state two conclusions, of which the first is this: The intellect could not attain happiness unless an act of will existed, which in this is more powerful than that act of intellect.

4>25. The second conclusion is this: Granted that an act of intellect formally attains the essence of an object bestowing happiness, because its act concerning that is an act of happiness, formally it possesses it from an act of will. (595)

4>24–25. Series starts at 2.12. On the intellect/will controversy in Pico, see my analysis above, pp. 105–110. Once again, the "common way" discussed here is not Pico's view. Cf. 3>43.

4>26. Persone in diuinis numero distinguuntur.

4>27. Personalitates in diuinis sunt primo diuersae.

4>28. Theologice loquendo dico quod in aeuo non est successio formaliter intrinseca continuatiua, sed bene terminatiua; secundum philosophos tamen aliter dicerem.

4>29. Rationabilius est credere Origenem esse saluum, quam credere ipsum esse damnatum.

4>28. 1486 Thelogice

4>26. Re Peter Lombard *Sentences* 1, *d.* 19, upholding views summarized there of John Damascene, last Greek church father (late seventh to early eighth century). Lombard's text clarifies that according to Augustine the three Persons are distinguished numerically not as something *triplex* (three separate entitities), but as *trinus* (something that is threefold). Cf. Pico's strategy in 3>24, etc. In the series beginning at 2.1. See also the following note.

4>27. Series starts at 2.1. Pico breaks here with Augustine, Hilarius, and Ambrose (as cited in *Sentences* 1, *d.* 23), who denied the applicability of the term "diversity" in distinguishing the divine Persons. Pico's thesis more directly opposes Thomas Aquinas *Sentences* 1, *d.* 24, *q.* 2, *art.* 1. As in the previous conclusion, Pico's position again reflects the views of the Greek as opposed to Latin fathers, breaking with the complex theology of Latin scholasticism concerning the "generation" and "procession" of Persons from the abstract essence of God. His motive was presumably to find the simplest possible way to uphold trinitarianism, which he was compelled to endorse not on systematic but on dogmatic grounds.

Theological Conclusions Opposed to the Common Mode of Speaking

4>26. Persons in God are distinguished numerically.

4>27. Personalities in God are at first diverse.

4>28. Theologically speaking, I say that in aeviternity succession formally speaking is not intrinsically continuative, but limited. According to the philosophers, however, I state the contrary.

4>29. It is more rational to believe that Origen is saved, than to believe that he is damned.

4>28. *Re* discussion of *Sentences* 2, *d.* 2. On "aeviturnity," see p. 61 n. 9 and 2.18 note. The double-truth illustrated in this thesis was too common a strategy to provoke any criticism from the papal commission.

4>29. In his oral response to the papal commission, Pico claimed that since Origen (third century CE) was not known to have erred "out of a pertinacity of will," it was probable and pious to believe that he was saved (Dorez and Thuasne 1897: 124–25). The commission declared that Pico's thesis was "rash and savoring of heresy, since it is opposed to the determination of the universal church" (p. 130). Pico responded in the *Apology*, in *Opera,* 199–224, 239, with a long discussion of canon law, apparently drawing on his early legal training at the University of Bologna. Excerpted from the *Apology*, Pico's response gained considerable popularity in the sixteenth century, admired by classicists for its analysis of problems of textual attribution and by church reformers for the limits it imposed on ecclesiastical authority. There is a personal ring to Pico's claim that Origen was not condemned for his heresies but for "the glory of his eloquence and knowledge." For an edition, French translation, and analysis of this section of the *Apology*, see Crouzel (1977).

CONCLVSIONES SECVNDVM PROPRIAM OPINIONEM NVMERO .LXII. IN DOCTRINA PLATONIS, DE QVA PAVCA HIC ADDVCVNTVR, QVIA PRIMA PARADOXA CONCLVSIO TOTAM SIBI ASSVMIT PLATONIS DOCTRINAM DISCVTIENDAM.

5>1. Per numeros triplares, qui a Platone in Timeo ponuntur in triangulo animam significante, admonemur quousque in formis numerandis sit progrediendum per naturam illius quod est prima forma formans. Per numeros uero duplares ibidem positos, admonemur quatenus, positis duobus extremis terminis, coordinanda sunt media per naturam eius, quod est medium in uniuerso.

PLATONIC CONCLUSIONS ACCORDING TO HIS OWN OPINION. Proclus's commentary on the *Timaeus* was again a major influence in this section. Pico apparently consulted Ficino's translations of Plato as well as the Greek text, but his quotations are not taken verbatim from Ficino's versions, and a number of theses here are aimed polemically at his older rival. There are also complex ties in this section to material in the *Commento*, which Pico planned as a sketch for a projected commentary on the *Symposium* opposed to Ficino's.

SIXTY-TWO CONCLUSIONS ACCORDING TO MY OWN OPINION ON THE DOCTRINE OF PLATO, OF WHICH FEW ARE BROUGHT FORWARD HERE, SINCE MY FIRST PARADOXICAL CONCLUSION TAKES IT UPON ITSELF TO DISCUSS THE ENTIRE DOCTRINE OF PLATO.

5>1. By the cubic numbers that Plato places in the *Timaeus* in the triangle signifying the soul, we are admonished as to how far to proceed in numbering forms through its nature, which is the first forming form. But by the square numbers found in the same place, we are reminded as to what extent, with the two extreme limits posited, middle things should be ordered through its nature, which is the middle nature in the universe. (600)

5>1. "first forming form" = world soul. "two extreme limits" = the intellectual nature and prime matter. On the proportions of the soul in *Timaeus* 35c–36a. Late-ancient and medieval commentators commonly placed the numbers mentioned in that text in "Crantor's diagram" (or the so-called Platonic lambda):

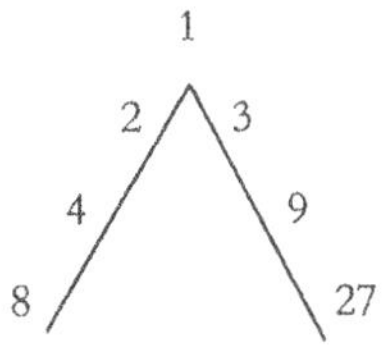

Note that the sum of the cubic numbers on the right side of the diagram—representing the number of forms in the world soul—is 40, suggesting why we find 40 forms in the lower world informed by the soul in thesis 25.12. For Pico's style in this thesis, see also 3>39 and note. Cf. Ficino's different approach towards this topic in his commentary on the *Timaeus*, in *Opera* (1576: 2:1458–60). Since 6 and any of its multiples by 10 had numerological significance for Pico (both are "perfect numbers"), it is difficult to believe that it is an accident that his first Platonic thesis is the 600th thesis in his final version of the text.

5>2. Cum quaeritur a Platone an ad exemplar genitum an ingenitum factus sit mundus, nihil aliud quaeritur nisi an ad animales rationes, an ad ideas intellectuales.

5>3. Qui nouerit modum illuminationis superiorum super media intelliget idem significare et Platonicos per congregationem animarum in Monte Ida, et hebreos per animarum congregationem in Monte Synao in auditione legis.

5>4. Qui sciuerit rationem causae praesupponere rationem perfecti, intelliget iuxta Platonicam doctrinam quare dixerit Pherecides non prius Iouem mundum fabricasse quam in amorem fuerit transformatus. <22v/23r>

5>5. Empedocles per spheram intelligibilem a Venere contentam, nihil aliud intelligit quam mundum archetipum ab ordine intra se manentis primae prouidentiae contentum.

5>6. Ideo amor ab Orpheo sine oculis dicitur, quia est supra intellectum.

5>7. Cum dicit Plato in Timao in medio mundi positam animam, quicquid dicant caeteri Platonici, ego per medium lunam intelligo.

5>8. Infra ambitum terminati entis recte quinque illa Platonis pro transcendentibus ponuntur: Ens, Idem, Alterum, Status, et Motus.

5>7. 1486 coeteri

5>8. 1486 ponuntur.Ens.Idem.Alterum.Status.&Motus.

5>2. Interpreting *Timaeus* 28c ff. The central question in Christian traditions lay in the sense in which the intellectual nature (or hypostatized realm of Platonic ideas) could be considered to be "uncreated." See my discussion of the relation between the ideas and the divine nature above, pp. 53–56.

5>3. Allegorizing Plato *Laws* 681e ff., Exodus 19, etc. For other examples of Pico's illuminationism, see note 5.1.

5>4. Drawn from Proclus *In Timaeum* 3 (here I used Taylor, trans., 1:431).

5>2. When Plato asks whether the world was made in accordance with a created or uncreated exemplar, nothing else is asked except whether it was made in accordance with animate reasons or intellectual ideas.

5>3. Whoever understands the way in which superior things illuminate middle things knows that the Platonists, by the congregation of souls on Mount Ida, and the Hebrews, by the congregation of souls on Mount Sinai in hearing the Law, mean the same thing.

5>4. Anyone who knows that the idea of a cause presupposes the concept of what is perfected understands why, according to Plato's teachings, Pherecydes said that Jove did not fabricate the world before he was transformed into love.

5>5. By the intelligible sphere extended from Venus, Empedocles meant nothing but the archetypal world extended from the order of first providence, which dwells in itself.

5>6. Love is said by Orpheus to be without eyes, because it is above the intellect. (605)

5>7. When Plato in the *Timaeus* says that the soul is placed in the middle of the world, whatever other Platonists say, by the middle, I understand the moon.

5>8. Beneath the limits of determined being, Plato correctly posited these five transcendentals: being, the same, the other, place, and motion.

5>5. Allegorizing Empedocles, Diels frag. 27. "archetypal world" = Pico's intellectual nature; "order of first providence" = God. In other sections of the theses, cf., e.g., 26.3.

5>6. In the series listed at 2.12 note. The open question is which modes of intellect and love Pico had in mind here. Cf., e.g., 5>14, 5>21, 5>24–25, 5>48, 5>49, etc.

5>7. Cf. 23.9 from Iamblichus. Cf. the disclaimer "whatever other Platonists say" with Pico's words in 11>1, etc., on the Cabalists.

5>8. Cf. 2>13 and note.

5>9. Platonice loquendo de anima, dico animam uiuere cum Saturno uitam contemplatiuam, cum Ioue politicam et practicam, cum Marte irascibilem et ambitiosam, cum Venere concupiscibilem et uoluptuosam, cum Mercurio uegetalem cum stupido sensu.

5>10. Ex precedenti conclusione habetur quae sit uirga Mercurii soporifera.

5>11. Primus septennarius uitae humanae est sub Mercurio, secundus sub Venere, tertius sub Marte, quartus sub Ioue, quintus sub Saturno, et reliqui septennarii secundum eum qui fuerit praedominatus in praecedentibus.

5>12. Predictis uitis cooperantur Sol et Luna ut causae uniuersales et per appropriationem: Luna Mercurio et Saturno, Sol Veneri et Marti, simul uterque Ioui.

5>13. Si Syriani theologiam sequamur, rationabile est ecclesiasticae hierarchiae sacerdotes in coelesti hierarchia anagogicis uirtutibus proportionari.

5>14. Cum Platonem audimus Palladem et amorem philosophos deos uocantem, ita intelligamus, ut amor sit philosophus ratione uiae, Pallas ratione termini.

5>12. 1486 appropriationem.Luna:Mercurio:&Saturno.Sol:Veneri & Marti.Simul uterque Ioui.

5>9–12. Other theses on astrology are listed in note 22.4–8. Following what we find there, the sun and the moon here apparently = the intellect and its inferior reflection located in "reason." It is important to note that no predictive or horoscopal astrology is involved in these conclusions. On this topic, see my discussion above, pp. 139–42.

5>9. Speaking Platonically of the soul, I say that the soul lives a contemplative life with Saturn, with Jove a political and practical life, with Mars an irascible and ambitious life, with Venus a sensual and voluptuous life, with Mercury a vegetative life with the dull senses.

5>10. From the preceding conclusion one can know what the sleep-inducing wand of Mercury is.

5>11. The first seventh of human life exists under Mercury, the second under Venus, the third under Mars, the fourth under Jupiter, the fifth under Saturn, and the remaining sevenths under whatever dominated in the preceding. (610)

5>12. To the preceding lives the sun and the moon cooperate as universal causes and through appropriation: the moon to Mercury and Saturn, the sun to Venus and Mars, both simultaneously to Jupiter.

5>13. If we follow the theology of Syrianus, it is rational [to claim] that priests in the ecclesiastical hierarchy correspond to the analogous powers in the celestial hierarchy.

5>14. When we hear Plato calling Pallas and Love philosopher gods, we should understand him this way: that Love is a philosopher by reason of the means, Pallas by reason of the end.

5>13. Syrianus = Proclus's master at the Platonic Academy, fifth century CE. Cf. Proclus *In Timaeum* 1 (here I used Taylor, trans. 1:128), which Pico interprets to agree with the *Celestial Hierarchies* of Pseudo-Dionysius the Areopagite. Given the historical links between Proclus's *henads* and Pseudo-Dionysius's orders of angels, Pico's thesis has a basis in fact. For further correlations with Dionysius's "powers," see also 10>9 on the Orphic hymns.

5>14. In the series listed in 2.12 note. "Pallas" shows up regularly in Pico as a symbol of the intellectual nature, e.g., in the *Commento* (Garin, *Scritti vari*, 498).

5>15. Per extremorum et medii rationem cognoscere possumus conuenienter uniuersi gradus sic in quinque posse diuidi: In super ens, uere ens, non uere ens, non uere non ens, uere non ens.

5>16. Per ipsum tale, uere tale, semper tale, in Platonis doctrina, debemus intelligere proprietatem intellectus, animae, et primorum corporum. <23r/23v>

5>17. Si Syriani doctrinam sequamur, conueniens est post unitatem totalis intellectionis, quae et trifariam diuiditur in substantialem, potentialem, et operatiuam, ponere trinarium intellectionis, partialis scilicet, participatae, et imaginariae.

5>18. Quicquid dicant caeteri Platonici de rationalis animae partium distinctione, assero ego si <   >, id est rationalem partem, in <   > et <   > diuidamus, eandem partem ut phantasiae coniungitur <   > dici, ut intellectui <   >, ut sibiipsi <   >.

5>19. Possibile est ut pars rationalis animae nostrae, quam secundum peripateticos possibilem intellectum uoco, ad hoc perueniat, ut sine coniunctione ad phantasmata discurrat et operetur.

5>15. 1486 diuidi.In super ens.uere ens.non uere ens. *etc.*

5>16. 1486 Per ipsum tale.vere tale.semper tale in Platonis

5>18. 1486 coeteri | 1487 *omits blank space after* sibiipsi

5>15. "method of the extremes and the middle" = cf. 3>52, 3>70, and my note to 3>53–54. The thesis takes us from God ("that-above-being") to prime matter ("truly-not-being"). Cf. also 8>1, ascribed to Zoroaster.

5>16. Interpreting *Timaeus* 49d ff. For the style of this thesis, cf. 24.1 from Proclus.

5>17. Presumably again drawn from or inspired by Proclus.

5>15. By the method of the extremes and the middle we can recognize that the grades of the universe can be appropriately divided like this in five ways: into that-above-being, truly-being, not-truly-being, not-truly-not-being, and truly-not-being.

5>16. By the self-such, truly-such, and always-such, in the doctrine of Plato, we should understand the property of the intellect, of the soul, and of the first bodies. (615)

5>17. If we follow the doctrine of Syrianus, it is appropriate after the unity of total intellection, which is also divided triply into substantial, potential, and operative intellection, to posit another triad of intellection, namely, partial, participated, and imagerial.

5>18. Whatever other Platonists say about the distinction of parts in the rational soul, I assert that if we divide < >, that is, the rational part, into < > and < >, that the same part as it conjoined to the phantasy is called < >, to the intellect < >, to itself < >.

5>19. It is possible that the rational part of our soul, which following the Peripatetics I call the possible intellect, can arrive at this: that it can discourse and operate without conjunction to phantasmata.

5>18. Apparently inspired by an exceedingly complex passage in Proclus *In Timaeum* 2 (cf. Taylor, trans. 1:207). Given Pico's disclaimer at the beginning of this thesis ("Whatever other Platonists say"), we cannot be certain what Greek terms he had in mind. Kieszkowski, followed by Biondi, unjustifiably fills in the blanks with some terms from the fifth-century anthologist Stobaeus. Following the 1487 reprint, all later editions (including Kieszkowski's and Biondi's) omit the blank-space after *sibiipsi*, rendering the last part of Pico's thesis meaningless. Cf. this thesis, among other possibilities, with 17.1 from Simplicius.

5>19. Drawn again from Proclus *In Timaeum* 2 (cf. Taylor, trans. 1:207–8). Pertinent to Pico's syncretic fusion of the Platonic and Aristotelian theories of knowledge. Cf. 1.6 and note and my discussion above, pp. 102–105.

5>20. Perfectius et uerius reperitur pulchritudo in intelligibilibus quam in sensibilibus.

5>21. Cum dicit Plato Amorem natum ex congressu Peniae et Pori in ortis Iouis, in natalibus Veneris, diis discumbentibus, nihil aliud intelligit quam in angeli mente tunc primum amorem, id est desiderium pulchritudinis, esse natum cum in eo idearum splendor, imperfectius tamen, refulxit.

5>22. Amor de quo in Symposio loquitur Plato, in deo nullo modo esse potest.

5>23. Per duplicem Venerem, de qua in Symposio Platonis, nihil aliud intelligere debemus quam duplicem pulchritudinem, sensibilem et intelligibilem.

5>24. Amor de quo Plotinus loquitur non est coelestis amor de quo Plato in Symposio, sed illius uera et proxima imago.

5>25. Pugnantia quae uidetur in dictis Orphei et Agathonis, quorum alter amorem antiquiorem omnibus diis dicit, alter iuniorem, perfecte soluemus si ad duplex deorum esse, intelligibile et naturale, respexerimus.

5>21. 1486 discmnbentibus

5>20. Cf. 5>23, 5>26.

5>21. Interpreting *Symposium* 203b–c. Cf. *Commento* (Garin, *Scritti vari*, 499, 501ff.), where Pico attacks Ficino's reading of this material, and Plotinus's allegorical account of this myth in *Enneads* 3.5.

5>22. The implied distinction is between so-called acquisitive and nonacquisitive love, *eros* and *agape*. In the *Commento* (Garin, *Scritti vari*, 488), Pico likewise argues (vs. Ficino) that in God there can be no "desire of things besides himself." Cf. again *Enneads* 3.5.

5>20. Beauty is found more perfectly and more truly in intelligible than in sensible things.

5>21. When Plato says that Love was born from the union of Poverty and Plenty in the garden of Jove, on the birthday of Venus while the gods feasted, he means only this, that then the first love, that is, the desire of beauty, was born in the angelic mind when in it the splendor of ideas, though imperfectly, began to shine. (620)

5>22. The love of which Plato speaks in the *Symposium* can in no way exist in God.

5>23. By the two Venuses in Plato's *Symposium* we should understand nothing but two kinds of beauty, sensible and intelligible.

5>24. The love of which Plotinus speaks is not the celestial love of which Plato writes in the *Symposium,* but its true and proximate image.

5>25. The conflict that appears in the words of Orpheus and Agathon, when one says that Love is more ancient than all the gods, the other that he is younger, we can perfectly resolve if we consider the twofold existence of gods, intelligible and natural.

5>23. *Re Symposium* 180d ff. Cf. 5>20, 5>26, *Commento* (Garin, *Scritti vari,* 498), Plotinus *Enneads* 3.5.

5>24. Cf. *Commento* (Garin, *Scritti vari,* 521ff.), Plotinus *Enneads* 3.5. A nice example of Pico's use of hierarchical distinctions to reconcile authorities.

5>25. *Re Symposium* 195a ff.

5>26. Pulchritudo est in deo per causam, in totali intellectu uere essentialiter totaliter, in particulari intellectu uere partialiter essentialiter, in anima rationali uere participaliter, in uisibilibus coeli accidentibus imaginarie essentialiter totaliter, in subcoelestibus qualitatibus uisibilibus imaginarie partialiter essentialiter, in quan/titatibus imaginarie participaliter. <23v/24r>

5>27. Cum dicit Plato Omne quod fit a causa fieri, referendum est per se ad per se, et per accidens ad per accidens.

5>28. Cum dixit Plato in Timeo ex indiuidua diuiduaque substantia conflatam animam, per indiuiduam substantiam animalem intellectum significauit, per diuiduam animalem rationem.

5>29. Non est credendum in doctrina Platonis animam quicquam intelligere per inspectionem ad ideas, nisi cum peruenit ad illum statum qui est supremus gradus contemplatiuae perfectionis.

Correlarium: Errant qui credunt secundum Platonem quod ea quae nos quotidie cognoscimus et intelligimus, in idearum lumine cognoscamus.

5>30. Modus cognoscendi per ideas est ille cuius dixit Plato in Timeo paucos homines esse participes, sed bene deos omnes.

5>31. Exponere in Fabula Critiae per quinque partus, quinque formas corporis omnino est inconueniens.

5>26. Systematizing material from Diotima's speech in the *Symposium* 210a ff. See above, pp. 66–67. When we compare this extraordinary thesis with Plotinus *Enneads* 1.6, which also distinguishes hierarchical "modes" of beauty, we see how far Pico goes beyond his Neo-Platonic sources in his proportional language.

5>27. Interpreting *Timaeus* 28a "modally." "what exists per se" = Pico's intellectual nature; "what exists accidentally" = lower levels of reality informed by "soul" and "reason." Cf. with 24.38–42 from Proclus and note.

5>28. Reading *Timaeus* 34c ff. to conform to Pico's system.

5>26. Beauty exists in God as its cause, in the total intellect truly essentially totally, in the particular intellect truly partially essentially, in the rational soul truly participationally, in the visible accidents of the heavens imagerially essentially totally, in subcelestial visible qualities imagerially partially essentially, in quantities imagerially participationally. (625)

5>27. When Plato says, *Everything that happens happens for a cause,* we should refer what exists per se to per se causes, and what exists accidentally to accidental causes.

5>28. When in the *Timaeus* Plato said that the soul is composed out of undivided and divided substance, by undivided substance he meant the animate intellect, by divided substance, animate reason.

5>29. It should not be believed that in Plato's teachings any soul understands through an inspection of ideas, except when it arrives at that state that is the supreme grade of contemplative perfection.

Corollary: They err who believe that according to Plato those things that we daily know and understand, we know in the light of the ideas.

5>30. The means of knowing through ideas is that of which Plato said in the *Timaeus* that few men are participants, but truly all gods.

5>31. To explain the five parts in the fable in the *Critias* as five forms of body is totally inappropriate. (630)

5>29–30. On Pico's harmonization of the Platonic and Aristotelian theories of knowledge. Cf. 1.6 and note, 20.12 from Plotinus, and my discussion above, pp. 102–103. Presumably, "all gods" in 5>30 = demons, intelligences, and souls in a mystic state. Cf. 24.3 from Proclus.

5>31. Aimed polemically at Ficino, who in his commentary on the *Critias* (Ficino *Opera,* 1576: 1486) equates the "five parts" with "five forms of body . . . namely, stones, metals, plants, animals lacking reason, and animals endowed with reason."

5>32. Per aliam uitam in Epinomide intelligere debemus connexionem partis cum suo toto, et credo idem esse quod apud Cabalistas dicitur saeculum uenturum.

5>33. Qualiter uerum sit quod in Epinomide dicitur, arithmeticam scientiam inter omnes speculatiuas maxime facere ad foelicitatem, intelligi potest per conclusiones nostras de mathematicis.

5>34. Per coelum in Epinomide, quod dicit Plato esse nobis causam omnium bonorum, non ideam coeli, sed ipsum coelum, quod est coeleste animal, intelligere debemus.

5>35. Per necessitatis regnum in Symposio Platonis, nihil aliud intelligere debemus quam superabundantiam naturae alterius supra naturam eiusdem, et infiniti supra terminum.

5>36. Per demonstrationem Platonis in Phedro de animae immortalitate, nec de nostris animis, ut Proclus, Hermias, et Syrianus credunt, nec de omni anima, ut Plotinus et Numenius, nec de mundi tantum anima, ut Posidonius, sed de coelesti qualibet anima, probatur et concluditur immortalitas.

5>32. 1486 soeculum

5>36. 1486 ut Proclus.Hermias. & Syrianus credunt

5>32. Correlating a casual reference in *Epinomis* 973c with an eschatological symbol common in medieval Hebrew thought. Wirszubski (1989: 190–91) claims that Pico took the concept of the "world to come" from Flavius Mithridates' translation for Pico of the *Bahir*, or possibly from two other translations by Mithridates that quote the *Bahir*, but the concept was also discussed in many other texts known to Pico.

5>33. Cf., e.g., *Epinomis* 976d ff., theses 7>1ff. The reference here is to mystic happiness.

5>32. By the other life in the *Epinomis*, we should understand the connection of the part with its whole, and I believe that this is identical to what the Cabalists call the world to come.

5>33. In what sense what the *Epinomis* says is true, that among all the speculative sciences arithmetic leads the most to happiness, can be understood through my conclusions on mathematics.

5>34. By heaven in the *Epinomis*, which Plato says is the cause of all our goods, we should not understand the idea of heaven, but heaven itself, which is a celestial animal.

5>35. By the rule of necessity in Plato's *Symposium*, we should understand nothing but the superabundance of the nature of the other over the nature of the same, and of the infinite over limit.

5>36. By Plato's demonstration in the *Phaedrus* concerning the immortality of the soul, the immortality of every celestial soul is proven and concluded—not of our souls, as Proclus, Hermias, and Syrianus believe, nor of every soul, as Plotinus and Numenius claim, nor only of the soul of the world, as Posidonius believes. (635)

5>34. Interpreting *Epinomis* 976e–977b. "heaven" in that text = the god Uranus. "celestial animal" in this thesis apparently = the world soul, although in Pico's theses from Proclus both "heaven" and the "per se animal," etc., correspond to particular *henads* in Proclus's "intelligible trinity." Cf., e.g., 24.50, 24.52. Other theses implying astrological views are listed in 22.4–8 note.

5>35. Correlating the mythopoeic language of *Symposium* 195c with abstract concepts found in other parts of the Platonic corpus. For the style of this conclusion, cf. 24.1 from Proclus. In the *Commento* (Garin, *Scritti vari*, 515–16), Pico identifies Plato's "rule of necessity" with prime matter. By implication, then, the "other"/"infinite" here = prime matter; the "same"/"limit" = the formal or intellectual principle.

5>36. Cf. *Phaedrus* 245c ff. Related conclusions are listed in 20.3 note. Cf. especially 5>42. It is interesting to note Pico's sharp criticism here of the Platonic exegeses of these late-ancient scholastics.

5>37. Tempus essentialiter est in incorporeis, participatiue in corporeis.

5>38. Tempus, ubi habet esse essentiale, habet esse totaliter extra animam. <24r/24v>

5>39. Tempus habet ab anima suum esse participatum: a prima quidem anima per modum effectiuae causalitatis, ab ultima uero per modum obiectiuae consecutionis.

5>40. Motus primi coeli, et uniuersaliter quilibet motus siue localis siue alterationis, secundario et per accidens tempore mensuratur.

5>41. Licet natura intellectualis simul omnia intelligat, non tamen hoc est per uirtualem et unitiuam continentiam, sed per mutuam penetrationem formarum, et indissociatam concatenationem totius esse participati, id est, formalis.

5>42. Per demonstrationem Platonis in Phedro de immortalite animae, firmius demonstratur aeternitas mundi quam per ullam rationem Aristotelis in .vii. Physicorum.

5>43. Sicut et uidetur et auditur homo ab homine per motionem sensus ad extra, ita et uidetur et auditur demon ab homine et a demone per motionem sensus ad intra.

5>44. Cur homo non possit non uideri si sit presens a recte disposito in potentia uisiua, demon autem tunc solum uideatur cum uult uideri, ex modo quo unusquisque eorum uidetur haberi potest.

5>39. colon retained from 1486 edition

5>37–40. For related theses, see 2.18 note.

5>41. Cf. 3>25, 6>6–7, etc. Pico normally associates "formal" (or "quidditative") existence with the intellectual nature. Cf. 3>1, 4>3.

5>37. Time exists essentially in incorporeal, participatively in corporeal things.

5>38. Time, where it has essential existence, has existence totally outside the soul.

5>39. Time has its participated existence from the soul: from the first soul through effective causality, from the last soul as an objective consequence.

5>40. The motion of the first heaven and universally every motion, whether local or of alteration, secondarily and accidentally is measured in time.

5>41. Granted that the intellectual nature simultaneously understands all things, this is not through its potential and unifying containment of them, but through the mutual penetration of forms, and the indissociable connection of all participated, that is, all formal, existence. (640)

5>42. Through Plato's demonstration in the *Phaedrus* of the immortality of the soul the eternity of the world is more firmly demonstrated than through any argument of Aristotle's in book 7 of the *Physics*.

5>43. Just as men are seen and heard by men through the motion of the senses outwards, so demons are seen and heard by men and demons through the motion of the senses inwards.

5>44. The reason why men cannot avoid being seen if they are properly situated in visual potentiality, while demons are seen only when they want to be seen, can be understood from the way in which both of them are visible.

5>42. Cf. 5>36 and note, *Commento* (Garin, *Scritti vari*, 468ff.).

5>43–44. See note 22.9–10.

5>45. Sensus naturae quem ponunt Alchindus, Bacon, Guilielmus Parisiensis, et quidam alii, maxime autem omnes magi, nihil est aliud quam sensus uehiculi quem ponunt Platonici.

5>46. Cum dicit Plato neminem nisi inuitum peccare, nihil aliud intelligitur quam illud quod Thommas tenet, scilicet non posse esse peccatum in uoluntate, nisi sit defectus in ratione.

5>47. Prouidentia est statuitiue in deo, ordinatiue in intelligentia, exequtiue in anima, denuntiatiue in coelo, terminatiue in toto uniuerso.

5>48. Non solum per dicta in Epinomide et Philebo a Platone, in quibus dialogis expresse ponit Plato foelicitatem in contemplatione, sed per dicta in Phedro de furore amatorio, constat secundum Platonem non esse foelicitatem in actu amoris, quia furor non est foelicitas, sed impetus et oestrum concitans, urgens et impellens ad foelicitatem.

5>49. Ex eo nomine quo dei nominant amorem, patet diligenter aduertenti quod in actu amoris non est foelicitas. <24v/25r>

5>45. 1486 Alchindus. Bacon Guilielmus Parisiensus:

5>48. 1486 aestrum | 1487 estrum

5>45. "*sense of nature*" = magical medium (discussed, e.g., in the *De legibus* of William of Paris [William of Auvergne]) through which telepathic powers and similar forces were said to be conducted. The Neo-Platonic "vehicle" was the quasi-material body of the soul (cf. thesis 2>70), through which the purified soul could travel through the world soul and hence through the whole of the material universe. Reference to its "sense" here seems to imply again the existence of telepathic powers or the ability of the soul to gather information at a distance. For the general history of the Neo-Platonic "vehicle," see Dodds (1963: 300, 304ff., 313–21). Cf. also 23.6, 5>50 and note.

5>45. The *sense of nature*, which al-Kindi, Bacon, William of Paris, and certain other, indeed nearly all, magicians posit, is nothing but the *sense of the vehicle* put forward by the Platonists.

5>46. When Plato says that only the unwilling sins, he only means what Thomas maintains, namely that there can be no sin in the will, unless there is a defect in reason. (645)

5>47. Providence exists statutorily in God, ordinatively in intelligence, executively in the soul, denunciatively in the heavens, determinatively in the whole universe.

5>48. It is evident not only though Plato's words in the *Epinomis* and *Philebus*, dialogues in which Plato expressly locates happiness in contemplation, but through the words in the *Phaedrus* on amatory frenzy, that according to Plato happiness does not exist in an act of love, since frenzy is not happiness but an inciting impulse and gadfly, urging and impelling us to happiness.

5>49. From that name which the gods call love, it is clear to anyone paying close attention that happiness does not exist in an act of love.

5>46. Cf. note 2.12, *Commento* (Garin, *Scritti vari*, 492), and my detailed discussion above, pp. 105ff.

5>47. Related theses on "modes" of providence and necessity, etc., are listed in note 24.2.

5>48–49. Again in the series beginning at 2.12. "name which the gods call love" = cf. *Phaedrus* 252b, where we find that mortals call love Eros, but the gods call it Pteros (from "wings"). Pico's point is that love carries us to our mystical goal but should not be confused with the goal itself. It is interesting that Pico does not closely associate himself with Plato's view (as Pico represents it) that the greatest happiness lies in contemplation or an act of intellect; on this see especially 3>43 and my discussion above, pp. 107–108.

5>50. Ista propositio in Phedro: Omnis anima totius inanimati curam habet, simpliciter de quacunque uere anima intelligenda est.

5>51. Ex dicto illo Platonis in Phedro, quod nisi anima hominis ea que uere sunt intuita esset, in hoc animal non uenisset, si recte intelligatur, intelligetur quod opinio Plotini ponens transmigrationem animarum in bruta non est ad mentem Platonis.

5>52. Ex oratione Socratis in Phedro ad pana, habetur complete opinio Platonis de foelicitate.

5>53. Opinio Cratyli de nominibus ita est intelligenda: non quod talia sint nomina, sed quod talia esse debent si sint recta.

5>54. Ideo dixit Socrates in Cratylo se somniare circa ideas, quia ideis non utimur in hoc statu, sed earum imaginibus proximis uel secundariis.

5>55. Per unum in Sophiste, intellige unum in alteritate.

5>51. 1486 Phedro: quod nisi . . . venisset. Si recte

5>53. colon retained from 1486 edition

5>50. Cf. *Phaedrus* 246b–c, which has obvious magical suggestions: "Every soul has care of everything inanimate and traverses the whole universe, though in ever-changing forms. Thus when it is perfect and winged it journeys on high and controls the whole world" (adapted from Hackforth's translation). Further affinities can be found here with Plotinus *Enneads* 4.8.1ff., especially 4.8.2. Cf. 20.2, 5>45, 9>14 from Pico's magical theses.

5>51. *Phaedrus* 249e–250a. Cf. 20.4, 21.8, 8>4. Cf., e.g., Plotinus *Enneads* 1.1.11. Pico would have presumably interpreted those sections of the Platonic corpus that discuss the transmigration of souls (in the *Phaedrus*, *Republic*, *Phaedo*, *Timaeus*, and elsewhere) allegorically.

5>50. That proposition in the *Phaedrus*, *Every soul has care for everything inanimate*, should be understood absolutely of truly every soul.

5>51. From that saying of Plato in the *Phaedrus*, *Unless the soul of man had contemplated those things that truly exist, it would not have entered into this animal*, if rightly understood, it will be known that the opinion of Plotinus placing the transmigration of souls into beasts does not conform to the mind of Plato. (650)

5>52. From Socrates's prayer to Pan in the *Phaedrus*, the opinion of Plato on happiness is completely known.

5>53. The opinion of the *Cratylus* on names should be understood this way: not that names are like that, but that they must be if they are to be correct.

5>54. In the *Cratylus* Socrates said that he *dreamt* about ideas, because we do not use ideas in this state, but their proximate or secondary images.

5>55. By the one in the *Sophist,* understand the one in otherness.

5>52. Pan (Greek for "all") = presumably a symbol for Pico's intellectual nature; cf. 10>28 and note. *Re Phaedrus* 279b–c: "Grant that I may become fair within, and that such outward things as I have may not war against the spirit within me" (trans. Hackforth). Series begins at 2.12.

5>53. On linguistic realism. Cf., e.g., *Cratylus* 383a–b, 387d. In the *Apology* (*Opera,* 175), Pico tells us that in the *Cratylus* Plato claimed that names had magical powers if they were "rightly imposed." In general, for Pico, that meant in Hebrew or languages "closely derived" from it; cf. 28.33, 28.47, 2>80, 3>55, 9>22, etc.

5>54. Cf. *Cratylus* 439a–d. Series begins at 1.6. On Pico's theory of knowledge, see pp. 102–105.

5>55. I.e., the one in the *Sophist* does not refer to God, as the Neo-Platonists claimed, but to the oneness or unity found in created things. For Pico's strategy in debating this point, cf. 3>70 and my discussion above, pp. 25–29.

5>56. Dictum illud in Sophiste: Qui unum non dicit nihil dicit, illud est quod ab Aristotele dicitur: Qui unum non intelligit nihil intelligit.

5>57. Dictum illud Platonis in Sophiste, de simulachris quae dicit demonica machinatione conficta, et si multis aliis modis possit uerificari, conueniens tamen est exponere per hoc: quod illa, ut gradum medium in entitate tenent, demonico ordini proportionantur.

5>58. Venatio illa Socratis, de qua in Protagora, conuenienter per sex gradus potest sic distribui: ut primus sit esse materiae extrinsecae, secundus esse particulare immateriale, tertius esse uniuersale, quartus esse rationale, quintus esse particulare intellectuale, sextus esse totale intellectuale; in septimo tanquam, in sabbato, cessandum est a uenatione.

5>59. Quod dicitur in Euthydemo, non in habitu, sed actu consistere foelicitatem, intellige de actu reflexo.

5>60. Per id quod in Lachete dicitur: Quorumcumque est scientia_non esse aliam eorundem ut preteritorum, aliam ut presentium, aliam ut futurorum, illud potest intelligi tritum apud peripateticos, non esse scientiam nisi uniuersalium.

5>57. colon retained from 1486 edition

5>58. colon retained from 1486 edition | 1486 immateriale. Tertius | 1487 potest sic describi | 1487 tanquam sabbato

---

5>56. Cf. *Sophist* 237e. Here and in 5>60 we see Pico's most direct way of harmonizing Plato and Aristotle. The *De ente et uno* 2 (Garin, *Scritti vari*, 394) tells us that this passage in the *Sophist* refers to the equivalence of being and the one.

5>57. Cf. *Sophist* 266b–c, referring to dream images, shadows, reflections, etc., associated with objects in the material world.

5>56. That saying in the *Sophist*, *Whoever does not say one thing, says nothing*, is the same as what Aristotle says, *Whoever does not understand one thing, understands nothing*. (655)

5>57. Even though that saying of Plato's in the *Sophist*, concerning the images he says were made by demonic contrivance, can be verified in many other ways, it is appropriate to explain it through this: that those images, since they hold the middle grade in being, correspond to the demonic order.

5>58. That hunt of Socrates in the *Protagoras* can be appropriately divided this way into six grades: so that the first is the existence of external matter, the second particular immaterial existence, the third universal existence, the fourth rational existence, the fifth particular intellectual existence, the sixth total intellectual existence. In the seventh, in the Sabbath, as it were, one must desist from the hunt.

5>59. What is said in the *Euthydemus*, that happiness does not consist in a habit but in an act, understand of a reflexive act.

5>60. Through what the *Laches* says, that knowledge of all things is not one way when those things are past, another when they are present, another when they are future, that common saying of the Peripatetics can be understood, that no knowledge exists except of universals.

5>58. *Re* the quietism that Pico posited at the height of the mystical ascent; see above, pp. 39ff., 112–14. The apparent reference here is to the myth in *Protagoras* 321b ff., which pertains to man's creation and education by the gods. This myth provided one of the main sources for the famous opening section on man in Pico's *Oration*.

5>59. "reflexive act" = see 2>74 note. Series starts at 2.12. Cf. especially 3>43.

5>60. Cf. *Laches* 198d, note 5>56.

5>61. Dictum illud Platonis in Gorgia, Si orator scit iusta, est iustus, dico absolute, secundum se non ut ad hominem tantum, posse saluari, si / unum ab alio esse intelligamus non formaliter, sed illatiue. <25r/25v>

5>62. Licet ratio Platonis in Phedone per uiam contrariorum absolute non concludat, expositis tamen a Cebete ad hominem aliquid concludit.

5>61. 1486 illativae | 1487 illative

5>61. Cf. *Gorgias* 460b. Again pertinent to Pico's (qualified) intellectualism. Cf. 2.12 note.

5>61. I say that that saying of Plato in the *Gorgias*, *If an orator knows just things, he is just*, can be saved absolutely, understood in itself and not just *ad hominem*, if we recognize that one follows from the other not formally but inferentially. (660)

5>62. Granted that Plato's argument through the method of opposites in the *Phaedo* proves nothing absolutely, with respect to those things put forward by Cebes, it proves something *ad hominem*.

5>62. "method of opposites" = cf. *Phaedo* 70d ff., which proposes a simple demonstration of the immortality of the soul: Everything is generated from its opposite; since life is the opposite of death, it must therefore follow it. Pico's point is that this demonstration, while not sufficient in itself, successfully answers the doubts about immortality previously raised by Cebes (70a ff.).

CONCLVSIONES SECVNDVM OPINIONEM PROPRIAM IN DOCTRINA ABVCATEN AVENAN, QVI DICITVR AVCTOR DE CAVSIS.

6>1. Cum dixit Abucaten Auenan animam esse supra tempus, intelligendum est de anima absoluta secundum substantiam, praescindendo ab omni operatione quae competit ei inquantum est anima.

CONCLUSIONS ON THE *BOOK OF CAUSES.* The *Book of Causes*, an adaptation of Proclus's *Elements of Theology*, was among the most commented upon metaphysical treatises of the later Middle Ages. The route that the work traced from its Greek to Arabic and Latin versions is still unknown; see the introduction to Pattin's edition (n.d. [1966]). Occasionally, as in the commentaries on the text by Thomas Aquinas and Giles of Rome, the work's ties to Proclus were explicitly recognized; more often, the treatise was attributed to Aristotle (like other Neo-Platonic texts including the so-called *Theology of Aristotle*) or was said to be the work or translation of various Arabic or Latin authors. Neither "Abucaten Avenan" nor any plausible variation of that name that I can think of is given as an author or translator of the text in any known manuscript. This section of the nine hundred theses is not listed in Pico's second preface and was apparently hastily added to replace other theses that Pico struck out when the book was in press. (Note that the title, unlike all others in the text, does not even include the number of theses.) It is interesting that Pico's choice for a replacement text was again based on Proclus's work.

CONCLUSIONS ACCORDING TO MY OWN OPINION ON THE DOCTRINE OF ABUCATEN AVENAN, WHO IS CALLED THE AUTHOR OF THE *BOOK OF CAUSES*.

6>1. When Abucaten Avenan said that the soul exists over time, this should be understood of the soul detached in substance, cut off from every operation that belongs to it insofar as it is a soul.

Note on the *editio princeps* and Pico's missing theses: The orthography of the *editio princeps* shifts in minor but revealing ways around this point that provide some hints concerning the text's history. The most obvious of these shifts (there are others) involves the text's use of the diphthong: In hundreds of cases before 5>47 the text consistently uses the diphthong *oe* in *coelum* or *coelestium*; thereafter (starting at 7a>10, where one of these words next appears), we just as consistently find *caelum* and *caelestium*. This trivial shift becomes noteworthy when we realize that it reflects changes starting near (and, in all probability, at exactly the same point) where Pico inserted these ten theses into his text. The most plausible explanation is that the printers began working here from a revised manuscript that was copied by a different scribe than the one who produced the original manuscript, explaining the sudden orthographical shifts. Presumably, the second manuscript included, or was delivered with instructions for making, revisions in other parts of the text. Discrepancies between counts of theses in several section titles and the number of theses in those sections, as well as faulty cross-referencing between theses in the text (see, e.g., thesis 9>4 and note) suggest that at a minimum the excluded conclusions included two theses from Pico's "theological conclusions" (theses 4>1–29) and one from his "paradoxical conclusions introducing new doctrines into philosophy" (theses 3>1–71). Miscounts of theses in other sections suggest that while the text was in press other parts of the work also had theses hastily added or subtracted—in the latter case, presumably due to theological dangers.

6>1. "soul detached in substance" = presumably the unparticipated or world soul. Cf. 23.9 from Iamblichus. This thesis attempts to reconcile the language of the *Book of Causes* with the views Pico supports in 5>37–40. Other theses on duration are listed in note 2.18.

6>2. Cum dicit Abucaten: Omnis anima nobilis tres habet operationes, diuinam, intellectualem, et animalem, ita est intelligendum, quod primam habeat per imaginem proportionalitatis, secundam per formalitatem participationis, tertiam per proprietatem essentialitatis.

6>3. Cum dixit Abucaten Omnem causam primariam plus influere, per plus intelligas eminentiam modi causandi et intimitatem eius quod in re producitur.

6>4. Quamuis dicat Abucaten quod esse, quod est primum creatum, est super intelligentiam, non credas tamen illud secundum hypostasim esse distinctum ab intelligentia.

6>5. Cum dixit Abucaten causam primam superiorem esse omni narratione, non tam propter id habet ueritatem quod primo affert, quia scilicet causam ante se non habet, quam propter id quod secundario innuit, quia omne intelligibile unialiter antecedit.

6>6. Quod dicit Abucaten, intelligentiam esse substantiam quae non diuiditur, maxime est uerum per indiscretam in ea intelligibilium ad inuicem penetrationem.

6>7. Ex praecedenti conclusione potest haberi quomodo intelligendum est dictum Abucaten, quod omnis intelligentia est plena formis.

6>2. 1486 operationes.diuinam:

6>2. Meant again to reconcile the *Book of Causes* with Pico's views. Cf., e.g., 3>1.

6>3. In the series starting at 2.17. Presumably "every primary cause" = both God and the intellectual nature. For the latter, cf. the wording here with 3>25. The apparent goal of this thesis was to prepare the way for a reconciliation of emanationism with creationism by distinguishing different "modes" of causation. On this strategy, see above, pp. 20–21.

6>2. When Abucaten says, *Every noble soul has three operations, divine, intellectual, and animate*, this should be understood this way: that it possesses the first through the likeness of proportionality, the second through the formality of participation, the third through the property of essentiality.

6>3. When Abucaten said *Every primary cause influences more*, by *more* understand the eminence of its mode of causation, and the intimation of itself that it produces in things.

6>4. Although Abucaten says that existence, which is the first created thing, exists above intelligence, do not believe that as a hypostasis it is distinct from intelligence. (665)

6>5. When Abucaten said that the first cause is superior to all speech, this is not true so much because of what he affirms first, namely since it has no cause before itself, but because of what he suggests second, because it is unially antecedent to everything intelligible.

6>6. What Abucaten states, that intelligence is a substance that is not divided, is principally true due to the undivided mutual penetration in it of intelligibles.

6>7. From the preceding conclusion one can know how to interpret Abucaten's saying, *Every intelligence is full of forms*.

6>4. Again an attempt to harmonize the *Book of Causes* with Pico's views, in which (1) no created being exists above the intellectual nature; and in which (2) some "mode" of existence (like everything else) is found on every level of reality.

6>5. Reflects Pico's metaphysical views of language. Cf. above, pp. 24, 37, 79–81.

6>6–7. Cf. 3>25, 5>41, etc. Pico is again attempting to harmonize the *Book of Causes* with his own correlative system.

6>8. Per ultimam propositionem Abucaten possumus intelligere quid sibi uelit illa diuisio_quam fecit Plato in principio tractatus Timei, et possumus scire quod sub ea non comprehenditur anima nisi / per uiam extremalis conbinationis. <25v/26r>

6>9. Ex antepenultima propositione Abucaten colligi potest quod declinare plus ad sensum quam ad intellectum non est animae ut anima est, sed ut cadens est.

6>10. Cum dicit Abucaten intelligentiam, ut diuina, est regere res, intelligendum est de regimine statuitiuo, non ordinatiuo qui ei competit ut intelligentia est.

6>8. Interpreting *Timaeus* 27c. Cf. 22.11 (attributed to Porphyry) and note.

6>9. Cf. the wording in 21.1–3, 9>12. Series begins at 1.6.

6>8. Through the final proposition of Abucaten we can understand the meaning of that division that Plato makes in the beginning of the *Timaeus*, and we can know that the soul is not included in that except through the method of the combination of extremes.

6>9. From the proposition of Abucaten that is second before last we can gather that to decline more to the senses than to the intellect does not pertain to the soul as it is a soul, but as it is falling. (670)

6>10. When Abucaten says that intelligence, as it is divine, rules things, this should be understood of statutory rule, not of the ordinative rule that belongs to it as it is intelligence.

6>10. Cf. the wording in 5>47. On modes of providence and necessity, etc., cf. the theses listed in note 24.2.

CONCLVSIONES DE MATHEMATICIS SECVNDVM OPINIONEM PROPRIAM NVMERO .LXXXV.

7>1. Mathematicae non sunt uerae scientiae.

7>2. Si foelicitas sit in speculatiua perfectione, mathematicae non faciunt ad foelicitatem.

7>3. Mathematicae scientiae non sunt propter se, sed ut uia ad alias scientias quaerendae.

7>4. Sicut subiecta mathematicorum, si absolute accipiantur, intellectum nihil perficiunt, ita si ut imagines accipiantur superiorum, immediate nos ad intelligibilium speculationem manu ducunt.

7>5. Sicut dictum Aristotelis de antiquis, dicentis quod ideo errarunt in physica contemplatione, quia mathematice res physicas tractarunt, uerum esset si illi materialiter mathematica non formaliter accepissent, ita est uerissimum modernos, qui de naturalibus mathematice disputant, naturalis philosophiae fundamenta destruere.

MATHEMATICAL CONCLUSIONS. Pico's numerological system fused the emanationist metaphysics of Neo-Pythagoreanism and Neo-Platonism found in Iamblichus, Syrianus, and Proclus, etc.—in which the "many" unfolded from the "one" in complex numerological patterns—with *gematria* and other formal and informal types of number symbolism in Scriptures, the Kabbalah, various patristic and scholastic sources (Augustine, Isidore of Seville, Rabanus, etc.), and in elementary textbooks like Nichomachus's *Introduction to Arithmetic* and Theon of Smyrna's *Mathematics Useful for Understanding Plato*. What we find in this section is hence not one but a syncretic collection of numerological methods—illustrating from every possible angle the biblical dictum that God created the universe "according to weight and number." In the sixteenth century Pico's promise in this section to debate "everything knowable" through numbers was hilariously satirized by Rabelais (2:18), who has Pantagruel achieving the same

EIGHTY-FIVE CONCLUSIONS ON MATHEMATICS ACCORDING TO MY OWN OPINION.

7>1. The mathematical sciences are not true sciences.

7>2. If happiness exists in speculative perfection, mathematics does not lead to happiness.

7>3. The mathematical sciences are not sciences per se, but a way to seek other sciences.

7>4. Just as the subjects of mathematics, if they are taken absolutely, do not perfect the intellect, so if they are taken as images of superior things, they lead us immediately by the hand to the investigation of intelligibles. (675)

7>5. Just as the saying of Aristotle concerning the ancients, which states that they erred in physical contemplation because they treated physical things mathematically, would be true if they had accepted mathematics materially, not formally, so it is very true that the moderns, who dispute mathematically concerning natural things, destroy the foundations of natural philosophy.

---

end using hand signals (many of them obscene). But this part of the nine hundred theses nevertheless had a powerful influence on sixteenth- and seventeenth-century thought and was drawn on heavily by Agrippa von Nettesheim, John Dee, Giordano Bruno, Robert Fludd, Athanasius Kircher, and scores of lesser-known writers.

7>1–5. Cf. 5>33. "materially"/"formally" = see note 7>9. The "moderns" here = the fourteenth-century *calculatores* (Bradwardine, Swineshead, Buridan, Oresme, etc.), who applied mathematics to problems treated qualitatively in traditional Aristotelian physics. The traditional claim that Renaissance Platonism helped promote the mathematical physics of the later scientific revolution finds little support in these theses, as we find especially in 7>5.

7>6. Nihil magis nociuum theologo quam frequens et assidua in mathematicis Euclidis exercitatio.

7>7. Sicut medicina mouet spiritus principaliter ut regunt corpus, ita musica mouet spiritus ut seruiunt animae.

7>8. Medicina sanat animam per corpus, musica autem corpus per animam.

7>9. Per arithmeticam non materialem, sed formalem, habetur optima uia ad prophetiam naturalem.

7>10. Ioachin in prophetiis suis alia uia non processit quam per numeros formales.

7>11. Per numeros habetur uia ad omnis scibilis inuestigationem et in/tellectionem; ad cuius conclusionis uerificationem polliceor me ad infrascriptas .lxxiiii. questiones per uiam numerorum responsurum. <26r/26v>

7>6. Since Euclidean mathematics, unlike Neo-Platonic and Neo-Pythagorean numerology, does not deal with "images of superior things" (7>4).

7>7–8. On the quasi-physical spirits of Greek medicine, see above, pp. 123–25. Belief in the curative powers of music was a commonplace in traditional thought in and outside the West. See also thesis 10>2 and note.

7>9. "Formal"/"material" arithmetic = mathematics symbolizing cosmological or metaphysical principles (intelligible things) and mathematics applied to the inferior realm of motion and change. On formal numbers, see also 3>26, 9>23, 11>57. In the *Oration* and *Apology*, following *Republic* 7 (525b), Pico disdainfully refers to applied mathematics as "mercantile arithmetic" (*Opera*, 327, 120; Garin, *Scritti vari*, 148).

7>6. Nothing is more harmful to the theologian than frequent and continuous exercise in Euclidean mathematics.

7>7. Just as medicine chiefly moves the spirits that rule the body, so music moves the spirits that serve the soul.

7>8. Medicine heals the soul through the body, but music the body through the soul.

7>9. Through formal, not material, arithmetic, the optimal way is had to natural prophecy. (680)

7>10. Joachim in his prophecies did not proceed in any other way than through formal numbers.

7>11. Through numbers a method exists to the investigation and understanding of everything knowable. To verify this conclusion I promise to respond to the following seventy-four questions through the way of numbers.

7>10. Joachim = Joachim of Fiore. See above, pp. 37, 73.

7>11. One of three or four methods mentioned in Pico's text that lead to knowledge "of everything knowable"—something that De Lubac (1974) denies that Pico claims anywhere. Cf. 3>54–55 and 11>2 (on the universal scope of Pico's Cabalistic methods) and 7a>74 and 11>72 on the universal knowledge discovered in astrological signs ("the book of God"). Pico would also claim that his "method of the extremes and the middle" (e.g., 3>52, 3>70, 5>15) led to an understanding of "everything knowable."

QVESTIONES AD QVAS POLLICETVR SE PER NVMEROS RESPONSVRVM.

7a>1. Vtrum sit deus.

7a>2. Vtrum sit infinitus.

7a>3. Vtrum sit causa omnium rerum.

7a>4. Vtrum sit simplicissimus.

7a>5. Vtrum sit intelligens.

7a>6. Quomodo deus intelligat.

7a> title. 1486 RESPONSVRVM:.

QUESTIONS TO WHICH HE PROMISES TO RESPOND THROUGH NUMBERS. While it is usually simple enough to guess Pico's answers to the questions in this section, it is not possible to reconstruct his arguments thesis by thesis; in most cases, in any event, he had several strategies available. For an illustration of how complex Pico's number symbolism could be, see 3>39 and note. Scholars since the nineteenth century have claimed that besides the more obvious writers that this section influenced (Agrippa, Dee, Fludd, Kircher, etc.), it had a major influence on Zwingli's thought. For references, see Kristeller (1965: 76), Kieszkowski (1973: 24–25 nn. 125, 127).

QUESTIONS TO WHICH HE PROMISES TO RESPOND THROUGH NUMBERS.

7a>1. Whether there is a God.

7a>2. Whether he is infinite.

7a>3. Whether he is the cause of all things. (685)

7a>4. Whether he is the most simple thing.

7a>5. Whether he has intellect.

7a>6. In what way God understands.

7a>1–4. The series of theses on proofs for the existence of God begins at 7.18. Pico presumably meant to play here with the Neo-Pythagorean view of the number "one" as a symbol of absolute unity (and hence as a symbol of "God," "simplicity," etc.), and simultaneously as the generative source of an infinite series of numbers (and hence as a symbol of the "many"). See also Pico's theses ascribed to Pythagoras, 25.1ff.

7a>5–6. Latin scholastics sometimes labeled God as *intellectus, intelligens, et intelligible*—e.g., in Latin translations of Maimonides' *Guide for the Perplexed* 1:68—but Pico normally reserved terms like these for the intellectual nature, claiming that God totally transcended the realm of understanding. Cf. 3>49 and note and the phrasing in 2>7, 7a>42. In respect to 7a>6: God understands all things through contemplation of his own nature; see, e.g., 4>6.

7a>7. An sit dare naturam superiorem natura intellectuali.

7a>8. An esse quiditatiuum rei sit intimius esse quod habeat res.

7a>9. Quid de humanitate in sua precisissima abstractione possit praedicari, et quid non.

7a>10. Quomodo elementa sint in caelo.

7a>11. Quis modus debeat teneri in inuestigatione uniuscuiusque scibilis.

7a>12. Vtrum supra naturam rerum corporalium sit dare naturam rationalem incorpoream.

7a>13. Vtrum supra naturam rationalem sit dare naturam intellectualem.

7a>14. Vtrum inter naturam rationalem et intellectualem sit aliqua natura media.

7a>15. Vtrum inter naturam intellectualem et deum sit aliqua natura media.

7a>7. Since God cannot be considered a nature per se—since he is the cause of all natures—no nature more perfect than the intellectual nature can exist. Thus, writing in reference to Avicenna, Pico tells us in the *Commento* (Garin, *Scritti vari*, 465–66) that from a perfect cause (God) there can only come a single perfect effect (the intellectual nature), from which the rest of reality emanates. In the series on emanationism that begins at 2.17. See especially 8.8 from Avicenna.

7a>8. A thing's "most intimate existence" is its "unial existence," which unites it to the intellectual nature and ultimately to all the rest of creation. Cf. 3>1–4, 3>8, 3>20, etc.

7a>9. Cf. the previous thesis and note. There is also a connection here with 1.2, etc.

7a>7. Whether one should posit a nature superior to the intellectual nature.

7a>8. Whether the quidditative existence of a thing is the most intimate existence that a thing has. (690)

7a>9. What can be predicated of humanity in its most separate state of abstraction and what cannot.

7a>10. In what way the elements exist in heaven.

7a>11. What method should be followed in the investigation of everything knowable.

7a>12. Whether above the nature of corporeal things one should posit a rational incorporeal nature.

7a>13. Whether above the rational nature one should posit an intellectual nature. (695)

7a>14. Whether between the rational and intellectual natures any middle nature exists.

7a>15. Whether between the intellectual nature and God any middle nature exists.

7a>10. Series on the *caelum* starts at 7.9, where we find that the elements exist in heaven in two "modes." The hints found in 23.4 suggest that in this thesis Pico's "way of numbers" involved Cabala and possibly *gematria*. See my note to that thesis. Cf. also 11>67.

7a>11. One based on proportion and correspondence. Cf., e.g., 3>52, 3>55, 5>15, etc. Pico apparently meant to use his "method of the extremes and the middle" in the following four theses.

7a>12–15. Cf. 3>36 and the preceding note. While Pico speaks at times of the rational nature as being incorporeal, as in 7a>12, on the grounds of cosmic correspondence he normally posited matter on some "mode" in every level of creation, even in the rational and intellectual natures. On matter in the soul, see 2>70.

7a>16. Vtrum in aliqua natura_contradictoria se compatiantur.

7a>17. Vtrum in aliqua natura coincidant contradictoria.

7a>18. Quis numerus annorum sit naturaliter debitus uitae boni hominis.

7a>19. Quis sit numerus annorum naturaliter debitus uitae mali hominis.

7a>20. Quot sint gradus principales naturarum uniuersi.

7a>21. Vtrum natura corporea ut talis sit actiua uel tantum sit passiua.

7a>22. Quid dicat corpus.

7a>23. Vtrum sint in materia dimensiones interminate.

7a>24. Vtrum sit melius deum causare res quam non causare.

7a>25. Vtrum creatio rerum ad extra_procedat necessario a diuina essentia in tribus personis hypostatizata.

7a>19. 1486 Qui

7a>16–17. Cf. 3>13–15, etc.

7a>18–19. Is there numerological significance in the fact that 7a>18 is Pico's 700th thesis? (In Western numerology, multiples of 10 of numerological symbols—like the traditional "three score and ten years" of human life—were generally viewed as having significance analogous to those symbols.) Probably involves the kinds of "good" and "bad" numbers that Pico discusses, citing patristic authorities, in the *Apology*, in *Opera*, 173. Thus "two" is an evil number (providing St. Jerome with an argument against bigamy and explaining why unclean animals went into Noah's ark by twos), and "seven" is a good number (explaining why clean animals went in by sevens).

7a>16. Whether in any nature contradictions are compatible.

7a>17. Whether in any nature contradictions coincide.

7a>18. What number of years is naturally owed to the life of a good man. (700)

7a>19. What is the number of years naturally owed to the life of a bad man.

7a>20. How many principal grades of natures exist in the universe.

7a>21. Whether corporeal nature as such is active or only passive.

7a>22. What body signifies.

7a>23. Whether unlimited dimensions exist in matter. (705)

7a>24. Whether it is better for God to cause things than not to cause them.

7a>25. Whether the creation of things beyond itself proceeds necessarily from the divine essence hypostatized in three Persons.

7a>20. A thesis again presumably based on Pico's "method of the extremes and the middle." Cf. 5>15, where we are given five "grades." In dealing with the mystical ascent, however, Pico usually distinguishes six levels below God, e.g., in 5>58.

7a>21. Apparently both, with its active aspect more evident in higher natures. Cf. 11>67.

7a>22. Cf. 1.14–15, etc.

7a>23. Pertains to the conflict between Thomas and Averroes that Pico planned to resolve in 1>13.

7a>24. Possibly linked to the series on emanationism that begins at 2.17.

7a>25. Cf. 2>14–15, etc.

7a>26. Vtrum inter causam et causatum necessario mediet aliquid.

7a>27. Vtrum recte multitudo scibilium ad decem praedicamentorum / numerum sit reducta. <26v/27r>

7a>28. Quae sit differentia inter modum intelligendi angelorum_et animarum rationalium.

7a>29. Quae sit differentia inter modum intelligendi dei et angelorum.

7a>30. Vtrum natura angelica sit quodammodo omnia.

7a>31. Vtrum natura rationalis sit quodammodo omnia.

7a>32. Vtrum possint esse plures dei.

7a>33. Vtrum detur infinitum in natura.

7a>34. Quomodo differat infinitas quam theologi attribuunt deo_ab illa quam dicunt philosophi impossibile esse dari.

7a>35. Vtrum deus sit omnia in omnibus.

7a>29. 1486 angelorum:

7a>26. Series on emanation begins at 2.17. See especially 8.8, 7a>7.

7a>27. Apparently not. Cf. 3>27–34.

7a>28–29. Cf. 3>5–7, etc.

7a>26. Whether between the cause and the caused something necessarily mediates.

7a>27. Whether the multitude of knowable things can be correctly reduced to ten categories.

7a>28. What is the difference between the mode of understanding of angels and of rational souls. (710)

7a>29. What is the difference between the mode of understanding of God and of angels.

7a>30. Whether the angelic nature is in some way all things.

7a>31. Whether the rational nature is in some way all things.

7a>32. Whether many gods can exist.

7a>33. Whether the infinite can exist in nature. (715)

7a>34. In what way the infinity that theologians attribute to God differs from the infinity that philosophers say cannot exist.

7a>35. Whether God is all things in all things.

7a>30–31. Cf. 3>35–36, etc.

7a>32–34. Pico's arguments here are not known, although (as in 7a>1–4) they would presumably concern "one" as a simultaneous symbol of absolute unity and as the source of an infinite series of numbers.

7a>35. Cf. 3>15.

7a>36. Quomodo differat esse creaturarum ab esse dei.

7a>37. Quae pertineant ad considerationem theologi.

7a>38. Quando futura sit saeculi consumatio.

7a>39. Quis et qualis erit rerum status in saeculi consumatione.

7a>40. Quae opinio uerior de trinitate: Arii, Sabellii, Eucliph, aut fidei catholicae.

7a>41. Vtrum formae sensibiles sint intelligibiliter in angelo.

7a>42. Vtrum in angelo sit aliud quam intelligens, intellectio, et intellectum.

7a>43. Vtrum haec in angelo realiter_an ratione distinguantur.

7a>44. Vtrum sit eadem natura mouentis et moti motu physico.

7a>40. 1486 Arii.Sabellii.Eucliph.

7a>36. God's existence is "unial." Cf. 3>1, 3>15.

7a>37. Theology pertains to that which is "unially one." See 3>8.

7a>38–39. Cf. 10>20, 11>9.

7a>40. Arius d. 336 CE/Sabellius fl. 215 CE/Wyclif d. 1384 CE = all judged to be heretics in part for their views of the Trinity. Cf. thesis 11>5.

7a>36. In what way the existence of creatures differs from the existence of God.

7a>37. What things pertain to the consideration of the theologian.

7a>38. When the world will end. (720)

7a>39. Who will exist, and what will be the state of things, at the end of the world.

7a>40. What opinion is truer concerning the Trinity: that of Arius, Sabellius, Wyclif, or the Catholic faith.

7a>41. Whether sensible forms exist intelligibly in the angel.

7a>42. Whether in the angel there exists anything besides intellect, intellection, and that intellected.

7a>43. Whether these are distinguished in the angel really or rationally. (725)

7a>44. Whether the nature of the mover and that which is physically moved is the same.

7a>41. Forms exist in the intellectual nature or angel in a "formal" mode. Cf., e.g., 3>23–26, etc.

7a>42–43. Cf. 2>7, 3>49, 7a>5 and notes. They are presumably distinguished through a "formal distinction." Cf. 2>66, 3>56, 3>58, etc. On formal distinctions, linked most closely to John Duns Scotus, see note 3.7.

7a>44. Series begins at 2.37–38. For Pico's views, see 2>36.

7a>45. Vtrum sit dare aliquid quod secundum suam naturam sit pura potentia, quam philosophi uocant materiam primam.

7a>46. Vtrum mediate uel immediate, et quomodo, materia prima dependeat a deo.

7a>47. Vtrum omne quod est infra deum sit compositum ex actu et potentia.

7a>48. Vtrum sit materia eiusdem rationis in omnibus.

7a>49. Vtrum aliqua res creata possit esse inmunis ab imperfectione.

7a>50. Quae naturae sint aptae foelicitari.

7a>51. Vtrum foelicitas consistat in intellectu an in uoluntate.

7a>52. Vtrum quantitas sit per se uel participatiue uisibilis.

7a>53. Vtrum natura intellectualis sit deo semper unita. <27r/27v>

7a>54. Vtrum in natura intellectuali plus sit imperfectionis quam perfectionis.

7a>52. 1486 participativae

7a>45. Cf. 3>53–54 and note.

7a>46. A question repeatedly raised but left unanswered in Pico's surviving works.

7a>47. On the grounds of cosmological proportion Pico would answer that in some "mode" this is true.

7a>48. Cf. the theses listed in 2.21 note.

7a>49. No, insofar as even the intellectual nature, the most perfect created thing (cf. 7a>7 note), has a material component.

7a>50. Angelic and rational natures. Series starts at 2.12.

7a>45. Whether something should be posited that by its nature is pure potentiality, which the philosophers call prime matter.

7a>46. Whether mediately or immediately, and in what way, prime matter depends on God.

7a>47. Whether everything that exists below God is composed out of act and potentiality.

7a>48. Whether matter of the same kind exists in all things. (730)

7a>49. Whether any created thing can be free from imperfection.

7a>50. What natures are fit for the bestowal of happiness.

7a>51. Whether happiness exists in the intellect or in the will.

7a>52. Whether quantity is visible per se or participatively.

7a>53. Whether the intellectual nature is always united to God. (735)

7a>54. Whether in the intellectual nature there is more imperfection than perfection.

7a>51. It exists in a union of both. See 3>43. Series starts again at 2.12.

7a>52. Participatively. Cf. the language in 5>26.

7a>53. Pico could invoke the logical tool that he introduces in 2>62 to solve such questions (see note). God is totally transcendent, but the perfection of the intellectual nature nevertheless depends on its continuous union with or relations to God.

7a>54. Undoubtedly argued from proportions of the type found in 5>15, etc.

7a>55. Cuius naturae propria sit uera mobilitas.

7a>56. Vtrum animae conueniat modus scientiae per uiam numerorum.

7a>57. Quis sit primus modus praedicandi per se.

7a>58. Quis sit secundus modus praedicationis per se.

7a>59. Vtrum diffinitio inuestigetur per demonstrationem.

7a>60. Quare solum de inherentia passionis ad subiectum habetur scientia.

7a>61. Vtrum anima rationalis sit materialis.

7a>62. Vtrum sit incorruptibilis.

7a>63. Vtrum uniuersaliter intelligat.

7a>64. Vtrum sicut est dare mundum sensibilem, ita sit dare mundum intelligibilem.

7a>65. Vtrum sit maior uel minor numerus separatarum specierum quam materialium.

7a>55. Undoubtedly some "mode" of corporeal nature. Cf., e.g., 23.3.

7a>56. Cf. 3>18, 3>36, etc.

7a>57–58. On "modes of predication" or "modes of speaking," see note 1.3. The first mode = something predicated of the essence of an object. The second mode = something predicated as a *passio propria* or "proper accident" of an object (cf. 2.24, 2.35, and notes).

7a>59. In the series beginning at 7.10–11.

7a>60. Cf. the language in 3>32. The "knowledge" here (*scientia*) = knowledge proper to human nature. Cf. 3>7.

7a>55. To what nature is true mobility proper?

7a>56. Whether the means of knowing through the way of numbers is appropriate to the soul.

7a>57. What is the first mode of predication per se.

7a>58. What is the second mode of predication per se. (740)

7a>59. Whether definition is investigated through demonstration.

7a>60. Why knowledge is had only of the inherence of a property in a subject.

7a>61. Whether the rational soul is material.

7a>62. Whether it is incorruptible.

7a>63. Whether it understands universally. (745)

7a>64. Whether just as one posits a sensible world, one should posit an intelligible world.

7a>65. Whether a greater or smaller number of separated images exists than of material images.

7a>61. Like everything else, in a certain "mode" it is. Cf. 2>70 and note.

7a>62. Cf., e.g., 3>47.

7a>63. Cf. 3>60–66.

72>64. Linked to Pico's correlative views of reality.

7a>65. Following Pico's emanational principles, a proportionally smaller number.

7a>66. Quare in opere secundae diei non est dictum: Et uidit deus quoniam bonum.

7a>67. Quare sexta numeratio homo dicitur.

7a>68. Quare sex diebus dicitur deus omnia perfecisse.

7a>69. Quid significet deum septima die quieuisse.

7a>70. Vtrum distinguatur irascibilis a concupiscibili.

7a>71. Quae sit distinctio inter potentias animae cognoscitiuas.

7a>72. Cur homines naturaliter appetant uictoriam.

7a>73. Cur naturalis sit homini modus cognoscendi per rationem phantasiae coniunctam.

7a>74. Vtrum in caelo sint descripta et significata omnia cuilibet scienti legere.

7a>66. Cf. Peter Lombard *Sentences* 2, *d*. 14. In the *Apology* (*Opera*, 173), Pico, citing St. Jerome, tells us that "On the second day it was not said, 'And God saw that it was good,' because the number two is an evil number." Cf. 7a>18–19 note. Pico could also add Cabalistic arguments to this one; cf. 28.23 and note.

7a>67. "sixth numeration" = sixth of the ten *sefirot* in the Kabbalah. On the sixth *sefirah* as the "great man" or "great Adam" (a symbol for Pico of Christ), see note 28.10. On Pico's methods here, see next note.

7a>68. Pico had numerous strategies available to answer this question using his *via numerorum*. One strategy connects this thesis with the previous one, since "days" in the Kabbalah were associated with particular *sefirot* and since Pico normally correlated the sixth *sefirah* or the "great man" with Christ, God's creative power. The symbolism of six as the first "perfect number"—the first number equal to the sum of its factors ($1 + 2 + 3 = 6$), a symbol of completion—would have presumably also figured here. The importance of the number six in Pico's numerology is further illustrated in those metaphysical and mystical theses in which the cosmos is divided into six hierarchical layers, in his acknowledgement of six "nations" of thinkers, etc. Cf., e.g., 24.55, 5>26, 5>58. Pico could also have used various esoteric methods like *gematria* to demonstrate this thesis.

7a>66. Why in the work of the second day it was not said, *And God saw that it was good.*

7a>67. Why the sixth numeration is called man.

7a>68. Why God is said to have perfected all things in six days. (750)

7a>69. What is meant by the fact that God rested on the seventh day.

7a>70. Whether the irascible passions are distinguished from the sensual passions.

7a>71. What distinction exists between the cognitive powers of the soul.

7a>72. Why men naturally desire victory.

7a>73. Why the means of knowing through reason conjoined to the phantasy is natural to man. (755)

7a>74. Whether in heaven all things are described and signified to anyone knowing how to read them.

7a>69. *Re* commentary on Peter Lombard *Sentences* 2, *d.* 15. In the *Apology*, in *Opera,* 174, Pico sings a paean to the number seven, one "worthy of great attention because the Lord rested on the seventh day, because of the seven gifts of the Holy Spirit, the seven seals in Revelation, the seven trumpets, seven eyes, seven angels, seven churches, seven stars, seven evil spirits, seven vices in Solomon, and seven days that the prophet David sang to God." The number seven as a symbol of the final "Sabbath" of the soul or of history also crops up regularly in the theses and in the *Heptaplus*. Cf. 5>58, 11>16, etc.

7a>70. Cf. the theses listed in 2.11 note. The links between various passions and Pythagorean numerology, seen in theses 25.1–14, probably figured here.

7a>71. Related to the series on the unity of soul beginning at 1.12.

7a>72. "Victory" in the usual scholastic sense = salvation, victory over the devil.

7a>73. Cf. 5>19, 5>29–30, etc., and my discussion above, pp. 103–4.

7a>74. Other theses pertinent to astrology are listed in note 22.4–8. Cf. also 11>72 and my discussion above, p. 139.

CONCLVSIONES NVMERO .XV. SECVNDVM PROPRIAM OPINIONEM DE INTELLIGENTIA DICTORVM ZOROASTRIS ET EXPOSITORVM EIVS CHALDEORVM.

<27v/28r>

8>1. Quod dicunt interpretes chaldei super primum dictum Zoroastris, de scala a Tartaro ad primum ignem, nihil aliud significat quam seriem naturarum uniuersi a non gradu materiae ad eum qui est super omnem gradum graduate protensum.

8>2. Ibidem dico interpretes nihil aliud per uirtutes mysteriales intelligere quam naturalem magiam.

CONCLUSIONS ON ZOROASTER AND HIS CHALDEAN COMMENTATORS. See above, p. 13. On the so-called *Chaldean Oracles* in the Renaissance, see Dannenfeldt (1960). Inexplicably, however, this standard review does not discuss Pico, whose influence on later interpreters of the *Oracles* was critical. Brief discussions can be found in an earlier study by Dannenfeldt (1957) and in Wirszubski (1989: 241ff.). For Pico's claim that he possessed the *Chaldean Oracles* in "Chaldean," cf. thesis 24.31 and Pico's letter to Marsilio Ficino (written in the fall of 1486) in *Opera*, 367–68. In that letter, Pico boasts of possessing books containing the oracles of "Ezre ["Ezte" in the Basel *Opera*], Zoroaster, and Melchiar of the *magi*" (Kristeller 1937: 2:272). Pico's claims were taken at face value by Francesco Patrizi and the other Renaissance editors of the *Oracles*, who assumed that the extant Greek collections of the *Oracles* made by Psellus (eleventh century) and Pletho (fifteenth century) from fragments in Plotinus, Proclus, and similar late-ancient sources derived from whatever "Chaldean" texts Pico had in hand. (It was Pletho, apparently, who first attributed the *Oracles* to Zoroaster.) In any event, it is noteworthy that this section of the nine hundred theses does contain material not found in Psellus or Pletho; nor does Pico's numbering of the *Oracles* coincide with the order found in those earlier collections. The issue of what commentaries Pico consulted in this section is as mysterious as what version of the *Oracles* he had in hand. In his letter to Ficino, Pico speaks of "libellus de dogmatis Chaldaicae theologiae tum Persarum, Graecorum, et Chaldaeorum in illa divina et locupletissima enarratione" [a little book on the teachings of Chaldean theology in that divine and opulent exposition of the Persians, Greeks, and Chaldeans] that had recently come into his hands. In the *Oration*, he speaks in passing of "Evantes the Persian, where he explains the Chaldean theology," followed by a strange text—found correctly only in the faded manuscript of the early draft of the *Oratio*—recorded in a mixture of Hebrew and Aramaic

FIFTEEN CONCLUSIONS ACCORDING TO MY OWN OPINION ON UNDERSTANDING THE SAYINGS OF ZOROASTER AND HIS CHALDEAN COMMENTATORS.

8>1. What the Chaldean interpreters say about the first saying of Zoroaster, concerning the ladder from Tartarus to the first fire, signifies nothing but the series of natures in the universe from ungraded matter to that which in gradation extends beyond all grades.

8>2. In the same place, I say that by mysterious powers the interpreters mean nothing but natural magic.

---

written, as Wirszubski notes, in Ethiopian letters. Leaving aside the remote possibility that some derivative Aramaic version of the *Oracles* with commentaries once existed (produced by some late-medieval Jewish scholar from Greek sources), there are only two likely explanations: (1) Either Flavius Mithridates, Pico's first tutor in Semitic languages, forged Chaldean materials based on those sources and represented them to Pico as genuine; or (2) Pico's claim of possessing a Chaldean version of the *Oracles* was his own fabrication, meant again to distinguish his work from that of Ficino, who years earlier had translated the *Oracles* from Pletho's Greek version and had added his own commentary. From what we know of Flavius's character, the forgery thesis seems by far the likeliest; nor would forging these texts be a difficult task, given Pico's slight knowledge of Aramaic in 1486 and the brevity of the *Oracles* as they exist in other forms. Strong evidence for the forgery thesis appears in the Aramaic quotation found in the early draft of the *Oration*, whose strange mix of Semitic languages and alphabets fits exactly what has long been known of Flavius's "Chaldean" (cf., e.g., Wirszubski 1963). Flavius's involvement is suggested as well by the clear links between the theses in this section (e.g., 8>8–9, 8>14, 8>15) and Pico's Cabalistic theses and by internal evidence (see my note to 8>11) that Pico did have some kind of Aramaic text in hand when he composed these theses. If the forgery thesis holds up, another fascinating chapter can be added to the story of Pico and his strange tutor.

8>1. Reading Pico's system into the symbolic language of the *Oracles*. Cf. especially 5>15 from Pico's Platonic theses.

8>2. In part attempting to naturalize demonic references in the *Oracles*. Cf. the wording in 10>3, ascribed to Orpheus.

8>3. Quod dicunt interpretes super dictum secundum Zoroastris, de duplici aere, aqua, et terra, nihil aliud sibi uult nisi quodlibet elementum quod potest diuidi per purum et impurum habere habitatores rationales_et irrationales; quod uero purum est tantum, rationales tantum.

8>4. Ibidem per radices terrae nihil aliud intelligere possunt quam uitam uegetalem, conuenienter ad dicta Empedoclis, qui ponit transanimationem etiam in plantas.

8>5. Ex dicto illo Zoroastris: Ha ha, hos terra deflet usque ad filios, sequendo expositionem Oziae chaldei, expressam habemus ueritatem de peccato originali.

8>6. Dicta interpretum Chaldeorum super .xi. amphorismo, de duplici ebriatione, Bacchi et Sileni, perfecte intelligentur per dicta cabalistarum de duplici uino.

8>7. Quae dicunt interpretes super .xiiii. amphorismo_perfecte intelligentur per ea quae dicunt cabaliste de morte osculi.

8>8. Magi in .xvii. amphorismo nihil aliud intelligunt per triplex indumentum ex lino, panno, et pellibus, quam triplex animae habitaculum, caeleste, spiritale, et terrenum.

8>3. Interesting clues are found in this thesis to parts of Pico's magic. For Pico, the locus of the "pure elements" was the *caelum*, where we find them existing only "according to their active power" (see 11>67). We know from many other places in Pico that this region is inhabited by totally rational "celestial souls." Below, in the terrestrial world, as suggested in this thesis, we find elements inhabited by both "rational" and "irrational" souls; magic works on the rational part of those elements through the mediation of the purified soul of the magician (cf. 9>10–14). Further on "pure elements" in Pico, see note to 10>12.

8>4. For Empedocles, see Diels frag. 117. Cf. 20.4, 21.8, 5>51. Pico normally interpreted transmigration as a symbol of men living the "vegetative" or "brutish" life, etc. Cf. *Oration*, in *Opera*, 315; Garin, *Scritti vari*, 108.

8>5. Hosea the Chaldean = Mithridates' invention?

8>3. What the interpreters say about the second saying of Zoroaster, concerning two kinds of air, water, and earth, simply means that every element that can be divided into the pure and impure has rational and irrational inhabitants. But that which is pure only has only rational inhabitants.

8>4. In the same place, by the roots of the earth they can only mean the vegetative life, which conforms to the words of Empedocles, who posits transanimation even into plants. (760)

8>5. From that saying of Zoroaster, *Ha! ha! The Earth weeps for them continuously to her sons*, following the exposition of Hosea the Chaldean, we have the express truth concerning original sin.

8>6. The sayings of the Chaldean interpreters over the eleventh aphorism, concerning two kinds of drunkenness, of Bacchus and Silenus, are perfectly understood through the words of the Cabalists concerning two kinds of wines.

8>7. What the interpreters say about the fourteenth aphorism is perfectly understood by what the Cabalists say about the death of the kiss.

8>8. In the seventeenth aphorism the *magi* understand nothing by the three garments of linen, cloth, and skins but the three habitations of the soul, celestial, spiritual, and terrestrial.

8>6. For the sense of this thesis, cf. 11>17. "two kinds of drunkenness"/"two kinds of wines" = symbols of higher and lower modes of love, will, or mystical frenzy. In the series on mystical happiness or beatitude starting at 2.12. As also seen in other late-medieval texts (cf., e.g., Kibre 1936: 179), there is an interesting conflation in Pico's Latin here and in the next few theses (cf. also 10>1, 11>57) of the words "aphorism" and "amphora," a vessel or pitcher; see further my note to thesis 11>57.

8>7. "death of the kiss" = see the *Commento* (Garin, *Scritti vari*, 558), where we find that among the Cabalists "*binsica*, namely, the 'death of the kiss,' occurs when the soul in its intellectual rapture is united so closely to separated things that, elevated from the body, it abandons it totally." Cf. 11>11, 11>13.

8>8. "garments" = see 28.35 and note. "celestial"/"spiritual" [or possibly "aerial"]/"terrestrial" = references to the natural habitats of celestial, demonic, and human souls.

8>9. Poteris ex praecedenti conclusione aliquid intelligere de pelliceis tunicis quas sibi fecit Adam, et de pellibus quae erant in Tabernaculo.

8>10. Per canem nihil aliud intelligit Zoroaster_quam partem inrationalem animae et proportionalia, quod ita esse uidebit qui diligenter dicta omnia expositorum considerauerit, qui et ipsi, sicut et Zoroaster, enigmatice loquuntur.

8>11. Dictum illud Zoroastris, ne exeas cum transit Lictor < >, / perfecte intelligetur per illud Exodi, quando sunt prohibiti Israhelite exire domos suas in transitu angeli interficientis primogenita aegyptiorum. <28r/28v>

8>12. Per Syrenam apud Zoroastrem nihil aliud intelligas quam partem animae rationalem.

8>13. Per puerum apud interpretes nihil aliud intellige quam intellectum.

8>11. 1486 ne ex eas | 1486 trasit | 1487 *omits* blank space

8>12. 1486 intrlligas

8>9. Cf. Gen. 3:21, Exod. 36:8ff., which were heavily glossed in the Middle Ages. The skins (Exod. 36:19) made up part of the veil in the tabernacle and were red rams' skins—for Pico, as we find in his Cabalistic theses, a symbol of Christ. In Christian mythology, the veil was torn asunder on Christ's death; the "skins" here are hence symbols of the Fall and Redemption. Cf. 11>22, 11>24, and 11>38 from Pico's second set of Cabalistic theses.

8>10. Cf. 8>12–13.

8>9. You can understand something from the preceding conclusion about the skin tunics that Adam made for himself and about the skins that were in the tabernacle. (765)

8>10. By the dog, Zoroaster simply means the irrational part of the soul and corresponding things, which anyone will see is true who carefully considers all the sayings of the commentators, who themselves, just like Zoroaster, speak enigmatically.

8>11. That saying of Zoroaster, *Do not go out when the attendant <   > passes*, is perfectly understood through that saying in Exodus, when the Israelites were forbidden to leave their homes while the angel passed, killing the first born of the Egyptians.

8>12. By the Siren in Zoroaster understand nothing but the rational part of the soul.

8>13. By the boy in the interpreters understand nothing but the intellect.

8>11. Cf. Exod. 12:1ff. A space exists here in the *editio princeps*—it is omitted in all later editions—which was apparently left for insertion of an Aramaic word (see Plate 5). It is not likely that the space arose from sloppy typesetting, since no similar end-of-page breaks exist anywhere else in the 1486 edition. Assuming that this space was left intentionally, as seems to be the case, we have *prima facie* evidence that Pico *did* have some kind of Aramaic text in hand when he compiled this section—for reasons discussed earlier, most likely a forgery by Mithridates.

8>12–13. Cf. 8>10. Designation of the intellectual nature as the "first born," "child," "boy," "son of God," etc., was a commonplace in the esoteric traditions of late antiquity. Cf., e.g., 11>10.

8>14. Per dictum illud Zoroastris, adhuc tres dies sacrificabitis et non ultra, apparuit mihi per arithmeticam superioris merchiaue illos computandi dies, esse in eo dicto expresse praedictum aduentum Christi.

8>15. Quid sit intelligendum per capras apud Zoroastrem intelliget qui legerit in libro Bair quae sit affinitas capris et quae agnis cum spiritibus.

8>14. "superior *merkabah* (chariot)" = the speculative part of the Cabala that concerns "divine" things; cf. 28.22 and note, 11>2. Wirszubski (1989: 193–94) provides a conjectural reading: Since "days" in the Kabbalah symbolize particular *sefirot* (cf. 28.6, 26.8, etc.), if we assume that Pico began counting at the first *sefirah* and moved downwards, the third day would be *Binah*, which medieval kabbalists sometimes referred to as the "son of God." For Pico, however, *Binah* (as well as the phrase "son of God" in non-Christian traditions) symbolized the intellectual nature (see previous thesis and note, also 11>10); nor is it clear that counting *sefirot* is what Pico had in mind by the "arithmetic of the superior *merkabah*," which could have involved a number of other Cabalistic techniques.

8>14. Through that saying of Zoroaster, *For three days still you will sacrifice and no more*, it became clear to me, computing those days through the arithmetic of the superior *merkabah*, that in that saying the coming of Christ is expressly predicted. (770)

8>15. What should be understood by she-goats in Zoroaster anyone will understand who reads in the book *Bahir* what the affinity is of she-goats and what of lambs with spirits.

8>15. Scholem (1954: 167) noted that the passages referred to here are not found in the *Bahir* itself but in a collection of fragments attached in one family of manuscripts to the end of that text. Scholem remarks that Flavius Mithridates began his translation of these fragments on the same line that he ended his version of the *Bahir* (in Cod. Vatic. 191), possibly leading to Pico's confusion concerning their source. Scholem's conjecture is a reasonable one; however, it is not known whether Mithridates' translation of that text was finished before Pico published his theses, leaving it uncertain whether the confusion was Pico's or his tutor's; on dating Mithridates' translations, see my introductory note to theses 28.1–47.

CONCLVSIONES MAGICAE NVMERO .XXVI. SECVNDVM OPINIONEM PROPRIAM.

9>1. Tota Magia quae in usu est apud modernos, et quam merito exterminat ecclesia,_ nullam habet firmitatem, nullum fundamentum, nullam ueritatem, quia pendet ex manu hostium primae ueritatis, potestatum harum tenebrarum, quae tenebras falsitatis male dispositis intellectibus obfundunt.

9>2. Magia naturalis licita est et non prohibita, et de huius scientiae uniuersalibus theoricis fundamentis pono infrascriptas conclusiones secundum propriam opinionem.

9>3. Magia est pars practica scientiae naturalis.

9>4. Ex ista conclusione_et conclusione paradoxa dogmatizante .xlvii. sequitur quod magia sit nobilissima pars scientiae naturalis.

TWENTY-SIX MAGICAL CONCLUSIONS. On Pico's magic, see above, pp. 115–32. To develop a full understanding of that magic, a number of theses outside this section—especially, but not exclusively, in Pico's conclusions from Proclus (24.1–55) and the Cabala (28.1–47) in the first part of his work and in sections 5>, 8>, 10>, and 11> given "according to his own opinion"—must be integrated with the evidence found here.

TWENTY-SIX MAGICAL CONCLUSIONS ACCORDING TO MY OWN OPINION.

9>1. All magic that is in use among the moderns, and which the church justly exterminates, has no firmness, no foundation, no truth, because it is depends on the enemies of the first truth, *those powers of darkness*, which pour the darkness of falsehood over poorly disposed intellects.

9>2. Natural magic is permitted and not prohibited, and concerning the universal theoretical foundations of this science I propose the following conclusions according to my own opinion.

9>3. Magic is the practical part of natural science.

9>4. From that conclusion and the forty-seventh paradoxical dogmatizing conclusion, it follows that magic is the noblest part of natural science. (775)

9>1–2. "*those powers of darkness*" (Col. 1:13) = cf. 22.9–10. Medieval magical treatises regularly began by protesting that their magic was of the natural and not demonic variety.

9>3–4. Discussed above, pp. 130–31. The reference in 9>4 is actually to the forty-sixth "paradoxical dogmatizing conclusion," suggesting that one thesis was dropped from that section at a late date; see my introductory note to theses 6>1–10. The claim in these theses is that it is our obligation to operate magic in the world.

9>5. Nulla est uirtus in caelo_aut in terra seminaliter et separata quam et actuare et unire magus non possit.

9>6. Quodcunque fiat opus mirabile, siue sit magicum, siue cabalisticum, siue cuiuscunque alterius generis, principalissime referendum est in deum gloriosum et benedictum, cuius gratia supercaelestes mirabilium uirtutum aquas super contemplatiuos homines bonae uoluntatis quotidie pluit liberaliter. <28v/29r>

9>7. Non potuerunt opera Christi uel per uiam magiae uel per uiam cabalae fieri.

9>8. Miracula Christi non ratione rei factae, sed ratione modi faciendi, suae diuinitatis argumentum certissimum sunt.

9>9. Nulla est scientia quae nos magis certificet de diuinitate Christi_quam magia et cabala.

9>5. Cf. 9>11. "Heaven" (*caelum*) throughout Pico's magical theses refers to the celestial or astronomical realm and not to heaven in the religious sense.

9>5. No power exists in heaven or earth seminally and separated that the magician cannot actuate and unite.

9>6. Whatever miraculous work is performed, whether it is magical or Cabalistic or of any other kind, should be attributed principally to God the glorious and blessed, whose grace daily pours supercelestial waters of miraculous power liberally over contemplative men of good will.

9>7. The works of Christ could not have been performed through either the way of magic or the way of Cabala.

9>8. The miracles of Christ are the most certain argument of his divinity, not because of the things that he did, but because of the way in which he did them.

9>9. There is no science that assures us more of the divinity of Christ than magic and Cabala. (780)

9>6. This thesis and 9>12 and 9>20, etc., suggest that for Pico operations in imitative magic, or at least a major part of it, did not work mechanically but depended on the mediation of the purified soul.

9>7–9. Discussed above, pp. 126–28.

9>10. Quod magus homo facit per artem, fecit natura naturaliter faciendo hominem.

9>11. Mirabilia artis magicae non sunt nisi per unionem et actuationem eorum quae seminaliter et separate sunt in natura.

9>12. Forma totius magicae uirtutis est ab anima hominis stante, et non cadente.

9>13. Magicam operari non est aliud quam maritare mundum.

9>14. Siqua est natura immediata nobis quae sit uel simpliciter_uel saltem ut multum rationaliter rationalis, magicam habet in summo, et eius participatione potest in hominibus esse perfectior.

9>15. Nulla potest esse operatio magica alicuius efficaciae nisi annexum habeat opus cabalae, explicitum uel implicitum.

9>10–14. Discussed above, pp. 131–32. Cf. theses 5>45, 5>50. The point here is that the purified soul of the magician can gather up all the rational forces distributed in the celestial and terrestrial worlds (cf. 8>3, 10>3) and elevate them: *homo magus* functions as a cosmic priest. In 9>14 we find that magic involves "rational" natures; in 11>12 we find that "pure Cabala" (there are also inferior varieties) involves the "intellectual part" of the rational soul.

9>10. What man the *magus* makes through art, nature made naturally making man.

9>11. The miracles of the magical art exist only through the union and actuation of those things that exist seminally and separated in nature.

9>12. The form of all magical power comes from the soul of man standing, and not falling.

9>13. To operate magic is nothing other than to marry the world.

9>14. If there is any nature immediate to us that is either simply rational, or at least exists for the most part rationally, it has magic in its summit, and through its participation in men can be more perfect. (785)

9>15. No magical operation can be of any efficacy unless it has annexed to it a work of Cabala, explicit or implicit.

9>15. Given the fact that Pico distinguished a number of different types of magic and of Cabala (see above, pp. 126–28), it is not possible to know for certain his meaning here. In general, I take it that Pico's primary sense is that since the rational part of the soul (which is pertinent to "natural magic") derives from the intellectual part of the soul (which is pertinent to "pure Cabala"), Cabala is implicit in any magical act. Pico's view that certain parts of Cabala drew on powers higher than those of natural magic is also affirmed in the next three theses. For still another link between *magia* and Cabala, see 9>25.

9>16. Illa natura quae est orizon temporis aeternalis est proxima mago, sed infra eum.

9>17. Illius naturae quae est orizon temporis et aeternitatis propria est magia, inde est petenda per modos debitos, notos sapientibus.

9>18. Illius natura quae est orizon aeternitatis temporalis est mago proxima, sed super eum, et ei propria est cabala.

9>19. Ideo uoces et uerba in magico opere efficaciam habent, quia illud in quo primum magicam exercet natura, uox est dei.

9>20. Quaelibet uox uirtutem habet in magia, inquantum dei uoce formatur.

9>21. Non significatiuae uoces plus possunt in magia quam significatiue; et rationem conclusionis intelligere potest qui est profundus ex praecedenti conclusione.

9>22. Nulla nomina ut significatiua, et inquantum nomina sunt singula et per se sumpta, in magico opere uirtutem habere possunt, nisi sint hebraica, uel inde proxime deriuata.

9>17. 1487 per modos debitos notus

9>22. 1486 significativa.& inquantum

9>16–18. "horizon of eternal time"/"horizon of time and eternity"/"horizon of temporal eternity" = apparent references, respectively, to the realms of corporeal, rational, and intellectual natures. (Wirszubski's view [1989: 194] that all three refer to the same durational state is clearly mistaken.) For Pico's association between magic and the rational part of the soul—the "proper" nature of man—see 9>14. For his association of "pure Cabala" with the intellectual part of the soul, see 11>12. Other theses on duration are listed in note 2.18.

9>19–20. The obvious association is between word magic and God's creation of the world through speech in Gen. 1:1ff.—according to the kabbalists, mediated by the powers of the divine names and Hebrew alphabet.

9>16. That nature that is the horizon of eternal time is next to the *magus*, but below him.

9>17. Magic is proper to the nature of that which is the horizon of time and eternity, from whence it should be sought through due modes known to the wise.

9>18. The nature of that which is the horizon of temporal eternity is next to the *magus*, but above him, and proper to it is the Cabala.

9>19. Voices and words have efficacy in a magical work, because in that work in which nature first exercises magic, the voice is God's. (790)

9>20. Every voice has power in magic insofar as it is shaped by the voice of God.

9>21. Voices that mean nothing are more powerful in magic than voices that mean something. And anyone who is profound can understand the reason for this conclusion from the preceding conclusion.

9>22. No names that mean something, insofar as those names are singular and taken per se, can have power in a magical work, unless they are Hebrew names, or closely derived from Hebrew.

9>21. Cf. Iamblichus *De mysteriis* 7.4–5. Tied to Pico's view that language can only adequately describe the inferior world.

9>22. Again drawn from *De mysteriis* 7.4, with Pico replacing barbarian languages, and in particular Egyptian, as Iamblichus had it, with Hebrew! On the magic in Hebrew, see the theses listed in note 28.33. By names "closely derived" from Hebrew, Pico presumably had "Chaldean" names in mind, although in his theses from the *Orphic Hymns* he also implies that magic lay hidden in Greek.

9>23. Quilibet numerus praeter ternarium et denarium sunt materiales / in magia; isti formales sunt, et in magica arithmetica sunt numeri numerorum. <29r/29v>

9>24. Ex secretioris philosophiae principiis necesse est confiteri plus posse caracteres et figuras in opere Magico, quam possit quaecunque qualitas materialis.

9>25. Sicut caracteres sunt proprii operi magico, ita numeri sunt proprii operi cabalae, medio existente inter utrosque et appropriabili per declinationem ad extrema usu litterarum.

9>26. Sicut per primi agentis influxum, si sit specialis et immediatus, fit aliquid quod non attingitur per mediationem causarum, ita per opus cabale, si sit pura cabala et immediata, fit aliquid ad quod nulla magia attingit.

9>23. "ternarius"/"denarius" = the most sacred numbers in the Christian and Pythagorean traditions respectively. "material"/"formal" numbers = see note 7>9. In the *Apology* (*Opera*, 172), we find that 3 and 10 are "more formal" than others since 3 is the "first odd number," and "the first in each genus is the most perfect in that genus" (the latter concept appears to have been a scholastic commonplace and was not an innovation of Ficino's, as P. O. Kristeller [1943] argued); and 10 is "every number," since beyond it we count "by repetition." From Pico's discussion in the *Apology*, it seems likely that the magical arithmetic found here is simply the *via numerorum* of theses 7>1ff.—that is, magic used for contemplative or prophetic ends.

9>24. In the *Apology* (*Opera*, 172, 175), Pico tells us that "characters" and "figures" refer to words and numbers (not to figures on astrological talismans, as Yates [1964: 88] argued; cf. also opening note to theses 11>1–72). We also find that the "more secret philosophy" refers to Pythagorean mathematics, as is also suggested in the previous thesis. Pico's association of Pythagorean "formal numbers" with the creative powers of the intellectual nature—making them superior to the "material qualities" of Aristotelian physics—is further suggested in 3>25–26. Thomas Aquinas and the authors of the infamous *Malleus Maleficarum*, which was published shortly before Pico's text, explicitly associated magic using "characters" and "figures" with demonic magic, as Pico was surely aware. I suspect that no matter how innocent his underlying meaning, Pico intentionally chose his language for its provocative effect.

9>23. Every number besides the ternarius and denarius [3 and 10] are material numbers in magic. Those are formal numbers, and in magical arithmetic are the numbers of numbers.

9>24. Out of the principles of the more secret philosophy it is necessary to acknowledge that characters and figures are more powerful in a magical work than any material quality. (795)

9>25. Just as characters are proper to a magical work, so numbers are proper to a work of Cabala, with a medium existing between the two, appropriable by declination between the extremes through the use of letters.

9>26. Just as through the influence of the first agent, if that influence is individual and immediate, something is achieved that is not attained through the mediation of causes, so through a work of Cabala, if it is the pure and immediate Cabala, something is achieved to which no magic attains.

9>25. Here again characters = magical words in general, not words on astrological talismans, as Yates argued. Pico's point is simply that magical words can be translated into numbers, and numbers into magical words, apparently through the word/number equations of *gematria*. As in the previous two theses, the "works" Pico has in mind here are evidently those of contemplative or prophetic magic.

9>26. "pure Cabala" = Cabala involving the intellectual part of the soul, as opposed to "natural magic," which uses the rational part of the soul. Cf. 11>12, 9>16–18 and note. There is also apparently an implied contrast here with the inferior astrological forms of Cabalistic magic discussed in the *Apology*. On these, see above, pp. 126–28.

CONCLVSIONES NVMERO .XXXI. SECVNDVM PROPRIAM OPINIONEM DE MODO INTELLIGENDI HYMNOS ORPHEI SECVNDVM MAGIAM, ID EST, SECRETAM DIVINARVM RERVM NATVRALIVMQVE SAPIENTIAM A ME PRIMVM IN EIS REPERTAM.

10>1. Sicut secretam magiam a nobis primum ex Orphei hymnis elicitam fas non est in publicum explicare, ita nutu quodam, ut in infrascriptis fiet conclusionibus, eam per amphorismorum capita demonstrasse, utile erit ad excitandas contemplatiuorum mentes.

10>2. Nihil efficacius hymnis Orphei in naturali magia, si debita musica, animi intentio, et caeterae circumstantiae quas norunt sapientes, fuerint adhibitae.

10>3. Nomina deorum quos Orpheus canit non decipientium demonum, a quibus malum et non bonum prouenit. Sed naturalium uirtutum diuinarumque sunt nomina, a uero deo in utilitatem maxime hominis, si eis uti sciuerit, mundo distributarum.

Section title. 1486 REPERTAM:.

CONCLUSIONS ON THE ORPHIC HYMNS. On the Orphic tradition in the Renaissance, see Walker (1972). For the *Orphic Hymns*, see Quandt, ed. (1955). Pico interpreted the *Hymns* in part through the further Orphic fragments embedded in Proclus and similar figures, collected today in *Orphicorum Fragmenta*, ed. Kern (1922). His interpretations were also conditioned by his understanding of the Kabbalah and by his own cosmological and magical systems. Few sections of the nine hundred theses illustrate better than this one the complexity of Pico's symbolism. Pico here was apparently using the Greek text of the *Hymns* found in his library (Kibre 1936: 148); his translations of the names of a number of gods, in any case, are not the same as those found in the translation of the *Hymns* and commentary in MS Laur. Lat. Plut. 36, cod. 35, which have been attributed to Ficino.

The Magic in the Orphic Hymns

THIRTY-ONE CONCLUSIONS ACCORDING TO MY OWN OPINION ON UNDERSTANDING THE ORPHIC HYMNS ACCORDING TO MAGIC, THAT IS, THE SECRET WISDOM OF DIVINE AND NATURAL THINGS FIRST DISCOVERED IN THEM BY ME.

10>1. Since it is not permitted to explain in public the secret magic first drawn out by me from the Orphic hymns, so to have demonstrated it with certain aphoristic hints, as is done in the following conclusions, will be useful to excite the minds of contemplatives.

10>2. Nothing is more effective in natural magic than the Orphic hymns, if there is added the due music, intention of the soul, and other circumstances known to the wise.

10>3. The names of the gods that Orpheus sings are not the names of deceiving demons, from whom evil and not good comes, but of natural and divine powers, distributed in the world by the true God for the great utility of man—if he knows how to use them. (800)

10>1. Pico's stress on his originality here was again aimed at Ficino, who years earlier had composed his own commentary on the *Hymns* (see previous note). On Pico's esoteric use of the word "aphorism," see note to 8>6, 11>57.

10>2. Walker (1975: 22ff.), who like Yates confused Pico's natural magic with Ficino's, assumed that this thesis referred to the music used by Ficino to draw down celestial powers, discussed in Ficino's later *De vita coelitus comparanda*. However, there is no reason to assume that celestial magic is what Pico had in mind here. The thesis can equally apply to prophetic or mystical exegesis (cf. 10>7, etc.) or to control of noncelestial "powers" scattered in the world (cf. 10>3, etc.).

10>3. That is, the gods are symbols of whatever material or spiritual "powers" lay hidden in the sublunary, celestial, and (probably) angelic worlds. On divine and demonic powers in nature, cf. also 8>3, 9>1–2, and associated notes.

10>4. Sicut hymni Dauid operi Cabalae mirabiliter deseruiunt, ita hymni Orphei operi uerae, licitae, et naturalis magiae.

10>5. Tantus est numerus hymnorum Orphei, quantus est numerus cum quo deus triplex creauit saeculum, sub quaternarii pythagorici forma numeratus. <29v/30r>

10>6. Quarumcunque uirtutum naturalium uel diuinarum eadem est proprietatis analogia, idem etiam nomen, idem hymnus, idem opus, seruata proportione. Et qui tentauerit exponere uidebit correspondentiam.

10>7. Qui nescierit perfecte sensibiles proprietates per uiam secretae analogiae intellectualizare, nihil ex hymnis Orphei sanum intelliget.

10>5. 1486 qnaternarii

10>4. "hymns of David" = the Psalms. Discussion of the magic in the Psalms normally revolved around 1 Sam. 16:14–23, where we find David using music to cure Saul of demonic possession. On the healing powers of music, see also 7>7–8. In the *Apology* (*Opera*, 172), Pico cites St. Hilary's view (fourth century CE) that the traditional numbering of the Psalms reflected their magical "power and efficacy." It would be interesting to know how much of this idea survived in the original version of Pico's *Commentary on the Psalms*, which was suppressed by his Savonarolan editors and which today only survives in fragmentary form. See above, pp. 165–70.

10>5. Most Renaissance manuscripts included eight-six Orphic hymns; how many Pico recognized is anyone's guess. The "Pythagorean quaternarius" = the first four natural numbers, the numerical correspondents of the point, line, plane, and solid—the four building blocks of the Pythagorean world. The sum of these numbers (1 + 2 + 3 + 4 = 10) adds up to the denarius or "decad," whose symbolism permeates Pico's thought (cf., e.g., 11>56 and note). By the "method of the Pythagorean quaternarius," Pico presumably had in mind the addition of some

10>4. Just as the hymns of David miraculously serve a work of the Cabala, so the hymns of Orpheus serve a work of the true, permitted, and natural magic.

10>5. The number of Orphic hymns is the same as the number with which the threefold god created the world, calculated according to the method of the Pythagorean quaternarius.

10>6. For each natural or divine power the analogy of properties is the same, the name is the same, the hymn the same, the work the same, with proportion observed. And whoever tries to explain this will see the correspondence.

10>7. Anyone who does not know how to intellectualize sensible properties perfectly through the method of secret analogizing understands nothing sound from the Orphic hymns.

---

series of numbers in a similar way. Unfortunately, what these numbers were, as well as what Pico meant by "the number with which the threefold god created the world," are unknown; clues here may be found in theses 25.1ff. and 5>1, however. Wirszubski (1989: 197) identifies Orpheus's *deus triplex* or "threefold god" with the Christian Trinity and attempts an involved reading of this thesis using *gematria* and various kabbalistic names of God. Cf. Copenhaver (1997: 229), who repeats Wirszubski's calculations. In 10>3, however, Pico tells us that Orpheus's gods represent "natural and divine powers, distributed in the world by the true God," suggesting that *deus triplex* here does not refer to the Christian Trinity or to kabbalistic names but to some triadic emanational principle in the world; cf. the many other trinities of gods symbolizing such principles in Pico's theses, e.g., concerning Jove in 24.23, 24.26, 10>27. In 5>1, moreover, Pico explicitly associates numerical limits in creation with such an emanational triad. Readings like this illustrate the dangers of approaching Pico's work exclusively through a single tradition; indeed, no evidence suggests that thesis 10>5, which Wirszubski labels the "most Kabbalistic of all Orphic theses," involves Cabala in any way.

10>6–7. *Re* Pico's extreme correlative system.

10>8. Qui profunde et intellectualiter diuisionem unitatis uenereae in trinitatem gratiarum, et unitatis fatalis in trinitatem parcarum, et unitatis Saturniae in trinitatem Iouis, Neptunni, et Plutonis, intellexerit, uidebit modum debite procedendi in orphica theologia.

10>9. Idem sunt curetes apud Orpheum, et potestates apud Dionysium.

10>10. Qui praecedentis conclusionis opus attentauerit, adhibeat opus cabalae secundum appropriata timori Isaac.

10>11. Frustra Palemonem et Leucotheam adibit, qui Nereum non attraxerit, nec Nereum attrahet qui circa primariam animalem trinitatem operatus non fuerit.

10>12. Per octonarium numerum hymnorum maritimorum corporalis naturae nobis proprietas designatur.

10>11. 1487 palimonem

10>8. "method of duly proceeding in Orphic theology" = split monads or "unities" into trinities and then correlate them, as we find in the previous two theses. Cf. 24.1–55 from Proclus, 25.1–14 from Pythagoras, etc. Combining Pico's suggestions in the *Commento* (Garin, *Scritti vari*, 508–17) and *Heptaplus* 1.3 (*Opera*, 14; Garin, *Scritti vari*, 214): "Venus"/"trinity of Graces" = the beauty of the intellectual nature and its correspondents on lower levels of reality; "Fate"/ "trinity of Parcae" = the unity of divine providence and three modes of fate in the lower world; "Saturn"/"trinity of Jove, Neptune, and Pluto" = the intellectual nature and its division into the world soul and sublunary and subterranean realms.

10>9. "guardians" = an order of gods in the *Orphic Hymns*; "powers" = sixth of the nine angelic orders in Pseudo-Dionysius's *Celestial Hierarchies*. Cf. 5>13 and the following thesis and note. Pico would have presumably further correlated these with Proclus's "trinity of guardians" in 24.13–14, etc.

10>8. Anyone who profoundly and intellectually understands the division of the unity of Venus into the trinity of Graces, and of the unity of Fate into the trinity of Parcae, and of the unity of Saturn into the trinity of Jove, Neptune, and Pluto, will perceive the method of duly proceeding in Orphic theology. (805)

10>9. Guardians in Orpheus and powers in Dionysius are the same.

10>10. Anyone who attempts the work of the preceding conclusion should add a work of Cabala according to those things ascribed to the fear of Isaac.

10>11. Anyone who does not attract Nereus approaches Palaemon and Leucothea in vain, nor will anyone attract Nereus who has not operated around the primary animate trinity.

10>12. Through the eight maritime hymns the property of corporeal nature is represented to us.

10>10. "fear of Isaac" (Gen. 31:42) = standard kabbalistic symbol of the fifth *sefirah*, one of whose alternate names was *Gevurah* or "power." Combining this with the previous thesis, we find that "guardians" in Orpheus, "powers" in Dionysius, and *Gevurah* in the Kabbalah are the same. It is not clear what "the work of the preceding conclusion" refers to in 10>10. Was mystical exegesis the only thing at stake here? Since the fifth *sefirah* is also associated with magic in 28.40 and 11>47 (see notes), it appears as if Pico believed that these powers could be called down in some fashion. This was very dangerous material to be debating at Rome.

10>11–12. Palaemon/Leucothea/Nereus = sea gods of progressively increasing power, apparently (as suggested in 10>12) to be correlated with three levels of corporeal nature. In *Heptaplus* 1.3 (*Opera,* 13–14; Garin, *Scritti vari,* 213–15), we again find corporeal nature divided triply: into a region of "pure" and "unmixed" elements extending from the highest part of the air to the realm of fire (presumably Nereus in 10>11); an intermediate region associated with the middle of the air (presumably Leucothea); and a region of the "mixed" elements made from the dregs of terrestrial matter (presumably Palaemon). Cf. the three similar levels Pico proposes in 24.27–29 from Proclus, which are ruled by the trinity of "leaders" or "supermundane gods" (presumably correlated with the "first animate trinity" in 10>11). The magical functions of the supermundane gods are further suggested in 24.21ff. However we read these particular symbols, the point is clear that magical operations on each lower level of reality depend on the forces flowing from higher ones. Cf. here also 9>6, 9>15, 10>10, etc.

10>13. Idem est Typhon apud Orpheum, et Zamael in Cabala.

10>14. Siquis in opere precedentis conclusionis intellectualiter operabitur, per meridiem ligabit septentrionem; si uero mundialiter per totum operabitur, iudicium sibi operabitur.

10>15. Idem est nox apud Orpheum et ensoph in Cabala.

10>16. Ex praecedenti conclusione potest quis rectius exponere quam exponat Proclus quid sibi uelit illud dictum theologi inducentis opificem mundi noctem consulentem de opificio mundano.

10>17. Ex eisdem dictis potest intelligi cur in Symposio a Diotima Porus consilii filius, et Iesus in sacris litteris angelus magni consilii, nominetur.

10>18. Anima aquea, ut inferiora generat, superiora contemplatur in seipsa se sistit, triplici hymno maris, Neptunni, et oceani ab orpheo decantatur.

10>19. Nihil habebit firmum in opere qui vestam non attraxerit. <30r/30v>

10>17. 1486 nominetur:

10>13. Typhon = hundred-headed monster who rebelled against Zeus. Samael = Satan; cf. Scholem (1974: 385–88).

10>14. "north"/"judgment" = common symbol/alternate name of the fifth kabbalistic *sefirah*, *Din*, associated alternately with the origins of evil in the divine nature (cf. Scholem 1941: 237) or with God's stern judgment. "south" here = apparent symbol of the fourth *sefirah*, *Hesed* ("love" or "piety" in Pico). The sense of this thesis is clarified in 11>12–13, where we find suggestions that this magic involved meditative states.

10>15–16. "*Ein-Sof*" = God's transcendent nature in the Kabbalah, source of his manifested nature in the *sefirot*. Cf. 11>4, 11>35–36 and note. In his commentary on the *Timaeus*, Proclus places "night" below the pinnacle of his "intelligible trinity," presumably explaining Pico's disagreement with him here.

10>13. Typhon in Orpheus and Samael in the Cabala are the same. (810)

10>14. If anyone in the work of the preceding conclusion operates intellectually, he will bind the north through the south. But if he operates wholly in a worldly way, he will bring judgment upon himself.

10>15. Night in Orpheus and *Ein-Sof* in the Cabala are the same.

10>16. From the preceding conclusion one can explain more correctly than Proclus what that saying of the theologian means representing the demiurge of the world consulting night on the creation of the world.

10>17. From the same words one can know why in the *Symposium* Porus is named the son of counsel by Diotima, and Jesus in Sacred Scriptures is named the angel of great counsel.

10>18. As it generates inferior things, the aquatic soul contemplates the superior things present in itself, as sung by Orpheus in the three hymns to sea, Neptune, and ocean. (815)

10>19. Anyone who does not attract Vesta will possess nothing firm in his work.

10>17. On Porus ("plenty" in thesis 5>21) as "son of counsel," see *Symposium* 203b. Pico discusses this question again in the *Commento*, in Garin, *Scritti vari*, 513ff. Wind (1965; cf. 1968) provides long interpretations of this thesis, although not in the context of Pico's Roman plans.

10>18. The "aquatic soul" = the world soul, which "informs" the lower world with the reflections of ideas it receives from the intellectual nature or angelic mind. The *Commento* (Garin, *Scritti vari*, 510–11) also correlates the intellectual or angelic realm with ocean, Neptune, and the seas. For the style of this thesis, cf. 24.39ff. from Proclus, which involve similar emanational principles.

10>19. Drawn from Proclus *Theologia Platonica* 6 (here I used Taylor, trans. 2:73ff.). Vesta = symbol of the principle of unity and stability found on different levels of reality.

10>20. Per septennarium hymnorum paternae menti attributorum, Protogoni, Palladis, Saturni, Veneris, Rheae, Legis, Bacchi, potest intelligens et profundus contemplator de saeculi consumatione aliquid coniectare.

10>21. Opus praecedentium hymnorum nullum est sine opere Cabale, cuius est proprium practicare omnem quantitatem formalem, continuam et discretam.

10>22. Qui heroas in duplices non diuiserit, natiuos et aduentitios, saepe errabit.

10>23. Qui Apollinem adibit, mediabit opus per Bacchum triethericum, et consumabit per nomen ineffabile.

10>24. Non inebriabitur per aliquem Bacchum, qui suae musae prius copulatus non fuerit.

10>20. 1486 Veneris | 1487 generis

10>22. 1487 et ad ventiticos

10>23. 1486 adibit.mediabit

10>20–21. Discussed above, p. 129. Pico obviously intended to correlate the properties of each of these gods with one of his seven historical ages, ending in an age of mystic frenzy (the age of "Bacchus"). Thus "Protogonos" in Greek = "first born," etc. There are many methods of numerological prophecy in the Kabbalah, a number of which Pico planned to demonstrate in theses 7a>1–74; the exact methods that he had in mind here are unknown. For other theses involving the calculation of the date of the end of the world, see 7a>38 (to be answered through the "way of numbers") and 11>9. Wirszubski (1989: 141ff.) ignores the obvious links between 10>21 and the preceding thesis and conjectures that the phrase *quantitas formalis continua et discreta* (formal quantity, continuous and discrete) in 10>21 might be a symbol of one of the *sefirot*—illustrating the dangers of reading Pico's theses in isolation.

10>22. "heroes" in the Neo-Platonic tradition = a lower order of demons just below rational souls. Cf. 24.36–37 note. Cf. also 22.9–10.

10>20. Through the seven hymns attributed to the paternal mind—to Protogonos, Pallas, Saturn, Venus, Rhea, Law, and Bacchus—a knowledgeable and profound contemplator can predict something about the end of the world.

10>21. The work of the preceding hymns is nothing without a work of Cabala, whose property it is to practice every formal quantity, continuous and discrete.

10>22. Anyone who does not divide heroes into two, native and foreign, will often err.

10>23. Anyone who approaches Apollo will mediate a work through triennial Bacchus, and will complete it through the ineffable name. (820)

10>24. No one will be made drunk by any Bacchus, who has not first copulated with his muse.

10>23. In the series on mystical happiness or beatitude listed in 2.12 note. The most probable reading: "Apollo" here = God himself (cf. *Oratio*, in *Opera* 320; Garin, *Scritti vari*, 124); "triennial Bacchus" = the most elevated form of mystical frenzy, love, etc. (cf. 8>6, 11>17); "ineffable name" = YHVH, the divine name associated in the Kabbalah with the sixth *sefirah*, the archetypal "great Adam" or "great man" that unites all the rest (cf. 28.10 and note, 7a>67). Interpreted tentatively: The mystic approaches God through love, but his journey is only completed when he "takes himself up into the center of his unity" and is fully absorbed into God's absolute unity (*Oration*, in *Opera*, 315; Garin, *Scritti vari*, 106). Cf. 3>43 and my discussion on Pico's mystic thought on pp. 39ff., 105–14. A specifically Christian reading of the thesis follows when we recall that in other theses Pico correlated both the "ineffable name" and "great Adam" with Christ.

10>24. Series starts at 2.12. The "Bacchae" in general in the theses = different modes of will, divine frenzy, love, etc. Cf., besides the preceding thesis, 8>6, 11>17. The thesis expresses in symbolic language Pico's view that in the lower realms of reality acts of will require the direction of some cognitive power. On the intellectualist symbolism of the "muses" in the nine hundred theses, see the quotation from Pico above, p. 40.

10>25. Per quaternarium hymnorum primae formae mundanae attributorum, sui formabilis natura nobis designatur.

10>26. Qui perfecte in animam redierit, primae formae suam formam aequauerit.

10>27. Qui praecedentis conclusionis opus tentauerit, Iouem adibit tertium ut uiuentem, non ut uiuificantem.

10>28. Frustra adit naturam et protheum, qui pana non attraxerit.

10>29. Sicut post uniuersalem animationem est particularis animatio, ita post uniuersalem prouidentiam est particularis prouidentia.

10>30. Ex praecedenti conclusione sciri potest cur Ouidius, in execratione in Ibin, postquam inuocauit numen quod terram regit et aquam, terram inuocat et Neptunnum.

10>31. Qui annotauerit diligenter dicta ab aristotele in expositione definitionis de anima, uidebit cur Orpheus Palladi et Veneri uigilantiam attribuerit.

10>25. "first worldly form" = the world soul. Cf. the phrasing in 5>1, etc.

10>26. "first form" = the "total intellect," the highest level of reality attained by the mystic before the Sabbath of the soul (union with God). Cf. the phrasing in 7.3 from Averroes, 20.7 from Plotinus, etc.

10>27. "third Jove as living, not as vivifying" = cf. the phrasing in 24.24. The idea is that in its mystic state the soul reaches the "first form" (the total intellect) viewed transcendentally and not as it functions as the source of forms in the lower world. On the foundations of this distinction, cf., e.g., 3>19 and note.

10>28. Pan ("All" in Greek) = the intellectual nature (the "first form" in 10>26)? (cf. 5>52). "Proteus" = man? (cf. *Oration*, in *Opera*, 315; Garin, *Scritti vari*, 106). Athanasius Kircher interpreted Pan in this thesis as the "one" uniting the "many" in his *Oedipus Aegyptiacus* (1652–54: 2:428), one of the last major European works that owed anything to Pico's direct influence.

10>25. Through the four hymns attributed to the first worldly form, its formable nature is represented to us.

10>26. Whoever returns perfectly into the soul will equate his form with the first form.

10>27. Whoever attempts the work of the preceding conclusion approaches the third Jove as living, not as vivifying.

10>28. Whoever does not attract Pan approaches nature and Proteus in vain. (825)

10>29. Just as after universal animation there exists particular animation, so after universal providence there exists particular providence.

10>30. From the preceding conclusion it can be known why Ovid, in his *Curse against the Ibis*, after he has invoked the spirit that rules the earth and the water, invokes earth and Neptune.

10>31. Whoever carefully notes the words of Aristotle in his exposition of the definition of the soul will see why Orpheus attributes wakefulness to Pallas and Venus.

10>29–30. On different modes of providence, necessity, etc., see the theses listed in note 24.2. Neptune in the *Commento* (Garin, *Scritti vari*, 510) = the intellectual nature, although Pico sometimes used that symbol differently (cf. 10>8 and note). Ovid's poem against the Ibis can be found in his *Art of Love*; for the source of this thesis, see lines 67–71 in the Loeb edition.

10>31. Pallas/Venus = symbols here of intellect and will. In the series listed in note 2.12. The Aristotelian definition referred to in this thesis appears in *De anima* 2.1, where the soul is defined as the "act of the body." Further, there are "two kinds of act corresponding to knowledge and to reflecting . . . , and of these waking corresponds to reflecting, sleeping to knowledge possessed but not employed" (adapted from the revised Oxford translation). The hortatory intent of Aristotle's commentary here on Orpheus, as Pico saw it, is clear.

CONCLVSIONES CABALISTICAE NVMERO .LXXI. SECVNDVM OPINIONEM PROPRIAM, EX IPSIS HEBREORVM SAPIENTVM FVNDAMENTIS CHRISTIANAM RELIGIONEM MAXIME CONFIRMANTES.

Section title. 1486 FVNDANENTIS

CABALISTIC CONCLUSIONS CONFIRMING THE CHRISTIAN RELIGION. On my use of the terms "Kabbalah" and "Cabala," etc., see p. 11 n. 30. On Pico's sources, see the opening note to theses 28.1–47. Medieval texts throw far less light on these theses than on Pico's first set of Cabalistic conclusions, since his explicit aim here was to break from earlier traditions. Pico's plans for converting the Jews fit in nicely with the eschatological goals of his debate; on these, see pp. 39–46. The discrepancy in the number of theses in Pico's title and in his text suggests again that last minute revisions were made in the work.

Pico presumably meant to associate his final count of theses in this section with God's "name of seventy-two letters" (11>56)—a probability that has given rise to one of the most interesting claims ever made about any medieval or Renaissance text. In a recent paper, Brian Copenhaver (1997: 229ff.) argues that Pico may have intended these seventy-two theses (taken collectively and linked to God's secret name) as an "angelic amulet" meant to call down the angel Metatron (actually a symbol for Pico of the abstract intellectual nature; see 11>10 and note) and to repulse the evil demon Azazel (thesis 11>13). While nothing in Pico's text suggests such a spectacular reading, which derives from Copenhaver's interpretation of medieval kabbalism, we are told (p. 232) that Pico's silence may have simply reflected his esoteric concerns. Interesting as this speculation is, the evidence that amulets (or talismans) are nowhere mentioned in the nine hundred theses, the fact that Pico attacks their use in the *Heptaplus* (p. 119 n. 55 above), and the fact that the *Apology* angrily denounces those who "say they have the secret names of God and the powers by which they bind demons" (*Opera*, 181; cf. 175) argue strongly against this claim. In the *Apology* (*Opera*, 172–75), Pico tells us that his use of the terms "figures" and "characters" (which Professor Copenhaver, like Yates earlier, associates with sym-

Cabalistic Conclusions Confirming the Christian Religion

SEVENTY-ONE [SEVENTY-TWO] CABALISTIC CONCLUSIONS ACCORDING TO MY OWN OPINION, STRONGLY CONFIRMING THE CHRISTIAN RELIGION USING THE HEBREW WISEMEN'S OWN PRINCIPLES.

---

bols on amulets) refer to numbers read out symbolically and to ordinary words; it is conceivable that Pico is being deceptive, but the long list of examples that he gives us in the *Apology* perfectly matches what he says in his mathematical theses about the symbolic meanings of "formal numbers," which he identifies in that section (e.g., 7>9) with speculative prophecy and later labels "magical arithmetic" (9>23). The only theses that mention "characters" and "figures" in Pico's text also clearly suggest that they are not talismanic symbols but words and numbers translated back and forth via the word/number equations of *gematria* (see 9>24–25 and notes). When we look at Pico's only reference anywhere to God's "name of seventy-two letters" (theses 11>56–57), we find that name again linked to secrets revealed through word/number equations—associated with Pythagorean numerology and "formal arithmetic"—but not to anything remotely resembling talismanic magic. Finally, the claim that any part of Pico's text was intended as an "angelic amulet" to draw down the intellectual nature would conflict with Pico's religious views, which emphasized that philosophical studies were needed in any mystical ascent to that nature; this idea, in fact, lay at the center of the elaborate formal defense of philosophy that constitutes the main theme of Pico's famous *Oration* (above, pp. 33, 39ff.).

As we have seen earlier, the tendency to confuse Pico's thought with medieval kabbalism—usually with the most spectacular parts of that tradition—has distorted a great deal of Pico scholarship in the past five centuries. As we find in the following section, far from passively abandoning himself to medieval kabbalism, Pico radically transformed it by extensively correlating it with pagan and Christian ideas—finding in this syncretic fusion the ultimate Christian tool needed "to pierce the Jews with their own weapons" (see note 11>72).

11>1. Quicquid dicant caeteri Cabaliste, ego prima diuisione scientiam Cabalae in scientiam sephiroth et semot, tanquam in practicam / et speculatiuam, distinguerem. <30v/31r>

11>1. Since in medieval traditions "divine names" and "practical Kabbalah" were associated with magic, Scholem and Wirszubski (followed now by Copenhaver [1997: 217ff.])—reversing the natural order of Pico's thesis—tried to identify Pico's "science of *sefirot*" with speculative science and his "science of names" with practical science or magic. However, given Pico's disclaimer at the start of this thesis ("Whatever other Cabalists say . . ."), as well as the content of the theses that follow, no justification exists for inverting his sense: Practical science for Pico was the "science of *sefirot*" and speculative science the "science of names," and not the reverse. Indeed, a number of his theses explicitly associate practical or magical operations with the *sefirot* or emanated states of God (see, e.g., 28.40 and note). As so often in syncretic systems, however, such distinctions were not absolute: Since most of Pico's magic was not concerned with material operations but with mystical issues, and since he represented the first stages of the mystical ascent as intellectualist in nature (see pp. 105ff.), it is impossible to divide his thought neatly into practical and speculative spheres; indeed, it is precisely *through* speculative processes that the mystic begins his practical ascent to God. It should be noted that in the *Apology* (*Opera*,

Cabalistic Conclusions Confirming the Christian Religion

11>1. Whatever other Cabalists say, in a first division I distinguish the science of Cabala into the science of *sefirot* and *shemot* [names], as it were into practical and speculative science.

176, 180–81) Pico divided the Cabala differently than he does here. One division included the "first and true Cabala," which taught the "true sense of the Law received from the mouth of God" on the mountain (cf. thesis 11>72). It was this science that Pico meant to use to convert the Jews. Another division included those sciences that the Jews called Cabala "by transference" (*transumptive*), since these too were concerned with secret things. One of these was the *ars combinandi,* which involved anagrammatic manipulations of Scripture (see next note); another was "the supreme part of natural magic," which concerned "the powers of superior things that exist over the moon." The phrase "superior things that exist over the moon" was apparently meant to be ambiguous; the claim of Wirszubski (1989: 144) that the phrase refers exclusively to the *sefirot* is in error, since in the same section Pico speaks at length of "that part of the Cabala that concerns the powers of celestial bodies" (*Opera,* 168). The *Apology* ends its division of the Cabala with an attack on "false Cabalists" who claimed that they had the secret names of God by which they could bind demons and perform miracles.

11>2. Quicquid dicant alii cabaliste,_ ego partem speculatiuam cabalae quadruplicem diuiderem,_ conrespondenter quadruplici partitioni philosophiae quam ego solitus sum affere. Prima est scientia quam ego uoco alphabetariae reuolutionis, conrespondentem parti philosophiae_quam ego philosophiam catholicam uoco. Secunda, tertia,_ et quarta pars est triplex merchiaua,_ conrespondentes triplici philosophiae particularis,_ de diuinis, de mediis,_ et sensibilibus naturis.

11>3. Scientia quae est pars practica cabalae_practicat totam methaphysicam formalem et theologiam inferiorem.

11>4. Ensoph non est aliis numerationibus connumeranda, quia est illarum numerationum unitas abstracta et incommunicata, non unitas coordinata.

11>2. 1486 alphabecariae | 1487 alphabecarie | 1487 merchiana

---

11>2. "revolution of the alphabet" = Pico's anagrammatic method of reading the Torah, apparently the same as the *ars combinandi* mentioned in the previous note. On this and related methods, see above, pp. 63–66. Whether Pico classified *gematria* with this part of speculative Cabala is an open question. On *merkabah* (chariot), see my note to thesis 28.22; cf. 8>14, 11>50. On Pico's four divisions of philosophy: What Pico refers to here as "universal philosophy" pertains to reasoning based on cosmic proportion or correspondences (see theses 3>53–54 and note). The three chariots corresponding to the science of "divine, middle, and sensible natures" can be interpreted variously; using the data elsewhere, the most natural interpretation is that they refer to the intellectual, animate, and corporeal realms. In 28.22, however, we are cautioned against too narrow an interpretation by Pico's warning that "many orders" (*multiplex coordinatio*) of chariots exist. Wirszubski's interpretation of the chariots as symbols of triadic divisions in the *sefirot* system may coincide with medieval usage, but it conflicts sharply with Pico's thesis, whose Latin Wirszubski misreads (cf. Pico's thesis with Wirszubski 1989: 136–38). On Pico's rejection of traditional views of the chariots, note also Pico's disclaimer at the start of this thesis ("Whatever other Cabalists say . . .").

11>2. Whatever other Cabalists say, I divide the speculative part of the Cabala [the science of names] four ways, corresponding to the four divisions of philosophy that I generally make. The first is what I call the science of the revolution of the alphabet, corresponding to the part of philosophy that I call universal philosophy. The second, third, and fourth is the threefold *merkabah* [chariot], corresponding to the three parts of particular philosophy, concerning divine, middle, and sensible natures. (830)

11>3. The science that is the practical part of the Cabala practices all formal metaphysics and inferior theology.

11>4. *Ein-Sof* should not be counted with the other numerations, because it is the abstract and uncommunicated unity of those numerations, not the coordinated unity.

11>3. "practical part of the Cabala" = the "science of *sefirot*"; see note 11>1. "formal metaphysics"/"inferior theology" = science concerning the intellectual nature/science concerning the manifest nature of God in the *sefirot* (or similar concepts outside the Cabala)—the highest realm attained by the practical theology of the *viator*. Cf. 2>27, 3>8–9.

11>4. *Ein-Sof* = God's transcendent nature, the source of his manifest nature in the kabbalistic *sefirot* or "numerations." Cf. 10>15, 11>35–36 and note. Roughly speaking, *Ein-Sof* is equivalent to the abstract essence of God in Latin scholasticism. Cf. in the historical theses 3.1–2, 6.1, etc., which Pico apparently meant to correlate with theses like this one.

11>5. Quilibet hebreus cabalista, secundum principia et dicta scientiae Cabalae, cogitur ineuitabiliter concedere de trinitate_et qualibet persona diuina, patre, filio, et spiritu sancto, illud precise sine additione, diminutione, aut uariatione, quod ponit fides catholica christianorum.

Correlarium: Non solum qui negant trinitatem, sed qui aliomodo eam ponunt quam ponat catholica ecclesia, sicut Arriani, Sabelliani, et similes, redargui possunt manifeste si admittantur principia cabalae.

11>6. Tria magna dei nomina quaternaria, quae sunt in secretis cabalistarum, per mirabilem appropriationem tribus personis trinitatis ita debere attribui, ut nomen <אהיה> sit patris, nomen <יהוה> sit filii, nomen <אדני> sit spiritus sancti, intelligere potest qui in scientia cabalae fuerit profundus.

11>7. Nullus hebraeus cabalista potest negare quod nomen Iesu, si eum secundum modum et principia cabalae interpretemur, hoc totum precise_et nihil aliud significat, id est, deum dei filium patrisque sapientiam per tertiam diuinitatis personam, quae est ardentissimus amoris ignis, naturae humanae in unitate suppositi unitum.

11>8. Ex praecedenti conclusione intelligi potest cur dixerit Paulus / datum esse Iesu nomen quod est super omne nomen, et cur in nomine Iesu dictum sit: Omne genu flecti caelestium, terrestrium, et infernorum, quod etiam est maxime cabalisticum; et potest ex se intelligere qui est profundus in cabala. <31r/31v>

11>6. 1486 sit patris. Nomen . . . filii. Nomen . . . sancti. intelligere

---

11>5. One of many similar theses to follow. Pico's planned methods here are unknown, although in 7a>40 he planned to dispatch Arius and Sabellius using his *via numerorum*, parts of which involved *gematria*.

11>6. Kieszkowski's edition fills in the blanks with three Hebrew names, *none* of which have four letters. In line with medieval tradition, which Pico is apparently adhering to here, the "three great four-letter names of God" are Ehyeh, YHVH, and Adonai. The "ineffable name"

Cabalistic Conclusions Confirming the Christian Religion

11>5. Every Hebrew Cabalist, following the principles and sayings of the science of the Cabala, is inevitably forced to concede, without addition, omission, or variation, precisely what the Catholic faith of Christians maintains concerning the Trinity and every divine Person, Father, Son, and Holy Spirit.

Corollary: Not only anyone who denies the Trinity, but anyone who proposes it in a different way than the Catholic church does, like the Arians, Sabellians, and similar men, can be clearly refuted if the principles of the Cabala are admitted.

11>6. Whoever is profound in the science of the Cabala can understand that the three great four-letter names of God, which exist in the secrets of the Cabalists, through miraculous appropriation should be attributed to the three Persons of the Trinity like this: so that the name <אהיה Ehyeh> is that of the Father, the name <יהוה YHVH> of the Son, the name <אדני Adonai> of the Holy Spirit.

11>7. No Hebrew Cabalist can deny that the name Jesus, if we interpret it following the method and principles of the Cabala, signifies precisely all this and nothing else, that is: *God the Son of God and the Wisdom of the Father, united to human nature in the unity of assumption through the third Person of God, who is the most ardent fire of love.* (835)

11>8. From the preceding conclusion we can know why Paul says that Jesus was given the *name that is over every name,* and why it is said that *all in heaven, earth, and hell kneel in the name of Jesus,* which is also highly Cabalistic. And anyone who is profound in the Cabala can understand this by himself.

YHVH is correlated with the "Son," since Pico himself makes that connection in 11>15. Ehyeh and Adonai are the usual names associated with the first and last of the *sefirot* ("crown" and "kingdom"), and are almost surely paired here with the "Father" and the "Holy Spirit."

11>7. On the name "Jesus," cf. 11>14. Pico probably meant to generate the part of the thesis that I have italicized in my translation using his anagrammatic *revolutio alphabetariae.*

11>8. Cf. Phil. 2: 9–10.

11>9. Siqua est de nouissimis temporibus humana coniectura, inuestigare possumus per secretissimam uiam cabalae futuram esse consumationem saeculi hinc ad annos quingentos et quatuordecim, et dies uigintiquinque.

11>10. Illud quod apud Cabalistas dicitur <מטטרון>, illud est sine dubio quod ab Orpheo Pallas, a Zoroastre paterna mens, a Mercurio dei filius, a Pythagora sapientia, a Parmenide sphera intelligibilis, nominatur.

11>11. Modus quo rationales animae per archangelum deo sacrificantur, qui a Cabalistis non exprimitur, non est nisi per separationem animae a corpore, non corporis ab anima nisi per accidens, ut contingit in morte osculi, de quo scribitur: praeciosa in conspectu domini mors sanctorum eius.

11>12. Non potest operari per puram Cabalam, qui non est rationaliter intellectualis.

11>13. Qui operatur in Cabala sine admixtione extranei, si diu erit in opere, morietur ex binsica, et si errabit in opere aut non purificatus accesserit, deuorabitur ab Azazele per proprietatem iudicii.

11>13. 1486, 1487 ab a zazele

11>9. Cf. 7a>38, 10>20. We get 1 January 2000 by starting on the publication date of the theses (7 December 1486) and ignoring calendar changes. Pico's caution in producing such calculations should be noted; cf. above, p. 44. Some clues as to Pico's methods may be gleaned from *Heptaplus* 7.4, which, dating the world's origin using biblical genealogies, makes much of the correspondence between the six days of creation and the six ages of history before the final historical Sabbath.

11>10. All these symbols correspond to Pico's intellectual or angelic nature. See above, pp. 69–70. The fact that *Metatron* is what Pico had in mind for the blanks finds strong internal support in 19.2. Wirszubski offers further backing for this reading using external evidence (1989: 198–200).

Cabalistic Conclusions Confirming the Christian Religion

11>9. If any human prediction can be made concerning the Last Things, we can discover through the most secret way of the Cabala that the end of the world will occur five hundred and fourteen years and twenty-five days from now [1 January 2000].

11>10. That which among the Cabalists is called <מטטרון *Metatron*> is without doubt that which is called Pallas by Orpheus, the paternal mind by Zoroaster, the son of God by Mercury, wisdom by Pythagoras, the intelligible sphere by Parmenides.

11>11. The way in which rational souls are sacrificed by the archangel to God, which is not explained by the Cabalists, only occurs through the separation of the soul from the body, not of the body from the soul except accidentally, as happens in the death of the kiss, of which it is written: *Precious in the sight of the Lord is the death of his saints.*

11>12. Whoever is not rationally intellectual cannot operate through the pure Cabala. (840)

11>13. Whoever operates in the Cabala without the mixture of anything extraneous, if he is long in the work, will die from *binsica* [the death of the kiss], and if he errs in the work or comes to it unpurified, he will be devoured by Azazel through the property of judgment.

11>11. Cf. 28.1, 11>13. "death of the kiss" = see the quotation in note 8>7. "*Precious in the sight*" = Psalm 116:15.

11>12. "pure Cabala" = cf. 9>26 note. The pure Cabala works in the intellectual part of the soul, natural magic in the rational part (cf. 9>14). Further light is thrown on this thesis by 9>16–18.

11>13. *binsica* = see note 8>7; cf. 11>11. Azazel = demon in the scapegoat ritual in Lev. 16:8–10. "property of judgment" = *Din*, the fifth *sefirah*, the stern retribution of God. The thesis further suggests that Pico associated Cabalistic works with mystical states. Cf. this and the preceding thesis further with 10>14.

11>14. Per litteram <ש>,_ id est,_ scin,_ quae mediat in nomine Iesu,_ significatur nobis cabalistice quod tum perfecte quieuit,_ tanquam in sua perfectione,_ mundus cum Iod coniunctus est cum Vau, quod factum est in Christo,_ qui fuit uerus dei filius et homo.

11>15. Per nomen Iod he uahu he, quod est nomen ineffabile_quod dicunt Cabaliste futurum esse nomen messiae, euidenter cognoscitur futurum eum deum dei filium per spiritum sanctum hominem factum, et post eum ad perfectionem humani generis super homines paraclytum descensurum.

11>16. Ex mysterio trium litterarum quae sunt in dictione sciabat,_ id est, <שבת>, possumus interpretari cabalistice tunc sabbatiza/re mundum cum dei filius fit homo, et ultimo futurum sabbatum cum homines in dei filium regenerabuntur. <31v/32r>

11>17. Qui sciuerit quid est uinum purissimum apud Cabalistas,_ sciet cur dixerit Dauid: Inebriabor ab ubertate domus tuae, et quam ebrietatem dixerit antiquus uates Museus esse foelicitatem, et quid significent tot Bacchi apud Orpheum.

11>15. 1487 jod he vahu he

11>14. *yod, shin, vav* = the consonants in the name "Jesus." Pico presumably meant to read out these secrets from the shapes of these letters using the approach suggested in 28.22, where we find that each stroke in Hebrew has symbolic significance. There is presumably a connection between this thesis and the next, since *yod* and *vav*, the first and last letters in the name "Jesus," are also part of the "ineffable name" YHVH that Pico associated with the Messiah.

11>15. See preceding note. Like most of Pico's longer Cabalistic secrets, this one is presumably to be demonstrated through his *revolutio alphabetariae* or through a combination of that method with pure letter symbolism. "Paraclete" = the Holy Spirit.

Cabalistic Conclusions Confirming the Christian Religion

11>14. By the letter <ש>, that is, *shin*, which mediates in the name Jesus, it is indicated to us Cabalistically that the world then rested perfectly, as though in its perfection, when *Yod* was conjoined with *Vav*—which happened in Christ, who was the true Son of God, and man.

11>15. By the name *Yod he vav he*, which is the ineffable name that the Cabalists say will be the name of the Messiah, it is clearly known that he will be God the Son of God made man through the Holy Spirit, and that after him the Paraclete will descend over men for the perfection of mankind.

11>16. From the mystery of the three letters in the word *shabbat*, that is, <שבת>, we can interpret Cabalistically that the world will sabbatize when the Son of God becomes man, and that ultimately the Sabbath will come when men are regenerated in the Son of God.

11>17. Whoever knows what the purest wine is among the Cabalists, understands why David says, *I will be made drunk by the abundance of your dwelling*, and what drunkenness the ancient seer Musaeus says is happiness, and what so many Bacchae mean in Orpheus. (845)

11>16. "*shabbat*" = Sabbath, "sabbatize" = to rest. Pico's precise methods here are again unknown, although there is presumably a connection with 11>14 via the mystical symbolism of the letter *shin*.

11>17. Tied to the series on mystical happiness or beatitude beginning at 2.12. Musaeus = purported pre-Homeric poet, often identified as a follower (or son) of Orpheus and closely associated with the Orphic mysteries. Pico's apparent source here was *Republic* 363c–d. "purest wine"/"drunkenness"/"so many Bacchae" = superior modes of will, love, or mystical frenzy. Cf. 8>6, 10>23–24.

11>18. Qui coniunxerit Astrologiam Cabalae uidebit quod sabbatizare et quiescere conuenientius fit post Christum die dominico, quam die sabbati.

11>19. Si dictum illud Prophetae: Vendiderunt iustum argento, cabalistice exponamus, nihil aliud nobis significat quam hoc, scilicet, Deus ut redemptor uenditus fuit argento.

11>20. Si interpretationem suam aduerterint Cabaliste super hac dictione, <אז>, quae significat tunc, de trinitatis mysterio multum illuminabuntur.

11>21. Qui coniunxerit dictum Cabalistarum dicentium quod illa numeratio quae dicitur iustus et redemptor_dicitur etiam ze, cum dicto Thalmudistarum dicentium quod Isaac ibat sicut ze, portans Crucem suam, uidebit quod illud quod fuit in Isaac praefiguratum_fuit adimpletum in Christo, qui fuit uerus Deus uenditus Argento.

11>22. Per dicta Cabalistarum de rubedine Esau, et dictum illud quod est in Libro Bresit Rhaba, quod Esau fuit rubeus, et Rubeus eum ulciscetur, de quo dicitur: Quare rubeum uestimentum tuum? Habetur expresse quod Christus, de quo nostri Doctores eundem textum exponunt, ille erit qui ultionem faciet de uirtutibus immundis.

11>18. "Lord's day"/"day of the Sabbath" = Sunday and Saturday, but since days are associated with particular *sefirot* (cf., e.g., 28.6, 28.8, 11>37, etc.), and different *sefirot* with particular planets or Christ (cf., e.g., 11>46, 11>48), there is obviously more here than meets the eye. Given the flexibility of Pico's Cabalistic symbolism, it is possible to generate several plausible readings of the thesis.

11>19. Cf. Amos 2:6, Matt. 26:14–16. "the just"/"redeemer" = alternate terms for the ninth *sefirah*; a typological bond is thus established between the Old and New Testaments via Pico's Cabalistic symbolism. Cf. 11>21.

11>20. The equivalent for *tunc* that Pico has in mind here is apparently *az*, a common kabbalistic symbol. Wirszubski (1989: 174–75) points out that in medieval kabbalism the *alef* in *az* was sometimes taken as a symbol for the first three *sefirot* and the second letter (*zayin*) for the lower seven. It is not clear how this relates to the "mystery of the Trinity" in Pico's thesis, however.

11>18. Whoever joins astrology to Cabala will see that to sabbatize and rest becomes more appropriate after Christ on the Lord's day than on the day of the Sabbath.

11>19. If we explain Cabalistically that saying of the Prophet, *They have sold the just for silver,* it signifies to us only this, namely, God as Redeemer was sold for silver.

11>20. If the Cabalists turn their interpretation to this word, <אז *az*>, which signifies *then,* they will be greatly illuminated concerning the mystery of the Trinity.

11>21. Whoever joins the saying of the Cabalists stating, *That numeration which is called just and redeemer is also called ze,* with the saying of the Talmudists stating, *Isaac departed just like ze, carrying his cross,* will see that that which was prefigured in Isaac was fulfilled in Christ, who was the *true God sold for silver.*

11>22. Through the words of the Cabalists concerning the redness of Esau, and that saying that is in the book *Bereshit Rabbah,* that *Esau was red, and red, avenged him*—of whom it it is said, *Why are your garments red?*—it is expressly known that Christ, concerning whom our doctors expound the same text, will be *he who takes vengeance on impure powers.* (850)

11>21. "*ze*" = pronoun meaning "this" or "this one" = "just"/redeemer" = common name/symbol for the ninth *sefirah.* The association of Christ with the "the just" appears often in the New Testament, e.g., in Acts 3:14. Just as in 11>19, here Pico ties Jewish and Christian traditions through a complex series of symbolic equations linking snippets of unrelated texts; on this syncretic method, see above, pp. 67–68.

11>22. *Bereshit Rabbah* = the best-known Midrashic text, cited frequently by Moses Maimonides, Recanati, and other medieval sources known to Pico. "impure powers" = cf. with 28.31 and 11>27 for an extraordinary example of Pico's Christian Cabalism.

11>23. Per illud dictum Hieremiae: Lacerauit uerbum suum, secundum expositionem Cabalistarum, habemus intelligere quod deum sanctum et benedictum lacerauit deus pro peccatoribus.

11>24. Per responsionem Cabalistarum ad quaestionem quare in libro numerorum coniuncta est particula mortis Mariae particu/lae uitulae ruffae, et per expositionem eorum super eo passu ubi Moyses, in peccato uituli, dixit: Dele me; et per dicta in libro Zoar super eo textu: Et eius liuore sanati sumus, redarguuntur ineuitabiliter Hebrei dicentes non fuisse conueniens ut mors Christi satisfaceret pro peccato humani generis. <32r/32v>

11>25. Quilibet cabalista habet concedere quod messias eos a captiuitate Diabolica et non temporali erat liberaturus.

11>26. Quilibet Cabalista habet concedere ex dictis doctorum huius scientiae hoc manifeste dicentium, quod peccatum originale in aduentu messiae expiabitur.

11>27. Ex principiis cabalistarum euidenter elicitur quod per aduentum messiae tolletur circumcisionis necessitas.

11>24. 1487 particula vitule ruffe | 1486 Dele me. Et | 1486 dicentes.non

---

11>23. Cf. Lam. 2:17 (as rendered in the Vulgate). Wirszubski (1989: 163) points out that the "word" = a regular kabbalistic symbol of the tenth *sefirah*. Christ's identification in John 1:1ff., etc., with the "Word of God" also obviously comes into play here.

11>24. Cf. Num. 19:2–10, 20:1 (Pico, following the Vulgate, is syncretically associating the Old Testament Miriam with the New Testament Mary); Exod. 32:32; Isa. 53:5. On the *Zohar*, the key text of late-medieval kabbalism, see Scholem (1941). Whether Pico knew parts of it directly or only through Recanati, as Wirszubski and others have suggested, is unknown. Pico evidently planned a straightforward typological interpretation of the passages mentioned in this thesis. The "red calf" and other red things in the nine hundred theses (cf. 8>8, 11>38, and notes) predictably all stand for Christ and his redeeming blood.

Cabalistic Conclusions Confirming the Christian Religion

11>23. By that saying of Jeremiah, *he lacerated your word*, according the exposition of the Cabalists, we have to understand that *God lacerated God the holy and blessed on behalf of sinners.*

11>24. By the response of the Cabalists to the question of why in the Book of Numbers the section on the death of Mary is joined to the section on the red calf, and by their exposition of that passage where Moses, in the sin involving the golden calf, said *Destroy me!*, and by the words in the *Zohar* on that text, *And we were healed by his bruises*, those Hebrews claiming that it was not fitting that the death of Christ should satisfy mankind's sin are inevitably refuted.

11>25. Every Cabalist has to concede that the Messiah was to have liberated them from diabolical and not temporal captivity.

11>26. Every Cabalist has to concede, from the words of those learned in this science clearly saying this, that original sin will be expiated by the coming of the Messiah.

11>27. From the principles of the Cabalists it can be clearly deduced that the necessity for circumcision is removed by the coming of the Messiah. (855)

11>25–26. Views that could be drawn directly from a wide range of kabbalistic, Midrashic, or Talmudic texts.

11>27. Ties theses 28.31 and 11>22 together nicely.

11>28. Per dictionem <את>, quae bis ponitur in illo textu, in principio creauit deus Caelum et Terram, ego credo significari a Moyse creationem naturae intellectualis et naturae animalis, quae naturali ordine praecessit creationem caeli et terrae.

11>29. Quod dicitur a Cabalistis, quod linea uiridis gyrat uniuersum, conuenientissime dicitur ad conclusionem quam ultimam diximus ex mente Porphyrii.

11>30. Necessario habent concedere Cabaliste secundum sua principia quod uerus Messias futurus est talis, ut de eo uere dicatur quod est Deus et dei filius.

11>31. Cum audis Cabalistas ponere in Thesua informitatem, intellige informitatem per antecedentiam ad formalitatem, non per priuationem.

11>32. Si duplex Aleph quod est in textu: Non auferetur sceptrum, etc., coniunxerimus ad duplex Aleph quod est in textu: Deus possedit me ab initio, et ad duplex Aleph quod est in textu: Terra autem erat inanis, per uiam Cabalae intelligemus ibi Iacob de illo uero Messia locutum, qui fuit Iesus Nazarenus.

11>31. 1487 per accidentiam ad formalitatem

11>32. 1487 ab initio . et duplex aleph

11>28. Gen. 1:1. Since *et* is simply a definite article in Hebrew, Pico apparently planned to employ pure word/letter symbolism here. Pertinent to Pico's correlative cosmology.

11>29. Cf. 22.12 from Porphyry, 28.7 and note. The "*green line*" = *Binah* (intelligence), the third *sefirah*, associated in this thesis with Porphyry's "intellect." The implication here, also hinted at in a number of other theses, is that in Pico's mind the kabbalistic *sefirot* were more naturally correlated with distinctions in the Neo-Platonic intellectual nature than with God's nature.

11>30. See 11>39 and note.

Cabalistic Conclusions Confirming the Christian Religion

11>28. By the word <את · *et*>, which is placed twice in that text, *In the beginning God created the heavens and the earth*, I believe that Moses is referring to the creation of the intellectual nature and the animate nature, which in the natural order preceded the creation of the heavens and the earth.

11>29. What the Cabalists say, that a *green line circles the universe*, speaks appropriately to the final conclusion that I stated from the mind of Porphyry.

11>30. Following their own principles, the Cabalists must necessarily concede that the true Messiah will be such that of him it is truly said that he is God and the Son of God.

11>31. When you hear that the Cabalists posit formlessness in *Teshuvah*, by formlessness understand antecedence to form, not privation of it.

11>32. If we join the two *alefs* that are in the text, *The scepter shall not be taken away*, etc., to the two *alefs* that are in the text, *God possessed me from the beginning*, and to the two *alefs* that are in the text, *The earth was empty*, through the way of the Cabala we understand that there Jacob spoke of that true Messiah, who was Jesus of Nazareth. (860)

11>31. Pico's Latin transliteration may be corrupt. He apparently has in mind *Teshuvah* = "penitence" or "return," alternate name for the third *sefirah*. The sense of the thesis is clarified when we recognize that Pico associated that *sefirah*—whose more common name was *Binah*, "intelligence"—with the intellectual nature, the source of worldly forms. See note 11>29. Cf. also Pico's language in 6>7 from the *Book of Causes* and 28.23 and note. Wirszubski (1989: 176–77) again discusses this conclusion from the point of view of medieval kabbalism, but by ignoring its links to Pico's non-Cabalistic theses, he misreads its sense in Pico's thought.

11>32. Cf. Gen. 49:10 (spoken by Jacob), Prov. 8:22, Gen. 1:2. Pico here is correlating three unconnected passages from the Old Testament to read out their collective Christian message. On this syncretic technique, see above, pp. 67–68. As Wirszubski (1989: 177) puts it, each *alef* in these texts "is no more than a kind of code number or punched card by means of which three different verses are linked, each carrying latent Messiological connotations."

11>33. Per hanc dictionem <איש>; quae scribitur per Aleph, Iod, et / Scin, et significat Virum, quae deo attribuitur cum dicitur Vir belli, de trinitatis mysterio per uiam Cabalae perfectissime admonemur. <32v/33r>

11>34. Per nomen <הוא>, id est Vir, quod tribus litteris scribitur he, uau, et aleph, quod nomen deo propriissime attribuitur, et maxime conuenienter non solum ad Cabalistas, qui hoc expresse sepius dicunt, sed etiam ad theologiam Dionysii Areopagitae, per uiam Cabalae trinitatis mysterium, cum possibilitate incarnationis, nobis declaratur.

11>35. Si deus in se ut infinitum, ut unum, et secundum se intelligatur, ut sic nihil intelligimus ab eo procedere, sed separationem a rebus, et omnimodam sui in seipso clausionem, et extremam in remotissimo suae diuinitatis recessu profundam ac solitariam retractionem, de eo intelligimus ipso penitissime in abysso suarum tenebrarum se contegente, et nullo modo in dilatatione ac profusione suarum bonitatum ac fontani splendoris se manifestante.

11>36. Ex praecedenti conclusione intelligi potest cur dicatur apud cabalistas quod deus induit se decem uestimentis quando creauit saeculum.

11>33. 1486 dicitur. Vir belli

11>34. 1486 V (=Vir) | 1487 U

11>33. "*man of war*" = Exod. 15:3. Each of these letters presumably stands for one of the three Persons of the Trinity. Cf., e.g., the association of the letter *shin* and Christ in 11>14.

11>34. The reference here is to Pseudo-Dionysius's *Divine Names*, where the names of God and his "attributes" mentioned in Scripture are assigned to different Persons in the Trinity, just as they are assigned to different *sefirot* in the Kabbalah. As in the previous thesis, Pico presumably meant to assign each of the three letters in הוא (which means "he," not "man") to one Person in the Trinity.

Cabalistic Conclusions Confirming the Christian Religion

11>33. By this word <איש>, which is written Alef, Yod, and Sin, and signifies *man*—which is attributed to God when he is called a *man of war*—through the way of the Cabala we are perfectly admonished as to the mystery of the Trinity.

11>34. Through the name <הוא>, that is, *man*, which is written with the three letters he, vav, and alef, which name is very properly attributed to God—something in harmony not only with the Cabalists, who often expressly declare this, but as well with the theology of Dionysius the Areopagite—through the way of the Cabala the mystery of the Trinity, with the possibility of the Incarnation, is revealed to us.

11>35. If God is known in himself as infinite, as one, and as existing through himself, we recognize that nothing proceeds from him, but know his separation from things, and his total closure of himself in himself, and his extreme, profound, and solitary retraction in the remotest recess of his divinity; and we recognize him as he conceals himself inwardly in the abyss of his darkness, in no way revealing himself in the dilation and profusion of his goodness and fontal splendor.

11>36. From the preceding conclusion we can know why the Cabalists say that God dressed himself in ten garments when he created the world.

11>35–36. Distinguishing God's transcendent nature (the *Ein-Sof*) from his manifested nature (the *sefirot*). "ten garments" = ten *sefirot*; cf. 28.35 and note. The idea that the abstract essence of the "one," "absolute," etc., dressed itself in inferior garments (often identified with foreign religious concepts or conflicting concepts in a tradition) was a handy syncretic device. The technique shows up in a number of ancient Eastern and Western pagan traditions as well as in the Kabbalah; it is similar in many ways to the Eastern concept of avatars.

11>37. Qui intellexerit in dextrali coordinatione subordinationem pietatis ad sapientiam, perfecte intelliget_per uiam Cabalae quomodo Abraam in die suo per rectam lineam uidit diem Christi,_ et gauisus est.

11>38. Effectus qui sunt sequuti post mortem Christi debent conuincere quemlibet Cabalistam quod Iesus Nazarenus fuit uerus Messias.

11>39. Ex hac conclusione et trigesima superius posita sequitur quod quilibet Cabalista habet concedere quod interrogatus Iesus quis esset,_ rectissime respondit,_ dicens: Ego sum principium qui loquor uobis.

11>40. Hoc habent ineuitabiliter concedere Cabaliste, quod uerus messias per aquam homines purgabit.

11>41. Sciri potest in Cabalam per mysterium mem clausi cur post se Christus miserit paraclytum. <33r/33v>

11>37. "piety"/"wisdom" = the fourth and second *sefirot*, correlated here with the "day of Abraham" and the "day of Christ" respectively. For Christ as God's "Wisdom," cf. 1 Cor. 1:24. The "right-hand order" = the *sefirot* proper, as opposed to the "emanation of the left-hand" composed of evil forces; cf. on this note 28.14. "right line" presumably = the third *sefirah* (*Binah*, "intelligence"), which Pico elsewhere symbolizes by the "green line" and associates with the intellectual nature (see 11>29 and note; cf. also 25.7, where the intellectual nature is symbolized by the "right" or "straight ray"). Pico's thesis is meant to provide a commentary on John 8:56, where Christ declares that Abraham in his day rejoiced when he prophesized Christ's coming. Interpreted briefly: Abraham (the fourth *sefirah*) prophesized the arrival of Christ (the second *sefirah*) via the intellectual nature (the third *sefirah*), from which man obtains his prophetic knowledge. The thesis conforms to Pico's views on prophecy expressed in the series beginning at 7.1.

11>38. "The effects that followed the death of Christ" = there was an eclipse of the sun, and the veil of the temple was torn asunder (Luke 23:44–46, Mark 15:33–39). Matt. 27:45–54 adds an earthquake, with the dead rising from their tombs. In the *Heptaplus*, second preface (*Opera,* 6; Garin, *Scritti vari,* 188), Pico interprets the tearing of the veil as a sign that following Christ's

Cabalistic Conclusions Confirming the Christian Religion

11>37. Anyone who understands the subordination of piety to wisdom in the right-hand order, understands perfectly, through the way of the Cabala, in what way Abraham in his day saw the day of Christ through the right line, and rejoiced. (865)

11>38. The effects that followed the death of Christ should convince every Cabalist that Jesus of Nazareth was the true Messiah.

11>39. From this conclusion and the thirtieth, stated above, it follows that every Cabalist has to concede that Jesus, when asked who he was, responded very rightly, saying, *I am the beginning who speaks to you.*

11>40. The Cabalists inevitably have to concede this: that the true Messiah will purify men through water.

11>41. It can be known in the Cabala through the mystery of the closed *mem* why after himself Christ sent the Paraclete.

---

death the intelligible world was no longer mystically divided from the lower world—the reverse of the "severing of the shoots" found in 28.4 and 28.36. *Re* the eclipse of the sun, see 11>46 and note. Further on the veil in the temple, see 8>9 and note.

11>39. *Re* John 8:25 (as given approximately in certain variations of the Vulgate). Pico here is correlating Christ with *Hokhmah* ("wisdom"), the second *sefirah*, as we see when we compare this thesis with 28.25.

11>40. Cf. 11>44–45 and note.

11>41. "mystery of the closed *mem*" = reference to the fact that *mem* has both open (מ) and closed (ם) forms, the latter used at the end of a word. Pico apparently intended to read out the letter symbolism of the closed *mem* through the means suggested in 28.33. It was a commonplace in Hebrew commentary traditions that the closed *mem* showed up only once in the Hebrew bible in a nonfinal position (Isa. 9:6); the verse has a strong Messianic character and was much discussed by both Jewish and Christian commentators. "Paraclete" = the Holy Spirit.

11>42. Scitur per fundamenta cabale quam recte dixerit Iesus: Antequam nasceretur Abraam, ego sum.

11>43. Per mysterium duarum litterarum uau et iod scitur quomodo ipse messias ut deus fuit principium suiipsius ut homo.

11>44. Scitur ex cabala per mysterium partis septentrionalis cur iudicabit deus saeculum per ignem.

11>45. Scitur in cabala apertissime cur dei filius cum aqua baptismi uenerit, et spiritus sanctus cum igne.

11>46. Per eclipsationem solis quae accidit in morte Christi sciri potest secundum fundamenta cabalae quod tunc passus est filius dei et uerus messias.

11>47. Qui sciet proprietatem Aquilonis in cabala, sciet cur sathan Christo promisit regna mundi, si cadens eum adorasset.

11>42. colon retained from 1486 edition

11>42. John 8:58. See 11>37 and note. The thesis can presumably be explained by the fact that "Jesus," associated with the second *sefirah* (as in 11>37, 11>39, etc.), precedes "Abraham," a standard symbol of the fourth *sefirah*.

11>43. *vav* and *yod* = first and last letters in the name "Jesus"; cf. 11>14. Pico presumably planned to demonstrate this using pure letter symbolism of the sort seen in 28.33, etc.

11>44–45. The "north" and "fire" in medieval kabbalism were most often associated with the fifth *sefirah* (God's "judgment" or "power"), and "water" with the fourth ("love" or "piety" for Pico). Cf. 11>67 and note.

CABALISTIC CONCLUSIONS CONFIRMING THE CHRISTIAN RELIGION

11>42. It is known through the principles of the Cabala that Jesus correctly said, *Before Abraam was born, I am.* (870)

11>43. Through the mystery of the two letters *vav* and *yod*, it is known in what way the Messiah as God was the beginning of himself as man.

11>44. Through the mystery of the northern part, it is known from the Cabala why God will judge the world through fire.

11>45. It is known very openly in the Cabala why the Son of God comes with baptismal waters and the Holy Spirit with fire.

11>46. Through the eclipse of the sun that occurred at the death of Christ, it can be known following the principles of the Cabala that then the Son of God and the true Messiah suffered.

11>47. Anyone who knows the property of the north in the Cabala, knows why Satan promised Christ the kingdoms of the world, if falling he adored him. (875)

11>46. For the correlation between Christ and the sun, cf. 11>51.

11>47. "north" (or "north wind") = standard symbol of the fifth *sefirah*, one of whose properties was "power." The fifth *sefirah* was regularly associated with Satan and the origins of evil (cf. Scholem 1941: 237), but Pico also associates it with magical power (cf. 10>10 note). Whether "kingdoms of the world" here is intended symbolically ("kingdom" = *Malkhut*, the lowest *sefirah*) is an open question.

11>48. Quicquid dicant caeteri cabalistae, ego decem spheras sic decem numerationibus correspondere dico, ut ab aedificio incipiendo, Iupiter sit quartae, Mars quintae, Sol sextae, Saturnus septimae, Venus octauae, Mercurius nonae, Luna decimae; tum supra aedificium, firmamentum tertiae, Primum mobile secundae, caelum empyreum decimae.

11>49. Qui sciuerit correspondentiam decem preceptorum ad prohibentia per coniunctionem ueritatis astrologicae cum ueritate theologica, uidebit ex fundamento nostro praecedentis conclusionis, quicquid alii dicant Cabalistae, primum preceptum primae numerationi correspondere, Secundum secundae, Tertium tertiae, Quartum septimae, Quintum quartae, Sextum quintae, Septimum nonae, Octauum octauae, Nonum sextae, Decimum decimae.

11>50. Cum dicunt cabalistae a septima et octaua petendos filios, ita dicas in merchiaua inferiori accipi, ut ab una petatur ut det, ab altera ne prohibeat. Et quae det et quae prohibeat potest intelligere ex praecedentibus conclusionibus qui fuerit intelligens in astrologia et cabala.

11>51. Sicut fuit luna plena in Salomone, ita fuit plenus Sol in uero Messia qui fuit Iesus. Et de conrespondentia ad diminutionem / in sedecia potest quis coniectare, si profundat in cabala. <33v/34r>

11>48–50. "numerations" = the *sefirot*. "edifice" = the fourth through tenth *sefirot* (cf. 28.9). On *merkabah* (chariot), see 28.22, 11>2 and notes. Wirszubski (1989), who took Pico's inferior chariot as a symbol of a lower triad of the ten *sefirot*, sees 11>50 as an example of magical use of the *sefirot* system. But as Pico tells us clearly in 11>2, for him the "inferior chariot" referred to the realm of "sensible natures"; thus the magical "petitions" in 11>50 are not directed immediately to the seventh and eighth *sefirot* but either to the astrological bodies corresponding to them in 11>48 (Saturn and Venus) or to lower sensible natures. How Pico believed that these "petitions" were to be directed is unknown. Pico's correlation in 11>48 of the empyrean heaven with the tenth *sefirah*—rather than with the first, as we would expect—was probably a slip.

Cabalistic Conclusions Confirming the Christian Religion

11>48. Whatever other Cabalists say, I say that the ten spheres correspond to the ten numerations like this: so that, starting from the edifice, Jupiter corresponds to the fourth, Mars to the fifth, the sun to the sixth, Saturn to the seventh, Venus to the eighth, Mercury to the ninth, the moon the tenth. Then, above the edifice, the firmament to the third, the *primum mobile* to the second, the empyrean heaven to the tenth [*sic*].

11>49. Anyone who knows the correspondence of the Ten Commandments through conjunction of astrological truth with theological truth will see from the foundation that I set out in the preceding conclusion, whatever other Cabalists say, that the first commandment corresponds to the first numeration, the second to the second, the third to the third, the fourth to the seventh, the fifth to the fourth, the sixth to the fifth, the seventh to the ninth, the eighth to the eighth, the ninth to the sixth, the tenth to the tenth.

11>50. When the Cabalists say that sons should be sought from the seventh and the eighth, those petitions in the inferior *merkabah* are to be interpreted this way: so that one is asked to grant them, the other not to prohibit them. And which one grants and which one prohibits anyone who is knowledgeable in astrology and Cabala can understand from the preceding conclusions.

11>51. Just as the full moon was in Solomon, so the full sun was in the true Messiah, who was Jesus. And concerning the diminished correspondence in Zedekiah anyone can conjecture, if he is profound in the Cabala.

11>51. Zedekiah = King of Judah when it fell to the Babylonians, explaining his "diminished correspondence" with Christ. Cf., e.g., 2 Kings 24:18ff (Vulgate Malachim 24:18ff.). Correlating this thesis with 11>48, we find Jesus (the "sun" here) further associated with the sixth *sefirah* (the "great Adam").

11>52. Ex praecedenti conclusione intelligi potest cur euangelista Matheus, in quatuordecim illis generationibus ante Christum, quasdam dimiserit.

11>53. Cum fieri lucem nihil sit aliud quam participare lucem, conueniens est ualde illa cabalistarum expositio ut in ly fiat lux, per lucem, speculum lucens intelligamus, et in ly facta est lux, speculum non lucens.

11>54. Quod dicunt Cabalistae, beatificandos nos in speculo lucente reposito sanctis in futuro saeculo, idem est praecise, sequendo fundamenta eorum, cum eo quod nos dicimus, beatificandos sanctos in filio.

11>55. Quod dicunt Cabalistae, lumen repositum in septuplo lucere plus quam lumen relictum, mirabiliter conuenit arithmeticae pythagoricae.

11>56. Qui sciuerit explicare quaternarium in denarium habebit modum, si sit peritus Cabalae, deducendi ex nomine ineffabili nomen .lxxii. litterarum.

11>53. 1486 ly fiat lux.per lucem

11>52. Cf. Matt. 1:1–17, which divides the lineage from Abraham to Christ into three symmetrical sets of fourteen generations each. Matthew apparently omitted "certain persons" from the last fourteen generations between the Babylonian exile and Christ because of their "diminished correspondence" (like Zedekiah's) with Christ.

11>53. Cf. Gen. 1:3. "shining mirror"/"mirror not shining" = symbols of the sixth and tenth *sefirot* respectively. An eschatological sense is implied here when we link this thesis with 28.20, which uses the same symbols. This reading is supported by the fact that Pico often correlates the sixth *sefirah* with Christ. See also the following thesis.

11>54. See the preceding note. They presumably mean the same thing since the "shining mirror" = the sixth *sefirot* = "the great Adam," one of Pico's regular Cabalistic symbols for Christ.

Cabalistic Conclusions Confirming the Christian Religion

11>52. From the preceding conclusion it can be known why the evangelist Matthew omitted certain persons in those fourteen generations [he names] before Christ. (880)

11>53. Since for light to be made is nothing but to participate light, that exposition of the Cabalists is very appropriate: that in *Let there be light*, by light we should understand the shining mirror, and in *Light was made*, the mirror not shining.

11>54. What the Cabalists say, that we will be beatified in the shining mirror restored to the saints in the future world, is exactly the same, following their principles, as that which we say, that the saints will be beatified in the Son.

11>55. What the Cabalists say, that the light restored in the seventh shines more than the light left behind, miraculously agrees with Pythagorean arithmetic.

11>56. Anyone who knows how to unfold the quaternarius into the denarius will have the method, if he is skilled in the Cabala, of deducing the name of seventy-two letters from the ineffable name.

11>55. "seventh" = the seventh *sefirah*, corresponding to the seven ages of history, seven stages of the mystical ascent, etc. Thus in 11>66 we find that the function of the seventh *sefirah* as it is reflected in the soul is the conversion to "superior things." The miraculous correspondence with Pythagorean arithmetic is clarified in 25.5, where we find that the number seven is a Pythagorean symbol for the "beatifying power of the intellect."

11>56. "To unfold the quaternarius into the denarius" = 1 + 2 + 3 + 4 = 10. Pico is saying that you can take the ineffable name YHVH, add the numerical equivalents of its letters (10 + 5 + 6 + 5 = 26), and through further operations known to those "skilled" in Cabala derive the name of seventy-two letters. Copenhaver (1997: 224) discusses two ways that such calculations were made in medieval kabbalism, but we have no textual evidence concerning Pico's methods. The inspiration behind the name of seventy-two letters is supposedly Exod. 14:19–21, each verse of which has seventy-two letters.

11>57. Per praecedentem conclusionem potest intelligens in arithmetica formali intelligere quod operari per *scemamphoras* est proprium rationalis naturae.

11>58. Rectius foret illud Becadmin, quod ponit glosa chaldaica super dictione Bresit, exponere de sapientialibus ideis_quam de trigintaduabus uiis‸ ut dicunt alii Cabalistae; utrunque tamen est rectum in Cabala.

11>59. Qui profunde considerauerit quadruplicem rerum statum: Primo unionis et stabilitae mansionis, Secundo processionis, Tertio reuersionis, Quarto beatificae reunionis, videbit litteram Beth cum prima littera_primum, cum media_medium, cum ultimis_ultima‸ operari.

11>60. Ex praecedenti conclusione potest contemplatiuus homo intelligere cur lex dei a Beth littera incipit, de qua scribitur quod est immaculata, quod erat cum eo cuncta componens, quod est conuertens animas, quod facit dare fructum in tempore suo. <34r/34v>

11>58. 1486 Cabalistae.utrunque

11>59. 1486 reunionis.Videbit

11>57. "formal arithmetic" = cf. 7>9 note. "*shem ha-meforash*" = God's "proper name" YHVH, the ineffable name or tetragrammaton. Cf. Maimonides *Guide for the Perplexed* 1.61 ("On the Names of God"). I suspect that Pico's Latin transliteration scemamphoras may be related through folk etymology to his conflation of "aphorism" and "amphora" (a vessel, in Greek) in other esoteric sections of the text (cf. 8>6–8, 10>1). The suggestion is that the sacred aphorisms of *prisci theologi* like Zoroaster and Orpheus are "vessels" of esoteric knowledge—as is the proper name of God interpreted through pure letter symbolism, the "revolution of the alphabet," *gematria*, etc. Pico's transliteration was picked up by countless later Renaissance syncretists like Agrippa von Nettesheim.

11>58. Cf. 28.26. "*Becadmin*" as Pico translated it = "with eternal" or "through eternal" things. "*Bereshit*" = "in the beginning," the opening word of the Torah. Its normal associations were with "wisdom," the second *sefirah*—and for Pico, a symbol of Christ. "sapiential ideas" = the Platonic ideas existing on some unidentified level of reality—originating at the highest level in Christ or "Wisdom," the "mind of God" in Christian theology. "thirty-two paths = the combination of the twenty-two letters of the Hebrew alphabet and ten *sefirot* out of which the "Wisdom of God" created the world. The thesis thus refers to the eternity of the ideas or Christ or both. Cf. also thesis and note 3.5.

Cabalistic Conclusions Confirming the Christian Religion

11>57. From the last conclusion anyone knowledgeable in formal arithmetic can understand that to operate through the *shem ha-meforash* is proper to the rational nature. (885)

11>58. It will be more correct to explain that *Becadmin,* which the Chaldean gloss places over the word *Bereshit,* as concerning the sapiential ideas than the thirty-two paths, as other Cabalists say. Both, however, are correct in the Cabala.

11>59. Whoever profoundly considers the fourfold state of things—the first concerning the unity and stability of indwelling, the second concerning procession, the third concerning reversion, the fourth concerning beatific reunion—will see that the letter *Bet* operates the first with the first letter, the middle with the middle letter, the last ones with the last letters.

11>60. From the last conclusion a contemplative man can understand why the Law of God—of which it is written that it is *immaculate,* that it *was joined with him as he created,* that it *converts souls,* and that it *yields fruit in its time*—begins with the letter *Bet.*

11>59. Wirszubski's reading (1974: 150–51; 1989: 164–65) of this obscure thesis seems plausible. Counting as two letters those five consonants that change forms at the end of a word, medieval kabbalists could claim twenty-seven letters for the Hebrew alphabet. The first was *alef,* the middle *nun,* the last two were *shin* and *tav.* Combining (as Pico suggests) *bet* with the first letter gives us *av,* "Father." Combining it with the middle letter, we get *ben,* "Son." Combining it with the last two letters we get *shabbat,* "Sabbath." All these correspond neatly with "indwelling," "procession," and "reversion and beatific reunion" in Pico's thesis. On the association of Christ with "procession" in Latin theology, cf. 2.1 and note.

11>60. Cf. for these references Psalms 19:8 (Vulgate 18:8), Prov. 8:30, Psalms 1:3. The point here is that the whole of the Christian Trinity and salvation is implied in the first letter of the Hebrew bible.

11>61. Per eandem conclusionem sciri potest quod idem filius, qui est sapientia patris, est qui omnia unit in patre, et per quem omnia facta sunt, et a quo omnia conuertuntur, et in quo demum sabbatizant omnia.

11>62. Qui profunde considerauerit nouenarium beatitudinum numerum de quo apud Matheum in euangelio, uidebit illas mirabiliter conuenire nouenario nouem numerationum quae sunt infra primam, quae est inaccessibilis diuinitatis abyssus.

11>63. Sicut Aristoteles diuiniorem philosophiam, quam philosophi antiqui sub fabulis et apologis uelarunt, ipse sub philosophicae speculationis facie dissimulauit_et uerborum breuitate obscurauit, ita Rabi Moyses aegyptius, in libro qui a latinis dicitur dux neutrorum, dum per superficialem uerborum corticem uidetur cum Philosophis ambulare, per latentes profundi sensus intelligentias, mysteria complectitur Cabalae.

11>64. In textu, Audi Israhel, dominus deus noster dominus unus, rectius est ut intelligatur ibi collectio ab inferiori ad superius, et a superiori ad inferius, quam ab inferiori ad superius bis.

11>61. "Wisdom of the Father" = cf. 1 Cor. 1:25, etc. Pico here apparently planned some complex correspondences between the "Son" and the other terms generated in 11>59 (see note). On the association of Christ with the "Sabbath," cf. 11>16, 11>18.

11>62. Cf. Matt. 5:1–12. "inaccessible abyss of divinity" = not *Ein-Sof*, or God himself, who is above the *sefirot* system (cf. 11>4), but *Keter* ("crown"), the first *sefirah* or "numeration."

11>61. Through the same conclusion one can know that the same Son, who is the *Wisdom of the Father*, is he who unites all things in the Father, and through whom all things were made, and by whom all things are converted, and in whom at last all things sabbatize.

11>62. Whoever profoundly considers the nine beatitudes in the Gospel according to Matthew will see that those miraculously agree with the nine numerations which are below the first, which is the inaccessible abyss of divinity. (890)

11>63. Just as Aristotle disguised and concealed the more divine philosophy, which the ancient philosophers veiled under tales and fables, under the mask of philosophical speculation and in the brevity of words, so Rabbi Moses the Egyptian, in the book the Latins call the *Guide for the Perplexed*, while in the superficial shell of words appears to move with the philosophers, in hidden insights of a profound sense enfolds the mysteries of the Cabala.

11>64. In the text, *Hear O Israel, the Lord our God is one Lord*, it is more correct to understand the collection from inferior to superior, and from superior to inferior, than from inferior to superior twice.

11>63. An important thesis that tells us as much about Pico's views of Aristotle as about his views of Maimonides. Pico draws three philosophical conclusions from the *Guide for the Perplexed* in theses 12.1–3. Although written before the major kabbalistic texts, the *Guide* was often interpreted as a kabbalistic work by later writers in that tradition. Pico's library had several copies of the text in its medieval Latin translation (Kibre 1936: 152, 213).

11>64. "*Hear O Israel . . .*" = Deut. 6:4, opening words of the liturgical *Shema*, which like this thesis underscores the oneness of God. Pico's thesis apparently pertains to the underlying unity of the seven inferior and three superior *sefirot*. How the thesis pertains to Christianity is not clear, however.

11>65. Rectius est ut AMEN tipheret dicat et regnum, ut per uiam numeri ostenditur, quam quod dicat regnum tantum, ut quidam uolunt.

11>66. Ego animam nostram sic decem sephirot adapto, ut per unitatem suam sit cum prima, per intellectum cum secunda, per rationem cum tertia, per superiorem concupiscibilem cum quarta, per superiorem irascibilem cum quinta, per liberum arbitrium cum sexta, et per hoc totum ut ad superiora se conuertitur cum septima, ut ad inferiora cum octaua, et mixtum ex utroque, potius per indifferentiam uel alternariam adhesionem quam simultaneam continentiam, cum nona, et per potentiam qua inhabitat primum habitaculum cum decima.

11>67. Per dictum Cabalistarum quod Caeli sunt ex igne et aqua, simul et ueritatem Theologicam de ipsis sephirot nobis manifestat, et philosophicam ueritatem quod elementa in caelo sint tantum secundum actiuam uirtutem. <34v/35r>

11>65. 1487 Amen. thipheret

11>65. On "AMEN," cf. 28.47. Pico evidently planned to demonstrate the interconvertibility of AMEN, *Tiferet* (the sixth *sefirah*), and kingdom (the tenth *sefirah*) using some variation of *gematria*, as suggested by his reference to his "way of number." Since Pico also correlated *Tiferet*, the "great Adam," with Christ, his association of it here with AMEN would undoubtedly lead to secondary symbolic equations.

11>66. See my discussion above, pp. 81–82.

Cabalistic Conclusions Confirming the Christian Religion

11>65. It is more correct that AMEN should signify *Tiferet* and kingdom, as is shown through the way of number, than that it should signify kingdom only, as some would have it.

11>66. I adapt our soul to the ten *sefirot* thus: so through its unity it is with the first, through intellect with the second, through reason with the third, through superior sensual passion with the fourth, through superior irascible passion with the fifth, through free choice with the sixth, through all these as it converts to superior things with the seventh, through all these as it converts to inferior things with the eighth, through a mixture of both of these—more through indifferent or alternate adhesion than simultaneous inclusion—with the ninth, and through the power by which it inhabits the first habitation with the tenth.

11>67. Through the saying of the Cabalists, *The heavens are made from fire and water*, we are simultaneously shown both the theological truth of the *sefirot* themselves, and the philosophical truth that the elements in heaven exist only according to their active power. (895)

11>67. Pico explains this thesis in the *Heptaplus*, second proem (*Opera*, 5; Garin, *Scritti vari*, 184), invoking some traditional folk etymology: "The *caelum* is called *asciamaim* [*shamayim*] by the Hebrews, as though composed of *es* and *maim* [*mayim*], that is, out of fire and water." Wirszubski (1989: 180) interprets the "theological truth" in the thesis: The sixth *sefirah*, sometimes called "heaven," unites the fifth and fourth *sefirot*, associated with fire and water respectively. The "philosophical truth" in the thesis is suggested in *Disputations* 3.4, where we find that the elements only exist in the *caelum* in some pure and ineffable mode; see above, pp. 139–42. Cf. also 23.4, 7a>10 (to be answered through the "way of numbers").

11>68. Qui sciuerit quid sit denarius in Arithmetica formali, et cognouerit naturam primi numeri spherici, sciet illud quod ego adhuc apud aliquem Cabalistam non legi, et est quod sit fundamentum secreti magni Iobelei in Cabala.

11>69. Ex fundamento praecedentis conclusionis sciri pariter potest secretum quinquaginta portarum intelligentiae, et millesimae generationis, et regni omnium saeculorum.

11>70. Per modum legendi sine punctis in lege, et modus scribendi res diuinas, et unialis continentia per indeterminatum ambitum rerum diuinarum, nobis ostenditur.

11>71. Per id quod dicunt Cabalistae de aegypto, et attestata est experientia, habemus credere quod terra aegypti sit in analogia, et subordinatione proprietatis potentiae.

11>68. 1486 formabili. | *Emendationes errorum*, corrige: formali | 1487 text emended *sic*

11>71. 1487 subordinationis

11>68. "denarius" = 10. "formal arithmetic" = see note 7>9. "first spherical number" = 5. Spherical numbers were numbers like 5 or 6 which, when raised to any power, yield products that always end in that same number. Cf. Theon of Smyrna *Mathematics Useful for Understanding Plato* 1.24. Thus any multiple of 5 by itself always ends in 5: 5 x 5 = 25, 125 x 5 = 625, 1205 x 5 = 6025, etc. "great jubilee" = standard kabbalistic symbol of the third *sefirah*, one of whose names was *Teshuvah* ("penitence" or "return"). The "great jubilee" had eschatological significance (cf. 28.42 and note), which was clearly what Pico planned to emphasize in this thesis. The numbers 5 and 10 in Pico's mind were appropriate symbols of eschatological return due to the periodicity of 5 as a spherical number and since after 10 we count "by repetition," as he tells us in the *Apology* (*Opera*, 172). Since in Western numerology any multiple by 10 of a given number was usually said to have a symbolic significance analogous to that number itself, 500 (5 x 100) was likewise a symbol of return; this is apparently why Pico originally included 500 theses according to his own opinion, symbolizing the fact that his system was meant to return thought to its ancient unity.

Cabalistic Conclusions Confirming the Christian Religion

11>68. Whoever knows what the denarius is in formal arithmetic, and recognizes the nature of the first spherical number, knows that which up to now I have not read in any Cabalist, and that is what is the principle in the Cabala of the secret great jubilee.

11>69. From the principle in the preceding conclusion one can equally know the secret of the fifty gates of intelligence, and of the thousandth generation, and of the kingdom of all ages.

11>70. Through the method of reading without points [vowel signs] in the Law, we are shown both the method of writing divine things and the unial containment of divine things through an unlimited compass.

11>71. Through that which the Cabalists say about Egypt—and experience confirms it—we have to believe that the land of Egypt stands in analogy and in subordination to the property of power.

11>69. "fifty gates of intelligence"/"thousandth generation"/"kingdom of all ages" = further millennial and eschatological symbols tied to the numerology of the previous thesis. On the "fifty gates of intelligence" ("intelligence" or *Binah* = most common name of the third *sefirah*), see further Scholem (1974: 113); cf. also 28.13.

11>70. To read "without points" (vowel signs) in Hebrew effectively removes divisions between words. The underlying idea is that the Torah itself is the "great name of God," containing all real or possible existents in some undivided state. There may be a further allusion here to automatic writing, which was often said to be conducted in a trance. Cf. above, pp. 64–65.

11>71. "property of power" = *Gevurah*, the fifth *sefirah*. Hence any text discussing Egypt can be read symbolically as referring to God's power and, as suggested in 28.40 and 10>10 (see notes), to magic as well. The apparent inspiration here is from commentaries on Exod. 7:1ff.

11>72. Sicut uera astrologia docet nos legere in libro dei, ita Cabala docet nos legere in libro legis.

¶Finis

Impressum Romae opera Venerabilis uiri Eucharii Silber alias Franck. Anno ab incarnatione Domini .Mcccc.lxxxvi. die Septima Decembris. Sedente Innocentio .viii. Pont.Max.Anno Pontificatus eiusdem Tertio. <35r/35v>

CONCLVSIONES non disputabuntur nisi post Epiphaniam. Interim publicabuntur in omnibus Italiae Gymnasiis. Et siquis Philosophus aut Theologus etiam ab extrema Italia arguendi gratia Romam uenire uoluerit, pollicetur ipse Dominus disputaturus se uiatici expensas illi soluturum de suo.

Colophon 1486 punctuation *sic* | 1487 no colophon

Final announcement 1487 Et si quis Philosophos | 1486, 1487 .D. = Dominus | 1486 de suo:. . : . followed on the remainder of 35v by the printer's *registrum*. 36r contains the *Emendationes errorum*

11>72. "book of God"/"book of the Law" = nature/Torah. For the astrological reference here, cf. 7a>74, to be answered through Pico's *via numerorum*. According to the *Apology* (*Opera*, 178), the "first and true Cabala" pertained to the true interpretation of the Law that God revealed to Moses on the mountain—providing Christians with a means to "pierce the Jews with their own weapons" [unde Iudaeos suis telis confodiant]. Thus Pico's last thesis, like the last section of his text as a whole, contains suggestions for a final means to convert the Jews, a traditional sign of the beginning of the millennium.

COLOPHON. Found only in the original 1486 printed text and, partially, in two of the derivative manuscripts copied from that edition (see above, pp. 185–86). Kieszkowski (1973: 90) reports it in his apparatus; Biondi's edition (1995) omits it entirely.

11>72. Just as true astrology teaches us to read in the book of God, so the Cabala teaches us to read in the book of the Law. (900)

¶The End

Printed at Rome, the work of that venerable man Eucharius Silber, alias Franck, on the seventh day of December, in the 1486th year since the Incarnation of the Lord, with Innocent VIII, supreme Pontiff, sitting in the third year of his papacy.

THE CONCLUSIONS will not be disputed until after the Epiphany. In the meantime they will be published in all Italian universities. And if any philosopher or theologian, even from the ends of Italy, wishes to come to Rome for the sake of debating, his Lord the disputer promises to pay the travel expenses from his own funds.

FINAL ANNOUNCEMENT. The final announcement shows up only in the rare *editio princeps* and 1487 reprint. The announcement is reported in part, with some errors, in Kieszkowski's edition (1973: 90). Biondi's edition (1995: xii) gives the announcement in Italian only, not translating the phrase "etiam ab extrema Italia." Innocent VIII's bull ordering the destruction of the nine hundred theses complains that Pico had his text "affixed in diverse public places of the holy city, in which we reside with the Roman curia" and had them published "in other parts of the world" [et aliis mundi partibus publicare fecisset] (Garin, *Scritti vari*, 63). Whether this originally included territories outside Italy is unknown. The 1487 German reprint also included Pico's promise to pay the traveling expenses of debaters, but no evidence currently links Pico to that edition. Nor do we know how many philosophers or theologians, real or would-be, showed up at Rome demanding from Pico their traveling expenses. Scattered second-hand reports of Pico's Roman adventures, real and apocryphal, exist that warrant closer study, however.

Select Bibliography

The specialized literature on Pico is large and notoriously unreliable. Here I have only listed cited works and a handful of additional key studies. Unpublished manuscripts discussed in my text or notes are not listed. For the older literature and other editions of Pico's works, see the bibliographies in Garin (1937), Monnerjahn (1960), Di Napoli (1965), Kristeller (1965), Kieszkowski (1973), and Roulier (1989). For some of the newer literature, see the notes in the two-volume collection of symposium papers edited by Garfagnini (1997). For a list of Pico's manuscripts, see the appendix in Kristeller (1965). Relevant parts of studies reprinted in the supplemental volume to the important 1971 reprint of Pico's Basel *Opera* are marked with an asterisk (*). On occasion I have included some brief source notes.

1. Primary Sources in Western Thought

Adelard of Bath. See under "Gollancz" in this section.

Agrippa von Nettesheim, Henry Cornelius. *Opera.* Lyon, n.d. [1600]. Repr. Hildesheim, 1970.

Albareda, A. M. "Il vescovo di Barcellona Pietro Garsias bibliotecario della Vaticana, sotto Alessandro VI." *La Bibliofilia* 60 (1958): 1–18.

Albertus Magnus. *Opera omnia.* Ed. Auguste Borgnet. 38 vols. Paris, 1890–1895.

———. *Opera omnia.* Ed. Bernhard Geyer. Westphalia, 1951– .

Alexander of Aphrodisias. *Commentaria in Aristotelem Graeca*, vols. 1–3, and *Supplementum Aristotelicum*, vol. 2. Berlin, 1882–1909.

Apuleius. *The Golden Ass of Apuleius.* Loeb ed. London, 1922.

Aquinas, Thomas. *Opera omnia.* Parma, 1852–1873.

———. *Opera omnia.* Leonine edition. Rome, 1882–1995.

Archangelus de Burgonovo O.M. *Apologia pro defensione doctrinae cabalae contra Petrum Garziam episcopum Ussellensem Mirandulam impugnantem sed minime laedentem, et Conclusiones Cabalisticae lxxi secundum opinionem propriam eiusdem Mirandulae . . . per eundem . . . acutissime declaratae et elucidatae.* Bologna, 1564.

Aristotle. *The Complete Works of Aristotle.* Revised Oxford Translation. Ed. Jonathan Barnes. 2 vols. Princeton, 1984.

Averroes. *Opera Aristotelis cum Averrois commentariis.* 12 vols. in 14. Venice, 1562–1574. Repr. Frankfurt, 1962.

Barbaro, Ermolao. *Epistolae, Orationes et Carmina.* Ed. Vittore Branca. 2 vols. Florence, 1943.

Bellanti, Lucio [Bellantius, Lucas]. *Responsiones in disputationes Joannis Pici Mirandulae comitis adversus astrologos.* Florence, 1498.

Benignus, Georgius. *Septem et septuaginta in opusculo Magistri Nicolai de Mirabilibus reperta mirabilia praesenti opere annotavit.* Florence, 1497 [1489].

Benivieni, Girolamo. *Commento di Hieronymo Benivieni cittadino fiorentino sopra a più sue canzone et sonetti dello amore et della bellezza divina.* Florence, 1500.

———. *Opere.* Florence, 1519.

*Berti, Domenico. "Intorno a Giovanni Pico della Mirandola. Cenni e documenti inediti." *Rivista contemporanea* 16 (1859): 7–56. Contains important source materials.

Calori Cesis, F. *Giovanni Pico della Mirandola.* Mirandola, 1897. In *Memorie storiche della città e dell'antico ducato della Mirandola* 11 (1897). Contains essential documents.

Campanella, Tommaso. *Opere di Giordano Bruno e di Tommaso Campanella.* Eds. Augusto Guzzo and Romano Amerio. Milano, 1956.

*Ceretti, Felici. "Volgarizzamento Latino del Salmo LXVII, del conte Giovanni Pico della Mirandola." *La scuola cattolica e la scienza italiana.* Serie 2, anno 5, vol. 9 (Milan, 1895): 98–112.

Cicero. *De natura deorum and Academica.* Trans. H. Rackham. Vol. 19 of the Loeb editions of the works of Cicero. Cambridge, Mass., 1933.

Corpus Hermeticum. Ed. A. D. Nock, trans. A. J. Festugière. 4 vols. Paris, 1945–1954.

Crinito, Pietro. *De honesta disciplina.* Ed. Carlo Angeleri. Rome, 1955.

Diels, ed. *Die Fragmente der Vorsokratiker.* 6th ed., with additions by Walter Kranz. Berlin, 1952.

Pseudo-Dionysius. *Oeuvres complètes du Pseudo-Denys l'Aréopagite.* Ed. M. de Gandillac. Paris, 1943.

*Dorez, L. and L. Thuasne. *Pic de la Mirandole en France (1485–1488).* Paris, 1897. Contains the proceedings of the papal commission and other essential documents.

*Dorez, L. "Lettres inédites de Jean Pic de la Mirandole (1482–1492)." *Giornale storico della letteratura italiana* 85 (1895): 352–61.

———. See also in Section 2.

Duns Scotus, John. *Opera omnia.* Ed. Lucas Wadding. 26 vols. Paris, 1891–1895.

———. *Opera omnia.* Eds. C. Balic et al. Vols. 1–7, 16–19. Vatican City, 1950– .

Elia del Medigo. See under "John of Jandun" in this section.

Erasmus. *Opera.* 10 vols. Lyon, 1703–1706.

Ficinus, Marsilius. *Supplementum Ficinianum.* Ed. P. O. Kristeller. 2 vols. Florence, 1937.

———. *Commentaire sur le Banquet de Platon.* Ed. and trans. Raymond Marcel. Paris, 1956.

———. *Opera omnia.* 2 vols. Basel, 1576. Repr. Turin, 1959.

———. *Philebus Commentary.* Ed. and trans. Michael Allen. Berkeley, 1975.

———. *De vita coelitus comparanda.* Venice, 1498. Repr. with variant readings and notes by Martin Plessner. Hildesheim, 1978.

———. *Three Books on Life. A Critical Edition and Translation.* With introduction and notes. Ed. and trans. Carol V. Kaske and John R. Clark. Medieval & Renaissance Texts & Studies, vol. 57. Binghamton, N.Y., 1989.

Franciscus de Mayronis. *In quatuor libros sententiarum.* Venice, 1520.

Gaffarel, J. [Gaffarellus, J.] *Codicum Cabalisticorum Manuscriptorum quibus est usus Joannes Picus Comes Mirandulanus Index.* Paris, 1651. Repr. in J. C. Wolf. *Bibliotheca Hebraica.* Vol. 1. Hamburg, 1715.

Galilei, Galileo. *Dialogue Concerning the Two Chief World Systems.* Trans. Stillman Drake. Berkeley, Calif., 1967.

*Garin, Eugenio. *La cultura filosofica del Rinascimento italiano.* Florence, 1961. Contains fragments of Pico's commentary on the Psalms, the first draft of the *Oration*, some previously unpublished letters, and Garin's dating of Pico's letters.

———. See also under "Picus Mirandulanus, Johannes" in this section and under "Garin" in Section 2.

Garsias, Petrus. *Assertiones theologicales apud sanctum Eustachium XXVIII Aprilis disputandae per dominum Petrum Garcia.* Paris, n.d. [1478]. Repr. in Kieszkowski's edition of Pico's theses.

Garsias, Petrus. *Determinationes magistrales contra conclusiones Joannis Pici.* Rome, 1489.

Gollancz, Hermann. *Dodi Venechdi.* London, 1920. Texts of two Hebrew adaptations of Adelard of Bath's *Quaestiones naturales.*

Grant, Edward, ed. *A Sourcebook in Medieval Science.* Cambridge, Mass., 1974.

Iamblichus. *De mysteriis.* Ed. G. Parthey. Berlin, 1957.

———. *Iamblichi Chalcidensis in Platonis dialogos commentariorum fragmenta.* Ed. with trans. and commentary by John M. Dillon. Leiden, 1973.

John of Jandun. *Joannis de Gandavo Summi Averroiste subtilissime questiones in octo libros Aristotelis De physico auditu . . . his annectuntur questiones Helie Hebrei Cretensis De primo motore, De efficientia mundi, De esse et essentia et uno, eiusdem annotationes in plurima dicta Commentatoris.* Venice, 1544. Contains some texts of Elia del Medigo's used by Pico when preparing for his debate.

Kibre, Pearl. *The Library of Pico della Mirandola.* New York, 1936. Includes inventories of Pico's library.

Kircher, A. *Oedipus Aegyptiacus.* 3 vols. Rome, 1652–1654.

Kristeller, P. O. "Giovanni Pico della Mirandola and His Sources." *L'opera e il pensiero di Giovanni Pico della Mirandola nella storia dell'Umanesimo.* Vol. 1. Florence, 1965. Pp. 35–142. Contains important source materials and bibliographical data.

Landino, Cristoforo. *De vera nobilitate.* Ed. Maria Teresa Liaci. Florence, 1970.

Leibniz, Gottfried Wilhelm. *Opera omnia.* Ed. Louis Dutens. 6 vols. Geneva, 1768.

Liber de causis. Ed. A. Pattin. Louvain, n.d. [1966].

Maimonides. *The Guide for the Perplexed by Moses Maimonides.* Trans. M. Friedländer. 2d ed. London, 1904.

Mazzoni, Jacopo. *De triplici hominum vita, activa nempe, contemplativa et religiosa, methodi tres, quaestionibus quinque millibus centum et nonaginta septem distinctae, in quibus omnes Platonis et Aristotelis, multae verum aliorum Graecorum, Arabum et Latinorum in universo scientiarum orbe discordiae componuntur, quae omnia publice disputanda Romae proposuit anno salutis 1576.* Rome, 1576. Also apparently published with slight variations in Bologna, 1577.

Milanesi, Carlo. "Testamento olografo e codicillo di Giovanni Pico dei Conti della Mirandola," *Giornale storico delgli archivi Toscani* 1 (1857): 85–94.

De Mirabilibus, Nicolaus. *Disputatio nuper facta in domo Magnifici Laurentii Medices.* Florence, 1489.

Mithridates, Flavius. *Sermo de Passione Domini.* Ed. with introduction and commentary by Chaim Wirszubski. Jerusalem, 1963.

More, Thomas. *Giovanni Pico della Mirandola: His Life by His Nephew Giovanni Francesco Pico (and Other Writings).* Trans. Thomas More. Ed. with an introduction by J. M. Rigg. London, 1890. Highly abridged English version of Gianfrancesco Pico's *Vita* of his uncle.

Nag Hammadi Library. Ed. James M. Robinson. Leiden, 1978.

Nesi, Giovanni. *De oraculo novo.* Florence, 1497.

Orphei Hymni. Ed. G. Quandt. Berlin, 1955.

Orphicorum Fragmenta. Ed. Otto Kern. Berlin, 1922.

Peter of Spain (Johannes XXI). *Petri Hispani Summulae logicales.* Ed. I. M. Bochenski. Turin, 1947.

Petrus Lombardus. *Opera omnia.* Ed. J.-P. Migne. *Patrologia latina,* vols. 191–92. Paris, 1844–1891.

———. *Sententiae in IV libris distinctae.* Collegium S. Bonaventura. 2 vols. in 3. Rome, 1971–1982.

Picus Mirandulanus, Johannes. *Conclusiones.* Rome, 1486.

———. *Apologia.* Bologna, 1487.

———. *Conclusiones.* Ingolstadt, 1487 (?).

———. *Commentationes.* 2 vols. Bologna, 1496.

———. *Opera . . . novissime accurate revisa.* Strassburg, 1504. First edition to use the title *De hominis dignitate* for Pico's *Oratio.*

———. *Conclusiones.* Paris (?), 1532.

———. *Opera omnia.* Basel, 1557.

———. *Opera omnia.* Venice, 1557.

———. *Opera omnia.* Basel, 1572. Repr. Turin, 1971.

———. *Philosophia Epicurea, Democratica, Theophrastica,* etc. Ed. N. Hill of London. Paris, 1601; Geneva, 1619. Contains a reprint edition of the nine hundred theses.

———. *De hominis dignitate, Heptaplus, De ente et uno e scritti vari.* Ed. Eugenio Garin. Florence, 1942. [Cited in text as Garin, *Scritti vari.*]

———. *Disputationes adversus astrologiam divinatricem.* Ed. Eugenio Garin. 2 vols. Florence, 1946–1952.

———. *Conclusiones sive Theses DCCCC.* Ed. Bohdan Kieszkowski. Geneva, 1973.

———. *Une controverse sur Origène à la Renaissance: Jean Pic de la Mirandole et Pierre Garcia.* Ed. and trans. Henri Crouzel. Paris, 1977. French translation of parts of one section of the *Apology.*

———. *Commentary on a Canzone of Benivieni.* Trans. Sears Jayne. New York, 1984.

———. *Conclusiones nongentae: Le novecento Tesi dell'anno 1486.* Ed. and trans. Albano Biondi. Florence, 1995.

———. *Expositiones in Psalmos.* Ed. Antonino Raspanti. Italian trans. by Antonino Raspanti and Giacomo Raspanti. Florence, 1997.

———. See also in this section under "Berti," "Calori Cesis," "Ceretti," "Dorez," "Garin," "Kristeller," "Kibre," "Milanesi," and "Wirszubski."

Picus Mirandulanus, Johannes Franciscus. *Liber de providentia contra philosophrastos.* Modena, 1508.

———. *Opera omnia.* Basel, 1557.

———. See also under "Cavini" in Section 2.

Plato. *The Collected Dialogues.* Eds. Edith Hamilton and Huntington Cairns. Princeton, 1961.

Plotinus. *Enneads.* 3 vols. Eds. P. Henry and H. R. Schwyzer. Oxford, 1964–1982.

Plutarch. *De defectu oraculorum.* Trans. Frank C. Babbit. In vol 5. of the Loeb edition of Plutarch's *Moralia.* Cambridge, Mass., 1936.

Porphyry. *Porphyrii philosophi Platonici opuscula tria.* Ed. Augustus Nauck. Leipzig, 1860.

———. *Sententiae ad intelligibilia ducentes.* Ed. B. Mommert. Leipzig, 1907.
Proclus Diadochus. *In theologiam Platonis.* Ed. A. Portus. Frankfurt, 1618. Reprints Pico's theses *secundum Proclum* in an appendix.
———. *The Six Books of Proclus on the Theology of Plato.* Trans. Thomas Taylor. 2 vols. London, 1816.
———. *The Commentaries of Proclus on the Timaeus of Plato.* 2 vols. Trans. Thomas Taylor. London, 1820.
———. *In Timaeum.* Ed. Diehl. 3 vols. 1903–1906.
———. *Tria opuscula.* Ed. Helmut Boese. Berlin, 1960.
———. *The Elements of Theology.* Ed. and trans. E. R. Dodds. 2d ed. London, 1963.
———. *Théologie Platonicienne.* Eds. and trans. H. D. Saffrey and L. G. Westerink. 6 vols. Paris, 1968– .
Recanati, M. *Commentary on the Pentateuch.* Venice, 1523. (In Hebrew.)
Savonarola, Girolamo. *Prediche sopra Aggeo.* Ed. Luigi Firpo. Rome, 1965.
———. *Trattato contra li astrologi.* Vol. 1 of *Scritti filosofici.* Eds. G. Garfagnini and E. Garin. Rome, 1982.
Steuco, Agostino. *De perenni philosophia.* 1540. Repr. New York, 1972, with an introduction by Charles B. Schmitt.
Themistius. *Paraphrasis in posteriora Aristotelis, etc.* Trans. Ermolao Barbaro. Treviso, 1481.
Theon of Smyrna. *Mathematics Useful for Understanding Plato.* Trans. Robert and Deborah Lawler. San Diego, 1979.
Theophrastus. *Theophrasti Eresii opera quae supersunt omnia.* Ed. F. Wimmer. Leipzig, 1854–1862.
———. *Metaphysica.* Eds. W. D. Ross and F. H. Fobes. Oxford, 1929.
Wirszubski, Chaim. "Giovanni Pico's Book of Job." *Journal of the Warburg and Courtauld Institutes* 32 (1969): 171–99. Transcribes some notes of Pico's on prophetic magic.

2. Secondary Sources on Western Thought

Allen, Michael J. B. *Marsilio Ficino and the Phaedran Charioteer.* Berkeley, 1981.
———. "Ficino's Theory of the Five Substances and the Neo-Platonists's *Parmenides.*" *Journal of Medieval and Renaissance Studies* 12 (1983): 19–44.
———. *The Platonism of Marsilio Ficino.* Berkeley, 1984.
———. "Marsilio Ficino's Interpretation of Plato's *Timaeus* and Its Myth of the Demiurge." In James Hankins, John Monfasani, and Frederick Purnell, Jr., eds. *Supplementum Festivum: Studies in Honor of Paul Oskar Kristeller.* Medieval &

Renaissance Texts & Studies, vol. 49. Binghamton, N.Y., 1987. Pp. 399–439.

———. *Icastes: Marsilio Ficino's Interpretation of Plato's* Sophist (*Five Studies and a Critical Edition with Translation*). Berkeley, 1989.

Anagnine, Eugenio. *Giovanni Pico della Mirandola: Sincretismo religioso-filosofico.* Bari, 1937.

Armstrong, A. H., ed. *The Cambridge History of Later Greek and Early Medieval Philosophy.* Cambridge, 1967.

Atti del Convegno internazionale per la celebrazione del V centenario della nascita di Giovanni Manardo, 1462–1536. Ferrara, 1963.

Berti, Dominico. See under "Berti" in Section 1.

Biondi, Albano. See under "Picus Mirandulanus, Johannes" in Section 1.

Blau, Joseph L. *The Christian Interpretation of the Cabala in the Renaissance.* New York, 1944.

Breen, Q. "Giovanni Pico della Mirandola on the Conflict of Philosophy and Rhetoric." *Journal of the History of Ideas* 13 (1952): 384–426.

British Museum, Department of Printed Books. *Catalogue of Books Printed in the XVth Century Now in the British Museum.* London, 1908–1962.

Calori Cesis, F. See under "Calori Cesis" in Section 1.

Cassirer, Ernst. *Individuum und Kosmos in der Philosophie der Renaissance.* Berlin, 1927. English trans. Mario Domandi. New York, 1963.

———. "Giovanni Pico della Mirandola, A Study in the History of Renaissance Ideas." *Journal of the History of Ideas.* Vol. 3, no. 2–3 (1942): 123–44, 319–46. Repr. in P. O. Kristeller and Philip P. Wiener, eds. *Renaissance Essays.* New York, 1968. Pp. 11–60.

Cassuto, U. *Gli Ebrei a Firenze nell'età del Rinascimento.* Florence, 1918.

———. "Wer War der Orientalis Mithridates?" *Zeitschrift für die Geschichte der Juden in Deutschland* 5 (1934): 230–36.

Cavini, Walter. "Un inedito di Giovan Francesco Pico della Mirandola: La 'Quaestio de falsitate astrologiae.'" *Rinascimento* ser. 2 (1973): 133–71.

*Ceretti, Felice. "Il conte Antonmaria Pico della Mirandola, memorie e documenti." *Atti e memorie delle RR. deputazioni di storia patria per le provincie dell'Emilia.* N.s. 3, pt. 2 (1878): 237–87. Contains important documents.

Copenhaver, Brian P. "Iamblichus, Synesius, and the Chaldaean Oracles in Marsilio Ficino's *De Vita Libri Tres*: Hermetic Magic or Neoplatonic Magic?" In James Hankins, John Monfasani, and Frederick Purnell, Jr., eds. *Supplementum Festivum: Studies in Honor of Paul Oskar Kristeller.* Medieval & Renaissance Texts & Studies, vol. 49. Binghamton, N.Y., 1987. Pp. 441–55.

———. "Astrology and Magic." In Charles B. Schmitt, Quentin Skinner, Eckhard

Kessler, and Jill Kraye, eds. *Cambridge History of Renaissance Philosophy*. Cambridge, 1988. Pp. 264–300.

———. "L'occulto in Pico. Il mem chiuso e le fauci spalancate de Azazel: la magia cabalistica di Giovanni Pico." In Gian Carlo Garfagnini, ed. *Giovanni Pico della Mirandola: Convegno internazionale di studi nel cinquecentesimo anniversario della morte (1494–1994)*. Vol. 1. Florence, 1997. Pp. 213–36.

Cotton, Juliana Hill. "Alessandro Sarti e il Poliziano." *La Bibliofilia* 64 (1962): 225–46.

Cranz, F. Edward. "Alexander of Aphrodisias." *Catalogus translationum et commentariorum*. Vol. 1. Washington, D.C., 1960. Pp. 77–135; Vol. 2. Washington, D.C., 1971. Pp. 411–22.

Craven, William G. *Giovanni Pico della Mirandola, Symbol of His Age*. Geneva, 1981. Bibliographical study.

Crouzel. See under "Picus Mirandulanus, Johannes" in Section 1.

Dannenfeldt. "The Pseudo-Zoroastrian Oracles in the Renaissance." *Studies in the Renaissance* 4 (1957): 7–30.

———. "Hermetica Philosophica." *Catalogus translationum et commentariorum*. Vol. 1. Washington, D.C., 1960. Pp. 137–56. See also the *addenda et corrigenda* in Vol. 2, pp. 423–24 and Vol. 3, pp. 425–26.

———. "Oracula Chaldaica." *Catalogus translationum et commentariorum*. Vol. 1. Washington, D.C., 1960. Pp. 137–56.

Deferrari, Roy J. and M. Barry. *A Lexicon of St. Thomas Aquinas*. Washington, 1948.

Dell'Aqua, G., and L. Münster. "I rapporti di Giovanni Pico della Mirandola con alcuni filosofi ebrei." *L'opera e il pensiero di Giovanni Pico della Mirandola nella storia dell'Umanesimo*. Vol. 2. Florence, 1965. Pp. 149–68.

Dillon, John M. *The Middle Platonists, 80 B.C. to A.D. 220*. Ithaca, N.Y., 1977.

———. See also under "Iamblichus" in Section 1.

Dodds, E. R. See under "Proclus" in Section 1.

Dorez, L. "La mort de Pic de la Mirandole et l'édition Aldine des oeuvres d'Ange Politien (1494–1497)." *Giornale storico della letteratura italiana* 32 (1898): 360–64; 33 (1899): 180.

———. See also in Section 1.

Dulles, Avery. *Princeps Concordiae: Pico della Mirandola and the Scholastic Tradition*. Cambridge, Mass., 1941.

Eco, Umberto. "Rapporti tra 'revolutio alphabetaria' e lullismo." In Gian Carlo Garfagnini, ed. *Giovanni Pico della Mirandola: Convegno internazionale di studi nel cinquecentesimo anniversario della morte (1494–1994)*. Vol. 1. Florence, 1997. Pp. 13–28.

Eisenstein, Elizabeth L. *The Printing Press as an Agent of Change: Communications and Cultural Transformations in Early Modern Europe*. 2 vols. New York, 1979.

Eliade, Mircea. *From Primitives to Zen: A Thematic Sourcebook of the History of Religions*. New York, 1967.

Farmer, S. A. and John B. Henderson. "Commentary Traditions and the Evolution of Premodern Religious and Philosophical Systems: A Cross-Cultural Model." Papers for the Heidelberg Colloquium, Historische und methodologische Aspekte der Kommentierung von Texten, University of Heidelberg, July 1997. An updated version of this paper is posted at www.safarmer.com/pico/.

Garfagnini, Gian Carlo. "Savonarola tra Giovanni e Gianfrancesco Pico." In Gian Carlo Garfagnini, ed. *Giovanni Pico della Mirandola: Convegno internazionale di studi nel cinquecentesimo anniversario della morte (1494–1994)*. Vol. 1. Florence, 1997. Pp. 237–79.

Garin, Eugenio. *Giovanni Pico della Mirandola: Vita e dottrina*. Firenze, 1937.

———. *La filosofia*. 2 vols. Milan, 1947.

———. *Giovanni Pico della Mirandola*. Parma, 1963.

———. *Lo zodiaco della vita*. Rome, 1976.

———. See also under "Garin" and "Picus Mirandulanus, Johannes" in Section 1.

Gentile, Giovanni. "Il concetto dell'uomo nel Rinascimento." *Il pensiero italiano del Rinascimento*. 3d ed. Florence, 1955.

Gilbert, Neal W. "The Early Italian Humanists and Disputation." In Anthony Molho and John A. Tedeschi, eds. *Renaissance Studies in Honor of Hans Baron*. Florence, 1971. Pp. 201–26.

Gilmore, Myron. "More's Translation of Gianfrancesco Pico's Biography." *L'opera e il pensiero di Giovanni Pico della Mirandola nella storia dell'Umanesimo*. Vol. 2. Florence, 1965. Pp. 301–4.

Gilson, Etienne. *History of Christian Philosophy in the Middle Ages*. New York, 1955.

Glorieux, P. *La littérature quodlibétique*. 2 vols. Kain and Paris, 1925–1935.

———. "Où en est la question du Quodlibet?" *Revue du moyen âge latin* 2 (1946): 405–14.

———. "Quodlibeti." *Enciclopedia Cattolica*, vol. 10. Vatican City, 1953. Columns 436–38.

Gombrich, E. H. *Symbolic Images*. Oxford, 1978.

Goody, Jack. See in Section 3.

Harris, William V. *Ancient Literacy*. Cambridge, Mass., 1989.

Hatfield, Rab. "The Compagnia de' Magi." *Journal of the Warburg and Courtauld Institutes* 33 (1970): 107–61.

Havelock, Eric. *Preface to Plato*. Cambridge, Mass., 1963.

———. *The Greek Concept of Justice: From Its Shadow in Homer to Its Substance in Plato*. Cambridge, Mass., 1978.

———. *The Literate Revolution in Greece and Its Cultural Consequences*. Princeton, 1982.

Haydn, Hiram. *The Counter-Renaissance*. New York, 1950.

Heninger, S. K., Jr. *The Cosmographical Glass: Renaissance Diagrams of the Universe*. San Marino, Cal., 1977.

Hirsch, Rudolf. *Printing, Selling and Reading, 1450–1550*. Wiesbaden, 1967.

Jardine, Nicholas. "Epistemology of the Sciences." In Charles B. Schmitt, Quentin Skinner, Eckhard Kessler, and Jill Kraye, eds. *Cambridge History of Renaissance Philosophy*. Cambridge, 1988. Pp. 685–711.

Jayne, Sears. See under "Picus Mirandulanus, Johannes" in Section 1.

Kaske, Carol V. and John R. Clark. See under "Ficinus" in Section 1.

Kibre, Pearl. See in Section 1.

Kieszkowski, Bohdan. "Les rapports entre Elie del Medigo et Pic de la Mirandole." *Il Rinascimento* 15 (1964): 41–91. Contains important source materials concerning Pico's debate.

———. See also under "Picus Mirandulanus, Johannes" in Section 1.

Klibansky, R. "Plato's *Parmenides* in the Middle Ages and the Renaissance." *Medieval and Renaissance Studies* 1, no. 2 (1943): 281–330.

Kraye, Jill, W. F. Ryan, and C. B. Schmitt, eds. *Pseudo-Aristotle in the Middle Ages*. London, 1986.

Kristeller, P. O. *Renaissance Concepts of Man and Other Essays*. New York, 1972.

———. "The Latin Poems of Giovanni Pico della Mirandola: A Supplementary Note." In G. M. Kirkwood, ed. *Poetry and Poetics from Ancient Greece to the Renaissance: Studies in Honor of James Hutton*. Ithaca, N.Y., 1975. Pp. 185–206.

———. See also under "Kristeller" and "Ficinus" in Section 1.

Levi Della Vida, Giorgio. *Richerche sulla formazione del più antico fondo dei manoscritti orientali della Biblioteca Vaticana*. Vatican City, 1939. Pertinent to study of Pico's manuscripts.

Lewy, Hans. *Chaldaean Oracles and Theurgy*. New ed. Paris, 1978.

Lloyd, A. C. "The Later Platonists." In *Cambridge History of Later Greek and Early Medieval Philosophy*. Cambridge, 1967. Pp. 269–325.

Logan, R. K. *The Alphabet Effect: The Impact of the Phonetic Alphabet on the Development of Western Civilization*. New York, 1986.

Lovejoy, Arthur O. *The Great Chain of Being*. New York, 1936.

Lowry, Martin. *The World of Aldus Manutius*. Ithaca, N.Y., 1979.

De Lubac, Henri. *Pic de la Mirandole: Études et discussions*. Paris, 1974.

McGinn, Bernard. "Cabalists and Christians: Reflections on Cabala in Medieval and Renaissance Thought." In R. H. Popkin and G. M. Weiner, eds. *Jewish Christians and Christian Jews*. Dordrecht and Boston, 1994. Pp. 11–34.

Mack, Burton L. *The Lost Gospel: The Book of Q and Christian Origins*. New York, 1993.

Mahoney, Edward P. "Nicoletto Vernia and Agostino Nifo on Alexander of Aphrodisias: An Unnoticed Dispute." *Rivista critica di storia della filosofia* 23 (1969): 268–96.

———. "Metaphysical Foundations of the Hierarchy of Being according to Some Late-Medieval and Renaissance Philosophers." In Parviz Morewedge, ed. *Philosophies of Existence, Ancient and Modern*. New York, 1982. Pp. 165–257.

———. "Pico, Plato, and Albert the Great: The Testimony and Evaluation of Agostino Nifo." *Medieval Philosophy and Theology* 2 (1992): 165–92.

———. "Giovanni Pico della Mirandola and Elia del Medigo, Nicoletto Vernia and Agostino Nifo." In Gian Carlo Garfagnini, ed. *Giovanni Pico della Mirandola: Convegno internazionale di studi nel cinquecentesimo anniversario della morte (1494–1994)*. Vol. 1. Florence, 1997. Pp. 127–56.

Marcel, Raymond. *Marsile Ficin*. Paris, 1958.

———. "Pico de la Mirandole et la France." *L'opera e il pensiero di Giovanni Pico della Mirandola nella storia dell'Umanesimo*. Vol. I. Florence, 1965. Pp. 205–30.

Mercati, Giovanni Cardinale. *Codici latini Pico, Grimani, Pio e di altra biblioteca ignota del secolo xvi esistenti nell'Ottoboniana e i codici greci Pio di Modena*. Vatican City, 1938.

Monnerjahn, Engelbert. *Giovanni Pico della Mirandola: Ein Beitrag zur philosophischen Theologie des italienischen Humanismus*. Wiesbaden, 1960.

Moody, Ernest. *Studies in Medieval Philosophy, Science, and Logic. Collected papers, 1933–1969*. Berkeley, 1975.

Munk, Salomon. *Mélange de philosophie juive et arab*. Paris, 1859.

Di Napoli, Giovanni. *Giovanni Pico della Mirandola e la problematica dottrinale del suo tempo*. Rome, 1965.

Nardi, Bruno. *Sigieri di Brabante nel pensiero del Rinascimento italiano*. Rome, 1945.

———. "La mistica averroistica e Pico della Mirandola." In E. Castelli, ed. *Umanesimo e Machiavellismo*. Padua, 1949. Pp. 55–74.

———. *Saggi sull'Aristotelismo padovano dal secolo XIV al XVI*. Florence, 1958.

Nelson, John C. *Renaissance Theory of Love*. New York, 1958.

Oberman, Heiko. " 'Facientibus quod in se est Deus non denegat Gratiam': Robert Holcot, O.P., and the Beginnings of Luther's Theology." *Harvard Theological Review* 55, 8 (1962): 317–42.

———. *The Harvest of Medieval Theology*. Cambridge, Mass., 1963.

———. *Forerunners of the Reformation*. New York, 1966.

O'Malley, John W. *Praise and Blame in Renaissance Rome*. Durham, N.C., 1979. Some notes of interest relevant to Pico's debate.

Ong, Walter J. *Ramus, Method, and the Decay of Dialogue*. Cambridge, Mass., 1958.

Ozment, Stephen. "Luther and the Late Middle Ages: The Formation of Reformation Thought." In Robert M. Kingdon, ed. *Transition and Revolution: Problems and Issues of European Renaissance and Reformation History*. Minneapolis, 1974. Pp. 109–52.

Panofsky, Erwin, and Fritz Saxl. *Dürer's Melencolia I. Studien der Bibliothek Warburg* no. 2. Leipzig, 1923.

Pattin, see under *Liber de causis* in Section 1.

De Pina Martins, José V. *Jean Pic de la Mirandole: un portrait inconnu de l'humanisme*. Paris, 1976.

Poletti, Sergio. *Del modo tenuto da Cristoforo e Martino da Casalmaggiore nel sopprimere Giovanni Pico della Mirandola*. Mirandola, 1987. Contains an Italian translation of Pico's will, excerpts from Marin Sanudo's diary, and comments by Giovanni Spadolini and Sergio Poletti.

Popkin, Richard. *The History of Scepticism from Erasmus to Spinoza*. Revised and expanded version. Berkeley, 1979.

Randall, John Herman, Jr. *The Career of Philosophy. Vol. I: From the Middle Ages to the Enlightenment*. New York, 1962.

Raspanti, Antonino. *Filosofia, Teologia, Religione. L'unitá della visione in Giovanni Pico della Mirandola*. Palermo, 1991.

———. See also under "Picus Mirandulanus, Johannes" in Section 1.

Reeves, Marjorie. *The Influence of Prophecy in the Later Middle Ages: A Study in Joachimism*. London, 1969.

Reusch, Franz Heinrich. *Der Index der verbotenen Bücher*. 2 vols. Bonn, 1883–1885.

Rescher, Nicholas. *Al-Farabi's Short Commentary on Aristotle's Prior Analytics*. Pittsburgh, 1963.

———. *Studies in the History of Arabic Logic*. Pittsburgh, 1963.

———. *The Development of Arabic Logic*. Pittsburgh, 1964.

———. *Al-Kindi: An Annotated Bibliography*. Pittsburgh, 1964.

Rice, Eugene F. *The Renaissance Idea of Wisdom*. Cambridge, Mass., 1958.

Ridolfi, R. *Vita di Girolamo Savonarola*. 4th ed., enlarged. Florence, 1974.

Rosán, L. J. *The Philosophy of Proclus*. New York, 1949.

Roulier, Fernand. *Jean Pic de la Mirandole (1463–1494): humaniste, philosophe, et théologien*. Geneva, 1989.

Saffrey, H. D. "Pietro Balbi et la première traduction latine de la Théologie Platonicienne de Proclus." In *Recherches sur la tradition platonicienne au moyen âge et à la renaissance*. Paris, 1987. pp. 189–201.

———. See also under "Proclus" in Section 1.

Saggs, H. W. F. *Civilization before Greece and Rome*. New Haven, Connecticut, 1989.

Sarton, George. *Introduction to the History of Science*. 3 vols. in 5. Baltimore, 1927–1948.

Schmitt, Charles B. "Gianfrancesco Pico's Attitude toward His Uncle." *L'opera e il pensiero di Giovanni Pico della Mirandola nella storia dell'Umanesimo*. Vol. 2. Florence, 1965. Pp. 305–11.

———. "Perennial Philosophy: From Agostino Steuco to Leibniz." *Journal of the History of Ideas* 27, 4 (1966): 505–32.

———. *Gianfrancesco Pico della Mirandola*. The Hague, 1967.

———. "Theophrastus." *Catalogus translationum et commentariorum*. Vol. 2. Washington, D.C., 1971. Pp. 239–322.

———. See also under "Steuco" in Section 1.

Scholem, Gershom. *Major Trends in Jewish Mysticism*. Jerusalem, 1941.

———. "Zur Geschichte der Anfänge der Christlichen Kabbala." In *Essays Presented to Leo Baeck*. London, 1954. Pp. 158–93.

———. *Ursprung und Anfänge der Kabbala*. Berlin, 1962.

———. *Kabbalah*. New York, 1974.

Secret, François. "Pico della Mirandola e gli inizi della Cabala christiana." *Convivium* n.s. 25 (1957): 31–47.

———. "Qui était l'orientaliste Mithridate?" *Revue des Études Juives* 116 n.s. 16 (1957): 96–102.

———. *Le Zôhar chez les Kabbalistes chrétiens de la Renaissance*. Paris, 1958.

———. *Les Kabbalistes chrétiens de la Renaissance*. Paris, 1964.

———. "Nouvelles précisions sur Flavius Mithridates Maître de Pic de la Mirandole et traducteur de commentaires de Kabbale." *L'opera e il pensiero di Giovanni Pico della Mirandola nella storia dell'Umanesimo*. Vol. 2. Florence, 1965. Pp. 169–87.

Semprini, G. "Le novecento tesi di Pico della Mirandola." *Rivista di Psicologia* 20 (1920): 358–72.

Shumaker, Wayne. *The Occult Sciences in the Renaissance*. Berkeley, 1972.

Smalley, Beryl. *The Study of the Bible in the Middle Ages*. 3d ed. Oxford, 1983.

Spence, Jonathan D. *The Memory Palace of Matteo Ricci*. New York, 1985.

Starrabba, R. "Richerche storiche su Guglielmo Raimondo Moncada, ebreo convertito siciliano del secolo XV." *Archivio storico siciliano* n.s. 3 (1878): 15–91. Contains documents *re* Flavius Mithridates.

Thomas, Keith. *Religion and the Decline of Magic.* New York, 1971.

Thorndike, Lynn. *A History of Magic and Experimental Science.* 8 vols. New York, 1923–1958.

———. *University Records and Life in the Middle Ages.* New York, 1944.

Della Torre, Arnaldo. *Storia dell'Accademia Platonica di Firenze.* Florence, 1902.

Trinkaus, Charles. *In Our Image and Likeness: Humanity and Divinity in Italian Humanist Thought.* 2 vols. Chicago, 1970.

Valcke, Louis. "Jean Pic de la Mirandole (1463–1494): quatre ouvrages récents." *Dialogue* 34 (1995): 343–66.

Valenziani, Enrichetta. "Les incunables de Pic de la Mirandole." In Henri Bédarida, ed. *Pensée humaniste et tradition chrétienne aux XVe. et XVIe. siécles.* Paris, 1950. Pp. 333–58.

Vickers, Brian, ed. *Occult and Scientific Mentalities in the Renaissance.* Cambridge, 1984.

Walbank, F. W. *The Hellenistic World.* Rev. ed. Cambridge, Mass., 1993.

Walker, D. P. *Spiritual and Demonic Magic from Ficino to Campanella.* Notre Dame, Ind., 1958; repr. 1975.

———. *The Ancient Theology.* Ithaca, N.Y., 1972.

Weinstein, Donald. *Savonarola and Florence: Prophecy and Patriotism in the Renaissance.* Princeton, 1970.

Westman, Robert S., and J. E. McGuire. *Hermeticism and the Scientific Revolution.* Los Angeles, 1977.

Wind, Edgar. "The Revival of Origen." *Studies in Art and Literature for Belle da Costa Greene.* Ed. Dorothy Miner. Princeton, 1954. Pp. 412–24.

———. "Porus Consilii Filius (Notes on the Orphic 'Counsels of Night')." *L'opera e il pensiero di Giovanni Pico della Mirandola nella storia dell'Umanesimo.* Vol. 2. Florence, 1965. Pp. 198–203.

———. *Pagan Mysteries in the Renaissance.* Revised and Enlarged Edition. New York, 1968.

Wirszubski, Chaim. "Francesco Giorgio's Commentary on Giovanni Pico's Kabbalistic Theses." *Journal of the Warburg and Courtauld Institutes* 37 (1974): 145–56.

———. *Pico della Mirandola's Encounter with Jewish Mysticism.* Cambridge, Mass., 1989.

———. See also under "Wirszubski" and "Mithridates" in Section 1.

Yates, Frances. *Giordano Bruno and the Hermetic Tradition.* London, 1964.

———. "Giovanni Pico della Mirandola and Magic." *L'opera e il pensiero di Gio-*

vanni Pico della Mirandola nella storia dell'Umanesimo. Vol. 1. Florence, 1965. Pp. 159–203.

———. *The Art of Memory.* Chicago, 1966.

Zambelli, Paola. "Giovanni Mainardi e la polemica sull'astrologia." *L'opera e il pensiero di Giovanni Pico della Mirandola nella storia dell'Umanesimo.* Vol. 2. Florence, 1965. Pp. 205–79.

———, a. "Una disputa filosofica ereticale proposta nelle Università Padane nel 1519." In Paolo Rossi, ed. *Il rinascimento nelle corti padane: società e cultura.* Bari, 1977. Pp. 495–528.

———, b. *Une réincarnation de Jean Pic à l'époque de Pomponazzi: les thèses magiques et hérétiques d'un aristotélicien oublié, Tiberio Russiliano Sesto Calabrese (1519).* Mainz, 1977.

3. *Non-Western Primary and Secondary Sources*

Barth, Fredrik. *Cosmologies in the Making: A Generative Approach to Cultural Variation in Inner New Guinea.* Cambridge, 1987.

De Bary, William Theodore, et al., eds. *Sources of Chinese Tradition.* Vol. 1. New York, 1960.

Berling, Judith. *The Syncretic Religion of Lin Chao-en.* New York, 1980.

Bettray, Johannes, S.V.D. *Die Akkommodationsmethode des P. Matteo Ricci S.I. in China.* Rome, 1955.

Budge, E. A. Wallis, ed. and trans. *The Egyptian Book of the Dead.* London, 1895. Repr., New York, 1967.

Cabezón, José Ignacio, ed. *Scholasticism: Cross-Cultural and Comparative Perspectives.* Albany, 1998.

Chu Hsi. *Learning to Be a Sage. Selections from the Conversations of Master Chu, Arranged Topically.* Trans. Daniel K. Gardner. Berkeley, 1990.

Elman, Benjamin A. *From Philosophy to Philology: Intellectual and Social Aspects of Change in Late Imperial China.* Cambridge, Mass., 1984.

Farriss, Nancy M. *Maya Society under Colonial Rule.* Princeton, 1984.

Faulkner, Raymond, trans. *The Egyptian Book of the Dead: The Book of Going Forth By Day.* San Francisco, 1994.

Frazer, James George. *The Golden Bough.* 3d. ed. 13 vols. New York, 1935.

Freidel, David, Linda Schele, and Joy Parker. *Maya Cosmos: Three Thousand Years on the Shaman's Path.* New York, 1993.

Fung Yu-lan. *A History of Chinese Philosophy.* Trans. Derk Bodde. Vol. 2. Princeton, 1953.

Goody, Jack, ed. *Literacy in Traditional Societies*. Cambridge, 1968.
———. *The Domestication of the Savage Mind*. Cambridge, 1977.
———. *The Logic of Writing and the Organization of Society*. Cambridge, 1986.
———. *The Interface between the Written and the Oral*. Cambridge, 1987.
Goody, Jack, and Ian Watt. "The Consequences of Literacy." *Comparative Studies in Society and History* 5, no. 3 (April 1963): 304–45. Repr. in Jack Goody, ed. *Literacy in Traditional Societies*. Cambridge, 1968. Pp. 27–68.
Gregory, Peter. *Tsung-mi and the Sinification of Buddhism*. Princeton, 1991.
Griaule, Marcel. *Conversations with Ogotemmêli: An Introduction to Dogon Ideas*. London, 1965.
Henderson, John. *The Development and Decline of Chinese Cosmology*. New York, 1984.
———. *Scripture, Canon, and Commentary: A Comparison of Confucian and Western Exegesis*. Princeton, 1991.
———. *The Construction of Orthodoxy and Heresy: Neo-Confucian, Islamic, Jewish, and Early Christian Patterns*. Albany, 1998.
———. See also under "Farmer" in Section 2.
Karlgren, Bernhard. "Legends and Cults in Ancient China." *Bulletin of the Museum of Far Eastern Antiquities* 18 (1946): 199–365.
———. "Some Sacrifices in Chou China." *Bulletin of the Museum of Far Eastern Antiquities* 40 (1968): 1–32.
León-Portilla, Miguel. *Aztec Thought and Culture: A Study of the Ancient Nahuatl Mind*. Norman, Okla., 1963.
———. *Pre-Columbian Literatures of Mexico*. Norman, Okla., 1969.
Mumme, Patricia Y. "Haunted by Sankara's Ghost: The Srivaisnava Interpretation of *Bhagavad Gita* 18:66." In Jeffrey R. Timm, ed. *Texts in Context: Traditional Hermeneutics in South Asia*. Albany, 1992. Pp. 69–84.
Needham, Joseph. *Science and Civilization in China*. Cambridge. 1954– .
Popul Vuh. Trans. Dennis Tedlock. New York, 1985.
Porkert, Manfred. *The Theoretical Foundations of Chinese Medicine: Systems of Correspondence*. Cambridge, Mass., 1974.
Sandars, N. K. *The Epic of Gilgamesh: An English Version with an Introduction*. Rev. ed. London, 1972.
Spence, Jonathan D. See in Section 2.
Stewart, Charles, and Rosalind Shaw, eds. *Syncretism/Anti-Syncretism: The Politics of Religious Synthesis*. London, 1994.
Sutra of Hui Neng. In A. F. Price and Wong Mou-Lam, trans. *The Diamond Sutra and the Sutra of Hui Neng*. Berkeley, 1969.

Taube, Karl A. *The Major Gods of Ancient Yucatan.* Dumbarton Oaks Studies in Pre-Columbian Art and Archaeology. Washington, D.C., 1992.

Thompson, J. E. S. *Maya History and Religion.* Norman, Okla., 1970.

Toer, Pramoedya Ananta. *Footsteps.* Trans. Max Lane. New York, 1995.

Tsunoda, Ryusaku, et al., eds. *Sources of Japanese Tradition.* Vol. 1. New York, 1958.

Turner, Victor. *The Forest of Symbols: Aspects of Ndembu Ritual.* Ithaca, N.Y., 1967.

DeWoskin, Kenneth. *A Song for One or Two.* Ann Arbor, 1982. On Chinese magic.

4. Nonhistorical Studies

Bak, Per, Chao Tang, and Kurt Wiesenfeld. "Self-Organized Criticality." *Physical Review A* 38, no. 1 (1 July 1988): 364–74.

Bak, Per and Kan Chen. "Self-Organized Criticality." *Scientific American* 264, no. 1 (Jan. 1991): 46–53.

Baron–Cohen, Simon, and John E. Harrison, eds. *Synaesthesia.* Oxford, 1997.

Black, Ira B. *Information in the Brain: A Molecular Perspective.* Cambridge, Mass., 1991.

Brown, Peter. *The Hypnotic Brain.* New Haven, 1991.

Byrne, John H., and William O. Berry, eds. *Neural Models of Plasticity: Experimental and Theoretical Approaches.* San Diego, 1989.

Churchland, Patricia S. *Neurophilosophy: Toward a Unified Science of the Mind–Brain.* Cambridge, Mass., 1986.

Churchland, Patricia S., and Terrence J. Sejnowski. *The Computational Brain.* Cambridge, Mass., 1992.

Cytowic, Richard E. *Synesthesia: A Union of the Senses.* New York, 1989.

———. *The Man Who Tasted Shapes.* New York, 1993.

Deacon, Terrence W. *The Symbolic Species: The Co-Evolution of Language and the Brain.* New York, 1997.

Edelman, Gerald. *Neural Darwinism.* New York, 1987.

Gazzaniga, Michael S., ed. *The Cognitive Sciences.* Cambridge, Mass., 1995.

Glass, Leon, and Michael C. Mackey. *From Clocks to Chaos: The Rhythms of Life.* Princeton, 1988.

Goldberger, A. L. "Fractals and the Birth of the Gothic: Reflections on the Biologic Basis of Creativity." *Molecular Psychiatry* 1, 2 (1996): 99–104.

Goldman–Rakic, P. S. "Circuitry of the Pre-Frontal Cortex and the Regulation of Behavior by Representational Memory." In F. Blum and V. Mountcastle.

Higher Cortical Function: Handbook of Physiology. Washington, D.C., 1987. Pp. 373–417.

Kauffman, Stuart A. *The Origins of Order: Self-Organization and Selection in Evolution*. New York, 1993.

Luria, A. R. *The Mind of a Mnemonist: A Little Book about a Vast Memory*. Trans. Lynn Solotaroff. Cambridge, Mass., 1968.

Mandelbrot, Benoit. *The Fractal Geometry of Nature*. Updated and Augmented. New York, 1983.

Merzenich, M., G. H. Recanzone, W. M. Jenkins, and R. J. Nudo. "How the Brain Functionally Rewires Itself." In M. A. Arbib and J. A. Robinson, eds. *Natural and Artificial Parallel Computation*. Cambridge, Mass., 1990. Pp. 170–210.

Mountcastle, Vernon. "An Organizing Principle for Cerebral Function: The Unit Module and the Distributed System." In G. M. Edelman and V. B. Mountcastle. *The Mindful Brain*. Cambridge, Mass., 1978. Pp. 7–50.

Pellionisz, A., and R. Llinás. "Tensor Network Theory of the Metaorganization of Functional Geometries in the Central Nervous System." *Neuroscience* 16 (1985): 245–73.

Rumelhart, David E., et al. *Parallel Distributed Processing: Explorations in the Microstructure of Cognition*. 2 vols. Cambridge, Mass., 1986.

Stein, Barry E., and M. Alex Meredith. *The Merging of the Senses*. Cambridge, Mass., 1993.

Werner, Heinz. *Comparative Psychology of Mental Development*. New York, 1948.

Subject Index

This index lists major topics discussed in the introductory monograph, theses, and commentary. It does not list topics found in single theses nor the profusion of esoteric symbols in Pico's text. While a full concordance of the nine hundred theses might be of general interest, it would have limited use as a guide to Pico's thought, since he routinely correlated the concepts and symbols of radically different writers and traditions. Readers interested in pursuing specialized questions in depth should refer to the extensive cross-references in the text, to which this index is intended to provide shortcut access.

Page numbers in the index refer to the text or notes in the introductory study; thesis numbers refer to theses or linked notes. References to theses in topical series are usually provided only for the first conclusion in that series; the note to that thesis usually provides a brief general discussion of the series, a list of related theses, and when applicable cross-references to the introductory monograph.

Index of Names and Works

This index covers major references to names or texts in the introductory monograph, theses, and commentary. It does not include passing references to premodern writers or texts, citations to unpublished manuscripts, or references to modern scholars or their studies. Page numbers refer to the text or notes in the introductory study; thesis numbers refer to theses or linked notes. The index does not track individual sources used by Pico in compiling the theses; for data on this question, see the notes in the subsections of the text indicated in the index. Fuller references than normal are given to Pico's works and to Aristotelian texts, since citations in these cases are scattered widely in the text and commentary.

The purpose of this index is to provide shortcuts to the network of cross-references in the introductory study, theses, and commentary, where Pico's links to particular writers or traditions can be pursued in greater depth.

CPSIA information can be obtained
at www.ICGtesting.com
Printed in the USA
BVHW032234310122
627320BV00040B/251